P9-CAA-557

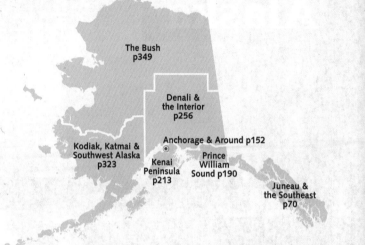

The Bush
p349

Denali &
the Interior
p256

Anchorage & Around p152

Kodiak, Katmai &
Southwest Alaska
p323

Kenai
Peninsula
p213

Prince
William
Sound p190

Juneau &
the Southeast
p70

🏃 Alaska's Best Hikes & Paddles ＞p50

Directory
A–Z

THIS EDITION WRITTEN AND RESEARCHED BY

Jim DuFresne,
Catherine Bodry, Robert Kelly

Wondrous Wilderness & Outdoor Playground

Wilderness – land free of strip malls, traffic jams and McDonald's restaurants – is the best attraction Alaska has to offer. Within Alaska is the largest national park in the country (Wrangell-St Elias), the largest national forest (Tongass), and the largest state park (Wood-Tikchik). This is where people play outdoors. During 20-hour days, they climb mountains, canoe wilderness rivers, strap on crampons and trek across glaciers. In July they watch giant brown bears snagging salmon; in November they head to Haines to see thousands of bald eagles gathered at the Chilkat River. They hoist a backpack and follow the same route

that the Klondike stampeders did a century earlier or spend an afternoon in a kayak, bobbing in front of a 5-mile-wide glacier continually calving icebergs into the sea around them. In Alaska these are more than just outdoor adventures. They are natural experiences that can permanently change your way of thinking.

The Biggest State of Them All

Alaska is big and so is everything about it. There are mountains and glaciers in other parts of North America, but few on the same scale or as overpowering as those in Alaska. At 20,320ft, Mt McKinley is not only the highest peak in North America,

Big, breathtakingly beautiful and wildly bountiful; there are few places in the world, and none in the USA, with the unspoiled wilderness, mountainous grandeur and immense wildlife that is Alaska.

(left) Northern lights (see boxed text, p294)
(below) Kenai Fjords National Park (p225)

it's also a stunning sight when you catch its alpenglow in Wonder Lake. The Yukon is the third-longest river in the USA, Bering Glacier is larger than Switzerland, and Arctic winters are one long night while Arctic summers are one long day. The brown bears on Kodiak Island have been known to stand 14ft tall; the king salmon in the Kenai River often exceed 70lb; in Palmer they grow cabbages that tip the scales at 127lbs. A 50ft-long humpback whale breaching is not something easily missed, even from a half mile away.

Far, Far Away

The 49th state is the longest trip in the USA and probably the most expensive. From elsewhere in the country it takes a week on the road, two to three days on a ferry, or a $700 to $900 airline ticket to reach Alaska. Once there, many visitors are overwhelmed by the distances between cities, national parks and attractions. Alaskan prices are the stuff of legends. Still, the Final Frontier is on the bucket list of most adventurous travelers, particularly those enamored of the great outdoors. Those who find the time and money to visit the state rarely regret it.

❯ Alaska

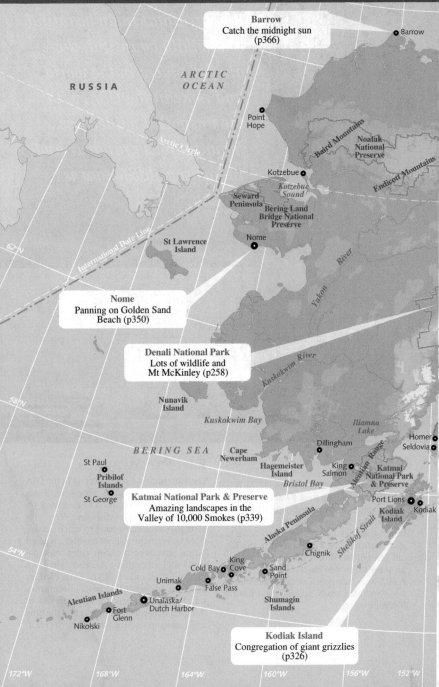

Barrow
Catch the midnight sun
(p366)

Barrow

*ARCTIC
OCEAN*

RUSSIA

Point
Hope

Baird Mountains

*Noatak
National
Preserve*

Endicott Mountains

Kotzebue

*Kotzebue
Sound*

Seward
Peninsula

*Bering Land
Bridge National
Preserve*

St Lawrence
Island

Nome

Yukon River

Nome
Panning on Golden Sand
Beach (p350)

Denali National Park
Lots of wildlife and
Mt McKinley (p258)

Kuskokwim River

Nunavik
Island

Kuskokwim Bay

*Iliamna
Lake*

Dillingham

Homer
Seldovia

BERING SEA

Cape
Newerham

St Paul

Pribilof
Islands

St George

Hagemeister
Island

Bristol Bay

King
Salmon

Aleutian Range

*Katmai
National Park
& Preserve*

Katmai National Park & Preserve
Amazing landscapes in the
Valley of 10,000 Smokes (p339)

Port Lions

Kodiak
Island

Kodiak

Shelikof Strait

Alaska Peninsula

Chignik

Cold Bay

King
Cove

Sand
Point

Unimak

False Pass

Shumagin
Islands

Aleutian Islands

Fort
Glenn

Unalaska/
Dutch Harbor

Nikolski

Kodiak Island
Congregation of giant grizzlies
(p326)

62°N

International Date Line

Arctic Circle

58°N

54°N

172°W   168°W   164°W   160°W   156°W   152°W

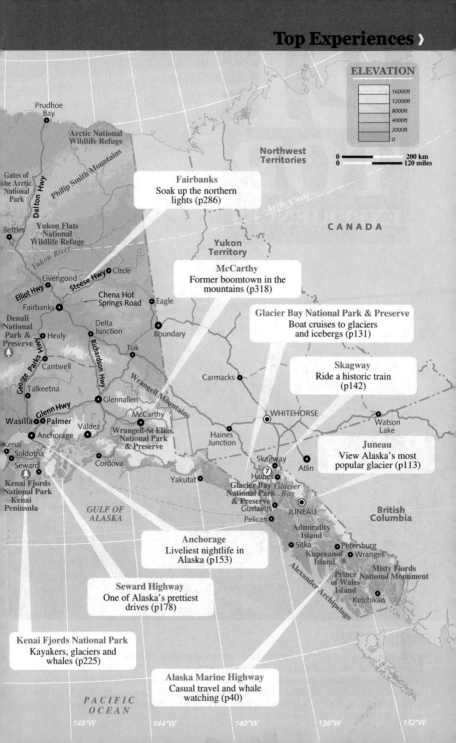

Top Experiences ›

ELEVATION

16000ft
12000ft
8000ft
4000ft
2000ft
0

0   200 km
0   120 miles

Northwest Territories

CANADA

Yukon Territory

Fairbanks
Soak up the northern lights (p286)

McCarthy
Former boomtown in the mountains (p318)

Glacier Bay National Park & Preserve
Boat cruises to glaciers and icebergs (p131)

Skagway
Ride a historic train (p142)

Juneau
View Alaska's most popular glacier (p113)

Anchorage
Liveliest nightlife in Alaska (p153)

Seward Highway
One of Alaska's prettiest drives (p178)

Kenai Fjords National Park
Kayakers, glaciers and whales (p225)

Alaska Marine Highway
Casual travel and whale watching (p40)

Prudhoe Bay

Arctic National Wildlife Refuge

Philip Smith Mountains

Gates of the Arctic National Park

Dalton Hwy

Bettles

Yukon Flats National Wildlife Refuge

Yukon River

Livengood

Circle

Elliot Hwy

Steese Hwy

Fairbanks

Chena Hot Springs Road

Eagle

Denali National Park & Preserve

Healy

Delta Junction

Boundary

Richardson Hwy

Tok

George Parks Hwy

Cantwell

Talkeetna

Glenn Hwy

Glennallen

Wasilla

Palmer

Wrangell Mountains

Carmacks

WHITEHORSE

Valdez

Anchorage

McCarthy

Wrangell-St Elias National Park & Preserve

Kenai

Soldotna

Seward

Cordova

Yakutat

Haines Junction

Watson Lake

Atlin

Kenai Fjords National Park

Kenai Peninsula

GULF OF ALASKA

Haines

Skagway

Glacier Bay National Park & Preserve

Glacier Bay

Gustavus

Pelican

JUNEAU

British Columbia

Admiralty Island

Sitka

Kupreanof Island

Petersburg

Wrangell

Prince of Wales Island

Misty Fiords National Monument

Ketchikan

Alexander Archipelago

PACIFIC OCEAN

148°W   144°W   140°W   136°W   132°W

Arctic Circle

21 TOP EXPERIENCES

Mt McKinley

1 The Athabascans call it the Great One, and few who have seen this 20,320ft bulk of ice and granite would disagree. Seen from the Park Rd of Denali National Park, McKinley (p260) chews up the skyline, dominating an already stunning landscape of tundra fields and polychromatic ridgelines. The mountain inspires a take-no-prisoners kind of awe. Climbers know that feeling well. As the highest peak in North America, McKinley attracts over a thousand alpinists every summer: less than 50% make it to the summit.

Riding the Alaska Ferry to the Aleutian Islands

2 There's no experience like it: three nights on a ferry that services remote Alaskan communities far along the tendril of the Aleutian chain. Commercial fishers with plastic bins full of gear, tourists lugging giant camera lenses searching for birds, and even a family or two returning from a visit to the doctor in Homer are all likely to be your new friends by the time you disembark in Unalaska. In port, more folks pile on just to take off stacks of hamburgers; the '*Tusty*' is the only restaurant most of these towns have.

Bear Viewing

3 Whether it's a black bear galloping across the road or a grizzly snapping salmon from a wild river, spotting your first bear never fails to get your heart racing. You can leave it to chance and hope to see one from your car or – at a distance – on a hike, or head to known bear-watching spots such as Ketchikan (p77), Kodiak Island (p331) or, for the elusive polar bear, even the Alaska Zoo (p160)!

Spotting Whales in Southeast Alaska

4 You're half asleep in the forward observation lounge of an Alaska Marine Highway ferry (see boxed text, p40), when suddenly there's a rush of passengers and an announcement that humpback whales have been spotted. You join the crowd outside and see a pair of black humps and spouts less than a quarter mile away. Suddenly one of the whales breaches, heaving its nearly 50ft-long body almost completely out of the water. It's such an unexpected sight that it has everybody buzzing until the ferry arrives in Wrangell.

RICHARD CUMMINS / LONELY PLANET IMAGES ©

Anchorage Nightlife

5 You've already taken in the Anchorage Museum (p153) and climbed Flattop Mountain (p159) but who can go to bed? It's still light at 11pm and there is a bolt of energy surging through downtown Anchorage. There are pushcart vendors hawking sausages on 4th Ave, horse-drawn carriages picking up passengers at Hotel Captain Cook, frisbees in the air at Delaney Park and a line out the door at Chilkoot Charlie's (p173), where a band must be rocking tonight.

McCarthy Road & McCarthy

6 When all you need is an open road, a funky town, and 13.2 million acres of wilderness to make you happy, the McCarthy Rd (p316) is waiting. Running atop a historic rail line, the road shakes and rattles you through the heart of America's largest national park, Wrangell-St Elias. Sixty miles in, the road dead-ends at a footbridge. On the other side is McCarthy (p318), a former red-light district that's now a handsome old boomtown and the perfect base for exploring this epic landscape of glaciers and reach-for-the-sky alpine ranges.

Icebergs in Glacier Bay

7 Passengers have already seen sea lions, horned puffins and even a pod of orcas when icebergs of all shapes, sizes and shades of blue begin to appear in Glacier Bay National Park & Preserve (p131). By lunchtime the tour boat reaches Margerie Glacier and for the next half hour passengers see and hear the ice fall off the face of the glacier in a performance that is nothing short of dramatic.

MEDIOIMAGES/PHOTODISC ©

Mt Roberts Tramway

8 The Mt Roberts Trail is not overly difficult, but it is steady. Within an hour most people break out of the trees to find stunning views of Juneau and Douglas. Even better is the nearby Mt Roberts Tramway station (p116), a great place to stop after an afternoon of alpine scrambling. For the price of a cold beer – and who couldn't use one after climbing a mountain? – you can ride the tramway back to Juneau.

MARK NEWMAN / LONELY PLANET IMAGES ©

Katmai National Park & Preserve

9 As your floatplane descends to Brooks Camp (p339), you're likely to see massive grizzlies ambling along the shore of Naknek Lake. Head inland less than a mile and you'll be treated to the quintessential photo op: brown bears atop a waterfall, catching salmon leaping upstream. Continue inland to the Valley of 10,000 Smokes – a surreal valley covered in 700ft of ash from a 1912 eruption – where rivers slice canyons that resemble those in Arizona or Utah rather than Alaska.

An Alaskan Salmon Bake

10 The floatplane takes off from a bustling waterfront, crosses three glaciers and 30 minutes later lands at Taku Glacier Lodge (p123). The lodge is classic Alaska: a low-slung log building adorned with moose antlers and bear skins. Staff are grilling king salmon caught just up the Taku River and you can smell the brown-sugar sauce they're basting the filets with. So can the bears. Two black bears pop out of the woods and are chased off before you sit down to a meal of a lifetime.

Salmon bake, Fairbanks, right

NIK WHEELER/CORBIS ©

Flying in a Bush Plane

11 Faster than the state bird (the mosquito), and almost as ubiquitous, the Alaskan bush plane (p421) really can get you there from here. But dropping off adventurers into the remotest corners of the state is only half of what these remarkable craft can do. They can land you on a glacier 7200ft above sea level, circle an area that's a mere ball toss away from the highest peak on the continent, and give a live satellite view of the top of the world.

White Pass & Yukon Route Railroad

12 The historic White Pass & Yukon Route train (p147) is snaking through the mountains when the conductor calls 'Glacier Station'. Only there's no town or depot – there's just a pair of backpackers, and when one waves a red bandana it brings the train to a halting stop. The hikers board the train and it's hard to tell what they are most excited about: the cold beer waiting for them in Skagway or the three days they spent climbing Laughton Glacier.

Watching the Midnight Sun

13 'There are strange things done under the Midnight Sun,' wrote Robert Service during the gold rush days, and it seems as true today as then. With near endless daylight in an all too short summer, Alaskans and visitors alike go into overdrive and push as much sport, travel, partying and adventure into the time they have. To catch the true midnight sun (that is, the sun above the horizon at midnight) head north to the Arctic Circle. In Barrow there are no sunsets at all for 84 days in a row.

The Magic of Mendenhall

14 Somebody says bears have begun feeding on spawning salmon in Steep Creek so you make a late evening run to Mendenhall Glacier (p129). There are no bears when you arrive but there are also no other visitors. So you plop down on the stone wall and take in this river of ice that tumbles out of the mountains and the parade of icebergs that it discharges into the Mendenhall River. Who needs bears when you have ice as beautiful as this?

15 Though Anchorage is now the biggest 'Native village' by population, and Western influences are seen everywhere, the essence of traditional culture lives on in settlements across the state. Most are just a bush-plane flight away, but the best way to begin your understanding is to visit an urban cultural center, run by Alaska Natives and largely for Alaskan Natives. Afterwards, consider a visit to the Iñupiat hub of Barrow for the whaling festival (p368).

Carving totem poles at the Alaska Native Heritage Center in Anchorage, left

Northern Lights

16 Natural spectacles don't get much better than this surreal solar-powered jig. And while a good glossy photo can do the colors of the aurora justice, it simply can't capture the magic of a live performance. Starting in late August, Fairbanks (see boxed text, p294) is the undisputed capital with 200 shows a year. Whistle when the aurora is out, some locals say, and you can influence its movements.

Nome

17 Famed for its connection to the classic Iditarod dogsled race, Nome was also the scene of one of the North's great gold rushes. Today prospectors still work Golden Sand Beach, and almost everywhere you'll find the remains of the boomtown days, including massive dredges and an old railway, rusting their way to oblivion on the tundra. Despite its isolation, Nome (p350) is also the center of three radiating highways that include Arctic scenery, great fishing and the chance to spot herds of musk ox and caribou.

A View of Juneau

18 You begin on S Franklin St, passing gift shops and saloons. Soon the street is climbing steadily, leaving the throngs of cruise-ship passengers behind as you pass within view of the state capitol and the onion domes of a Russian Orthodox church. You come to a pair of long stairways so you climb those as well. Finally you reach the top where there are views of mountains all around. You catch your breath for a moment while gazing at the prettiest state capital in the country.

Denali National Park

19 The centerpiece of this 6-million-acre national park (p258) may be lofty Mt McKinley, the highest peak in North America, but it's the chance to experience nature on its own terms that's the bigger attraction for many. Only one route, the 92-mile Park Rd, runs through Denali, and if there's any place in Alaska you're going to see megafauna roaming free and wild it's here. You don't even need to step off the bus, though that's certainly recommended. Most of Denali is trackless wilderness and discovering it yourself is the way to go.

Riding a Scenic Highway

20 The pull of the open road is forceful in a land as wide open as Alaska, and the highways here are as unique as the state. Make the 126-mile Seward Hwy (p214) a day trip, stopping to catch the bore tide, watch beluga whales or Dall sheep, or simply take a hike. Spin across one of the largest continual wetlands in North America on the Copper River Hwy (p201) or drive onto a ferry that pushes its way through the misty fjords of the Southeast on the Alaska Marine Hwy (p40).

Seward Hwy with Turnagain Pass and Kenai Mountains in the background, left

Kayaking Kenai Fjords National Park

21 As you paddle you might be treated to the thunder of calving tidewater glaciers, the honking and splashing of sea lions at a haul-out, or the cacophony of a kittiwake rookery. Near Peterson Glacier you might find plump harbor seals bobbing on glacier ice, or breaching whales at the mouth of Resurrection Bay. Getting an orca's-eye view of this rich marine ecosystem is just one of the many rewards of propelling yourself through the rocking waters of Kenai Fjords (p225).

need to know

Currency
» US dollars ($)

Language
» English

When To Go

■ Warm to hot summers, mild winters
■ Warm to hot summers, cold winters
■ Mild summers, cold winters
□ Cold climate

Fairbanks
GO Jun-Sep

Denali National Park
GO Jun-Aug

Anchorage
GO Jun-Oct

Homer
GO May-Oct

Juneau
GO May-Aug

Your Daily Budget

Budget less than
$70
» Hostel beds: $20-30 a night

» Large supermarkets have hot items and salad bars

» Hiking is free and trails are everywhere

Midrange
$150-200
» Double room, midrange motel: $150 a night

» Many restaurants feature mid-afternoon specials

» Continental breakfasts are common at motels

Top end, over
$250
» Double room, upscale hotel: $200 plus a night

» Dinner main $25-30 at top restaurants

» Rent a car ($55-70 per day) for out-of-town sights

High Season
(Jun–Aug)

» Solstice festivals and 20-hour days are enjoyed in June

» Salmon runs peak in July & August

» Mountain trails and passes are snow-free in August

» Room demand and prices peak in July

Shoulder
(May & Sep)

» Car rental rates 30% lower than in June

» Southeast Alaska is sunny during May, but rainy in September and October

» Northern lights begin to appear in late September

Low Season
(Jan–Mar)

» Brrrrr! Bundle up, it's cold

» Longer days and warmer temps make late February the best time for winter sports

» Even sourdoughs want to leave Alaska during spring break-up in March

Money
» 24hr ATMs widely available, especially in cities and larger towns.

Visas
» Most international visitors need a visa and should have a multiple entry one if coming from the Lower 48 through Canada.

Mobile Phones
» Coverage is surprisingly good, even in remote areas. Pre-paid SIM cards can be used in some international mobile phones for local calls and voicemail.

Driving
» Drive on the right; steering wheel is on the left side of the car.

Websites
» **Alaska Travel Industry Association** (www.travelalaska. com) Alaska's official tourism site.

» **Alaska Public Lands Information Centers** (www.alaskacenters. gov) Info on parks and activities.

» **Alaska Wilderness Recreation & Tourism Association** (www. awrta.org) Committed to sustainable travel.

» **Alaska Marine Highway** (www. ferryalaska.com) Booking state ferries.

» **Lonely Planet** (www. lonelyplanet.com) Pre-planning, hotel bookings and more.

Exchange Rates

Australia	A$1	$1.04
Canada	C$1	$0.99
Euro Zone	€1	$1.40
Japan	¥100	$1.30
New Zealand	NZ$1	$0.82
UK	£1	$1.60

For current exchange rates see www.xe.com

Important Numbers
Alaska shares a statewide area code of ☑907, except Hyder, which uses ☑250.

Country code	☑1
International dialing	☑011
Emergency	☑911
Road conditions	☑511 or 866-282-7577
Alaska Marine Highway	☑800-642-0066

Arriving in Alaska
» **Ted Stevens Anchorage International Airport** People Mover Bus ($1.75) to downtown hourly from South Terminal; 20-minute taxi ride to city ($25).

» **Alaska Marine Highway terminals** Shuttle vans or taxis greet ferries in the Southeast, except in Juneau.

» **Fairbanks International Airport** Seven MACS buses daily to downtown transit station ($1.50); 15-minute taxi ride to city ($18).

Bears in Alaska
One of the most common concerns for visitors arriving in Alaska, particularly those who plan to head outdoors, is encountering a bear. Alaska has more bears than the rest of the states combined, including more than 30,000 brown bears – 98% of the US population. But the reality is you have a far better chance of having a car accident on the way to Denali National Park than you do being charged by a bear once there. More people are killed by moose in Alaska every year (usually the result of hitting one with a car) than bears, and hypothermia is a far greater danger to those playing outdoors than wildlife. Always practice good bear precaution measures (see p414) but don't let the fear of bears prevent you from enjoying Alaska's great outdoors.

what's new

For this new edition of Alaska, our authors have hunted down the fresh, the transformed, the hot and the happening. These are some of our favorites. For up-to-the-minute recommendations, see lonelyplanet.com/alaska.

Ferries to Gustavus

1 The crown jewel of the cruise ship industry, Glacier Bay National Park just became easier to reach for those not traveling on a big ship. In 2011 the Alaska Marine Hwy added Gustavus as one of its Southeast Alaska ports of call, offering round-trip service from Juneau to the small community that serves as a gateway to one of Alaska's most popular national parks. (p134)

Anchorage Museum, Anchorage

2 Finally, it's finished! A $106 million, 10-year expansion has turned the Anchorage Museum into Alaska's best cultural center and one of its top attractions. (p153)

Triple Lakes Trail, Denali National Park

3 Experience what has become one of the park entrance area's best day hikes on this 8.6-mile trail, opened in 2011. (p264)

Juneau Arts and Culture Center, Juneau

4 You can't miss the new Juneau Arts and Culture Center. Outside is a huge humpback-whale statue; inside, galleries are devoted to local artists and their artwork. (p127)

Fountainhead Antique Auto Museum, Fairbanks

5 You don't have to be a car-lover to appreciate this collection of 70 working antique vehicles – with one-of-a-kind items, vintage clothing and great old photos. (p287)

Alaskan Sojourn Hostel, Skagway

6 Affordable accommodations arrived in Skagway in 2011 with the opening of the Alaskan Sojourn Hostel, an excellent place to stay after hiking the Chilkoot Trail. (p148)

Morris Thompson Cultural & Visitor Center, Fairbanks

7 Three different agencies offer cultural performances, movies and workshops, as well as information on Fairbanks and public lands in the area. (p289)

Saffron Project, Valdez

8 Finally, not just good Indian food, but great Indian food has arrived in Alaska. Here you'll use your hands to eat one of only three sumptuous dishes. (p200)

A Taste of Alaska, Fairbanks

9 Where else can you feast on traditional Athabascan cuisine without being invited to someone's home? (p295)

if you like...

Hiking

Alaska is a hiker's heaven, offering paved urban trails, bush-whacking wilderness routes, and everything in between. You're rarely far from a hiking trail, even in the state's capital or largest city.

Denali National Park Choose from ranger-led hikes or multi-day backcountry jaunts in this massive wilderness. (p258)

Juneau Dozens of trails climb the lush and vertical mountains behind Alaska's capital city. The trail up fog-enshrouded Mt Roberts commences in the heart of Juneau, or you can wander around Mendenhall Glacier. (p117)

Seward Surrounded by mountains and sparkling Resurrection Bay, it's a hiker's paradise, with beach walks, Mt Marathon and the excellent Lost Lake Trail. (p219)

Anchorage Chugach State Park serves as the dramatic backdrop to Alaska's biggest town, and is filled with stellar hiking along the front range; Flattop Mountain is the state's most-summited peak and offers panoramic views of the city below. (p159)

Paddling

Alaska has more coastline than the rest of the US combined, making kayaking a top choice for outdoor pursuits. Hidden coves, calving glaciers, waterfalls, sea-lion rookeries: the list of photographs you could take from a kayak is seemingly endless.

Prince William Sound A massive green cirque full of deep fjords and quiet coves, Prince William Sound covers 15,000 sq miles of wilderness. (p190)

Kenai Fjords National Park Accessible from the road system via Seward, Kenai Fjords National Park offers wildlife encounters and tidewater glaciers packed into its steep fjords. (p225)

Glacier Bay National Park Everywhere you turn, a tidewater glacier seems to be calving; with 11 of them, it's not surprising. Paddle among icebergs as you tour this grand park. (p131)

Misty Fiords National Monument An ethereal landscape, as the name implies: steep mountains and fjords topped by wispy fog, with waterfalls slicing down from beyond sight. It's magical. (p86)

Bear Watching

Most visitors come to Alaska to see bears, and many are lucky enough to walk away with at least one sighting. Increase your odds by visiting one of the spots below.

Katmai National Park & Preserve Brooks Falls is the place to get the quintessential photo of brown bears snapping salmon as they jump up the waterfall. (p339)

Steep Creek The cheapest place to spot bears is at this salmon-viewing platform outside Juneau. Here, brown and black bears come to feast on the spawning fish. (p129)

Denali National Park Brown and black bears patrol the wilderness beneath North America's tallest mountain. (p258)

Kodiak National Wildlife Refuge The world's largest bears live here, some pushing 1500lb. A bear-sighting flight will take you right to them. (p331)

Point Barrow If you're lucky, you just might spot a polar bear here. (p367)

» Sea kayaking in Kenai Fjords National Park (p225)

Glacier Viewing

These massive rivers of ice never fail to amaze when you see them up close. Whether they're calving into water or depositing moraines on land, their mighty presence is surprisingly powerful.

Mendenhall A snowball's throw from Juneau is the Mendenhall Glacier, the city's number one attraction. Its 1.5-mile-wide face is quite photogenic. (p129)

Exit The only glacier in Kenai Fjords National Park that's accessible by road, Exit Glacier is but a mere drip from the massive Harding Ice Field that looms from the mountains above. (p225)

Childs The rumble of calving ice is louder than thunder; you'll hear the glacier's presence before you even see it. Watch out for mini tsunamis created by the calves! (p201)

Matanuska Stop to gawk from the Glenn Hwy, or take a tour and walk on the ice. Either way, you'll be duly impressed by the size of this one. (p311)

Scenic Trips

Answer the call of the open road, stare out a train window at homesteaders' cabins or watch glaciers slide by from the deck of a ferry – all are options on Alaska's unique transportation system.

Copper River Highway An old railroad bed, this gravel road spins across one of the US's largest continual wetlands and ends at thundering Childs Glacier and the Million Dollar Bridge. (p201)

Alaska Marine Highway Drive onto the Alaska Ferry and go where no roads can: through narrow passages lined with foggy mountains, past glaciers and alongside marine life such as whales and Dall porpoises. (p40)

Denali Highway Winding through the foothills of the Alaska Range, the Denali Hwy is full of glacial valleys, alpine tundra, braided rivers and massive glaciers. (p284)

Hurricane Turn This two-car train runs from Talkeetna to Hurricane, servicing homesteaders, anglers and adventurers along rivers and valleys inaccessible by road. (p176)

Fishing

Hooking a big one is a major reason why folks visit Alaska, and you can take your pick from salmon, halibut, trout and more.

Russian & Kenai Rivers This is where 'combat fishing' gets its name: hundreds of fisherfolk yelling 'fish on!' and trying not to hook each other during the height of the red salmon run. (p229)

Ship Creek Watch massive salmon run right through downtown Anchorage and get shoulder to shoulder with anglers who are pulling in kings, with the city skyline as a backdrop. (p153)

Homer Take a halibut charter and bring home hundreds of pounds – of one fish. Don't forget to buy your Halibut Derby ticket, though. (p242)

Kodiak Alaska's largest fishing fleet resides here. Head out to remote salmon streams or charter a halibut boat – the limit here is twice what it is elsewhere! (p327)

If you like... Native art and heritage, the new Morris Thompson Cultural & Visitor Center in Fairbanks offers classes, demonstrations and even the chance to dine on Athabascan food. (p289)

River Running

Running Alaska's rivers is a great way to travel and is becoming more and more popular as packrafting takes off. Match your skill (and adrenaline) levels with guided trips or, if you're experienced, head out on an expedition.

Nizina River in Wrangell-St Elias National Park, the highlight of this float is cruising through the vertical-walled Nizina Canyon. (p321)

Denali National Park The Nenana River is the most-rafted river in Alaska, with wet-suited tourists bobbing through a scenic canyon. (p267)

Talkeetna River A placid, scenic float for the mellower folks, this one has forget-me-not views of Mt McKinley on a clear day. (p277)

Kenai River A shade of fluorescent glacial blue, the Kenai makes for a great float past anglers – and maybe a bear or two – on the Kenai Peninsula. (p228)

Whale Watching

Catching a whale breach never fails to make a crowd gasp, but seeing belugas bubble to the surface can be equally exciting. Check out the following places for a chance to spot these amazing marine mammals.

Glacier Bay NatiLEFTonal Park & Preserve Glaciers aren't the only draw: humpback whales performing acrobatics often steal the show on boat tours of Glacier Bay. (p133)

Kenai Fjords National Park Another spot where a boat tour will take you out into whale country. You might see humpbacks, orcas or gray whales. (p225)

Sitka You can choose from more than a dozen operators that will show you whales and other marine life; one company has a glass-bottomed boat. Head to Whale Park (just 4 miles out of town) in the fall for a cheaper whale-watching experience. (p109)

Camping

Peering from a tent out to a view of alpine flowers, glacial rivers, or even wildlife is a great way to sleep on a budget. Alaska is full of campsites: public, private, free and nonestablished – take your pick.

Wonder Lake At mile 84 of the Park Rd in Denali National Park, Wonder Lake reflects Mt McKinley on its surface. If the mountain is out, you'll never want to get back in your tent. (p268)

Golden Sands Beach Stretching a mile outside Nome, this sandy beach is an anomaly in Alaska. Pitch your tent next to miners hoping for a golden nugget. (p351)

Brooks Camp In Katmai National Park & Preserve – probably the only place your tent will be behind an electric fence, thanks to all those grizzlies running around. (p339)

Seward Highway This 126-mile scenic road offers more than a half dozen campgrounds within a few miles of the highway, and all are framed by the Chugach Mountains. (p214)

month by month

March

As the sun emerges from hibernation, so do Alaskans. Though the temperatures are still quite low, the sun gives off a welcome hint of warmth and brightness.

Iditarod

Cheer on the dogs and their mushers as they slice by in 'the last great race.' The ceremonial start is in downtown Anchorage, while the official race is from Wasilla or Willow all the way to Nome. (www.iditarod.com; p383)

April

What most folks call spring is 'breakup' in Alaska, and April is full-on breakup season. The air smells of water as snow and ice melt, and the energy level of Alaskans notably increases.

Alaska Folk Festival

Musicians from across Alaska and the Yukon descend on Juneau for a week of music and dancing. Who cares if it rains every day? Get wet and dance away. (www.akfolkfest.org; p122)

May

May is shoulder season and a great month to visit, with discounts on tickets, tours and accommodations. The weather's cool and trails are usually snow-covered, but the days are long and the crowds are thin.

Copper River Delta Shorebird Festival

Birders invade Cordova for four days of workshops, lectures, dinners and exhibitions, all in celebration of some of the greatest migrations in Alaska across one of North America's largest continual wetlands. (www.cordovachamber.com; p205).

Kachemak Bay Shorebird Festival

If the birders aren't gathering in Cordova, then they're nesting in Homer, enjoying workshops, field trips and birding presentations by keynote speakers. It wouldn't be Homer without an arts and crafts fair too. (www.homeralaska.org; p238).

Little Norway Festival

Be a Viking for a day in Petersburg and feast on seafood at night at one of Southeast Alaska's oldest festivals. There are parades and pageants, and the entire town appears to be dressed in Norwegian folk costumes. (www.petersburg.org; p101).

Kodiak Crab Festival

Celebrated since 1958, this festival includes survival-suit racers and seafood cook-offs. Grab a plate and dig in to as much of everyone's favorite shellfish as you can fit in your belly. (www.kodiak.org; p331).

(above and below) Alaska State Fair, Palmer (p24)

June

June marks the height of tourist season in Alaska. The longest day of the year is celebrated in solstice festivities across the state, and salmon begin their runs from sea to spawning grounds.

☆ Sitka Summer Music Festival

Since 1972 this festival has been a most civilized gathering, with chamber music, concerts and lots of culture by the sea in beautiful Sitka. You'll need to book tickets in advance. (www.sitkamusicfestival.org; p110)

Moose Pass Summer Solstice Festival

Join in some small-town fun and games, not to mention a short parade and major boogying, down on the Kenai Peninsula in tiny Moose Pass. (www.moosepass.net; p217)

Midnight Sun Festival

Celebrate summer solstice in Fairbanks with music from 40 bands on three stages, the Yukon 800 Power Boat Races and a baseball game that starts at midnight but doesn't need any lights. Held on the Sunday before Solstice. (www.explorefairbanks.com; p293)

Nalukataq (Whaling Festival)

Join Barrow residents in late June as they celebrate and give thanks for another successful whaling season with dancing and blanket tosses. You'll even get to taste your first *muktuk* (whale skin and blubber). (www.cityofbarrow.org; p368).

July

The days are still long, the mountains are green, salmon streams are full and everyone is in good spirits. Not surprisingly, this month is the busiest for festivals.

Fourth of July in Skagway

Soapy Smith, Alaska's most lovable scoundrel, headed up Skagway's first parade in 1898 and this small town has been staging a great one ever since. It not only includes an egg toss – it holds the Guinness World Record for it. (www.skag way.com; p147)

Fourth of July in Juneau

Head to the docks with Juneau residents after the cruise ships have slipped away and dress up in your Mardi Gras finest; build a giant sand castle on Douglas Island, or simply enjoy the colorful parade. (www.traveljuneau.com; p122).

Mt Marathon Race

Take in the exhausting Fourth of July 3.1-mile run up Seward's 3022ft-high peak, which started in 1915. Join the fans as they crane their necks at the racers, many of whom make it up and back in well under an hour. (p222).

Girdwood Forest Fair

Girdwood's magical arts fair is held in the rain forest over Fourth of July weekend. Come twirl Hula-Hoops to live music, shop for local art and relax in a rainy beer garden by a glacial stream. (www. girdwoodforestfair.com; (p178)

Southeast Alaska State Fair

Held in late July in Haines, this unique fair hosts a lively Fiddler Contest as well as the Most Lovable Dog Competition – but make sure you don't miss the pig races. (www.seakfair.org; p138)

August

Summer is in full swing at the beginning of August, but night and chillier temperatures return at the end. Berries are ripe, produce is ready for harvest and you might even spot the northern lights.

Blueberry Festival

Blue tongues aren't the only thing you'll see here: slug races, pie-eating contests, a parade and even a poetry slam are all events held at this celebration of everyone's favorite berry. (www. visit-ketchikan.com; p80)

Gold Rush Days

Five days of bed races, canoe races, dances, fish feeds and floozy costumes in Valdez, plus a boat race for dinghies made of cardboard and duct tape. Oh, and a little gold rush history

too. (www.valdgoldrushdays. org; p197)

Alaska State Fair

Palmer's showcase for 100lb cabbages and the best Spam recipes in the state, plus live music, logging shows and deep-fried Twinkies. It runs from late August through the first weekend in September. (www.alaskastate-fair.org; p188).

September

September is another shoulder month for tourism, with discounted prices and fewer crowds. Night is full-on here, but the hiking is still good and you have a good chance of seeing the northern lights.

Kodiak State Fair & Rodeo

Buckin' broncos and wrestling steers for the cowboys and cowgirls; for the non-cowboys, there are pie-eating and halibut-cleaning contests and plenty of other fair amusements. (www. kodiak.org; p331)

Seward Music & Arts Festival

This family-friendly festival incorporates artists and more than 20 musical acts and theatrical companies, including circus lessons for the kiddos. Every year the town gets together and paints a mural; come help them. (www.sewardfestival. com; p222).

October

In most of Alaska, winter is on. Winds blow the last of the leaves from trees, snow caps the mountains and days are noticeably long. That doesn't keep Alaskans from having a good time, though.

Great Alaska Beer Train

All aboard! The *Microbrew Express* is a special run of the Alaska Railroad from Anchorage to Portage; it's loaded with happy passengers sipping the best beer made in Alaska and taking in some of Alaska's finest scenery. (www.alaskarailroad.com).

Alaska Day Festival

Sitka dresses the part in celebrating the actual transfer ceremony when the United States purchased Alaska from Russia in 1867. You'll find community dances, a kayak race and an afternoon tea for kids to learn about life in 1867. (www.sitka.org; p110)

November

Bundle up and put on your bunny boots. You won't find many tourists here this time of year, but the nightlife is vibrant in larger towns and cities and there's a palpable sense of community.

Whalefest!

It's whales galore in Sitka – so many you don't even need a boat to view them. This scientific gathering will teach you everything you need to know about these amazing marine mammals. (www.sitkawhalefest.org; p110)

Alaska Bald Eagle Festival

This is the largest gathering of bald eagles in the world. There are more birds in Haines than tourists at this festival, when more than 3000 eagles gather along the Chilkat River. Simply spectacular. (www.baldeaglefestival.org; p140)

itineraries

Whether you've got six days or 60, these itineraries provide a starting point for the trip of a lifetime. Want more inspiration? Head online to lonelyplanet.com/thorntree to chat with other travelers.

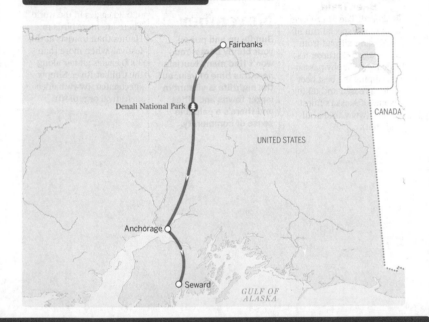

Five Days
Fairbanks to Seward by Train

> This land-based itinerary takes advantage of the scenic Alaska Railroad corridor. Start out in **Fairbanks**, the northernmost point of the Alaska Railroad, where you can spend a day exploring the museums and a night appreciating that the sun barely sets. Hop on the train to **Denali National Park**, and take a good day hike on the new Triple Lakes Trail. The next morning, take the extraordinarily scenic, eight-hour ride to **Anchorage**; along this stretch the tracks leave the road and probe into roadless wilderness, paralleling rivers instead of the highway. Spend two nights and one full day in Anchorage, taking advantage of its surprisingly sophisticated shopping and dining scene. Check out the world-class Anchorage Museum, or work off your salmon belly with a bike ride along the Coastal Trail. Then hop aboard for another scenic journey to **Seward**. Again, the train deviates from the road and takes you 10 miles into the Chugach Mountains. Seward is the southern terminus of the railroad, ending in spectacular Resurrection Bay. Be sure to take a tour of Kenai Fjords National Park to spot sea lions, sea otters and whales.

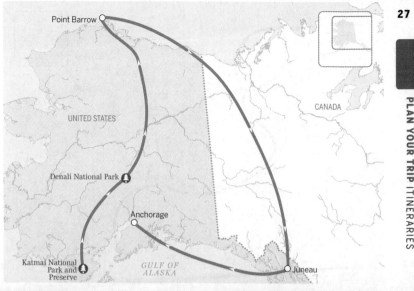

10 Days
Katmai National Park to Anchorage

One of the fastest growing activities in Alaska is bear viewing. There's no shortage of bears here, nor tourists wanting to see one – preferably catching and devouring a salmon. Make it to at least one of the following destinations and you're likely to spot one.

One of the most famous bear-viewing sites is Brooks Falls in **Katmai National Park & Preserve**. Here is where you'll catch the ultimate Alaskan photo: a dozen grizzlies perched on the edge of a waterfall, snapping salmon out of the air as they leap upstream. There are so many bears here in July, in fact, that the moment you step out of your float plane at Brooks Camp you are ushered into the National Parks office for a mandatory bear orientation, likely passing a grizzly or two ambling up the shore of Naknek Lake on your way.

A bit more accessible than Katmai National Park & Preserve is **Denali National Park**, which sits on the road system. Here you can jump onto a park shuttle bus and press your face against the glass as you scour the sweeping landscape for both brown and black bears. Though you're likely to spot one of these legendary beasts, you'll probably also catch sight of caribou and moose.

Keep heading north to **Point Barrow** for a chance to spot a polar bear at the top of the world. Photographing one of these massive white creatures is an experience few will ever have. A guided tour will take you out of town where you might also catch sight of a walrus.

For a more urban experience, fly to **Juneau**. The most affordable bear watching is found here, since you don't have to travel far from the city to catch brown and black bears feasting on salmon at the capital city's Steep Creek near Mendenhall Glacier.

Finally, if you haven't had the luck to be in the right spot at the right time, you can always head to **Anchorage** and see, all in the same hour, a black bear, a grizzly and the magnificent polar bear at the Alaska Zoo. It's not quite as cool as seeing a bear in its natural setting, but you can get much closer to them, and it's a lot safer.

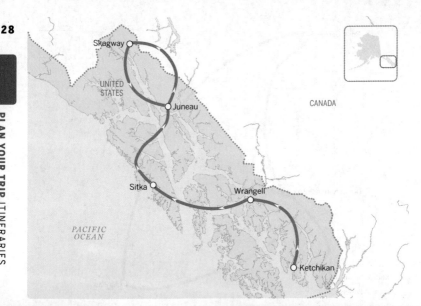

Two Weeks
Cruising Southeast Alaska

One of the most exciting trips is taking the Alaska Marine Highway from Bellingham, WA, to Skagway. It's an easy-to-plan journey through a scenic region of Alaska, although you should reserve space on the Alaska Marine Highway ferry if you want a cabin. Board the ferry in Bellingham and enjoy the coastal scenery of Canada – including staffed lighthouses – for a couple of days before disembarking for two days at **Ketchikan**. If it's not raining spend a day climbing Deer Mountain and enjoy lunch on the peak with panoramic views of the Inside Passage. Head out to Totem Bight State Park to see totems and a colorful community house. If it *is* raining, book a flightseeing tour of Misty Fiords National Monument, an almost mystical landscape of steep fjords and waterfalls running off foggy green mountains.

Catch the ferry to **Wrangell** and take a wild jet-boat tour up the Stikine River, North America's fastest navigable river. Be sure to visit Petroglyph Beach, where ancient rock carvings of faces and spirals emerge at low tide. Continue to **Sitka** on the ferry for an afternoon at Sitka National Historical Park and another on a whale-watching cruise.

Head to **Juneau** and sign up for a walk across the beautiful ice of Mendenhall Glacier. Top that off the next day by climbing Mt Roberts and then having a beer (or two) before taking the Mt Roberts tramway back to the city. In the evening enjoy one of the city's salmon bakes and indulge in the tourist trap that is the Red Dog Saloon.

Climb aboard high-speed catamaran MV *Fairweather* for two days in **Skagway**, the historic start of the Klondike Gold Rush. Board the White Pass & Yukon Route Railroad for a day trip to Lake Bennett and in the evening catch the rollicking *Days of '98 Show*. Take a hike in the Dewey Lakes Trail System, which originates right in town. After Skagway you'll need to backtrack to Juneau if you want to fly home. Spend your final day flying through the rainforest like an eagle on one of the city's two ziplines. Fly home from here or extend your trip and take the state ferry back.

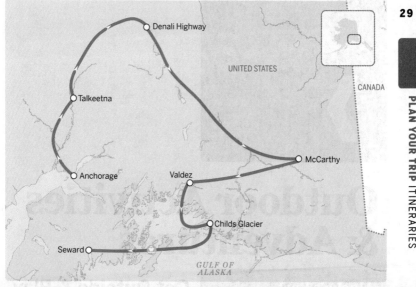

Two Weeks
Road Tripping

Driving the very open roads in such a dramatic land is what road tripping is all about. Get yourself a rental vehicle and crank up your tunes: you're in for an amazing ride. Fly into **Anchorage** and pick up your car (make sure you book well in advance). Stop at one of the city's large supermarkets, stock up with road-trip goodies and the local brew and then beat it out of town.

Head north out of town and take the George Parks Hwy through Wasilla. Turn at the Talkeetna Spur Rd and hang out in **Talkeetna**, a laid-back climbers' town. Spend the day on the last flagstop train in the US, the *Hurricane Turn*. In the evening, be sure to check out the antics at the historic Fairview Inn's bar.

Head back to the Parks Hwy and continue north to the **Denali Highway**. Open only in summer, this 135-mile dirt road traverses the foothills of the Alaska Range. Take your time; the road is rough and the scenery stunning. Pitch a tent along the road wherever it feels right – preferably next to a rushing stream – and then continue heading east in the morning until you hit the Richardson Hwy.

Travel south and then follow the McCarthy Rd east to the Kennecott River, 127 miles from Glennallen. Spend the next day exploring the quaint village of **McCarthy** and the amazing mining ruins at Kennecott. Return to the Richardson Hwy and head south.

Continue into **Valdez** and stay an extra day to splurge on a Columbia Glacier cruise. Drive onto the Alaska Marine Highway ferry (reserve this in advance) and sail across Prince William Sound to Cordova. Drive the amazing Copper River Hwy, which runs across one of the largest continual wetlands in North America, out to **Childs Glacier** and the Million Dollar Bridge. Spend a night camped across the river from the glacier, listening to the boom of calving ice. Drive back into Cordova and onto the ferry to Whittier. On the same day drive 90 miles south to **Seward**, passing through scenic Turnagain Pass. Stay two days in Seward; book a boat tour or kayak in Resurrection Bay, but on the afternoon of the second day hightail it back to Anchorage (127 miles) to turn in your car before the dealer closes.

Outdoor Activities & Adventures

Alaska's Best Campgrounds

Blueberry Lake State Recreation Site (p315)Ten sites in a scenic alpine setting north of Valdez.

Fort Abercrombie State Historical Park (p331) Near Kodiak; wooded sites, interesting WWII artifacts and intriguing tidal pools to explore.

Marion Creek Campground (p363) BLM facility along the Dalton Hwy, north of the Arctic Circle, with stunning views of the Brooks Range.

Mendenhall Lake Campground (p123) Near Juneau, a beautiful USFS campground with glacial views from some of the sites.

Ninilchik View State Campground (p238) Lots of sites overlooking Cook Inlet, Old Ninilchik and great clamming beaches.

Get Outside & Play

You didn't come all this way to sit in a theater watching three acts of *Hamlet*. Or to stand in a gallery staring at an impressionist painting of lord-knows-what. Or even to spend an evening consuming a six-course meal featuring more silverware and dishes than the last hostel you stayed at.

What unites all Alaskans, young and old, tall and small, is a desire to be out in the wilderness. You don't have to scale Mt McKinley to enjoy the Alaskan outdoors – there are plenty of ways to leave the pavement behind. Alaska is, after all, the USA's biggest playground. Now go outside and play!

Backpacking

Although much of Alaska's wilderness is hard to reach for visitors with limited time or small budgets, there are a number of trails throughout the state that serve as excellent avenues into the wilderness for unguided, multiday treks.

Denali National Park (p260) is the best-known destination for backpackers, but highlighted throughout the regional chapters are seven more trails well suited to overnight adventures:

» **Chilkoot Trail** (p52)

» **Petersburg Lake Trail** (p53)

» **Iditarod National Historic Trail** (p58)

Double-check your equipment before leaving home. Most towns in Alaska will have at least one store with a wall full of camping supplies, but prices will be high and by mid- to late summer certain items will be out of stock.

Absolutely essential equipment...

☐ a backpack

☐ a lightweight tent with rain fly and bug netting

☐ a three-season sleeping bag with a temperature range of -10°F to 40°F (-23°C to 4°C)

☐ sturdy, high-top hiking boots

☐ a water filter

☐ a compass or GPS unit

In your clothing bag...

☐ mittens

☐ a hat

☐ a fleece pullover (it can get cold at night, even in July)

☐ rain gear – both pants and parka (because it will definitely rain)

Equipment to consider packing...

☐ a self-inflating sleeping pad

☐ a reliable backpacker's stove

☐ a small cooking kit

☐ sports sandals for a change of footwear at night or for fording rivers and streams

» **Resurrection Pass Trail** (p61)

» **Dixie Pass Route** (p65)

» **Chena Dome Trail** (p66)

» **Pinnell Mountain Trail** (p67)

Cabins

Every agency overseeing public land in Alaska – from the Bureau of Land Management (BLM) and the National Park Service (NPS) to the Alaska Division of Parks – maintains rustic cabins in remote areas. The cabins are not expensive ($25 to $50 per night), but they are not easy to reach, either. Most of them are accessed via a floatplane charter. Others can be reached on foot, by boat or by paddling. By arranging a charter and reserving a cabin in advance you can sneak away into the wilderness, with half the effort and time that backpackers or paddlers put in, and reach remote corners of Alaska.

» **Tongass National Forest** (www.fs.fed. us/r10/tongass/cabins/cabins.shtml) and **Chugach National Forest** (www.fs.fed.us/ r10/chugach/cabins/index.html) have the most cabins available – almost 190 between them.

» Alaska Division of Parks has more than 40 cabins scattered from Point Bridget State Park near Juneau to Chena River State Recreation Area east of Fairbanks. Get a list of cabins and reserve them up to six months in advance through the **DNR Public Information Center** (☎269-8400; www.alaskastateparks.org).

» The BLM manages 12 cabins in the **White Mountain National Recreation Area** (☎474-2251, 800-437-7021; www.ak.blm.gov; per night $20-25), north of Fairbanks.

» The US Fish & Wildlife Service has seven cabins on Kodiak Island in the **Kodiak National Wildlife Refuge** (☎487-2600; kodiak.fws.gov; per night $45).

» The National Park Service maintains three cabins in **Kenai Fjords National Park** (☎224-3175; www.nps.gov/kefj; per night $50), which are reached by floatplane or water taxi and are reserved through the **Alaska Public Lands Information Center** (☎271-2737).

Camping

Camping isn't just cheap lodging in Alaska; it's a reason to be outside, soaking up the scenery while watching a freshly caught

BACKCOUNTRY CONDUCT

» Check in with the nearest USFS office or NPS headquarters before entering the backcountry. By telling them your intentions, you'll get peace of mind from knowing that someone is aware you're out there.

» Take time to check out the area before unpacking your gear. Avoid animal trails (whether the tracks be moose or bear), areas with bear scat, and berry patches with ripe fruit.

» Throughout much of Alaska, river bars and old glacier outwashes are the best places to pitch a tent. If you come along the coast stay well above the high-tide line – the last ridge of seaweed and debris on the shore – to avoid waking up with saltwater flooding your tent.

» Do not harass wildlife. Avoid startling an animal, as it will most likely flee, leaving you with a short and forgettable encounter. Never attempt to feed wildlife; it is not healthy for you or the animal.

» Use biodegradable soap and do all washing away from water sources.

» Finally, be thoughtful when in the wilderness. It is a delicate environment. Carry in your supplies and carry out your trash. Never litter or leave garbage smoldering in a fire pit. In short, leave no evidence of your stay. Only then can an area remain a true wilderness.

trout sizzling on your campfire. Camping is so popular that many communities have set up facilities on the edge of town.

But the best camping is away from towns at the public campgrounds operated by the Alaska Division of Parks, the US Forest Service (USFS) or the BLM in northern Alaska. The state park system maintains the most – more than 70 rustic campgrounds scattered throughout Alaska – with fees from free to $15 a night in the more popular ones. The majority do not take reservations.

For more on commercial campgrounds see p411.

Cycling

With its long days, cool temperatures, a lack of interstate highways and a growing number of paved paths around cities such as Anchorage, Juneau and Fairbanks, Alaska can be a land of opportunity for road cyclists.

Cyclists do have to take some extra precautions in Alaska. Other than cities and major towns, comprehensively equipped bike shops are rare, so it's wise to carry not only metric tools but also a tube-patch repair kit, brake cables, spokes and brake pads. Due to high rainfall, especially in the Southeast, waterproof saddle bags are useful, as are tire fenders. Rain gear, mittens and a woolen hat are also necessities.

Some roads do not have much of a shoulder, so cyclists should utilize the sunlight hours to pedal when traffic is light in such areas. It is not necessary to carry a lot of food, as you can easily restock on all major roads.

Good sources for cycling maps and news on events are Alaska's three major bike clubs:

» **Arctic Bicycle Club** (☎566-0177; www. arcticbike.org) In Anchorage.

» **Juneau Freewheelers** (www. juneaufreewheelers.com)

» **Fairbanks Cycle Club** (☎459-8008; www. fairbankscycleclub.org)

Fishing

Alaska has a fish-every-cast reputation, but serious anglers visiting the state carefully research the areas they plan to fish and arrive equipped with the right gear and tackle. They often pay for guides or book a room at remote camps or lodges where rivers are not fished out by every passing motorist.

Those planning wilderness trips should pack a backpacking rod that breaks down into four or five sections and is equipped with a light reel. In the Southeast and Southcentral backcountry, anglers can target cutthroat trout, rainbow trout and Dolly Varden. Further north, especially around Fairbanks, they can catch grayling, with its sail-like dorsal fin, and arctic char. In August, salmon seem to be everywhere.

An open-face spinning reel with light line – something in the 4lb to 6lb range – and a small selection of spinners and spoons will allow you to fish a wide range of waters, from streams and rivers to lakes. For fly-fishing, a 6-weight rod with a matching floating line or sinking tip is well suited for Dolly Vardens, rainbows and grayling. For salmon, a 7-weight or 8-weight rod and line are better choices. You can purchase the locally used lures and flies after you arrive.

You will also need a fishing license. A non-resident's fishing license costs $145 a year, but you can purchase a seven-/14-day license for $55/80. Every bait shop in the state sells them; you can also purchase one online through the **Alaska Department of Fish & Game** (☑465-4100; www.state.ak.us/adfg).

Many visiting anglers invest in a fishing charter. Joining a captain on his boat is $170 to $250 per person for four to six hours on the water, but local knowledge is the best investment you can make to put a fish on your line. Communities with large fleets of charter captains include Homer, Seward, Petersburg, Kodiak and Ketchikan, with halibut most in demand among visitors. Head to Soldotna to land a 50lb king salmon in the Kenai River.

If money is no object, fly-in fishing adventures are available from cities such as Anchorage and Fairbanks. These outings use small charter planes to reach wilderness lakes and rivers for a day of salmon and steelhead fishing. It's an expensive day trip – often $400 to $500 per person – but the fishing is legendary, sometimes even a catch per cast.

Glacier Trekking & Ice Climbing

The glaciers may be melting, but glacier trekking is still a popular activity in Alaska. Most first-time glacier trekkers envision a slick and slippery surface, but in reality the ice is very rough and embedded with gravel and rocks to provide surprisingly good traction. There are several roadside-accessible glaciers, the **Matanuska Glacier** (p313) being the best known, where you can walk a short distance on the gravel-laced ice in ordinary hiking boots.

For a more interesting afternoon, hook up with a guiding company that offers glacier treks. On such outings you'll be outfitted with a helmet, crampons and an ice axe and roped up for several miles of walking on the frozen surface. The beauty of the ice, sprinkled with azure pools, sliced by deep blue crevasses and surrounded by bare rock mountains, is stunning.

Glaciers are also the main destination in Alaska for ice climbers in the summer. Icefalls and ice faces, where the glacier makes its biggest vertical descents out of the mountains, are where climbers strap on crampons and helmets and load themselves with ropes, ice screws and anchors. Inexperienced climbers should sign up for a one-day ice climbing lesson, in which guides lead you to an ice fall and then teach you about cramponing, front pointing and the use of ice tools.

Outfitters that offer glacier trekking or ice climbing excursions:

» **Above & Beyond Alaska** of Juneau leads a seven-hour glacier trek and climb on Mendenhall Glacier. (p129)

» **St Elias Alpine Guides** is based in tiny McCarthy and offers half- and full-day treks on Root Glacier as well as ice climbing. (p321)

» **MICA Guides** of Sutton has a three-hour glacier walk ($45) and a harder icefall trek ($70) on the Matanuska Glacier. (p313)

» **Ascending Path** of Girdwood offers Midnight Sun Glacier Hikes that start at 8pm and uses Byron Glacier for its ice-climbing outings. (p180)

Mountain Biking

The mountain bike's durable design, knobby tires and suspension system may have been invented in California, but it was made for Alaska. With such a bike you can explore an almost endless number of dirt roads, miner's two-tracks and even hiking trails that you would never consider with a road bike. For many, the versatile mountain bike is the key and 4WD tracks are the avenue to escaping roads and RVers for the scenery and wildlife of the backcountry.

Just remember to pick your route carefully before heading out. Make sure the length of the route and the ruggedness of the terrain are within your capability, and that you have appropriate equipment. Always pack a lightweight, wind-and-water-resistant jacket and an insulating layer because the weather changes quickly in Alaska and so can the terrain. Even when renting a bike, make sure you can repair a flat with the proper spare tube and tools. Water, best carried in a hydration pack, is a must, as is energy food.

There is much mountain-bike activity around Anchorage, which has several places to rent bikes (p157). Within the city, mountain bikers head to Kincaid Park (p157) and

SEEING ALASKA FROM ABOVE

There isn't a bush pilot in Alaska who wouldn't be willing to take you on a flightseeing trip. Most flightseeing is done in small planes, holding three to five passengers, with the tour lasting, on the average, one to two hours. A much smaller number are given in helicopters due to the high costs of operating the aircraft. With the rising price of fuel, expect to pay anywhere from $250 to $350 per person for a one-hour flight.

The following are some of Alaska's most spectacular flights:

» **Glacier Bay National Park** From Haines, glaciers, Fairweather Mountains, maybe a whale or two.(p138)

» **Misty Fiords National Monument** Two-hour flights that include a rainforest walk in this wilderness near Ketchikan. (p87)

» **Mt McKinley** The bush pilots who fly climbers to the mountain will also take visitors around it for Alaska's most spectacular flightseeing tour. (p277)

» **Wrangell-St Elias National Park** From McCarthy you can view the stunning peaks and glaciers in the USA's largest national park. (p321)

Far North Bicentennial Park (p157) for their fill of rugged single track. In surrounding Chugach State Park, the Powerline Pass Trail is an 11-mile round-trip adventure into the mountains, while the popular 13.5-mile Lakeside Trail (p185) is a leisurely ride that skirts Eklutna Lake.

The Resurrection Pass, Russian River and Johnson Pass Trails in the Chugach National Forest have become popular among off-road cyclists in the Kenai Peninsula. North of Anchorage, Hatcher Pass (p187) is a haven of mountain-biking activity, with riders following Archangel Rd (also known as the Archangel Valley), Craggie Creek Trail and Gold Mint Trail to glaciers and old mines in the Talkeetna Mountains.

The most popular area for riders in Fairbanks is the Chena River State Recreation Area (p298), while in Juneau mountain bikers head to Perseverance Trail (p78) near downtown, and Montana Creek Trail (p119) out Egan Dr near the Mendenhall Glacier.

If you are able to travel with equipment on your bike (sleeping bag, food and tent), you can partake in a variety of overnight trips or longer bicycle journeys. The 92-mile Denali Park Rd (p266) is off-limits to vehicles, but you can explore it on a mountain bike. Another excellent dirt road for such an adventure is the 135-mile Denali Hwy (p284) from Paxson to Cantwell.

Paddling

The paddle is a way of life in Alaska, and every region has either canoeing or kayaking opportunities or both. Both the Southeast and Prince William Sound offer spectacular kayaking opportunities, while Fairbanks and Arctic Alaska are home to some of the best wilderness canoe adventures in the country.

Great paddling adventures:

» **Misty Fiords National Monument** A kayak adventure near Ketchikan. (p54)

» **Tracy Arm Kayak Route** South of Juneau. (p55)

» **Swan Lake Canoe Route** In the Kenai Peninsula. (p63)

» **Savonoski Loop** In Katmai National Park. (p69)

» **Beaver Creek** (p68)

Blue-water Paddling

In Alaska, 'blue water' refers to the coastal areas of the state, which are characterized by extreme tidal fluctuations, cold water and the possibility of high winds and waves. Throughout Southeast and Southcentral Alaska, the open canoe is replaced with the kayak, and blue-water paddling is the means of escape into coastal areas such as Muir Inlet (p131) in Glacier Bay National Park or Tracy Arm-Fords Terror (p55), south of Juneau.

Tidal fluctuations are the main concern in blue-water areas. Paddlers should always pull their boats above the high-tide mark and keep a tide book in the same pouch as their topographic map. Cold coastal water, rarely above 45°F (7°C) in the summer, makes capsizing worse than unpleasant. With a life jacket, survival time in the water is less than two hours; without one there is no time. If your kayak flips, stay with the boat and attempt to right it and crawl back in. Trying to swim to shore in Arctic water is risky at best.

Framed backpacks are useless in kayaks; gear is best stowed in duffel bags or small day packs. Carry a large supply of assorted plastic bags, including several garbage bags. All gear, especially sleeping bags and clothing, should be stowed in plastic bags, as water tends to seep in even when you seal yourself in with a cockpit skirt. Over-the-calf rubber boots are the best footwear for getting in and out of kayaks.

White-water Paddling

Throughout Alaska's history, rivers have been travel routes through the rugged terrain. Many rivers can be paddled in canoes; others, due to extensive stretches of white water, are better handled in rafts or kayaks.

Alaska's rivers vary, but they share characteristics not found on many rivers in the Lower 48: water levels tend to change rapidly, while many rivers are heavily braided and boulder-strewn. Take care in picking out the right channel to avoid spending most of the day pulling your boat off gravel. You can survive flipping your canoe in an Alaskan river, but you'll definitely want a plan of action if you do.

Much of the equipment for white-water canoeists is the same as it is for blue-water paddlers. Tie everything into the canoe; you never know when you might hit a whirlpool or a series of standing waves. Wear a life jacket at all times. Many paddlers stock their life jacket with insect repellent, waterproof matches and other survival gear in case they flip and get separated from their boat.

Rafting

Both white-water and expedition rafting are extremely popular in Alaska. The Nenana River just outside of Denali National Park is a mecca for white-water thrill-seekers with companies like the **Denali Outdoor Center** (p267) offering daily raft trips through the summer through Class IV rapids. The season climaxes on the second weekend after the Fourth of July holiday, when the Nenana River Wildwater Festival is staged as two days of river races and a wild-water rodeo. Other rivers that attract white-water enthusiasts include the Lowe River near Valdez (p196), Sixmile Creek (p216) with its Class V rapids near Hope, the Matanuska River (p313) east of Palmer, and Kennicott River near Kennecott (p321).

Expedition rafting tours are multiday floats through wilderness areas. While some white water may be encountered, the raft is mainly used as transportation. Thanks partly to publicity created by the oil-drilling controversy, the Arctic National Wildlife Refuge (ANWR) is very popular for people seeking this type of remote experience. But it's not cheap. Arctic Treks (p51), for example, offers a 10-day float through the ANWR of the Hulahula River costing $4400 per person. The Tatshenshini–Alsek River system is also a highly regarded wilderness raft trip that begins in the Yukon Territory and ends in Glacier Bay National Park (p138).

Rock Climbing & Mountaineering

Mt McKinley and the other high peaks in Alaska draw the attention of mountain climbers from around the world. But rock climbing has also been growing in popularity in recent years. On almost any summer weekend, you can watch climbers working bolt-protected sport routes just above Seward Hwy along Turnagain Arm. Canyons in nearby Portage are also capturing the attention of rock climbers. Off Byron Glacier, several routes grace a slab of black rock polished smooth by the glacier. Not far from Portage Lake, a short hike leads to the magnificent slate walls of Middle Canyon.

Fairbanks climbers head north of town to the limestone formations known as Grapefruit Rocks, or else pack a tent and sleeping bag for the Granite Tors Trail (p298) off the Chena Hot Springs Rd. A 7-mile hike from the trailhead leads to the tors, a series of 100ft granite spires in a wilderness setting.

For climbing equipment there's Anchorage's **Alaska Mountaineering & Hiking** (p175) or **Beaver Sports** (p297) in Fairbanks.

Information

» For information on scaling the state's loftiest peaks, start with the Anchorage-based **Mountaineering Club of Alaska** (☑272-1811; www.mcak.org). On its website is the excellent *Introduction to Alaskan Peaks*.

» The best climbing guidebooks to the state are *Alaska: A Climbing Guide*, by Michael Wood and Colby Coombs, and *Alaska Rock Climbing Guide*, by Kelsey Gray.

» An excellent website for climbing tips and inspiration is William Finley's **Akmountain. com** (www.akmountain.com).

PANNING FOR A FORTUNE

With gold prices reaching an all-time high of $1900 an ounce in 2011 and the economy slumping, more people are heading to Alaska in search of gold. But after all the previous gold rushes, is there any gold left for recreational gold panners? You bet! Geologists estimate that only 5% of what the state contains has been recovered.

Even short-term visitors can strike it rich. Alaska has more than 150 public prospecting sites where you can recreationally pan for gold without staking a claim. The best options are in the Interior. They include, on Taylor Hwy, the Jack Wade Dredge at Mile 86 and American Creek at Mile 151; the Petersville State Recreation Mining Area on Petersville Rd off the George Parks Hwy at Trapper Creek; and on Glenn Hwy, Caribou Creek at Mile 106.8 and Nelchina River at Mile 137.5.

When panning for gold, you must have one essential piece of equipment: a gravity-trap pan, which can be purchased at most hardware stores. Those who have panned for a while also show up with rubber boots and gloves to protect feet and hands from icy waters; a garden trowel to dig up loose rock; a pair of tweezers to pick up gold flakes; and a small bottle to hold their find.

Panning techniques are based on the notion that gold is heavier than the gravel it lies in. Fill your pan with loose material from cracks and crevices in streams, where gold might have washed down and become lodged. Add water to the pan, then rinse and discard larger rocks, keeping the rinsing in the pan. Continue to shake the contents toward the bottom by swirling the pan in a circular motion, and wash off the excess sand and gravel by dipping the front into the stream.

You should be left with heavy black mud, sand and, if you're lucky, a few flakes of gold. Use tweezers or your fingernails to transfer the flakes into a bottle filled with water.

Outfitters

» **Alaska Mountain Guides and Climbing School** (✆800-766-3396; www.alaskamountainguides.com) runs a climbing school in Haines and leads high-altitude climbing expeditions to Mt McKinley, Mt Fairweather and other peaks.

» **Alaska Mountaineering School** (✆733-1016; www.climbalaska.org) of Talkeetna specializes in Mt McKinley.

» **St Elias Alpine Guides** tackles Mt Blackburn and other peaks in Wrangell-St Elias National Park. (p321)

Surfing

Alaska has more coastline than any other state in the USA, but the last thing most people associate with the frozen north is surfing. Until now. Following a *Surfer* magazine cover story on surfing in Alaska, the state's first surf shop, **Icy Waves Surf Shop** (p149), opened in Yakutat. That caught the attention of CBS News, which sent a camera crew to the remote town for three days. Yakutat's 20-minute segment on the news show *Sunday Morning* with Charles Osgood propelled it into the limelight and transformed the small town into 'Surf City Alaska.'

Due to its big waves and uncrowded beaches, Yakutat was named one of the five best surf towns in the USA by *Outside* magazine. Today more than 100 surfers from all over the world will visit the surf capital of Alaska every summer to join 20 or so locals for 'surfing under St Elias,' the 18,000ft peak that overshadows the town. The best waves occur from mid-April to mid-June and from mid-August through September, and – to the surprise of non-Alaskan surfers – the water isn't all that cold. The Japanese current pushes summer water temperatures into the mid-60s, while the rest of the surfing season they range from the mid-40s to the mid-50s.

Surfers have also hit the beaches of Sitka and Kodiak. Alaska's 'Big Island' has an almost endless number of places to surf, but the majority of surfers head to the beaches clustered around Pasagshak Point, 40 miles south of town.

An Alaskan-style surfin' safari means packing a wet suit with hood, booties and gloves, and often wearing a helmet. You'll also need to watch for brown bears, which often roam the beaches in search of washed-up crabs, salmon and other meals. Surfers have been known to encounter gray whales, sea otters, and even chunks of ice if they hit the waves too soon after the spring breakup.

Cruising in Alaska

Best Ports of Call

Juneau The only state capital inaccessible by road, Juneau stuns with massive green walls of mountains and a big ol' glacier just out of town.

Skagway Experience gold-rush history – or at least reenactments – in this Southeast Alaskan town.

Seward The start (or end) of many cruises, Seward is a great place to wander for a day. Check out the excellent Alaska SeaLife Center.

Kodiak A fishing town before anything else, Kodiak's lack of tourist culture makes it a refreshing place to stop.

Ketchikan Walk cacophonous Creek St or check out the serene Totem Heritage Center, shrouded in pines.

Why Cruise?

There are plenty of reasons to take an Alaskan cruise, namely the two 'Cs': comfort and convenience. And in a state that could take months, if not years, to thoroughly explore, you get a chance to see many of the top sights in one convenient, all-inclusive package.

Most days, you'll get a chance to disembark in port for anywhere from four to eight hours, where you can bop around town, take in a hike or an excursion, or even a longer trip inland to Denali National Park, Talkeetna or Eagle. You also get to sit on deck and spot bald eagles hunting, humpback whales breaching and glaciers calving: not a bad little bit of sightseeing. On the smaller lines, you'll get more wildlife excursions and more stops.

Backpackers, independent travelers and spendthrifts can always hop on the Alaska Marine Highway ferry. You'll see the same sights, but you won't get a casino, heated pool, hot tub, all-you-can-eat buffet or cruise director.

When to Go

Cruises run May through September. For the best weather try going in July and August, but for a bit less traffic and cheaper tickets consider taking a cruise in the shoulder seasons of early May and late September.

SUSTAINABLE CRUISING

Although all travel comes with an environmental cost, by their very size, cruise ships have an outsize effect. Among the main issues:

» **Pollution** A large cruise liner like the *Queen Mary* emits 1lb (0.43kg) of carbon dioxide per mile, while a long-haul flight releases about 0.6lb (0.25kg). In Alaska, an 11-day cruise from Seattle to Juneau on a small boat with around 100 guests will burn about 71 gallons of fuel per passenger, releasing some 0.77 tons of carbon into the air per passenger. The flight from Seattle to Juneau releases some 0.17 tons of carbon per passenger. Cruise ships also release around 17% of total worldwide nitrogen oxide emissions, and create around 50 tons of garbage and a million tons of wastewater on a one-week voyage.

» **Cultural impact** Cruise lines generate much-needed money and jobs for their ports of call, thousands of people arriving at once can change the character of a town and seem overwhelming to locals and noncruising travelers. Some towns see five cruise ships a day – that's around 15,000 people. The cruise industry notes it complies with international regulations, and adapts to stricter laws in places such as Alaska and the US west coast. It's equipping some ships with new wastewater treatment facilities, LED lighting and solar panels. Princess Cruises partnered with Juneau, Alaska, to develop 'cold-ironing', whereby ships in port plug into electric power; this is also done in San Francisco, Vancouver and Seattle.

What You Can Do

If you're planning a cruise, it's worth doing some research. Email the cruise lines and ask them about their environmental policies – wastewater treatment, recycling initiatives – and whether they use alternative energy sources. Knowing that customers care about these things has an impact. There are also organizations that review lines and ships on their environmental records. These include the following:

» **Friends of the Earth** (www.foe.org/cruisereportcard) Letter grades given to cruise lines and ships for environmental and human health impacts.

» **US Centers for Disease Control & Prevention** (www.cdc.gov) Follow the travel links to the well-regarded sanitation ratings for ships calling into US ports.

» **World Travel Awards** (www.worldtravelawards.com) Annual awards for the 'World's Leading Green Cruise Line'.

Picking Your Ship
Cruise Ships

For the comfort of a floating all-inclusive hotel, you can't beat a large cruise ship. However, these resorts on the sea do have their limitations. You won't be able to stop in as many places as you can on a smaller ship, and you'll be sharing your Alaska wilderness experience with around 3000 other vacationers. Most large cruises stop only in the major ports of call, and generally start from Vancouver or Seattle. Excursions range from heli-seeing trips and zipline tours to guided hikes, kayaks and day trips to Denali National Park. Cruises cost around $120 a night, but that does not include your flight to the port of embarkation. You can save good money (sometimes as much as 50%) by hopping on a 'repositioning' cruise, which takes the boat back to its home port.

Here's how they break down:

» **Carnival** (☑888-227-64825; www.carnival.com) Young people rule on these ships.

» **Celebrity** (☑877-202-4345; www.celebritycruises.com; ⚓) Family friendly and laid back.

» **Holland America** (☑877-932-4259; www.hollandamerica.com) A classy option.

» **Norwegian** (☑866-234-7350; www.ncl.com) Works well for the older crowd.

» **Princess** (☑800-774-62377; www.princess.com) One of the larger cruise lines to visit Alaska.

» **Royal Caribbean** (☑866-562-7625; www.royalcaribbean.com) Despite the name, it offers more than 50 voyages to Alaska each summer.

» (above) A cruise ship in Yakutat Bay, near Hubbard Glacier
» (left) A cruise ship in Sitka Sound

ALASKA MARINE HIGHWAY:
THE INDEPENDENT TRAVELER'S CRUISE *JIM DUFRESNE*

Travel on the state ferries is a leisurely and delightful experience. The midnight sun is warm, the scenery stunning and the possibility of sighting whales, bald eagles or sea lions keeps most travelers at the side of the ship.

Alaska Marine Highway (☎465-3941, 800-642-0066; www.ferryalaska.com) runs ferries equipped with observation decks, food services, lounges and solariums with deck chairs. You can rent a stateroom for overnight trips – these aren't as 'stately' as they may sound, and are downright spartan compared with what you'll get on a cruise liner – but many travelers head straight for the solarium and unroll their sleeping bags on deck chairs. You can find information on specific ports of call and rates in the Juneau & Southeast (p70); Kodiak, Katmai & Southwest Alaska (p323); and Prince William Sound (p190) chapters.

The ferries have cafeterias or snack bars and a few have sit-down restaurants, but budget travelers can save money by bringing their own food and cooking it on board the ship. There are microwaves on every ship. Most ships have onboard naturalists who give a running commentary on the trip. Bring your headphones, warm clothes, some extra snacks and a good book.

Ferry schedules change almost annually, but the routes stretch from Bellingham, WA, to the Aleutian Chain, with possible stops including Prince Rupert, BC; Ketchikan; Wrangell; Petersburg; Sitka; Juneau; Haines; and Skagway. From Haines you can drive north and within a couple of hours pick up the Alcan. A trip from Bellingham to Juneau takes 2½ to four days, depending on the route.

Nine ships ply the waters of Southeast Alaska and once a month the MV *Kennicott* makes a special run from Southeast Alaska across the Gulf of Alaska to Whittier. This links the Southeast routes of the Alaska Marine Highway ferries to the Southcentral portion that includes such ports as Homer, Kodiak, Valdez and Cordova. This sailing is extremely popular because it allows travelers to skip the long haul over the Alcan. Book it long before you arrive in Alaska.

Along with the Southeast, the Alaska Marine Highway services Southcentral and Southwest Alaska. Three ferries, including the high-speed catamaran MV *Chenega* connect 16 communities, including Cordova, Valdez, Whittier, Homer and Kodiak.

Once a month from May through September the MV *Tustumena* makes a special run along the Alaska Peninsula to Aleutian Islands (p336).

If the Alaska Marine Highway ferries are full in Bellingham, head to Port Hardy at the north end of Vancouver Island, where **BC Ferries** (☎888-223-3779; www.bcferries.com) leave for Prince Rupert, BC. From this Canadian city you can transfer to the Alaska Marine Highway and continue to Southeast Alaska on ferries not as heavily in demand as those in Bellingham.

Reservations

The ferries are extremely popular during the peak season (June to August). If boarding in Bellingham, you absolutely need reservations for a cabin or vehicle space, and just to be safe you should probably have one even if you're just a walk-on passenger.

The summer sailing schedule comes out in December and can be seen online. Reservations can be made online or by calling the Alaska Marine Highway. When reserving space, you must know the ports you want to visit along the route, with exact dates. Stopovers are not free; rather, tickets are priced on a port-to-port basis.

All fares listed in this book are for adults (aged 12 and older) but do not include a fuel surcharge, generally around 10%, but that could change in these times of erratic diesel prices. A ticket from Bellingham to Juneau runs about $330 per person; a two-berth cabin will cost you an extra $300 or so.

Small Ships

Just 3% of Alaska cruisers take a small-ship voyage. While you'll have tighter quarters, bumpier seas and fewer entertainment options than on the big boys, these vessels offer better chances of seeing wildlife, more land and kayak excursions, onboard naturalists (most of the time), good food, a more casual atmosphere (you can leave that blue sports coat at the office where it belongs) and a more intimate portrait of Alaska.

These boats sleep anywhere from eight to 100 and are more likely to depart from within Alaska. While this is probably your best bet if you are looking to match comfort with quality and authentic experience, it does come with a steeper price tag: anywhere from $400 to $1200 a night.

Each small cruise ship is different. Here's a breakdown of some of our favorites:

» **AdventureSmith Explorations** (☑800-620-2875; www.adventuresmithexplorations.com; per person $1795-4500) This company offsets its carbon emissions and focuses on learning and adventure cruises in Southeast Alaska aboard its fleet of small boats, which range from intimate charters (accommodating just 12 people) to larger cruisers that can take around 100 people. The boats have kayaks and small skiffs for numerous excursions that include everything from kayaking in Glacier Bay National Park to wildlife watching near Tracy Arm, the ABC Islands, Icy Straight, Misty Fiords and Frederick Sound. Most trips depart from Juneau.

» **Adventure Life Voyages** (☑800-344-6118; www.alvoyages.com; per person $7599-20,000) Specializes in top-end trips up the Inside Passage. Carries 62 to 128 passengers.

» **America Safari Cruises** (☑888-862-8881; www.amsafari.com; per person $6395-9995) Offers themed cruises, carrying 12 to 36 passengers, that focus on whale watching, Glacier Bay, wildlife watching or adventure travel. The small boats (they call them yachts) have modern, elegant staterooms, and a naturalist is on board to teach you the ways of the Alaska wilderness. Most trips depart from Juneau, but one leaves from Seattle.

» **Discovery Voyages** (☑800-324-7602; www.discoveryvoyages.com; per person $2200-5550) While the quarters are tight on this small boat, Discovery Voyages offers some interesting five- to eight-day options, with trips focusing on whale watching, hiking and kayaking, photography, or wildlife exploration. It also offsets its carbon emissions. Carries up to 12 passengers with cabins sleeping six.

» **Lindblad Expeditions** (☑800-397-3348; www.expeditions.com; per person from $8990) Offers kayaking, wilderness walks, onboard naturalists and Zodiac excursions during eight-day cruises in the Southeast. Many trips include the airfare from Seattle, and take visitors from Juneau through the Inside Passage, past Tracy Arm, Petersburg, Frederick Sound, Chatham Strait, Glacier Bay National Park, Point Adolphus and Inian Pass. Carries up to 62 passengers, with cabins for 31.

Picking Your Route
Inside Passage

The classic, sailing from Seattle or Vancouver. The 'great land' coastal views don't start until Prince Rupert Island. Most trips stop in Ketchikan – with about as many bars as people and some fine totem poles – then continue to Juneau, home to a great glacier and heli-seeing tours; Skagway, a gold-rush port with good hiking close to town; and the granddaddy attraction of Alaska cruises, Glacier Bay, where you'll see 11 tidewater glaciers spilling their icy wares into the sea.

Gulf of Alaska

This trip includes the Inside Passage but then continues to the Gulf of Alaska, with stops in Seward, the Hubbard Glacier and Prince William Sound. While you get a broader picture of coastal Alaska on this one-way cruise, it also comes at a price, as you'll generally need to arrange flights from separate ports.

Bering Sea

These trips are more expensive and generally focus on natural and cultural history. Folks that enjoy learning on their vacations will like this trip, with stops in the Pribilof Islands, Nome and, on the really expensive cruises, King Island.

'Cruisetours'

These trips give you the chance to get off the boat for about half of your trip. Most begin with the Inside Passage cruise, then head out on a tour bus, with stops in Talkeetna, Denali National Park, Fairbanks, Eagle or the Copper River. Most cruise companies have all-inclusive hotels in these destinations (basically cruise ships without the rocking).

Travel with Children

Best Regions for Kids

Anchorage & Around
Packed with parks, urban salmon streams, bike paths and plenty of man-made amusements. Head south to ride the Alyeska Tram or take the whistle-stop train out to Spencer Glacier for unique ways into the backcountry.

Kenai Peninsula
Ice-blue rivers for floating and fishing, boat tours that cruise right up to calving glaciers and sea-lion rookeries, and wilderness cabins for roughing it – but not too much.

Denali & the Interior
A combination of intensely wild lands and the distractions of 'Glitter Gulch' or Fairbanks, the Interior entertains with big animals, huge mountains, hot springs and even an amusement park. Plus there's pizza readily available.

Southeast
Gold mines and glaciers, whales and salmon, hiking trails and boat tours: the Southeast has a little bit of everything but on an Alaskan-sized scale.

Everybody is a kid in Alaska. Whether it's a stream choking with bright red salmon or a bald eagle winging its way across an open sky, nature's wonders captivate five-year-olds just as much as their parents. A fourth grader might not fully appreciate, or even endure, a visit to Wall St like Dad would, but both will be equally stunned by the 8-mile-wide face of Hubbard Glacier from the deck of a cruise ship.

Alaska for Kids

The best that Alaska has to offer cannot be found in stuffy museums or amusement parks filled with heart-pounding rides. It's outdoor adventure, wildlife and scenery on a grand scale, attractions and activities that will intrigue the entire family – whether you're a kid or not.

Outdoor Activities

If your family enjoys the outdoors, Alaska can be a relatively affordable place once you've arrived. A campsite is cheap compared to a motel room, and hiking, backpacking and wildlife watching are free. Even **fishing** is free for children, since anglers under 16 don't need a fishing license in Alaska.

The key to any Alaskan **hike** is to match it to your child's ability and level of endurance. It's equally important to select one that has an interesting aspect to it – a glacier, ruined gold mine, waterfalls or a remote cabin to stop for lunch.

Paddling with children involves a greater risk than hiking due to the frigid temperature of most water in Alaska. You simply don't want to tip at any cost. Flat, calm water should be the rule. Needless to say, all rentals should come with paddles and lifejackets that fit your child.

Children marvel at **watching wildlife** in its natural habitat but may not always have the patience for a long wait before something pops out of the woods. In July and August, however, you can count on seeing a lot of fish in a salmon stream, a wide variety of marine life in tidal pools, and bald eagles where the birds are known to congregate. Marine wildlife **boat tours** work out better than many park shuttles because, let's face it, a boat trip is a lot more fun than a bus ride. **Nature tours** that are done in vans are also ideal for children as they stop often and usually include short walks.

Eating Out

Like elsewhere in the USA, most Alaskan restaurants welcome families and tend to cater to children, with high chairs, kids menus of smaller sizes and reduced prices, and waitresses quick with a rag when somebody spills their drink. Upscale places where an infant would be frowned upon are limited to a handful of places in Anchorage. Salmon bakes are a fun, casual and colorful way to introduce Alaska's seafood, especially since they often come with corn and potatoes – familiar items at any barbecue.

Children's Highlights

Hiking Trails

» **Flattop Mountain Trail** Anchorage's most popular family day hike

» **Tonsina** A mellow trail to a beach walk and salmon stream outside Seward

» **Perseverance Trail** A path into the heart of Juneau's mining history

» **Horseshoe Lake Trail** Near the entrance to Denali National Park, it leads to an oxbow lake where moose are often seen

For a Rainy Day

» **Imaginarium** Anchorage's wondrous and whimsical science center

» **Alaska SeaLife Center** Diving seabirds, swimming sea lions and a tide-pool touch tank are found in Seward's marine research center

» **Dimond Park Aquatic Center** Flume slides, a bubble bench, tumble buckets and interactive water sprays

» **Sitka Sound Science Center** Five aquariums, three touch tanks and a working hatchery

Outdoor Fun

» **Iditaride** Tour an Iditarod veteran's kennels, then take a 20-minute ride on a sled pulled by hard-working dogs in Seward

» **Chena Hot Springs** Has swimming pools that are cooled to kid-friendly temps

» **Matanuska Glacier** A self-guided trail leads families 200yd onto the ice

» **Petroglyph Beach** Search for ancient rock carvings and sea life at low tide in Wrangell

Planning
When to Go

Summer is by far the best time to visit: the odds of spotting wildlife are good, salmon are swimming upstream, hiking trails are free of snow and the weather is as good as it's going to get. Crowds and lines are rarely a problem, unless everyone is stopped and staring at the same large mammal, so traveling during high season doesn't pose too much of a problem crowd-wise. **Festivals** abound during the summer, and most are family-friendly.

Note that between May and September you're going to deal with bugs. A lot of them.

Accommodations

Many independently owned accommodations and lodges in small towns won't offer amenities such as roll-away beds or cribs, but chain motels will. If you absolutely need a crib at night either check in advance or bring your own travel crib.

Sleeping under the stars – or Alaska's midnight sun – can be a memorable experience and is easy on the budget. Numerous **campgrounds** are connected to the road system, which means you won't have to lug heavy backpacks around. For toddlers and children younger than five years, the best way to escape into the wilderness is to rent a **wilderness cabin**. Many are reached by floatplane, an exciting start to any adventure for a child. The rustic cabins offer secure lodging in a remote place where children often have a good chance of seeing wildlife or catching fish.

Transportation

Many national companies have safety seats for toddlers and young children for about $10 extra per day. Unfortunately the smaller, independent agencies away from the airports, which generally offer better rental rates, often do not have car seats.

One of the best ways to see Alaska with toddlers or young children is on a **cruise ship**. The larger the ship, the more family amenities and activities it will offer. Smaller cruise ships, those that hold fewer than 200 people, do not work as well as they are usually geared more towards adventurous couples. But the **Alaska Marine Highway System** is well suited for families. Children have the space to move around and large ferries such as the MV *Columbia,* MV *Kennicott,* MV *Malaspina* and MV *Matanuska* feature both current movies and ranger programs on marine life, birds and glaciers.

On the **Alaska Railroad** children can walk between passenger carriages and spend time taking in the scenery from special domed viewing cars.

What to Pack

You'll be able to find almost anything in the larger towns that you forgot to pack. The most important thing to remember is layers – you simply can't pack warm enough. High-quality outerwear, especially rain gear, is important on any hike or camping trip. Don't forget a hat. Finally, sunscreen and insect repellent are indispensible.

regions at a glance

The regions you visit in Alaska will depend on your budget and time. The bulk of travelers stick to the few areas that roads reach, as getting off the road can be pricey and plenty of excellent sites are within range of road and ferry, not to mention tourist infrastructure.

The majority of tourists visit Southeast Alaska on a cruise or the Alaska Ferry, or fly into Anchorage and explore the Kenai Peninsula, or head up to visit North America's tallest mountain. A fair number fly to remote streams and lodges for salmon fishing, bear viewing or simply an epic river float.

Juneau & the Southeast

Wildlife ✓✓✓
Glaciers ✓✓
Hiking ✓✓

Marine Life
The sea is the lifeblood of Southeast Alaska, and it teems with life. You'll have the chance to spot whales, seals, Dall porpoises, sea otters and more.

Rivers of Ice
The massive Mendenhall Glacier outside Juneau is the most visited in Alaska, and for good reason: easily accessible, the half-mile face stretches in a glowing line across an iceberg studded lake. Further north, Glacier Bay National Park & Preserve is the best place to witness calving tidewater glaciers.

Rainforest Walks
Hiking through the Tongass National Forest or up Mt Roberts, behind Juneau, in the green, sweet-smelling trees can be a divine experience, if a soggy one. Excellent trails meander out of almost every town, offering glimpses into an amazing rainforest ecosystem.

p70

Anchorage & Around

Hiking ✓✓✓
Urban Culture ✓✓✓
Cycling ✓✓✓

The Front Range
Anchorage is backed by the Chugach Mountains, a backyard playground for the state's largest city. Flattop Mountain is the most popular climb, but you can delve into the backcountry or simply take a boardwalk stroll at Potter Marsh.

Bistros & Boutiques
No longer a frontier tent city, Anchorage now serves up fancy cocktails, designer duds and is home to a world-class museum. Hit the trails, then hit the showers and enjoy an evening on the town.

Rolling Around
With over 120 miles of paved trails, most of them in urban greenbelts, Anchorage is a great place to explore by bike. If you fancy mountain biking, head to Girdwood, where you'll find an excellent mountain-bike course.

p152

Prince William Sound

Kayaking ✓✓✓
Hiking ✓✓✓
Glaciers ✓✓✓

Paddling
A 15,000-mile cirque with only three small towns to its name, Prince William Sound is packed with quiet coves, rainy islands, tidewater glaciers and remote wilderness cabins. Trips from Valdez, Cordova and Whittier are all worthwhile.

Hiking
The Copper River Delta has more than a half-dozen trails originating from the Copper River Hwy, while Valdez has several that originate right out of town and head into the steep peaks. Even more are just outside town off the Richardson Hwy.

Massive Calves
Outside Valdez, the giant Columbia Glacier emits huge chunks of ice, some that release under water and pop to the surface without warning. Outside Cordova, the colossal Childs Glacier rumbles louder than thunder as it releases pieces of ice the size of small houses.

p190

Kenai Peninsula

Paddling ✓✓
Fishing ✓✓✓
Road tripping ✓✓

Glacial Fjords
Kenai Fjords National Park, outside Seward, and Kachemak Bay, outside Homer, are two excellent kayaking spots, with opportunities for seeing marine life, access to remote hiking trails and cabins, and accessible tidewater glaciers.

Fish On
The Kenai Peninsula is where 'combat fishing' is at its fiercest: hundreds of anglers lined shoulder to shoulder, pulling fat, meaty salmon out of an icy blue river. The Russian and Kenai rivers are the most popular, but are by no means the only places to hook a salmon.

Highways & Byways
Two main roads splinter across the Peninsula, which is larger than Maryland. Running almost the entire length of both is winding, two-lane scenery overload, with mountains, glaciers and rivers rolling by outside your window.

p213

Denali & the Interior

Mountains ✓✓✓
Rivers ✓✓
Northern Lights ✓✓

The Big One(s)
This is the home of North America's tallest mountain: Mt McKinley, or Denali. But Mts Foraker and Hunter, perennial bridesmaids to Denali, are stunners too, as is Mt St Elias to the southeast.

Floating & Fishing
Giant mountains have giant glaciers, which in turn create giant rivers, filled with salmon, or perfect for bobbing down in a raft. You can choose between a seemingly endless number. The most popular are near Talkeetna and Denali National Park.

Rainbows in the Sky
It doesn't really get dark around Fairbanks during the summer, but when it does you're in for a laser show à la Mama Nature. The northern lights are actually out over 300 days a year here. Head to Chena Hot Springs for an awesome soak and a show.

p256

Kodiak, Katmai & Southwest Alaska

Bears ✓✓✓
Wilderness ✓✓✓
History ✓✓

Grizzlies
Kodiak is home to the world's largest bear, the Kodiak brown bear. It also has the highest concentration of these mighty creatures. In Katmai National Park & Preserve, grizzlies snap salmon as they jump up a waterfall, mere feet from where you stand.

Wide Open Spaces
The nation's largest state park (Wood-Tikchik) is found here, as well as the astounding Valley of 10,000 Smokes. There are very few developed trails and getting to these spots requires pricey flights, but the scenery and satisfaction are worth every dollar.

Alaska Natives & WWII
Head out to the Aleutian Chain for forgotten history: you'll see bunkers, pillboxes, Quonset huts and more, all remnants of WWII. Equally intriguing is the Native history, which is particularly accessible in Unalaska.

p323

The Bush

Wilderness ✓✓✓
Culture ✓✓
Wildlife ✓✓

Wild Lands
Here, places like Gates of the Arctic National Park & Preserve don't have trails or even visitor facilities. The Dalton Hwy scrapes through the Brooks Range and on to the North Slope, through mind-boggling space.

Small Towns & Villages
Small Alaska Native villages dot the Bush, some connected by the Yukon River; Kotzebue serves as a hub for many of these. Nome emits a Wild West vibe: a gold-rush town and the end of the Iditarod Trail, it's a good-times scene at the edge of the planet.

Musk Ox & Caribou
The Porcupine herd of caribou, whose calving grounds are in the Arctic National Wildlife Refuge, is a stunning sight to behold. Other Arctic animals in the region are musk ox, outside Nome, and polar bears, near Barrow.

p349

Look out for these icons:

 TOP CHOICE Our author's recommendation

 A green or sustainable option

FREE No payment required

On the Road

Alaska's Best Hikes & Paddles

Includes »

Hiking & Paddling in Alaska

Much of Alaska's wilderness is hard to reach for visitors with limited time or small budgets. The lack of specialized equipment, the complicated logistics of reaching remote areas and lack of backcountry knowledge keeps many out of the state's great wilderness tracts such as the Arctic National Wildlife Refuge (ANWR). To experience such a remote and pristine place you may need to turn to a guiding company and pay a premium price.

But that doesn't mean you can't sneak off on your own for a trek into the mountains or a paddle down an icy fjord. There are so many possible adventures in Alaska that even the most budget-conscious traveler can take time to explore what lies beyond the pavement. Do it yourself and save.

The best way to enter the state's wilderness is to begin with a day hike the minute you step off the ferry or depart from the Alcan. After the initial taste of the woods, many travelers forgo the cities and spend the rest of their trip on multiday adventures into the backcountry to enjoy Alaska's immense surroundings.

There are also a range of paddling opportunities, from calm rivers and chains of lakes for novice canoeists to remote fjords and coastlines whose rugged shorelines and tidal fluctuations are an attraction for more experienced open-water paddlers. Alaska is an icy paradise for kayakers. Double-bladed paddlers can easily escape into a watery wilderness, away from motorboats and cruise ships, and enjoy the unusual experience of gazing at glaciers or watching seal pups snuggle on icebergs from sea level.

This chapter covers 14 popular wilderness excursions. They are either maintained trails or natural paddling routes that backpackers can embark on as unguided journeys provided they have the proper equipment and sufficient outdoor experience.

☞ Tours

If you lack the expertise to head outdoors on your own – or the logistics of visiting remote wilderness, such as the Alaska National Wildlife Refuge, are too daunting – guiding companies will help you get there. Whether you want to climb Mt McKinley, kayak Glacier Bay or pedal from Anchorage to Fairbanks, there's an outfitter willing to put an itinerary together, supply the equipment and lead the way. Guide companies are also listed in regional chapters.

ABEC's Alaska Adventures (☑877-424-8907; www.abecalaska.com) Rafting and backpacking the Arctic National Wildlife Refuge and Gates of the Arctic National Park.

Alaska Mountain Guides (☑800-766-3396; www.alaskamountainguides.com) Week-long kayaking trips in Glacier Bay and mountaineering schools in Haines.

Alaskabike.com (☑245-2175, 866-683-2453; www.alaskabike.com) Fully supported cycle tours along the George Parks, Richardson and Glenn Hwys.

Arctic Treks (☑455-6502; www.arctictreksadventures.com) Treks and rafting in the Gates of the Arctic National Park and the Arctic National Wildlife Refuge.

Arctic Wild (☑888-577-8203; www.arcticwild.com) Floats and treks in the Brooks Range and Arctic National Wildlife Refuge.

CampAlaska (☑800-376-9438; www.campalaska.com) Camping tours with hiking, rafting and other activities.

Mt Sobek (☑888-831-7526; www.mtsobek.com) Kayaking Glacier Bay, bear viewing at Pack Creek and raft trips on the spectacular Tatshenshini River.

St Elias Alpine Guides (☑345-9048, 888-933-5427; www.steliasguides.com) Mountaineering, rafting, trekking and glacier-skiing at Wrangell-St Elias National Park.

Tongass Kayak Adventures (☑772-4600; www.tongasskayak.com) Kayaking LeConte Glacier and Tebenkof Bay Wilderness in Southeast.

ℹ Useful Websites

Alaska Hike Search (www.alaskahikesearch.com) Includes details on almost 100 trails around Anchorage and Southcentral Alaska.

Alaska Department of Natural Resources (www.dnr.state.ak.us/parks/aktrails) Has details on trails in every corner of the state.

RECOMMENDED READS

» *Denali National Park Guide to Hiking, Photography & Camping* (2005) – Longtime Alaskan Ike Waits has produced the most comprehensive guide to Alaska's best-known national park.

» *Klondike Trail: the Complete Hiking and Paddling Guide* (2001) – From the legendary Chilkoot Trail to a paddle down the Yukon River, this book by Jennifer Voss will lead you on an adventure of a lifetime.

» *55 Ways to the Wilderness in Southcentral Alaska* (1994) – Check out this book by Helen Nienhueser and John Wolfe for trails around the Kenai Peninsula, the Anchorage area and from Palmer to Valdez.

» *50 Hikes in Alaska's Chugach State Park* (2001) – Shane Shepherd and Owen Wozniak cover the state park's best trails and routes near Anchorage.

» *Hiking with Grizzlies* (2006) – Former Denali National Park bear observer Tim Rubbert tells you how to travel into grizzly country to make sure you come back out.

» *Hiking Alaska's Wrangell-St Elias National Park* (2008) – Greg Fensterman will keep you from getting lost on 50 hikes and backpacking treks in this book, which includes GPS waypoints.

» *The Alaska River Guide* (2008) – Karen Jettmar provides the complete river guide for Alaska, covering 100 trips, from the Chilkat in the Southeast to Colville on the Arctic slope.

» *The Kenai Canoe Trails* (1995) – Daniel L Quick's guide to Kenai National Wildlife Refuge's Swan Lake and Swanson River canoe routes, with maps, fishing information and photos.

Alaska Department of Fish & Game Wildlife Notebook (www.adfg.state.ak.us/pubs/notebook/notehome.php) The excellent Wildlife Notebook covers all the state's major species of animals and birds that you may encounter on the trail or while paddling.

Knik Canoers & Kayakers (www.kck.org) With its tips, safety advice and contacts, this website is a great start for anybody thinking about a paddling adventure in Alaska.

/ww.moosepass.net) Outlines
this small community in the
gach National Forest.

seatrails.org) SEATrails
criptions and downloadable
n 80 trails in 19 communities
theast Alaska.

Sitka Trail Works (www.sitkatrailworks.org)
Detailed coverage maps on almost 20 trails
around Sitka.

Trail Mix (www.juneautrails.org) Helps you find
a trail in Alaska's capital city.

Trails of Anchorage (www.trailsofanchorage.
com) This site focuses on the great hiking
found within the city limits of Anchorage.

CHILKOOT TRAIL

🏃 Hiking the Chilkoot Trail

The Chilkoot is the most famous trail in
Alaska and often the most popular as more
than 3000 people spend three to four days
following the historic route every summer.

This was the route used by the Klondike
gold miners in the 1898 gold rush, and walking the well-developed trail is not so much a
wilderness adventure as a full-on history lesson. The trip is a 34-mile trek and includes
the Chilkoot Pass – an extremely steep climb
up to 3525ft, where most hikers resort to
scrambling on all fours over the loose rocks
and boulders.

For many, the highlight of the hike is riding the historic White Pass & Yukon Route
(WP&YR) railroad from Lake Bennett to
Skagway. Experiencing the Chilkoot and returning on the WP&YR is probably the ultimate Alaska trek, combining great scenery,
a historical site and an incredible sense of
adventure.

It is possible to hike the Chilkoot Trail
starting from either direction but it is easier
and safer when you set off from Dyea in the
south and climb up the loose scree of the
Chilkoot Pass, rather than down it. First stop
is the Chilkoot Trail Center (📞983-9234;
Broadway St) to obtain backpacking permits
(adult/child $50/25).

Parks Canada allows only 50 hikers per
day on the trail and holds only eight permits
to be handed out each day at the Trail Center.
It is definitely wise to reserve your permits
($11.70 per reservation) in advance through
Parks Canada (📞867-667-3910, 800-661-0486;
www.pc.gc.ca/eng/lhn-nhs/yt/chilkoot/index
.aspx) if you intend walking mid-July to mid-

Chilkoot Trail

August. Also check with the staff at the Trail
Center to make doubly sure you have all
the right visas and paperwork to complete
the hike the Chilkoot into Canada and then
return to Skagway in the USA.

SECTION	DISTANCE
Dyea trailhead to Canyon City	7.5 miles
Canyon City to Sheep Camp	4.3 miles
Sheep Camp to Chilkoot Pass	3.5 miles
Chilkoot Pass to Happy Camp	4 miles
Happy Camp to Deep Lake	2.5 miles
Deep Lake to Lindeman City	3 miles
Lindeman City to Bare Loon Lake	3 miles
Bare Loon Lake to Lake Bennett	4 miles

ℹ️ Information

LEVEL OF DIFFICULTY Medium to hard
INFORMATION National Park Service
(☎983-2921; www.nps.gov/klgo).
FUN FACT The 33-mile-long Chilkoot Trail is considered the world's longest outdoor museum due to all the artifacts that the participants in the Klondike Gold Rush left behind.

ℹ️ Getting There & Away

For transport to the Dyea trailhead there's **Frontier Excursions** (☎877-983-2512, 983-2512; www.frontierexcursions.com; per person $15). At the northern end of the trail, hikers can return to Skagway via the **White Pass & Yukon Route** (☎800-343-7373; www.whitepassrailroad.com; adult/child $95/47.50; ⏲2pm Mon, Tue & Fri). White Pass & Yukon also offers hikers a train/bus combination (adult/child $99/44.50; from Sunday to Tuesday and Thursday to Friday) north to Whitehorse.

PETERSBURG LAKE TRAIL

🏃 Hiking the Petersburg Lake Trail

A short hop across the Wrangell Narrows from the fishing community of Petersburg is Petersburg Lake Trail and Portage Mountain Loop that can be combined for a trek to two US Forest Service cabins.

The Petersburg Lake Trail is well planked and provides backpackers with a wilderness opportunity and access to a USFS cabin without expensive bush-plane travel. Those planning to continue on to Portage Bay or Salt Chuck along Portage Mountain Loop should keep in mind that the trails are not planked or maintained and, at best, only lightly marked. The 7-mile trek to Portage Cove is very challenging and involves crossing wet muskeg areas or stretches flooded out by beaver dams.

Bring a fishing pole, as there are good spots in the creek for Dolly Varden and rainbow trout. In August and early September there are large coho and sockeye salmon runs throughout the area that attract both anglers and bears.

The trek begins at the Kupreanof Island public dock. From the dock a partial boardwalk heads south for a mile past a handful of cabins and then turns northwest up the tidewater arm of the creek, almost directly across Wrangell Narrows from the ferry terminal. A well-planked trail goes from the saltwater arm and continues along the freshwater creek to the Petersburg Lake USFS Cabin.

Petersburg Lake Trail

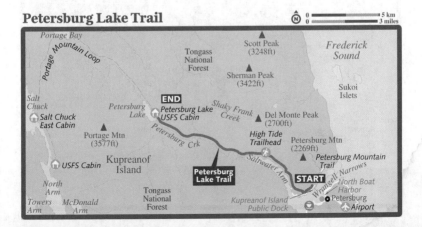

trip on which you'll want to
...terproof clothing and rubber
...nt or plan on reserving the
...abin at least two months in
... earlier if you want to tackle
...e in August during the salmon runs.
...eserve the USFS cabin through the **National Recreation Reservation System** (☎877-444-6777, 515-885-3639; www.recreation.gov).

SECTION	DISTANCE
Kupreanof Island dock to Saltwater Arm	2 miles
Saltwater Arm to Petersburg Creek	2.5 miles
Trail by creek to USFS cabin	6 miles
USFS cabin to Portage Bay	7 miles
Portage Bay to Salt Chuck East Cabin	4.5 miles

Information

LEVEL OF DIFFICULTY Medium
INFORMATION USFS Petersburg Ranger District (☎772-3871; www.fs.fed.us/r10/tongass).

Getting There & Away

For transportation across Wrangell Narrows to the public dock on Kupreanof Island contact **Tongass Kayak Adventures** (☎772-4600; www.tongasskayak.com; per trip $25).

MISTY FIORDS NATIONAL MONUMENT

Paddling Misty Fiords

The Misty Fiords National Monument encompasses 3594 sq miles of wilderness and lies between two impressive fjords – Behm Canal (117 miles long) and Portland Canal (72 miles long). The two natural canals give the preserve its extraordinarily deep and long fjords with sheer granite walls that rise thousands of feet out of the water. Misty Fiords is well named; annual rainfall is 14ft.

The destinations for many kayakers are the smaller but impressive fjords of Walker Cove and Punchbowl Cove in Rudyerd Bay, off Behm Canal. Dense spruce-hemlock rain forest is the most common vegetation type throughout the monument, and sea lions, harbor seals, brown and black bears, mountain goats and bald eagles can all be seen.

Misty Fiords has 15 **USFS cabins** (☎877-444-6777, 518-885-3639; www.recreation.gov; $25-45), which should be reserved in advance. Two paddles – Alava Bay and Winstanley Island in Behm Canal – allow kayakers to end the day at the doorstep of a cabin.

Misty Fiords National Monument

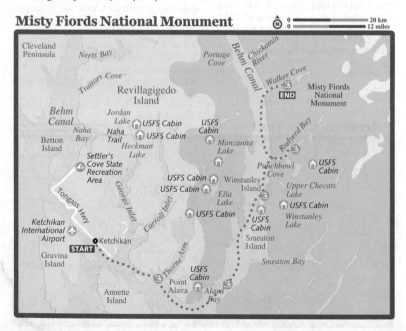

You can't do this trip without good rain gear and a backpacker's stove – wood in the monument is often too wet for campfires. Be prepared for extended rain periods and make sure all your gear is sealed in plastic bags.

SECTION	DISTANCE
Ketchikan to Thorne Arm	13 miles
Thorne Arm to Alava Bay	9 miles
Alava Bay to Winstanley Island	21 miles
Winstanley Island to Rudyerd Bay	9 miles
Rudyerd Bay to Walker Cove	10 miles

ⓘ Information

LEVEL OF DIFFICULTY Medium, open water
INFORMATION Southeast Alaska Discovery Center (☏228-6220; www.fs.fed.us/r10/tongass)

ⓘ Getting There & Away

Experienced kayakers can paddle out of Ketchikan (a seven- to 12-hour day trip) but most paddlers arrange to be dropped off at Alava Bay or deep in Behm Canal near the protected water of Rudyerd Bay. **Southeast Sea Kayaks** (☏225-1258, 800-287-1607; www.kayakketchikan.com) has single/double kayaks for $49/59 per day and discounts apply for longer rentals. This wonderful outfitter can assist in all aspects of a self-guided trip, including boat transportation. Water-taxi rates begin at $290 for transport one way to Alava Bay for one to six paddlers; with advance notice they can often combine groups to make the service more affordable.

TRACY ARM-FORDS TERROR WILDERNESS

🏃 Paddling Tracy Arm-Fords Terror Wilderness

Endicott Arm, Tracy Arm and Fords Terror form the Tracy Arm-Fords Terror Wilderness, a 653,000-acre preserve, where you can spend weeks paddling to a backdrop of glaciers, icebergs and 2000ft granite walls.

Popular Tracy Arm makes a pleasant two- to three-day (30-mile) paddle, ideal for novice kayakers. Calm water is the norm due to the protection of the steep granite walls. Camping is limited, however; the only spots in the first half are two valleys almost opposite each other, 8 miles north along the arm, and a small island at the head of the fjord.

Tracy Arm attracts cruise ships and tour boats, which detract from the wilderness experience. Experienced kayakers could consider Endicott Arm, a 30-mile fjord created by Dawes and North Dawes glaciers. Extending from Endicott Arm is Fords Terror, a narrow water chasm named after a US sailor who found himself battling whirlpools and grinding icebergs when he tried to row out against the incoming tide in 1899.

SECTION	DISTANCE
Juneau to Sawyer Glaciers drop-off	77 miles
Sawyer Glaciers to mid-fjord camping spots	8 miles
Mid-fjord camping spots to Harbor Island	21 miles
Pick-up to Juneau (tour boat)	48 miles

Tracy Arm-Fords Terror Wilderness

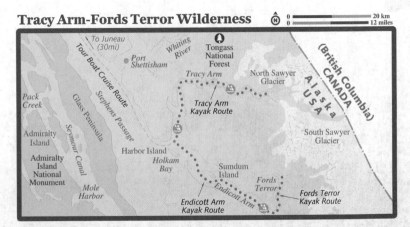

1. Sea Kayaking Around Icebergs
Tracy Arm-Fords Terror Wilderness area (p55) is a paddling paradise.

2. Hiking near Lake Clark
Less than 5000 visitors a year make it to Lake Clark National Park & Preserve (p338), where the hiking is phenomenal.

3. Paddling Past Cascades
Misty Fiords National Monument (p54) is a mystical landscape of fjords and waterfalls.

4. Backpacking
The Chugach Mountains (p59) form a backyard playground for the state's largest city.

NEIL RABINOWITZ/CORBIS ©

ⓘ Information

LEVEL OF DIFFICULTY Easy, open water
INFORMATION USFS Juneau Ranger District
(☎586-8800; www.fs.fed.us/r10/tongass)

ⓘ Getting There & Away

The departure point for Tracy Arm is Juneau, where drop-offs and pickups can be arranged to make the trip considerably easier. Otherwise it's a two- or three-day paddle in open water to reach the fjords. Kayaks can be rented from **Alaska Boat & Kayak Shop** (☎364-2333; www.juneaukayak.com; single/double per day $50/70), which also offers a water-taxi service for drop-offs at the entrance of Endicott Arm. **Adventure Bound Alaska** (☎463-2509, 800-228-3875; www.adventureboundalaska.com) provides drop-off and pick-up services deep inside Tracy Arm for $183 per person.

IDITAROD NATIONAL HISTORIC TRAIL

🏃 Hiking the Iditarod National Historic Trail

One of the best backpacking adventures near Anchorage is the 26-mile Iditarod National Historic Trail that was once used by gold miners and mushers. This classic alpine crossing begins at Crow Pass Trailhead, 37 miles east of Anchorage, climbs Crow Pass and wanders past Raven Glacier. You then enter Chugach State Park and descend Eagle River Valley, ending north of Anchorage at the Eagle River Nature Center. The trail is well maintained and well marked but requires fording Eagle River, which is tricky in rain.

Armed with a decent light backpack and blessed with some reasonably good weather you could potentially cover this 26-mile trail in one long, challenging, adventurous Alaskan summer day. Heck, they stage a mountain race here every summer with the winner usually smashing it out in less than 3½ hours. But why would you rush? The alpine scenery is remarkable, the mining ruins along the trail are interesting, and the hike is reasonably demanding. Plan on taking two days, or even three, because this is why you come to Alaska – to wander in the mountains.

You must have a stove; campfires are not allowed in the state park. Near Mile 3 of the trail is a **USFS cabin** (☎877-444-6777, 518-

Iditarod National Historic Trail

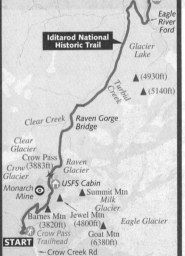

885-3639; www.recreation.gov; $35) in a beautiful alpine setting. At the other end of the trail are yurts and a cabin ($65) rented out by the **Eagle River Nature Center** (☎694-2108; www.ernc.org).

Even if you don't have any desire to hoist a hefty backpack, don't pass up an opportunity to spend a day hiking one of the hundreds of well-maintained and easy-to-follow trails scattered across the state. How good is the day hiking in Juneau? The trailhead for the Mt Roberts Trail (p117) is only five blocks from the state capitol, while the USFS maintains 29 other trails accessible from the Juneau road system. Anchorage is also blessed with numerous close-to-home trails. A 15-minute drive from downtown and you can be at a treeline trailhead in Chugach State Park, where a path quickly leads into the alpine. Skagway, Girdwood, Seward and Sitka also have numerous trails close to main streets.

For the state's best close-to-town day hikes, hit the trail on one of these:

» **Crow Pass Trail** (p179) From Girdwood a round-trip hike of 8 miles takes you past gold-mining artifacts, an alpine lake and Raven Glacier.

» **Deer Mountain Trail** (p77) Just arrived in Alaska? This 2.5-mile trail from downtown Ketchikan to the top of Deer Mountain will whet your appetite to tie up your hiking boots at every stop.

» **West Glacier Trail** (p119) This 3.4-mile-long trail near Juneau hugs a mountainside while providing a bird's-eye view of the Mendenhall Glacier.

» **Williwaw Lakes Trail** (p160) Within minutes of the heart of Anchorage, this easy 13-mile hike leads you to a series of alpine lakes in the Chugach State Park and offers the possibility of seeing Dall sheep.

» **Mt Marathon Trail** (p219) There are several ways to climb 3022ft-high Mt Marathon, which overlooks downtown Seward, but all end at a heavenly alpine bowl just behind the peak.

SECTION	DISTANCE
Crow Pass trailhead to Crow Pass	4 miles
Crow Pass to Eagle River Ford	9 miles
Eagle River Ford to Icicle Creek	7.3 miles
Icicle Creek to Eagle River Nature Center	5.7 miles

ℹ Information

LEVEL OF DIFFICULTY Medium

INFORMATION Eagle River Nature Center
(☑694-2108; www.ernc.org); **Alaska Division of Parks** (☑345-5014; www.alaskastateparks.org); **USFS Glacier Ranger District** (☑783-3242; www.fs.fed.us/r10/chugach)

ℹ Getting There & Away

The Crow Pass trailhead is reached 7 miles from Mile 90 Seward Hwy, via Alyeska Hwy and Crow Creek Rd. The northern trailhead is at the end of Eagle River Rd, 12 miles from the Glenn Hwy. There is transportation to Girdwood (p182). To return to Anchorage you can catch bus 102 of the **People Mover** (☑343-6543; www.people mover.org) from the Eagle River Transit Center near Glenn Hwy.

RUSSIAN LAKES TRAIL

🏃 Hiking the Russian Lakes Trail

This 21-mile, two-day trek is ideal for hikers who do not want to overextend themselves in Chugach National Forest. The trail is well-maintained and well-marked, and most of the hike is a pleasant forest walk broken up by patches of wildflowers, ripe berries, lakes and streams.

Highlights of the hike include getting an eyeful of the supremely impressive glaciated mountains that stab the sky across from Upper Russian Lake, the possibility of experiencing a firsthand encounter with moose or bears – or both – and the chance to catch your own fish-shaped dinner. The trek offers excellent angling opportunities for fishing folk who are willing to carry in a rod and reel. Dolly Varden, rainbow trout and salmon are found in the upper portions of the Russian River; rainbow trout in Lower Russian Lake, Aspen Flats and Upper Russian Lake; and Dolly Varden in Cooper Lake near the Cooper Lake trailhead.

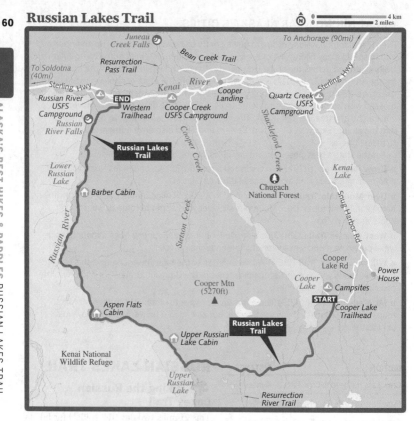

Three **USFS cabins** (☎877-444-6777, 515-885-3639; www.recreation.gov; $35-$45) are on the trail on Upper Russian Lake (9 miles from the Cooper Lake trailhead), Aspen Flats (12 miles from the Cooper Lake trailhead) and Barber Cabin (3 miles from the western trailhead).

SECTION	DISTANCE
Cooper Lake trailhead to junction of Resurrection River Trail	5 miles
Trail junction to Upper Russian Lake Cabin	4 miles
Upper Russian Lake to Aspen Flats	3 miles
Aspen Flats to Lower Russian Lake	6 miles
Lower Russian Lake to Russian River USFS Campground	3 miles

ℹ Information

LEVEL OF DIFFICULTY Easy

INFORMATION USFS Seward Ranger District (☎224-3374; www.fs.fed.us/r10/chugach)

ℹ Getting There & Away

It is easiest to begin this trek from the Cooper Lake trailhead, the higher end of the trail. To get there, turn off at Mile 47.8, Sterling Hwy onto Snug Harbor Rd; the road leads south 12 miles to Cooper Lake and ends at a marked parking lot and the trailhead.

The western trailhead is on a side road marked 'Russian River USFS Campground' at Mile 52.7, Sterling Hwy. From there it's just under a mile's hike to the parking lot at the end of the campground road – the beginning of the trail. There is a small fee if you leave a car here. If you're planning to camp at Russian River the night before starting the hike, keep in mind that the campground is extremely popular during the salmon season in June and July.

RESURRECTION PASS TRAIL

🏃 Hiking Resurrection Pass Trail

Located in the Chugach National Forest, this 39-mile trail was carved by prospectors in the late 1800s and today is the most popular hiking route on the Kenai Peninsula. Resurrection Pass Trail's mild climb from 500ft to only 2600ft has made it an increasingly popular trail for mountain bikers, who can ride the entire route in one day. For those on foot, the trip can be done in three days by a strong hiker but most people prefer to do it in four to five days to make the most of the immense beauty of the region.

The trail is also the first leg of a trek across the Kenai Peninsula. By linking Resurrection Pass, Russian Lakes and Resurrection River Trails in Chugach National Forest, you can hike 71 miles from Hope to Seward and cross only one road.

There are eight USFS cabins (☎877-444-6777, 518-885-3639; www.recreation.gov; $35-45) along the route but they must be reserved in advance. Most hikers take a tent and stay in designated backcountry campsites at Mile 4, Wolf Creek (Mile 5.3), Caribou Creek (Mile 7), Mile 9.6, Mile 12.6 and East Creek (Mile 14.6). Most sites have bear-resistant food lockers but pack a camp stove, as fallen wood is scarce during summer.

SECTION	DISTANCE
Northern trailhead to Caribou Creek Cabin	6.9 miles
Caribou Creek Cabin to Fox Creek Cabin	4.7 miles
Fox Creek Cabin to East Creek Cabin	2.8 miles
East Creek Cabin to Resurrection Pass	4.9 miles
Resurrection Pass to Devil's Pass Cabin	2.1 miles
Devil's Pass Cabin to Swan Lake Cabin	4.4 miles
Swan Lake Cabin to Trout Lake Cabin	6 miles
Trout Lake Cabin to southern trailhead	6.7 miles

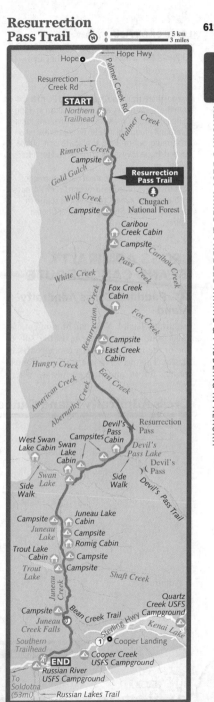

ℹ️ **Information**
LEVEL OF DIFFICULTY Easy
INFORMATION USFS Seward Ranger District
(📞224-3374; www.fs.fed.us/r10/chugach)

ℹ️ **Getting There & Away**

The northern trailhead can be found 20 miles from the Seward Hwy and 4 miles south of Hope on Resurrection Creek Rd. Hope, a historic mining community founded in 1896 by gold seekers, is a charming, out-of-the-way place to visit, but be warned, Hope Hwy is not an easy road for hitch-hiking.

From Hope Hwy, go south at the Resurrection Pass trail signs onto Resurrection Creek Rd, passing the fork to Palmer Creek Rd. The southern trailhead is on the Sterling Hwy, near Cooper Landing.

CROSS ADMIRALTY ISLAND CANOE ROUTE

🏃 **Paddling Cross Admiralty Island**

Admiralty Island National Monument, 50 miles southwest of Juneau, is the site of one of the most interesting canoe routes in Alaska. This preserve is a fortress of dense coastal forest and ragged peaks, where brown bears outnumber anything else on the island, including humans. The Cross Admiralty Canoe Route is a 32-mile paddle that spans the center of the island from the village of Angoon to Mole Harbor.

Although the majority of it consists of calm lakes connected by streams and portages, the 10-mile paddle from Angoon to Mitchell Bay is subject to strong tides that must be carefully timed. Avoid Kootznahoo Inlet as its tidal currents are extremely difficult to negotiate; instead, paddle through the maze of islands south of it. Leave Angoon at low tide, just before slack tide so that the water will push you into Mitchell Bay.

The traditional route is to continue on to Mole Harbor via Davidson Lake, Lake Guerin, Hasselborg Lake, Beaver Lake and Lake Alexander, all connected by portages. Because of the logistics and cost of being picked up at Mole Harbor with a canoe, most paddlers stop in the heart of the chain and after a day or two of fishing backtrack to Angoon to utilize the Alaska Marine Hwy for a return to Juneau.

There are good camping spots at Tidal Falls on the eastern end of Salt Lake, on the islands at the south end of Hasselborg Lake and on the portage between Davidson Lake

Cross Admiralty Island Canoe Route

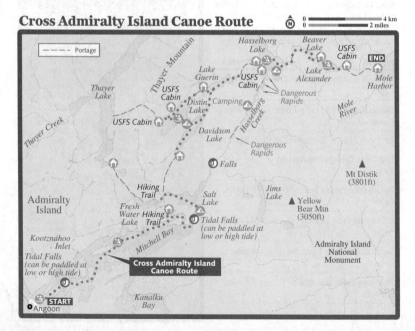

and Distin Lake. For those who can plan in advance, there are several USFS cabins (📞877-444-6777, 515-885-3639; www.recreation.gov; $35-45) along the route, including those on Hasselborg Lake, Lake Alexander and Distin Lake.

SECTION	DISTANCE
Angoon to Salt Lake Tidal Falls	10 miles
Tidal Falls to Davidson Lake portage	2.5 miles
Portage to Davidson Lake	3.5 miles
Davidson Lake to Hasselborg Lake portage	6 miles
Portage to Hasselborg Lake	1.7 miles
Hasselborg Lake to Beaver Lake portage	2 miles
Portage to Beaver Lake	0.5 miles
Beaver Lake to Mole Harbor portage	3 miles
Portage to Mole Harbor	2.5 miles

ⓘ Information

LEVEL OF DIFFICULTY Medium; mostly Class 1 water

INFORMATION Admiralty Island National Monument (📞586-8800; www.fs.fed.us/r10/tongass/districts/admiralty)

ⓘ Getting There & Away

This adventure begins with a ferry trip to the village of Angoon onboard the **Alaska Marine Highway** (📞800-642-0066; www.ferryalaska.com). One-way fare from Juneau to Angoon is $37, plus another $22 to carry a canoe onboard. Carefully set up your trip around the ferry schedule; a boat arrives at Angoon roughly every two to three days.

Rent your canoe in Juneau from **Alaska Boat & Kayak Shop** (📞789-6886; www.juneaukayak.com), which is conveniently located near the ferry terminal in Auke Bay. Canoes are $50 a day with discounts for rentals of three days or more.

SWAN LAKE CANOE ROUTE

🏃 Paddling the Swan Lake Canoe Route

In the northern lowlands of the Kenai National Wildlife Refuge there is a chain of rivers, lakes, streams and portages that make up the Swan Lake canoe route. The trip is perfect for novice canoeists, as rough water is rarely a problem and portages do not exceed half a mile. Fishing for rainbow trout is good in many lakes, and wildlife is plentiful; a paddle on this route could result in sightings of moose, bears, beavers and a variety of waterfowl.

This easy and popular route connects 30 lakes with forks in the Moose River for 60 miles of paddling and portaging. The entire route would take only a week but a common three-day trip is to begin at the west entrance on Swan Lake Rd and end at Moose River Bridge on Sterling Hwy.

SECTION	DISTANCE
West Entrance to Marten Lake	2.6 miles
Marten Lake to Otter Lake	2.4 miles
Otter Lake to Camp Island Lake	4.5 miles
Camp Island Lake to Moose River	5 miles
Moose River to Sterling Hwy	4.5 miles

ⓘ Information

LEVEL OF DIFFICULTY Easy; Class I water

INFORMATION Kenai National Wildlife Refuge (📞262-7021; kenai.fws.gov)

ⓘ Getting There & Away

To reach the Swan Lake canoe route, travel to Mile 84, Sterling Hwy, east of Soldotna, and turn north on Robinson Lake Rd, just west of the Moose River Bridge. Robinson Lake Rd turns into Swanson River Rd, which leads to Swan Lake Rd, 17 miles north of the Sterling Hwy. East on Swan Lake Rd are two entrances for the canoe route. The west entrance for the Swan Lake route is at Canoe Lake, and the east entrance is another 6 miles beyond, at Portage Lake.

Throughout the summer months, **Alaska Canoe & Campground** (📞262-2331; www.alaskacanoetrips.com) rents canoes and runs a shuttle service for people paddling the Swan Lake canoe route. It costs $32 per day for canoe rental for three days or longer, $50 for a drop-off at the west entrance and $55 for the east entrance. Alaska Canoe's campground (tent sites/cabins $13/150) is near the takeout along Sterling Hwy and it makes a nice place to stay overnight if you find yourself arriving late on the last day.

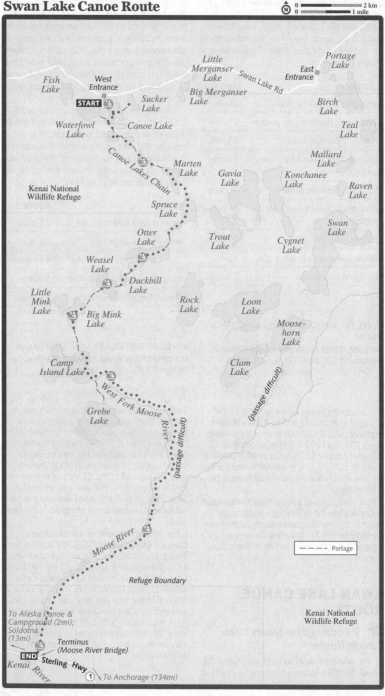

DIXIE PASS ROUTE

🏃 Hiking the Dixie Pass Route

Even by Alaskan standards, Wrangell-St Elias National Park is a large tract of wilderness. At 20,625 sq miles, it's the largest US national park, contains the most peaks over 14,500ft in North America and has the greatest concentration of glaciers on the continent.

Within this huge, remote park, Dixie Pass provides the best wilderness adventure that doesn't require a bush-plane charter. The trek from the trailhead up to Dixie Pass and return is 24 miles. Plan to camp there at least one or two additional days to take in the alpine beauty and investigate the nearby ridges. Such an itinerary requires three or four days and is moderately hard.

You reach the Dixie Pass trailhead by hiking 2.5 miles up Kotsina Rd from Strelna and then another 1.3 miles along Kotsina Rd after the Nugget Creek Trail splits off to the northeast. The trailhead is on the right-hand side of Kotsina Rd; look for a marker.

The route begins as a level path for 3 miles to Strelna Creek, and then continues along the west side of the creek for another 3 miles to the first major confluence. After fording the creek, it's 5 to 6 miles to the pass; along the way you'll cross two more confluences and hike through an interesting gorge. The ascent to Dixie Pass is fairly easy to spot, and once there you'll find superb scenery and alpine ridges to explore.

SECTION	DISTANCE
McCarthy Rd to Dixie Pass trailhead	3.8 miles
Dixie Pass trailhead to Strelna Creek	3 miles
Strelna Creek to Dixie Pass	8.5 miles

ℹ️ Information

LEVEL OF DIFFICULTY Hard

INFORMATION Wrangell-St Elias National Park (☎822-5234; www.nps.gov/wrst)

ℹ️ Getting There & Away

For transportation into the park, there's **Kennicott Shuttle** (☎822-5292; www.kennicottshuttle.com), which runs a daily bus from Glennallen to McCarthy. With a round-trip Glennallen-to-McCarthy ticket ($139) the company will also drop off and pickup hikers at the Dixie Pass trailhead. Stop at the park headquarters in Copper Center to complete a backcountry trip itinerary and pickup USGS quadrangle maps.

Dixie Pass Route

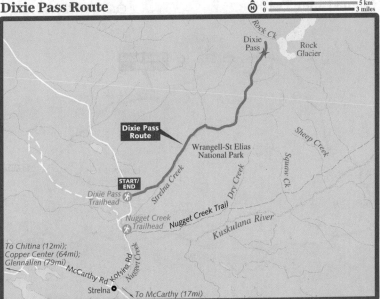

CHENA DOME TRAIL

🏃 Hiking the Chena Dome Trail

Fifty miles east of Fairbanks in the Chena River State Recreation Area, this 29.5-mile loop trail makes an ideal three- or four-day alpine romp. The trail circles the Angel Creek drainage area, with the vast majority of it along tundra ridgetops above the treeline. That includes climbing Chena Dome, a flat-topped peak near Mile 10 that, at 4421ft, is the highest point of the trail.

An intriguing aspect of the trek is the remains of a military plane that crashed into the ridge in the 1950s. The trail winds pass the site near Mile 8.5. Other highlights are views from Chena Dome, picking blueberries in August, and a free-use shelter at Mile 17. In clear, calm weather you can even see Mt McKinley from spots along the trail.

Pack a stove (open fires aren't permitted), and carry at least 3 quarts (3L) of water per person (refill bottles from small pools in the tundra). There's a free-use shelter at Mile 17, while a 1.5-mile and 1900ft descent from the main trail will bring you to **Upper Angel Creek Cabin** ($25 per night), which can be used as a place to stay on the third night; reserve online with **Alaska Division of Parks** (www.dnr.state.ak.us/parks/cabins/onlineres.htm).

SECTION	DISTANCE
Northern trailhead to treeline	3 miles
Treeline to military airplane wreck	5.5 miles
Airplane wreck to Chena Dome summit	2 miles
Chena Dome summit to free-use shelter	6.5 miles
Free-use shelter to final descent off ridge	10 miles
Final descent to southern trailhead	2.5 miles

ℹ️ Information

LEVEL OF DIFFICULTY Hard
INFORMATION Alaska Division of Parks (☎451-2705; www.alaskastateparks.org)

ℹ️ Getting There & Away

It's easier to hike the loop by beginning at the northern trailhead at Mile 50.5, Chena Hot Springs Rd. The trailhead is 0.7 miles past Angel Creek Bridge. The southern trailhead is at Mile 49. You can rent a car, hitchhike or call **Chena Hot Springs Resort** (☎451-8104; www.chena hotsprings.com), which will provide round-trip van transportation for $65 per person (minimum two people).

Chena Dome Trail

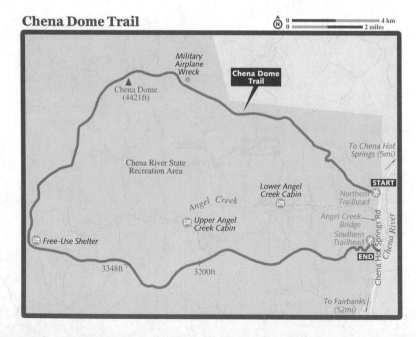

PINNELL MOUNTAIN TRAIL

Hiking Pinnell Mountain Trail

The outstanding sight on this trail is the midnight sun. Pinnell Mountain Trail is a 27.3-mile trek, 86 miles northeast of Fairbanks on the Steese Hwy, and from June 18 to June 25 the sun doesn't set on the trail. You can view the sun sitting just above the horizon at midnight from several high points on the trail, including at the Eagle Summit trailhead.

The route is mostly along tundra ridgetops that lie above 3500ft and can be steep and rugged, but the tundra wildflowers and views are spectacular, with the Alaska Range visible to the south. Water is scarce in the alpine sections, so bring plenty and refill at snow patches, springs or tundra pools

This is a three-day trek, covering 8 to 10 miles a day. Most hikers start at the Eagle Summit trailhead on Mile 107.3, Steese Hwy, the higher end of the trail. The Twelvemile Summit trailhead is closer to Fairbanks, at Mile 85, Steese Hwy. Two free-use shelters (North Fork shelter and Ptarmigan Creek shelter) along the trail are great places to wait out a storm or cook a meal, but bring a tent with good bug netting.

SECTION	DISTANCE
Eagle Summit trailhead to Porcupine Dome	6 miles
Porcupine Dome to Ptarmigan Creek shelter	4 miles
Ptarmigan Creek shelter to North Fork shelter	8 miles
North Fork shelter to Twelvemile Summit trailhead	9.5 miles

ℹ️ Information

LEVEL OF DIFFICULTY Medium to hard
INFORMATION Bureau of Land Management (BLM; ☎474-2200; www.ak.blm.gov)

ℹ️ Getting There & Away

Traffic on the Steese Hwy this far out of Fairbanks is a steady trickle. Hitchhiking is possible if you are willing to give up a day getting there. Even those who bring a car will end up hitchhiking back to the trailhead where they began.

The best alternative to hitchhiking is to rent a car and take the opportunity to explore Central or even Circle on the Yukon River. Check with the **Fairbanks Visitors Bureau** (☎456-5774; www.explorefairbanks.com) to see who is renting cars that are allowed on the Steese Hwy.

ALASKA'S BEST HIKES & PADDLES PINNELL MOUNTAIN TRAIL

Pinnell Mountain Trail

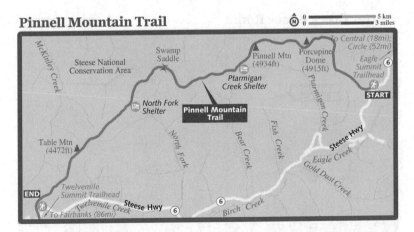

BEAVER CREEK

🏃 Paddling Beaver Creek

Beaver Creek is *the* adventure for budget travelers with time and a yearning to paddle through a roadless wilderness. The moderately swift stream, with long clear pools and frequent rapids, is rated Class I and can be handled by canoeists with expedition experience. The 111-mile creek flows past hills forested in white spruce and paper birch below the jagged peaks of the White Mountains.

A day's paddle beyond Nome Creek, Beaver Creek spills into Yukon Flats National Wildlife Refuge, where it meanders through a marshy area. Eventually it flows north into the Yukon River, where, after two or three days, you'll pass under the Yukon River Bridge on the Dalton Hwy and can be picked up here. This is a 399-mile paddle and a three-week expedition – the stuff great Alaskan adventures are made of.

The scenery is spectacular, the chances of seeing another party remote and you'll catch so much grayling you'll never want to eat another one. You can also spend a night in the Borealis-Le Fevre Cabin, a BLM cabin on the banks of Beaver Creek.

SECTION	DISTANCE
Nome Creek to Beaver Creek	16 miles
Beaver Creek to Victoria Creek	111 miles
Victoria Creek to Yukon River	162 miles
Yukon River to Dalton Hwy	110 miles

ℹ️ Information

LEVEL OF DIFFICULTY Medium, Class I water
INFORMATION Bureau of Land Management (BLM; ☎474-2200; www.ak.blm.gov)

ℹ️ Getting There & Away

To get there, at Mile 57, Steese Hwy go north on US Creek Rd for 6 miles, then northwest on Nome Creek Rd to the Ophir Creek Campground. You can put in at Nome Creek and paddle to its confluence with Beaver Creek. Most paddlers plan on six to nine days to reach Victoria Creek, a 127-mile trip, where gravel bars are used by bush planes to land and pick up paddlers.

Rent a canoe from **7 Bridges Boats & Bikes** (☎479-0751; www.7gablesinn.com/7bbb; daily/weekly $50/150). They'll take you to Mile 57 of the Steese Hwy, where US Creek Rd reaches Nome Creek Rd. For pickup at Yukon River Bridge, 175 miles north of Fairbanks, call **Dalton Hwy Express** (☎474-3555; www.daltonhighwayexpress.com).

Beaver Creek Canoe Route

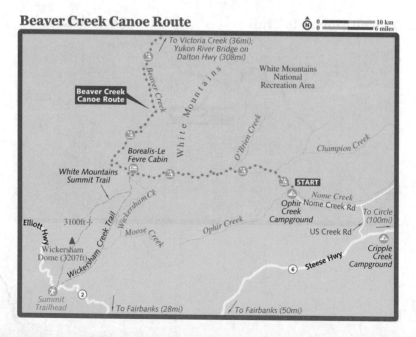

SAVONOSKI LOOP

🏃 Paddling Savonoski Loop

This 80-mile, six- to eight-day paddle begins and ends at Brooks Camp and takes paddlers into remote sections of Katmai National Park & Preserve, offering the best in wilderness adventure without expensive bush-plane travel.

Although there's no white water, the trip is still challenging, with the hardest section being the 12-mile run of the Savonoski River, which is braided and has many deadheads and sweepers. The Savonoski is also prime brown-bear habitat and for this reason park rangers recommend paddling the river in a single day and not camping along it.

The first section through Naknek Lake is especially scenic and well protected at the end where you dip in and out of the Bay of Islands. You're then faced with a mile-long portage along a trail (often a mud-hole) before continuing on to Lake Grosvenor and the Grosvenor River. Then head down the Savonoski River, which brings you to the last leg, a 20-mile paddle along the south shore of the Iliuk Arm back to Brooks Camp.

Paddlers have to remember that Katmai is famous for its sudden and violent storms, some lasting days. The preferred mode of travel here is a kayak, due to the sudden winds and rough nature of the big lakes.

SECTION	
Brooks Camp to Lake Grosvenor portage	30
Portage to Lake Grosvenor	1 mile
Lake Grosvenor to Grosvenor River	14 miles
Grosvenor River to Savonoski River	3 miles
Savonoski River to Iliuk Arm	12 miles
Iliuk Arm to Brooks Camp	20 miles

ℹ Information

LEVEL OF DIFFICULTY Medium to hard, Class I water

INFORMATION Katmai National Park (☑246-3305; www.nps.gov/katm)

ℹ Getting There & Away

See Katmai National Park & Preserve (p339) for information on reservations and getting to the area. Most visitors either fly in with a folding kayak or rent a kayak from **Lifetime Adventures** (☑800-952-8624; www.lifetimeadventures.net) in Brooks Camp. Folding kayaks are $45/55 a day for a single/double or $245/280 per week. The Anchorage-based outfitter will also arrange an unguided trip that includes airfare from Anchorage to King Salmon, floatplane charter to Brooks Camp and folding kayaks for $950 per person per week.

Savonoski Loop

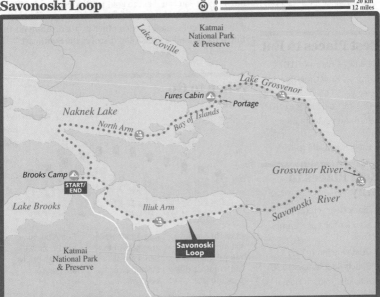

Juneau & the Southeast

Includes »

Best Places to Eat

» Ludvig's Bistro (p111)

» Tracy's King Crab Shack (p124)

» Coastal Cold Storage (p102)

» Ruth Ann's Restaurant (p91)

» Stowaway Café (p149)

Best Places to Stay

» Black Bear Inn (p80)

» Mendenhall Lake Campground (p123)

» Gustavus Inn (p133)

» Beach Roadhouse (p138)

» Alaskan Sojourn Hostel (p148)

Why Go?

Southeast Alaska is so *unAlaska*. While much of the state is a treeless expanse of land with a layer of permafrost, the Southern Panhandle is a slender, long rainforest that stretches 540 miles from Icy Bay south to Portland Canal and is filled with ice-blue glaciers, rugged snowcapped mountains, towering Sitka spruce and a thousand islands known as the Alexander Archipelago.

Before WWII, the Southeast was Alaska's heart and soul, and Juneau was not only the capital but the state's largest city. Today the region is characterized by big trees and small towns. Each community here has its own history and character: from Norwegian-influenced Petersburg to Russian-tinted Sitka. You can feel the gold fever in Skagway and see a dozen glaciers near Juneau. Each town is unique and none of them are connected to each other by road. Jump on the state ferry or book a cruise and discover the Southeast.

When to Go
Juneau

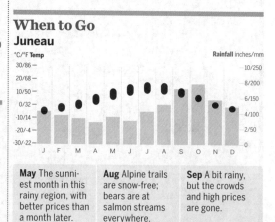

May The sunniest month in this rainy region, with better prices than a month later.

Aug Alpine trails are snow-free; bears are at salmon streams everywhere.

Sep A bit rainy, but the crowds and high prices are gone.

History

Petroglyphs lying along the shoreline in Wrangell, Petersburg and other locations indicate that human habitation in Southeast Alaska dates back at least 8000 to 10,000 years. The Russians arrived in 1741, entered Sitka Sound and sent two longboats ashore in search of fresh water. The boats never returned, and the Russians wisely departed.

What the unfortunate shore party encountered were members of Tlingit tribes, who over time had developed the most advanced culture – in terms of food gathering, art and the construction of large clan houses – of any Alaska Native group. The Tlingits were still there in 1799 when the Russians returned and established the Southeast's first nonindigenous settlement. Aleksandr Baranov built a Russian fort near the present ferry terminal to continue the rich sea-otter fur trade. He was in Kodiak three years later when Tlingits, armed with guns from British and American traders, overwhelmed the fort, burned it to the ground and killed most of its inhabitants.

Baranov returned in 1804, this time with an imperial Russian warship and, after destroying the Tlingit fort, established the headquarters of the Russian-American Company at the present site of Sitka. Originally called New Archangel, Sitka flourished both economically and culturally on the strength of the fur trade and in its golden era was known as the 'Paris of the Pacific.'

In an effort to strengthen their grip on the region and protect their fur-trading interests, the Russians built a stockade near the mouth of the Stikine River in 1834. They named it Redoubt St Dionysius. But in 1840 the political winds shifted and the Russians leased the entire Southeast coastline to the British, who renamed the new outpost Fort Stikine. After purchasing Alaska from the Russians, the Americans formally took control of the territory in Sitka in 1867. A year later Fort Stikine was renamed Wrangell and raised its third national flag in less than 30 years.

In 1880, at the insistence of a Tlingit chief, Joe Juneau and Dick Harris went to Gastineau Channel to try their luck and prospect for gold. They hacked their way through the thick forest to the head of Gold Creek, and there they found, in the words of Harris, 'little lumps as large as peas and beans.' The news spurred the state's first major gold strike, and within a year a small town named Juneau appeared, the first to be founded after Alaska's purchase from the Russians. After the decline in the whaling and fur trades reduced Sitka's importance, the Alaskan capital was moved to Juneau in 1906.

The main gold rush, the turning point in Alaska's history, occurred in Skagway when more than 40,000 gold-rush stampeders descended on the town at the turn of the century as part of the fabled Klondike Gold Rush. Most made their way to the Yukon gold fields by way of the Chilkoot Trail until the White Pass & Yukon Route Railroad was completed in 1900.

In 1887 the population of Skagway was two; 10 years later, 20,000 people lived there and the gold-rush town was Alaska's largest city. A center for saloons, hotels and brothels, Skagway became infamous for its lawlessness. For a time, the town was held under the tight control of crime boss Jefferson Randolph 'Soapy' Smith and his gang, who conned and swindled naive newcomers out of their money and stampeders out of their gold dust. Soapy Smith was finally removed from power by a mob of angry citizens. In a gunfight between Smith and city engineer Frank Reid, both men died, ending Smith's reign as the 'uncrowned prince of Skagway' after only nine months.

At the time, Wrangell was also booming as the supply point for prospectors heading up the Stikine River to the Cassiar Gold District of British Columbia in 1861 and 1874, and then using the river again to reach the Klondike fields in 1897. Wrangell was as ruthless and lawless as Skagway. With miners holding their own court, it was said 'that a man would be tried at 9am, found guilty of murder at 11:30am and hung by 2pm.'

Just as gold fever was dying out, the salmon industry was taking hold. One of the first canneries in Alaska was built in Klawock on Prince of Wales Island in 1878. Ketchikan was begun in 1885 as a cannery, and in 1897 Peter Buschmann arrived from Norway and established Petersburg as a cannery site because of the fine harbor and a ready supply of ice from nearby LeConte Glacier.

After WWII, with the construction of the Alcan (Alaska Hwy) and large military bases around Anchorage and Fairbanks, Alaska's sphere of influence shifted from the Southeast to the mainland further north. In 1974 Alaskans voted to move the state capital again, this time to the small town of Willow,

Southeast Alaska Highlights

1 Strapping on crampons and hiking across the icy blue world of Juneau's **Mendenhall Glacier** (p129)

2 Ziplining down a mountain and spending the afternoon viewing bears at Ketchikan's **Herring Creek** (p77)

3 Visiting the **Wrangell Museum** (p92) to discover why two presidents and Wyatt Earp passed through town

4 Following the Klondike gold rush by hiking Skagway's **Chilkoot Trail** (p52)

5 Heading deep into **Glacier Bay National Park** (p131) to see seals, sea lions and glaciers calving icebergs the size of small houses

6 Meeting the locals and soothing sore muscles at the **Tenakee Springs Bathhouse** (p118)

7 Viewing totems in a mystical rainforest at **Sitka National Historical Park** (p106)

8 Hanging 10 with surfer dudes in **Yakutat** (p149)

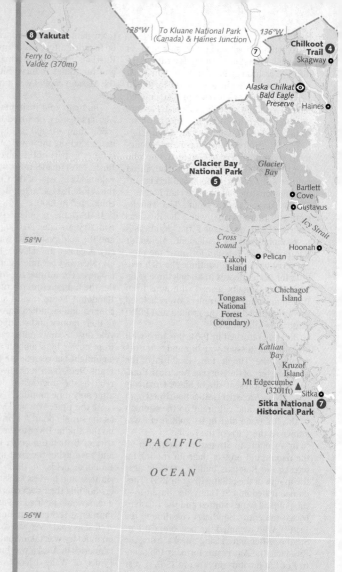

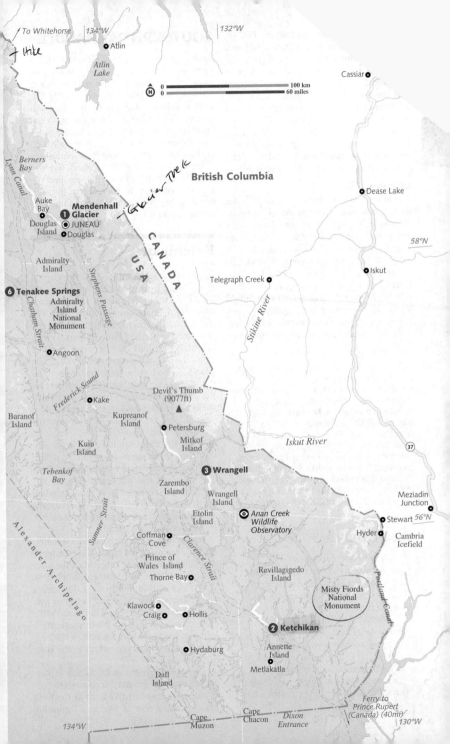

:horage. The so-
hung over Juneau
ening to turn the
The issue became
etween Anchorage
l voters, faced with
g to construct a new
nding in 1982.

ll the capital and the
ss, lightly populated
area where ...uents make a living fishing
and catering to tourists and cruise ships.

Climate

The Southeast has Alaska's mildest climate. Greatly affected by warm ocean currents, the region has warm summer temperatures averaging 69°F (20°C), with an occasional heat wave that sends temperatures to 80°F (27°C). Winters are also relatively mild, and subzero days are rare. Residents, who have learned to live with an annual rainfall of 60in to 200in, call the frequent rain 'liquid sunshine.' The heavy precipitation creates the dense, lush rainforests and numerous waterfalls most travelers come to cherish.

ⓘ Getting There & Around

Most of the Southeast may be road-less, but getting there and getting around is easy. Ketchikan is only 1½ hours away from Seattle by air on **Alaska Airlines** (☑800-426-0333; www.alaskaair. com) or 37 hours on the **Alaska Marine Highway** (☑800-642-0066; www.ferryalaska.com) from Bellingham, WA. The state ferries, North America's longest public ferry system, also provide transportation between the regions, cities, towns and little fishing ports. Separate ferries link Prince of Wales Island with Ketchikan, Wrangell and Petersburg (p91), Haines with Skagway (p142), and Juneau and Glacier Bay (p128).

HAVE YOUR SAY

Found a fantastic restaurant that you're longing to share with the world? Disagree with our recommendations? Or just want to talk about your most recent trip?

Whatever your reason, head to lonelyplanet.com, where you can post a review, ask or answer a question on the Thorntree forum, comment on a blog, or share your photos and tips on Groups. Or you can simply spend time chatting with like-minded travelers. So go on, have your say.

SOUTHERN PANHANDLE

Residents like to call this region of Alaska 'rainforest islands': lush, green, watery, remote and road-less to the outside world. This is the heart of Southeast Alaska's fishing industry, and the region's best wilderness fishing lodges are scattered in the small coves of these islands. Cruise ships pass through, but they only inundate Ketchikan; the other communities receive few if any vessels. Best of all, two ferry systems, the Alaska State Marine Highway and the Inter-Island Ferry Authority, serve the area, so island hopping, even in this remote rainforest, is easy.

Ketchikan

POP 13,477

Once known as the 'Canned Salmon Capital of the World', today Ketchikan settles for 'First City', the initial port for Alaska Marine ferries and cruise ships coming from the south. It could also be called the 'Thin City'. Just 90 miles north of Prince Rupert, Ketchikan hugs the bluffs that form the shoreline along the southwest corner of Revillagigedo Island. Several miles long but never more than 10 blocks wide, Ketchikan centers on the single main drag of Tongass Ave, which sticks to the shore of Tongass Narrows like a bathtub ring. On one side of Tongass, many businesses and homes are built on stilts out over the water, while on the other side they cling to the steep slopes and often have winding wooden staircases leading to their doors. Space is so scarce here that the airport had to be built on another island. Extending north and south from the downtown area is Tongass Hwy, which wraps around the south end of Revillagigedo Island.

Founded as a cannery site in 1885, Ketchikan's mainstay for most of its existence was salmon, and then timber when the huge Ketchikan Pulp Mill was constructed at Ward Cove in 1954. But in the 1970s strikes and changes in public policy began to mar the logging industry. Louisiana-Pacific closed its sawmill in the city center after a strike in 1983 and its pulp mill in 1997, resulting in hundreds of workers losing their high-paying jobs.

There is still commercial fishing in Ketchikan and the industry accounts for 30% of the local economy. What rings the local cash registers now is tourism. Beginning

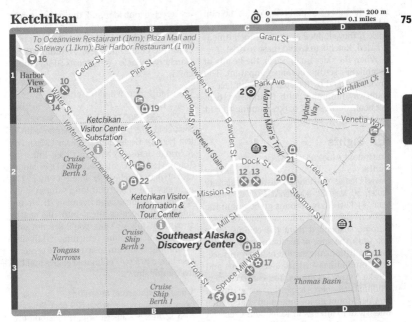

Ketchikan

in the mid-1990s Ketchikan transformed itself into a cruise-ship capital, with up to six ships visiting a day, bringing 650,000 passengers to the shores of Thin City from May to October.

If you stay in Ketchikan longer than an hour, chances are good that it will rain at least once if not several times. The average annual rainfall is 162in, but in some years it has been known to be more than 200in. Local residents never use umbrellas or let the rain interfere with daily activities, even outdoor ones. If they stopped everything each time it drizzled, Ketchikan would cease to exist.

When the skies finally clear, the beauty of Ketchikan's setting becomes apparent. The town is backed by forested hills and faces a waterway humming with floatplanes, fishing boats, ferries and barges hauling freight to other Southeast ports.

◉ Sights

Southeast Alaska Discovery Center
MUSEUM
(www.fs.fed.us/r10/tongass/districts/discovery center; 50 Main St; adult/child $5/free; ⊙8am-5pm; ⊛) Three large totems greet you in the lobby of the center while a school of silver salmon, suspended from the ceiling, leads you toward a slice of nicely re-created rainforest. Upstairs, the exhibit hall features sections on Southeast Alaska's ecosystems and Alaska Native traditions. You can even view wildlife here: there's a spotting scope trained on Deer Mountain for mountain goats, while underwater cameras in Ketchikan Creek let you watch thousands of salmon struggling upstream to spawn.

Dolly's House
HISTORIC BUILDING
(24 Creek St; adult/child $5/free; ⊙8am-5pm or when cruise ships are in) Departing from Stedman St is Creek St, a boardwalk built over Ketchikan Creek on pilings – a photographer's delight. This was Ketchikan's famed red-light district until prostitution became illegal in 1954. During Creek St's heyday, it supported up to 30 brothels and became known as the only place in Alaska where 'the fishermen and the fish went upstream to spawn.' The house with bright red trim is Dolly's House, the parlor of the city's most famous madam, Dolly Arthur. Now it's a museum dedicated to this notorious era. You can see the brothel, including its bar, which was placed over a trapdoor to the creek for quick disposal of bootleg whiskey.

Totem Heritage Center
CULTURAL CENTER
(www.ketchikanmusuems.org; 601 Deermount St; adult/child $5/free; ⊙8am-5pm) A 15-minute walk east from the cruise-ship docks is Totem Heritage Center, where totem poles brought from deserted Tlingit communities are kept to prevent further deterioration. Inside the center 17 totems are on display in an almost spiritual setting that shows the reverence Alaska Natives attach to them. More

are erected outside, and the entire center is shrouded in pines and serenaded by the gurgling Ketchikan Creek. A combined ticket for the Center and Deer Mountain Tribal Hatchery & Eagle Center costs $15/5 (adult/child).

Deer Mountain Tribal Hatchery & Eagle Center
HATCHERY
(⌨228-5533, 800-252-5158; 1158 Salmon Rd; adult/child $12/5, combined admission with Totem Heritage Center $15/5; ⊙8am-4:30pm; ⊛) A bridge across Ketchikan Creek links the Totem Heritage Center with the Deer Mountain Tribal Hatchery & Eagle Center. The hatchery raises 350,000 king salmon, coho salmon, steelhead and rainbow trout annually and releases them into the nearby stream. In July or later, you'll see not only the salmon fry but returning adult fish swimming upstream to spawn. The center is also home to a pair of injured eagles and has live raptor shows.

Tongass Historical Museum
MUSEUM
(www.ketchikanmusuems.org; 629 Dock St; adult/child $2/free; ⊙8am-5pm) Sharing a building with the Ketchikan Public Library is the Tongass Historical Museum, which houses a collection of local historical and Alaska Native artifacts, many dealing with Ketchikan's fishing industry. More interesting is the impressive Raven Stealing the Sun totem just outside and an observation platform overlooking the Ketchikan Creek falls.

Thomas Basin
HARBOR
If you thought Creek St was photogenic, cross Stedman St and be ready to burn some megapixels. Thomas Basin is home to Ketchikan's fishing fleet and the city's most picturesque harbor. When the boats come in, you can photograph them unloading their catch and then follow the crews to the colorful Potlatch Bar (126 Thomas St) nearby, a classic fishers' pub.

Stairways & Boardwalks
LOOKOUTS
All over Ketchikan there are stairways leading somewhere higher. Sure, they're knee-bending climbs, but the reward for your exertion is great views from the top. Heading back west along Dock St, just past the Ketchikan Daily News Building, is Edmond St, also called the Street of Stairs for obvious reasons. Heading down Park Ave from the hatchery, you'll pass the Upland Way stairs that climb to a viewpoint. Nearby is a bridge across Ketchikan Creek, the site of a

The biggest bears – browns tipping the scale at 1000lbs or more – are seen at such exotic locations as Katmai National Park and the Kodiak National Wildlife Refuge. But for sheer numbers, ease of transportation and affordable bear watching it's hard to pass up Southeast Alaska. Like elsewhere in Alaska, bear watching in the Southeast is best in July and August, and each location corresponds with particular salmon runs:

» **Fish Creek Hyder** (Hyder; p88) It may be hard to reach, but once there it's easy to spend an afternoon watching brown bears.

» **Naha Bay** (Ketchikan; p78) It's an 8-mile paddle by kayak to Naha River National Recreation Trail, where in August black bears are snagging salmon at a small waterfall.

» **Herring Creek** (Ketchikan; p77) After ziplining down a mountain you can watch black bears catching salmon.

» **Margaret Creek** (Ketchikan; p77) Bears gather at this creek, located 26 miles north of Ketchikan on Revillagigedo Island, in late August and the first two weeks in September. Most visitors arrive on a charter float plane and then walk a quarter-mile trail to a viewing platform.

» **Anan Creek** (Wrangell; p92) You can rent a USFS cabin and spend your entire day watching black and brown bears.

» **Pack Creek** (Admiralty Island; p130) This wilderness island has one of the highest densities of bears in Alaska; you can see them from the safety of an observation tower.

» **Steep Creek** (Juneau; p129) It's a short hike in Mendenhall Valley to reach Steep Creek Fish Viewing Site and watch black bears feeding on salmon.

---

fish ladder and one end of **Married Man's Trail** – a delightful series of boardwalks and stairs leading up to the Cape Fox Lodge or back to Creek St.

Ketchikan's newest boardwalk is the **Waterfront Promenade**, which begins near Berth 4, passes **Harbor View Park** (a city park that is composed entirely of decking and pilings), follows the cruise ship docks and then wraps around Thomas Basin Harbor. Along the way there are plenty of whale-tail and halibut benches where you can take a break and admire the maritime scenery.

🏃 Activities

Bear Watching

As in much of Alaska, Ketchikan's charter pilots have met the public's interest in bear watching. The most affordable way to see bears, though, is to paddle a kayak to Nada Bay, where black bears feed on salmon in August, or visit Alaska Canopy Adventures (p79), which provides access to the bears feeding in Herring Creek.

Alaska Seaplane Tours   BEAR WATCHING
(☎225-1974, 866-858-2327; www.alaskaseaplanetours.com; tours $339) Flies to Prince of Wales Island to watch bruins on a two-hour tour.

Promech Air   BEAR WATCHING
(☎225-3845, 800-860-3845; www.promechair.com; tours $339) Its three-hour tour includes a flight to the Neet's Bay Hatchery and 1½ hours watching black bears.

Seawind Aviation   BEAR WATCHING
(☎225-1206, 877-225-1203; www.seawindaviation.com; tours $350) A 2½-hour tour to Margaret Creek north of Ketchikan, where a short hike brings you to a viewing spot of feeding black bears.

Hiking

Most Ketchikan area trails are either out of town or must be reached by boat.

Deer Mountain Trail   HIKING
Within walking distance of downtown is Deer Mountain Trail, Ketchikan's most popular hike. The well-maintained 2.5-mile trail can be reached by taking the Bus' Green Line to the corner of Deermount and Fair Sts and then heading south on Ketchikan Lakes Rd. The trail is a climb to the 3000ft summit of Deer Mountain and along the way overlooks provide panoramic views – the first only a mile up the trail. Toward the top of the mountain are more trails that extend into the alpine region and a free-use shelter.

ℹ NOT GETTING LOST

For peace of mind while hiking or paddling in Ketchikan, pick up a free **personal locator beacon** from the Ketchikan Visitor Information & Tour Center. If you became lost it can be activated to send a distress signal and your GPS location to the Ketchikan Volunteer Rescue Squad. When your adventure is over you simply return it.

But keep in mind this is a steady climb and a more challenging hike beyond the shelter.

Rainbird Trail   HIKING

Dedicated in 2010, this 1.3-mile trail is also within town, stretching from the University of Alaska-Southeast campus off 7th Ave to a trailhead off Third Ave Bypass. You can ride the Bus' Green Line to UAS and follow this delightful trail as it winds through a rainforest along a bluff before giving way to striking views of the city and Tongass Narrows below.

Ward Lake Nature Walk   HIKING

The easy 1.3-mile Ward Lake Nature Walk, an interpretive loop around Ward Lake, begins near the parking area at the lake's north end. Beavers, birds and the occasional black bear might be seen. To reach the lake, follow N Tongass Hwy, 7 miles from downtown to Ward Cove; turn right on Revilla Rd and continue up 1.5 miles to Ward Lake Rd.

Perseverance Trail   HIKING

The 2.3-mile (one-way) Perseverance Trail from Ward Lake to Perseverance Lake passes through mature coastal forest and muskeg. The view of Perseverance Lake with its mountainous backdrop is spectacular and the hiking is moderately easy. The trailhead is on Ward Lake's east side, just past CCC Campground.

Dude Mountain Trail   HIKING

Ketchikan's other alpine trek is Dude Mountain Trail, reached from Revilla Rd by turning right on Brown Mountain Rd, 5 miles from N Tongass Hwy. At the end of Brown Mountain Rd is the trailhead for Dude Mountain Trail, which begins as a boardwalk through stands of old-growth spruce and becomes a trail as you follow a narrow ridge to the 2848ft peak. It's a 1-mile trek and a gain of 1200ft to the top, but once there you're in open alpine and can easily ridge-walk to Diana Mountain (3014ft) or Brown Mountain (2978ft). Plan on two hours for the round-trip to Dude Mountain.

Paddling

Ketchikan serves as the base for some of the best kayaking in the Southeast. Possibilities include anything from an easy paddle around the waterfront to a weeklong trip in Misty Fiords National Monument. Pick up charts and topographic maps from the Southeast Alaska Discovery Center, and outdoor supplies from **Tongass Trading Company** (☏225-5101; 201 Dock St).

For kayak rentals there's **Southeast Sea Kayaks** (☏225-1258, 800-287-1607; www.kayakketchikan.com; Westflight Bldg, 1621 Tongass Ave; single/double kayaks per day $49/59) The outfitter, located north of the downtown area on Tongass Ave, also offers tours, including a 2½-hour paddle of Ketchikan's waterfront (adult/child $94/59). A much better paddling experience, however, is its Orcas Cove trip (adult/child $154/134), a four-hour adventure that begins with a boat ride across the Tongass Narrows and then paddling among protected islands looking for sea lions, orcas and seals.

Betton Island   KAYAKING

Due west of Settler's Cove State Park at the north end (Mile 18.2) of N Tongass Hwy is this island and several smaller islands nearby, making it an excellent day paddle if you're staying at the campground. Although Clover Pass is a highly trafficked area, the backside of Betton Island offers a more genuine wilderness setting. Pack a tent and sleeping bag and you can turn this into an overnight excursion by camping on the great beaches of the Tatoosh Islands on the west side of Betton Island.

Naha Bay   KAYAKING

Also from Settler's Cove State Park, it's an 8-mile paddle to Naha Bay, the destination of an excellent three- or four-day adventure. At the head of the bay is a floating dock where you can leave your kayak and set off down the Naha River National Recreation Trail. The scenic 5.4-mile trail follows the river up to Jordan and Heckman Lakes, both of which have **USFS cabins** (☏877-444-6777, 518-885-3639; www.recreation.gov; cabins $35). The fishing here is good and black bears are plentiful – in August you might see them catching salmon at a small waterfall 2 miles up the trail from Roosevelt Lagoon.

A narrow outlet connects Naha Bay with Roosevelt Lagoon. You don't have to enter the lagoon to access the trail. Kayakers wishing to paddle into the lagoon must either portage around the outlet or enter it at high slack tide, as the narrow pass becomes a frothy, roaring chute when the tide is moving in or out.

George & Carroll Inlets   KAYAKING

From Hole in the Wall Bar & Marina (p86), 7.5 miles southeast of Ketchikan down the South Tongass Hwy, you can start an easy one- to four-day paddle north into George or Carroll Inlets or both. Each inlet is protected from the area's prevailing southwesterlies, so the water is usually calm (although north winds occasionally whip down George Inlet). From Hole in the Wall to the top of George Inlet is a 26-mile paddle.

Snorkeling

Snorkel Alaska   SNORKELING

(247-7783; www.snorkelalaska.com; per person $99) They scuba dive in Alaska, why not snorkel? This company hands you a wet suit, complete with hood, gloves and boots, and then leads you into the water at Mountain Point for a fascinating underwater wildlife tour that includes sea stars, urchins, sea cucumbers and every fish that swims by. The three-hour tour includes transport from the downtown area.

Wilderness Cabins

Some 30 USFS cabins (877-444-6777, 518-885-3639; www.recreation.gov; cabins $25-45) dot the Ketchikan area. It's best to reserve them in advance but often early in the summer and midweek something will be available. Some cabins can be reached by boat but most visitors fly to them. Within about 20 miles of Ketchikan are Alava Bay Cabin ($35), on the southern end of Behm Canal in Misty Fiords National Monument; Fish Creek Cabin ($45), connected by a short trail to Thorne Arm; and two Patching Lake Cabins ($25), which offer good fishing for cutthroat trout and grayling.

Ziplining

Ketchikan has everything needed to be the zipline capital of Alaska: lush rainforests and elevation. There are three zipline operations now; more are bound to come.

Alaska Canopy Adventures   EXTREME SPORTS

(225-5503; www.alaskacanopy.com; 116 Wood Rd; per person $190) Operating two of the lines is Alaska Canopy Adventures. Eagle Zipline is the main one, with eight lines, three suspension bridges and a 4WD vehicle to transport you up a mountain so you can zip 6200ft to the bottom. Also on-site is the Alaska Rain Forest Sanctuary, where visitors can view wildlife, including salmon runs in Herring Creek and bears that feast on them.

👉 Tours

Being the cruise-ship port that it is, more tours operate in and around Ketchikan than can possibly be done in a two-week vacation, much less a six-hour stopover. The standard is a two-hour tour of the city that includes a run out to Totem Bight; a half-dozen operators offer it for around $45 per person. The best place to see what's available and to sign up is the **Ketchikan Visitor Information & Tour Center** building on City Dock, where a whole wing is devoted to a gauntlet of tour providers touting their services.

Alaska Amphibious Tours   SCENIC DRIVE

(225-9899, 866-341-3825; www.akduck.com; tours adult/child $38/24) Uses amphibian vehicles that double as a bus and a boat to provide 1½-hour tours of the downtown area and the harbor. The top-heavy vehicle puts you 8ft above anything on the road for a great view, but the time spent cruising the harbor is shorter than most would like.

Bering Sea Crab Fishermen's Tour   BOAT TOUR

(888-239-3816; www.56degreesnorth.com; tours adult/child $159/99) Ketchikan is a long way from the Bering Sea and they don't catch many king crabs here, but you can experience both on the *Aleutian Ballad*. The crab boat, which once featured on the TV show *The Deadliest Catch*, has a 100-seat amphitheater for a 3½-hour, on-the-water tour of commercial fishing. Bering Sea crabbers pull up huge pots full of tanner, Dungeness and even giant king crabs as well as bait lines to catch rockfish and shark. This seemingly out-of-place tour is extremely interesting.

Wilderness Exploration & Crab Feast   BOAT TOUR

(225-6077; www.catchcrabs.com; tours per person $99) Another catch-a-crab tour but smaller and more affordable than the Bering Sea boat. The three-hour tour begins at George Inlet Lodge, a historic cannery bunkhouse 8 miles south of town, where you board a vessel for a boat cruise that includes pulling up pots filled with Dungeness crabs. It ends back at the lodge with an all-you-can-eat crab feast. The meal is excellent and is truly all-you-can-eat; you can even skip the boat ride and just show up for the crab feed ($42).

🎆 Festivals & Events

Ketchikan's Fourth of July celebration includes a parade, contests, softball games, an impressive display of fireworks and a logging show. The smaller Blueberry Festival, held at the State Office Building and the Main Street Theater on the first weekend in August, consists of arts and crafts, singers, musicians, and food stalls serving blueberries every possible way. During most of April the Alaska Hummingbird Festival is staged at the Southeast Alaska Discovery Center to celebrate those tiny birds winging their way back to Ketchikan.

🛏 Sleeping

Ketchikan charges 13% on lodging in city and bed taxes. There are no public campgrounds close to town; the closest are 4.5 miles north of the ferry terminal at Ward Lake Recreation Area (p86).

TOP CHOICE Black Bear Inn   B&B $$

(📞225-4343; www.stayinalaska.com; 5528 N Tongass Hwy; r $160-230; ⊕@) This incredible B&B offers a range of waterfront accommodations 2.5 miles north of the downtown madness and next to a Blue Line bus stop. There are four bedrooms in the home and a small apartment on the 2nd floor with a private entrance. Outside is a logger's bunkhouse that was floated to Ketchikan and renovated into a charming honeymooner's cabin. Every room in the house has been beautifully put together by the proprietor, who is also an artist. Among the many amenities is a covered hot tub outside where you can soak while watching eagles soaring and whales swimming in the narrows.

New York Hotel   BOUTIQUE HOTEL $$

(📞225-0246, 866-225-0246; www.thenewyork hotel.com; 207 Stedman St; r $149-189, ste $209; ⊕@🛜) A historic boutique hotel in a great location between Creek St and Thomas Basin. The eight rooms are filled with antiques and colorful quilts but have been updated with cable TV, small refrigerators and a private bath. The hotel also has seven suites a short walk away, five of them on Creek St, which feature comfortable living rooms,

small kitchen areas and sleeping accommodations for four. The 2nd-floor perch means you can watch the salmon spawn in Ketchikan Creek below and the seals that follow them on high tides.

Cape Fox Lodge   HOTEL $$$

(📞225-8001, 866-225-8001; www.capefoxlodge; 800 Venetia Way; r $195-229; 🛜) This is Ketchikan's splashiest lodging. Perched atop the hill behind Creek St, it offers the best views in town and can be reached by a high-tech funicular tram from the Creek St boardwalk. The opulent lodge has 72 amenity-filled rooms and suites and an acclaimed restaurant overlooking the city. There is so much Native art in the lobby – baskets, totems, an 1880 ceremonial shirt – it's like walking through a gallery. Also on site is a coffee shop and gift store, and staff can arrange almost any tour possible.

Super 8 Motel   MOTEL $$

(📞225-9088; 800-800-8000; 2151 Sea Level Dr; r $109-121; 🛜) Overlooking the waterfront but behind Plaza Mall, the nicest aspect about this motel isn't its location but its amenities. Breakfast, shuttle service to/from the ferry or airport, free wi-fi and recently updated rooms make it a bargain in the land of high motel prices.

Landing Best Western   HOTEL $$$

(📞225-5166, 800-428-8304; www.landingho tel.com; 3434 Tongass Ave; s/d from $186/216; ⊕@🛜) Across the street from the ferry terminal is this sprawling hotel with 107 rooms and suites that have cable TV, microwaves, coffeemakers and small refrigerators. On site are a pub, a restaurant and a fitness center, just in case walking the 2 miles downtown isn't enough exercise for you.

Narrows Inn   LODGE $$

(📞247-2600, 888-686-2600; www.narrowsinn. com; 4871 N Tongass Hwy; r $145-170, ste $230-245; ⊕@🛜) A mile north of the airport ferry on the waterfront, it offers 44 standard rooms that are well kept and very clean. You pay extra for the ocean-view rooms, which feature balconies, despite the fact that the view includes the airport runway on the other side of the Narrows. The inn also includes a bar, restaurant and a marina where a fishing charter can be booked.

Ketchikan Hostel   HOSTEL $

(📞225-3319; www.ketchikanhostel.com; 400 Main St; dm $20; ⊙Jun-Aug; ⊕@) The best of Ketchikan's two hostels is right downtown spread out in a Methodist church complex that includes a large kitchen, three small common areas and separate-sex dorm rooms. The friendly hostel is spotlessly clean, but doors are locked after curfew. Reservations are recommended in July.

Gilmore Hotel HOTEL **$$**
(225-9423, 800-275-9423; www.gilmorehotel. com; 326 Front St; r $115-155; @) Built in 1927 as a hotel and renovated several times since, the Gilmore has 34 rooms that still retain a historical flavor. The rooms are 'historically proportioned' (ie small) but comfortable, with cable TV, coffeemakers and hair dryers. The entire 2nd floor is nonsmoking.

✗ Eating

Ketchikan has many places to eat, but the expensive Alaskan prices usually send the newly arrived visitor into a two-day fast. If this is your first Alaskan city, don't fret – it only gets worse as you head north!

TOP CHOICE Bar Harbor Restaurant MODERN AMERICAN **$$$**
(225-2813; 2813 Tongass Ave; mains $18-34; dinner Tue-Sun;) A small cozy place between downtown and the ferry terminal with an intriguingly eclectic menu that is constantly changing. Yeah, they serve seafood here, but there are also a lot of things on the menu that didn't start life in the water, such as the signature dish, Ketchikan's best prime rib. The wine list is nice and so is the back deck with its covered tables and watery view. Reservations recommended.

Annabelle's SEAFOOD **$$$**
(326 Front St; lunch mains $10-17, dinner mains $23-34; lunch & dinner) At the Gilmore Hotel, this keg and chowder house has a seafood-heavy menu, a wonderful bar and 1920s decor. The chowder is good, and the keg half of the restaurant even better, with its long polished bar, brass footrest and antique slot machine. Where are the spittoons?

Diaz Café ASIAN **$$**
(335 Stedman St; mains $11-16; lunch & dinner Tue-Sun) Located on the south side of Ketchikan Creek, this longtime cafe dates back to the 1920s, when Filipinos and Japanese weren't allowed to live north of the creek. Today the eatery is a favorite among locals looking for affordable Asian and Filipino

dishes ranging from *pansit* (fried n. to bowls of green soup heaped with noo

Ketchikan Coffee Co COFFEE HOUSE **$**
(225-0246; 207 Stedman St; breakfast mains $5-7, lunch mains $9-13; breakfast & lunch; @) The historic ambience of the New York Hotel spills over into its coffee bar. Along with lattes and espressos, there are beers and wines on the blackboard menu along with a few veggie options, like black bean nachos. In the morning you can enjoy a bagel sandwich or surf the internet.

Heen Kahidi Restaurant AMERICAN **$$$**
(800 Venetia Way; breakfast mains $9-15, lunch mains $11-17, dinner mains $19-42; breakfast, lunch & dinner;) Generally regarded as Ketchikan's best dining experience, the Cape Fox Lodge restaurant offers hilltop dining with floor-to-ceiling windows, providing a view of the world below and eagles at eye level. The dinner menu is split evenly between seafood, steaks and pasta.

Burger Queen BURGERS **$**
(518 Water St; burgers $6-9; 11am-3pm Mon, to 7pm Tue-Sat) Ketchikan's favorite burger joint. Ten varieties, including one with a Polish sausage *and* a hamburger patty, plus 30 flavors of milkshake. Order a burger and fries and have it delivered to the Arctic Bar across the street where you can be sipping a beer.

Sushi Harbor SUSHI **$**
(629 Mission St; lunch mains $9-11, rolls $7-14; lunch & dinner). This Japanese restaurant bustles all day with locals, tourists and cruise-ship workers. There are almost 40 types of roll on the menu, but even just a bowl of shrimp tempura udon (noodle soup) will keep you going all afternoon.

Oceanview Restaurant MEXICAN **$$**
(1831 Tongass Ave; lunch mains $10-11, dinner mains $12-22; lunch & dinner) Ketchikan's best Mexican restaurant offers 10 types of burritos, nine sizzling fajita dishes and, in that great Alaskan tradition, pasta, pizza and a decent veal marsala. It's all served in pleasant surroundings overlooking the Narrows.

Pioneer Café CAFE **$$**
(619 Mission St; breakfast mains $6-13, lunch mains $9-14, dinner mains $11-20; breakfast, lunch & dinner) One of the few downtown restaurants that was around in the time of the lumber mills and the only one open 24 hours on Friday and Saturday, it serves the best breakfast in town and serves it all day.

u & east a Highlights

You can't drive to Juneau, or most of Southeast Alaska, and that seems only proper. This watery, mountainous region, filled with fjords, thousands of islands, impressive glaciers and small but interesting ports, is best explored at the casual pace of a cruise ship or state ferry.

Russian Culture

1 St Michael's Cathedral (p104) not only anchors downtown Sitka but it could be one of the most beloved churches in Southeast Alaska. When the original burnt down in 1966 residents immediately built a replica.

Icing on the Lake

2 It's big, it's blue and it's still active, tossing icebergs into Menhenhall Lake. No wonder Mendenhall Glacier (p129) is Juneau's most popular attraction. View it, hold a piece of it, walk on it; this glacier will amaze you.

Rustic Cabins

3 The floatplane lands on an isolated lake and you step out to a small A-frame cabin. It's one of the 150 US Forest Service cabins scattered across Southeast Alaska, your personal slice of wilderness for the next three days.

Gold Rush Town

4 It's a mob scene in downtown Skagway (p142) with crowded wooden sidewalks, horse-drawn carriages, trains announcing their arrival and salesmen hawking their goods from false-front shops. Just like it was during the Klondike Gold Rush at the turn of the century.

Clockwise from top left
1. St Michael's Cathedral, Sitka 2. Mendenhall Glacier
3. Managed cabin 4. Skagway

2

3

H. D. KIRMS
PIONEER JEWELL
AS ORIGINAL CUI
EST. 1897
SKAGWAY, AK

Alaska Fish House   SEAFOOD $$
(Spruce Mill Way; sandwiches $12-16; ☻10am-4:30pm) Located at ground zero of the cruise-ship strip, this outdoor seafood stand has good salmon chowder, halibut tacos and even fish burgers. Even better than the grub is the quiet seating area in the back that's literally perched over Thomas Basin Harbor.

Safeway   SUPERMARKET $
(2417 Tongass Ave; ☻5am-midnight; 🛜) This grocery store on the side of Plaza Mall has a salad bar ($7 per lb), Starbucks, deli and ready-to-eat items, including Chinese food, and a dining area overlooking the boat traffic on Tongass Narrows.

Drinking & Entertainment

Arctic Bar   BAR
(509 Water St) Just past the tunnel on downtown's northwest side, this local favorite has managed to survive 70 years by poking fun at itself and tourists. On the back deck overlooking the Narrows is a pair of fornicating bears. And hanging below the wooden bruins, in full view of every cruise ship that ties up in front of the bar, is the sign 'Please Don't Feed the Bears.'

Fat Stan's   COCKTAIL BAR
(Salmon Landing Market) A small and surprisingly mellow place considering it's located in the heart of cruise-ship central. Maybe that's because it makes 20 different types of martini, including key lime pie and watermelon Jolly Roger. Sip some gin and watch the crowds.

First City Saloon   BAR
(830 Water St; 🛜) This sprawling club now has two bars, pool tables and comfortable lounge areas with sofas, ottomans and wi-fi. Its dance floor features a 1970s disco ball and a stripper's pole. This is the one place in Ketchikan that rocks, with live music at least twice a week during the summer, often impromptu when cruise-ship bands are looking to let loose.

Great Alaskan Lumberjack Show   SPECTATOR SPORT
(☏225-9050, 888-320-9049; www.lumberjacksports.com; off Spruce Mill Way; adult/child $35/17.50) When the lumberjacks are at the peak of their axe-and-saw battles, you can hear the crowd cheering throughout downtown. A favorite of cruise ships, the hour-long show features 'rugged woodsmen' using handsaws and axes, climbing poles, log rolling and engaging in other activities that real loggers haven't engaged in since the invention of the chainsaw. There are three to four shows daily, depending on how many cruise ships are in.

Shopping
Ketchikan has a rich artist community and between all the jewelry shops are galleries that display local work.

Main Street Gallery   ARTS & CRAFT
(www.ketchikanarts.org; 330 Main St; ☻9am-5pm Mon-Fri, 11am-3pm Sat) Operated by Ketchikan Area Arts & Humanities Council, this wonderful gallery stages a reception on the first Friday of every month, unveiling the work of a selected local or regional artist. It's an evening of refreshments and presentations by the artist and extended hours by other galleries downtown.

Soho Coho   ARTS & CRAFT
(www.trollart.com; 5 Creek St) The home gallery of Ketchikan's most noted artist, Ray Troll, whose salmon- and fish-inspired work is seen all around town, including on the sides of buses.

Alaska Natural History Association   BOOKS
(50 Main St; ☻8am-5pm) The Southeast Alaska Discovery Center bookstore offers an extensive selection of Alaska titles and comfortable sitting areas in which to thumb through them.

Parnassus Books   BOOKS
(105 Stedman St; ☻8:30am-6pm) This longtime bookstore is a delightful place to spend a rainy afternoon browsing Alaskan books, cards and local art.

Information
INTERNET ACCESS Seaport Cyber (5 Salmon Landing; per hr $6; ☻8:30am-5pm) Internet, wi-fi, phone cards and phones for international calls. **Ketchikan Public Library** (629 Dock St; ☻10am-8pm Mon-Wed, to 6pm Thu-Sat; @🛜) The library has wi-fi and internet computers – both free – but clamps a 30-minute limit on wi-fi and 15 minutes on the terminals.

MEDICAL SERVICES Creekside Family Health Clinic (☏220-9982; creeksidehealth.com; 320 Bawden St, Ste 313; ☻8am-5pm Mon-Fri) A walk-in clinic downtown. **Ketchikan General Hospital** (☏225-5171; 3100 Tongass Ave) Near the ferry terminal.

MONEY First Bank (☎228-4474; 331 Dock St) Its 24-hour ATM is less than a block from the one at Wells Fargo. **Wells Fargo** (☎225-2184; 306 Main St) One of a handful of banks mixed in with the gift shops downtown.

POST Main post office (3609 Tongass Ave) Near the ferry terminal. **Postal substation** (422 Mission St) Conveniently located downtown.

TOURIST INFORMATION Ketchikan Visitor Information & Tour Center (☎225-6166, 800-770-3300; www.visit-ketchikan.com; City Dock, 131 Front St; ⊙7am-6pm) You can pick up brochures and free maps, ask the friendly staff questions, use courtesy phones, and even book tours from here. **Ketchikan Visitor Center Substation** Near Berth 3 of the cruise-ship dock and open when ships are in. **Southeast Alaska Discovery Center** (☎228-6220; www.fs.fed.us/r10/tongass/districts/discoverycenter; 50 Main St; ⊙8am-5pm) You don't need to pay the admission to get recreation information at this Alaska Public Lands Information Center. Separate from the displays is a trip-planning room containing an information desk and computer access to reserve USFS cabins.

ⓘ Getting There & Away

AIR Flights to Ketchikan from Seattle (one way $380, two hours), Anchorage (one way $400, 4½ hours) and major Southeast communities are all possible with **Alaska Airlines** (☎800-252-7522; www.alaskaair.com). **Promech Air** (☎225-3845, 800-860-3845; www.promechair.com; 1515 Tongass Ave) offers scheduled floatplane flights between Ketchikan and Prince of Wales Island, including Hollis (one way $105), Craig/Klawock ($130) and Thorne Bay ($105). Ketchikan has many bush-plane operators for charter trips, including **Taquan Air** (☎225-8800, 800-770-8800; www.taquanair.com; 4085 Tongass Ave).

BOAT Northbound **Alaska Marine Highway** ferries leave almost daily in summer, heading north for Wrangell ($37, six hours), Petersburg ($60, nine hours), Sitka ($83, 20 hours), Juneau ($107, 29 hours) and Haines ($134, 33½ hours). Heading south, the MV Columbia departs Ketchikan once a week for Bellingham ($239, 37 hours). The MV Lituya provides service to Metlakatla ($21, 1½ hours) Thursday through Monday. For sailing times call the **ferry terminal** (☎225-6181; 3501 Tongass Ave).

  Inter-Island Ferry Authority (☎225-4838, 866-308-4848; www.interislandferry.com) vessels are capable of holding vehicles and depart Ketchikan at 3:30pm daily, bound for Hollis on Prince of Wales Island (one way adult/child $37/18, three hours). Rates for the ferry vary and are based on your vehicle's length; a subcompact one way costs $50.

ⓘ Getting Around

TO/FROM THE AIRPORT The Ketchikan airport is on one side of Tongass Narrows, the city is on the other. A small car-and-passenger **ferry** ($5 for walk-on passengers) runs between the airport and a landing off Tongass Ave, just northwest of the main ferry terminal. From there you can catch the Bus or a taxi. There isn't a better way to arrive at the First City than on the **Tongass Water Taxi** (☎225-8294): Richard Schuerger meets all flights at the baggage-claim area and then gives you a lift on his boat to the dock nearest your destination. The cost downtown is $19 for the first person and $8 for every additional person.

CAR For two to four people, renting a car is a good way to spend a day seeing sights out of town. There's unlimited mileage with either of the following but a 16% tax.

Alaska Car Rental (☎225-5123, 800-662-0007; 2828 Tongass Ave; compacts $57)

First City Car Rental (☎225-7368; www.firstcitycarrental.com; 1417 Tongass Ave; mid-size $59)

PUBLIC TRANSPORTATION Ketchikan's excellent public bus system is called **the Bus** (☎225-8726; one way $1), but don't worry, there's more than one of them. There are several lines, with the Green Line circling through the heart of the city from the airport ferry to Thomas Basin, the Red Line heading south past Saxman Village to Rotary Beach and the Blue Line heading south all the way to Totem Bight State Park. The Bus also has a free downtown loop called Salmon Run. You can't miss the bus: famed artist Ray Troll painted spawning salmon all over it. The 20-minute loop goes from Berth 4 of the cruise-ship dock to the Totem Heritage Center.

TAXI Cab companies in town include **Sourdough Cab** (☎225-5544) and **Yellow Taxi** (☎225-5555). The fare from the ferry terminal or the airport ferry dock to downtown is $15.

BICYCLE Ketchikan has an expanding system of bike paths that head north and south of downtown along Tongass Ave. Rent Trek hybrids at **Southeast Exposure** (☎225-7746; 1224 Tongass Ave; 4hr/full-day rentals $20/30).

Around Ketchikan

SOUTH TONGASS HIGHWAY

On South Tongass Hwy, 2.5 miles south of Ketchikan, is Saxman Native Village & Totem Park (☎225-4421; www.capefoxtours.com; ⊙8am-5pm), an incorporated Tlingit village of 430 residents. The village is best known for its Saxman Totem Park, which holds 24 totem poles brought here from abandoned

Southeast and restored ~~~ 1930s. Among the col-~~~ f the Lincoln Pole (the ~~~ ska State Museum in ~~~ arved in 1883, using a ~~~ incoln, to commemo-~~~ f white people.

~~~und the Totem Park ~~~ .___ $5) or, if cruise ships are in, join an Alaska Native–led two-hour village **tour** (adult/child $35/17), which includes a Tlingit language lesson, a traditional drum-and-dance performance, a narrated tour of the totems and a visit to the carving shed. Independent travelers can join this tour by calling the village a day in advance.

From Saxman, South Tongass Hwy continues another 12 miles, bending around Mountain Point and heading back north to George Inlet. This route is more scenic than North Tongass Hwy, but holds little in the way of stores, restaurants or campgrounds. One exception is **Hole in the Wall Bar & Marina** (7500 S Tongass Hwy; ⊙noon-2am), a funky little hangout that feels light years away from the tourist madness of Ketchikan in summer. There's not much inside other than a handful of stools, a woodstove, a pool table and a lot of friendly conversation usually centered on fishing. But the bar is in a beautiful location, perched above a small marina in a narrow cove off George Inlet. There's also a good kayaking route that starts here (p79).

In Herring Bay there is a hatchery and Alaska Canopy Adventures (p79), a zipline operation. The South Tongass Hwy then ends at Beaver Falls Hatchery; the Silvis Lake Trail begins nearby.

NORTH TONGASS HIGHWAY

The closest campgrounds to Ketchikan are in Ward Lake Recreation Area; take North Tongass Hwy 4.5 miles north of the ferry terminal and turn right onto Revilla Rd, then continue 1.5 miles to Ward Lake Rd. **CCC Campground** (sites $10), basically an overflow area, is on Ward Lake's east shore, while **Signal Creek Campground** (sites $10) has 24 sites on the south shore. **Last Chance Campground** (sites $10) is in a beautiful area with four scenic lakes, 19 sites and three trails that run through the lush rainforest.

Ten miles northwest of Ketchikan is **Totem Bight State Park** (☏247-8574; 9883 N Tongass Hwy; admission free), which contains 14 restored or recarved totems and a colorful

community house. Just as impressive as the totems are the park's coastline and wooded setting. A viewing deck overlooks Tongass Narrows. Next door to the state park is the equally intriguing **Potlatch Park** (☏225-4445; www.potlatchpark.com; 9809 Totem Bight Rd; admission free; ⊙7:30am-4pm). Walk behind its huge gift shop to enter the park; it's home to a dozen totems, one of which is 42ft high, five beautiful tribal houses and an on-site carver who is usually working on a totem in the carving shed. Best of all, the only charge to experience both parks is $1 – for a ride on the Bus' Blue Line.

Tongass Hwy ends 18 miles north of Ketchikan at **Settler's Cove State Recreation Area** (sites $10), a scenic coastal area with a lush rainforest bordering a gravel beach and rocky coastline. Its campground has 14 sites, a quarter-mile trail to a waterfall and observation deck, and is rarely overflowing like those at Ward Lake.

Misty Fiords National Monument

This spectacular, 3570-sq-mile national monument (p54), just 22 miles east of Ketchikan, is a natural mosaic of sea cliffs, steep fjords and rock walls jutting 3000ft straight out of the ocean. Brown and black bears, mountain goats, Sitka deer, bald eagles and a multitude of marine mammals inhabit this drizzly realm. The monument receives 150in of rainfall annually, and many people think Misty Fiords is at its most beautiful when the granite walls and tumbling waterfalls are veiled in fog and mist. Walker Cove, Rudyerd Bay and Punchbowl Cove – the preserve's most picturesque areas – are reached via Behm Canal, the long inlet separating Revillagigedo Island from the mainland.

Kayaking is *the* best way to experience the preserve. Ketchikan's **Southeast Sea Kayaks** (p78) offers a five-day guided paddle ($1699), with transportation by boat to the fjords and back, and a three-day paddle designed for families (adult/child $999/659). It also rents kayaks and provides transport for boats and paddlers.

You can also view the area on sightseeing flights or day cruises. Flightseeing may be the only option if you're in a hurry, and most tours include landing on a lake. But keep in mind that this is a big seller on the cruise ships and when the weather is nice

My Haida name is Nun Sleenas, which roughly translates to 'Woman Who Works With Her Hands.' I am a member of the Eagle-Frog Clan and have been carving for almost 20 years. I began in my late 20s as an apprentice, and one of the first things I was taught was how to make my (carving) tools.

The Tree

We like to use western red cedar because it's light and carves very easily, like balsa wood. We call it the 'tree of life' because during your entire life you're surrounded by red cedar. The totems in your village, your house, your boat, even your rain hat, they're all made from red cedar. It can take up to a year to find the right tree, to strip the bark and for the log to cure. Many of the trees I carve are more than 400 years old.

The Plan

You begin with a hand-drawn plan on how to carve the totem based on the story you want to tell. This is not something you can do with a computer program. It has to come from the heart.

The Carving

You start with rough cuts and then move on to the finish work and end with the painting. At some point as a carver you take on apprentices to help you (with the carving) and because you have an obligation to pass this tradition on. A 32ft pole will take me almost a year to carve.

The Heritage

Cedar lasts a long time so it is important I do the best I can with every totem I carve. I will be gone someday but the quality of my work will still be seen.

it is an endless stream of floatplanes flying to the same area: Rudyerd Bay and Walker Cove. Throw in the tour boats and one local likened such days to 'the Allied invasion of Omaha Beach.'

If you plan ahead, you can rent one of 13 **USFS Cabins** (☎877-444-6777, 515-885-3639; www.recreation.gov; cabins $25-45) in the area. The cabins must be reserved in advance, usually several months. A 14th cabin, at Big Goat Lake, is free and available on a first-come, first-served basis, as are four Adirondack shelters (three-sided free-use shelters) in the preserve.

For more on the monument, contact the **USFS Ketchikan Ranger District** (☎225-2148; www.fs.fed.us/r10/tongass; 3031 Tongass Ave).

ⓘ Getting There & Around

AIR There isn't an air charter in Ketchikan that doesn't do Misty Fiords. The standard offering is a 1½-hour flight with a lake landing for $230 to $260, and it's easily booked at the visitors center. The following air charters offer tours and cabin drop-offs.

Alaska Seaplane Tours (☎225-1974, 866-858-2327; www.alaskaseaplanetours.com)

Family Air Tours (☎247-1305, 800-380-1305; www.familyairtours.com)

Seawind Aviation (☎225-1206, 877-225-1203; www.seawindaviation.com)

Southeast Aviation (☎225-2900, 888-359-6478; www.southeastaviation.com)

BOAT Cruises on a speedy catamaran are another option. **Allen Marine Tours** (Map p75; ☎225-8100, 877-686-8100; www.allenmarine tours.com; 5 Salmon Landing, Suite 215; adult/child $159/109) is the main operator, offering four-hour tours on an 80ft catamaran through the monument that include narration, snacks and use of binoculars to look at wildlife.

Prince of Wales Island

POP 3360

For some tourists, the Alaska they come looking for is only a three-hour ferry ride away from the crowds of cruise-ship tourists they encounter in Ketchikan. At 140 miles long and covering more than 2230 sq miles, Prince of Wales Island (POW) is the USA's third-largest island, after Alaska's Kodiak and Hawaii's Big Island.

HYDER

On the eastern fringe of Misty Fiords National Monument, at the head of Portland Canal, is Hyder (population 87), a misplaced town if there ever was one. It was founded in 1896 when Captain DD Gailland explored Portland Canal for the US Army Corps of Engineers and built four stone storehouses, the first masonry buildings erected in Alaska, which still stand today. Hyder and its British Columbian neighbor Stewart boomed after major gold and silver mines were opened in 1919, and Hyder became the supply center for more than 10,000 residents. It's been going downhill ever since, the reason it now calls itself 'the friendliest ghost town in Alaska.'

A floatplane or a long drive from Prince Rupert are the only options for getting here. Because of Hyder's isolation from the rest of the state, it's almost totally dependent on larger Stewart (population 700), just across the Canadian border. Hyder's residents use Canadian money, set their watches to Pacific time (not Alaska time), use Stewart's area code and send their children to Canadian schools. When there's trouble, the famed Canadian Mounties step in. All this can make a sidetrip here a little confusing.

The most famous thing to do in Hyder is drink at one of its 'friendly saloons.' The historic **Glacier Inn** (☎250-636-9092) is the best known and features an interior papered in signed bills, creating the '$20,000 Walls' of Hyder. Next door is First and Last Chance Saloon, and both bars hop at night.

But the best reason to find your way to this out-of-the-way place is for bear viewing. From late July to September, you can head 6 miles north of town to Fish Creek Bridge and watch brown and black bears feed on chum salmon runs. The USFS has constructed a viewing platform here, and there are interpreters on-site during summer. Continue along the road and you cross back into British Columbia at Mile 11. At Mile 23 is a point from which to view the impressive **Bear River Glacier**, Canada's fifth largest.

For lodging there is **Ripley Creek Inn** (☎250-636-2344; www.ripleycreekinn.com; 306 5th Ave, Stewart; s C$85-115, d C$105-135; ☺☎) and **Bear River RV Park** (☎250-636-9205; www.stewartbc.com/rvpark; Hwy 37A, Stewart; tent/RV sites C$19/34; ☎), with 68 sites along the Bear River a mile from Stewart.

Unfortunately, if you're in Ketchikan, the only way to reach Hyder is to fly with **Taquan Air** (☎225-8800, 800-770-8800; www.taquanair.com), which makes the run on Monday and Thursday ($370 round-trip). That may seem expensive, but consider that a day trip to Admiralty Island's Pack Creek to see brown bears is around $500. For information on either town, contact the **Stewart/Hyder International Chamber of Commerce** (☎250-636-9224, 888-366-5999; www.stewart-hyder.com; 222 5th Ave, Stewart).

This vast, rugged island is a destination for the adventurous at heart, loaded with hiking trails and canoe routes, Forest Service cabins and fishing opportunities. The 990-mile coastline of POW meanders around numerous bays, coves, saltwater straits and protective islands, making it a kayaker's delight. And, for anyone carrying a mountain bike through Alaska, a week on the island is worth all the trouble of bringing the two-wheeler north. The island has the most extensive road system in the Southeast, 1300 miles of paved or maintained gravel roads that lead to small villages and several hundred miles more of shot-rock logging roads that lead to who-knows-where.

There are no cruise ships on POW, but there are clear-cuts and you must be prepared for them. Blanketing the island is a patchwork quilt of lush spruce-hemlock forest and fields of stumps where a forest used to be. They are a sign that you have reached real Alaska, a resource-based state where people make a living from fishing, mining and cutting down trees.

The Inter-Island Ferry Authority ferry from Ketchikan lands at Hollis (population 112), which has few visitor facilities and no stores or restaurants. The towns best set up for tourism are Craig (population 1201) and Klawock (population 755), only 7 miles apart and a 31-mile drive across the island along the paved Hollis–Klawock Hwy. Founded as a salmon-canning and cold-storage site in 1907, Craig is the island's largest and most interesting community, with its mix of commercial fishers and loggers.

Also supporting lodging, restaurants, small grocery stores and other visitor amenities are Thorne Bay (population 471), 38 miles northeast from Klawock, and Coffman Cove (population 176), 55 miles north of Klawock. POW now has 150 miles of paved roads that connect all of these towns, with the exception of Coffman Cove.

⊙ Sights

FREE Klawock Totem Park   PARK
(Bayview Blvd) Of the three totem parks on POW, the Klawock Totem Park is by far the most impressive and obviously a great source of community pride. Situated on a hill overlooking the town's cannery and harbor, Klawock's 21 totems comprize the largest collection in Alaska and make for a scenic, almost dramatic setting. Some totems are originals from the former village of Tukekan , the rest are replicas.

FREE Prince of Wales Hatchery   HATCHERY
(☎755-2231; Mile 9, Hollis–Klawock Hwy; ⊘8am-noon & 1-4pm; ♿) The Prince of Wales Hatchery was established in 1897 and today is the second-oldest one in Alaska. The present facility was built in 1976 and raises coho, king and sockeye salmon, with many released into the adjacent Klawock River. Inside the visitors center is an aquarium and gift shop where fresh coho is often for sale; outside you can occasionally see black bears feeding across the river.

Fish Ladders   LOOKOUT
On the island's southern half, you can watch salmon attempt to negotiate a couple of fish ladders during the summer spawning season. Both Cable Creek Fish Pass and Dog Salmon Fish Pass have viewing platforms, from which you might also see hungry black bears.

🏃 Activities

Hiking
The USFS maintains more than 20 hiking trails on POW, the majority of them being short walks to rental cabins, rivers or lakes. In the south, a good hike can be made to One Duck Shelter from a trailhead on the road to Hydaburg, 2 miles south of Hollis junction. The trail is steep, climbing 1400ft in 1.2 miles, but it ends at a three-sided free-use shelter that sleeps four. To spend the night in the open alpine area with panoramic views of the Klawock Mountains is worth the knee-bending climb. To the north

the Balls Lake Trail begins in the Balls Lake Picnic Area just east of Eagle's Nest Campground and winds 2.2 miles around the lake.

Cycling
Mountain bikers have even more opportunities than hikers. Bikes can be rented in Coffman Cove from A5 Outdoor Recreation (☎329-2399; www.a5outdoorrec.com; 103A Sea Otter Dr; per day $25) and then taken on any road to explore the island. One of the most scenic roads to bike is South Beach Rd (also known as Forest Rd 30) from Coffman Cove to Thorne Bay. It's a 37-mile ride along the narrow, winding dirt road that is often skirting Clarence Strait. Along the way is Sandy Beach Picnic Area (Mile 6, Sandy Beach Rd), an excellent place to see humpback whales, orcas and harbor seals offshore or examine intriguing tidal pools at low tides.

Paddling
Opportunities for paddlers are almost as limitless as they are for mountain bikers. At the north end of POW off Forest Rd 20 is the Sarkar Lakes Canoe Route, a 15-mile loop of five major lakes and portages along with a USFS cabin and excellent fishing. For a day of kayaking, depart from Klawock and paddle into Big Salt Lake, where the water is calm and the birding is excellent. A5 Outdoor Recreation (see above) also rents kayaks (single/double $50/60 per day) and will provide transportation for an additional fee.

RAINFOREST ISLAND FERRY

Presently tourism on Prince of Wales Island is light due to limited ferry service. But that could change with the launch of the Rainforest Islands Ferry. The proposed ferry would restore the Inter-island Ferry Authority service between Coffman Cove, Wrangell and South Mitkof Island that was discontinued in 2008 and link Coffman Cove directly to Ketchikan. Such a service would allow you to continue north onto Wrangell or Petersburg after visiting POW, eliminating the need to backtrack to Ketchikan. Contact the City of Coffman Cove (☎329-2233; www.ccalaska.com) for the latest of the new ferry that originally was supposed to be in service by 2012.

CAVING ON PRINCE OF WALES ISLAND

One of the most unusual aspects of POW's geology is the broad cave system found in the north end of the island. The karst formation is an area of eroded limestone concealing underground streams and caverns, and it includes more than 850 grottos and caves. The caves received national attention in the mid-1990s when paleontologists from the University of South Dakota discovered the remains of a man dating back 9500 years in one cave, and the almost perfect remains of a brown bear that dated back 45,000 years in another. Both allowed scientists to speculate on how the last ice age affected animal and human migration from Asia.

The two most popular caves are northwest of Thorne Bay, a 94-mile drive from Hollis, and can be easily viewed even if you've never worn a headlamp. At **El Capitan Cave** (Forest Rd 15), 11 miles west of Whale Pass, you can take a free, two-hour, ranger-led cave tour daily in summer at 9am, noon and 2:30pm. Tours are limited to six people and involve a 370-step stairway trail. Contact the **Thorne Bay USFS Ranger Station** (✆828-3304) for reservations (required at least two days in advance; no children under seven). Nearby **Cavern Lake Cave**, on the road to Whale Pass, features an observation deck, allowing visitors to peer into the cave's mouth at the gushing stream inside.

Also in the area is the short, wheelchair-accessible **Beaver Falls Karst Trail**, on the main road between the two turnoffs for Whale Pass, which offers an above-ground experience as its boardwalk leads past sinkholes, pits, underground rivers and other typical karst features.

🛏 Sleeping

There are 18 USFS cabins, one Adirondack shelter and two campgrounds on the island. Two cabins can be reached by rowing across a lake, thus eliminating the floatplane expense required with many others.

TOP CHOICE **Inn of the Blue Heron**   B&B $$
(✆826-3608; www.littleblueheroninn.com; 406 9th St, Craig; s $79-99, d $99-115, ste $155; ☕🐾) A delightful B&B overlooking South Cove Boat Harbor and only a five-minute walk to shops and restaurants in Craig. The inn has three upstairs rooms and an apartment suite on the 1st floor, all featuring TVs, small refrigerators and microwaves.

Dreamcatcher B&B   B&B $$
(✆826-2238; www.dreamcatcherbedandbreakfast. com; 1405 Hamilton Dr, Craig; r $125; ☕🐾) Three guest rooms in a beautiful seaside home. Big picture windows and a wraparound deck give way to a wonderful view of water, islands, mountains and, of course, clear-cuts.

Ruth Ann's Hotel   HOTEL $$
(✆826-3378; cnr Main & Water Sts, Craig; r $105-130; ☕🐾) Across the street from Ruth Ann's renowned restaurant (p91) is her hotel which has 14 rooms in two buildings.

Cabins in Alaska   CABINS $$
(✆888-648-7277; www.cabinsinalaska.com; Hollis–Craig Rd; bunkhouses/cabins $100/200) Less than 6 miles west of the Hollis Ferry Terminal is this resort with cabins that sleep four and bunkhouses that sleep two. Both have kitchens, while nearby is a bathhouse with showers and laundry facilities.

Log Cabin Resort & RV Park   CABINS $
(✆755-2205, 800-544-2205; www.logcabinresor tandrvpark.com; Big Salt Lake Rd, Klawock; sites per person $10, cabins $95-170) Located a half-mile up Big Salt Rd in Klawock, this park offers condos, three rustic beachfront cabins and tent space with showers and a community kitchen. It also rents canoes (per day $25) for use on Big Salt Lake or Klawock Lake.

Coffman Cove Cabin Rentals   CABINS $
(✆329-2251; www.coffmancove.org/cccabins.html; cabins per person $40) A pair of self-contained cabins with fully equipped kitchens and within walking distance of the ferry terminal.

USFS Cabins   CABINS $
(✆877-444-6777, 518-885-3639; www.recreation. gov; cabins $35-65) Control Lake Cabin is reached from State Hwy 929, where a dock and rowboat are kept on the west end of the lake. Red Bay Lake Cabin is at the north end of the POW, off Forest Rd 20, and reached with a half-mile hike to a boat and then a 1.5-mile row across the lake.

Harris River Campground   CAMPGROUND $
(sites $8) This campground is near the Hollis Rd junction. The 14-site USFS campground

has fire rings, BBQ grills and picnic tables; seven sites have tent pads.

Eagle's Nest Campground
CAMPGROUND $

(sites $8) This 11-site campground, 18 miles west of Thorne Bay, overlooks a pair of lakes. It has a canoe-launching site and a half-mile shoreline boardwalk.

✕ Eating

TOP CHOICE/ Ruth Ann's Restaurant
SEAFOOD $$$

(✆826-3377; 300 Front St, Craig; dinner mains $16-53; ⊙lunch & dinner Mon-Sat; ⊕) This would be a favorite no matter which Alaskan city it was located in, but in Craig it becomes one of those unexpected joys. The small restaurant with an even smaller bar offers quaint waterfront dining with views of the bay, weathered wharfs and fishing boats returning with their catch that often ends up on your plate: salmon, oysters, steamer clams and giant prawns stuffed with crab.

Dockside Restaurant
BREAKFAST $

(Front St, Craig; breakfast mains $6-13, lunch mains $9-12; ⊙breakfast & lunch) This wonderful cafe serves the best breakfast on POW, but it's the pies that make it legendary among locals. There's usually a half-dozen different kinds in the cooler, and a $5 slice is money well spent.

Klawock Diner
DINER $$

(6648 Big Salt Rd, Klawock; lunch mains $6-11, dinner mains $11-20; ⊙lunch & dinner) This rambling diner has a sloping floor and an attached bus that serves as the kitchen. The burgers are good and the onion rings are great; just don't let them roll off the table.

Wheelhouse Coffee Roasters
CAFE $

(✆826-2333; 801 Water St; ⊙7am-5pm Mon-Fri, 8am-4pm Sat, 9am-3pm Sun; ⊛) An espresso bar in Craig with a small but wonderful bookstore dedicated to Alaska titles.

ℹ Information

Alicia Roberts Medical Center (✆755-4800; Hollis–Klawock Hwy, Klawock; ⊙walk-ins 9am-4pm Mon-Fri) Main medical facility on the island.

Craig Library (✆826-3281; 504 3rd St, Craig; ⊙noon-5pm Mon, 10am-5pm Tue-Fri, 7-9pm Mon-Thu, noon-4pm Sat; @) Free internet access and used books for sale.

Post office (Craig–Klawock Hwy, Craig) Next to Thompson House Supermarket.

Prince of Wales Chamber of Commerce (✆755-2626; www.princeofwalescoc.org; Klawock Bell Tower Mall, Hollis–Klawock Hwy;

⊙8:30am-4:30pm Mon-Fri; ⊛) Operates a visitors center in Klawock.

USFS office (⊙8am-5pm Mon-Fri) Craig (✆826-3271; 900 9th St); Thorne Bay (✆828-3304; 1312 Federal Way) Head to the Craig office for information on trails, cabins and paddling adventures.

Wells Fargo (301 Thompson Rd, Craig) Next to the post office and equipped with a 24-hour ATM.

ℹ Getting There & Away

The **Inter-Island Ferry Authority** (✆866-308-4848, Hollis Terminal 530-4848, Ketchikan Terminal 225-4848; www.interislandferry.com) operates a pair of vessels that depart from Hollis at 8am and from Ketchikan at 3:30pm daily (one way adult/child $37/18).

ℹ Getting Around

For lengthy stays it's best to rent a car in Ketchikan and take it over on the ferry. You can also rent a compact in Craig through **Wilderness Rent-A-Car** (✆826-5200; www.wildernesscar-rental.com); it's $70 per day with unlimited mileage, but you have to keep it on the pavement.

Island Ride (✆401-1414) connects with ferries in Hollis, but you have to call them in advance to reserve a seat. The one-way fare to Craig is $30 per person.

Wrangell & Around

POP 2369

Strategically located near the mouth of the Stikine River, Wrangell is one of the oldest towns in Alaska and the only one to have existed under three flags and ruled by four nations – Tlingit, Russia, Britain and America.

In Wrangell's heyday it was a jumping-off point for three major gold rushes up the Stikine River from 1861 to the late 1890s. Back then Wrangell was as lawless and ruthless as Skagway, and at one point Wyatt Earp,

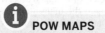

POW MAPS

For a quick visit, the map inside the free *Prince of Wales Island Guide* is sufficient. For an extended stay or if you're planning to explore the logging roads, purchase the *Prince of Wales Island Road Guide* ($10) published by the USFS. Either is available at the POW Chamber of Commerce or USFS Ranger Station.

the famous Arizona lawman, filled in as a volunteer marshal for 10 days before moving on to Nome. Wrangell's most famous visitor, however, was John Muir, who came in 1879 and again in 1880. Muir wrote that 'Wrangell village was a rough place. It was a lawless draggle of wooden huts and houses, built in crooked lines, wrangling around the boggy shore of the island for a mile or so.'

Eventually Wrangell became a fishing and lumber town typical of Southeast Alaska, and when the timber industry crashed in the early 1990s the town was hit harder than most. For years the town was seen as a bitter, dying community, but many believe Wrangell has since turned the corner. Unlike Petersburg, the 2010 censuses showed that Wrangell gained residents. Its economy is also more stable, with an emerging dive fishery, which harvests sea urchins, sea cucumbers and geoducks, and the Marine Service Center, a shipyard that provides repair and haul-out for commercial vessels

Of all the Alaska Marine Highway's major stops, Wrangell is the least gentrified. Cruise ships are only a once-a-week occurrence here, so the town is rarely inundated and isn't ritzy. You don't come to Wrangell for posh luxury hotels or well-developed tourist attractions. Instead, use Wrangell as a home base for exploring the surrounding wilds.

The island offers great mountain biking and bike-camping opportunities; kayakers can explore the Stikine River or myriad islands and waterways around the river's mouth; and local guides lead boat trips to Anan Creek bear observatory and other places of interest.

◉ Sights

Wrangell Museum　　　　　　MUSEUM
(296 Outer Dr; adult/child/family $5/3/12; ☺10am-5pm Mon-Sat) This impressive museum in the Nolan Center is what the colorful history and characters of Wrangell deserves. As you stroll through the many rooms, an audio narration automatically comes on and explains that chapter of Wrangell's history, from Tlingit culture and the gold-rush era to the time Hollywood arrived in 1972 to film the movie *Timber Tramps*. You can marvel at a collection of Alaskan art that includes a Sidney Laurence painting or be amused that this rugged little town has had two presidential visits (Warren Harding and Ronald Reagan).

FREE **Chief Shakes Island**　　　PARK
(Shakes St) This island is the most enchanting spot in Wrangell. The small grassy islet is in the middle of the boat harbor and reached by a pedestrian bridge. The tiny island, with its totems, tall pines and the half-dozen eagles usually perched in the branches, is a quiet oasis compared to the hum of the fishing fleet that surrounds it. In the middle is Shakes Community House, an excellent example of a high-caste tribal house that contains tools, blankets and other cultural items. It's open only to accommodate cruise ships (call the Wrangell Museum for times). Just as impressive are the six totems surrounding the tribal house, all duplicates of originals carved in the late 1930s.

FREE **Petroglyph Beach**　ARCHAEOLOGICAL SITE
(Evergreen Ave; ♿) Located on the town's north side is a state historic park where you can see primitive rock carvings believed to be at least 1000 years old. The best set is located 0.7 miles from the ferry terminal and can be reached by heading north on Evergreen Ave; a sign here marks the boardwalk that leads to a viewing deck with interpretive displays and petroglyph replicas. Follow the stairway to the beach and then turn right and walk north about 50yd. Before you reach the wrecked fishing vessel (photographers will love it), look for the carvings on the large rocks, many of them resembling spirals and faces. There are almost 50 in the area and you need to hunt around to find most of them. The majority are submerged at high tide so check a tide book before you leave and bring a bottle of water. The carvings are easier to see when wet.

Totems　　　　　　　MONUMENTS
For its size, Wrangell has an impressive collection of totems, with more than a dozen scattered through town. Pick up the free *Wrangell Guide* at the visitors center and spend an afternoon locating them all. Along with Chief Shakes Island, make sure you stop at Totem Park (Front St) and Chief Shakes Grave (Case Ave) to see the killer-whale totems.

🏃 Activities

Bear Watching

Thirty miles southeast of Wrangell on the mainland, Anan Creek is the site of one of the largest pink salmon runs in Southeast Alaska. From the platforms at Anan Creek

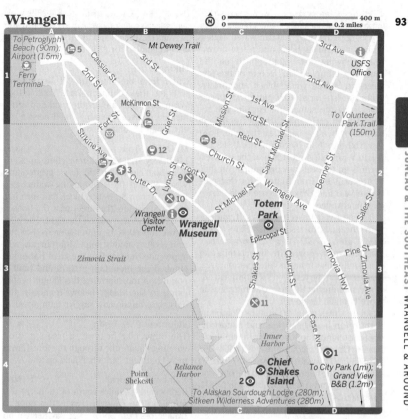

Wrangell

Top Sights

Sights

Activities, Courses & Tours

Sleeping

Eating

Drinking

JUNEAU & THE SOUTHEAST WRANGELL & AROUND

Wildlife Observatory (www.fs.fed.us/r10/tongass/recreation/wildlife_viewing/ananobservatory.shtml; permits $10), you can watch eagles, harbor seals, black bears and a few brown bears chowing down gluttonously on the spawning humpies. This is one of the few places in Alaska where black and brown bears coexist – or at least put up with each other – at the same run. Permits are required from early July through August, or basically when the bears are there, and are reserved online or by calling the USFS Office in Wrangell. Almost half of the daily 60 permits go to local tour operators. Another 18 are available from March 1 for that particular year and 12 permits are issued three days in advance.

The best way to see the bears, if you can plan ahead, is to reserve the USFS Anan Bay Cabin (☑877-444-6777; www.recreation. gov; $35), which comes with four permits and is a 1-mile hike from the observation area. This cabin can be reserved six months in advance, and during the bear-watching season it pretty much has to be.

Anan Creek is a 20-minute floatplane flight or an hour boat ride, and almost every tour operator in town offers a trip there. Alaska Charters & Adventures (☑874-4157, 888-993-2750; www.alaskaupclose.com; 7 Front St) offers an eight-hour boat trip to the observatory ($278), and Alaska Waters Inc (☑874-2378, 800-347-4462; www.alaskawaters.com), at the Stikine Inn, has a six-hour boat tour

---

MUSKEG MEADOWS

Completed in 1998 atop the sawdust and wood chips left behind by local sawmill operations, Wrangell's nine-hole Muskeg Meadows Golf Course (☑874-4653; www.wrangellalaskagolf.com; Ishiyama Dr; per round $22), half a mile east of Bennet St, may be the first certified course in the Southeast, but it's uniquely Alaskan. Surrounded by wilderness, members are rarely alarmed when a bear comes bounding across a fairway. Then there is the club's Raven Rule: if a raven steals your ball you may replace it with no penalty provided you have a witness. Finally, the course's narrow fairways and tangled roughs of spruce and muskeg have resulted in this warning posted in the clubhouse: 'You got to have a lot of balls to play Muskeg Meadows.'

($265). Sunrise Aviation (☑874-2319; www.sunriseflights.com; Wrangell Airport) will provide permits ($23 each) and fly up to four passengers in and out for $360 each way.

Hiking

Other than the climb up Mt Dewey and walking the Volunteer Park Trail, all of Wrangell's trails are off the road and often include muskeg, meaning you'll need a car and a pair of rubber boots.

Mt Dewey Trail   HIKING
Mt Dewey Trail is a half-mile climb up a hill to a small clearing in the trees, overlooking Wrangell and the surrounding waterways. From Mission St, walk a block and turn left at 3rd St. Follow the street past the houses to the posted stairway on the right. The hike to the top takes 15 minutes or so, but the trail is often muddy. John Muir fanatics will appreciate the fact that the great naturalist climbed the mountain in 1879 and built a bonfire on top, alarming the Tlingit people living in the village below. Ironically, the only signs on top now say 'No Campfires.'

Volunteer Park Trail   HIKING
The other hike in town: a pleasant stroll winding a half-mile through the forest from near Volunteer Park's ball field off 2nd Ave.

Rainbow Falls Trail   HIKING
Signposted 4.7 miles south of the ferry terminal on the Zimovia Hwy is this popular trail across from Shoemaker Bay Recreation Area. It's 0.7 miles to the waterfalls, where you'll find an observation platform above the cascade and great views of Chichagof Pass and Zimovia Strait.

Institute Creek & North Wrangell
Trails   HIKING
These two trails create a route across Wrangell Island, passing a series of three-sided shelters along the way that make an overnight adventure possible. Institute Creek Trail begins towards the end of Rainbow Falls Trail and then climbs 1500ft in 2.7 miles to the Shoemaker Bay Overlook Shelter. The lower section of the trail can be soggy at times, the upper section steep.

A half-mile before the shelter, North Wrangell Trail veers off and leads 1.3 miles to High Country Shelter and, in 2.3 miles, to Pond Shelter. Eventually the trail descends to Spur Rd Extension, on the east side of Wrangell Island 4 miles from town. The entire hike from the west side to the east is 6.5 miles.

Thoms Lake Trail
HIKING

A 1.4-mile path to the lake, Thoms Lake Trail is reached by following Zimovia Hwy to its paved end and then turning east on Forest Rd 6267. About halfway across the island, just before crossing Upper Salamander Creek, turn right on Forest Rd 6290 and follow it 4 miles to the trailhead. The first half-mile of the trail is planked, but the rest cuts through muskeg and can get extremely muddy during wet weather. There are plans to resurface the trail.

Paddling

One look at a nautical chart of Wrangell will have kayakers drooling and dreaming. Islands and protected waterways abound, though many are across the vast Stikine River flats, where experience is a prerequisite due to strong tides and currents. Novices can enjoy paddling around the harbor, over to Petroglyph Beach or to Dead Man's Island.

Alaska Vistas
KAYAKING

(☑874-3006, 866-874-3006; www.alaskavistas. com; 106 Front St) Inside the Java Junkies espresso shed, a wi-fi hot spot at City Dock, Alaska Vistas rents kayaks (per day single/double $55/65). The company also runs guided kayak tours, including a full-day East West Cove paddle ($200) on the well-protected east side of Wrangell Island. Vans are used to transport you to the east shore and a jet boat returns you to Wrangell at the end of the day.

☆ Festivals & Events

The summer's biggest event is the Fourth of July celebration. All of Wrangell gets involved in the festival, which features a parade, fireworks, live music, a logging show, street games, food booths and a salmon bake.

In the third week of April, Wrangell hosts its Stikine River Birding Festival, when boat tours head up the river to witness the largest springtime concentration of bald eagles in Alaska.

🛏 Sleeping

Wrangell levies a 13% sales and bed tax on all lodging.

TOP CHOICE Rooney's Roost
B&B $$

(☑874-2026; www.rooneysroost.com; 206 McKinnon St; r $125; ☻🛜) Wrangell's best B&B is within easy walking distance of the ferry, just a short way up 2nd St. There are four antique-filled guest rooms with queen-size beds, TV and private baths. In the morning you enjoy a delicious breakfast, and in the afternoon you can relax on the deck with view of Wrangell.

Stikine Inn
MOTEL $$

(☑874-3388, 888-874-3388; www.stikineinn.com; 107 Stikine Ave; s $115-143, d $134-151; 🛜) Wrangell's largest motel is on the waterfront near the ferry dock, and in 2011 it completed a three-year renovation that included its bar, lobby and most of the 34 rooms. The waterview rooms cost more, but they are now among the best in town.

Grand View B&B
B&B $$

(☑874-3225; www.grandviewbnb.com; Mile 1.9, Zimovia Hwy; r $105-135; ☻@🛜) Next to City Park, this seaside B&B does have the grandest view in town. From the living room a row of picture windows frame a scene of Zimovia Strait and the mountains that surround it. The entire ground floor is devoted to guests and includes three spacious rooms, private baths, a large kitchen and an impressive collection of Alaska art and artifacts.

Alaskan Sourdough Lodge
LODGE $$

(☑874-3613, 800-874-3613; www.akgetaway. com; 1104 Peninsula St; s/d $114/124; ☻@🛜) This family-owned lodge was hosting visitors when there were still lumber mills in Wrangell. It offers 16 large rooms, a sauna, steam bath, free transportation to/from the ferry or airport and outdoor decks full of wicker furniture, some with a view of the harbor.

City Park
CAMPGROUND $

(☑874-2444, Mile 1.7, Zimovia Hwy; tent sites free) For those with a tent, the closest campground is this delightful waterfront park, 1 mile south of town and immediately south of a historic cemetery. Within the pleasant wooded setting are eight sites, shelters and restrooms. Only tent campers are allowed to stay here and there is no fee for camping. There's a one-night limit if you have a car, but that's overlooked if you arrive on foot.

Wrangell Hostel
HOSTEL $

(☑874-3534; 220 Church St; dm $20; ☻) In the First Presbyterian Church, this basic place has separate-sex dorm rooms with inflatable mattresses, showers and a large kitchen and dining room. It has no curfew and will graciously let you hang out there during an all-day rain.

WORTH A TRIP

THE STIKINE RIVER

A narrow, rugged shoreline and surrounding mountains and glaciers characterize the beautiful, wild Stikine River, which begins in the high peaks of interior British Columbia and ends some 400 miles on in a delta called the Stikine Flats, just north of Wrangell. The Stikine is North America's fastest navigable river, and its most spectacular sight is the Grand Canyon of the Stikine, a steep-walled gorge where violently churning white water makes river travel impossible. John Muir called this stretch of the Stikine 'a Yosemite 100 miles long.'

Trips from below the canyon are common among rafters and kayakers. They begin with a charter flight to Telegraph Creek in British Columbia and end with a 160-mile float back to Wrangell.

Travelers arriving in Wrangell with a kayak but insufficient funds to charter a bush plane can paddle from the town's harbor across the Stikine Flats (where there are several USFS cabins) and up one of the Stikine River's three arms. By keeping close to shore and taking advantage of eddies and sloughs, experienced paddlers can make their way 30 miles up the river to the Canadian border – or even further, passing 12 USFS cabins (☑877-444-6777; www.recreation.gov), and the two bathing huts at Chief Shakes Hot Springs and Shakes Glacier inside Shakes Lake along the way. But you must know how to line a boat upstream and navigate a highly braided river and, while in the lower reaches, accept the fact that you'll encounter a lot of jet-boat traffic.

Wrangell's USFS office can provide information on the Stikine River, including two helpful publications: *Stikine River Canoe/Kayak Routes* ($5) and *Lower Stikine River Map* ($5), the latter covering the river up to Telegraph Creek.

Wrangell charter boats that run trips on the Stikine or offer drop-off services for kayakers:

» Breakaway Adventures (☑874-2488, 888-385-2488; www.breakawayadventures.com) Day trips up the river by jet boat take in Shakes Glacier and the hot springs ($175).

» Stikeen Wilderness Adventures (☑800-874-2085; www.akgetaway.com; Alaskan Sourdough Lodge, 1104 Peninsula St) Provides a water-taxi service for kayakers and rafters.

» Sunrise Aviation (☑874-2319; www.sunriseflights.com; Wrangell Airport) Has an hour-long flightseeing tour of the Stikeen River and LeConte Glacier for $525 for up to five passengers.

Fennimore's B&B　　　　　　　　B&B $

(☑874-3012; www.fennimoresbbb.com; 321 Stikine Ave; r $90; ⊜) The easiest lodging for late-night ferry passengers to reach, Fennimore's is a five-minute walk (if that) across the street from the ferry terminal. Four rooms, basic but clean, on the 1st floor have private bath and private entrances. All have cable TV, a refrigerator, microwave and queen-size bed. To top it off there are bikes for guests to tool around town on.

Shoemaker Bay Recreation Area　　　　　　CAMPGROUND $

(☑874-2444; Mile 4.5, Zimovia Hwy; tent sites free, RV sites $15-25) This campsite is across from the Rainbow Falls trailhead in a wooded area near a creek. There are 25 sites, 15 with hookups for RVers, and a tent-camping area for everybody sleeping in ripstop nylon. All sites have a good view of Zimovia Strait.

Nemo Point　　　　　　　　CAMPGROUND $

(☑874-2323; Forest Rd 6267; sites free) This offers the best camping on Wrangell Island, but unfortunately it is 14 miles from town. Each of the six free wheelchair-accessible sites has a picnic table, outhouse and a stunning view of Zimovia Strait. Take Zimovia Hwy/Forest Hwy 16 south to Forest Rd 6267. The sites stretch along 4 miles of Forest Rd 6267.

✖ Eating

Stikine Inn　　　　　　　　AMERICAN $$

(107 Stikine Ave; lunch mains $10-14, dinner mains $16-30; ⊙lunch & dinner) Every table at Stikine Inn's new restaurant faces the water and the fishing boats passing by. The dinner menu is split between steaks, chops and seafood, but it's hard to pass up the halibut strips and hand-cut fries because you just know somebody caught that fish yesterday.

Diamond C Café
CAFE $

(223 Front St; breakfast mains $6-12, lunch mains $8-16; ☺breakfast & lunch) Eat what the locals eat – eggs and hash browns, biscuits and gravy, deep-fried fish-and-chips – and listen to the conservative pulse of the community from the tables around you.

Alaskan Sourdough Lodge
SEAFOOD $$

(☎874-3613; 1104 Peninsula St; mains $19-24; ☺dinner) If you call ahead, the lodge will allow you to join its guests for home-style meals that include a salad bar and often crab, halibut and salmon during the summer.

Marine Bar
PIZZA $

(Shakes St; lunch mains $4-11, pizzas $18-25; ☺lunch & dinner) A smoky hangout for deckhands, but there's outdoor seating and a pizza counter serving Wrangell's beloved pie: taco pizza with refried beans, seasoned hamburger and cheese, baked and then loaded with lettuce, tomatoes, salsa and sour cream. It comes with the fantasy of spending the winter in Mexico.

IGA Supermarket
SUPERMARKET $

(223 Brueger St; ☺8am-6pm Mon-Sat) It has an in-store bakery, espresso and a deli with some ready-to-eat items and sandwiches.

🍷 Drinking

Stikine Inn
BAR

(107 Stikine Ave) The Stikine Inn's lounge is a small and quiet place to have a drink. If the evening is nice there's an outdoor patio where you can watch vessels disappear into the mist on Zimovia Strait.

Diamond C Coffee Shop
COFFEE HOUSE

(223 Front St) Next to the Diamond C restaurant, this latte shop offers a caffeinated 'happy hour' all afternoon just when you need it.

Totem Bar
BAR

(Front St) Wrangell's redneck bar, where the sign on the front door says 'Hippies Use Backdoor. No Exceptions.'

🛍 Shopping

Wrangell Museum
BOOKS

(296 Outer Dr) The gift shop in this fine museum has the best selection of Alaskan books in town.

ⓘ Information

First Bank (224 Brueger St) Across from IGA Supermarket, it maintains a 24-hour ATM on Front St.

Irene Ingle Public Library (☎874-3535; 124 2nd St; ☺10am-noon & 1-5pm Mon & Fri, 1-5pm & 7-9pm Tue-Thu, 9am-5pm Sat; @🛜) A wonderful facility for such a small town; has free wi-fi and a paperback exchange.

Post office (112 Federal Way) At the town's north end with an impressive totem out front.

USFS Office (☎874-2323; 525 Bennett St; ☺8am-4:30pm Mon-Fri) Located three-quarters of a mile north of town; has information on regional USFS cabins, trails and campgrounds.

Wrangell Medical Center (☎874-7000; 310 Bennett St) For anything from Aspirin to Zoloft.

Wrangell Visitor Center (☎874-3699, 800-367-9745; www.wrangell.com; 296 Outer Dr; ☺10am-5pm Mon-Sat) In the Nolan Center, it stocks the free *Wrangell Guide* and shows a 10-minute film on the area in a small theater. It also offers internet access ($5/10 per 20 minutes/hour).

ⓘ Getting There & Around

Daily northbound and southbound flights are available with **Alaska Airlines** (☎874-3308, 800-426-0333). Many claim the flight north to Petersburg is the 'world's shortest jet flight,' since the six- to 11-minute trip (one way $126) is little more than a takeoff and landing.

Alaska Marine Highway (☎874-3711) services run almost daily both northbound and southbound from Wrangell in summer. To the north is Petersburg ($33, three hours) via the scenic, winding Wrangell Narrows, to the south Ketchikan ($37, six hours). There are plans for a new service called Rainforest Island Ferry to run between Wrangell and Mitkof Island. Check with the **City of Coffman Cove** (☎329-2233; www.ccalaska.com) for the status of it.

Practical Rent-A-Car (☎874-3975), at the airport, rents compacts for $49 per day plus a 17% rental tax, while **Klondike Bike** (☎874-2553; www.klondikebike.com; 502 Wrangell Ave) rents bikes for $35 per day. Running around town in yellow vans is **Northern Lights Taxi** (☎874-4646).

A CABIN IN THE WOODS

There are 22 USFS cabins in the Wrangell District of Tongass National Forest and until recently all of them were reached via floatplanes, boats or on foot. But in 2010 the USFS opened **Middle Ridge Cabin** (☎877-444-6777; www.recreation.gov; cabin $35), the first road-accessible cabin. It's still an adventurous retreat. The cabin is 20 miles south of Wrangell along Forest Rd 50050, which is recommended for 'high-clearance vehicles. Once out there you'll feel like you're miles from civilization. And you will be.

Petersburg

POP 2948

From Wrangell, the Alaska Marine Highway ferry heads north to begin one of the Inside Passage's most scenic sections. After crossing over from Wrangell Island to Mitkof Island, the vessel threads through the 46 turns of Wrangell Narrows, a 22-mile channel that is only 300ft wide and 19ft deep in places. So winding and narrow is the channel that locals call it 'pinball alley.' Others refer to it as 'Christmas tree lane' because of the abundance of red and green navigational lights.

At the other end of this breathtaking journey lies Norwegian-influenced Petersburg, one of Southeast Alaska's hidden gems. Peter Buschmann arrived in 1897 and found a fine harbor, abundant fish and a ready supply of ice from nearby LeConte Glacier. He built a cannery in the area, enticed his Norwegian friends to follow him here, and gave his first name to the resulting town. Today, a peek into the local phone book reveals the strong Norwegian heritage that unifies Petersburg.

The waterfront of this busy little fishing port is decorated with working boats and weathered boathouses, while tidy homes and businesses – many done up with distinctive Norwegian rosemaling, a flowery Norwegian art form – line the quiet streets. Petersburg has Alaska's sixth-largest fishing fleet and sends more than 55 million pounds of salmon, halibut, black cod, shrimp and crab annually to the town's four canneries and two cold-storage plants. The canneries sit above the water on pilings, overlooking boat harbors bulging with vessels, barges, ferries and seaplanes. Even at night, you can see small boats trolling the nearby waters for somebody's dinner.

The town lies across Frederick Sound from a spectacular glaciated wall of alpine peaks – including the distinctive Devil's Thumb – that form a skyline of jagged snow-capped summits. Nearby LeConte Glacier discharges icebergs to the delight of visitors.

Without a heavy dependency on timber, Petersburg enjoys a healthier economy than Wrangell or Ketchikan, so it doesn't need to pander to tourists. Thus the lack of a hostel or even a camping area within town but also the heavy cruise-ship traffic that Juneau and Skagway experience. That makes Petersburg a joy for most independent travelers, who will quickly discover the locals are friendly and their stories interesting.

◎ Sights

Clausen Memorial Museum   MUSEUM
(203 Fram St; adult/child $3/free; ⊘10am-5pm Mon-Sat) This museum holds an interesting collection of artifacts and relics, mostly related to local fishing history. Exhibits include the largest king salmon ever caught (126lbs), a giant lens from the old Cape Decision lighthouse, a Tlingit dugout canoe and the 30-minute film, *Petersburg; The Town Fish Built.* Outside is *Fisk*, the intriguing fish sculpture that was commissioned in 1967 to honor the Alaska Centennial.

FREE **Sing Lee Alley**   HISTORIC SITE
Heading south, Harbor Way passes Middle Boat Harbor and turns into Sing Lee Alley. This was the center of old Petersburg, and much of the street is built on pilings over Hammer Slough. On the alley, **Sons of Norway Hall** is the large white building with the colorful rosemaling built in 1912 and the center for Petersburg's Norwegian culture. Come on down and play bingo at 7pm on Friday; 'O-32,' ja shore you betcha.

Also along Sing Lee Alley is **Bojer Wikan Fishermen's Memorial Park.** This deck-of-a-park is built on pilings over Hammer Slough and features an impressive statue of a fisher that honors all his fellow crew members lost at sea. Also on display is the *Valhalla*, a replica of a Viking ship that was built in 1976 and purchased by Petersburg two years later.

North Boat Harbor   LANDMARK
(Excel St, at Harbor Way) The North Boat Harbor is the best one for wandering the docks, talking to crews and possibly even scoring some fresh fish. Begin at the Harbormaster Office; a wooden deck here provides a picturesque overview of the commercial fleet and has a series of interpretive panels that will teach you the difference between purse seine and a long-liner. Continue north along the waterfront to see **Petersburg Fisheries** (Dolphin St, at Nordic Dr), the original outfit founded by Peter Buschmann in 1900; today it's a subsidiary of Seattle's Icicle Seafoods.

Sandy Beach Recreation Area   PARK
From downtown, Nordic Dr heads north on a scenic route that ends at Sandy Beach Recreation Area, a beautiful day-use area 2 miles from downtown. There are 2000-year-old Tlingit fish traps snaking the mudflats and a rock with petroglyphs carved on it. Both the traps and the carvings are hard to spot, but

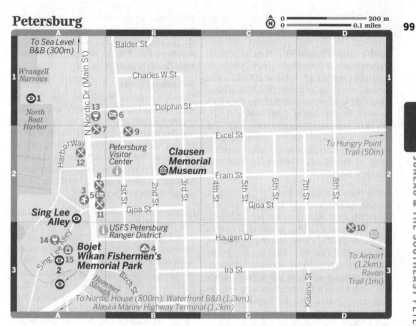

Petersburg

the Petersburg Ranger District (p103) organizes guided interpretive walks to them during the summer here. Call for times.

🏃 Activities

Hiking

Hungry Point Trail   HIKING

Within town is the 0.7-mile Hungry Point Trail that begins at the ball field at the end of Excel St and cuts across muskeg. The gravel path keeps your feet dry, but surrounding you are stunted trees so short you have a clear view of Petersburg's mountainous skyline. The trail ends at Sandy Beach Rd; head right a quarter-mile to reach **Outlook Park**, a marine wildlife observatory with free binoculars to search Frederick Sound for humpbacks, orcas and sea lions.

Raven Trail
HIKING

The 4-mile Raven Trail begins at the water tower on the airport's southeast side (accessible from Haugen Dr). It crosses muskeg areas on a boardwalk, then climbs to beautiful open alpine areas at 2000ft. Some sections are steep and require a little scrambling. The trail eventually leads to the USFS Raven's Roost Cabin (877-444-6777, 515-885-3639; www.recreation.gov; cabins $35). The cabin is above the treeline, providing easy access to good alpine hiking and spectacular views of Petersburg, Frederick Sound and Wrangell Narrows.

Petersburg Mountain Trail
HIKING

On Kupreanof Island, the 3.5-mile Petersburg Mountain Trail climbs to the top of Petersburg Mountain (2750ft), which offers views of Petersburg, the Coast Mountains, glaciers and Wrangell Narrows. Plan on five hours for the round-trip. To get across the channel, go to the skiff float at the North Boat Harbor and hitch a ride with somebody who lives on Kupreanof Island. On the Kupreanof side, head right on the overgrown road toward Sasby Island. You can also call Tongass Kayak Adventures (p100), which runs hikers across the channel for $25 per trip.

Petersburg Lake Trail
HIKING

Petersburg Lake Trail is a 10.5-mile trail in the Petersburg Creek-Duncan Salt Chuck Wilderness on Kupreanof Island; it leads to the USFS Petersburg Lake Cabin (877-444-6777, 515-885-3639; www.recreation.gov; cabins $35). See p53 for details.

Blind River Rapids Boardwalk
HIKING

At Mile 14.5 of the Mitkof Hwy is the mile-long Blind River Rapids Boardwalk that winds through muskeg to the rapids, a scenic area that's busy in June for king salmon fishing.

Three Lakes Loop Trails
HIKING

Along Three Lakes Rd, a USFS road heading east off Mitkof Hwy at Mile 13.6 and returning at Mile 23.8, are Three Lakes Loop Trails, a series of four short trails that total 4.5 miles. At Mile 14.2 is a 3-mile loop with boardwalks leading to Sand, Crane and Hill Lakes, all known for good trout fishing. Sand Lake has a free-use shelter. From the Sand Lake Trail, a 1.5-mile trail leads to Ideal Cove on Frederick Sound.

Paddling

Petersburg offers interesting possibilities for kayakers, LeConte Glacier and Tebenkof Bay Wilderness among them, but many of the trips require a week or more. Kayak rentals are available from Tongass Kayak Adventures (772-4600; www.tongasskayak.com; single/double kayaks $55/65).

Petersburg Creek
KAYAKING

This outstanding steelhead and sockeye stream is across from Petersburg on Kupreanof Island and makes for an easy day paddle, beginning from the South Harbor. During high tide you can paddle more than 4 miles up the creek and reach a trailhead for the Petersburg Lake Trail. Tongass Kayak Adventures offer a guided four-hour paddle up the creek ($95 per person).

LeConte Glacier
KAYAKING

The most spectacular paddle in the region is to LeConte Glacier, 25 miles east of Petersburg. It's North America's southernmost tidewater glacier. From town, it takes one to two days to reach the frozen monument, including crossing Frederick Sound north of Coney Island. The crossing should be done at slack tide, as winds and tides can cause choppy conditions. If the tides are judged right, and the ice is not too thick, it's possible to paddle far enough into LeConte Bay to camp within view of the glacier.

Tongass Kayak Adventures offers an easier outing. Its 10-hour tour begins with a cruise to the glacier, then paddling among the icebergs ($265 per person).

Thomas Bay
KAYAKING

Almost as impressive as LeConte Glacier is Thomas Bay, 20 miles from Petersburg and north of LeConte Bay on Frederick Sound's east side. The bay has a pair of glaciers, including Baird Glacier, where many paddlers go for day hikes. The mountain scenery around the bay is spectacular, and the area has three USFS cabins: Swan Lake Cabin (per night $35), Spurt Cove Cabin (per night $25) and Cascade Creek Cabin (per night $35). All require reservations. Paddlers should allow four to seven days for the round-trip out of Petersburg.

Whale Watching

Petersburg offers some of the best whale watching in Southeast Alaska. From mid-May to mid-September humpback whales migrate through, and feed in, Frederick Sound, 45 miles northwest of Petersburg, with the peak feeding period in July and August. Other wildlife that can be spotted includes Steller's sea lions, orcas and seals.

A handful of charter-boat operators offer eight-hour whale-watching tours that range from $275 to $325 per person. **Kaleidoscope Cruises** (☏772-3736, 800-868-4373; www.petersburglodgingandtours.com), which has a four-person minimum, is run by Barry Bracken, a marine biologist who focuses on eco-education, while **Whale Song Cruises** (☏772-9393, 772-3724; whalesongcruises.com), with a two-person minimum, is equipped with a hydrophone so you can listen to the whales as well as see them.

☞ Tours

For a large selection of area tours, head to **Viking Travel** (☏772-3818, 800-327-2571; 101 Nordic Dr), which acts as a clearinghouse for just about every tour in town. Possibilities include a four-hour boat tour to LeConte Glacier ($196), an eight-hour whale-watching tour ($300) and a helicopter flightseeing tour with a glacier walk ($402).

Most of the charter operators that do whale watching also have sightseeing trips to view LeConte Glacier, and that includes Kaleidoscope Cruises, whose five-hour tour is $190 per person. **Pacific Wings** (☏772-4258; www.pacwing.com), **Nordic Air** (☏772-3535; www.nordicairflying.com) and **Kupreanof Flying Service** (☏772-3396; www.kupreanof.com) offer flightseeing trips to the glacier ($150 to $165 per person).

Also available, either through Viking or directly, is a combination rainforest hike and LeConte Glacier cruise with Tongass Kayak Adventures (p100) for $225 per person. The full-day outing begins with a hike along Three Lakes Loop Rd and then another to Ideal Cove, where a charter boat picks you up for an afternoon at the glacier.

★★ Festivals & Events

The community's best event, famous around the Southeast, is the **Little Norway Festival**, held the third full weekend in May. The festival celebrates Norwegian Constitution Day (May 17). The locals dress in traditional costumes, there's a foot race in the morning and Nordic Dr is filled with a string of craft booths and beer tents. But best of all are the fish and shrimp feeds at night, all-you-can-manage-to-eat affairs.

Other festivals is a lively **Fourth of July** celebration and the **Tongass Rainforest Festival** (tongassrainforestfestival.org) on the second weekend of September.

🛏 Sleeping

Petersburg already desperately needed budget lodging and campsites in town, and then its only hostel closed in 2011. The city adds 10% sales and bed tax on accommodations.

TOP CHOICE **The Lucky Loon**   GUESTHOUSE $$
(☏772-2345; www.theluckyloon.com; 181 Frederick Dr; d $150; 🖥📶) If you've had it with the cruise-ship crowds, this is your escape: a beautiful home in its own wooded retreat, 3 miles from downtown Petersburg. From the deck, kitchen and living room you enjoy a spectacular view of Frederick Sound, watching an assortment of wildlife pass by every day – from bald eagles and sea lions to humpback whales. For what you pay for a room in town, you get the entire home. The only drawback is a five-night minimum, but what a way to spend five days.

Scandia House   HOTEL $$
(☏772-4281, 800-722-5006; www.scandiahousehotel.com; 110 Nordic Dr; s/d $110/120, ste $195; 📶) The most impressive place in town, this hotel has 33 bright and modern rooms, some with kitchenettes, and a main-street location. Rates include courtesy shuttle service from the airport/ferry and muffins and coffee in the morning – though it's hard to pass up the jolting espresso in the adjoining Java Hus.

Sea Level B&B   B&B $$
(☏772-3240; www.sealevelbnb.com; 913 N Nordic Dr; r $100-130; 🖥📶) This B&B is built on

ADVENTUROUS KAYAKING

One of the best kayaking adventures in Southeast Alaska is the paddle from the Alaska Native village of Kake to Petersburg. This 90-mile route follows Kupreanof Island's west side through Keku Strait, Sumner Strait and up the Wrangell Narrows to Petersburg. The highlight of the trip is Rocky Pass, a remote and narrow winding waterway in Keku Strait that has almost no boat traffic other than the occasional kayaker. This seven- to 10-day trip is easy to put together – kayaks can be rented in Petersburg and transported on the state ferry to Kake – but is not an outing for novice paddlers. Caution has to be used in Sumner Strait, which lies only 40 miles away from open ocean and has its share of strong winds and waves.

pilings over the Wrangell Narrows, making it look more like a boathouse than a home. Two guest rooms have private bath and large picture windows filled with the boat traffic cruising past Mt Petersburg. On the outside deck there are chairs and rod holders so you can catch your dinner when the tides are in.

Waterfront B&B
B&B $$

(772-9300, 866-772-9301; www.waterfrontbedandbreakfast.com; 1004 S Nordic Dr; r $110-145; @) The closest place to the ferry terminal – it's practically next door. It has an outdoor hot tub where you can soak while watching the ferry depart. Five bright and comfortable rooms have private bath and share a living room that overlooks the Petersburg Shipwrights. For many guests, watching a boat being repaired on dry dock is far more interesting than whatever is on TV.

Nordic House
B&B $$

(772-3620; www.nordichouse.net; 806 S Nordic Dr; r with shared bath $82-149;) Within an easy walk of the ferry terminal, this place offers seven rooms that are large and clean. Guests have use of a kitchen/common area that overlooks the boat harbor.

Ohmer Creek Campground
CAMPGROUND $

(information 772-3871; Mile 22, Mitkof Hwy; campsites $6) The USFS campground is 22 miles southeast of town, but it's cheap and very scenic. It has 15 sites (for tents or RVs), an interpretive trail and fishing in the creek.

Tides Inn
MOTEL $$

(772-4288, 800-665-8433; www.tidesinnalaska.com; 307 1st St; s $100-110, d $115-130; @) The largest motel in town has 45 rooms, some with kitchenettes. Rates include a (very) light continental breakfast.

RV Staging Park
CAMPGROUND $

(772-3392; 2nd St, at Haugen Dr; P) For those who arrive in a RV or van, the city maintains the RV Staging Park, a gravel parking area where you can park for the night before moving on. No amenities and unfortunately no place to pitch a tent, but free parking.

 Eating

TOP CHOICE **Coastal Cold Storage**
SEAFOOD $

(306 N Nordic Dr; breakfast mains $4-8, lunch mains $8-12; breakfast & lunch Mon-Sat;) You're in Petersburg – indulge in what they catch. Stop at this processor/seafood store/restaurant for a shrimp burger, salmon-halibut chowder or the local specialty, halibut beer bits. Or purchase whatever is swimming in the tanks: steamer clams, oysters or Dungeness crab. In the coolers you find just-made salmon sandwiches, shrimp salads, halibut cheeks and even squid bait. Need a beer with those bits? The staff will deliver your order next door to the Harbor Bar.

Beachcomber Inn
AMERICAN $$$

(772-3888; 384 Mitkof Hwy; mains $19-30; dinner Tue-Sat) Built on pilings over the sea, this rambling inn is all restaurant and bar. Every seat has a fabulous maritime-and-mountain view, but the small tables on the covered outdoor deck are an especially nice place to kick back. The inn is 4 miles south of town but runs a free shuttle van from hotels and B&Bs in Petersburg. So even if you don't want to feast on smoked black cod or a bowl of halibut ceviche, come for a drink as an excuse to gather in the view while chatting up the locals.

Inga's Galley
SEAFOOD $

(104 N Nordic Dr; sandwiches $10, dinner mains $8-12; lunch & dinner Mon-Sat) From this parking-lot shack next to the Scandia House comes creative food and good prices. Inga's Mitkof sandwich is seasoned and seared halibut topped with pesto, prosciutto and melted provolone. The fish-and-chips is fresh rockfish rolled in Panko (Japanese breadcrumbs). There are also nonseafood items on the menu and a large tent with heaters where you can mingle with locals while staying dry and warm.

El Rincon
MEXICAN $

(114 N Nordic Dr; lunch mains $8-10, dinner mains $12-14 lunch & dinner Mon-Sat) This shack is on the other side of Scandia House and offers up Petersburg's best Mexican grub, from carne asada tacos and chile relleno to an excellent *camarones à la diabla* (shrimp marinated in habanero sauce). Takeaway only.

Elk & Emblem Club
AMERICAN $$

(772-4601; 1st Ave & Excel St; mains $21-24; dinner Thu-Sat) Almost everybody in Petersburg is an Elk & Emblem member just so they can eat at the club restaurant. The tableside views of Petersburg below are paired up with good food and weekly specials. You can also eat there as a guest: just introduce yourself to whoever answers the buzzer at the door.

Pappa Bear's Pizza
PIZZA $

(219 N Nordic Dr; pizzas $18-25; lunch & dinner Mon-Sat) This place hops at lunchtime, serving

pizza whole or by the slice, along with subs and burger baskets. If you're ready to ditch your vegetarian ways, order the Carnivore pizza that comes topped with pepperoni, Italian sausage, Canadian bacon and an assortment of other animal parts.

Hammer & Wikan SUPERMARKET **$**
(1300 Howkan; ⊙7am-8pm Mon-Sat, 8am-7pm Sun) Off Haugen Dr on the way to the airport, this is Petersburg's main supermarket.

🍷 Drinking

Java Hus COFFEE HOUSE
(Nordic Dr; ⊙6am-6pm Mon-Sat, 7am-4pm Sun; 🖥) This is where Petersburg gets buzzed first thing in the morning. Next to Scandia House.

Harbor Bar BAR
(310 N Nordic Dr; 🛜) The classic place of deckhands and cannery workers, with pool tables, free popcorn and an excellent beer selection. In that great Alaskan tradition, patrons have started pinning dollar bills to the walls.

Kito's Kave BAR
(Sing Lee Alley; 🛜) This bar has regular live music and dancing and can be a rowdy place that hops until well after midnight. In the afternoon it's quieter and you can tap into its wi-fi for the price of a beer.

🛍 Shopping

Sing Lee Alley Books BOOKS
(11 Sing Lee Alley; ⊙9:30am-5:30pm) In a former 1929 boardinghouse, this delightful bookstore has five rooms of books and a well-read proprietor.

ℹ Information

First Bank (103 N Nordic Dr) Has a 24-hour ATM.
Petersburg Medical Center (✆772-4299; 103 Fram St) Has a 24-hour emergency room, and on Saturday operates as a drop-in health clinic.
Petersburg Public Library (12 S Nordic Dr, at Haugen; ⊙noon-9pm Mon-Thu, 10am-5pm Fri & Sat; @🛜) Upstairs in the Municipal Building. There's free, no-hassle internet.
Petersburg Visitor Center (✆772-4636; www.petersburg.org; cnr Fram & 1st Sts; ⊙9am-5pm Mon-Sat, noon-4pm Sun) A good first stop, with both tourist and USFS information; its free *Petersburg Map* will lead you straight.
Post office (1201 Haugen Dr) Half a mile east of downtown on the way to the airport.
USFS Petersburg Ranger District (✆772-3871; 12 N Nordic Dr; ⊙8am-5pm Mon-Fri)

For information about hiking trails, paddling, camping or reserving cabins.

ℹ Getting There & Around

There are daily northbound and southbound flights with **Alaska Airlines** (✆772-4255, 800-426-0333).The airport is on Haugen Dr, a quarter-mile east of the post office.

The **Alaska Marine Highway Terminal** (✆772-3855; www.ferryalaska.com) is a mile south of downtown; in the summer there is a ferry passing through in one direction or the other almost daily. On Tuesday and Friday the high-speed MV *Fairweather* makes a straight run between Juneau and Petersburg ($66, 4½ hours).

The Inter-Island Ferry Authority ferry service between Wrangell and the south end of Mitkof Island was cancelled in 2008, but there are plans to replace it with Rainforest Island Ferry. Check with the **City of Coffman Cove** (✆329-2233; www.ccalaska.com) for the latest.

Scandia House rents midsize cars for $60 a day. For 24-hour taxi service, there's **Midnight Rides Cab** (✆772-2222). **Life Cyclery** (✆650-7387; 402 N 2nd Ave; ⊙10am-5pm Mon-Sat) rents hybrid bicycles ($30 for four hours).

NORTHERN PANHANDLE

Southeast Alaska gets serious when you enter the northern half of the Panhandle. The mountains get higher, the glaciers are more numerous, fjords seem steeper and there's more snow in the winter that lingers on the mountains longer into the summer. You have the current capital and a former one. You have Alaska's most famous gold rush and two roads that actually go somewhere else. Most of all, the dramatic scenery you witness in the Northern Panhandle leads to great wilderness adventures, whether it's canoeing across Admiralty Island, kayaking in Glacier Bay or hiking on Mendenhall Glacier.

Sitka

POP 8881
Fronting the Pacific Ocean on Baranof Island's west shore, Sitka is a sparkling gem in a beautiful setting. Looming on the western horizon, across Sitka Sound, is the impressive Mt Edgecumbe, an extinct volcano with a graceful cone similar to Japan's Mt Fuji. Closer in, a myriad of small, forested islands out in the Sound turns into beautiful ragged silhouettes at sunset, competing for attention with the snowcapped mountains and

JUNEAU & THE SOUTHEAST SITKA

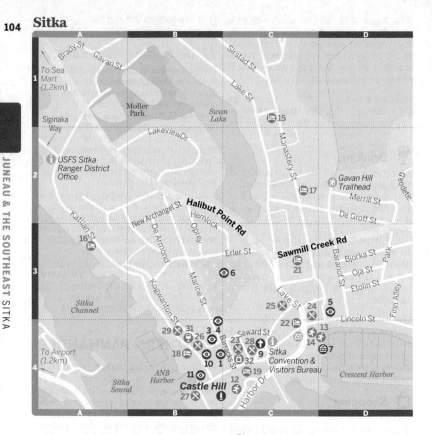

sharp granite peaks flanking Sitka on the east. And in town, picturesque remnants of Sitka's Russian heritage are tucked around every corner.

Sitka is the heart of the Russian influence in Southeast Alaska. The Russians may have landed here as early as 1741 and they stayed for more than a century – until 1867, when the Americans arrived after purchasing Alaska from them.

Today Sitka's Russian history, the main attraction for tourists, is as interesting and as well preserved as the Klondike Gold Rush era is in Skagway. The heart of Sitka's downtown is St Michael's Cathedral, the city's beloved Russian Orthodox church, with Lincoln St serving as Main St. From here you're within easy walking distance of almost all of Sitka's attractions, including Sitka National Historical Park that is filled with totems and Russian artifacts.

⊙ Sights

Sitka Historical Society Museum   MUSEUM
(www.sitkahistory.org; 330 Harbor Dr; admission $2; ⊙9am-5pm Mon-Fri, to 4pm Sat & Sun) Within the Centennial Building is this museum, which is one room with a good portion of it a gift shop. The rest is crammed with a collection of relics, a model of the town as it appeared in 1867 and displays on Russian Alaska. Outside between the museum and the library is an impressive handcarved Tlingit canoe, made from a single log.

St Michael's Cathedral   CHURCH
(☎747-8120; Lincoln St; suggested donation $5; ⊙9am-4pm Mon-Fri when cruise ships are in) Two blocks west of the Centennial Building is the cathedral. Built between 1844 and 1848, the church stood for more than 100 years as Alaska's finest Russian Orthodox cathedral. When a fire destroyed it in 1966, the church had been the oldest religious structure from

on longtime Alaska resident William 'Skagway Bill' Fonda.

Blockhouse & Princess Maksoutoff's Grave   HISTORIC SITES

Still more of Sitka's Russian background guards the hill north of the Alaska Pioneers Home. The blockhouse (cnr Kogwanton & Marine Sts) is a replica of what the Russians used to protect their stockade from the Indian village.

Across Marine St, at the top of Princess St, is Princess Maksoutoff's Grave, marking the spot where the wife of Alaska's last Russian governor is buried. But for a strategically placed chain-link fence, the grave would be in the Russian Cemetery. But a bright and shiny sign proclaims this tiny three-grave site as the Lutheran Cemetery. Cynics might postulate that the princess probably lost her status as a bona fide Lutheran when she married the Russian Orthodox governor, but now that she's a bona fide tourist attraction the Lutherans want her back. More old headstones and Russian Orthodox crosses can be found in the overgrown and quintessentially creepy Russian Cemetery (located at the north end of Observatory St, or just squeak through the gap in the chain-link fence behind the princess' grave), where the drippy verdure seems poised to swallow up the decaying graves.

Russian Bishop's House   HISTORIC BUILDING

(☑747-6281; Lincoln St, at Monastery St; adult/child $4/free; ☉9am-5pm) East of downtown along Lincoln St, the Russian Bishop's House is the oldest intact Russian building in Sitka. Built in 1843 out of Sitka spruce, the two-story log house is one of the few surviving examples of Russian colonial architecture in North America. The National Park Service (NPS) has restored the building to its condition in 1853, when it served as a school, bishop's residence and chapel. The 1st-floor museum is free, while the tours to the 2nd floor are well worth the price of admission.

Sheldon Jackson Museum   MUSEUM

(www.museums.state.ak.us; 104 College Dr; adult/child $4/free; ☉9am-5pm) Further east along Lincoln St on the former campus of Sheldon Jackson College is Sheldon Jackson Museum. The college may be gone, but this fine museum survived because the state of Alaska purchased it in 1983. The unusual building, built to look like a tribal community house, is home to a small but excellent collection of indigenous artifacts gathered

the Russian era in Alaska. Luckily the priceless treasures and icons inside were saved by Sitka's residents, who immediately built a replica of their beloved church.

Castle Hill & Totem Square   HISTORIC SITES

Continue west on Lincoln St for the walkway to Castle Hill. Kiksadi clan houses once covered the hilltop site, but in 1836 the Russians built 'Baranov's Castle' atop the hill to house the governor of Russian America. It was here, on October 18, 1867, that the official transfer of Alaska from Russia to the USA took place. The castle burned down in 1894.

More Russian cannons and a totem pole can be seen in Totem Sq, near the end of Lincoln St. Across Katlian St from the square is the prominent, yellow Alaska Pioneers Home. Built in 1934 on the old Russian Parade Ground, the home is for elderly Alaskans. The 13ft-tall bronze prospector statue in front of the state home is modeled

Sitka

between 1888 and 1898 by Dr Sheldon Jackson, a minister and federal education agent in Alaska. Among the artifacts are Alaska Native masks, hunting tools and baskets, and a collection of boats and sleds used in Alaska – from reindeer sleds and dogsleds to *umiaks* (kayaks).

Sitka Sound Science Center   HATCHERY
(www.sitkasoundsciencecenter.org; 801 Lincoln St; donation $5; ⊙8am-5pm; ⚓) Sitka's best children's attraction is this hatchery and science center. Inside the science center are five aquariums, including the impressive 800-gallon 'Wall of Water' and three touch tanks where kids can get their hands wet handling anemones, sea cucumbers and starfish. Outside is a working hatchery where tanks are filled with 60,000 king-salmon fryling.

Sitka National Historical Park   PARK
Lincoln St ends at this 113-acre park, Alaska's smallest national park, at the mouth of Indian River. The park preserves the site where the Tlingits were finally defeated by the Russians in 1804 after defending their wooden fort for a week. The Russians had arrived with four ships to revenge a Tlingit raid on a nearby outpost two years earlier. The Russians' cannons did little damage to the walls of the Tlingit fort and, when the Russian soldiers stormed the structure with the help of Aleuts, they were repulsed in a bloody battle. It was only when the Tlingits ran out of gunpowder and flint, and slipped away at night, that the Russians were able to enter the deserted fort.

Begin at the park's **visitors center** (www.nps.gov/sitk; adult/child $4/free; ⊙8am-5pm), where Russian and indigenous artifacts are displayed and a 12-minute video in the theater will provide an overview of the battle. Outside is Totem Trail, a mile-long path that leads you past 18 totems first displayed at the 1904 Louisiana Exposition in St Louis and then moved to the newly created park.

It is these intriguing totems, standing in a beautiful rainforest setting by the sea and often enveloped in mist, that have become synonymous with the national park and even the city itself. Eventually you arrive at the site of the Tlingit fort near Indian River, where its outline can still be seen. You can either explore the trail as a self-guided tour or join a ranger-led 'Battle Walk.'

Alaska Raptor Center
WILDLIFE RESERVE

(☎747-8662, 800-643-9425; www.alaskaraptor.org; 1101 Sawmill Creek Rd; adult/child $12/6; ⏰8am-4pm; ♿) For an eye-to-eye encounter with an eagle, head to this raptor center, reached by turning left on the first gravel road after crossing Indian River. The 17-acre center treats 200 injured birds a year, with its most impressive facility being a 20,000-sq-ft flight-training center that helps injured eagles, owls, falcons and hawks regain their ability to fly. In the center eagles literally fly past you, only 2ft or 3ft away, at eye level; it's so close you can feel the wind from their beating wings – amazing.

🏃 Activities

Hiking

Sitka offers superb hiking in the beautiful but tangled forest surrounding the city. A complete hiking guide is available from the USFS Sitka Ranger District office. Sitka Trail Works (www.sitkatrailworks.org), a nonprofit group that raises money for trail improvements, has additional trail information on its website and arranges hikes on weekends throughout the summer.

Indian River Trail
HIKING

This easy trail is a 5.5-mile walk along a clear salmon stream to Indian River Falls, an 80ft cascade at the base of the Three Sisters Mountains. The hike takes you through typical Southeast rainforest and offers the opportunity to view brown bears, deer and bald eagles. The trailhead, a short walk from the town center, is off Sawmill Creek Rd, just east of Sitka National Cemetery. Pass the driveway leading to the Public Safety Academy parking lot and turn up the gated dirt road. This leads back to the city water plant, where the trail begins left of the pump house. Plan on four to five hours round-trip to the falls.

Gavan Hill Trail
HIKING

Also close to town is this popular mountain climb, a trail that ascends almost 2500ft

over 3 miles to Gavan Hill peak. The trail offers excellent views of Sitka and the surrounding area. From the trail's end, the adventurous hiker can continue to the peaks of the Three Sisters Mountains.

Gavan Hill is also linked to Harbor Mountain Trail. Halfway across the alpine ridge is a free-use USFS shelter available on a first-come, first-served basis; it's 3.5 miles from the Gavan Hill trailhead, a hike of three to four hours.

The trailhead and a small parking area are just before the cemetery gate at the end of Baranof St. Camping is good in the trail's alpine regions, but bring drinking water as it is unavailable above the treeline.

Sitka Cross Trail
HIKING

Rather than leading up out of town, this easy, well-used 2.2-mile trail runs roughly parallel to civilization, from one end of town to the other. The west end starts by the water tower at the intersection of Charteris St and Georgeson Loop, but you can pick it up from the high school off of Verstovia Rd. The trail leads east there, crossing Gavan Hill Trail and ending at Indian River Trailhead. Along the way you'll pass peat bogs and old-growth forests.

Harbor Mountain Trail
HIKING

This trail is reached from Harbor Mountain Rd, one of the few roads in the Southeast providing access to a subalpine area. Head 4 miles northwest from Sitka on Halibut Point Rd to the junction with Harbor Mountain Rd. A parking area and picnic shelter are 4.5 miles up the rough dirt road.

Another half-mile further is the parking lot at road's end, where an unmarked trail begins on the lot's east side. The trail ascends 1.5 miles to alpine meadows, knobs and ridges with spectacular views. From here a trail follows the tundra ridge to the free-use shelter on the saddle between Harbor Mountain and Gavan Hill, where you can pick up Gavan Hill Trail. Plan on spending two to four hours if you are just scrambling through the alpine area above Harbor Mountain Rd.

Mosquito Cove Trail
HIKING

At the northwest end of Halibut Point Rd, 0.7 miles past the ferry terminal, Starrigavan Recreation Area offers a number of short but scenic trails. One of them, Mosquito Cove Trail, is an easy and scenic 1.25-mile loop over gravel and boardwalk.

Mt Verstovia Trail
HIKING

This 2.5-mile trail is a challenging climb of 2550ft to the 'shoulder,' a compact summit that is the final destination for most hikers, although it is possible to continue climbing to the peak of Mt Verstovia (3349ft). The panorama from the shoulder on clear days is spectacular, undoubtedly the area's best.

The trailhead is 2 miles east of Sitka, along Sawmill Creek Rd and is posted across from Jamestown Bay. The Russian charcoal pits (signposted) are reached within a quarter-mile, and shortly after that the trail begins a series of switchbacks. It's a four-hour round-trip to the shoulder, from where a ridgeline leads north to the peak (another hour each way).

Beaver Lake–Herring Cove Loop
HIKING

Dedicated in 2010, the Herring Cove Trail is a 1.3-mile route that begins just past the gate at the eastern end of Sawmill Creek Rd and extends north to Beaver Lake Trail, which loops around the lake from Sawmill Creek Campground. Together the two trails make for a 3.6-mile hike from the Herring Cove Trailhead, featuring three waterfalls, outstanding views of the surrounding mountains and boardwalks that wind through an interesting muskeg. This is a popular trail for families.

Mt Edgecumbe Trail
HIKING

The 6.7-mile trail begins at the USFS Fred's Creek Cabin (☏877-444-6777, 518-885-3639; www.recreation.gov; cabins $35) and ascends to the crater of this extinct volcano. Views from the summit are spectacular on a clear day. About 3 miles up the trail is a free-use shelter (no reservations required).

Mt Edgecumbe (3201ft) is on Kruzof Island, 10 miles west of Sitka, and can only be reached by boat because large swells from the ocean prevent floatplanes from landing. Contact Sitka Sound Ocean Adventures (p108), which offers water taxi service to the USFS cabin for $300 round-trip for two passengers. Actual hiking time is five to six hours one way, but by securing Fred's Creek Cabin you can turn the walk into a three-day adventure with two nights spent in shelters. That would be Sitka's best backpacking adventure by far.

Paddling

Sitka also serves as the departure point for numerous blue-water trips along the protected shorelines of Sitka Sound, Baranof and Chichagof Islands. You can rent kayaks in town at Sitka Sound Ocean Adventures (☏752-0660; www.kayaksitka.com), which operates from a blue bus in the parking lot near the main harbor. Kayaks are available (single/double $65/80 per day), as are guided trips. The company's most popular is a 'paddle and cruise,' a 4½-hour tour that includes one-way boat transportation back so you can paddle further into the Sound.

Katlian Bay
KAYAKING

This 45-mile round-trip from Sitka Harbor to scenic Katlian Bay (on Kruzof Island's north end) and back is one of the area's most popular paddles. The route follows narrow straits and well-protected shorelines in marine traffic channels, making it an ideal trip for less experienced blue-water paddlers, who will never be far from help.

A scenic sidetrip is to hike the sandy beach from Katlian Bay around Cape Georgiana to Sea Lion Cove on the Pacific Ocean. Catch the tides to paddle the Olga and Neva Straits on the way north and return along Sukot Inlet, staying overnight at the USFS Brent's Beach Cabin (☏877-444-6777, 518-885-3639; www.recreation.gov; cabins $35). Plan on four to six days for the paddle.

Shelikof Bay
KAYAKING

You can combine a 10-mile paddle to Kruzof Island with a 6-mile hike across the island from Mud Bay to Shelikof Bay along an old logging road and trail. Once on the Pacific Ocean side, you'll find a beautiful sandy beach for beachcombing and the USFS Shelikof Cabin (☏877-444-6777, 518-885-3639; www.recreation.gov; cabins $35).

West Chichagof
KAYAKING

Chichagof Island's western shoreline is one of Southeast Alaska's best blue-water destinations for experienced kayakers. Unfortunately, the trip often requires other transportation, because few paddlers have the experience necessary to paddle the open ocean around Khaz Peninsula (which forms a barrier between Kruzof Island's north end and Slocum Arm, the south end of the West Chichagof-Yakobi Wilderness). For most paddlers that means a water-taxi service to take you there.

The arm is the southern end of a series of straits, coves and protected waterways that shield paddlers from the ocean's swells and extend over 30 miles north to Lisianski Strait. With all its hidden coves and inlets, the trip is a good two-week paddle. Travelers with even more time and a sense of adventure could continue another 25 miles through Lisianski Strait to the fishing village of Pelican, where the ferry stops twice a month in summer. Such an expedition would require at least two to three weeks.

Snorkeling

Island Fever Diving & Adventures
SNORKELING

(747-7871; www.islandfeverdiving.com; 213 Harbor Dr) is a full-service dive shop, but its most popular offerings are snorkeling trips. It provides all the gear, including dry suits and transportation for either a 2½-hour adventure to Magic Island ($118) or a four-hour trip to No Thorofare Bay ($150). The water may be cold, but the giant kelp forests and colorful sea stars, anemones and fish are stunning.

Whale Watching

More than a dozen companies in Sitka offer boat tours to view whales and other marine wildlife, and most of them swing past St Lazaria Island National Wildlife Refuge, home to 1500 pairs of breeding tufted puffins.

TOP CHOICE Sitka's Secrets
WILDLIFE TOUR

(747-5089; www.sitkasecret.com) The 27ft boat that Sitka's runs to St Lazaria Island carries only six passengers, for a far more personal adventure. Its three-hour cruise ($120 per person, minimum three persons) to view seabirds and whales is operated by a married couple, both biologists and former national wildlife refuge managers.

Sea Life Discovery Tours
WILDLIFE TOUR

(966-2301, 877-966-2301; www.sealifediscovery tours.com; tours adult/child $89/65;) Operates a glass-bottomed boat that gives visitors views of the area's underwater marine life from 10ft below the surface. The narrated two-hour tours includes a touch tank onboard, making it an excellent choice for children.

Sitka Wildlife Quest/Allen Marine Tours
WILDLIFE TOUR

(747-8100, 888-747-8101; www.allenmarinetours. com) Offers wildlife cruises whenever cruise ships are in. On Saturday the three-hour tour (adult/child $99/69) departs 1:30pm from the Crescent Harbor dock to view whales, sea otters, puffins and other wildlife. Reservations are not needed for the Saturday special.

Whale Park
WHALE WATCHING

(Sawmill Creek Rd) If you can't afford a wildlife cruise, try Whale Park, 4 miles south of town,

which has a boardwalk and spotting scopes overlooking the ocean. Fall is the best time to sight cetaceans; as many as 80 whales – mostly humpbacks – have been known to gather in the waters off Sitka between mid-September and the end of the year.

Wilderness Cabins

A number of USFS cabins lie within 30 minutes' flying time of Sitka. Among the most popular cabins are Redoubt Lake Cabin, at the northern end of Redoubt Lake, about 10 miles south of Sitka; Baranof Lake Cabin, which enjoys a scenic (though reportedly buggy) mountainous setting on the island's east side; barrier-free Lake Eva Cabin, also on Baranof Island's east shore, north of the Baranof Lake Cabin; and White Sulphur Springs Cabin, on the west shore of Chichagof Island, which is popular with locals because of the adjacent hot-springs bathhouse.

All cost $35 per night and should be reserved in advance through the USFS (877-444-6777, 518-885-3639; www.recreation.gov). For air-taxi service, try Harris Aircraft Services.

Tours

Sitka Tours
BUS

(747-8443; adult/child $12/6) If you're only in Sitka for as long as the ferry stopover, don't despair: Sitka Tours runs a two-hour bus tour just for you. The tour picks up and returns passengers to the ferry terminal, making brief visits to Sitka National Historical Park and St Michael's Cathedral. Time is allotted for the obligatory T-shirt-shopping experience.

Fortress of the Bear
BEAR WATCHING

(747-3550; www.fortressofthebear.com; adult/child $10/5) If you haven't seen a bear in the wild – or don't want to – this attraction offers an opportunity to observe five brown bears that were abandoned as cubs. The walls of the 'fortress' are actually wastewater treatment pools left over after the lumber mill near the end of Sawmill Creek Rd closed in 1993. The setting is a little strange and these are captive bears, but they are incredibly active swimming, wrestling and just being bears. Bus transportation from downtown included.

Tribal Tours
CULTURAL

(747-7290, 888-270-8687; sitkatours.com; Tlingit Clan House, 204 Katlian St) A wide array of local tours with an Alaska Native perspective. Tribal Tours' 2½-hour bus tour (adult/child

THESE BOOTS ARE MADE FOR RUNNING

Slip on your rubber boots and run. That is what Sitkans have been doing since 1995 during their annual Running of the Boots Celebration (www.runnin goftheboots.org). The half-mile boot race to the harbor is held in late September and marks the transition from tourism to fishing season when residents com memorate taking back their town. The only requirement to run is you have to wear rubber boots, but in a place as rainy as Southeast Alaska you're prob ably already wearing them.

$53/42) includes Sitka National Historical Park, Sheldon Jackson Museum and a Tlingit Native dance performance. It also has a two-hour coach and hiking tour that includes driving out to Old Historic Sitka and hiking Starrigavan Trail (per person $58).

★☆ Festivals & Events

Sitka Summer Music Festival (747-6774; www.sitkamusicfestival.org) extends Sitka's reputation as the Southeast's cultural center at this three-week event in June, which brings together professional musicians for chamber-music concerts and workshops. The evening concerts are truly a treat for the senses: classical music filling Centennial Hall, where the glass backdrop of the stage gives way to views of the harbor, snow-covered mountains and eagles soaring in the air. The highly acclaimed event is so popular you should purchase tickets in advance of your trip.

On the weekend nearest October 18, **Alaska Day Festival** sees the city re-enact, in costumes (and even beard styles) of the 1860s, the transfer of the state from Russia to the USA.

The city stages the **WhaleFest!** (747-7964; www.sitkawhalefest.org) during the first weekend of November to celebrate the large fall gathering of humpbacks with whale-watching cruises, lectures, craft shows and more.

⌨ Sleeping

Sitka levies a 12% city and bed tax on all lodging. Two USFS campgrounds are in the area, but neither is close to town.

TOP CHOICE **Fly-in Fish Inn**   BOUTIQUE HOTEL **$$**
(747-7910; www.flyinfishinn.com; 485 Katlian St; r $159-179;) In the middle of the bustling harbors and canneries of Katlian is Sitka's most unusual inn. Fly-in Fish Inn is gracious luxury, with 10 large rooms featuring refrigerators, wet bars, microwaves, cable TV – you name it. There's also a dining room (serving a full breakfast), a small bar and a seaplane dock, so arranging a flightseeing or fly-in fishing trip is as easy as calling the front desk and then stepping out of your room.

Shee Atiká Totem Square Inn   HOTEL **$$**
(747-3693; 866-300-1353; www.totemsquare inn.com; 201 Katlian St; r $154-194;) This is Sitka's finest hotel, with 68 large, comfortable rooms featuring the traditional (Alaska Native art and prints on the walls) and the modern (flat-screen TVs, hair dryers and wi-fi). There's a work-out facility, breakfast room, laundry, business center and free airport shuttle. Its best feature, however, is still the views from the rooms, overlooking either the historic square or a harbor bustling with boats bringing in the day's catch.

Ann's Gavan Hill B&B   B&B **$**
(747-8023; www.annsgavanhill.com; 415 Arrow-head St; s/d $75/95;) An easy walk from downtown is this lovely Alaskan home, with a wraparound deck that includes two hot tubs. The three bedrooms are spacious, comfortable and equipped with TV and DVD. The delightful proprietor is a former commercial fisher and still an avid hunter – the reason for the bearskin and marine charts on the walls.

Starrigavan Recreation Area   CAMPGROUND **$**
(reservations 877-444-6777, 518-885-3639; www. recreation.gov; Mile 7.8, Halibut Point Rd; campsites $12-16) Sitka's finest campground has 35 sites spread along three loops for three types of campers: RVers, car-and-tent campers, and backpackers and cyclists. You're 7 miles north of town, but the coastal scenery is beautiful and nearby is Old Sitka State Historic Site, which features trails and interpretive displays dedicated to the site of the original Russian settlement. There are numerous amenities, such as bird- and salmon-viewing decks, and several hiking trails and Nelson Logging Rd for mountain bikers depart from the campground. Sites can be reserved in advance.

Sitka International Hostel
HOSTEL **$**

(☎747-8661; www.sitkahostel.org; 109 Jeff Davis St; dm/r $20/60; ☺@☎) Sitka's new hostel is downtown in the historic Tillie Paul Manor, which once served as the town's hospital. The building has been totally renovated and now features a men's room upstairs with its own kitchen and three women's rooms on the 1st floor along with a family room, another small kitchen and a lovely sun porch with a mountain view. The hostel is locked from 10am to 6pm, but hostel managers are good about greeting late-night arrivals who call ahead.

Westmark Sitka Hotel
HOTEL **$$$**

(☎747-6241, 800-544-0970; www.westmarkhotels.com; 330 Seward St; r/ste $199/279; ☺@☎) The business traveler's favorite, it has 106 rooms and suites, a central location, a fine restaurant and bar with views of the harbor and room service.

Cascade Inn
INN **$$**

(☎747-6804, 800-532-0908; www.cascadeinnsitka.com; 2035 Halibut Point Rd; r $125-160; ☺☎) Perched right above the shoreline, all 10 rooms in this inn face the ocean and have a private balcony overlooking it. Sure, you're 2.5 miles north of town, but the inn's oceanfront deck with its sauna and BBQ is worth the ride on the downtown bus.

Hannah's B&B
B&B **$$**

(☎747-8309; www.hannahsbandb.com; 504 Monastery St; r $110-120; ☺) This long-time B&B proprietor believes that if you're coming to Alaska you're trying to escape, so there are no phones, no TVs and no computers. What she does have is location – only four blocks from Lincoln St – and two beautiful rooms that include microwave, mini-refrigerator and private entrance.

Sitka Hotel
HOTEL **$**

(☎747-3288; www.sitkahotel.com; 118 Lincoln St; s/d $99/105; @☎) Sitka's oldest hotel was extensively renovated after a fire, and now the new rear-facing rooms, many with views of Sitka Sound, are large and comfortable. The rest of the rooms are smaller but well kept, and all have cable TV. A few even have kitchenettes. The location and services (laundry, luggage storage, wi-fi) makes the Sitka Hotel a good value.

Super 8 Motel
MOTEL **$$**

(☎747-8804, 800-800-8000; www.the.super8.com/sitka03097; 404 Sawmill Creek Rd; r $139) This is a Super 8 Motel so you know what you're getting: large, clean, utilitarian rooms. The rate is higher than most accommodations in Sitka, but its downtown location, indoor hot tub, free continental breakfast and 24-hour laundromat make it a popular choice.

Sawmill Creek Campground
CAMPGROUND **$**

(Blue Lake Rd; campsites free) Southeast of town, via Sawmill Creek Rd and Blue Lake Rd, is this free 11-site campground that features mountain scenery, the Beaver Lake Trail and fishing opportunities in nearby lakes.

✖ Eating

TOP CHOICE **Ludvig's Bistro**
MEDITERRANEAN **$$$**

(☎966-3663; www.ludvigsbistro.com; 256 Katlian St; tapas $12-16, mains $24-34; ☺dinner; ☺) Sitka's boldest restaurant is Southeast's best. Too bad it's so quaint. Ludvig's is as colorful as the commercial fishing district that surrounds it, but there are only seven tables and a handful of stools at its brass-and-blue-tile bar. But an evening here is well worth the wait or even a reservation. The menu is described as 'rustic Mediterranean fare,' and almost everything is local, even the sea salt. If seafood paella is on the menu, order it. The traditional Spanish rice dish comes loaded with scallops, king crab, salmon, calamari, prawns and whatever else the local boats netted that day.

Kenny's Wok & Teriyaki
CHINESE **$**

(210 Katlian St; mains $7-12; ☺lunch & dinner) Practically next door to Ludvig's is this Chinese restaurant that always seems packed. That's because it has only nine tables, and the locals love the portions and the prices. You might have to share a table, but the lunch-bowl specials ($7) are the best meal deal in Sitka.

Bayview Pub
PUB **$$**

(www.sitkabayviewpub.com; 407 Lincoln St; sandwiches $12-16; ☺lunch Tue-Sun, dinner Mon-Sun) Head upstairs in the MacDonald Bayview Trading Company Building for the best view of any restaurant in town. Soak in that scene of boat traffic in Sitka Sound with a pint of Alaskan microbrew beer, including Sitka's own Baranof Island Brewing Co. The Bayview also has a nice list of wines that can be enjoyed by the glass and daily specials that feature locally caught fish.

Larkspur Café
CAFE $$

(2 Lincoln St; sandwiches $8-12, dinner mains $8-20; ⊘lunch & dinner Tue-Sat, brunch Sunday) In the back of the Raven Radio Building is this laid-back cafe that has beer on tap, wine by the glass, great desserts and occasional live music at night. It has a blackboard menu that changes daily, but if the smoked salmon soup is listed, order it and then enjoy a bowl of it on the pleasant outdoor porch.

Two Chicks & a Kabob Stick
FAST FOOD $

(www.chickskabob.com; 124 Lincoln St; kabobs $10 ⊘lunch Tue-Fri) These chicks know how to grill a tasty kabob. From a cart behind Brenners Clothing Store, they take spice-rubbed or honey-glazed shrimp or salmon, grill it on a stick and serve it with brown rice. It's so good you don't even realize it's healthy.

Little Tokyo
SUSHI $

(315 Lincoln St; lunch specials $8-10; fish & tempura rolls $7-13; ⊘lunch & dinner; ⊜) Even crewmembers from the commercial fleet, who know a thing or two about raw fish, say this sushi bar is a good catch.

Victoria's
BREAKFAST $$

(118 Lincoln St; breakfast & lunch mains $9-14, dinner mains $15-29; ⊘4:30am-9pm; ⊜) Sitka's early-morning breakfast joint, it's open no matter when your charter captain decides to shove off to chase kings and cohos. If you're a late riser, come back in the evening for a good selection of seafood.

Back Door Café
COFFEE HOUSE $

(✎104 Barracks St; snacks $1-5; ⊘6:30am-5pm Mon-Sat, to 2pm Sun; ⊜⊚) Enter this small coffee house through either Old Harbor Books on Lincoln St or the...you guessed it...which is off Barracks St. The cruise-ship hordes parading endlessly down Lincoln St can't immediately see it so they go elsewhere. As a result, this cafe is as local as it gets and possibly the only place in Alaska where you can get a cup of coffee for less than $1. That includes a refill.

Highliner Coffee
COFFEE HOUSE $

(Seward Square Mall, 327 Seward St; snacks $1-5; ⊘breakfast & lunch; ⊜@⊚) At the Highliner they like their coffee black and their salmon wild, which explains why the walls are covered with photos of local fishing boats or political stickers like 'Invest in Wild Salmon's Future: Eat One!' Come here to catch the buzz from a latte and the local issues. Indulge in a bagel sandwich.

Sea Mart
SUPERMARKET $

(1867 Halibut Point Rd; ⊘24hr) Sitka's main supermarket is northwest of town and never closes. Inside it has an ATM, bakery, deli, ready-to-eat items and a dining area overlooking Mt Edgecumbe.

🍷 Drinking

Baranof Island Brewing Co
BREWERY

(www.baranofislandbrewing.com; 212 Smith St; ⊘11am-8pm) Off Sawmill Creek Rd, past the main post office, is Sitka's new microbrewery, producing such beers as Halibut Point Hefeweisen and Redoubt Red Ale. The brewery is such a hit with locals that there are already plans to move across the street into a larger facility that will have a taproom with food service.

Pioneer Bar
BAR

(212 Katlian St) The 'P-Bar' is Alaska's classic maritime watering hole. The walls are covered with photos of fishing boats, their crews and big fish and a blackboard with messages like, 'Experienced deckhand looking for seine job.' Don't ring the ship's bell over the bar unless you're ready to buy every crew-member a drink.

Fly-in Fish Inn Bar
BAR

(485 Katlian St) A delightful little six-stool bar at the back of the inn. On the covered deck outside you can watch deckhands unload the day's catch.

Victoria's Pourhouse
BAR

(118 Lincoln St) A friendly pub inside the Sitka Hotel with the largest TV screen in town.

☆ Entertainment

New Archangel Russian Dancers
TRADITIONAL DANCE

(✎747-5516; www.newarchangeldancers.com; adult/child $10/5) Whenever a cruise ship is in port, this troupe of more than 30 dancers in Russian costumes takes the stage at Centennial Hall for a half-hour show. A schedule is posted in the hall.

Sheet'ka Kwaan Naa Kahidi Dancers
TRADITIONAL DANCE

(✎747-7290; sitkatours.com; 204 Katlian St; adult/child $10/5) Not to be outdone, these dancers also perform traditional Tlingit dances when the cruise ships are in at the Tlingit Clan House, next to the Pioneers' Home.

Shopping

Old Harbor Books BOOKS
(201 Lincoln St; ⊘Mon-Sat) A fine bookstore with a large Alaska section.

Information

INTERNET ACCESS Using a head tax on cruise-ship passengers, the city of Sitka has set up free wi-fi throughout the downtown area. It can be picked up in most cafes, stores, bars and hotels along Lincoln St and Harbor Dr. **Kettleson Memorial Library** (320 Harbor Dr; ⊘10am-9pm Mon-Fri, 1-9pm Sat & Sun; @🔊) Next door to the Centennial Building and overlooking the harbor is the city's impressive library with 10 computers for internet access and free wi-fi.

MEDICAL SERVICES Sitka Community Hospital (☑747-3241; 209 Moller Dr) By the intersection of Halibut Point Rd and Brady St.

MONEY First National Bank of Anchorage (318 Lincoln St) Downtown, with a 24-hour ATM.

POST Pioneer substation (336 Lincoln St) Conveniently located downtown. **Post office** (1207 Sawmill Creek Rd) Main center is 1 mile east of town.

TOURIST INFORMATION Sitka Convention & Visitors Bureau (☑747-5940; www.sitka. org; 303 Lincoln St, Suite 4; ⊘8am-5pm Mon-Fri) Across the street from the cathedral. The bureau also staffs a visitor-information desk in the Centennial Building next to Crescent Harbor. **USFS Sitka Ranger District Office** (☑747-6671, recorded information 747-6685; 204 Siginaka Way, at Katlian St; ⊘8am-4:30pm Mon-Fri) Has information about local trails, camping and USFS cabins.

Getting There & Away

AIR Alaska Airlines (☑966-2926, 800-426-0333; www.alaskaair.com) Sitka is served by Alaska Airlines, with flights to/from Juneau ($126, 45 minutes) and Ketchikan($160, one hour). Its airport is on Japonski Island, 1.8 miles west, or a 20-minute walk, of downtown. In 2011 there was no airport shuttle meeting jet flights, and taxis were the only way to reach downtown.

Harris Aircraft Services (☑966-3050, 877-966-3050 in Alaska; www.harrisaircraft.com) Floatplane air-taxi service to small communities and USFS cabins.

BOAT The Alaska Marine Highway **ferry terminal** (☑747-8737) is 6.5 miles northwest of town; ferries depart in both directions almost daily to Juneau ($45, nine hours), Angoon ($35, six hours), Petersburg ($45, 11 hours) and Tenakee Springs ($35, nine hours).

Getting Around

BOAT For water-taxi service to contact **Esther G Sea Taxi** (☑74 6481) or **Sitka Sound Ocean Adv** (☑752-0660; www.kayaksitka.con

CAR At the airport, **Northstar Rent** (☑966-2552, 800-722-6927) rents for $55 per day, but there is a 20% ta.. Hey, you get unlimited mileage (like you need that in Sitka).

BUS Sitka's public bus system, **Community Ride** (☑747-7103; adult/child $2/1; ⊘6:30am-7:30pm Mon-Fri), has expanded significantly in recent years and now offers hourly service from downtown to as far south as Whale Park and as far north as the ferry terminal. **Ferry Transit Bus** (☑747-8443; one way/round-trip $8/12), operated by Sitka Tours, meets all ferries year-round for the trip to and from town.

TAXI For a ride around Sitka, try **More's Taxi Service** (☑738-3210).

BICYCLE Yellow Jersey Cycle Shop (☑747-6317; www.yellowjerseycycles.com; 329 Harbor Dr; per 2hr/day $20/30), across the street from the library, rents quality mountain bikes.

Juneau

POP 31,275

Juneau is a capital of contrasts and conflicts. It borders a waterway that never freezes but lies beneath an ice field that never melts. It was the first community in the Southeast to slap a head tax on cruise-ship passengers but draws more of them (almost a million) than any other town. It's the state capital but since the 1980s Alaskans have been trying to move it. It doesn't have any roads that go anywhere, but half its residents and its mayor opposed a plan to build one that would.

Welcome to America's strangest state capital. In the winter it's a beehive of legislators, their loyal aides and lobbyists locked in political struggles. They no sooner leave than, in May, the cruise ships arrive with swarms of passengers. It's the most geographically secluded state capital in the country, the only one that cannot be reached by car – only boat or plane.

But Juneau is also the most beautiful city in Alaska and arguably the nation's most scenic capital. The city center, which hugs the side of Mt Juneau and Mt Roberts, is a maze of narrow streets running past a mix of new structures, old storefronts and slanted houses, all held together by a network of staircases. The waterfront is bustling with cruise ships, fishing boats and floatplanes buzzing

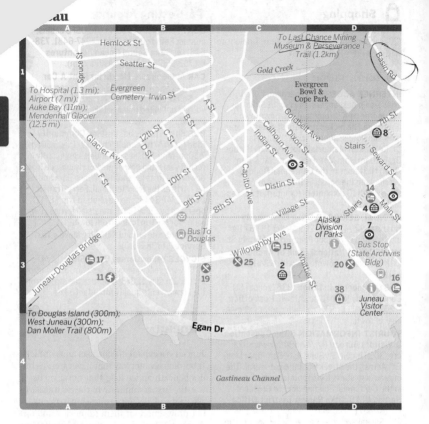

in and out. High above the city is the Juneau Ice Field, covering the Coastal Range and sending glaciers down between the mountains like marshmallow syrup on a sundae.

The state's first major gold strike and the first town to be founded after Alaska's purchase from the Russians, Juneau became the territorial capital in 1906. Juneau's darkest hour occurred in the late 1970s after Alaskans voted to move the state capital again. The so-called 'capital move' put a stranglehold on the growth of Juneau until Alaskans defeated its billion-dollar price tag in a statewide vote in 1982. The referendum gave Juneau new life and the town burst at its seams, booming in typical Alaskan fashion.

While the downtown area clings to a mountainside, the rest of the city 'officially' sprawls over 3100 sq miles to the Canadian border, making it one of the largest cities (in area) in the USA. The city center is the busi-

est and most popular area among visitors in summer. From downtown, Egan Dr, the Southeast's only four-lane highway, heads northwest to Mendenhall Valley, home to the city's growing residential section, much of its business district and world-famous Mendenhall Glacier. In the Valley, Egan Dr turns into Glacier Hwy, a two-lane road that leads to Auke Bay, site of the Alaska Marine Highway terminal. Across Gastineau Channel is Douglas, a small town that was once the major city in the area.

Considering it's still a state capital, Juneau isn't the hive of cultural activity you might expect. Entertainment venues are minimal and good restaurants are rare. But many find it a refreshing haven of liberalism in a state that is steadily marching to the right. Spend a morning eavesdropping in cafes and coffee houses and you'll hear the environmental and social conscience of Alaska.

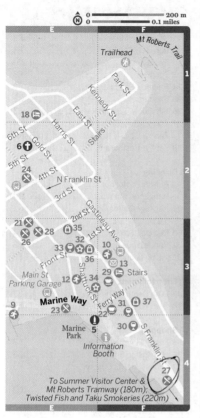

a hostile land into an art form with a display of items ranging from waterproof gut parkas and a century-old *umiak* to tomcod fishing rods. Beautifully effective. The top floor is devoted to the state's Russian period and major gold strikes, and connecting the two is a circular ramp that winds around the museum's most popular exhibit: a diorama of a full-size eagle's nest in a two-story-high tree.

Juneau-Douglas City Museum MUSEUM
(www.juneau.org/parkrec/museum; 114 W 4th St; adult/child $4/free; ⊙9am-5pm Mon-Fri, from 10am Sat & Sun) This museum focuses on gold with interesting mining displays and the video *Juneau: City Built On Gold*. It is also home to the 1922 Sydney Laurence painting, *Early Morning, Juneau, Alaska* and if you love to hike in the mountains, the museum's 7ft-long relief map is the best overview of the area's rugged terrain other than a helicopter ride. Tuesday to Thursday the staff leads a historical walking tour (adult/child $15/10) of the downtown area beginning at 1:30pm at the museum.

FREE Alaska State Capitol HISTORIC BUILDING
(120 4th St; ⊙8:30am-5:30pm Mon-Fri, from 10am Sat & Sun) Next to the City Museum is the Alaska State Capitol. Built in 1929–31 as the territorial Federal Building, the capitol looks more like an overgrown high school. Stuffed inside are legislative chambers, the governor's office, and offices for the hundreds of staff members who arrive in Juneau for the winter legislative session. Free 30-minute tours are held every half-hour and start from the visitor desk in the lobby; a self-guided tour pamphlet is also available.

Last Chance Mining Museum MUSEUM
(1001 Basin Rd; adult/child $4/free; ⊙9:30am-12:30pm & 3:30-6:30pm; ⊡) Amble out to the end of Basin Rd, a beautiful half-mile walk from the north end of Gastineau Ave, to the intriguing Last Chance Mining Museum. The former Alaska-Juneau Gold Mining Company complex is now a museum where you can view the remains of the compressor house and examine tools of what was once the world's largest hard-rock gold mine. There is also a re-created mining tunnel and a 3D glass map of shafts that shows just how large it was. Nearby is the Perseverance Trail, and combining the museum with a hike to more mining ruins is a great way to spend an afternoon.

For visitors who come to Alaska for outdoor adventure, what really distinguishes the state capital from other Alaskan towns – and certainly other state capitals – is the superb hiking. Dozens of great trails surround the city; some begin downtown, just blocks from the capitol. Juneau also serves as the departure point for several wilderness attractions, including paddling paradises such as Glacier Bay National Park, Tracy Arm-Fords Terror Wilderness Area and Admiralty Island National Monument.

◉ **Sights**

Alaska State Museum MUSEUM
(www.museums.state.ak.us; 395 Whittier St; adult/child $5/free; ⊙8:30am-5:30pm; ⊡) The Alaska State Museum is near Centennial Hall and on its 1st floor features artifacts from Alaska's six major indigenous groups. The most intriguing exhibit, 'Art of Survival,' shows how Alaska Natives have turned living in

Juneau

Mt Roberts Tramway   CABLE CAR
(www.goldbelttours.com; 490 S Franklin St; adult/child $27/13.50; ◷noon-9pm Mon, 9am-9pm Tue-Sun; ♿) As far as trams go, this tramway is rather expensive for a five-minute ride. But from a marketing point of view its location couldn't be better. It whisks you right from the cruise-ship dock up 1800ft to the treeline of Mt Roberts, where you'll find a restaurant, gift shops and a small theater with a film on Tlingit culture. Or skip all that and just use the tram to access the Mt Roberts alpine area.

Waterfront Area & South Franklin Street   PLAZA
Between the cruise ships and Willoughby Ave, **Marine Park** is an open space where kids practice their skateboard tricks, state workers enjoy a sack lunch and tired tourists occasionally take a nap in the sun. Spotting scopes let you search Mt Juneau for moun-

tain goats, while on the dock is a **sculpture of Patsy Ann**, the late faithful Fido who became known as the 'Official Greeter of Juneau' for her tendency to rush down to the docks to meet arriving cruise ships. A block inland from the waterfront is **South Franklin Street**, a refurbished historical district where many buildings date from the early 1900s and have since been turned into bars, gift shops and restaurants.

Museums & Historic Sites   HISTORIC BUILDINGS
Overlooking downtown Juneau is **Wickersham State Historical Site** (☎586-9001; 213 7th St), which preserves the 1898 home of pioneer judge and statesman James Wickersham. In 2011, the museum was closed for extensive renovation. Call to see if it has reopened.

Two blocks downhill is **St Nicholas Russian Orthodox Church** (☎586-1023; 326 5th St; admission by donation; ◷noon-5pm Mon-Fri, to 4pm Sat & Sun). Built in 1893 against the backdrop of Mt Juneau, the onion-domed church is the oldest original one in Alaska. From a small gift shop filled with *matreshkas* (nestling dolls) and other handcrafted items from Russia, you enter the church where, among the original vestments and religious relics, a row of painted saints stare down at you. Playing softly in the background are the chants from a service. If you weren't spiritual before, you probably are now.

Across from the Juneau-Douglas City Museum is the State Office Building (400 Willoughby Ave), known locally as the SOB. From the outdoor court on the 8th floor there is a spectacular view of the channel and Douglas Island, while in the lobby is a massive Kimball organ dating back to 1928. Every Friday at noon a performance is given, a good reason to join state workers for a brown-bag lunch. West of the SOB along 4th Ave is the pillared Governor's Mansion (716 Calhoun Avenue). Built and furnished in 1912 at a cost of $44,000, the mansion is not open to the public.

🏃 Activities

Cycling

Bike paths run between Auke Bay, Mendenhall Glacier and downtown, and from the Juneau-Douglas Bridge to Douglas. Pick up a route guide at the Centennial Hall's main visitors center. Because most of Juneau's trails are steep, mountain biking is limited, but the Windfall Lake and Peterson Lake trails are popular with off-road cyclists.

Cycle Alaska   BICYCLE RENTAL
(☑321-2453; www.cycleak.com; 1107 W 8th St; per 4/8hr $35/45; ⊙10am-5pm Mon-Fri, 9am-5pm Sat & Sun) Rents quality road and mountain bikes along with children's bikes and tandems. The company offers a Bike & Brew (adult/child $99/75), a four-hour bicycle tour that includes Auke Bay, Mendenhall Glacier and finishes off at the Alaskan Brewing Co.

Driftwood Lodge   BICYCLE RENTAL
(435 W Willoughby Ave; rentals incl helmet & lock per hr/day $5/25) Rents basic mountain bikes.

Gold Panning

Juneau was built on gold or, more realistically, the tailings from its gold mines, and for many visitors that's the most fascinating part of its history. Two of the Juneau area's most successful historic mines were

the Alaska-Juneau Mine, on the side of Mt Roberts, and the Treadwell Mine, across Gastineau Channel near Douglas. The Alaska-Juneau Mine closed in 1944 after producing more than $80 million in gold, then valued at $20 to $35 per ounce. The Treadwell Mine closed in 1922 after a 1917 cave-in caused the company's financial collapse. During its heyday at the turn of the 20th century, the Treadwell made Douglas the channel's major city, with a population of 15,000. For more information about these mines and what you can see of them today, stop by the Juneau-Douglas City Museum.

AJ/Gastineau Mill Enterprises   MINE
(☑463-5017; adult/child $59/30) Offers a three-hour tour of the Gastineau Mill ruins at Sheep Creek, once the world's largest gold mill. The highlight of the tour is following a 360-foot-long conveyor tunnel carved into the mountainside where a miner demonstrates the equipment that was used. Gold panning at the end of course.

Hiking

Few cities in Alaska have such a diversity of hiking trails as Juneau. A handful of these trails are near the city centre, the rest are out the road. All five hike-in USFS cabins (☑877-444-6777, 518-885-3639; www.recreation.gov; cabins $35) should be reserved. See p129 for information on hiking at Mendenhall Glacier.

TOP
CHOICE Juneau Parks & Recreation   HIKING
(☑586-5226, recorded information 586-0428; www.juneau.org/parksrec; 155 S Seward St) Offers volunteer-led hikes every Wednesday (adults) and Saturday (kids OK) in 'rain, shine or snow.' Call or check the website for a schedule and the trails.

Gastineau Guiding   HIKING
(☑586-8231; www.stepintoalaska.com) Offers a number of guided hikes that include snacks, ponchos if needed and transportation. Among the offerings is West Glacier Trail (per person $189), a six-hour tour which includes Steep Creek Trail to look for bears.

CITY CENTER TRAILS

Perseverance Trail off Basin Rd is Juneau's most popular. The trail is a path into Juneau's mining history but also provides access to two other popular treks, Mt Juneau Trail and Granite Creek Trail, and together the routes can be combined into a rugged 10-hour walk for hardy hikers, or an

For an unusual sidetrip into rural Southeast Alaska you can board the Alaska Marine Highway (800-642-0066; www.ferryalaska.com) for a cruise to seven small villages. Most stopovers by the ferry last an hour, enough time to walk around. But for a better cultural experience, spend a night or two, even if it means paying for a charter flight back to Juneau or Ketchikan. Here are three of the most interesting:

Tenakee Springs

Since the late 19th century when it served as a winter retreat for fishers and prospectors, Tenakee Springs (population 131) has evolved into a village known for its relaxed pace. On the east side of Tenakee Inlet, the settlement is basically a ferry dock, a row of houses on pilings and the hot springs, the main attraction, which bubble out of the ground at 107°F.

Tenakee's alternative lifestyle centers on the free public bathhouse at the end of the ferry dock. The building encloses the principal spring, which flows through the concrete bath at 7 gallons per minute. Bath hours, separate for men and women, are posted, and most locals take at least one good soak per day, if not two.

The ferry MV *Le Conte* stops at Tenakee Springs twice a week (six hours; $35), allowing you to arrive on Friday from Juneau and depart on Sunday. Stay at Tenakee Hot Springs Lodge (736-2400, 364-3640; tenakeehotspringslodge.com; 1407 1st Street, Douglas; s/d $90/150;), or pitch a tent at the rustic campground a mile east of town, at the mouth of the Indian River. For more information on lodging and services check the website for the Tenakee Springs Business Association (www.tenakeespringssak.com).

Pelican

Juneau's has a twice-monthly state ferry to Pelican (population 88), a lively little fishing town on Chichagof Island. The cruise through Icy Straits is scenic, with regular humpback spottings, and the two hours in port is enough to see one of Southeast Alaska's last boardwalk communities. Pelican is a photographer's delight. Most of it built on pilings over tidelands, and its main street, dubbed Salmon Way, is a mile-long wooden boardwalk.

The town was established in 1938 by a fish packer and named after his boat. Fishing is Pelican's raison d'être. It has the closest harbor to Fairweather's salmon grounds – the reason its population swells during the summer. You can mingle with trollers, longliners and Pelican seafood workers at Rose's Bar & Grill, a classic Alaskan fishers' bar.

You can stay at Highliner Lodge (735-2476, 877-386-0397; www.highlinerlodge.com; Boat Harbor; s/d with shared bath $165/195;). Alaska Seaplane Service (735-2244 in Juneau, 789-3331 in Pelican, 888-350-8277; www.akseaplanes.com) fly people back to Juneau for $170. For more contact Pelican Visitors Association (www.pelican.net).

Metlakatla

Founded in 1887 when Anglican missionary William Duncan arrived at Annette Island with 823 Tsimsheans from British Columbia, Metlakatla became a federally recognized Indian Reservation four years later and today is the only one in Alaska. The 20-mile-long island is reserved for the Metlakatla Indians, whose village (population 1405) is the antithesis to Ketchikan just across the Tongass Narrows. While much in Ketchikan is made for cruise ships, Metlakatla is an authentic slice of Native Alaska, from its totems scattered throughout the town and its artists' village to its award-winning Tsimshean dancers.

The heart of the scenic town is Annette Island Packing Company, perched on stilts overlooking a beautiful harbor dotted with small islands. Graveyard and Yellow Hill Trails lead to overlooks. The MV *Lituya* makes two runs a day between Metlakatla and Ketchikan ($25, 1½ hours) Thursday to Monday, but that leaves only two hours, so it's best to arrange a personally narrated tour through MIC Tourism (886-8687; per person $40). You can stay at Tuckem Inn (886-1074; email winter@atpalaska.net; Western Ave; r $95;), and Promech Air (225-3845, 800-860-3845; www.promechair.com) will fly you back to Ketchikan for $49.

overnight excursion into the mountains surrounding Alaska's capital city.

To reach Perseverance Trail, take 6th St one block southwest to Gold St, which turns into Basin Rd, a dirt road that curves away from the city into the mountains as it follows Gold Creek. The trailhead is at the road's end, at the parking lot for Last Chance Mining Museum. The trail leads into Silverbow Basin, an old mining area that still has many hidden and unmarked adits and mine shafts; be safe and stay on the trail.

From the Perseverance Trail, you can pick up Granite Creek Trail and follow it to the creek's headwaters basin, a beautiful spot to spend the night. From there, you can reach Mt Juneau by climbing the ridge and staying left of Mt Olds, the huge rocky mountain. Once atop Mt Juneau, you can complete the loop by descending along the Mt Juneau Trail, which joins Perseverance Trail a mile from its beginning. The hike to the 3576ft peak of Mt Juneau along the ridge from Granite Creek is an easier but longer trek than the ascent from the Mt Juneau Trail. The alpine sections of the ridge are serene, and on a clear summer day you'll have outstanding views. From the trailhead for the Perseverance Trail to the upper basin of Granite Creek is 3.3 miles one-way. Then it's another 3 miles along the ridge to reach Mt Juneau.

Mt Roberts Trail is a 4-mile climb up Mt Roberts that begins at a marked wooden staircase at the northeast end of 6th St. It starts with a series of switchbacks, then breaks out of the trees at Gastineau Peak and comes to the tram station. From here it's a half-mile to the Cross, where you'll have good views of Juneau and Douglas. The Mt Roberts summit (3819ft) is still a steep climb away through the alpine brush. If you hike up, you can ride down the Mt Roberts Tramway to S Franklin St for only $10. And if you purchase $10 worth of food or drink at the visitors center on top, like a beer that you well deserve, the ride down is free.

Dan Moller Trail is a 3.3-mile trail leading to an alpine bowl at the crest of Douglas Island, where you'll find the recently rebuilt Dan Moller Cabin. Just across the channel in West Juneau, the public bus conveniently stops at Cordova St and from there, you turn left onto Pioneer Ave and follow it to the end of the pavement to the trailhead. Plan on six hours for the round-trip.

East Glacier Loop is one of many trails near Mendenhall Glacier, a 3-mile round-trip providing good views of the glacier from a scenic lookout at the halfway point. Pick up the loop along the Trail of Time, a half-mile nature walk that starts at the Mendenhall Glacier Visitor Center.

Nugget Creek Trail begins just beyond the East Glacier Loop's scenic lookout. The 2.5-mile trail climbs 500ft to Vista Creek Shelter, a free-use shelter that doesn't require reservations, making the round-trip to the shelter from the Mendenhall Glacier Visitor Center an 8-mile trek. Hikers who plan to spend the night at the shelter can continue along the creek toward Nugget Glacier, though the route is hard to follow at times.

West Glacier Trail is one of the most spectacular hikes in the Juneau area. The 3.4-mile trail begins off Montana Creek Rd past Mendenhall Lake Campground and hugs the mountainside along the glacier, providing exceptional views of the icefalls and other glacial features before ending at a rocky outcropping. Within 1.2 miles is a spur to a small shelter and bench now half-hidden in brush. From here an unmaintained trail, marked by cairns, heads for the face of the glacier. It involves more scrambling over rocks but is as popular as the main trail. Allow four to five hours for the West Glacier Trail.

For information on Mendenhall Glacier trails, see above.

JUNEAU AREA TRAILS

Point Bishop Trail is at the end of Thane Rd, 7.5 miles southeast of Juneau. This 8-mile trail leads to Point Bishop, a scenic spot overlooking the junction of Stephens Passage and Taku Inlet. The trail is flat but can be wet in many spots, making waterproof boots the preferred footwear. The hike makes for an ideal overnight trip, as there is good camping at Point Bishop.

Montana Creek Trail and Windfall Lake Trail connect at Windfall Lake and can be combined for an interesting 11.5-mile overnight hiking trip. It is easier to begin at the trailhead at Montana Creek and follow the Windfall Lake Trail out to the Glacier Hwy. The 8-mile Montana Creek Trail, known for its high concentration of bears, begins near the end of Montana Creek Rd, 2 miles from its junction with Mendenhall Loop Rd. The 3.5-mile Windfall Lake Trail begins off a gravel spur that leaves the Glacier Hwy just before it crosses Herbert River, 27 miles northwest of Juneau. The trail has been improved considerably in recent years and now features an USFS cabin, Windfall Lake Cabin, which sleeps six and is open as a warming shelter during the day.

Spaulding Trail is primarily used for cross-country skiing, but can be hiked in summer. The 3-mile route provides access to the Auke Nu Trail, which leads to the John Muir Cabin. The trailhead is off Glacier Hwy just past and opposite Auke Bay Post Office, 12.3 miles northwest of Juneau.

Peterson Lake Trail is a 4-mile route along Peterson Creek to its namesake lake, a favorite among hike-in anglers for the good Dolly Varden fishing. The trailhead is 20ft before the Mile 24 marker on Glacier Hwy, north of the Shrine of St Terese. Wear rubber boots, as it can be muddy during summer. The Peterson Lake Cabin turns this trail into a delightful overnight adventure.

Herbert Glacier Trail extends 4.6 miles along the Herbert River to Herbert Glacier, a round-trip of four to five hours. The trail is easy with little climbing, though wet in places, and begins just past the bridge over Herbert River at Mile 28 of Glacier Hwy.

Amalga Trail, also known as the Eagle Glacier Trail, is a level route that winds 7.5 miles to the lake formed by Eagle Glacier and the Eagle Glacier Cabin. Less than a mile from the glacier's face, the view from the cabin is well worth the effort of reserving it in advance. The trailhead is beyond the Glacier Hwy bridge, across Eagle River, 0.4 miles past the trailhead for the Herbert Glacier Trail. Plan on a round-trip of seven to eight hours (15 miles) to reach the impressive Eagle Glacier and return to the trailhead.

Paddling

Day trips and extended paddles are possible out of the Juneau area in sea kayaks.

Alaska Boat & Kayak   KAYAKING
(☎789-6886, 364-2333; www.juneaukayak.com; 11521 Glacier Hwy; single/double kayaks $50/70) Kayak rentals are available from this place, which is based in the Auke Bay Harbor and offers transportation services and multiday discounts. The company also offers half-day and full-day guided paddles.

Mendenhall Lake   KAYAKING
This lake at the foot of Mendenhall Glacier is an excellent destination for a paddle. Alaska Boat & Kayak offers a self-guided package to Mendenhall Lake ($99), which includes

kayaks, transportation and a waterproof map that leads you on a route among the icebergs in this relatively calm body of water. It also shows you where to land for a short hike to view the glacier up close.

Auke Bay   KAYAKING
The easiest trip is out to and around the islands of Auke Bay. You can even camp on the islands to turn the adventure into an overnight trip.

Taku Inlet   KAYAKING
This waterway is an excellent four- to five-day trip, with close views of Taku Glacier. Total paddling distance is 30 to 40 miles, depending on how far you travel up the inlet. It does not require any major crossing, though rounding Point Bishop can be rough at times. It is possible to camp at Point Bishop and along the grassy area southwest of the glacier, where brown bears are occasionally seen.

Berners Bay   KAYAKING
At the western end of Glacier Hwy, 40 miles from Juneau, is Echo Cove, where kayakers put in for paddles in the protected waters of Berners Bay. The bay, which extends 12 miles north to the outlets of the Antler, Lace and Berners Rivers, is ideal for an overnight trip or longer excursions up Berners River. The delightful USFS Berners Bay Cabin (☎877-444-6777, 518-885-3639; www.recreation. gov; cabins $35) is an 8-mile paddle from Echo Cove. Alaska Boat & Kayak charges $150 round-trip for transporting two kayaks to Echo Cove.

Whale Watching

The whale watching in nearby Stephens Passage is so good that some tour operators will refund your money if you don't see at least one. The boats depart from Auke Bay, and most tours last three to four hours. Some operators offer courtesy transportation from downtown.

TOP
CHOICE Orca Enterprises   WHALE WATCHING
(☎789-6801, 888-733-6722; www.alaskawhale watching.com; adult/child $119/89) Uses jet boats, that are fully wheelchair-accessible, to look at sea lions, orcas and harbor seals as well as humpback whales.

Gastineau Guiding   WHALE WATCHING
(☎586-8231; www.stepintoalaska.com; adult/ child $198/138) Five-hour tours that combine whale watching with an hour-long hike in the rainforest.

Harv & Marv's WHALE WATCHING
(☎209-7288, 866-909-7288; www.harvandmarvs.com; per person $149) Small, personalized tours with no more than six passengers in the boat.

Wilderness Cabins

Numerous **USFS cabins** (☎877-444-6777, 518-885-3639; www.recreation.gov) are accessible from Juneau, but all are heavily used, requiring advance reservations. If you're just passing through, check with the USFS Juneau Ranger District Office (p128) for a list of what's available. The following cabins are within 30 minutes' flying time from Juneau; air charters will cost around $500 to $600 round-trip from Juneau, split among a planeload of up to five passengers. **Alaska Seaplane Service** (☎789-3331; www.flyalaskaseaplanes.com) can provide flights on short notice.

West Turner Lake Cabin (cabins $35) is one of the most scenic and is by far the Juneau area's most popular cabin. It's 18 miles east of Juneau on the west end of Turner Lake, where the fishing is good for trout, Dolly Varden and salmon. A skiff is provided.

Admiralty Island's north end has three popular cabins, all $35 a night. **Admiralty Cove Cabin** is on a scenic bay and has access to Young Lake along a rough 4.5-mile trail. Brown bears frequent the area. The two **Young Lake Cabins** have skiffs to access a lake with good fishing for cutthroat trout and landlocked salmon. A lakeshore trail connects the two cabins.

There are also three rental cabins in Point Bridget State Park that rent for $45 a night. **Cowee Meadow Cabin** is a 2.5-mile hike into the park, **Blue Mussel Cabin** is a 3.4-mile walk and **Camping Cove Cabin** a 4-mile trek. Both Blue Mussel and Camping Cove overlook the shoreline and make a great destination for kayakers.

In 2012 a pair of cabins will be available at Eagle Beach State Recreation Area campground. Reserve them through the **DNR Public Information Center** (☎269-8400; www.dnr.state.ak.us/parks/cabins).

Ziplining

Juneau has a pair of ziplines where you can harness up and fly through 100ft trees like an eagle on the prowl.

Alaska Zipline Adventures ZIPLINING
(☎321-0947; www.alaskazip.com; adult/child $149/99) Located at beautiful Eaglecrest Ski Area on Douglas Island, this course includes seven ziplines and a sky bridge that zigzag across Fish Creek Valley. Transportation is included.

Alaska Canopy Adventures ZIPLINING
(☎523-0947; www.alaskacanopy.com; per person $199) At the other end of Douglas Island is this zipline course reached by boat from downtown Juneau. The course includes nine lines, two sky bridges and a 40ft rappel down a Sitka spruce at the end.

JUNEAU FOR CHILDREN

Macauley Salmon Hatchery (☎463-4810, 877-463-2486; www.dipac.net; 2697 Channel Dr; adult/child $3.25/1.75; ☺10am-6pm Mon-Fri, to 5pm Sat & Sun) The best attraction for kids visiting Juneau is this hatchery, 3 miles northwest of downtown. The visitors center has huge seawater aquariums loaded with local marine life, from tanner crabs to octopus, while the interpretive displays explaining the life cycle of salmon are museum quality. Underwater viewing windows and a 450ft fish ladder allow children to witness, from July to September, the amazing sight of thousands of salmon fighting their way upstream to spawn. You can also wander the outside grounds and pier to watch people catching lunker salmon.

Twin Lakes Park (Old Glacier Hwy) The City of Juneau maintains a wonderful system of parks including Twin Lakes Park, just past the hospital. The heart of the park is Project Playground, an amazing playscape that includes a mini climbing wall, a four-story Swiss chalet and a stairway that makes kids feel like they're salmon spawning upstream. There's also a solar-system trail around the lake that provides a realistic idea of how far each planet is from the sun.

Dimond Park Aquatic Center (☎586-2782; www.juneau.org/parkrec; 3045 Riverside Dr; adult/child $6.50/3.50; ☺6am-9pm Mon-Fri, 9am-8pm Sat, noon-6pm Sun) Juneau's newest attraction is this wonderful aquatic center that has flume slides, bubble benches, tumble buckets and interactive water sprays for children – and a hot tub for their parents.

☞ Tours

The easiest way to book a tour in Juneau is to head to the cruise-ship terminal, near the Mt Roberts Tram, where most of the operators will be hawking their wares from a line of booths like sideshow barkers at a carnival.

City & Glacier

Juneau Steamboat Co BOAT
(☏723-0372; www.juneausteamboat.com; 90-minute tours adult/child $40/35) Uses a unique 30ft, 16-passenger steamboat to gain a view of Juneau and the surrounding gold mines from the middle of the Gastineau Channel.

Experience Juneau TOUR
(☏723-6195; www.junotours.com; per person $19) A trolley tour that departs from the Mount Roberts Tram Station and in a 45-minute loop includes the Capitol, Governor's Mansion and even Douglas Island.

Mendenhall Glacier Transport/Mighty Great Trips BUS
(☏789-5460; www.mightygreattrips.com; per person $30) Offers a city-and-glacier tour.

★Juneau Ice Field

The hottest tour in Juneau is a helicopter ride to the Juneau Ice Field for a 20-minute ride in the basket of a dogsled. These tours last less than two hours and are $500 a pop, but when the weather is nice, people (primarily cruise-ship passengers) are waiting to hand over their money.

TOP CHOICE NorthStar Trekking HIKING
(☏790-4530; www.glaciertrekking.com) Skip the dogsled and strap on the crampons. NorthStar offers several glacier treks that begin with a helicopter ride and include all equipment and training. On its two-hour glacier trek ($399), you cross 2 miles of frozen landscape riddled with crevasses for a hike that is as stunning as it is pricey.

Era Helicopters SCENIC FLIGHTS
(☏586-2030, 800-843-1947; www.eraflightseeing.com) You spend an hour on Middle Branch Glacier as part of Era's glacier dogsled adventure ($489). For something more affordable, book its hour-long, four-glacier tour ($279), which includes a 20-minute glacier landing.

Temsco Helicopters SCENIC FLIGHTS
(☏789-9501, 877-789-9501; www.temscoair.com) Its mushing and glacier flightseeing tour ($489) lasts 1½ hours and lands at a dog camp on Denver Glacier. The company also has a 55-minute Mendenhall Glacier tour ($259), which includes 25 minutes walking around high up on the glacier.

Alaska Fly 'n' Fish Charters SCENIC FLIGHTS
(☏790-2120; www.alaskabyair.com) Its hour-long glacier flightseeing adventure ($600 for up to five passengers) is the most affordable way to get into the air for a peek at the ice field.

Tracy Arm

This steep-sided fjord, 50 miles southeast of Juneau, has a pair of tidewater glaciers and a gallery of icebergs floating down its length. Tracy Arm makes an interesting day trip, far less expensive and perhaps even more satisfying than a visit to Glacier Bay. You're almost guaranteed to see seals inside the Arm, and you might spot whales on the way there.

TOP CHOICE Adventure Bound Alaska BOAT
(☏463-2509, 800-228-3875; www.adventureboundalaska.com; 76 Egan Dr; adult/child $150/95) This longtime tour operator uses a pair of boats that leave daily from the Juneau waterfront. Reserve a seat in advance if you can – the full-day tour is popular with cruise ships – and pack a lunch along with your binoculars. Alternatively, get there under your own steam; see p55.

Allen Marine Tours BOAT
(☏789-0081, 888-289-0081; www.allenmarinetours.com; adult/child $199/149) Offers a Tracy Arm tour that includes lunch, but can you afford it?

✦ Festivals & Events

Alaska Folk Festival MUSIC
(☏463-3316; www.alaskafolkfestival.org) Attracts musicians from around the state for a week of performances, workshops and dances at Centennial Hall in mid-April.

Juneau Jazz & Classics Festival MUSIC
(☏463-3378; www.jazzandclassics.org) Jazz and classical music concerts and workshops during the third week in May. Similar to the Alaska Folk Festival.

Gold Rush Days CULTURAL
A late-June festival of logging and mining events in Douglas.

Fourth of July CULTURAL
Parades, carnival, outdoor food booths and a huge fireworks show over the Gastineau Channel.

DON'T MISS

TAKU GLACIER LODGE

The most popular tours in Juneau are flightseeing, glacier viewing and salmon bakes, and a trip to Taku Glacier Lodge allows you to combine all three. Built in 1923 as a hunting and fishing camp, the lodge is classic Alaska – a sturdy log structure with a front porch overlooking its namesake glacier. You reach it via a floatplane through Wings Airways (☑586-6275; www.wingsairways.com; Suite 175, 2 Marine Way; adult/child $280/225) that flies along the edge of the Juneau Ice Field and across a half-dozen glaciers. At the lodge you enjoy an incredible meal of wild king salmon caught in the nearby Taku River and then can wander the grounds, where visitors occasionally see black bears pop out of the woods. The tour lasts three hours and includes 45 minutes of flying, making it a much better and cheaper experience than taking a helicopter to the ice field. Sign up at the Wings Airways office behind Merchant's Wharf on Juneau's waterfront.

🛌 Sleeping

Juneau tacks on 12% in bed and sales taxes to the price of lodging.

Juneau International Hostel　　　HOSTEL $
(☑586-9559; www.juneauhostel.net; 614 Harris St; dm $10; ⊜@⊗) Alaska's best hostel and certainly its most affordable. One of the eight bunk rooms is a family room, while amenities include laundry, storage and free internet access and wi-fi. In the lounge area, the overstuffed sofas are strategically placed around a large bay window with a view of snowy peaks and Douglas Island. Best of all is the downtown location. You're only a few blocks from the Mt Roberts Trail. The only gripes are a strict locking-up (9am to 5pm) and chores.

Silverbow Inn　　　BOUTIQUE HOTEL $$$
(☑586-4146, 800-586-4146; www.silverbowinn. com; 120 2nd St; r $189-219; ⊜@⊗) A boutique inn on top of the best (and only) bagel shop downtown. The 11 rooms as well as the inn itself are filled with antiques but come with private bath, king and queen beds and flat-panel TVs. A 2nd-floor deck features a hot tub with a view of the mountains of Douglas Island. Breakfast is served in the morning, wine and cheese in the evening.

Mendenhall Lake Campground　　　CAMPGROUND $
(☑reservations 877-444-6777, 518-885-3639; www. recreation.gov; Montana Creek Rd; tent sites $10, RV sites $26-28) One of Alaska's most beautiful USFS campgrounds. The 69-site area (17 sites with hookups) is on Montana Creek Rd, off Mendenhall Loop Rd, and has a separate seven-site walk-in area. The campsites are alongside Mendenhall Lake, and many have spectacular views of the icebergs or even the glacier that discharges them. All the sites are well spread out in the woods, and 20 can be reserved in advance.

Alaska's Capital Inn　　　B&B $$$
(☑586-6507, 888-588-6507; www.alaskacapital inn.com; 113 W 5th St; r incl breakfast $259-$339; ⊜@⊗) Political junkies will love this place: it's across the street from the state capitol. In the gorgeously restored home of a wealthy gold rush–era miner, who obviously found color, this inn has seven rooms with private bath, phone and TV, and has hardwood floors covered by colorful Persian rugs. The backyard doesn't have a blade of grass, but rather multiple decks, gardens and a secluded hot tub that even the governor can't spy on. In the morning there's a full breakfast, and in the evening wine and cheese is served on the back deck, which overlooks the city. A Mount Roberts Tram pass comes with every room.

Auke Lake B&B　　　B&B $$
(☑790-3253, 800-790-3253; www.aukelakebb.com; 11595 Mendenhall Loop Rd; r $125-165; ⊜@⊗) Located 10 minutes from Mendenhall Glacier, this valley B&B has five luxurious rooms with phone, TV, refrigerator and coffeemaker. In the living room is a stuffed giant brown bear, while outside is a beautiful deck and hot tub overlooking a floatplane tied up on Auke Lake. So Alaskan.

Driftwood Lodge　　　MOTEL $$
(☑586-2280, 800-544-2239; www.driftwoodalas ka.com; 435 Willoughby Ave; r $95-110, ste $125-135; ⊜⊗) Near the Alaska State Museum, this lodge is the best value in accommodations downtown. The 63 rooms are clean and updated regularly, the motel offers 24-hour courtesy transportation to the airport and the ferry, and it's hard to top the location unless you're willing to spend twice as much.

Beachside Villa Luxury Inn
B&B $$

(463-5531, 888-879-0858; www.beachsidevilla.com; 3120 Douglas Hwy; r $169-239; ☺☎) This luxurious B&B has five rooms with amenities that range from balconies and private entrances to fireplaces and in-room Jacuzzis. But what makes it stand out is its Douglas Island location and views. Perched just above the Gastineau Channel, its porches and neatly landscaped backyard overlook downtown Juneau, Mt Roberts and the parade of floatplanes and vessels entering the capital city harbors. Why would you spend any time in your room?

Juneau Hotel
HOTEL $$$

(586-5666; www.juneauhotels.net; 1200 W 9th St; ste $189; ☺@☎) Located within easy walking distance of downtown attractions, this all-suites hotel is Juneau's best deal in top-end accommodations. The 73 suites have full kitchens, sitting areas, two TVs each and even washers and dryers.

Auke Village Campground
CAMPGROUND $

(Glacier Hwy; sites $10) Located 2 miles from the ferry terminal on Glacier Hwy, this first-come, first-served USFS campground has 11 sites in a beautiful wooded location overlooking Auke Bay.

Eagle Beach State Recreation Area
CAMPGROUND $

(586-2506; Mile 28, Glacier Hwy; sites $10) This state campground, 15 miles from the ferry terminal and 28 miles from downtown Juneau, is worth the drive. Eagle Beach includes a ranger station, wildlife viewing area and 17 wooded campsites ideal for tents. It's within walking distance of three trails: Amalga (Eagle Glacier), Herbert Glacier and Windfall Lake.

Alaskan Hotel
HOTEL $

(586-1000, 800-327-9347; www.thealaskanhotel.com; 167 S Franklin St; r with/without shared bath $90/$60, ste $120; ☎) The smallish rooms in this historical hotel are a little worn, but you accept that for the price and the gold-rush ambience. Most rooms have small refrigerators, sinks and cable TV, but avoid the ones overlooking Franklin St unless you plan to join the revelry below.

Goldbelt Hotel Juneau
HOTEL $$$

(586-6900, 888-478-6909; www.goldbelthotel.com; 51 Egan Dr; r $199-209; ☺@☎) Alaska Native–owned and centrally located downtown, the Goldbelt has big rooms with big,

comfortable beds and such amenities as room service, cable TV and courtesy pickup from the airport. The waterfront rooms are $10 extra but face a view of the cruise ships sailing in and the floatplanes taking off.

Super 8 Motel
MOTEL $$

(789-4858, 800-800-8000; 2295 Trout St; s/d $120/130) Your run-of-the-mill Super 8, but of the handful of chain motels clustered around the airport it's by far the most affordable. It offers free airport and ferry shuttle and a fish freezer big enough to hold that trophy halibut you landed. It's north of the airport, next to the McDonald's off Glacier Hwy.

Spruce Meadow RV Park
CAMPGROUND $

(789-1990; www.juneaurv.com; 10200 Mendenhall Loop Rd; tent sites $20-26, RV sites $30-34; ☎) Practically next door to Mendenhall Lake Campground but not nearly as nice is this full-service campground with laundromat, cable TV and tent sites as well as full hook-ups. It's right on the city bus route.

Thane Public Campground
CAMPGROUND $

(586-0617; 1585 Thane Rd; tent sites $5) Located a mile south of downtown on Thane Rd is the city-operated, tent-only place that tends to draw transients and seasonal workers.

✖ Eating

Juneau struggles to serve up a restaurant scene worthy of a state capital. Even fast-food fanatics find a limited menu here: basically there's a McDonald's and a Taco Bell. Thankfully, all restaurants and bars in the capital city are smoke-free.

TOP CHOICE Tracy's King Crab Shack
SEAFOOD $$

(www.kingcrabshack.com; 356 S Franklin St; crabs $8-17; ☺lunch & dinner) Squeezed between the Library Parking Garage and the Cruise Ship Dock is a row of food booths, with the best by far being Tracy's shack. From this little hut she serves up outstanding crab bisque, crab rolls and mini crab cakes. If there are two of you, grab an outdoor table and split a bucket of king crab pieces ($60), 2lb of the sweetest seafood you'll ever have.

Island Pub
PIZZA $$

(www.theislandpub.com; 1102 2nd St, Douglas; pizzas $13-20; ☺dinner) Across the channel from the capital city, this relaxing, unhurried restaurant serves firebrick-oven focaccia and gourmet pizza with a mountainous view. Before the pie arrives you can enjoy a drink from an impressive list of cocktails, ranging from Rick's Island Cosmo to Blue Iguana Margarita. Don't worry about a Red Dog Saloon mob scene. You're on Douglas Island.

Zephyr Restaurant — MEDITERRANEAN $$$
(780-2221; zephyrrestaurant.com; 200 Seward St; dinner mains $14-29; dinner) Easily Juneau's most innovative restaurant. The Italian restaurant ladens its Mediterranean menu with fresh Alaskan seafood (who doesn't?), and its seafood stew, infused with clams, spot prawns and smoked salmon, is wonderful. But Zephyr also offers such classic mains as oregano-and-lemon-marinated lamb and adventurous dishes like grilled stuffed calamari. Its interior of muted colors and hardwood floors is soothing, and its wine list is extensive enough to complement the menu.

Twisted Fish — SEAFOOD $$
Dinner
(550 S Franklin St; burgers $9-17, dinner mains $16-40; lunch & dinner) Beef be gone. Located between Taku Smokeries (www.takustore.com), which sells the best smoked salmon in Juneau, and a wharf where commercial fishers unload their catch, this restaurant is all about seafood. Indulge yourself by ordering salmon grilled on a cedar plank or salmon baked in a puff pastry. Even half the pizzas on the menu have something from the sea on them.

Hot Bite — BURGERS $
(11465 Auke Bay Harbor Dr; hamburgers $9-13; lunch & dinner) You have to drive out to the Auke Bay Harbor for the best milkshakes and burgers in Juneau. The small cafe is housed in the one-time ticket office of Pan American Airways but has seating outside for when the weather is nice. It offers up almost 40 flavors of milkshake and, as if three scoops of ice cream wasn't enough, its cheesecake shake also has cream cheese and graham-cracker crumbs mixed in.

Zen — ASIAN $$
(Goldbelt Hotel Juneau, 51 Egan Dr; lunch specials $10-13, dinner mains $12-30; breakfast, lunch & dinner) Zen calls itself an Asian fusion restaurant, taking what's readily available – Alaska seafood – and infusing it with a touch of the oriental. You end up with mains such as ginger halibut, black-cod stir fry or Thai coconut curry shrimp. If the dinner prices are too steep for you then come before 3pm – many of the lunch specials are the same dishes at half the price.

Silverbow Bagel Bakery — BAKERY $
(120 2nd St; bagel sandwiches $8-9; breakfast & lunch;) This downtown place bakes bagels daily, serving them au naturel, with a variety of spreads and toppings, or using them as bookends for breakfast and lunch sandwiches. Lots of seating.

Thane Ore House — SALMON BAKES $$
(586-3442; 4400 Thane Rd; adult/child $24/12; lunch & dinner;) Four miles south of town is this all-you-can-eat affair of grilled salmon and halibut that takes place in a rambling log lodge full of Alaskan memorabilia. When you've pushed your plate away, you can stroll the grounds and watch bald eagles feed in Gastineau Channel. There is van transportation from major downtown hotels.

Sandpiper — *Breakfast* — BREAKFAST $$
(429 Willoughby Ave; breakfast mains $10-17, lunch mains $11-14; breakfast & lunch Wed-Mon) Juneau's best breakfast. Skip the eggs and try one of their Belgian waffles, blueberry buttermilk pancakes or specialty French toasts such as mandarin orange and mascarpone cheese. Upstairs is its sister restaurant, the Pasta Shop, with fresh pastas, raviolis and gnocchi along with a great view of Mt Juneau.

Douglas Café — CAFE $$
(916 3rd St, Douglas; breakfast mains $8-12, burgers $12-16, dinner mains $19-24; breakfast Sat & Sun, lunch & dinner) Douglas' other fine eatery serves up 15 different types of burgers, including a Boring Burger. But if it's dinner, skip the bun and go for one of its tempting mains, which range from tarragon-lime chicken to Cajun prawn fettuccine.

Southeast Waffle Co — BREAKFAST $
(11806 Glacier Hwy; waffles $5-7; 6am-midnight Mon-Fri, 7am-midnight Sat, 7am-10pm Sun;) All you campers in the Mendenhall Valley and out on the road, here's where you head to in Auke Bay for a latte, free wi-fi and a blackboard menu of great waffles, stuffed with ham, cheese, sausage, blueberries, even chocolate chip and peanut butter.

Pel'Meni — FAST FOOD $
(Merchant's Wharf, Marine Way; dumplings $6; 11:30am-1:30am Sun-Thu, to 3:30am Fri & Sat) The only things on the menu – well, there is no menu – are authentic, homemade Russian dumplings, filled with either potato or sirloin, spiced with hot sauce, curry and cilantro and served with a piece of bread to

clean the bowl afterwards. The perfect end to a night of drinking – the reason Pel'Meni is open until the wee hours. Record buffs will be amazed by the wall full of LPs and the turntable that provides the proper late-night atmosphere.

Olivia's de Mexico
MEXICAN $$

(222 Seward St; lunch mains $7-9, dinner mains $11-16; ☺lunch Mon-Fri, dinner Mon-Sat) This is a friendly family-run *cocina* whose spicy aroma and Mexican music spills onto the street, enticing you into its brightly colored restaurant downstairs. In the summer you can order halibut tacos and burritos.

Bullwinkle's
PIZZA $

(318 Willoughby Ave; pizzas $13-21; ☺lunch & dinner; 🛜🍴) There's been a moose and a flying squirrel pitching pizza in Juneau for 40 years. The beer hall–like restaurant has changed little in that time and neither has the pizza: it's as tasty as ever. Bullwinkle's also has good sandwiches and a decent little salad bar for the veggie-deprived. Enjoy a pitcher of beer and free popcorn while waiting for your garlic veggie supreme pizza.

Paradise Café
BAKERY $

(245 Marine Way; breakfast mains $5-9, lunch mains $7-9; ☺breakfast & lunch Mon-Fri) Facing whatever cruise ship is in port is this colorful bakery, with four tables inside and four outside. Lots of art adorns the walls, while the aroma of freshly baked scones, savories and croissants fill the air. Its menu features some interesting sandwiches and soups, and the cafe's proximity to the docks makes it prime for people-watching.

🍃 Rainbow Foods
HEALTH FOOD $

(www.rainbow-foods.org; 224 4th St; food bar per lb $8; ☺9am-7pm Mon-Fri, 10am-6pm Sat, noon-6pm Sun) Practically right next door to the dig-and-drill politicians in the state capitol is this natural-food store, a hangout for liberals and environmentalists. Along with a large selection of fresh produce and bulk goods, the store has a hot- and cold-food bar for lunch, espresso and fresh baked goods and a bulletin board with the latest cultural happenings.

A&P Juneau Market
SUPERMARKET $

(615 W Willoughby Ave; salad bar per lb $7) Near the Federal Building, this supermarket has a good selection of local seafood, an espresso counter, salad bar, deli and small seating area.

🍷 Drinking

Nightlife centers on S Franklin and Front Sts, a historic, quaint (but not quiet) main drag attracting locals and tourists alike.

Red Dog Saloon
BAR

(200 Admiral Way, at S Franklin St) A sign at the door says it all – 'Booze, Antiques, Sawdust Floor, Community Singing' – and the cruise-ship passengers love it! Most don't realize, much less care, that this Red Dog is but a replica of the original, a famous Alaskan drinking hole that was across the street until 1987. Now *that* was a bar. The duplicate is interesting, but the fact that it has a gift shop should tell you who the clientele is during summer.

Alaskan Hotel Bar
BAR

(Alaskan Hotel, 167 S Franklin St) In keeping with the gold-rush atmosphere of the hotel, this low-key, half-hidden bar has red velvet sofas, Tiffany lamps, an impressive back bar and even a cigar room. There are often bands on Friday and Saturday.

Viking Lounge
LOUNGE

(218 Front St; @🛜) In this classic tin-ceiling building are actually three bars. At street level is a sports pub with four giant TV screens and almost 20 beers on tap, while half-hidden in the back is a lounge featuring a small dance floor and DJs on Friday and Saturday. Upstairs is a billiards hall with seven tables, sofas and free internet. Surf while indulging in a pint.

Hangar on the Wharf
BAR

(www.hangaronthewharf.com; 2 Marine Way) Housed in Merchant's Wharf, a renovated floatplane hangar that sits on pilings above Juneau's waterfront, the Hangar is mediocre and overpriced as a restaurant but great as a place to have a beer...or two. Your table is perched right over a seaplane dock, and the unobstructed view of the channel includes all the activity buzzing and floating downtown. Much better than the food is the restaurant's 20 beers on tap.

Rendezvous
BAR

(184 S Franklin St; 🛜) A South Franklin mainstay with cheap pitchers of beer (or as cheap as you can get in Juneau), rowdy bands on the weekend and karaoke on Wednesday.

🍃 Heritage Coffee Co & Café
COFFEE HOUSE

(www.heritagecoffee.com; 174 S Franklin St; ☺6:30am-7pm Mon-Fri, 7am-6pm Sat & Sun; @🛜)

Juneau's most popular coffee house, almost from the day it opened in 1977. The coffee is roasted locally, the sofas are comfortable and the wi-fi is free. The company also has a cafe at 216 2nd St that is a bit quieter and features outdoor seating.

☆ Entertainment

FREE Concerts in the Park   LIVE MUSIC
(www.jahc.org) Ranging from local folk singers to Tlingit dancers, these concerts are staged from June through mid-August and are accessible no matter which side of the channel you are on. The Friday evening concerts are 7pm to 8:30pm at Marine Park downtown, while the Sunday concerts start at 4pm and go through to 5:30pm at Savikko Park in Douglas.

Gold Town Nickelodeon   CINEMA
(☑586-2875; www.goldtownnick.com; 171 Shattuck St; adult/child $9/5) This delightful art-house theater presents small-budget and foreign films and documentaries. On Thursday the popcorn is free.

Perseverance Theater   THEATER
(☑364-2421; www.perseverancetheatre.org; 914 3rd St, Douglas) Founded in 1979, this is Alaska's only genuine full-time professional theater company. Sadly the theatre season begins in September and ends in May.

20th Century Theatre   CINEMA
(☑463-3549; www.juneaumovies.com; 222 Front St) Shows two current releases (or current by Alaskan standards) a night.

🛍 Shopping

Despite all the cruise-ship jewelry stores and gift shops, the Juneau art scene is alive and vibrant. The best time to sample it is during First Friday (www.jahc.org; ⏱4-7:30pm 1st Fri of the month), a free event when a reception is held for a local artist at the Juneau Arts & Culture Center while the Alaska State Museum and a dozen local art galleries are also open late.

Juneau Arts and Culture Center   ARTS & CRAFTS
(www.jahc.org; 350 Whittier St) You can't miss the impressive Juneau Arts and Culture Center (JACC), a statue of breaching humpback whale stands out front while its shadow is painted on the side of the building. Inside, the JACC gallery features the work of a local artist every month, while the adjacent Lob-

by Shop is a place for Southeast Alaskans to sell their artworks and books.

Juneau Artists Gallery   ARTS & CRAFTS
(www.juneauartistsgallery.com; Senate Bldg, 175 S Franklin St) Also downtown is the Juneau Artists Gallery, a co-op of 26 local artists who have filled the store with paintings, etchings, glass work, jewelry, pottery and quilts. The person behind the counter ready to help you is that day's 'Artist On Duty.'

Rie Munoz Gallery   ARTS & CRAFTS
(www.riemunoz.com; 2101 Jordan Ave) Out in the Valley, near Nugget Mall, is the Rie Munoz Gallery, featuring a large selection of Rie Munoz prints as well as some by Dale DeArmond, Byron Birdsall and several other noted Alaskan artists.

Foggy Mountain Shop   OUTDOOR EQUIPMENT
(www.foggymountainshop.com; 134 N Franklin St) For packs, outdoorwear, USGS topo maps and anything else you need for backcountry trips, stop at Foggy Mountain Shop. This is the only outdoor shop in town with top-of-the-line equipment, and the prices reflect that.

Hearthside Books   BOOKS
(www.hearthsidebooks.com; 254 Front St) Juneau's best bookstore also has a store in Nugget Mall in the Valley.

ℹ Information

INTERNET ACCESS Library (www.juneau.org/library; 292 Marine Way; ⏱11am-8pm Mon-Thu, noon-6pm Fri, noon-5pm Sat & Sun; @🛜) Juneau's main public library sits atop a four-story parking structure and offers free internet access and wi-fi. It's worth a stop here just for the views of downtown Juneau.

Universe Cyber Lounge (109 S Franklin St; per hr $6; @🛜) This cybercafe offers wi-fi, internet terminals and phonecards and shares space with Latinos, a Latin American restaurant. You can check your email while devouring a Cuban sandwich.

MEDICAL SERVICES Bartlett Regional Hospital (☑796-8900; 3260 Hospital Dr) Southeast Alaska's largest hospital is off Glacier Hwy between downtown and Lemon Creek.

Juneau Urgent Care (☑790-4111; 8505 Old Dairy Rd; ⏱8am-7:30pm Mon-Fri, 9am-5pm Sat & Sun) A walk-in medical clinic near Nugget Mall in the Valley.

MONEY There's no shortage of banks in Juneau. Most have ATMs and branches both downtown and in the Valley.

First Bank (605 W Willoughby Ave)

First National Bank of Anchorage (238 Front St)

Wells Fargo (123 Seward St)

POST Post office (cnr 9th St & Glacier Ave) On the 1st floor of the Federal Building.

Postal contract station (145 S Franklin St) Conveniently located downtown in the Seward Building.

TOURIST INFORMATION Juneau Visitor Center (☑586-2201, 888-581-2201; www.traveljuneau.com; 101 Egan Dr; ☺9am-5pm) The main visitors center is in Centennial Hall and has all the information you need to explore Juneau, find a trail or book a room. Among the racks of brochures is an USFS information area with a direct phone line to the Juneau Ranger District Office and courtesy phone for accommodations. The center also maintains smaller information booths at the airport, the marine ferry terminal and two where the cruise ships dock.

Alaska Division of Parks (☑465-4563; 400 Willoughby Ave; ☺8am-4:30pm Mon-Fri) Head to the 5th floor of the Natural Resources Building for state park information or the availability of cabins at Point Bridget State Park (p130).

USFS Juneau Ranger District Office (☑586-8800; 8510 Mendenhall Loop Rd; ☺8am-5pm Mon-Fri) This impressive office is in Mendenhall Valley and is the place for questions about cabins, trails, kayaking and Pack Creek bear-watching permits. The USFS office is also linked to the Centennial Hall visitors center via a free-use phone.

ⓘ Getting There & Away

AIR Alaska Airlines (☑800-252-7522; www.alaskaair.com) Offers scheduled jet service to Seattle ($400, two hours), all major Southeast cities, Glacier Bay ($100, 30 minutes), Anchorage ($30, two hours) and Cordova ($250, 2½ hours) daily in summer.

Alaska Seaplane Service (☑789-3331, 888-350-8277; www.flyalaskaseaplanes.com) Flies floatplanes from Juneau airport to Angoon ($140), Elfin Cove ($180), Pelican ($180) and Tenakee Springs ($140).

Wings of Alaska (☑789-0790; www.wingso falaska.com; 8421 Livingston Way) Flies to Gustavus ($93, 30 minutes, three per day), Haines ($108, 30 minutes, five per day), Hoonah ($69, 20 minutes, two per day) and Skagway ($118, 45 minutes, five per day).

BOAT Alaska Marine Highway (☑465-3941, 800-642-0066; www.ferryalaska.com) Ferries dock at Auke Bay Ferry Terminal, 14 miles northwest of downtown. In summer, the main-line ferries traversing the Inside Passage depart daily southbound for Sitka ($45, nine hours), Petersburg ($66, eight hours) and Ketchikan ($107, 18 hours).

You can shorten the sailing times on the high-speed MV *Fairweather*, which connects Juneau and Petersburg twice a week and Juneau and Sitka five times a week. There are also daily northbound sailings for Haines ($37, 4½ hours) and Skagway ($50, 5½ hours). Several shorter routes also operate in summer. The smaller MV *LeConte* regularly connects Juneau to the secondary ports of Hoonah ($33, four hours), Tenakee Springs ($35, eight hours) and Angoon ($37, 12 hours). Two times a month, the MV *Kennicott* departs Juneau for a trip to Yakutat ($85, 15½ hours) then across the Gulf of Alaska to Whittier ($221, 39 hours); reservations are strongly suggested.

ⓘ Getting Around

Good luck.

TO/FROM THE AIRPORT & FERRY A taxi to/from the airport costs around $25. The city bus express route runs to the airport, but only from 7:30am to 5:30pm Monday to Friday. On weekends and in the evening, if you want a bus you'll need to walk 10 minutes to the nearest 'regular route' stop behind Nugget Mall. The regular route headed downtown stops here regularly from 7:15am until 10:45pm Monday to Saturday, and from 9:15am until 5:45pm Sunday. The fare on either route is $1.50/1 per adult/child.

Unbelievable but true: no buses or regularly scheduled shuttles go to the ferry terminal in Auke Bay, an ungodly long 14-mile distance from downtown. A few taxis, including **Glacier Taxi** (☑796-2300), show up for most ferry arrivals, charging $35 for downtown. You can stick out your thumb (hitchhiking is commonplace) or take the city bus to/from the end of the line, which is 1.6 miles south of the ferry terminal at DeHart's Store in Auke Bay.

BUS Juneau's sadistic public bus system, **Capital Transit** (☑789-6901), stops way short of the ferry terminal and a mile short of the Mendenhall Glacier Visitor Center. Even getting to/from the airport can be problematic: only the 'express' route goes right to the terminal, and it only runs during business hours on weekdays. At other times, you'll have to schlep your bags between the airport and the 'regular' route's stop at Nugget Mall, a 10-minute walk. The 'regular' route buses start around 7am and stop before midnight, running every half-hour after 8am and before 6:30pm. The main route circles downtown then heads out to the Valley and Auke Bay Boat Harbor via Mendenhall Loop Rd, where it travels close to Mendenhall Lake Campground. Routes 3 and 4 make stops in the Mendenhall Valley either from downtown or Auke Bay, while a bus runs every hour from city stops to Douglas. Fares are $1.50/1 each way per adult/child, and exact change is required. Major stops downtown include the Federal Building and the Main St

Parking Garage, the closest thing to a bus terminal in Juneau, at the corner of Egan Hwy and Main St.

CAR Juneau has many car-rental places, and renting a car is a great way for two or three people to see the sights out of the city or to reach a trailhead. For a $59 special, call **Rent-A-Wreck** (☑789-4111, 888-843-4111; 2450 Industrial Blvd), a mile from the airport, which provides pickup and drop-off service between 7am and 5pm. You can also rent a car at the airport, but will have to stomach a 26% tax as opposed to a 15% tax elsewhere.

Around Juneau

FREE **Alaskan Brewing Company** BREWERY
(www.alaskanbeer.com; 5429 Shaune Dr; ⊗11am-6pm) Alaska's largest brewery also makes some of its best beer. Established in 1986, the brewery is in the Lemon Creek area and reached from Anka St, where the city bus will drop you off, by turning right on Shaune Dr. The beermaker's gift shop downtown, **Alaskan Brewing Co Depot** (219 S Franklin St), also runs a van out to the brewery every hour for $6 per person.

The tour includes viewing the small brewery and a free sampling of lagers and ales plus an opportunity to purchase beer in the gift shop, even 5-gallon party kegs. The brewery's beer-bottle collection from around the world is amazing. So many beers, so little time to drink them.

**Glacier Gardens Rain Forest
Adventure** GARDENS
(www.glaciergardens.com; 7600 Glacier Hwy; adult/child $25/16; ⊗9am-6pm) This 50-acre garden, near the brewery, includes ponds, waterfalls and lots of ferns and flowers on the side of Thunder Mountain. You hop on electric carts for a guided tour of the gardens, which ends at a viewing point almost 600ft up the mountain.

Mendenhall Glacier GLACIER
The most famous of Juneau's ice floes, and the city's most popular attraction, is Mendenhall Glacier, Alaska's famous drive-in glacier. The river of ice is 13 miles from downtown, at the end of Glacier Spur Rd. From Egan Dr at Mile 9 turn right onto Mendenhall Loop Rd, staying on Glacier Spur Rd when the loop curves back toward Auke Bay.

The Mendenhall Glacier flows 13 miles from its source, the Juneau Ice Field, and has

a half-mile-wide face. It's still ends in Mendenhall Lake, the reason for all the icebergs, but naturalists estimate that within five years it will retreat onto land and within 25 years retreat out of view entirely from the observation area. On a sunny day it's beautiful, with blue skies and snowcapped mountains in the background. On a cloudy and drizzly afternoon it can be even more impressive, as the ice turns shades of deep blue.

Near the face of the glacier is the **Mendenhall Glacier Visitor Center** (☑789-0097; adult/child $3/free; ⊗8am-7:30pm), which houses various glaciology exhibits, including a fabricated ice face of the glacier along with a large relief map of the ice field, spotting scopes that let you look for mountain goats, and a theater that shows the 11-minute film *Magnificent Mendenhall*.

Outside you'll find seven hiking trails, ranging from a 0.3-mile photo-overlook trail to a trek of several miles up the glacier's west side (p119). The newest is the **Nugget Falls Trail** that leads a half-mile to the impressive cascade near the face of the glacier. For many the most interesting path is **Steep Creek Trail**, a 0.3-mile boardwalk that winds past viewing platforms along the stream. From July through September you'll not only see sockeye and coho salmon spawning from the platforms but also brown and black bears feasting on them. This is Southeast Alaska's most affordable bear-viewing site.

The cheapest way to see the glacier is to hop on a Capital Transit bus (p128), but that leaves you a mile short of it. It's easier to jump on a bus from **Mendenhall Glacier Transport** (MGT; ☑789-5460; mightygreatrips. com; round-trip $16). MGT picks up from the cruise-ship docks downtown for the glacier, making a run every 30 minutes. The last bus of the day depends on the cruise-ship schedule.

One of the most unusual outdoor activities in Juneau is glacier trekking: stepping into crampons, grabbing an ice axe and roping up to walk on ice 1000 years or older. The scenery and the adventure is like nothing you've experienced before as a hiker. The most affordable outing is offered by **Above & Beyond Alaska** (☑364-2333; www.beyondak. com). Utilizing a trail to access Mendenhall Glacier, it avoids expensive helicopter fees on its guided seven-hour outing. The cost is $189 per person and includes all mountaineering equipment and transportation.

FREE **Shrine of St Terese** SHRINE

At Mile 23.3 Glacier Hwy is the Shrine of St Terese, a natural stone chapel on an island connected to the shore by a stone causeway. As well as being the site of numerous weddings, the island lies along the Breadline, a well-known salmon-fishing area in Juneau. The island is perhaps the best place to fish for salmon from the shore.

Point Bridget State Park PARK

(Mile 39, Glacier Hwy) Juneau's only state park is 2850-acre Point Bridget State Park, which overlooks Berners Bay and Lynn Canal; salmon fishing is excellent off the Berners Bay beaches and in Cowee Creek. Hiking trails wander through rainforest, along the park's rugged shoreline and past three rental cabins (p121). The most popular hike is Point Bridget Trail, a 3.5-mile, one-way walk from the trailhead on Glacier Hwy to Blue Mussel Cabin at the point, where often you can spot sea lions and seals playing the surf. Plan on six to seven hours for the round-trip with lunch at the cabin.

Admiralty Island & Pack Creek

Only 15 miles southeast of Juneau is Admiralty Island National Monument, a 1493-sq-mile preserve, of which 90% is designated wilderness. The monument has a wide variety of wildlife – from Sitka black-tailed deer and nesting bald eagles to harbor seals, sea lions and humpback whales – but more than anything else, Admiralty Island is known for bears. The 96-mile-long island has one of the highest populations of bears in Alaska, with an estimated 1500 brown bears, more than all the Lower 48 states combined. It's the reason the Tlingit called Admiralty Kootznoowoo, 'the Fortress of Bears.'

The monument's main attraction for visitors is Pack Creek, which flows from 4000ft mountains before spilling into Seymour Canal on the island's east side. The extensive tide flats at the mouth of the creek draw a large number of bears in July and August to feed on salmon, making the spot a favorite for observing and photographing the animals.

Bear viewing at Pack Creek takes place at Stan Price State Wildlife Sanctuary, named for an Alaskan woodsman who lived on a float house here for almost 40 years. The vast majority of visitors to the sanctuary are day-trippers who arrive and depart on floatplanes. Upon arrival, all visitors are met by a ranger who explains the rules and then each party hikes to an observation tower – reached by a mile-long trail – that overlooks the creek.

Pack Creek has become so popular that the area buzzes with planes and boats every morning from early July to late August. Anticipating this daily rush hour, most resident bears escape into the forest, but a few bears hang around to feed on salmon, having long since been habituated to the human visitors. Seeing five or six bears would be a good viewing day at Pack Creek. You might see big boars during the mating season from May to mid-June; otherwise it's sows and cubs the rest of the summer.

Some visitors fly into the monument to stay at one of the 14 USFS cabins (☎877-444-6777, 518-885-3639; www.recreation.gov; cabins $25-35) or to paddle the Cross Admiralty Island canoe route, a 32-mile paddle that spans the center of the island from the village of Angoon to Mole Harbor. Although the majority of the route consists of calm lakes connected by streams and portages, the 10-mile paddle from Angoon on Admiralty Island's west coast to Mitchell Bay is subject to strong tides that challenge even experienced paddlers.

Angoon (pop 459) is the only community on Admiralty Island and serves as the departure point for many kayak and canoe trips into the heart of the monument, including the Cross Admiralty canoe route. Because of the difficulty getting a canoe out of Mole Harbor, many people are content to just spend a few days exploring and fishing Mitchell Bay and Salt Lake or paddling to a USFS cabin and then backtracking.

From June to mid-September, the USFS and Alaska Department of Fish and Game operate a permit system for Pack Creek and only 24 people are allowed per day from July to the end of August. Guiding and tour companies receive half the permits, leaving 12 for individuals who want to visit Pack Creek on their own. As of 2012, National Recreation Reservation Service (☎877-444-6777, 518-885-3639; www.recreation.gov), the people who handle USFS cabin reservations, are also handling Pack Creek permits. For the latest on the permit changes, particularly the date they become available each year, contact the Admiralty Island National Monument office (☎586-8800; www.fs.fed.us/r10/tongass/districts/admiralty) in Juneau.

In Angoon you can rent a canoe or kayak at **Favorite Bay Inn** (☏788-3234; email favoritebayinn@gmail.com), which charges $60 a day, less for a rental of six days or longer. You can also rent a canoe from **Alaska Boat & Kayak** (☏789-6886, 364-2333; www.juneau kayak.com; 11521 Glacier Hwy; canoes per day $50) at Auke Bay near Juneau and then place it on the Alaska Marine Ferry.

🛏 Sleeping

Services are limited in Angoon as tourism seems to be tolerated only because the village is a port of call for the ferry. It's also important to remember Angoon is a dry community.

Favorite Bay Inn   B&B **$$**
(☏788-3234, 800-423-3123; favoritebayinn@gmail. com; s/d/tr $149/159/169; ◍🕿) By far the best place to stay: a large, rambling log home 2 miles from the ferry terminal where you can get a bed and a hearty breakfast.

Kootznahoo Inlet Lodge   LODGE **$**
(☏788-3501; s/d $99/109; 🕿) Within town is this lodge with 10 rooms featuring private baths and coffee service.

ⓘ Getting There & Away

PACK CREEK Most visitors arrive at Pack Creek via a guided air-charter trip from Juneau. **Alaska Fly 'N' Fish** (☏790-2120; www.alaskabyair.com) holds permits and offers a guided 5½-hour, fly-in tour ($600). They will also transport you (for $170 to $400 per person depending on the size of your party) if you're lucky enough to snare a permit.

ANGOON Alaska Marine Highway (☏800-642-0066; www.ferryalaska.com) provides ferry service between Juneau and Angoon ($37, five hours) on Thursday and Saturday. **Alaska Seaplane Service** (☏789-3331, 888-350-8277; www.akseaplanes.com) offers three flights a day between Juneau and Angoon ($130 one way).

Glacier Bay National Park & Preserve

Eleven tidewater glaciers that spill out of the mountains and fill the sea with icebergs of all shapes, sizes and shades of blue have made Glacier Bay National Park and Preserve an icy wilderness renowned worldwide.

When Captain George Vancouver sailed through the ice-choked waters of Icy Strait in 1794, Glacier Bay was little more than a dent in a mountain of ice. In 1879 John Muir made his legendary discovery of Glacier Bay and found that the end of the bay had retreated 20 miles from Icy Strait. Today, the glacier that bears his name is more than 60 miles from Icy Strait, and its rapid retreat has revealed plants and animals that continue to fascinate modern-day naturalists.

Apart from its high concentration of tide-water glaciers, Glacier Bay is the habitat for a variety of marine life, including whales. The humpbacks are by far the most impressive and acrobatic, as they heave their massive bodies in spectacular leaps (called 'breaching') from the water. Adult humpbacks often grow to 50ft and weigh up to 40 tons. Other marine life seen at Glacier Bay includes harbor seals, porpoises, killer whales and sea otters, and other wildlife includes brown and black bears, wolves, moose, mountain goats and more than 200 bird species.

Glacier Bay is also where the cruise-ship industry and environmentalists have squared off. After the number of whales seen in the park dropped dramatically in 1978, the NPS reduced ship visits to 79 during the three-month season. But the cruise-ship industry lobbied the US Congress and the NPS in 1996 to OK a 30% increase in vessels allowed in the bay – almost 200 cruise ships a season. Environmentalists sued, and eventually a compromise of two large cruise ships per day was hammered out.

But the whales aren't the only area of concern here. Glacier Bay's ice, like glaciers all over Alaska, is rapidly melting. This is particularly true in Muir Inlet, or the East Arm as it's commonly called. Twenty years ago it was home to three active tidewater glaciers, but now there is only one, McBride. Only two glaciers in the park are advancing; Johns Hopkins and Lamplugh. The rest are receding and thinning.

Still, Glacier Bay is the crowning jewel of the cruise-ship industry and the dreamy destination for anybody who has ever paddled a kayak. The park is an expensive sidetrip, even by Alaskan standards. Plan on spending at least $400 for a trip from Juneau, but remember that the cost per day drops quickly after you've arrived. Of the more than 300,000 annual visitors, more than 90% arrive aboard a ship and never leave the boat. The rest are a mixture of tour-group members who head straight for the lodge and backpackers who wander toward the free campground.

Although the park headquarters, campground and visitors centers are located in Bartlett Cove, the gateway to Glacier Bay is Gustavus (gus-*tay*-vus), located nine miles away. This interesting backcountry community (pop 442) is where the state ferry and Alaska Airlines lands, but it has no downtown. Most of the area businesses are either spread out along the Salmon River or half-hidden in the woods. Electricity only arrived in the early 1980s, and residents still maintain a self-sufficient lifestyle. For visitors who rush through to see the glaciers, Gustavus is little more than an airstrip left over from WWII and a road to Bartlett Cove. For those who spend a little time poking around and meeting locals, Gustavus can be an interesting place and a refreshing break from cruise-ship ports like Skagway.

◉ Sights & Activities

Glaciers

The glaciers are 40 miles up the bay from Bartlett Cove. If you're not on a cruise ship or don't want to spend a week or two kayaking, the only way to see them is onboard a tour boat.

Glacier Bay Lodge & Tours BOAT TOUR
(☏264-4600, 888-229-8687; www.visitglacierbay. com) The *Fairweather Express* operated by Glacier Bay Lodge & Tours is a high-speed catamaran that departs at 7:30am for an eight-hour tour into the West Arm and returns by 4pm, in time for the Alaska Airlines flight back to Juneau. The tour costs $190/95 per adult/child and includes lunch and narration by an onboard park naturalist.

Gustavus Marine Charters BOAT TOUR
(☏697-2233; www.gustavusmarinecharters.com) For a more personal and leisurely experience there's the *Kahsteen*, operated by Gustavus Marine Charters. The 42ft yacht heads up with four to six passengers, a pair of kayaks, a skiff for shore excursions and Mike Nigro, a former backcountry ranger, as your captain. A three-/four-day trip to the glaciers, which includes gourmet meals, is $1350/1800.

Hiking

Glacier Bay has few trails and in the backcountry foot travel is done along riverbanks, on ridges or across ice remnants of glaciers. The only developed trails are in Bartlett Cove.

The mile-long Forest Trail is a nature walk that begins and ends near the Bartlett Cove dock and winds through the pond-studded spruce and hemlock forest near the campground. Rangers lead walks on this trail daily in summer; inquire at the Glacier Bay Visitor Center.

Bartlett River Trail, a 1.5-mile trail, begins just up the road to Gustavus, where there is a posted trailhead, and ends at the Bartlett River estuary. On the way, it meanders along a tidal lagoon and passes through a few wet spots. Plan on two to four hours for the 3-mile round-trip.

The Point Gustavus Beach Walk, along the shoreline south of Bartlett Cove to Point Gustavus and Gustavus, provides the only overnight trek from the park headquarters. The total distance is 12 miles, and the walk to Point Gustavus, an excellent spot to camp, is 6 miles. Plan on hiking the stretch from Point Gustavus to Gustavus at low tide, which will allow you to ford the Salmon River, as opposed to swimming across it. Point Gustavus is an excellent place to sight orcas and whales in Icy Strait.

Paddling

Glacier Bay offers an excellent opportunity for people who have some experience on the water but not necessarily as kayakers, because the Fairweather Express (☏264-4600, 888-229-8687; www.visitglacierbay.com; one way adult/child $114/57) drops off and picks up paddlers at two spots, usually at the entrance of the Muir Inlet (East Arm) and inside the West Arm. By using the tour boat, you can skip the long and open paddle up the bay and enjoy only the well-protected arms and inlets where the glaciers are located. The most dramatic glaciers are in the West Arm, but either one will require at least four days to paddle to glaciers if you are dropped off and picked up. With only a drop-off, you need a week to 10 days to paddle from either arm back to Bartlett Cove.

Paddlers who want to avoid the tour-boat fares but still long for a kayak adventure should try the Beardslee Islands. While there are no glaciers to view, the islands are a day's paddle from Bartlett Cove and offer calm water, protected channels and pleasant beach camping. Wildlife includes black bears, seals and bald eagles, and the tidal pools burst with activity at low tide.

TOP CHOICE Glacier Bay Sea Kayaks KAYAKING
(☏697-2257; www.glacierbayseakayaks.com; single/double kayaks per day $45/50) Glacier Bay rents kayaks as well as leads guided

trips to the Beardslee Islands (half-/full-day $95/150).

Alaska Mountain Guides   KAYAKING
(☎800-766-3396; www.alaskamountainguides.com) Has a field office in Gustavus to run several guided kayak trips into Glacier Bay. A seven-day paddle to the West Arm, which includes tour transportation as well as all equipment and food, is $1925 per person, and an eight-day paddle up the East Arm that begins from Bartlett Cove is $2200.

Spirit Walker Expeditions   KAYAKING
(☎697-2266, 800-529-2537; www.seakayakalaska.com) Spirit Walker runs paddling trips to Point Adolphus where humpback whales congregate during the summer. Trips begin with a short boat ride with the kayaks across Icy Strait to Point Adolphus and run $435 for a day paddle and $1085 for a three-day paddle.

Whale Watching
Cross Sound Express   WHALE WATCHING
(☎697-2726, 888-698-2726; www.taz.gustavus.com; tours adult/child $120/60) Its 47ft MV *Taz* carries up to 23 passengers and departs the Gustavus dock daily during the summer at 8:30am and 12:30pm for a 3½-hour whale-watching tour.

Woodwind Sailing Adventures   WHALE WATCHING
(☎697-2282; sailglacierbay.homestead.com) Wood wind's spacious 40ft sailing catamaran offers a whale-watching trip to Icy Point ($160) and an excellent kayaking-with-the-whales day trip to Point Adolphus ($250).

☞ Tours
You can see Glacier Bay in a hurry, though you have to ask yourself if that is a wise use of your travel funds. For a quickie flightseeing tour, Haines is the closest community and thus offers cheaper flights.

Glacier Bay Lodge & Tours   BOAT
(☎264-4600, 888-229-8687; www.visitglacierbay.com) Has an inclusive package that includes two nights at Glacier Bay Lodge, meals and a day tour to see the glaciers up bay on the *Fairweather Express*. The cost is $480 per person but does not include air transportation from Juneau.

Gray Line   BOAT
(☎586-3773, 800-544-2206; www.graylineofalaska.com) Offers a two-day package from Juneau that includes round-trip flight to Gustavus, a

night at Glacier Bay Lodge and a boat tour of the West Arm ($699 per person).

🛏 Sleeping & Eating
Most of the accommodations are in Gustavus, which adds a 7% bed-and-sales tax.

BARTLETT COVE
NPS campground   CAMPGROUND $
This NPS facility 0.25 miles south of Glacier Bay Lodge is set in a lush forest just off the shoreline, and camping is free. There's no need for reservations, there always seems to be space for another tent. It provides a bear cache, eating shelter and pleasant surroundings. Coin-operated showers are available in the park, but there aren't any places selling groceries or camping supplies.

Glacier Bay Lodge   LODGE $$$
(☎697-2225, 888-229-8687; www.visitglacierbay.com; 199 Bartlett Cove Rd; r $199-224; ⊜) This is the only hotel and restaurant in Bartlett Cove. The lodge has 55 rooms, a crackling fire in a huge stone fireplace and a dining room that usually hums in the evening with an interesting mixture of park employees, backpackers and locals from Gustavus. Nightly slide presentations, ranger talks and movies held upstairs cover the park's natural history.

GUSTAVUS
Gustavus Inn   INN $$$
(☎697-2254, 800-649-5220; www.gustavusinn.com; Mile 1, Gustavus Rd; s/d $205/410, with shared bath $195/$390; ⊜🤶) This longtime Gustavus favorite is a charming family homestead lodge mentioned in every travel book on Alaska, with good reason. It's thoroughly modern and comfortable but without being sterile or losing its folksy touch. The all-inclusive inn is well known for its gourmet dinners, which feature homegrown vegetables and fresh local seafood served family-style. Guests have free use of bicycles, and courtesy transportation to/from Bartlett Cove and the airport is cheerfully provided. Even if you can't afford to stay at the inn, book a seat at its dinner table one night.

Aimee's Guest House   GUESTHOUSE $$
(☎697-2330; www.glacierbayalaska.net; Gustavus Rd; ste $105-160; ⊜) A former smokehouse on the Salmon River (the reason for the colorful fish mural outside) has been converted into three bright, airy and comfortable vacation rentals featuring one or two bedrooms, full kitchens, and everything you would need to spend a few days in Gustavus. The upper-level

deck, with its hammock, wicker furniture and bed outside, is classic Alaska.

Blue Heron B&B
B&B **$$**

(☑697-2337; www.blueheronbnb.net; State Dock Rd; r/cottages $145/185; ☻) Surrounded by 10 acres of fields and gardens is this B&B with two rooms and two cottages with kitchenettes. All are modern, bright and clean, and each has a TV/VCR and private bath. In the morning everybody meets in the sun room for a full breakfast ranging from organic rolled oats with blueberries to omelets. Everything you need to enjoy Gustavus – rubber boots, rain pants, bikes, transportation anywhere – is provided.

Annie Mae Lodge
LODGE **$$**

(☑697-2346, 800-478-2346; www.anniemae.com; Grandpa's Farm Rd; s $120-150, d $170-200; ☻☎) This large rambling lodge has wraparound porches and 11 rooms, most with private bath. On the 2nd level all seven rooms have a private entrance off the porch, while a large dining room and common area is where a continental breakfast is served in the morning; dinners are available in the evening for an additional charge.

Glacier Bay Bear Track Inn
LODGE **$$$**

(☑697-3017, 888-697-2284; www.beartrackinn.com; 255 Rink Creek Rd; per person 1/2/3 nights $475/$749/$989; ☻☎) Another massive log lodge situated on 97 acres east of the airport with views of Icy Straits. The all-inclusive inn has 14 comfortable bedrooms, a walk-around fireplace, overstuffed chairs and moose-antler chandeliers in the lobby, and a dining room that serves mains such as fresh Dungeness crab and grilled Caribou medallion.

Homeshore Café
CAFE **$$**

(Gustavus Rd, at Wilson Rd; pizzas $11-15; ☻lunch & dinner Tue-Sat) Gustavus' only restaurant that's open year-round serves salads, sandwiches and surprisingly good pizza with beer to wash it down.

Beartrack Mercantile
MARKET **$**

(State Dock Rd; ☻9am-7pm Mon-Sat) On the way to the ferry dock, Gustavus' only market has limited groceries, camping supplies and hardware.

ℹ Information

The best source of information is the NPS in Bartlett Cove.

Glacier Bay Visitor Center (☑697-2661; www.nps.gov/glba; ☻11:30am-9pm) On the 2nd floor of Glacier Bay Lodge, it has exhibits, a bookshop and an information deck.

Gustavus Visitors Association (☑697-2454; www.gustavusak.com) Has loads of information on its website.

Visitor Information Station (☑697-2627; ☻6am-9pm) Campers, kayakers and boaters can stop at the park's Visitor Information Station at the foot of the public dock for backcountry permits, logistical information and a 20-minute orientation video.

ℹ Getting There & Around

TO/FROM THE AIRPORT If you arrive at the Gustavus airport, you're still 9 miles from Bartlett Cove. The Glacier Bay Lodge bus meets all Alaska Airline flights and charges $15 for the ride. **TLC Taxi** (☑697-2239) meets all ferry arrivals and also charges $15 for a trip to Bartlett Cove.

AIR Alaska Airlines (☑800-252-7522; www.alaskaair.com) Offers the only jet service, but it's rarely the cheapest airfare, with a round-trip ticket running $194 for the daily 25-minute trip from Juneau to Gustavus.

Wings of Alaska (☑in Juneau 789-0790; in Gustavus 697-2201; www.wingsofalaska.com) Scheduled flights to Juneau for $92/184 one way/round-trip or less if you book online.

Air Excursions (☑697-2375; www.airexcursions.com) flies to Gustavus for $100/200 one way/round-trip.

BOAT The cheapest way to reach Gustavus is via the **Alaska Marine Highway** (☑800-642-0066; www.ferryalaska.com), which began service in 2011. On Monday and Wednesday the MV Le-Conte makes the round-trip run from Juneau to Gustavus (one way $33; 3½ hours) along a route that often features numerous whale sightings.

Haines

POP 2508

Heading north of Juneau on the state ferry takes you up Lynn Canal, North America's longest and deepest fjord. Along the way, Eldred Rock Lighthouse stands as a picturesque sentinel, waterfalls pour down off the Chilkoot Range to the east, and the Davidson and Rainbow Glaciers draw 'oohs' and 'aahs' as they snake down out of the jagged Chilkat Mountains to the west. You end up in Haines, a scenic departure point for Southeast Alaska and a crucial link to the Alaska Hwy. Every summer thousands of travelers, particularly RVers, pass through this slice in the mountains on their way to Canada's Yukon Territory and Interior Alaska.

Haines is 75 miles north of Juneau on a wooded peninsula between the Chilkat and Chilkoot Inlets. Originally a stronghold of the wealthy Chilkat Tlingit Indians, it was put on the map by a gun-toting entrepreneur named Jack Dalton. In 1897 Dalton turned an old Indian trade route into a toll road for miners seeking an easier way to reach the Klondike. The Dalton Trail quickly became such a heavily used pack route to mining districts north of Whitehorse that the army arrived in 1903 and established Fort William H Seward, Alaska's first permanent post. For the next 20 years it was Alaska's only army post and then was used as a rest camp during WWII.

WWII led to the construction of the Haines Hwy, the 159-mile link between the Southeast and the Alcan. Built in 1942 as a possible evacuation route in case of a Japanese invasion, the route followed the Dalton Trail and was so rugged it would be 20 years before US and Canadian crews even attempted to keep it open in winter. By the 1980s, the 'Haines Cut-off Rd' had become the paved Haines Hwy, and now more than 50,000 travelers in cars and RVs follow it annually.

After logging fell on hard times in the 1970s, Haines swung its economy towards tourism and it's still surviving. And it should. Haines has spectacular scenery, quick access to the rivers and mountains where people like to play, and is comparatively dry (only 53in of rain annually). All of this prompted *Outside* magazine to plaster a photo of Haines on its cover in 2004 and call it one of the country's '20 best places to live and play.'

You'll immediately notice that this town is different from what you've experienced elsewhere in the Southeast. Maybe it's the relative lack of cruise-ship traffic that gives Haines a tangible sense of peace and tranquility; as a port Haines receives less than 40,000 cruise-ship passengers in a season – it is lucky to reach the number that Juneau sees in a good weekend. Or maybe it's the fact that there isn't a restaurant, gift shop or tour operator along Main St that is owned by a corporate conglomerate. Haines' businesses are uniquely Haines, and most likely the person behind the counter is the one who owns the store. The town isn't especially well developed for tourism: you won't find a salmon bake here and, no doubt for many travelers, that's part of its charm.

◉ Sights

Sheldon Museum
MUSEUM

(www.sheldonmuseum.org; 11 Main St; adult/child $5/free; ◷10am-5pm Mon-Fri, 1-4pm Sat & Sun) The Sheldon Museum houses a collection of indigenous artifacts upstairs, including a particularly interesting display on rare Chilkat blankets. Downstairs is devoted to Haines' pioneer and gold-rush days and even includes the sawed-off shotgun that Jack Dalton used to convince travelers to pay his toll.

Hammer Museum
MUSEUM

(www.hammermuseum.org; 108 Main St; adult/child $3/free; ◷10am-5pm Mon-Fri) The Hammer Museum is a monument to Dave Pahl's obsession with hammers. He has 1500 on display, a 20ft-high one outside and several hundred more in storage. In the world's only hammer museum you learn world history through the development of the hammer, from one less than ¼oz to another weighing more than 40lb.

American Bald Eagle Foundation
MUSEUM

(www.baldeagles.org; 113 Haines Hwy; adult/child $10/5; ◷10am-5pm Mon-Fri, 1-5pm Sat & Sun) An impressive wildlife diorama is featured at the American Bald Eagle Foundation – it displays more than 180 specimens and almost two dozen eagles. Two live raptors are always on display, with handlers giving demonstrations.

Fort Seward
HISTORIC BUILDINGS

Alaska's first permanent military post is reached by heading uphill (east) at the Front St–Haines Hwy junction. Built in 1903 and decommissioned after WWII, the fort is now a national historical site, with a handful of restaurants, lodges and art galleries in the original buildings. A walking-tour map of the fort is available at the visitors center, or you can just wander around and read the historical panels that have been erected there.

Alaska Indian Arts Center
ARTS CENTER

(www.alaskaindianarts.com; 24 Fort Seward Dr; ◷9am-5pm Mon-Fri) Indigenous culture can be seen in Fort Seward in the former post hospital, home of the Alaska Indian Arts Center. During the week you can watch artists carve totems, weave Chilkat blankets or produce other works of art. You can even order a totem.

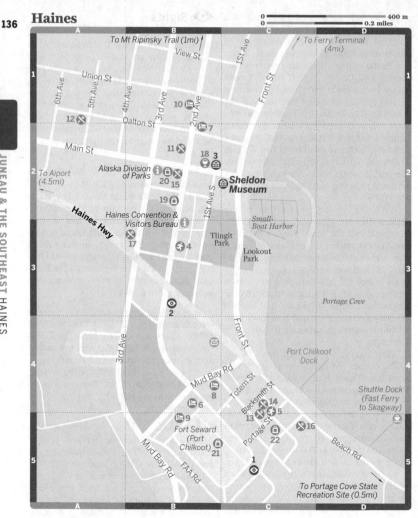

🏃 Activities

Cycling

You can discover some great road trips or what little single-track mountain biking there is in Haines by visiting **Sockeye Cycle** (📞766-2869, 877-292-4154; www.cyclealaska.com; 24 Portage St; bicycles per 2/4/8hr $14/25/35; ⊙9am-5:30pm Mon-Fri, to 4pm Sat), which rents a variety of top-of-the-line bicycles. The most popular road trip is the scenic 22-mile ride out to Chilkoot Lake. The shop also offers bike tours, with its best being an eight-hour ride on dirt roads through the alpine of the newly created Tatshenshini-Alsek

Provincial Park. The cost is $206 per person and includes mountain bikes, guide, transport and lunch.

Hiking

Two major trail systems are within walking distance of Haines. South of town are the Chilkat Peninsula trails, including the climb to Mt Riley. North of Haines is the path to the summit of Mt Ripinsky. Stop at the visitors bureau and pick up the brochure *Haines is for Hikers*, which describes the trails in more detail. For outdoor gear or a guided hike, stop by **Alaska Backcountry Outfitter** (📞766-2876; 111 2nd Ave; ⊙10am-5pm).

JUNEAU & THE SOUTHEAST HAINES

Mt Ripinsky Trail · HIKING

The trip to the 3690ft summit of Mt Ripinsky offers a sweeping view of the land from Juneau to Skagway. The route, which includes South Summit (3573ft), Peak 3920 and a descent from 7 Mile Saddle to Haines Hwy, is either a strenuous 10-hour journey for experienced hikers or an overnight trip.

To reach the trailhead, follow 2nd Ave north to where Young Rd, posted with a Mt Ripinsky Trail sign, splits from Lutak Rd (the road to the ferry terminal) and heads up the hill. Signs will direct you to the old pipeline road, where parking and the trail are clearly posted.

You can camp in the alpine area between Mt Ripinsky and the South Summit and then continue the next day west along the ridge to Peak 3920. From here you can descend to 7 Mile Saddle and then to the Haines Hwy, putting you 7 miles northwest of town. In recent years the trail has been greatly improved, but this is still a challenging overnight hike with spectacular views. For a 3-mile day hike, trek to the AT&T tower on Ridge Trail, a spur off the east end of the main trail.

Battery Point Trail · HIKING

This 2-mile trail is a flat walk along the shore to Kelgaya Point, where you can cut across to a pebble beach and follow it to Battery Point for excellent views of Lynn Canal.

The trail begins a mile beyond Portage Cove Recreation Site at the end of Beach Rd. Plan on a two-hour round-trip.

Mt Riley Trails · HIKING

This climb to a 1760ft summit is considerably easier than the one to Mt Ripinsky, but it still provides good views in all directions, including vistas of Rainbow and Davidson Glaciers. One trail up the mountain begins at a junction 2.2 miles up the Battery Point Trail out of Portage Cove Recreation Site. From here, you hike 3 miles over Half Dome and up Mt Riley.

Another route, closer to town, begins at the end of FAA Rd, which runs behind Officers' Row in Fort Seward. From the road's end, follow the water-supply access route for 2 miles to a short spur that branches off to the right and connects with the trail from Mud Bay Rd. The hike is 3.9 miles one way and eliminates the need to find a ride out to the third trailhead to Mt Riley, 3 miles out on Mud Bay Rd. The trailhead off Mud Bay Rd is posted, and this 2.8-mile route is the steepest but easiest to follow and the most direct to the summit. Plan on a five- to six-hour round-trip.

Seduction Point Trail · HIKING

This trail begins at Chilkat State Park Campground and is a 6.5-mile (one-way) hike to the point separating Chilkoot and Chilkat

Inlets. The trail swings between forest and beaches, and provides excellent views of Davidson Glacier.

If you have the equipment, this trail can be turned into an excellent overnight hike by setting up camp at the cove east of Seduction Point. Carry in water and check the tides before departing, as the final stretch along the beach after David's Cove should be walked at low- or mid-tide. The entire round-trip takes nine to 10 hours.

River Running

Haines is also a departure point for numerous raft trips. Chilkat Guides (☎766-2491; www.raftalaska.com; adult/child $94/65) offers a four-hour float daily down the Chilkat River through the bald-eagle preserve, with opportunities to view eagles and possibly brown bears; there is little or no white water.

On a much grander scale of adventure is the exciting nine- to 10-day raft trip down the Tatshenshini-Alsek River system, from Yukon Territory to the coast of Glacier Bay. This river trip is unmatched for its scenic mix of rugged mountain ranges and dozens of glaciers. Chilkat Guides and Alaska Discovery/Mt Sobek (☎888-687-6235; www.mtsobek.com) both run the trip, which costs between $3000 and $3300 per person.

☞ Tours

Other than Gustavus, Haines is the closest community to Glacier Bay National Park, making flightseeing tours much more reasonable here than in Skagway or Juneau.

TOP CHOICE Alaska Nature Tours WILDLIFE
(☎766-2876; www.alaskanaturetours.net; 109 2nd Ave) Offers excellent environmentally focused tours with knowledgeable guides for activities that range from birding and bear watching to easy hikes to Battery Point. Its Twilight Wildlife Watch is a 2½-hour tour (adult/child $75/60) that departs at 6pm and heads up the Chilkoot River, stopping along the way to look for eagles, mountain goats and brown bears who emerge at dusk to feed on spawning salmon.

Jilkaat Kwaan Cultural Tours CULTURAL
(☎766-4000, 855-766-4001; www.visitklukwan. com, www.chilkatferry.com; Mile 22, Haines Hwy; adult/child $149/99) This tour takes place in Klukwan, a Native village north of Haines and home of the Jilkaat Kwaan Cultural Heritage Center. The center was due to be finished in 2012 and includes a museum housing the village's treasured artworks, an arts studio, a replica tribal house and an eagle observatory along the Chilkat River. The four-hour tour includes everything from cultural dances and songs to meeting artists at the Carving Shed and watching villagers preparing fish for brining and storage at the smokehouse. Lunch and transportation is included.

Haines–Skagway Fast Ferry BOAT
(☎766-2100, 888-766-2103; www.hainesskagway fastferry.com; Beach Rd) If you don't have time for Skagway, the Fast Ferry has a Rail & Sail Tour (adult/child $170/85) that includes round-trip transportation to the Klondike city and the Summit Excursion on the White Pass & Yukon Railroad.

Mountain Flying Service SCENIC FLIGHTS
(☎766-3007, 800-954-8747; www.flyglacierbay. com; 132 2nd Ave) Offers an hour-long tour of the Glacier Bay's East Arm for $159 per person and an 80-minute tour of the more dramatic West Arm for $199. On a clear day, it's money well spent.

✯ Festivals & Events

Haines stages the Great Alaska Craft Beer & Home Brew Festival in the third week of May when most of the state's microbrews compete for the honor of being named top suds.

Like every other Alaskan town, Haines has a festive celebration for Fourth of July, but the town's biggest event is the Southeast Alaska State Fair. Staged at the end of July, the fair is five days of live music, an Ugliest Dog Contest, logging and livestock shows and the famous pig races that draw participants from all Southeast communities.

🛏 Sleeping

Haines tacks 9.5% tax onto the price of lodging.

TOP CHOICE Beach Roadhouse B&B $$
(☎766-3060, 866-741-3060; www.beachroad house.com; Mile 1, Beach Rd; r/cabins $105/145; ❂🖧) This B&B is what Alaska is all about and well worth the 2-mile trek out Beach Rd. The large cedar home is perched above Lynn Canal and surrounded by impressive pines for a tranquil, woodsy setting. Four rooms are large and include kitchenettes. The two cabins are even larger with full kitchens and lofts that sleep three to four persons. Perhaps the best amenity of this roadhouse

is just a few yards away: the start of scenic Battery Point Trail.

Alaska Guardhouse Lodging   B&B $$
(☑766-2566, 866-290-7445; www.alaskaguard house.com; 15 Fort Seward Dr; s/d $105/135; ◉🛜) What used to jail misbehaved soldiers is now housing visitors in comfort and luxury. Four large bedrooms, a pleasant living room and an enclosed sun porch with rocking chairs all give way to views of mountains and water.

Fort Seward Lodge   MOTEL $
(☑766-2009, 877-617-3418; www.ftsewardlodge. com; 39 Mud Bay Rd; r with/without shared bath $110 /75; ◉🛜) The former Post Exchange of Fort Seward is now one of Haines' best places to spend a night. The rooms are simple but clean and outside are surrounded by a wraparound deck with mountainous views. Along with affordable accommodations, the lodge offers free shuttle service from the ferry terminal.

Hotel Halsingland   HOTEL $$
(☑766-2000, 800-542-6363; www.hotelhalsing land.com; 13 Fort Seward Dr; r $79-119; ◉@🛜) The grand dame of Haines hotels is the former bachelor officers' quarters and overlooks Fort Seward's parade ground. A National Historic Landmark, the hotel is a little worn around the edges, but every year a few more of the 32 rooms are renovated. Many still have fireplaces and classic claw-foot bathtubs, while Room No 4, a corner room on the 2nd floor, has unbelievable views.

Portage Cove State Recreation Site   CAMPGROUND $
(Beach Rd; tent sites $5) Half a mile southeast of Fort Seward or a 2-mile walk from downtown, this scenic campground overlooks the water and has nine sites that are for backpackers and cyclists only. Follow Front St south; it becomes Beach Rd near Fort Seward.

Lynn View Lodge   B&B $$
(☑766-3713; www.lynnviewlodge.com; Mile 6.5, Lutak Rd; r $95-135, cabins $95; ◉🛜) A mile from the ferry terminal northeast of town, this B&B has a great view of Lynn Canal and a long, covered porch to relax on and soak up the scenery. Accommodations range from two rooms with shared bath and two suites with private bath to two small cabins. Cars are also available for $79 a day.

Captain's Choice Motel   MOTEL $$
(☑766-3111, 800-478-2345; www.capchoice.com; 108 2nd Ave; s/d $123/133; ◉@🛜) Haines' largest motel has the best view of the Chilkat Mountains and Lynn Canal and a huge sundeck to enjoy it on. Rooms are spacious enough to include a microwave, small refrigerator, coffee-maker and TV. A light breakfast is offered in the morning, and courtesy transportation to the ferries is available.

Summer Inn B&B   B&B $
(☑766-2970; www.summerinnbnb.com; 117 2nd Ave; s/d with shared bath incl breakfast $80/100; ◉) Built in 1912 in the heart of town by Tim Vogel, a member of Soapy Smith's gang in Skagway, this B&B has five bedrooms along with an enclosed porch where you can watch life in Haines come and go. Soapy Smith fanatics can take a soak in Vogel's original bathtub.

Chilkat State Park Campground   CAMPGROUND $
(Mud Bay Rd; sites $10) Seven miles southeast of Haines toward the end of Chilkat Peninsula, this campground has good views of Davidson and Rainbow Glaciers spilling out of the mountains into the Lynn Canal. There are 15 woodsy campsites and a beach to explore at low tide.

Haines Hitch-Up RV Park   CAMPGROUND $
(☑766-2882; www.hitchuprv.com; 851 Main St; RV sites $33-45; 🛜) Wedged between two major roads, this open but beautifully tended park is for RVs only, no tents. It has 92 sites with hookups, some with cable TV, as well as laundry and shower facilities.

Bear Creek Cabins & Hostel   HOSTEL $
(☑766-2259; www.bearcreekcabinsalaska.com; Mile 1.5, Small Tract Rd; dm/cabins $20/68; ◉) A 20-minute walk outside town – follow Mud Bay Rd near Fort Seward and when it veers right, continue straight onto Small Tract Rd for 1½ miles – this hostel has no lockout or curfew. A number of cabins surround a well-kept, grassy common area. Two of the cabins are used as the hostel dorms. A restroom/ shower building also has laundry facilities, and there is a common kitchen area.

Chilkoot Lake State Recreation Site   CAMPGROUND $
(Lutak Rd; sites $10) Five miles north of the ferry terminal and nine miles north of town, the campground has 32 sites and picnic shelters. The fishing for Dolly Varden is good

A VALLEY FULL OF EAGLES

The Alaska Chilkat Bald Eagle Preserve was created in 1982 when the state reserved 48,000 acres along the Chilkat, Klehini and Tsirku Rivers to protect the largest known gathering of bald eagles in the world. Each year from October to February, more than 4000 eagles congregate here to feed on spawning salmon. They come because an upwelling of warm water prevents the river from freezing, thus encouraging the late salmon run. It's a remarkable sight – hundreds of birds sitting in the bare trees lining the river, often six or more birds to a branch.

The best time to see this wildlife phenomenon is during the Alaska Bald Eagle Festival (baldeagles.org/festival). The five-day event in the second week of November attracts hundreds of visitors from around the country to Haines for speakers and presentations at the Sheldon Museum and the American Bald Eagle Foundation Center. But the basis of the festival is trooping out to the Chilkat River on 'expedition buses' with naturalists on board and encountering numbers of eagles that you cannot see anywhere else in the country at any other time of the year.

If the rain, snow and sleet of November is not on your Alaskan agenda, then you can still see eagles during the summer from the Haines Hwy, where there are turnouts for motorists to park and look for birds. The best view is between Mile 18 and Mile 22, where you'll find spotting scopes, interpretive displays and viewing platforms along the river. The numbers are not as mind-boggling as in early winter but 400 eagles live here year-round and more than 80 nests line the rivers.

Among guides who conduct preserve tours is Alaska Nature Tours (p238), which conducts four-hour tours (adult/child $75/60) daily in summer. The tours cover much of the scenery around the Haines area but concentrate on the river flats and river mouths, where you usually see up to 40 eagles, many of them nesting.

There is also River Adventures (766-2050, 800-478-9827; www.jetboatalaska.com), which uses jet boats for its Eagle Preserve River Adventure. The tour includes bus transportation 24 miles up the river to the jet boats and then a 1½-hour boat ride to look for eagles and other wildlife. The price is $100 per person.

---

on Chilkoot Lake, a turquoise blue body of water surrounded by mountains.

Salmon Run Campground & Cabins
CABINS $

(766-3240; Mile 6.5, Lutak Rd; sites $17, cabins $75-85;) Situated near the campground are two small cabins that come with heating and bunks but no indoor plumbing or kitchen facilities.

✗ Eating

If you're craving fresh seafood, check the bulletin boards around town to see if any commercial fishers are selling fish or Dungeness crab off their boats in the harbor. For fresh veggies, there's the Haines Farmer's Market held every other Saturday and some Wednesdays during the summer at the Southeast Alaska State Fairground from 10am to noon.

TOP CHOICE Mosey's Cantina
MEXICAN $$

(www.moseyscantina.com; 31 Tower Rd; lunch mains $8-14, dinner mains $16-24; lunch Mon-Fri, dinner Wed-Mon;) This may be Haines, but Mosey's offers some of the best Mexican fare outside of Anchorage. The mole sauce is outstanding, the salsa is fire roasted and the tacos are filled with everything from applewood-grilled chicken and carne asada to locally caught rockfish. While you're waiting for a table – there are only seven inside – enjoy a locally brewed beer on the porch outside.

Fireweed Restaurant
CALIFORNIAN $$

(37 Blacksmith St; sandwiches $8-13, pizzas $25; mains $13-17; lunch Wed-Sat, dinner Tue-Sat;) This clean, bright and laid-back bistro looks as if it belongs in California, not Haines. On its menu are words like 'organic', 'veggie' and 'grilled' as opposed to 'deep fried' and 'captain's special'. Vegetarians actually have a choice here (try the grilled portobello mushroom); everybody else can indulge in sandwiches, burgers and the town's best pizza, all washed down with beer served in icy mugs.

Commander's Room
MODERN AMERICAN $$$

(766-2000; 13 Fort Seward Dr; mains $27-32; dinner;) Located in Hotel Halsingland is Haines' most upscale restaurant. Begin the evening with a drink in its cozy Officer's Club Lounge and then venture into the Commander's Room, where you'll find white tablecloths, a fine wine list and a chef who has a herb garden out back. In July and August the salmon and halibut are flown in daily, or try the Moroccan-spiced braised lamb shank served on a bed of Israeli couscous.

Mountain Market & Cafe   DELI $
(3rd Ave, at Haines Hwy; breakfasts $6-9, sandwiches $7-9; ⊙7am-7pm Mon-Fri, 8am-5pm Sat, 9am-5pm Sun; ⊕🍴) The center of Haines hipness and healthy eating. The market stocks health foods, while its deli is loaded with vegetarian options, baked goods, great homemade soup, espresso drinks and indoor seating. Adjoining the store is Mountain Spirits, the best wine shop in town.

Klondike   PIZZA $$
(Fair Dr; pizzas $14-18; ⊙dinner) Wood-fired pizza has arrived in Haines and locals love it. Located in Dalton City, the Klondike serves pizza pies, salads and beer that's brewed only two doors down. Eat inside or outside on a deck overlooking horseshoe and beach volleyball courts.

Dejon Delights   SEAFOOD $$
(☎766-2505; 37 Portage St; ⊙10am-6pm) This shop in Fort Seward turns out some of the best smoked fish in the Southeast, such as salmon that is first marinated in stout beer. If camping at Portage Bay, pick up a fillet of just-caught salmon and grill it on your campfire against the view of mountainous Lynn Canal.

Chilkat Restaurant & Bakery   CAFE $
(Dalton St, at 5th Ave; breakfasts $6-10, sandwiches $9-11, mains 11-20; ⊙breakfast & lunch Mon-Sat, dinner Fri, Sat & Mon; ⊕) A local favorite that has been baking goodies and serving breakfast for 25 years. For a nice break from eggs and potatoes, try the homemade granola with blueberries...but first you have to get past that display case filled with the daily offering of muffins and pastries. Heck with the granola, have a slice of rhubarb-strawberry pie for breakfast.

Bamboo Room   CAFE $$
(2nd Ave; breakfasts $7-15, lunch mains $8-15, dinner mains $15-25; ⊙6am-9pm) CBS newsman Charles Kuralt once ate breakfast at this cafe and loved it. No doubt he had the blueberry pancakes with whipped cream. [...] likes to claim it has the best sandwich in the Southeast, but it [...] pass up a plate of steamed Dungeness served whole.

Howsers IGA   SUPERMARKET $
(211 Main St) The main supermarket in Haines.

🍷 Drinking

Fort Seward Lodge   BAR
(39 Mud Bay Rd; ⊕) Tucked away upstairs in the Fort Seward Lodge's two-level restaurant is this small bar that's a refreshing break from the smoky, main-street watering holes. Dangling from the ceiling in the middle is the original red-velvet swing that ladies swung on to the delight of the soldiers.

Captain's Lounge   BAR
(Captain's Choice Motel, 108 2nd Ave; ⊕) Another small, half-hidden bar in the back of a motel. It offers casual atmosphere, cheap bar snacks and one of the best mountainous views of any bar in Southeast Alaska.

Fogcutter Bar   BAR
(Main St) Haines is a hard-drinking town, and this is where a lot of them belly up to the bar and spout off.

🔒 Shopping

Despite a lack of cruise-ship traffic, or maybe because of it, Haines supports an impressive number of local artists and has enough galleries to fill an afternoon.

TOP⟩ Extreme Dreams Fine
CHOICE
Arts   ARTS & CRAFTS
(www.extremedreams.com; Mile 6.5, Mud Bay Rd) Near the entrance of Chilkat State Park, south of town, is this wonderful gallery packed with the work of 20 local artists, from watercolors and weavings to hand-blown glass, cast silver and beautiful beads. The gallery also has a climbing wall because it's the studio of artist John Svenson, a renowned mountain climber who has scaled the highest peak on every continent except Mt Everest.

Wild Iris   ARTS & CRAFTS
(22 Tower Rd) This art gallery is the most impressive of a growing number on the edge of Fort Seward. Outside the home is a beautiful Alaskan garden; inside, a fine selection of original jewelry, silk-screened prints, cards, pastels and other local art.

The Bamboo
'libut steak
hard to
'rabs

141

NG COMPANY

was the movie set
m, *White Fang*. After
nes, the set was
outheast Alaska State
is now a destination
ior b. among the false-front
buildings and wooden sidewalks is the
Haines Brewing Company (haines
brewing.com; Fair Dr; ☉1-6pm Mon-Sat),
the maker of such beer as Dalton Trail
Ale, Elder Rock Red and the potent
Black Fang (9% alcohol content). Tours
are short – hey this is a one-room
brewery – but pints are available and
you can have a half-gallon growler
($10 to $13) filled for later. Most of the
restaurants in town also serve the local
brew and, frankly, why drink anything
else? As local author Heather Lende
says on a sign in the brewery, 'Life is too
short to waste my alcohol consumption
on cheap beer.'

Sea Wolf Art Studio   ARTS & CRAFTS
(www.tresham.com; Ft Seward Parade Ground)
Housed in a log cabin is Tresham Gregg's
gallery. Gregg is one of Haines' best-known
Alaska Native artists, and he combines the
imagery of the spiritism, animism and sha-
manism of Northwest Coast Indians to create wood carvings, totems, masks, bronze
sculpture and talismanic silver jewelry.

Babbling Book   BOOKS
(☏766-3356; 223 Main St; ☉11am-5pm Mon-Sat)
Stocks a great selection of Alaska books,
cards and calendars, while its walls serve as
the notice board for Haines' cultural scene.

ⓘ Information

Alaska Division of Parks (☏766-2292; 219
Main St, Suite 25; ☉8am-5pm Mon-Fri) For
information on state parks and hiking.
First National Bank of Anchorage (123 Main
St) For all your presidential-portrait needs.
Haines Borough Public Library (111 S 3rd Ave;
☉10am-9pm Mon-Thu, 10am-6pm Fri, 12:30-
4:30pm Sat & Sun; @) The cultural jewel of the
community. This impressive facility has a book
exchange, six computers for internet access
(by donation), a beautiful reading area with
rocking chairs and a two-story window overlooking the mountains. Curl up and read before
the majestic view.

Haines Convention & Visitors Bureau (☏766-
2234, 800-458-3579; www.haines.ak.us; 122
2nd Ave; ☉8am-5pm Mon-Fri, 9am-4pm Sat
& Sun) Has restrooms, free coffee and racks
of free information for tourists. There is also a
lot of information on Canada's Yukon for those
heading up the Alcan.
Haines Medical Clinic (☏766-6300; 131 1st
Ave S) For whatever ails you.
Post office (Haines Hwy) Close to Fort Seward.

ⓘ Getting There & Around

AIR There is no jet service to Haines, but **Wings
of Alaska** (☏766-2030; www.wingsofalaska.
com) has daily flights to Juneau ($114) and
Skagway ($65).
BOAT State ferries depart daily from the **ferry
terminal** (☏766-2111; 2012 Lutak Rd) 4 miles
north of town for Skagway ($31, one hour) and
Juneau ($37, 5½ hours). **Haines-Skagway
Fast Ferry** (☏766-2100, 888-766-2103; www.
hainesskagwayfastferry.com; Beach Rd) uses
a speedy catamaran to cruise down Taiya Inlet
to Skagway in 45 minutes. The 80ft cat departs
Haines from the Fast Ferry shuttle dock at 6am,
1pm and 7pm and more often if cruise ships are
packing Skagway. One-way fares are adult/child
$35/18, round-trip $68/34. In 2012 the **Chilkat
Express** (☏766-4000, 855-766-4001; www.
chilkatferry.com) will begin offering ferry passage between the two towns.
BUS Amazingly no buses serve Haines. You'll
need to either thumb it north or take the ferry to
Skagway and get a bus north from there.
CAR To visit Alaska Chilkat Bald Eagle Preserve
on your own, you can rent a car at **Captain's
Choice Motel** (☏766-3111, 800-478-2345),
which has compacts for $79 a day with unlimited
mileage. **Eagle Nest Car Rentals** (☏766-2891,
800-354-6009; 1183 Haines Hwy), in the Eagle
Nest Motel, has cars for $57 a day with 100 miles
included.
TAXI Ms Lucy Taxi Service (☏303-8000)
meets most ferries and charges $10 for the
trip into town. You can also arrange for a ride
out to the ferry terminal. If the weather is nice,
consider taking **Z Taxi** (☏314-0959), an electric
bicycle cart that holds two passengers and
makes for an extremely pleasant 15-minute ride
into town ($15).

Skagway
POP 968

Situated at the head of Lynn Canal is Skagway, one of the driest places in an otherwise
soggy Southeast. While Petersburg averages
more than 100in of rain a year and Ketchikan a drenching 154in, Skagway gets only
26in annually.

Much of Skagway is within Klondike Gold Rush National Historical Park, which comprises downtown Skagway, the Chilkoot Trail, the White Pass Trail corridor and a Seattle visitors center. Beginning in 1897, Skagway and the nearby ghost town of Dyea were the starting places for more than 40,000 gold-rush stampeders who headed to the Yukon primarily by way of the Chilkoot Trail. The actual stampede lasted only a few years, but it produced one of the most colorful periods in Alaskan history, that of a lawless frontier town controlled by villainous 'Soapy' Smith who was finally removed from power in a gunfight by town hero Frank Reid.

At the height of the gold rush, Michael J Heney, an Irish contractor, convinced a group of English investors that he could build a railroad over the White Pass Trail to Whitehorse. The construction of the White Pass & Yukon Route was nothing short of a superhuman feat, and the railroad became the focal point of the town's economy after the gold rush and during the military build-up of WWII.

The line was shut down in 1982 but was revived in 1988, to the delight of cruise-ship tourists and backpackers walking the Chilkoot Trail. Although the train hauls no freight, its rebirth was important to Skagway as a tourist attraction. Today Skagway survives almost entirely on tourism, and bus tours and more than 400 cruise ships a year turn this village into a boomtown again every summer. Up to five ships a day stop here and, on the busiest days, more than 9000 tourists – 10 times the town's resident population – march off the ships and turn Broadway into something of an anthill. It's the modern-day version of the Klondike Gold Rush and the reason why Skagway had more jewelry shops per capita than any place in Alaska and possibly the country.

Unlike the majority of Southeast towns, Skagway is a truly delightful place to arrive in by sea. Cruise-ship and state-ferry passengers alike step off their boats and are funneled to Broadway St, Skagway's main avenue and the heart of Klondike Gold Rush National Park Historic District. Suddenly you find yourself in a bustling town, where many people are dressed as if they are trying to relive the gold-rush days and the rest are obviously tourists from the luxury liners.

◉ Sights

FREE **Klondike Gold Rush National Historical Park Visitor Center** HISTORIC BUILDING
(☑983-9223; www.nps.gov/klgo; Broadway St, at 2nd Ave; ⊘8am-6pm; 🖼) The first stop of the day should be this **NPS center** in the original 1898 White Pass & Yukon Route depot. The center features displays – the most impressive being a replica of the ton of supplies every miner had to carry over the Chilkoot Pass – ranger programs and a small bookstore. The 30-minute film *Gold Fever: Race to the Klondike*, an excellent introduction to the gold rush, is shown on the hour. Rangers lead a 50-minute walking tour of the historic district on the hour from 9am to 4pm.

Skagway Museum MUSEUM
(7th Ave, at Spring St; adult/child $2/1; ⊘9am-5pm Mon-Fri, 10am-5pm Sat, to 4pm Sun) Skagway Museum is not only one of the finest in a town filled with museums but one of the finest in the Southeast. It occupies the entire 1st floor of the venerable century-old McCabe Building, a former college, and is devoted to various aspects of local history, including Alaska Native baskets, beadwork and carvings, and, of course, the Klondike Gold Rush. The display that draws the most looks is the small pistol Soapy Smith kept up his sleeve.

FREE **Mascot Saloon Museum** MUSEUM
(Broadway St, at 3rd Ave; ⊘8am-6pm) This is the only saloon in Alaska that doesn't serve beer, wine or a drop of whiskey – but it did during the gold rush, and plenty of it. Built in 1898, the Mascot was one of 70 saloons during Skagway's heyday as 'the roughest place in the world.' The park service has since turned it into a museum that looks into the vices – gambling, drinking, prostitution – that followed the stampeders to the gold-fields, encouraging visitors to belly up to the bar for a shot of sinful history.

FREE **Junior Ranger Activity Center** MUSEUM
(Broadway St, at 4th Ave; 10am-3pm Mon-Fri; 🖼) At the Pantheon Saloon, built in 1903, kids are the customers. The historic bar is now home to the park's new Junior Ranger Program where children and their parents examine artifacts that they can touch, dress up as stampeders and shoulder a miner's pack on their way to earning a Junior Ranger badge.

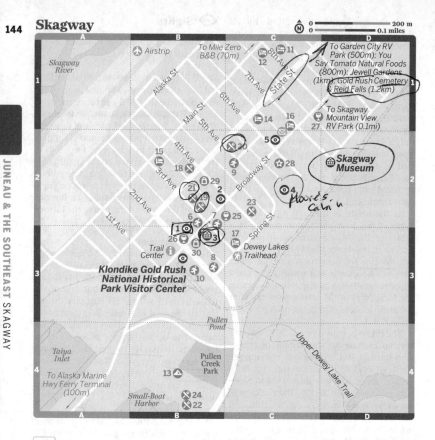

FREE Moore's Cabin & Bernard
Moore House   HISTORIC BUILDING
(5th Ave, at Spring St; ⊙10am-5pm) A block
southeast of the city museum is Skagway's
oldest building. Captain William Moore and
his son, Bernard, built the cabin in 1887,
when they staked out their homestead as the
founders of the town. Moore had to move
his home to its present location when gold-
rush stampeders overran his homestead.
The NPS has since renovated the building
and, in doing so, discovered that the famous
Dead Horse Trail that was used by so many
stampeders actually began in the large lawn
next to the cabin. Adjacent to the cabin is
the restored Bernard Moore House, which
features exhibits and furnishings depicting
family life during the gold rush.

FREE Wells Fargo Bank   HISTORIC BUILDING
(Broadway St, at 6th Ave; ⊙9:30am-5pm Mon-Fri)
This bank dates back to 1916 when a group
of East Coast businessmen founded the National Bank of Alaska and built the bank a
year later. In 1981 the bank underwent an
extensive historic renovations, and today it
is an interesting place to visit even if you're
not short on cash. Two of the five brass teller gates are originals, there are spittoons
in case you're chewing tobacco, and on
display everywhere are banking artifacts,
from a classic 'Cannonball' safe to an old
coin machine.

Arctic Brotherhood Hall   HISTORIC BUILDING
(Broadway St, at 2nd Ave) The most outlandish
building of the seven-block historical corridor along Broadway St, and possibly the
most photographed building in Alaska, is
this defunct fraternal hall, now home of the
Skagway Convention & Visitors Bureau. The
original driftwood, 8833 pieces of it, that
covers the facade were attached in 1899 and
extensively renovated, piece-by-piece, in
2005.

Gold Rush Cemetery & Reid Falls CEMETERY
Visitors who become infatuated with Smith and Reid can walk out to this cemetery, a 1.5-mile stroll northeast on State St. Follow State until it curves into 23rd Ave and just before crossing the bridge over the Skagway River look for the 'Gold Rush Cemetery' signs. They'll lead you to Soapy's grave across the railroad tracks and the rest of the cemetery, the site of many stampeders' graves as well as the plots of Reid and Smith. From Reid's gravestone, it's a short hike uphill to lovely Reid Falls, which cascades 300ft down the mountainside.

Jewell Gardens GARDENS
(☏983-2111; jewellgardens.com; Klondike Hwy; adult/child $12/6; ☺9am-5pm) If the crowds are overwhelming you, cross the Skagway River to Jewell Gardens. Located where Henry Clark started the first truck farm in Alaska, the garden is a quiet spot of flowerbeds, ponds, giant vegetables and a miniature train. There is also a pair of glassblowing studios where artists give fascinating demonstrations while making beautiful glassware. Call for times of the glassblowing and then hop on a SMART bus that will drop you off at the entrance.

Dyea HISTORIC SITE
In 1898 Skagway's rival city, Dyea (*die*-yee), at the foot of the Chilkoot Trail, was the trailhead for the shortest route to Lake Bennett, where stampeders began their float to Dawson City. After the White Pass & Yukon Route was completed in 1900, Dyea quickly died. Today the town is little more than a few old crumbling cabins, the pilings of Dyea Wharf and Slide Cemetery, where 47 men and women were buried after perishing in an avalanche on the Chilkoot Trail in April 1898.

To explore the ghost town, you can pick up the *Dyea Townsite Self-Guided Walking Tour* brochure from the NPS center. The guide will lead your along a mile loop from the townsite parking area past what few ruins remain. Or join a ranger-led walk, which meets at the parking area at 10am and 2pm daily.

Dyea is a 9-mile drive along winding Dyea Rd, whose numerous hairpin turns are not for timid RVers. But it's a very scenic drive, especially at **Skagway Overlook**, a turnoff with a viewing platform 2½ miles from Skagway. The overlook offers an excellent view of Skagway, its waterfront and the peaks above the town. Just before crossing the bridge over the Taiya River, you pass the Dyea Campground.

🏃 Activities

Hiking

The 33-mile Chilkoot Trail (p52) is Southeast Alaska's most popular hike, but other good trails surround Skagway. There is no USFS office in Skagway, but the NPS Visitor Center has a free brochure entitled *Skagway Trail Map*. You can also get backcountry information and any outdoor gear you need (including rentals) at the excellent **Mountain Shop** (www.packerexpeditions.com; 355 4th Ave).

Dewey Lakes Trail System HIKING
This series of trails leads east of Skagway to a handful of alpine and subalpine lakes, waterfalls and historic sites. From Broadway, follow 3rd Ave southeast to the railroad tracks. On the east side of the tracks are the trailheads to Lower Dewey Lake (0.7 miles), Icy Lake (2.5 miles), Upper Reid Falls (3.5 miles) and Sturgill's Landing (4.5 miles).

Plan on taking an hour round-trip for the hike to Lower Dewey Lake, where there are picnic tables, camping spots and a trail circling the lake. At the lake's north end is an alpine trail that ascends steeply to Upper Dewey Lake, 3.5 miles from town, and Devil's Punchbowl, another 1.25 miles south of the upper lake.

The hike to Devil's Punchbowl is an all-day trip or an ideal overnight excursion, as the views are excellent and there is a free-use shelter on Upper Dewey Lake that is in rough condition but does not require reservations. There are also campsites at Sturgill's Landing.

Yakutania Point & AB Mountain Trails HIKING
The Skagway River footbridge, reached by following 1st Ave west around the airport runway, leads to two trails of opposite caliber. For an easy hike to escape the cruise-ship crowds turn left from the bridge and follow the mile-long trail to picnic areas and lovely views at Yakutania Point and Smugglers Cove.

Nearby on Dyea Rd is AB Mountain Trail, also known as the Skyline Trail. This route ascends 5.5 miles to the 5100ft summit of AB Mountain, named for the 'AB' that appears on its south side when the snow melts every spring. The first 30 minutes is along a well-defined trail through a hemlock forest to a view of Skagway. After that the trail is considerably more challenging, especially above the treeline, requiring a full day to reach the summit.

Denver Glacier Trail HIKING
This trail begins at Mile 6 of the White Pass & Yukon Route, where the USFS has renovated a White Pass & Yukon Route caboose into the **Denver Caboose** (☎877-444-6777; www.recreation.gov; cabins $35), a rental cabin of sorts. White Pass & Yukon Route will drop hikers off at the caboose (round-trip adult/child $31/16). The trail heads up the east fork of Skagway River for 2 miles, then swings south and continues another 1.5 miles up the glacial outwash to Denver Glacier. Most of the trail is overgrown with brush, and the second half is particularly tough hiking.

Laughton Glacier Trail HIKING
At Mile 14 of the White Pass & Yukon Route is a 1.5-mile hike to the USFS **Laughton Glacier Cabin** (☎877-444-6777; www.recreation.gov; cabins $35). The cabin overlooks the river from Warm Pass but is only a mile from Laughton Glacier, an impressive hanging glacier between the 3000ft walls of the Sawtooth Range. The alpine scenery and ridge walks in this area are well worth the ticket on the White Pass & Yukon Route (round-trip adult/child $66/33). There are two excursion trains from Skagway, so this could be a possible day hike. But it's far better to carry a tent and spend a night in the area.

Cycling

Sockeye Cycle MOUNTAIN BIKING
(☎983-2851; www.cyclealaska.com; 381 5th Ave; bikes per 2/4/8hr $14/25/35) Rents hybrids and mountain bikes and offers several bike tours out of Skagway. Its 2½-hour Klondike Tour ($83) begins with van transportation to Klondike Pass (elevation 3295ft) on the Klondike Hwy. From there it's a 15-mile downhill ride back to town, with plenty of stops to view waterfalls. The same trip is also offered with a ride up on the White Pass & Yukon Route ($188).

Rafting

Skagway Float Tours RAFTING
(☎983-3688; www.skagwayfloat.com) Offers a three-hour tour of Dyea that includes a

45-minute float down the placid Taiya River (adult/child $75/55). Its Hike & Float Tour ($90/70) is a four-hour outing that includes hiking 1.8 miles of the Chilkoot Trail then some floating back.

Ziplining

Mammoth Waterfalls & Ultra Zipline   EXTREME SPORTS

(☑983-4444; www.alaskaexcursions.com; adult/child $169/149) With as many cruise ship as Skagway gets, you just knew a zipline wasn't far behind. It's here – actually in Dyea: 11 lines, one 750ft long, and four suspension bridges that take you down a forested mountain and across waterfalls. Tour includes transportation from Skagway.

☞ Tours

White Pass & Yukon Route Railroad   TRAIN

(☑983-2217, 800-343-7373; www.wpyr.com; Depot 2nd Ave) Without a doubt the most spectacular tour from Skagway is a ride aboard the historic railway of the White Pass & Yukon Route. Two different narrated sightseeing tours are available; reservations are required for both.

The premier trip is the Yukon Adventure. At Skagway's railroad depot you board parlor cars for the trip to White Pass on the narrow-gauge line built during the 1898 Klondike Gold Rush. This segment is only a small portion of the 110-mile route to Whitehorse, but it contains the most spectacular scenery, including crossing Glacier Gorge and Dead Horse Gulch, viewing Bridal Veil Falls and then making the steep 2885ft climb to White Pass, only 20 miles from Skagway. You make a whistle stop at the historic 1903 Lake Bennett Railroad Depot for lunch and then board the train to follow the shoreline of stunning Lake Bennett to Carcross. At this small Yukon town, buses take you back to Skagway. The Yukon Adventure departs from Skagway at 7:45am Sunday, Wednesday and Thursday; the fare is $229/115 per adult/child. Note that Lake Bennett is across the border in British Columbia, Canada, so passengers will need to carry passports or other proof of citizenship.

The White Pass Summit Excursion (three to 3½ hours, adult/child $112/56) is a shorter tour to White Pass Summit and back. The tour is offered at 8:15am and 12:45pm daily mid-May to mid-September and at 4:30pm Tuesday and Wednesday until early September.

Summit & City Tour

This is the standard tour in Skagway and includes Gold Rush Cemetery, White Pass Summit and Skagway Overlook, including a lively narration that might be historically accurate. The cost is $40 to $50 per person for a three-hour outing. Companies offering such a tour, among others:

Frontier Excursions (☑983-2512, 877-983-2512; www.frontierexcursions.com; cnr Broadway St & 3rd Ave)

Gray Line (☑983-2241, 800-544-2206; cnr Spring St & 3rd Ave, at Westmark Inn)

Klondike Tours (☑983-2075, 866-983-2075; www.klondiketours.com; cnr Broadway St & 2nd Ave)

M&M Tours (☑983-3900, 866-983-3900; www.skagwayadventures.com; cnr 2nd Ave & Spring St)

Other Tours

Some cruise tourist–oriented attractions are a short way out on the Klondike Hwy.

Red Onion Saloon   MUSEUML

(☑983-2222; redonion1898.com; cnr Broadway St & 2nd Ave) Skagway's beloved saloon was once a house of sin, the reason for its tours of the upstairs bedrooms, now a brothel museum. Tours are '$5 for 15 minutes just like in 1898' and are offered throughout the day.

Klondike Gold Dredge Tours   TOUR

(☑983-3175, 877-983-3175; www.klondikegoldfields.com; Mile 1.7, Klondike Hwy; 2hr tours $20) Offers tours of a former working gold dredge that was in Dawson before being moved to Skagway, where it has hit the mother lode. There is also a gold-panning show with a crack at finding dust yourself ($25) and a brewpub onsite.

Gold Rush Trail Camp   GOLD PANNING

(☑983-3333; Mile 3, Klondike Hwy; adult/child $49/33) Offers a miner's show, a turn at gold panning and Skagway's salmon bake. You book it and pick up the bus at Skagway Mountain View RV Park.

⭐ Festivals & Events

Skagway's **Fourth of July** celebrations feature a footrace, parade, street dance and the Ducky Derby, when a thousand plastic ducks are raced down a stream. But the town's most unusual celebration is **Soapy Smith's Wake**, on July 8. Locals and the cast of the *Days of '98 Show* celebrate with a hike out to the grave and a champagne toast, with champagne often sent up from California by Smith's great-grandson.

🛌 Sleeping

Skagway levies an 8% sales and bed tax on all lodging.

TOP CHOICE Alaskan Sojourn Hostel HOSTEL **$**
(☑907-983-2040; www.alaskansojourn.net; 488 8th Ave; dm/r $25/75; ➲🖧) Skagway's newest hostel is one of the finest in Southeast Alaska. Its lounge is an open and sun-filled room attached to an enclosed front porch where you could whittle away a rainy afternoon with a good book. There are mixed and single-sex dorms, as well as a private room and even a cute and very cozy two-person cabin. This is a relaxed and pleasant place away from the hustle of Broadway.

At the White House INN **$$**
(☑983-9000; www.atthewhitehouse.com; 475 8th Ave, at Main St; r incl breakfast $120-160; ➲@🖧) A very comfortable 10-room inn filled with antiques, remembrances of the Klondike and colorful comforters on every bed. Rooms are spacious and bright, even on a rainy day, and have cable TV and phone. In the morning you wake up to a breakfast of fresh-baked goods and fruit served in a sun-drenched dining room.

Mile Zero B&B B&B **$$**
(☑983-3045; www.mile-zero.com; 901 Main St; r incl breakfast $135-145; ➲🖧) This B&B is more like a motel with the comforts of home, as the six large rooms have their own private entrance on the wraparound porch. If you hook the fish of your dreams, there's a BBQ area where you can grill it for dinner.

Cindy's Place CABINS **$$**
(☑983-2674, 800-831-8095; www.alaska.net/~croland; Mile 1, Dyea Rd; cabins $65-125; ➲🖧) Two miles from town are two large log units with private baths and a small, cozy one without a shower. Each of them has refrigerator, microwave and coffee-maker, and they are tucked away into the forested ridge. In the morning fresh-baked goods magically appear on your doorstep. Ferry terminal transportation provided.

Skagway Inn INN **$$**
(☑983-2289, 888-752-4929; www.skagwayinn.com; Broadway St, at 7th Ave; r incl breakfast $119-199; ➲@🖧) In a restored 1897 Victorian building that was originally one of the town's brothels – what building still standing in

Skagway wasn't? – the inn is downtown and features 10 rooms, four with shared baths. All are small but filled with antique dressers, iron beds and chests.

Sergeant Preston's Lodge MOTEL **$$**
(☑983-2521, 866-983-2521; sgtprestons.eskagway.com; 370 6th Ave; s $85-115, d $90-125; ➲@🖧) This sprawling motel is one of the best bargains in Skagway. All 38 rooms are modern, clean and equipped with TVs, small refrigerators and microwaves. Other perks include courtesy transportation, complimentary coffee in the lobby and very accommodating proprietors.

Skagway Mountain View RV Park CAMPGROUND **$**
(☑983-3333, 888-778-7700; 12th Ave, at Broadway St; tent sites $15, RV sites $18-26; 🖧) The town's best campground for tenters. It has 60 RV sites and a limited number of tent sites. Amenities include firepits, laundry facilities, coin-operated showers, and dump stations for both humans and RVs. It's easy walking distance from downtown, but you won't feel trampled by tourists.

Chilkoot Trail Outpost CABINS **$$**
(☑983-3799; www.chilkoottrailoutpost.com; Mile 8.5, Dyea Rd; cabins $145-175; ➲🖧) Hitting the 'Koot? Start the big adventure with a good night's sleep at this resort located a half-mile from the trailhead. The cabins are very comfortable and equipped with microwaves, refrigerators and coffee-makers. In the morning you can fuel up on a buffet breakfast at the main lodge. There are bicycles available, and the screened-in gazebo is strategically located at a waterfall.

Westmark Inn HOTEL **$$**
(☑983-6000, 800-544-0970; 3rd Ave, at Spring St; r $135-145; ➲@🖧) Skagway's largest hotel is more of a sprawling complex with 151 rooms on both sides of 3rd Ave.

Skagway Home Hostel HOSTEL **$**
(☑983-2131; www.skagwayhostel.com; 456 3rd Ave; dm $15-20; ➲@) A home in a quiet residential neighborhood a half mile from the ferry terminal. It's a relaxed, if somewhat cluttered, hostel with 20 bunks and kitchen and laundry facilities. You can reserve a bunk online.

Dyea Campground CAMPGROUND **$**
(☑983-2921; sites $10) Located near the Chilkoot trailhead in Dyea, about 9 miles north of Skagway, this 22-site campground

is operated by the NPS on a first-come, first-served basis. There are vault toilets and tables but no drinking water. A mile away past the Dyea Townsite, the city of Skagway operates a free campground.

Pullen Creek RV Park   CAMPGROUND $
(☑983-2768, 800-936-3731; www.pullencreekrv.com; tent sites $25, with car/electricity & water $30/38) Squeezed between the ferry terminal and cruise-ship docks, an area crawling with tourists, is this city-operated campground with 46 sites, most with hookups but some for tents.

✖ Eating

Skagway has more than 20 restaurants operating during the summer, and some would say they're better than those you find in that capital city just to the south. And like Juneau, Skagway's eateries and bars are now a smoke-free zone.

TOP CHOICE Stowaway Café   CAJUN $$$
(☑983-3463; 205 Congress Way; lunch mains $9-12, dinner mains $20-24; ☉lunch & dinner) Just past the harbormaster's office, this place is fun, funky and fantastic. Outside is a beautiful mermaid and the restaurant's artfully cluttered front and back yards. The small cafe has a handful of tables, a view of the boat harbor, and excellent fish and Cajun-style steak dinners. Skagway's best dish is Stowaway's wasabi salmon.

Starfire   THAI $$
(4th Ave, at Spring St; lunch mains $12-15, dinner mains $14-19; ☉lunch Mon-Fri, dinner daily; ☑) Skagway's restaurants are among the best in the Southeast, so why wouldn't its Thai be authentic and good? Order spicy drunken noodles or curry dishes in five colors (purple is *Fire with Flavor!*) and enjoy it with a beer on the outdoor patio – so pleasant and secluded you would never know Skagway's largest hotel is across the street.

YAKUTAT: ON THE EDGE OF NOWHERE

Isolated on the strand that connects the Southeast to the rest of Alaska, Yakutat – of all places – is now something of a tourist destination, admittedly a minor one. The main reason is improved transportation. You still can't drive to the most northern Southeast town, but in the late 1990s, it became a port for the **Alaska Marine Highway** (☑800-642-0066; www.ferryalaska.com) when the MV *Kennicott* began its cross-Gulf trips. Now the ferry stops twice a month during the summer, headed to either Juneau or Whittier, while **Alaska Airlines** (☑800-252-7522; www.alaskaair.com) stops daily both northbound and southbound.

What does Yakutat have to offer curious tourists? Big waves, a big and very active glacier and a lot of USFS cabins next to rivers with big salmon.

The waves rolling in from the Gulf of Alaska have made Yakutat the surf capital of the Far North. This town of 662 even has its own surf shop, the **Icy Waves Surf Shop** (☑907-784-3226; www.icywaves.com).

Just 30 miles north of Yakutat is **Hubbard Glacier**, the longest tidewater glacier in the world. The 76-mile-long glacier captured national attention by galloping across Russell Fjord in the mid-1980s, turning the long inlet into a lake. Eventually Hubbard receded, reopening the fjord, but in 2002 it again surged across Russell Fjord and came close to doing it a third time in 2011. The 8-mile-wide glacier is easily Alaska's most active. The rip tides and currents that flow between Gilbert Point and the face of the glacier, a mere 1000ft away, are so strong that they cause Hubbard to calve almost continuously at peak tides. The entire area, part of the 545-sq-mile **Russell Fjord Wilderness**, is one of the most interesting places in Alaska and usually visited through flightseeing or boat tours. The **Yakutat Charter Boat Co** (☑888-317-4987; www.alaska-charter.com) runs a four-hour tour of the area for $140 per person.

Yakutat has a dozen lodges and B&Bs, including the **Glacier Bear Lodge** (☑784-3202, 866-425-6343; www.glacierbearlodge.com; r $195; ☎). There are also 12 **USFS cabins** (☑877-444-6777, 518-885-3639; www.recreation.gov; cabins $25-35) in the area, five of them accessible via Forest Hwy 10, which extends east from Yakutat. Many are near rivers and lakes that are renowned, even by Alaskan standards, for sport fishing for salmon, steelhead trout and Dolly Varden.

For more information contact the **Yakutat Chamber of Commerce** (www.yakutataslaska.com) or the **USFS Yakutat Ranger Station** (☑784-3359).

Skagway Fish Company SEAFOOD $$$
(☎983-3474; Congress Way; lunch mains $10-17, dinner mains $16-36; ☺lunch & dinner) Located next to the Stowaway Café is this restaurant overlooking the harbor, with a horseshoe bar in the middle and crab traps on the ceiling. You can certainly feast on fish, such as halibut stuffed with cream cheese, shrimp and veggies or king-crab bisque, but surprisingly, what many locals rave about are its baby back ribs.

Glacial Smoothies & Espresso COFFEE HOUSE $
(336 3rd Ave; breakfasts $4-7, sandwiches $7-9; ☺6am-6pm; ☝) Skagway's favorite for breakfast bagels, healthy sandwiches and smoothies with names like Gold Rush (peaches, pineapple, banana) and Cabin Fever (peanut butter, chocolate, banana). This is where you come to idle away a rainy afternoon with a white-chocolate mocha.

Olivia's Bistro SEAFOOD $$
(Broadway St, at 7th Ave; breakfast & lunch mains $9-15, dinner mains $14-27; ☺breakfast & lunch Mon-Fri, dinner Thu-Sun; ☝) Creative cuisine has returned to the Skagway Inn. This trendy cafe builds its menu around fresh seafood and what grows in its gardens next to the inn. For breakfast you can order a crab-and-gouda omelet, for lunch a crock of rich halibut chowder and for dinner smoked salmon in a pastry puff. How can you top that? With a serving of homegrown rhubarb crisp for dessert.

Lemon Rose Bakery BAKERY $
(cnr of State St & 5th Ave; light fare $3-10; ☺breakfast & lunch) This bakery is so small, the line in the morning for its giant cinnamon rolls ($3) covered with glaciers of icing snakes out to the sidewalk. They're worth the wait.

Poppies ORGANIC $$
(Klondike Hwy; mains $9-16; ☺lunch; ☝) Located within Jewell Gardens, this restaurant has the best salads in town because the greens are grown just outside and probably picked that afternoon. Most of the other dishes also begin with organic ingredients and, best of all, are served with a view of the gardens in full bloom and AB Mountain looming overhead.

Northern Lights PIZZERIA $$
(3rd Ave btwn Broadway & State Sts; pizzas $18-24, pastas $13-22; ☺lunch & dinner) When you need to carbo-load for the Chilkoot, here's where

you come. Northern Lights has Skagway's best pizza, with dough made fresh daily, as well as pasta, including a great lasagna. Specialty pies range from vegetarian to Greek but, thank goodness, none with halibut or salmon on them.

You Say Tomato Natural Foods ORGANIC $
(21st Ave, at State St; ☺2-6:30pm Tue-Sat) Located in a replica of the Whitehorse Railroad Depot is this natural-foods store with organic produce.

Fairway Market SUPERMARKET $
(4th Ave, at State St) Skagway's lone grocer.

🍴 Drinking & Entertainment

Red Onion Saloon BAR
(Broadway St, at 2nd Ave) Skagway's beloved brothel at the turn of the century is now its most famous saloon. The 'RO' is done up as a gold-rush saloon, complete with mannequins leering down at you from the 2nd story to depict pioneer-era working girls. When bands are playing here, it'll be packed, noisy and rowdy.

Skagway Brewing Co BREWERY
(☎983-2739; Broadway St, at 7th Ave) Skagway's microbrew offers stampeders such choices as Prospector Pale Ale, Boomtown Brown and Chilkoot Trail IPA. There are also nightly dinner specials under $10 and a quiet outdoor deck in the back to escape the rowdiness at the front.

Bonanza Bar & Grill SPORTS BAR
(☎983-6214; Broadway St) With Guinness, Newcastle and many other excellent beers on tap and TVs on the wall, this is the closest thing Skagway has to a sports bar. Only this one serves a two-fisted Alaskan crab melt.

Days of '98 Show THEATER
(☎983-2545; Eagle's Hall, 598 Broadway, at 6th Ave; adult/child $22/11) This is Southeast Alaska's longest-running melodrama. The evening show begins with 'mock gambling,' then moves on to a show focusing on Soapy and his gang. Up to four shows are offered daily, but call as the schedule is heavily dependent on the cruise ships.

🛍 Shopping

Skaguay News Depot BOOKS
(www.skagwaybooks.com; 264 Broadway St; ☺9am-6pm) A small bookstore with an excellent selection on the Klondike Gold Rush.

ℹ️ Information

**Klondike Gold Rush National Historical Park
Visitor Center** (☑983-9223; www.nps.gov/
klgo; Broadway St, at 2nd Ave; ⊙8am-6pm)
For everything outdoors – local trails, public
campgrounds, NPS programs – head to the
NPS' center.

Post office (641 Broadway St) Next door to
Wells Fargo bank.

Skagway Convention & Visitors Bureau
(☑983-2854, 888-762-1898; www.skagway.
com; Broadway St, at 2nd Ave; ⊙8am-6pm
Mon-Fri, to 5pm Sat & Sun) For information on
lodging, tours or what's new, visit this bureau
housed in the can't-miss Arctic Brotherhood
Hall (think driftwood).

Skagway Library (8th Ave, at State St; ⊙noon-
9pm Mon-Fri, 1-5pm Sat & Sun; @🛜) Wi-fi
access is free, but its two internet computers
are heavily used.

Skagway Medical Clinic (☑983-2255; 340
11th Ave; ⊙9am-5pm) If gold fever strikes,
head to this clinic.

Skagway Port of Call (221 2nd Ave; internet
per 15 min/hr $1.25/5; ⊙9am-6:30pm Mon-
Thu, 9am-5pm Fri, 10am-4pm Sat, 8:30am-
4pm Sun) Makes a living, and probably a decent
one, selling cruise-ship workers high-speed
internet access on 20 computers, along with
phone cards and every brand of instant noodles
made in Asia.

Trail Center (☑983-9234, 800-661-0486;
Broadway St, at 2nd Ave; ⊙8am-5pm) If you're
stampeding to the Chilkoot Trail, first stop here
in the restored Martin Itjen House at the foot
of Broadway. The center is a clearinghouse for
information on permits and transportation.

Wells Fargo (Broadway St, at 6th Ave) Occupies
the original office of National Bank of Alaska.

ℹ️ Getting There & Away

AIR Regularly scheduled flights from Skagway
to Juneau ($118) and Haines ($59) are available
from **Wings of Alaska** (☑983-2442; www.wing
sofalaska.com).

BOAT There is a daily run of the **Alaska Marine
Highway** (☑983-2229, 800-642-0066; www.
ferryalaska.com) from Skagway to Haines ($31,
one hour) and Juneau ($50, 6½ hours) and back
again. In Skagway, the ferry departs from the
terminal and dock at the southwest end of Broadway St. **Haines-Skagway Fast Ferry** (☑888-
766-2103; www.hainesskagwayfastferry.com)
provides speedy transportation on a catamaran
to Haines. The boat departs from the Skagway
small-boat harbor at 8am, noon and 6pm Monday through Thursday in summer, with additional
trips if needed by the cruise ships. One-way fares
are adult/child $35/18; round-trip $68/34. In

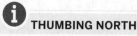

Hitchhiking the Klondike Hwy out of
Skagway is best just after a state ferry
pulls in, and even then it's challenging.
Backpackers thumbing north would do
better buying a $31 ferry ticket to Haines
and trying the Haines Hwy instead, as it
has considerably more traffic.

2012 the **Chilkat Express** (☑766-4000, 855-
766-4001; www.chilkatferry.com) will start running ferry services between the two towns.

BUS Yukon-Alaska Tourist Tours (☑866-
626-7383, in Whitehorse 867-668-5944; www.
yukonalaskatouristtours.com) offers a minibus
service to Whitehorse (one way $60), departing
the train depot in Skagway at 2pm daily except
Sunday. **Alaska Direct Bus Line** (☑800-770-
6652, 867-668-4833 in Whitehorse; www.
alaskadirectbusline.com) runs a bus on Sunday,
Wednesday and Friday from Whitehorse for
either Anchorage ($240) or Fairbanks ($210).

TRAIN It's possible to travel part way to Whitehorse, Yukon Territory, on the **White Pass &
Yukon Route** (☑983-2217, 800-343-7373; www.
whitepassrailroad.com), then complete the trip
with a bus connection at Carcross, Yukon Territory. The northbound train departs from the
Skagway depot at 7:30am Sunday, Wednesday
and Thursday in summer, and passengers arrive
in Whitehorse by bus at 5pm Yukon time. The
one-way fare is adult/child $195/97; it's three
times what the Yukon-Alaska Tourist Tours bus
costs, but many feel the ride on the historic,
narrow-gauge railroad is worth it.

ℹ️ Getting Around

CAR Sourdough Car Rental (☑983-2523; 6th
Ave, at Broadway St) has compacts for $69 a day
with unlimited miles. In Skagway, there's a 14%
tax on rental cars.

PUBLIC TRANSPORTATION The city operates
the **SMART bus** (☑983-2743; single ride/day
pass $2/5) that moves people (primarily cruise-
ship passengers) from the docks up Broadway
St and to Jewell Gardens and the Klondike Gold
Dredge on the edge of town.

TAXI Just about every taxi and tour company in
Skagway will run you out to Dyea and the trailhead for the Chilkoot Trail, and the price hasn't
gone up in years – $10 per person. **Frontier
Excursions** (☑983-2512, 877-983-2512; www.
frontierexcursions.com; Broadway St, at 7th
Ave) has trips daily.

BICYCLE Several places in town rent bikes, but
Sockeye Cycle (p146) has the best bikes.

Anchorage & Around

Best Places to Eat

» Snow City Café (p167)

» Maxine's Glacier City Bistro (p181)

» Bear Tooth Grill (p171)

» Turkey Red (p189)

» Modern Dwellers Chocolate Lounge (p167)

Best Places to Stay

» Copper Whale Inn (p164)

» Anchorage Downtown Hotel (p165)

» Hatcher Pass Lodge (p187)

» Wildflower Inn (p164)

» Eklutna Lake State Recreation Area (p185)

Why Go?

Once you realize that Anchorage isn't simply a big city on the edge of the wilderness but rather a big city in the wilderness, it starts to make sense. The town manages to mingle hiking trails and traffic jams, small art galleries and Big Oil, like no other city. Among big box stores and mini-malls, there's more than 100 miles of city trails meandering in hidden greenbelts and a creek splitting downtown where anglers line up to catch trophy salmon.

Towering behind the municipality is the nation's third-largest state park, the half-million-acre Chugach. The wilderness is never far, which is why Anchorage's young population (the average age is 32) is an active one. Stay for a few days, explore the cycle trails, patronize the art galleries and dine in Alaska's best restaurants, and you'll understand why half the state's population chooses to live in and around this city.

When to Go
Anchorage

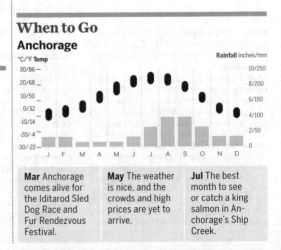

Mar Anchorage comes alive for the Iditarod Sled Dog Race and Fur Rendezvous Festival.

May The weather is nice, and the crowds and high prices are yet to arrive.

Jul The best month to see or catch a king salmon in Anchorage's Ship Creek.

ANCHORAGE

POP 291,826

History

Though British explorer Captain James Cook sailed past the site in 1779 in search of the elusive Northwest Passage, and hopeful gold prospectors had been visiting Ship Creek since the 1880s, Anchorage wasn't founded until 1915. That was the year the Alaska Railroad called the area home and the 'Great Anchorage Lot Sale' was held. A tent city of 2000 people popped up in no time.

Anchorage soon became the epicenter for Alaska's fledgling rail, air and highway systems. The Depression-era colonizing of the Matanuska Valley, WWII and the discovery of Cook Inlet oil in the 1950s all added to the explosive growth of these years. Anchorage's population, 8000 before WWII, then jumped to 43,000. After the 1964 Good Friday Earthquake, which dumped more than 100 homes into Knik Arm, the city was rebuilding itself when another opportunity arose: the discovery of a $10 billion oil reserve in Prudhoe Bay.

Although the Trans-Alaska Pipeline doesn't come within 300 miles of Anchorage, the city took its share of the wealth, growing a further 47% between 1970 and 1976. As the headquarters of various petroleum and service companies, Anchorage still manages to gush with oil money.

This city of stage plays and snowy peaks also has serious pork-barrel power. During the late 1970s, when a barrel of crude oil jumped more than $20 and Alaska couldn't spend its tax revenue fast enough, Anchorage received the lion's share. It used its political muscle to revitalize downtown Anchorage with the Sullivan Arena, Egan Civic Center and stunning Alaska Center for the Performing Arts.

◉ Sights

DOWNTOWN ANCHORAGE

Anchorage Museum   MUSEUM
(Map p162; ☑929-9200; www.anchoragemuseum. org; 625 C St; adult/child $12/7; ☺9am-6pm; ⬛) What was once simply Alaska's best museum is now a world-class facility thanks to a $106 million expansion of Anchorage's cultural jewel that was completed with much anticipation in 2010. The new West Wing, a four-story, shimmering, mirrored facade, added 80,000 sq ft to what was already the largest museum in the state. Its flagship exhibit is the Smithsonian Arctic Studies Center with more than 600 Alaska Native objects – art,

tools, masks and household implements – which was previously housed in Washington DC. It's the largest Alaska Native collection anywhere and it's surrounded by large video screens showing contemporary Native life. Nearby is the Listening Space where you can listen to storytellers and natural sounds from Arctic Alaska.

The museum now also contains the Imaginarium Discovery Center, a hands-on science center for children that was previously housed in a separate downtown location. On the 1st floor of the original East Wing you will still find the Art of the North Gallery, with entire rooms of Alaskan masters Eustace Ziegler and Sydney Laurence. On the 2nd floor, the Alaska History Gallery is filled with life-size dioramas that trace 10,000 years of human settlement, from early subsistence villages to modern oil dependency.

There are also galleries devoted to traveling art exhibits, a planetarium and the Kid-Space Gallery designed for young children (and their parents) to explore the worlds of art, history and science through hands-on play. Clearly, this is a place where you can spend an entire afternoon.

FREE Ship Creek Viewing Platform   LOOKOUT
(off Map p162) From mid- to late summer, king, coho and pink salmon spawn up Ship Creek, the historical site of Tanaina Indian fish camps. At the overlook you can cheer on those love-starved fish humping their way toward destiny, and during high tide see the banks lined with anglers trying to hook them in what has to be one of the greatest urban fisheries anywhere in the USA. Follow C St north as it crosses Ship Creek Bridge and then turn right on Whitney Rd. Nearby is the Bait Shack (off Map p162; ☑522-3474; www.the baitshackak.com; 212 N Whitney Rd; ☺6am-10pm) that will rent you the rod, reel, waders and tackle needed to catch a trophy king.

Oscar Anderson House   HISTORIC BUILDING
(Map p162; www.anchoragehistoricproperties.org; 420 M St; adult/child $5/3; ☺noon-5pm Mon-Wed) Housed in the city's oldest wooden-framed home, this little museum overlooks the delightful Elderberry Park. Anderson was the 18th person to set foot in Anchorage, and he built his house in 1915. Today it's the only home museum in Anchorage, and despite past budget problems it's open June to mid-September as a reminder that there's not a single building in this city a century old.

Anchorage & Around Highlights

1 Spending an afternoon at the new **Anchorage Museum** (p153), soaking up Alaskan culture and art

2 Pedaling the scenic **Tony Knowles Coastal Trail** (p158) with views of the Alaska Range on the way to Kincaid Park

3 Checking out the artistic salmon spawning in Anchorage during **Wild Salmon on Parade** (p166)

4 Enjoying a microbrew and sunset at the outdoor deck of **Snow Goose Restaurant** (p170) in Anchorage

5 Watching the amazing bore tide fill Turnagain Arm in one swoop near **Beluga Point** (p179)

6 Riding the **Alyeska Resort Tram** (p179) for an alpine hike and lunch above the treeline

7 Exploring **Eklutna Lake** (p185) by combining a day of kayaking and mountain biking

8 Seeing 100lb cabbages and softball-sized radishes at the **Alaska State Fair** (p188) in Palmer

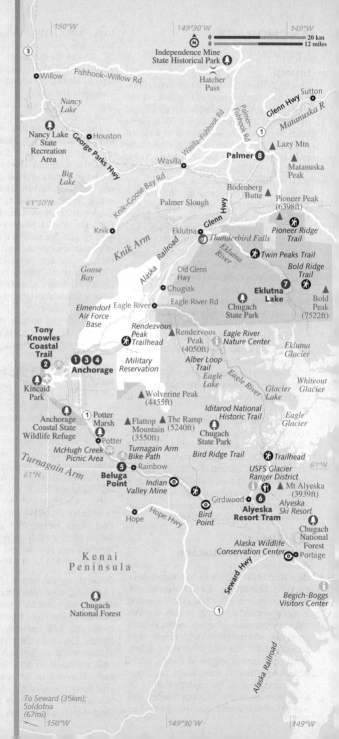

FREE **4th Avenue Market Place/Village of Ship Creek Center** MARKET
(Map p162; 333 W 4th Ave; ⊙10am-7pm Mon-Sat, 11am-6pm Sun) This shopping mall contains the usual gift shops, but also a lot of history. Painted on the walls outside is a historic timeline of Anchorage, while inside are displays devoted to the 1964 Good Friday Earthquake.

Resolution Park MONUMENT
(Map p162) At the west end of 3rd Ave, this small park is home to the **Captain Cook Monument**, built to mark the 200th anniversary of the English captain's 'discovery' of Cook Inlet. If not overrun by tour-bus passengers, this observation deck has an excellent view of the surrounding mountains. Nearby, on 2nd Ave, is the **Alaska Statehood Monument**, marking the original 1915 town site with a bust of oft-ignored President Ike Eisenhower.

Delaney Park PARK
(Map p162) Known locally as the Delaney Park Strip, this narrow slice of well-tended grass stretches from A to P Sts between W 9th and W 10th Aves; there's an impressive **playground** near the corner of E St. The park was the site of the 50-ton bonfire celebrating statehood in 1959 and Pope John Paul II's 1981 outdoor mass. Today it hosts festivals like Summer Solstice and Pridefest, not to mention Frisbee games any time the weather's nice.

MIDTOWN ANCHORAGE & SPENARD

FREE **Alaska Heritage Museum** MUSEUM
(Map p158; 301 W Northern Lights Blvd; ⊙noon-4pm Mon-Fri) Inside the midtown Wells Fargo bank, this museum is home to the largest private collection of Alaska Native artifacts in the state and includes costumes, baskets and hunting weapons. There are also original paintings covering the walls, including several by Sydney Laurence, and lots of scrimshaw. The museum's collection is so large that there are displays in the elevator lobbies throughout the bank.

Alaska Aviation Heritage Museum MUSEUM
(off Map p158; www.alaskaairmuseum.org; 4721 Aircraft Dr; adult/child $10/6; ⊙9am-5pm) Ideally located on the south shore of Lake Hood, the world's busiest floatplane lake, this museum is a tribute to Alaska's colorful bush pilots and their faithful planes. Housed within are 25 planes along with historic photos and dis-

ℹ **CULTURE PASS JOINT TICKET**

Anchorage's top two attractions, the Alaska Native Heritage Center and the Anchorage Museum, can both be enjoyed at a 22% discount with a special joint-admission ticket. The **Culture Pass Joint Ticket** is $29 per person and includes admission to both museums as well as shuttle transportation between them. You can purchase the joint pass from the ticket offices at either location.

plays of pilots' achievements, from the first flight to Fairbanks (1913) to the early history of Alaska Airlines. You can view early footage of bush planes in the museum's theater or step outside to its large observation deck and watch today's pilots begin their own quest for adventure with a roar on Lake Hood.

GREATER ANCHORAGE

Alaska Native Heritage Center CULTURAL CENTER
(Map p156; ☑330-8000, 800-315-6608; www.alaskanative.net; 8800 Heritage Center Dr; adult/child $25/17; ⊙9am-5pm) To experience Alaska Native culture firsthand, you can travel to the Bush or come to this 26-acre center and see how humans survived – and thrived – before central heating.

The main building houses meandering exhibits on traditional arts and sciences – including kayaks and rain gear that rival outdoors department store REI's best offerings. It also features various performances, among them the staccato Alaghanak song, lost for 50 years: the center collected bits and pieces of the traditional song from different tribal elders and reconstructed it. Outside, examples of typical structures from the Aleut, Yupik, Tlingit and other tribes are arranged around a picturesque lake. Docents explain the ancient architects' cunning technology: check out wooden panels that shrink in the dry summers (allowing light and air inside) but expand to seal out the cold during the wet winter.

This is much more than just a museum; it represents a knowledge bank of language, art and culture that will survive no matter how many sitcoms are crackling through the Alaskan stratosphere. It's a labor of love, and of incalculable value.

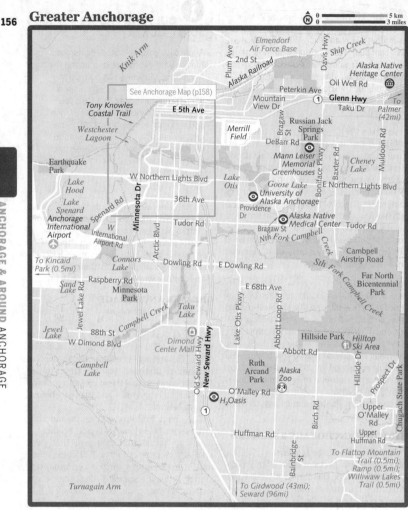

△ 0 ─── 5 km
Ⓝ 0 ─── 3 miles

Knik Arm

Elmendorf
Air Force Base

Plum Ave
2nd St
Alaska Railroad

Davis Hwy · Ship Creek

Alaska Native
Heritage Center ⊕

Oil Well Rd

Peterkin Ave

Mountain ① **Glenn Hwy**
View Dr
Taku Dr   To
Palmer
(42mi)

Tony Knowles
Coastal Trail

*Westchester
Lagoon*

See Anchorage Map (p158)

E 5th Ave

Merrill
Field

Russian Jack
Springs
Park

DeBarr Rd ◎

Mann Leiser
Memorial
Greenhouses

Cheney
Lake

*Earthquake
Park*

*Lake
Hood*

*Lake
Spenard*

Anchorage
International
Airport ✈

W Northern Lights Blvd

36th Ave

Tudor Rd

Lake
Otis

Goose Lake
University of
Alaska Anchorage

E Northern Lights Blvd

Providence
Dr

Alaska Native
Medical Center   Tudor Rd

Bragaw St
Nth Fork Campbell Creek

Sth Fork Campbell Creek

Campbell
Airstrip Road

To Kincaid
Park (0.5mi)

Connors
Lake

Dowling Rd

E Dowling Rd

*Sand
Lake*

Raspberry Rd
Minnesota
Park

E 68th Ave

Far North
Bicentennial
Park

*Jewel
Lake*

88th St
W Dimond Blvd

Campbell Creek

Taku
Lake

Dimond
Center Mall

Lake Otis Pkwy

Abbott Loop Rd

Hillside Park   Hilltop
Ski Area ⛷

*Campbell
Lake*

Abbott Rd

Ruth
Arcand
Park

Alaska
Zoo

O'Malley Rd
① H₂Oasis

Birch Rd

Upper
O'Malley
Rd

Upper
Huffman Rd

Huffman Rd

Bainbridge St

Prospect Dr

Chugach State Park

To Flattop Mountain
Trail (0.5mi);
Ramp (0.5mi);
Williwaw Lakes
Trail (0.5mi)

Turnagain Arm

To Girdwood (43mi);
Seward (96mi)

Alaska Botanical Garden   GARDENS
(www.alaskabg.org; 4601 Campbell Airstrip Rd;
adult/child $5/free; ☺daylight hr) The gar-
den is a colorful showcase for native species, where gentle paths lead you through
groomed herb, rock and perennial gardens
in a wooded setting. The mile-long Lowen-
fels Family Nature Trail – built for tanks
during WWII – is a great place to learn your
basic Alaskan botany or just to stroll and
watch the bald eagles pluck salmon from
Campbell Creek. Guided tours are offered
daily at 1pm.

FREE **Alaska Native Medical
Center**   GALLERY
(Map p156; 4315 Diplomacy Dr; ☺24hr) This hospital has a fantastic collection of Alaska Native art and artifacts: take the elevator to
the top floor and wind down the staircase
past dolls, basketry and tools from all over
Alaska.

Earthquake Park   PARK
(Map p156) For decades after the 1964 earthquake, this park remained a barren moon-
scape revealing the tectonic power that
destroyed nearby Turnagain Heights. Today

Earthquake Park, at the west end of Northern Lights Blvd on the Knik Arm, is being reclaimed by nature; you'll have to poke around the bushes to see evidence of tectonic upheaval.

University of Alaska Anchorage UNIVERSITY
(Map p156; www.uaa.alaska.edu; Providence Dr) UA-Anchorage is the largest college campus in the state, but there is far less to do here than at its sister school, UA Fairbanks. The Campus Center is home to a small art gallery and the bookstore, which has a good selection of Alaskana, clothing that says 'Alaska' on it and used microbiology texts. Take buses 1, 3, 13, 36, 45 or 102. There are trails from the campus that connect UA to Goose Lake, Chester Creek Greenbelt and Earthquake Park.

Goose Lake PARK
(Map p156; UA Dr) You'll stop complaining about global warming once you experience an 85°F Anchorage afternoon at Goose Lake. Just off Northern Lights Blvd (buses 3 and 45), this is the city's most developed lake for swimming, with lifeguards, paddleboat rentals and a small cafe, which serves fresh-baked pizza.

Russian Jack Springs Park PARK
(Map p156) Named after the original homesteader of the site, this 300-acre park is south of Glenn Hwy on Boniface Pkwy and can be reached by buses 8, 45 and 15. The park has tennis courts, hiking and cycling trails, and a picnic area. Near the DeBarr Rd entrance, you'll find the Mann Leiser Memorial Greenhouses (343-4717; 8am-3pm), a toasty oasis of tropical plants, exotic birds and fish.

Far North Bicentennial Park PARK
(Map p156) Comprising 4000 acres of forest and muskeg in east central Anchorage, this park features 20 miles of trails. In the center of the park is the Bureau of Land Management's (BLM's) Campbell Tract, a 700-acre wildlife preserve where it's possible to see moose and bears in the spring and brilliant fall colors in mid-September. Take O'Malley Rd east to Hillside Dr and follow the signs. There is an active grizzly population, and it's wise to steer clear of salmon streams during the twilight hours.

Kincaid Park PARK
(off Map p156) At the western 'nose' of the peninsula and southern terminus of the

First time in Anchorage? Not to worry. Alaska's largest city has a pedestrian-friendly downtown that is arranged in a regular grid: numbered avenues run east–west and lettered streets north–south. East of A St, street names continue alphabetically, beginning with Barrow. The grid begins to break down as you leave downtown, but numbered streets remain reliable.

When it's time to leave, 5th Ave heads northeast from downtown and becomes Glenn Hwy, the route to Fairbanks and Valdez. To the south, C St becomes New Seward Hwy that continues on to the Kenai Peninsula. Flying home? Heading due south, L St becomes Spenard Rd, which runs through midtown and Spenard en route to the airport.

Tony Knowles Coastal Trail is this beloved 1400-acre park populated by mountain bikers in the summer and Nordic skiers in the winter. Trails wind through a rolling terrain of forested hills where there are views of Mt Susitna and Mt McKinley on a clear day and fiery sunsets in the evening. From certain spots on the coastal trail you can stand directly under incoming jets. Follow Raspberry Rd west to the parking lot and trailheads.

Activities

Cycling

Anchorage has 122 miles of paved paths that parallel major roads or wind through the greenbelts, making a bicycle the easiest and cheapest way to explore the city. If you run out of gas before the end of the ride, all People Mover buses are equipped with bike racks.

Downtown Bicycle Rental BICYCLE RENTAL
(Map p162; 279-5293; www.alaska-bike-rentals. com; 333 W 4th Ave; per 3/24hr $16/32; 8am-8pm) Has road, hybrid and mountain bikes as well as tandems, trailers and even clip-in pedals and shoes. Locks, helmets and bike maps are free and the staff is a wealth of information on where to ride.

Pablo's Bicycle Rental BICYCLE RENTAL
(Map p162; www.pablobicyclerentals.com; 5th & L St; per 3/24hr $15/30; 8am-7pm) Bicycles and hotdogs to go.

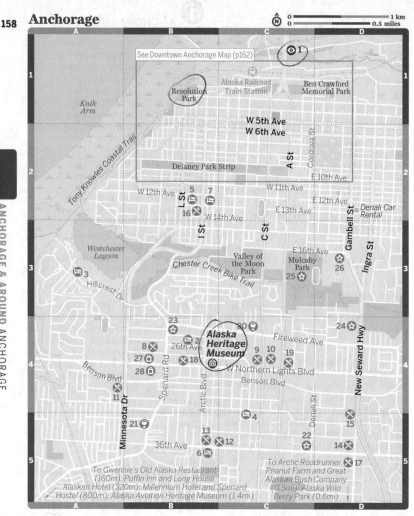

CYCLE TRAILS

Anchorage is a haven for mountain biking, with the most popular areas being Kincaid Park, Far North Bicentennial Park and Powerline Pass Trail in Chugach State Park.

Tony Knowles Coastal Trail CYCLING
(Map p162) Anchorage's favorite trail is the Tony Knowles Coastal Trail, 11 scenic miles that begin at the west end of 2nd Ave downtown and reach Elderberry Park a mile away. From there, the trail winds through Earthquake Park, around Point Woronzof and finally to Point Campbell in Kincaid Park. There are good views of Knik Arm and the Alaska Range along the way, and the Anchorage Lightspeed Planet Walk.

Ship Creek Bike Trail CYCLING
(Map p162) The newest ribbon of asphalt for cyclists runs 2.6 miles from the Alaska Railroad depot along the namesake creek and into the Mountain View neighborhood. Here you can watch aggressive anglers fish for salmon as you wind through woods and industry.

Chester Creek Bike Trail CYCLING
(Map p158) This scenic 6-mile path through the Chester Creek Greenbelt connects with the

coastal trail at Westchester Lagoon and follows a mountain-fed stream to Goose Lake.

Campbell Creek Trail CYCLING
Campbell Creek Trail features some of the newest paved path in Anchorage, stretching 8 miles from Far North Bicentennial Park to the Seward Hwy, with most of the ride in the Campbell Creek Greenbelt.

Hiking

Though there are dozens of trails in town, outdoors enthusiasts head to 773-sq-mile Chugach State Park for the mother lode.

Flattop Mountain Trail HIKING
(off Map p156) In Los Angeles, you cruise the Sunset Strip; in Paris, you stroll the Champs-Élysées; and in Anchorage, you climb Flattop Mountain. This is the first mountain every Anchorage youth scales on the way to higher things. The very popular 3-mile round-trip hike to the 3550ft peak is easy to follow, though you'll be scrambling at the summit. Allow three to five hours. Another trail continues 3 more miles along the ridgeline to Flaketop Peak. From the same parking area, you can also access the 2-mile Blueberry Loop (perfect for kids) and 11-mile Powerline Pass Trail, popular with mountain bikers.

From Seward Hwy, head 4 miles east on O'Malley Dr and make a right on Hillside Rd; after 1 mile make a left on Upper Huffman Rd and follow the signs to the Glen Alps park entrance. Parking is $5. For transportation there's **Flattop Mountain Shuttle** (🕿279-5293; www.hike-anchorage-alaska.com; round-trip adult/child $22/15) which leaves Downtown Bicycle Rental on 4th Ave at 1pm and 7pm daily.

Ramp HIKING
(off Map p156) The 14-mile round-trip hike to the Ramp starts close to the Flattop Mountain trailhead and takes you past alpine summits and through tranquil tundra. Rather than following the upper trail to Flattop Mountain, hike half a mile to the Powerline Pass Trail. Turn right and follow the power line for 2 miles, where an old jeep trail crosses over from the left and heads downhill to the south fork of Campbell Creek.

The trail then crosses the creek and continues to a valley on the other side. Hike up the alpine valley to Ship Lake Pass, which lies between the 5240ft Ramp and the 4660ft Wedge, with great camping and climbing. Allow eight to 10 hours.

Williwaw Lakes Trail   HIKING
(off Map p156) This easy 13-mile hike also begins close to the Flattop Mountain trailhead, leading to the handful of alpine lakes at the base of Mt Williwaw. The trail makes a pleasant overnight hike and many consider it the most scenic outing in the Hillside area of Chugach State Park.

Walk half a mile to the Powerline Pass Trail and then turn right, continuing 300yd to the Middle Fork Loop Trail. Follow it down and across the south fork of Campbell Creek, then north for 1.5 miles to the middle fork of the creek. Here you reach a junction; make a right on Williwaw Lakes Trail. You can make this an overnight trek or a seven- to nine-hour day hike.

Wolverine Peak Trail   HIKING
This strenuous but rewarding 14-mile round-trip ascends the 4455ft triangular peak, visible from Anchorage. The marked trail begins at an old homesteader road that crosses the south fork of Campbell Creek. Keep heading east and the road will become a footpath that ascends above the treeline and eventually fades out (mark it for the return trip). From there, it's 3 miles to Wolverine Peak.

From Seward Hwy, go 4 miles east on O'Malley Rd, turn left on Hillside Dr and follow signs to the Prospect Heights entrance of Chugach State Park. Parking costs $5.

Rendezvous Peak Route   HIKING
The 4-mile trek to this 4050ft peak is an easy three- to five-hour trip, rewarding hikers with incredible views of Mt McKinley, Cook Inlet, Turnagain and Knik Arms, and the city far below. From the parking lot, a short trail leads along the right-hand side of the stream up the valley to the northwest. It ends at a pass where a short ascent to Rendezvous Peak is easily seen and climbed.

From Glenn Hwy, exit Arctic Valley Rd (Fort Richardson) and follow signs to Arctic Valley; a 7-mile gravel road leads to the Alpenglow Ski Area parking lot. Parking costs $5.

McHugh Lake Trail   HIKING
This 13-mile trail originates at McHugh Creek Picnic Area, 15 miles south of Anchorage at Mile 111.8 of the Seward Hwy. The route follows the McHugh Creek valley, and in 7 miles reaches Rabbit and McHugh Lakes, two beautiful alpine pools reflecting the 5000ft Suicide Peaks.

The first 3 miles feature some good climbs, and the round-trip trek makes for a long day. It's better to haul in a tent and then spend the afternoon exploring the open tundra country and nearby ridges.

Anchorage for Children
Anchorage is exceptionally kid-friendly – more than 40 city parks boast playscapes. Close to downtown, Frontierland Park (Map p162; 10th Ave & E St) is a local favorite, while Valley of the Moon Park (Arctic Blvd & W 17th St) makes a delightful picnic spot. Entice your family to the Anchorage Museum by promising to first explore Imaginarium, the wonderful hands-on science center for children.

Alaska Zoo   ZOO
(Map p156; www.alaskazoo.org; 4731 O'Malley Rd; adult/child $12/6; ☺9am-6pm Sat-Mon, Wed & Thu, to 9pm Tue & Fri) The unique wildlife of the Arctic is on display at this zoo, the only one in North America that specializes in northern animals, including snow leopards, Amur tigers and Tibetan yaks. Alaskan native species, from wolverines and moose to caribou and Dall sheep, are abundant. What kids will love watching, however, are the bears. The zoo has all four Alaskan species (brown, black, glacier and polar) but Ahpun, the polar bear, is clearly the star attraction.

FREE Anchorage Lightspeed Planet Walk   WALK
(Map p162) A massive sun sits at the corner of 5th Ave and G St, marking the start of this built-to-scale model of the solar system. There are colorful interpretive displays for each of the planets; the first four planets can be reached within a few blocks of the sun but Pluto is out in Kincaid Park. The scale is set so that walking pace mimics the speed of light, but it'll take you all day to reach marble-sized Pluto at that pace. Travel faster than the speed of light by renting a mountain bike.

Bear & Raven Adventure Theatre   AMUSEMENT PARK
(Map p162; www.bearsquare.net; 315 E St; adult/child $12.50/10.50; ☺10am-8:30pm) This mini-amusement park is a cheesy but easy downtown break from shopping. The littlest ones will likely be bored with the 30-minute

video, but the virtual 'rides' (reeling in a salmon, for example) ought to satisfy them.

H2Oasis
SWIMMING

(Map p156; www.h2oasiswaterpark.com; 1520 O'Malley Rd; adult/child $24/19; ⊙10am-9pm Mon-Sat, to 8pm Sun) Qualifying as surreal, Anchorage's original water park is a $7 million, three-level amusement zone with palm trees, water slides, a wave pool and the 505ft Master Blaster, one very wet roller coaster. Feel free to just watch from the grown-ups-only hot tubs.

FREE Alaska Wild Berry Park
PARK

(off Map p158; www.alaskawildberryproducts.com; 5525 Juneau St; ⊙11am-7pm) If the Flattop Mountain hike is overly ambitious for your kids, head to this giant jam and gift shop with chocolate falls. It's definitely a tourist trap, but who can resist a 20ft chocolate waterfall? Outside there's a short nature trail leading to a handful of reindeer that kids can feed and pet.

☞ Tours

City Tours

Anchorage City Trolley Tours
BUS

(Map p162; (☏775-5603, 888-917-8687; www.alaskatrolley.com; 612 W 4th Ave; adult/child $15/7.50; ⊙9am-5pm) One-hour rides in a bright red trolley past Lake Hood, Earthquake Park and Cook Inlet, among other sights. Tours depart on the hour.

Anchorage Historical Tours
WALK

(Map p162; www.anchoragehistoricproperties.org; 524 W 4th Ave; adult/child $5/1) This hour-long downtown walking tour begins in the lobby of the Historic City Hall at 1pm, Monday to Friday.

Gray Line
BUS

(Map p162; ☏277-5581, 800-544-2206; www.graylineofalaska.com; Hilton Anchorage, 500 West 3rd Ave) A three-hour bus tour covers downtown plus the Alaska Native Heritage Center (adult/child $54/27).

Flightseeing Tours

They're costly and never as long as you wish, but they're a stunning way to spend an hour or two. If you've got the cash – lots of it – flightseeing tours provide an eagle-eye view of the wilderness and mountains, imparting a sense of scale that's difficult to appreciate from the ground.

Regal Air
SCENIC FLIGHTS

(☏243-8535; www.regal-air.com) Flying out of Lake Hood, this has some of the best rates for flightseeing. Its three-hour Mt McKinley tour is only $375, while a 1½-hour tour of Knik Glacier is $225.

Rust's Flying Service
SCENIC FLIGHTS

(☏243-1595, 800-544-2299; www.flyrusts.com) Offers a three-hour Mt McKinley flight that includes flying the length of Ruth Glacier ($375) and a three-hour Columbia Glacier tour ($335).

Day Tours

Have a leftover day? Have an adventure. There are few places in Alaska that somebody in Anchorage isn't willing to whisk you off to in a day.

Alaska Railroad
GLACIERS

(Map p162; ☏265-2494, 800-544-0552; www.akrr.com; 411 W 1st Ave) Has a number of one-day tours from Anchorage that begin with a train ride. Its nine-hour Spencer Glacier Float Tour (per person $202) includes a ride

---

GHOSTLY TOURS OF ANCHORAGE

In Anchorage you can sign up for a city tour, a tour on a trolley or a walking tour with a guide dressed (somewhat) like Captain Cook. Or you can be really brave and join Ghost Tours of Anchorage (☏274-4678; per person $15; ⊙7:30pm).

Oooooh! Now that's scary.

First offered in 2011, the tours have been a hit with out-of-towners who can't seem to get enough grizzly Alaskan tales of murder and mayhem. Among the stops during the 90-minute downtown walk is the Anchorage Club, where the staff will only go into the basement in pairs; the Gaslight Lounge with its unexplained noises, seismic activity and a jukebox that kicks on by itself; and the Historic Anchorage Hotel, which is said to have at least 32 'entities' as permanent guests.

The ghost tours take place nightly from mid-May to mid-September. To join, just show up in front of Snow City Café at 4th Ave and L St – site of perhaps the most notorious murder in Anchorage's history.

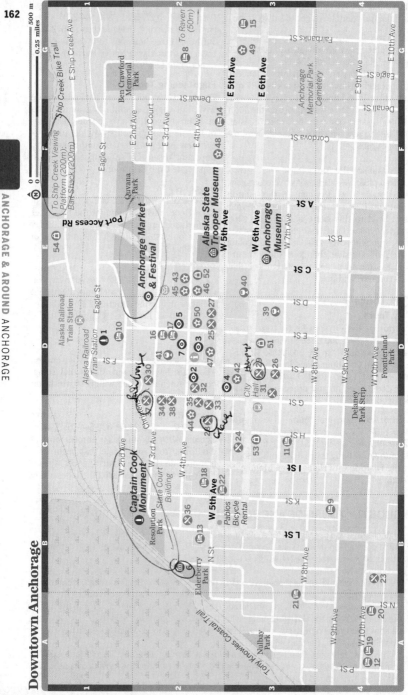

Downtown Anchorage

0.25 miles
500 m

To Ship Creek Viewing
Platform (200m);
Bait Shack (200m)

Ship Creek Bike Trail

E Ship Creek Ave

To Raven (50m)

Ben Crawford
Memorial Park

Quyana Park

Anchorage Market & Festival

Port Access Rd

Captain Cook Monument

Resolution Park

State Court Building

Pablos Bicycle Rental

Elderberry Park

Tony Knowles Coastal Trail

Nuluv Park

Alaska Railroad Train Station

Alaska Railroad Train Station

City Hall

Alaska State Trooper Museum
W 5th Ave

Anchorage Museum
W 6th Ave

Delaney Park Strip

Frontierland Park

Anchorage Memorial Park Cemetery

W 2nd Ave
W 3rd Ave
W 4th Ave
W 5th Ave
W 8th Ave
W 9th Ave
W 10th Ave

E 2nd Ave
E 2nd Court
E 3rd Ave
E 4th Ave
E 5th Ave
E 6th Ave
E 9th Ave
E 10th Ave

N St
L St
K St
A St
B St
C St
D St
E St
F St
H St
I St
P St
N St

Eagle St
Denali St
Cordova St
Fairbanks St
Eagle St

to Spencer Lake and a gentle raft trip among the glacier's icebergs. The Glacier Adventure Cruise ($199) is a train ride to Whittier and a four-hour boat cruise in Prince William Sound to watch glaciers calve while feasting on king crab cakes for lunch.

Phillips Cruises & Tours   BOAT

(Map p162; ☎276-8023, 800-544-0529; www.26glaciers.com; 519 W 4th Ave) Takes you by bus to Whittier and then on a boat past

26 glaciers in Prince William Sound. The eight-hour tour (adult/child $189/104) is offered daily and includes lunch.

Alaska's Finest Tours   BUS

(☎764-2067; www.akfinest.com) Several companies will take you on a six-hour tour of Turnagain Arm that will include a boat cruise to the face of Portage Glacier and the Alaska Wildlife Conservation Center. This one will do it for $99 per person.

⚜ Festivals & Events

These are just a few of Anchorage's more popular events; contact the **Anchorage Convention & Visitors Bureau** (✆276-3200; www.anchorage.net/events) to see what's on while you're here.

Anchorage Fur Rendezvous CULTURAL
(www.furrondy.net) The place to get fresh-trapped furs is still the 'Rondy,' but most folks prefer to sculpt ice, ride the Ferris wheel in freezing temperatures in February or March, or watch the 'Running of the Reindeer.' When the Rondy ends, the famed 1100-mile Iditarod Trail sled dog race to Nome begins. Better stay another week.

Three Barons Renaissance Fair CULTURAL
(www.3barons.org; 3400 E Tudor Rd; adult/child $8/3) Duchesses, counts, knights and wenches gather for revelry, merriment and drinking at the Crooked Toad Tavern for a week in early June at Tozier Track.

Spenard Jazz Fest JAZZ
(www.spenardjazzfest.org) For 10 days in early June, cool, trendy and local jazz musicians stage concerts and workshops throughout Anchorage.

🛌 Sleeping

Several new hostels in town are helping bring the cost of sleeping down, but Anchorage is expensive. Tack on the city's 12% sales-and-bed tax to the prices given here.

Chugach State Park has several public campgrounds, but none are close to town.

DOWNTOWN ANCHORAGE

TOP CHOICE Copper Whale Inn INN $$$
(Map p162; ✆258-7999; www.copperwhale.com; W 5th Ave & L St; r $185-220; ❀@🛜) An ideal downtown location, recently remodeled rooms and a bright and elegant interior make this gay-friendly inn one of the best top-end places in Anchorage. There are two relaxing waterfall courtyards in which to consume that novel, while many rooms and the breakfast lounge give way to views of Cook Inlet. Are those beluga whales out there?

Anchorage Downtown Hotel BOUTIQUE HOTEL $$$
(Map p162; ✆907-258-7669, 886-787-2423; www.anchoragedowntownhotel.com; 826 K St; r $189-212; ❀🛜) Recently remodeled, this not-so-downtown hotel is a very pleasant place to stay, with 16 colorful and comfortable rooms that feature private baths, coffeemakers and small refrigerators. In the morning you're handed a newspaper, in the evening a glass of wine.

Alaska Backpackers Inn HOSTEL $
(Map p162; ✆277-2770; www.alaskabackpackers.com; 327 Eagle St; dm $25-30, s/d $60/70; ❀@🛜) Anchorage's newest hostel is roomy, comfortable and professional, and has a different painting on every dorm-room floor. Most rooms have only four or two beds and the dayroom features everything from a 50in TV to a foosball table. A bit east of central downtown, it's still within walking distance of restaurants and bars.

Wildflower Inn B&B $$
(Map p158; ✆274-1239; www.alaska-wildflower-inn.com; 1239 I St; r $129-139; ❀🛜@) Housed in a historic home, a duplex built in 1945 for Federal Aviation Administration (FAA) families, this B&B offers three large rooms, pleasant sitting areas and a full breakfast in the morning featuring treats such as caramelized French toast. For anybody who packed their walking shoes, the location is ideal, just three blocks south of Delaney Park.

Historic Anchorage Hotel BOUTIQUE HOTEL $$$
(Map p162; ✆272-4533, 800-544-0988; www.anchoragehistorichotel.com; 330 E St; r/ste from $199/249; ❀@🛜) This boutique hotel was established only a year after the city was founded, in 1916, though the current building is from 1936. It's luxurious, loaded with amenities from an excellent continental breakfast to free newspapers, and has an ideal downtown location.

Inlet Tower HOTEL $$
(Map p158; ✆276-0110, 800-544-0786; www.inlettower.com; 1200 L St; r/ste $180/200; ❀@🛜) Fifteen floors of spacious rooms and suites with kitchenettes, gourmet coffee for the coffeemaker and large TVs with in-room movies. The views are amazing and the 24-hour shuttle to the airport, downtown or train station is another nice perk.

Hilton Anchorage HOTEL $$$
(Map p162; ✆272-7411, 800-245-2527; www.hiltonanchorage.com; 500 W 3rd Ave; r $300; ❀@🛜) The Hilton has the best location of any of the luxury hotels, right in the heart of the downtown scene. Three restaurants, a fitness center with a pool, two 1000lb bears in the lobby, and lots of elegance. If you're

going to pay this much, ask for a room with a view of Cook Inlet.

Parkside Guest House
B&B $$

(Map p162; ☑278-2290; www.parksideanchorage. com; 1302 W 10 Ave; r $165-195; ☺☎) This elegant B&B has four large rooms that lead out to a spacious 2nd-floor sitting area with a fireplace, rocking chairs and a view of the city skyline and Cook Inlet. Relax in a hot tub, do your laundry or store your luggage here.

Susitna Place
B&B $$

(Map p162; ☑274-3344; www.susitnaplace.com; 727 N St; r $110-140, ste $170-195; ☺☎) On the edge of downtown, this 4000-sq-ft home sits on a bluff overlooking Cook Inlet and Mt Susitna in the distance. Four rooms have shared baths while the Susitna suite comes with a fireplace, hot tub and a private deck.

Anchorage Grand Hotel
LUXURY HOTEL $$$

(Map p162; ☑929-8888, 888-800-0640; www.anchoragegrand.com; 505 W 2nd Ave; r $199; ☺@☎) This converted apartment building rests on a quiet street with 31 spacious suites that include full kitchens and separate living and bedroom areas. Many overlook Ship Creek and Cook Inlet, and its downtown location is convenient to everything.

Hotel Captain Cook
HOTEL $$$

(Map p162; ☑276-6000, 800-843-1950; www. captaincook.com; 939 W 5th Ave; s/d $255/265; ☺@☎≋) The grand dame of Anchorage accommodations still has an air of an Alaskan aristocrat right down to the doormen with top hats. There are plenty of plush services and upscale shops: hot tubs, fitness clubs, beauty salon, jewelry store and four restaurants including the famed Crow's Nest bar on the top floor.

Voyager Hotel
HOTEL $$

(Map p162; ☑277-9501, 800-247-9070; 501 K St; r $150-170; ☺@☎) A 40-room hotel with a great location downtown. Each room comes with a kitchenette, and some have peek-a-boo inlet views.

City Garden B&B
B&B $$

(Map p162; ☑276-8686; www.citygarden.biz; 1352 W 10th Ave; r $100-150; ☺☎) One of several B&Bs located on a two-block stretch of 10th Ave, this is an open, sunny, gay- and lesbian-friendly place with more cutting-edge art than antiques. The nicest of the three rooms has a private bath.

Oscar Gill House
B&B $$

(Map p162; ☑279-1344; www.oscargill.com; 1344 W 10th Ave; r $115-135; ☺) This historic clapboard home was built in 1913 in Knik by former Anchorage Mayor Oscar Gill and later moved to its midtown location. The B&B offers three guest rooms (two that share a bath), a fantastic breakfast that ranges from sourdough French toast to smoked salmon quiche, and free bicycles.

Anchorage International Hostel
HOSTEL $

(Map p162; ☑276-3635; www.anchoragehostel.org; 700 H St; dm/r $25/60; ☺☎) Though somewhat regimented with lockout times (noon to 4pm) and curfews (1am), this hostel's location is hard to beat; it's downtown, practically across from the bus terminal. It also has laundry facilities, common areas and luggage storage.

Days Inn
MOTEL $$

(Map p162; ☑276-7226; www.daysinnalaska.com; 321 E 5th Ave; r $179; @☎) Clean, utilitarian and small, with a 24-hour restaurant and a free shuttle to the train station or airport.

Econo Inn
MOTEL $

(Map p162; ☑274-1515; 642 E 5th Ave; r/ste $85/99; ☺☎) Shabby but adequate, with a free airport shuttle to sweeten the deal.

MIDTOWN ANCHORAGE & SPENARD

Qupqugiaq Inn
HOSTEL $

(Map p158; ☑563-5633; www.qupq.com; 640 W 36th Ave; dm $25, s/d without bath $80/90, s/d with bath $96/106; ☺@☎) This colorful establishment has curved hallways, tiled floors, granite windowsills and a continental breakfast that includes French-pressed coffee and roll-your-own oats. The large dorms sleep eight, and the private rooms are bright and clean. On the 1st floor is Serrano's Mexican Grill for a cold beer or a spicy taco.

Puffin Inn
MOTEL $$

(off Map p158; ☑243-4044, 800-478-3346; www. puffininn.net; 4400 Spenard Rd; r $119-159; ☺☎) Anchorage's best late-night-airport-arrival motel. It has four tiers of fine rooms, from 26 sardine-can, economy rooms ($119) to full suites with hot tubs and hideaway kitchens, all accessible via free 24-hour airport shuttle.

Anchorage Guest House
HOSTEL $

(Map p158; ☑907-274-0408; www.akhouse.com; 2001 Hillcrest Dr; dm $35, r from $89; ☺@☎) This spacious suburban home feels more like

OFFBEAT ANCHORAGE

The wildest salmon in Anchorage are nowhere near Ship Creek. They're found spawning along downtown streets as part of the Wild Salmon on Parade, an annual event in which local artists turn fiberglass fish into anything but fish. The first run of fish art was organized in 2003 and modeled after Chicago's Cows on Parade and Seattle's Pigs on Parade – Anchorage doesn't have too many cows or pigs but it does have plenty of salmon.

Over the years this art competition has spawned an 'Alaska Sarah Salmon'; a fish with boxing gloves titled 'Socked Eye Salmon'; 'Marilyn MonROE' and 'Vincent Van Coho.' The 30 or so colorful fish appear on the streets in early June and stick around until September. To see them all, pick up a fish tour map at the Log Cabin Visitors Center.

Most of us would rather avoid the police. But who can resist the Alaska State Trooper Museum (Map p162; www.alaskatroopermuseum.com; 245 W 5th Ave; admission free; ◉10am-4pm Mon-Fri, from noon Sat). Displays are dedicated to law enforcement, starting from when Alaska was a territory, the storefront museum has exhibits that range from a beautifully restored 1952 Hudson Hornet cop car to state-issued sealskin cop boots. Stop by its gift shop to buy a T-shirt that proclaims 'Alaska: 367 Troopers, 570,000 square miles.' That will impress the next cop who pulls you over at home.

a B&B than a hostel, which is why it costs a bit more. Owner and singer/songwriter Andy Baker offers laundry ($5), bag storage ($1 per day) and bike rentals ($5 per hour) for the nearby coastal cycle trail. Buses 3, 7 and 36 cruise within easy walking distance; exit at West High School.

Millennium Hotel HOTEL $$$
(off Map p158; ☎243-2300, 800-544-0553; 4800 Spenard Rd; r $249-340; ❀@❀❀❀) A large, 248-room resort with a woodsy lodge feel overlooking Lake Spenard. PETA members take note: there are stuffed animals, trophy mounts and large fish everywhere. All rooms have been recently renovated, and are large with king or queen beds.

Long House Alaskan Hotel HOTEL $$
(off Map p158; ☎243-2133, 888-243-2133; www.longhousehotel.com; 4335 Wisconsin St; s/d $143/153; ❀) A block off Spenard Rd, this log hotel has 54 huge rooms and lots of amenities. There's continental breakfast, guest laundry facilities, in-room fridges, microwaves, TV and coffee service, and 24-hour shuttle service to the airport. And to top it off, the staff are really friendly.

Lake Hood Inn B&B $$
(☎258-9321, 866-663-9322; www.lakehoodinn.com; 4702 Lake Spenard Dr; r $169-189; ❀❀) If you're infatuated with floatplanes and bush pilots, book a room here. This spotless upscale home, with four guest rooms, is adorned with airplane artifacts, from a Piper propeller that doubles as a ceiling fan to a row of seats from a Russian airline. Outside

are two decks where you can watch a parade of floatplanes lift off the lake.

Spenard Hostel HOSTEL $
(off Map p158; ☎248-5036; www.alaskahostel.org; 2845 W 42nd Pl; sites/dm/r $20/25/88; ❀@❀) Two blocks from Spenard Rd, this relaxed hostel has been an Anchorage mainstay for more than 20 years. You'll find laundry, no lockout and three kitchens to avoid mealtime madness. Campsites are a little cramped on the side of the house, but you can rent one of its tents if you don't have your own. Guests can also rent mountain bikes ($3 per hour) and store bags ($1/15 per day/month). Reservations are highly recommended for July and August. Take bus 7 or 36 to get here.

Arctic Adventure Hostel HOSTEL $
(Map p158; ☎562-5700; www.arcticadventure hostel.com; 337 W 33rd Pl; dm/r $25/50; ❀@❀) There are only six dorm beds at this midtown joint; the rest of the accommodations are private rooms that are minuscule but tidy and, for Anchorage, great value. The kitchen is huge – a great place to cook a big spread. The friendly owner will rent you bicycles and camping gear, and internet, storage and even a freezer for that 40lb king salmon you landed are free.

26th Street International Hostel HOSTEL $
(Map p158; ☎274-1252; www.26streethostel.com; 1037 W 26th Ave; dm/r $25/67; ❀❀@) This hostel is close to all the midtown action, plus it has free internet, continental breakfast, luggage storage and not one but two TV

lounges. Buses 3 and 7 stop on Spenard Rd, a block away.

GREATER ANCHORAGE

Golden Nugget RV Park
CAMPGROUND $

(☑333-5311, 800-449-2012; www.goldennugget camperpark.com; 4100 DeBarr Rd; sites $38, RV sites $47-52; @⑦) If you're pulling a trailer or packing a tent, this is Anchorage's largest commercial campground, with 215 sites in all. Everything you could possibly need is there: showers, laundry, souvenir shop, bus stop (bus 15).

Centennial Park
Campground
CAMPGROUND $

(☑343-6986; 8300 Glenn Hwy; sites $25) It's 5 miles from downtown but is pleasant, with 100 sites, good rates and 'the hottest showers in town.' People Mover buses 3 and 75 stop nearby.

✗ Eating

Anchorage has lots of fast food, espresso stands and, of course, more fried halibut and grilled salmon than you can shake a rod and reel at. But the bustling city also boasts a variety of international cuisines, from Polynesian to Mexican to Vietnamese, that you'll be hard-pressed to find in the Bush. Best of all, Anchorage restaurants and bars are smoke-free.

Scattered along 4th Ave downtown are so many pushcart vendors selling brats and reindeer sausage ($5), they ought to rename the road Hot Dog Blvd.

DOWNTOWN ANCHORAGE

TOP CHOICE Snow City Café
BREAKFAST $

(Map p162; www.snowcitycafe.com; 1034 W 4th Ave; breakfast $7-15, lunch $9-13; ⊙breakfast & lunch; ⑦) Consistently voted best breakfast by *Anchorage Press* readers, this busy cafe serves healthy grub to a mix of clientele that ranges from the tattooed to the up-and-coming. For breakfast, skip the usual eggs and toast and try a bowl of Snow City granola with dried fruit, honey and nuts.

Ginger
FUSION $$

(Map p162; ☑929-3680; www.gingeralaska.com; 425 W 5th Ave; lunch $9-16, dinner $17-28; ⊙lunch Mon-Fri, dinner daily) Ginger and curry rule at Anchorage's newest restaurant, whose menu is a fusion of Pacific Rim cuisine and classic Asian dishes. The end result is an artistic endeavor like banana and lemongrass soup or Spicy Tuna Tower served

in surroundings that are elegant but still Alaskan casual. The bar stocks fine wines and locally brewed beer, as well as a wide selection of sake.

Orso
MEDITERRANEAN $$

(Map p162; ☑222-3232; www.orsoalaska.com; 737 W 5th Ave; lunch $9-16, dinner $16-27; ⊙lunch & dinner) The walls are smoked salmon and the wooden floors are covered with oriental rugs, there's modern art all around and soft jazz floating into both dining levels and the bar. Mains are Mediterranean grill with an Alaskan twist, and the lamb osso buco served with creamy polenta has stayed on the menu from the day it opened.

Sack's Café
FUSION $$$

(Map p162; ☑274-4022; www.sackscafe.com; 328 G St; lunch $12-16, dinner $24-34; ⊙lunch & dinner) An upscale, chic restaurant serving elegant fare that is consistently creative. It is always bustling (reservations recommended) and has the best weekend brunch in town.

Marx Bros Café
MODERN AMERICAN $$$

(Map p162; ☑278-2133; 627 W 3rd Ave; dinner $36-38; ⊙dinner Tue-Sat) They woo you into this historic (1916) home promising views of Cook Inlet but let's face it, you're looking at fuel tanks along Ship Creek. Some of Anchorage's most innovative cooking and a 500-bottle wine list are the real reasons this 14-table restaurant is so popular. The menu changes nightly, but the beloved halibut macadamia always stays put. In the summer, book your table a week in advance.

Humpy's Great Alaskan Alehouse
PUB $$

(Map p162; www.humpys.com; 610 W 6th Ave; dinner $15-21; ⊙lunch & dinner; ⑦) Anchorage's most beloved beer place, with almost 60 beers on tap. There's also ale-battered halibut, gourmet pizzas, outdoor tables and live music most nights.

Modern Dwellers Chocolate
Lounge
CHOCOLATE $

(Map p162; www.moderndwellers.com; 423 G St; ⊙6am-10pm Mon-Sat, 8am-9pm Sun) There are dozens of coffee houses in Anchorage but none like this. Modern Dwellers is a cross between a chocolate shop, art gallery and an espresso bar, serving drinking chocolate and lattes and showcasing art and homemade sweets like Alaskan Wild Smoked Salmon Chocolate. There is also a midtown location at 751 E 36th Ave.

1. Maxine's Glacier City Bistro
Live music keeps the crowds warm on Friday and Saturday nights at this colorful venue (p181) in Girdwood.

2. Frozen River
The glaciers might be melting but ice climbing and glacier trekking (p33) are still popular activities.

3. Totem pole, Alaska Native Heritage Center

This 26-acre center (p175) is a knowledge bank of language, art and culture.

4. Anchorage Skyline

Towering behind Anchorage (p153) is the nation's third largest state park, the Chugach.

5. Downtown Anchorage

Visited during historic walking tours (p161), Fourth Avenue boasts some of the city's oldest buildings.

Snow Goose Restaurant
BREWERY $$

(Map p162; www.alaskabeers.com; 717 W 3rd Ave; lunch $11-17, dinner $11-27; ⊗lunch Tue-Sat, dinner daily) The outdoor deck on the 2nd floor is positioned to look onto Cook Inlet, Mt Susitna and the sunsets whenever they occur. The menu ranges from pizza and local fish to reindeer meatloaf but there are few things nicer than simply enjoying their homebrewed IPA on a sunny evening.

Glacier Brewhouse
BREWERY $$$

(Map p162; 274-2739; www.glacierbrewhouse.com; 737 W 5th Ave; lunch $11-18, dinner $19-30; ⊗lunch & dinner) Grab a table overlooking the three giant copper brewing tanks and enjoy wood-fired pizzas and rotisserie-grilled ribs and chops with a pint of oatmeal stout. But be prepared to wait for that table, as this place is unbelievably popular.

McGinley's Pub
IRISH PUB $$

(Map p162; www.mcginleyspub.com; 645 G St; sandwiches $10-11, dinner $12-16; ⊗lunch & dinner) We're all Irish, at least on St Patrick's Day, and in Anchorage this is where you come for corned beef and cabbage, bangers and mash, shepherd's pie and a pint of Smithwick's.

Club Paris
STEAKHOUSE $$$

(Map p162; 277-6332; www.clubparisrestaurant.com; 417 W 5th Ave; lunch $10-13, dinner $20-42; ⊗lunch Mon-Sat, dinner daily) This longtime restaurant – it survived the 1964 earthquake – is old-school fine dining and serves the best steaks in Anchorage. If there's room on your credit card, try the 4in-thick filet mignon.

Cafe 817
DELI $

(Map p162; 817 W 6th Ave; breakfast $6-12, sandwiches $9-11; ⊗breakfast & lunch Mon-Sat) In a funky tiled building, this cafe serves break-

ED FOGELS: STATE LAND MANAGER

Our state park system encompasses more than 3.3 million acres or an area larger than Connecticut. At 495,000 acres, Chugach State Park is the second-largest state park in Alaska and third largest in the country. But what makes it so incredibly unique is that it borders Anchorage. On the doorstep of our largest city we have a wilderness where you can mountain bike, camp, raft, scale a peak and hit the trail for a weekend of backpacking.

Hiking & Cycling Flattop

Flattop Mountain is our most popular trail in the park, and a different way to enjoy it is as a hike-and-bike adventure. Downtown Bicycle Rental (Map p162; 279-5293; www.alaska-bike-rentals.com; 333 W 4th Ave; ⊗8am-8pm) offers a hike/bike rental combo in which it places a mountain bike on its shuttle van and takes you to the trailhead. After hiking Flattop Mountain you get to enjoy a ride back to the city in the best direction to pedal – downhill.

Cheering on the Runners

One of Alaska's best mountain races is the Crow Pass Crossing (www.alaskamountainrunners.org), a 24-mile run held in July along the Iditarod National Historic Trail from Girdwood to Eagle River. Almost all of it takes place in Chugach State Park, and features an elevation gain of 3888ft and fording of glacier-fed Eagle River. If you're not up for the run, then hike the 4 miles to the Crow Pass to cheer on the runners at the highest point of the race.

Dinner at Pepe's House

My favorite mountain-bike outing is Powerline Pass Trail, a 12-mile ride that ends near Pepe's Turnagain House (http://turnagainhouse.com; Mile 103 Seward Hwy; ⊗dinner). Spot a car or arrange a ride and at the end of the trail you can indulge in fresh Alaskan seafood and a well-deserved martini.

A Bunk in the Backcountry

Lakeside Trail at Eklutna Lake State Recreation Area is an easy and beautiful way to reach the backcountry of Chugach State Park. To spend a night at the end of the trail, reserve a bunk at Serenity Falls Hut (269-8400; http://dnr.alaska.gov/parks/cabins/anch.htm; dm $10-15), our first multiple-party public-use hut in any state park.

fast, a wide variety of sandwiches and the best muffins in the city.

Urban Greens
SANDWICHES $

(Map p162; www.urbangreensak.com; 304 G St; sandwiches $8-9; ☺9am-3pm Mon-Fri) Tell Jared to take a hike. The freshest and tastiest subs in Anchorage are not at Subway but this small downtown sandwich shop.

Dark Horse Coffee Company
COFFEE HOUSE $

(Map p162; www.darkhorsecoffee.com; 646 F St; sandwiches $4-6; ☺breakfast & lunch; @🛜) It has lots of lattes, big pastries, even bigger waffles, and savory quiches and sandwiches. And the wireless is free. Surf and sip.

Side Street Espresso
COFFEE HOUSE $

(Map p162; 412 G St; light fare $4-7; ☺7am-3pm Mon-Sat) Serves espresso, bagels and muffins within walls covered in art.

New Sagaya City Market
MARKET $

(Map p158; www.newsagaya.com; 3900 W 13th Ave; ☺6am-10pm Mon-Sat, 8am-9pm Sun) Eclectic and upscale, this is a grocery store with lots of organic goodies, a great deli specializing in Asian fare and seating indoors and outdoors. There's also a second midtown location at 3700 Old Seward Hwy.

10th & M Seafoods
MARKET $

(Map p162; www.10thandmseafoods.com; 1020 M St; ☺8am-6pm Mon-Fri, from 9am Sat) This market sells the freshest seafood in a city that loves its seafood fresh. Staff will also butcher and ship your freshly killed moose or 200lb halibut.

MIDTOWN ANCHORAGE & SPENARD

TOP CHOICE Bear Tooth Grill
TEX-MEX $$

(Map p158; http://beartooththeatre.net; 1230 W 27th St; burgers $10-14, dinner $12-20; ☺lunch & dinner) A popular hangout with an adjacent theater, serving excellent burgers and seafood as well as Mexican and Asian fusion dishes. The microbrews are fresh and the cocktails are the best in town – if you're up for a splurge, lash out on *el Cielo* (the sky) margarita.

Moose's Tooth Brewpub
PIZZERIA $$

(Map p158; www.moosestooth.net; 3300 Old Seward Hwy; large pizza $16-25; ☺lunch & dinner; 🖉) An Anchorage institution serving a dozen custom-brewed beers including monthly specials. This is *the* place to refuel after climbing Flattop, with 40 gourmet pizzas on the menu, including 10 veggie pies.

Jen's Restaurant
EUROPEAN $$$

(Map p158; ☎561-5367; www.jensrestaurant.com; 701 W 36th Ave; lunch $13-26, dinner $18-40; ☺lunch Mon-Fri, dinner Tue-Sat) This fine restaurant in midtown has dazzled the critics with innovative, Scandinavian-accented cuisine emphasizing fresh ingredients and elaborate presentation. The dining room features a constantly changing exhibition of Alaskan artists while the wine bar stays open to midnight with music and a menu of tapas.

Organic Oasis
JUICE BAR $$

(Map p158; www.organicoasis.com; 2610 Spenard Rd; mains $11-16; ☺11am-9pm Mon-Sat, 1-6pm Sun; 🖉) Anchorage's hippest juice bar. Not into puréed carrots? It also serves pizza, wraps, pasta and burgers with loads of veggie choices, and even organic beer and wine.

Ray's Place
VIETNAMESE $

(Map p158; www.raysplaceak.com; 32412 Spenard Rd; dinner $8-15; ☺lunch & dinner Mon-Fri; 🖉) Leave Chilkoot Charlies early and cross the street to this Vietnamese restaurant that does great cold noodle salads and stir-fries, and stocks Vietnamese beer.

City Diner
DINER $

(Map p158; www.citydiner.org; 3000 Minnesota Dr; breakfast $7-14, sandwiches $10-14; ☺6am-11pm) You can't miss the gleaming silver facade of this nouveau diner. It's *American Graffiti* inside with all-day breakfast and huge sandwiches like the Lenny's Reuben. If you don't want a giant milkshake, you can always order a Diner Bloody Mary.

Greek Corner
GREEK $$

(Map p158; 201 E Northern Lights Blvd; lunch $7-11, dinner $13-23; ☺lunch & dinner) The best moussaka, souvlaki and stuffed grape leaves in Alaska just changed corners. The longtime Anchorage favorite now serves up its traditional Greek and Italian dishes in a larger, more open dining room or, if the sun is shining, on an outdoor deck.

Middle Way Café
CAFE $

(Map p158; 1200 W Northern Lights Blvd; breakfast $5-10, lunch $6-12; ☺breakfast & lunch; 🖉) This veggie-friendly cafe serves healthy breakfasts and organic salads, soups and sandwiches in a cozy, artsy atmosphere.

Sweet Basil Café
CAFE $

(Map p158; 1201 E Northern Lights Blvd; sandwiches $9-12; ☺lunch Mon-Sat; 🖉) Housed in a former Taco Bell, this cafe passes on the grande burritos and offers inexpensive, healthy cuisine (and decidedly unhealthy, but recommended, desserts), fruit smoothies and coffee.

Taco King
MEXICAN $

(Map p158; www.tacokingak.com; 113 W Northern Lights Blvd; dinner $7-9; ☺lunch & dinner) Anchorage's beloved taco shop is so good and so affordable there are now two more locations (1330 Huffman Rd and 3561 E Tudor Rd). The original is still the busiest.

Charlie's Bakery
CHINESE $$

(Map p158; 2729 C St; mains $10-15; ☺lunch & dinner Mon-Sat) The most authentic Chinese food you'll find in Anchorage, sold next to French baguettes.

Gwennie's Old Alaska Restaurant
BREAKFAST $$

(off Map p158; 4333 Spenard Rd; breakfast $7-12, dinner $16-30; ☺breakfast, lunch & dinner) An Alaskan gem: lots to look at (totems, stuffed bears, a gurgling stream) and big portions. Most non-Alaskans can share a reindeer sausage omelet and not be hungry for two days.

Bombay Deluxe
INDIAN $$

(Map p158; www.bombaydeluxe.com; 555 W Northern Lights Blvd; mains $12-22; ☺lunch & dinner) Skip the mediocre lunch buffet and order straight off the menu. Loads of vegetarian dishes and such exotic ones as goat curry.

Europa Bakery & Café
BAKERY $

(Map p158; 601 W 36th Ave; lunch $8; ☺breakfast & lunch) Come here for the soup-and-sandwich lunch, but don't leave without a fresh-baked French pastry.

Momma O's
SEAFOOD $

(Map p158; 2636 Spenard Rd; sandwiches $9-10, mains $9-14; ☺lunch & dinner Mon-Sat) The place for a halibut fix – have it fried or, better, Cajun style – but don't discount the excellent onion rings or udon noodles.

New Central Market
MARKET $

(Map p158; www.newcentralmarket.com; 555 W Northern Lights Blvd; ☺9am-9pm) A touch of Asia in the heart of Anchorage.

GREATER ANCHORAGE

Southside Bistro
MODERN AMERICAN $$$

(☎348-0001; www.southsidebistro.com; 1320 Huffman Park Dr; lunch $11-20, dinner $18-34; ☺lunch & dinner Tue-Sat) On the south side of town, this trendy bistro is beloved by all those living in the hills above it. The menu incorporates

Alaskan seafood, guaranteeing less than 24 hours from the net to the dish, along with Mat-Su veggies and Anchorage-area berries. Freshness never tasted so good, at least not in Alaska.

Arctic Roadrunner
BURGERS $

(off Map p158; 5300 Old Seward Hwy; burgers $5-7; ☺lunch & dinner Mon-Sat) Since 1964 this place has been turning out beefy burgers and great onion pieces and rings. If your timing is right you can eat outdoors while watching salmon spawn up Campbell Creek.

Peanut Farm
SPORTS BAR $$

(off Map p158; www.wemustbenuts.com; 5227 Old Seward Hwy; breakfast $10-13, sandwiches $10-12, mains $17-27; ☺6-2am) What was once a small, funky drinking hole is now a shockingly large sports bar complex with TVs at every booth. There are two entrances so take your choice of the original, cozy Peanut Farm or the new Sports Addition. Or skip both and head for the creekside deck, the best place in town to eat chicken wings and watch salmon spawn.

Thai Kitchen
THAI $

(www.thaikitchenak.com; 3405 Tudor Rd; lunch special $8, dinner $9-12; ☺lunch Mon-Sat, dinner daily; ☺Ⓟⓐ) This is where a hungry vegetarian comes. The lunch special is three mains and rice; the dinner lists more than 30 veggie choices like fried tofu with peanut sauce.

ⓧ Drinking

With its young and lively population, Anchorage has a lot to do after the midnight sun finally sets. The free *Anchorage Press* has events listings.

Bernie's Bungalow Lounge
LOUNGE

(Map p162; 626 D St) Pretty people, pretty drinks: this is the place to see and be seen. Its outdoor patio, complete with a waterspewing serpent, is the best in Anchorage and on the summer weekends it rocks late into the night with live music.

Crush
WINE BAR

(Map p162; www.crushak.com; 343 W 6th Ave) This swanky wine bar serves 'bistro bites,' a menu of appetizers, salads and small plates as well as more than 40 wines by the glass. Nibble and sip.

SubZero
COCKTAIL BAR

(Map p162; 610 6th Ave; ☺) Cool and jazzy, this wi-fi hot spot has two pages of cocktails including almost a dozen martinis and affordable 'Microlounge Micro-plates,' nibbles that range from crab cake sliders to macadamia nut seared goat cheese.

Reilly's
IRISH PUB

(Map p158; 317 W Fireweed Ave) A friendly pub with the goodness of Ireland on tap: Guinness Extra Stout, Murphy's Irish Stout and Harp Irish Ale.

F Street Station
PUB

(Map p162; 325 F St) This is the place where everybody knows your name. The only thing missing in this friendly, music-free drinking hole is Norm sitting at the end of the bar.

Crow's Nest
LOUNGE

(Map p162; 5th Ave & K St) There's upscale dining at the Crow's Nest, at the top of the Hotel Captain Cook, but most come for a drink and a million-dollar view of Cook Inlet.

☆ Entertainment

Clubs

TOP CHOICE **Chilkoot Charlie's**
LIVE MUSIC

(Map p158; www.koots.com; 2435 Spenard Rd) More than just Anchorage's favorite meat market, 'Koots,' as the locals call it, is a landmark. The sprawling, wooden edifice has 22 beers on tap, 10 bars, four dancefloors and a couple of stages where almost every band touring Alaska ends up. Its newest addition is a replica of the legendary Bird House. The original was a log-cabin bar on Seward Hwy that was still standing but drunkenly slanted after the 1964 earthquake before burning down in 2002.

Tap Root
LIVE MUSIC

(Map p158; www.taprootalaska.com; 3300 Spenard Rd) With the addition of Tap Root, Spenard cemented its reputation as the heart of Anchorage nightlife. The lively bar has 20 microbrews on tap, an impressive list of single malt Scotch whiskeys and more than 25 types

of bourbon. In the summer they pack them in with live bands every night of the week.

Anchor Pub
DJ

(Map p162; www.anchorak.com; 712 4th Ave) This clean joint serves soups and sandwiches, has a dancefloor and a lounge, and proudly displays the largest Blue Ocean TV screen on the west coast. Most nights it's DJs, on the weekends there are live bands.

Rum Runners
DJ

(Map p162; www.rumrunnersak.com; 415 W E St) Packed when DJs are spinning after 10pm Friday and Saturday, and it now boasts a mojito bar.

Club Soraya
DANCE

(Map p162; 4th Ave & D St; cover $5-10) If you can find this huge Latin dance club (hint: the entrance is through the Ship Creek Center), this is the place to shake. And if you can't shake it or swing it, dance lessons are on offer most nights of the week, including salsa from 9pm to 10pm on Friday followed by live music and tango on Wednesday.

Gay & Lesbian Venues

Several straight bars are regarded as gay and lesbian friendly: try Bernie's Bungalow Lounge and the Moose's Tooth Brewpub.

Mad Myrna's
GAY

(Map p162; www.madmyrnas.com; 530 E 5th Ave; cover Sat & Sun $5-10) A fun, cruisy bar with line dancing on Thursday, Drag Divas shows on Friday and dance music most nights after 9pm.

Kodiak Bar & Grill
GAY

(Map p162; 225 E 5th Ave; cover $3) A gay bar whose lunch counter in the back serves a surprising good taco burger until 5am on Friday and Saturday.

GAY & LESBIAN ANCHORAGE

It's not West Hollywood, but Anchorage does have a handful of gay- and lesbian-friendly bars and lodgings. The city is becoming more gay- and lesbian-friendly, but consider the situation carefully before revealing your sexual orientation.

The weeklong **Pridefest** (mid-June) is a gay-pride celebration that includes a Queer Film Festival, Drag Queen Bingo, a parade through downtown and a party at Delaney Park.

The **Gay & Lesbian Community Center of Anchorage** (GLCCA; ☎929-4528; www.identityinc.org; 336 E 5th Ave; ☉3-9pm Mon-Fri, noon-6pm Sat & Sun) has a community bulletin board and lots of info, including gay-friendly doctor recommendations. It also helps organize Pridefest and carries a newsletter, *North View*.

Bent Alaska (www.bentalaska.com) covers news and events that involve Alaskan gay, lesbian and transgender issues. For advice or help, call the **Gay & Lesbian Helpline** (☎258-4777, 888-901-9876; ☉6-11pm).

Raven GAY

(708 E 4th Ave) The other gay and lesbian bar in town.

Live Music

For jazz and blues, head to Blues Central at the Chef's Inn (Map p158; www.bluescentral.org; 825 W Northern Lights Blvd), an intimate venue with live blues and jazz nightly.

For other music, check out Humpy's Great Alaskan Alehouse, which features live music Thursday to Sunday at around 9pm, with a mix of acoustic, bluegrass and blues throughout the summer. The Snow Goose Restaurant also offers an open mic as well as local acoustic artists, and its small theatre often hosts musicians from out of state. Organic Oasis has live jazz, bluegrass or acoustic alternative music most evenings.

If line dancing is your thing, mosey down to the Long Branch Saloon (1737 E Dimond Blvd). It has pool tables, stiff drinks and live country and western music almost nightly. If you'd rather hear Irish jigs, head to McGinley's Pub, where there is live music Thursday and Saturday and open mic on Wednesday.

Cinemas

Fireweed Theatre (Map p158; 800-326-3264, ext 101; cnr Fireweed Ave & Gambell Rd) and Century 16 Theatre (Map p158; 770-2602; 301 E 36th Ave), across from the library, are both fine places for a flick.

Bear Tooth Theatrepub CINEMA

(Map p158; 276-4200; www.beartooththeatre. net; 1230 W 27th Ave) Cruise into this very cool venue (check out the mural on the lobby ceiling) where you can enjoy great microbrews, wine or even dinner while watching first-run movies as well as foreign and independent films ($3.50 to $5).

Alaska Experience Center CINEMA

(Map p162; 272-9076; www.alaskaexperiencethe atre.com; 333 W 4th Ave; adult/child $6/5; 10am-7pm) More a tourist trap than movie house, with IMAX nature films and a 15-minute theatrical simulation of the 1964 Good Friday Earthquake.

Theater & Performing Arts

Anchorage had an orchestra before it had paved roads, which says a lot about priorities around here.

Alaska Center for the Performing Arts PERFORMING ARTS

(Map p162; 263-2900, tickets 263-2787; www.my alaskacenter.com; 621 W 6th Ave) Impresses tourists with the film *Aurora: Alaska's Great Northern Lights* (adult/child $11.75/8.75), screened on the hour from 9am to 9pm during summer in its Sydney Laurence Theatre. It's also home to the Anchorage Opera (279-2557; www.anchorageopera.org), Anchorage Symphony Orchestra (274-8668; www. anchoragesymphony.org), Anchorage Concert Association (272-1471; www.anchorageconcerts.org) and Alaska Dance Theatre (277-9591; www.alaskadancetheatre.org).

Egan Civic Center CONCERT VENUE

(Map p162; 263-2800; www.anchorageconven tioncenters.com; 555 W 5th Ave) Try this place for top-drawer musical groups and other big events.

Sullivan Arena CONCERT VENUE

(Map p158; 279-0618; www.sullivanarena.com; 1600 Gambell St) Also hosts musical events.

Cyrano's Theatre Company THEATER

(Map p162; 274-2599; www.cyranos.org; 413 D St; tickets $12-15) This off-center playhouse is the best live theater in town, staging everything from *Hamlet* to *Archy and Mehitabel* (comic characters of a cockroach and a cat), Mel Brooks' jazz musical based on the poetry of Don Marquis. Only in Anchorage...

Other Entertainment

Great Alaskan Bush Company CABARET

(off Map p158; akbushcompany.com; 631 E International Airport Rd) It's about as beloved as a strip club gets. The cozy landmark is woman-owned and -operated, and everyone agrees that the truly moral thing to do is tip well.

Anchorage Bucs BASEBALL

(561-2827; www.anchoragebucs.com; general admission $5) This semipro team of the Alaska Baseball League plays at Mulcahy Ball Park, where living legend Mark McGuire once slammed a few homers. Also taking the same field is archrival Anchorage Glacier Pilots (274-3627; www.glacierpilots.com).

Shopping

Outdoor Gear

With so much wilderness at its doorstep you'd expect Anchorage to have a wide variety of outdoor shops – and it does.

REI OUTDOOR EQUIPMENT

(Map p158; www.rei.com/stores/16; 1200 Northern Lights Blvd) Anchorage's largest outdoor store has everything you might ever need, from wool socks to backpacks to kayaks to camp chairs. Besides being able to repair your camp stove or bicycle tire, it will also rent canoes, bear containers, tents and bicycles.

Alaska Mountaineering & Hiking
OUTDOOR EQUIPMENT

(AMH; Map p158; www.alaskamountaineering. com; 2633 Spenard Rd) Staffed by experts and stocked with high-end gear, AMH is the place for serious adventurers.

Army/Navy Store
OUTDOOR EQUIPMENT

(Map p162; www.army-navy-store.com; 320 W 4th Ave) One of the cheapest places in town to buy hardy military gear.

Souvenirs

Moose-dropping jewelry and thin T-shirts are available downtown at a variety of cheesy tourist shops.

Anchorage Market & Festival
ARTS & CRAFTS

(Map p162; www.anchoragemarkets.com; W 3rd Ave & E St; ◎10am-6pm Sat & Sun; ⊞) This was called the 'Saturday Market' until it became so popular they opened it on Sundays. A fantastic open market with live music and more than 300 booths stocked with cheap food, Mat-Su Valley veggies and souvenirs from birch steins to birch syrup.

Ulu Factory
HANDICRAFTS

(Map p162; www.theulufactory.com; 211 W Ship Creek Ave) The *ulu* (oo-loo) is to Alaska what the rubber alligator is to Florida: everybody sells them. Still, this shop is interesting, with demonstrations that will teach you how to use the cutting tool.

Dos Manos
ARTS & CRAFTS

(Map p158; www.dosmanosgallery.com; 1317 W Northern Lights Blvd) Across from Title Wave Books, it sells locally crafted art and jewelry, and very cool Alaska-themed T-shirts.

Northway Mall Wednesday Market
ARTS & CRAFTS

(3101 Penland Pkwy; ◎9am-4pm Wed) Many vendors head to this market on Wednesday.

Alaska Native Arts & Crafts

TOP CHOICE ANC Auxiliary Craft Shop
ARTS & CRAFTS

(4315 Diplomacy Dr; ◎10am-2pm Mon-Fri, 1st & 3rd Sat of month) Located on the 1st floor of the Alaska Native Medical Center (Map p156), it has some of the finest Alaska Native arts and crafts available to the public. But it has limited hours and does not accept credit cards.

Alaska Native Arts Foundation Gallery
ARTS & CRAFTS

(Map p162; www.alaskanativearts.org; 500 W 6th Ave) The gallery showcases Native art in a bright, open space.

Oomingmak Musk Ox Producers Co-op
CLOTHING

(Map p162; www.qiviut.com; 604 H St) Handles a variety of very soft, very warm and very expensive garments made of arctic musk-ox wool, hand-knitted in isolated Inupiaq villages.

Alaska Native Heritage Center
ARTS & CRAFTS

(Map p156; www.alaskanative.net; 8800 Heritage Center Dr) Stocks a gift shop with artifacts of questionable authenticity, but also features booths where craftspeople make fresh knickknacks while you watch.

ⓘ Information

BOOKSTORES Title Wave Books (www. wavebooks.com; 1360 W Northern Lights Blvd; ⊜) A fabulous, (mostly) used bookstore, with more than 30,000 sq ft of books, including many on Alaska.

LAUNDRY Dondee's Laundromat (2701 Minnesota Dr) Clean your dirty clothes or just drop them off.

K-Speed Wash (600 E 6th Ave) To clean your clothes at the speed of 'K,' whatever that means, try this place.

LEFT LUGGAGE In town many hotels and hostels will store excess luggage either free or for a small fee.

Anchorage International Baggage Storage (☏248-0373; Baggage Area, South Terminal; per bag per day $6-8; ◎5-2am) A bit pricey, but it's conveniently located at Anchorage International Airport.

LIBRARY & INTERNET ACCESS Internet access and wi-fi are widely available all over Anchorage at hotels, restaurants, bars and even gift shops.

Kaladi Bros Café (www.kaladi.com; 621 West 6th Ave; ⊜) Has nine locations in Anchorage with free wi-fi, including this downtown cafe attached to the performing arts center.

Sourdough Tobacco & Internet (☏277-7601; 735 4th Ave; per hr/ 20min $4/2; @) You get both high-speed internet and a walk-in humidor.

ZJ Loussac Public Library (☏343-2975; www. anchoragelibrary.org; Denali St at W 36th Ave; ◎10am-9pm Mon-Thu, to 6pm Fri & Sat, 1-5pm Sun) Has free internet terminals (one hour per day) as well as wi-fi.

MEDIA Tourist freebies are available everywhere: the *Official Anchorage Visitors Guide* and

RIDING THE ALASKA RAILROAD

In a remote corner of the Alaskan wilderness, you stand along a railroad track when suddenly a small train appears. You wave a white flag in the air – actually yesterday's dirty T-shirt – and the engineer acknowledges you with a sound of his whistle and then stops. You hop onboard to join others fresh from the Bush: fly fishermen, backpackers, a hunter with his dead moose, locals whose homestead cabin can be reached only after a ride on the *Hurricane Turn,* one of America's last flag-stop trains.

This unusual service between Talkeetna and Hurricane along the Susitna River is only one aspect that makes the Alaska Railroad so unique. At the other end of the rainbow of luxury is the railroad's Gold Star Service, two lavishly appointed cars that in 2005 joined the *Denali Star* train as part of the Anchorage–Fairbanks run. The 89ft double-decked dome cars include a glass observation area on the 2nd level with 360-degree views and a bartender in the back serving your favorite libations. Sit back, sip a chardonnay and soak in the grandeur of Mt McKinley.

Take your pick, rustic or relaxing, but don't pass up the Alaska Railroad. There's not another train like it.

The railroad was born on March 12, 1914, when the US Congress passed the *Alaska Railroad Act,* authorizing the US president to construct and operate the line. With the exception of the train used at the Panama Canal, the US government had never before owned and operated a railroad.

It took eight years and 4500 men to build a 470-mile railroad from the ice-free port of Seward to the boomtown of Fairbanks, a wilderness line that was cut over what were thought to be impenetrable mountains and across raging rivers. On a warm Sunday afternoon in 1923, President Warren Harding – the first US president to visit Alaska – tapped in the golden spike at Nenana.

The Alaska Railroad has been running ever since. The classic trip is to ride the railroad from Anchorage to Fairbanks, with a stop at Denali National Park. Many believe the most scenic portion, however, is the 114-mile run from Anchorage to Seward, which begins by skirting the 60-mile-long Turnagain Arm, climbs an alpine pass and then comes within a half-mile of three glaciers.

There are far cheaper ways to reach Seward, Fairbanks or points in-between. But in the spirit of adventure, which is why many of us come to Alaska, a van or bus pales in comparison to riding the Alaska Railroad.

Anchorage Daily News' Alaska Visitor's Guide are all packed with useful information.

Anchorage Daily News (www.adn.com) This daily has the largest circulation in the state but is a shell compared to the paper that won a Pulitzer Prize in the 1970s.

Anchorage Press (www.anchoragepress. com) A hip, free weekly with events listings and social commentary.

MEDICAL SERVICES Alaska Regional Hospital (☎276-1131; 2801 DeBarr Rd; ⏰24hr emergency service) Near Merrill Field. Take bus 13 or 15.

First Care Medical Center (☎248-1122; 3710 Woodland Dr, ste 1100; ⏰7am-midnight) Walk-in clinic just off Spenard Rd in midtown. Bus 7 stops there.

Providence Alaska Medical Center (☎562-2211; 3200 Providence Dr) The largest medical center in the state. Buses 1, 3, 13, 36, 45 and 102 will get you there.

MONEY Key Bank (☎257-5500, 800-539-2968; 601 W 5th Ave)

Wells Fargo (☎800-869-3557; 301 W Northern Lights Blvd) The main bank is in midtown.

POST Post office (344 W 4th Ave) This one's downtown in the Village of Ship Creek Center, but there are nearly a dozen more in town.

TOURIST INFORMATION Alaska Public Lands Information Center (APLIC; ☎644-3661; www.nps.gov/anch, www.alaskacenters. gov; 605 W 4th Ave; ⏰9am-5pm) In the Federal Building (you'll need photo ID to get in). The center has handouts for hikers, mountain bikers, kayakers, fossil hunters and just about everyone else, on almost every wilderness area of the state. Start here, go there. There are also excellent wildlife displays, free movies, fun dioramas, and at 11am and 2:30pm daily a guided Captain Cook walk to Resolution Park, covering the sea captain's travels in Alaska.

Log Cabin Visitor Center (☎257-2342; www. anchorage.net; 524 W 4th Ave; ⏰8am-7pm)

Has pamphlets, maps, bus schedules, city guides in several languages and a lawn growing on its roof.

Visitors center (☎266-2437; Anchorage International Airport) Several are located in the baggage-claim areas of both terminals; the south-terminal desk is staffed 9am to 4pm daily in summer.

TRAVEL AGENCIES New World Travel (☎276-7071; 3901 Old Seward Hwy) In the University Center a few blocks from the ZJ Loussac Public Library.

ℹ️ Getting There & Away

AIR Ted Stevens Anchorage International Airport (www.dot.state.ak.us/anc/index. shtml), Alaska's largest airport, is 6.5 miles west of the city center and handles 130 domestic and international flights daily from more than a dozen major airlines.

Alaska Airlines (☎800-252-7522; www.alas kaair.com) Provides the most intrastate routes to travelers, generally through its contract carrier, ERA Aviation, which operates services to Valdez, Homer, Cordova, Kenai, Iliamna and Kodiak. You can book tickets either online or at the airport.

PenAir (☎800-448-4226; www.penair.com) Flies smaller planes to 27 difficult-to-pronounce destinations in Southwest Alaska, including Unalakleet, Aniak and Igiugig.

BUS Anchorage is a hub for various small passenger and freight lines that make daily runs between specific cities. Always call first; Alaska's volatile bus industry is as unstable as an Alaska Peninsula volcano.

Alaska Direct Busline, Inc (☎800-770-6652; www.alaskadirectbusline.com) Has regular services between Anchorage and Glennallen ($75, three hours), Tok ($115, eight hours) and Whitehorse ($240, 17 hours), and points in-between.

Alaska Park Connection (☎800-266-8625; www.alaskacoach.com) Offers daily service from Anchorage north to Talkeetna ($65, 2½ hours) and Denali National Park ($90, six hours), and south to Seward ($65, three hours).

Alaska/Yukon Trails (☎800-770-7275; www. alaskashuttle.com) Runs a bus up the George Parks Hwy to Denali ($75, six hours) and Fairbanks ($99, nine hours).

Homer Stage Lines (☎235-2252; stagelinein-homer.com) Will take you to Homer ($90, 4½ hours) and points in-between.

Seward Bus Line (☎563-0800, 888-420-7788; www.sewardbuslines.net) Runs between Anchorage and Seward ($50, three hours) twice daily in summer.

TRAIN From its downtown depot, the **Alaska Railroad** (☎265-2494, 800-544-0552; www. akrr.com; 411 W 1st Ave) sends its *Denali Star*

north daily to Talkeetna (adult/child $89/45), Denali National Park ($146/73) and Fairbanks ($210/105). The *Coastal Classic* stops in Girdwood ($59/30) and Seward ($75/38), while the *Glacial Discovery* connects to Whittier ($65/33). You can save 20% to 30% traveling in May and September.

ℹ️ Getting Around

TO/FROM THE AIRPORT People Mover bus 7 offers hourly service between downtown and the airport (adult/child $1.75/1, 6:15am to 10:40pm Monday to Friday, 8:35am to 7:35pm Saturday, 10:35am to 5:35pm Sunday). Pick-up is at the south (domestic) terminal. You can call **Alaska Shuttle** (☎338-8888, 694-8888; www. alaskashuttle.net) for door-to-door service to downtown and South Anchorage (one to three people $30) or Eagle River ($45). Plenty of the hotels and B&Bs also provide a courtesy-van service. Finally, an endless line of taxis will be eager to take your bags and your money. Plan on a $25 fare to the downtown area.

BUS Anchorage's excellent bus system, **People Mover** (☎343-6543; www.peoplemover.org; Downtown Transit Center, 700 W 6th Ave; ☺8am-5pm Mon-Fri), runs from 6am to 11:30pm Monday to Friday, 8am to 9pm Saturday and 10am to 7pm Sunday. Pick up a schedule ($1) at the Downtown Transit Center or call for specific route information. One-way fares are $1.75/1 per adult/child; an unlimited day pass ($4) is available at the transit center. **Mascot** (☎376-5000; www.matsutransit.com), the Mat-Su Community Transit, has service between Anchorage and Wasilla and Palmer. Three runs a day depart from the Downtown Transit Center Monday through Friday (one way/day pass $2.50/6).

CAR & MOTORCYCLE All the national concerns (Avis, Budget, Hertz, Payless, National etc) have counters in the airport's south terminal.

ℹ️ **MORE AFFORDABLE CAR RENTALS**

Avoid renting a car at the Anchorage Airport if at all possible as you will be hit with a 34% rental tax. Rental agencies within Anchorage will tack on only an 18% tax and generally have cheaper rates. And while they can't pick you up at the airport, if you drop the car off during business hours some rental places will provide you with a ride to the airport.

Also keep in mind that if you can rent a vehicle in May or September as opposed to June, July or August, you will usually save an additional 30%.

Denali Car Rental (✆276-1230, 800-757-1230; 1209 Gambell St) Has subcompacts for $65/390 per day/week with 150 daily miles included.

Midnight Sun Car & Van Rental (✆243-8806, 888-877-3585; 4211 Spenard Rd) The best of the Spenard cheapies, with compacts for $61/370 per day/week.

House of Harley-Davidson (✆246-5300; www.harleyalaska.com; 4334 Spenard Rd) Rents out Harley-Davidsons (per day $200-250) and even offers a Fly-Buy-Ride program so you can hit the road in the Last Frontier on your new Harley. Sure, it's pricey, but still much better value than traditional psychotherapy.

TAXI If you need to call a cab, try either **Anchorage Yellow Cab** (✆222-2222) or **Anchorage Checker Cab** (✆276-1234).

SOUTH OF ANCHORAGE

The trip out of Anchorage along Turnagain Arm is well worth the price of a train ticket or rental car. Sure, it might be quicker (and probably cheaper) to fly, but staying on the ground will make you appreciate just how close to the wilderness Anchorage really is.

Seward Highway

Starting at the corner of Gambell St and 10th Ave in Anchorage, Seward Hwy parallels the Alaska Railroad south 127 miles to Seward. Once it leaves Anchorage proper, the highway winds along massive peaks dropping straight into Turnagain Arm. Expect lots of traffic, a frightening percentage of which involves folks who have (1) never seen a Dall sheep before, and (2) never driven an RV before; it's a frustrating and sometimes deadly combination. Mile markers measure the distance from Seward.

If you're lucky (or a planner), you'll catch the bore tide, which rushes along Turnagain Arm in varying sizes daily.

Potter Marsh (Mile 117) was created in 1916, when railroad construction dammed several streams; at the time of writing, it was in the process of being filled with eroded earth. You can stretch your legs along the 1500ft boardwalk while spying on ducks, songbirds, grebes and gulls.

Chugach State Park Headquarters (✆345-5014; Mile 115; ☉10am-4:30pm Mon-Fri) is housed in the Potter Section House, a historic railroad workers' dorm that also includes a free museum with a snowplow train and other era artifacts.

Turnagain Arm Trail, an easy 11-mile hike, begins at Mile 115. Originally used by Alaska Natives, the convenient route has since been used by Russian trappers, gold miners and happy hikers. The trail, with a mountain goat's view of Turnagain Arm, alpine meadows and beluga whales, can also be accessed at the McHugh Creek Picnic Area (Mile 112), Rainbow (Mile 108) and Windy Corner (Mile 107).

Indian Valley Mine (www.indianvalleymine. com; Mile 104; admission $1; ☉9am-9pm), a lode mine originally blasted out in 1901, still produces gold. You can buy bags of ore ($10 to $50) and see for yourself. The wonderful proprietors are extremely knowledgeable on the history and science of Alaskan gold mining; ask about the potato retort.

Indian Valley Trail (Mile 103) is a mellow 6-mile path that starts 1.3 miles along the gravel road behind Turnagain House. You can also access Powerline Pass Trail for much longer hiking or cycling. Nearby is the **Brown Bear Motel** (✆653-7000; Mile 103 Seward Hwy; r $59) with clean rooms and cheap beer in the adjoining Brown Bear Saloon that can get hopping at night.

Bird Ridge Trail starts with a wheelchair-accessible loop at Mile 102, then continues with a steep, popular and well-marked path that reaches a 3500ft overlook at Mile 2; this is a traditional turnaround point for folks in a hurry. Or you can continue another 4 miles to higher peaks and even better views from sunny Bird Ridge, a top spot for rock climbing.

Bird Creek State Campground (Mile 101; campsites $10) is popular for fishing, hiking and, best of all, the sound of the bore tide rushing by your tent. Remind children and morons to stay off the deadly mud flats.

Girdwood

POP 1800

Some 37 miles south of Anchorage, Alyeska Hwy splits off at Mile 90 Seward Hwy and heads 3 miles east to Girdwood, a small hamlet with a city list of things to do and see. Encircled by mighty peaks brimming with glaciers, Girdwood is a laid-back antidote to the bustle of Anchorage. Home to the luxurious Alyeska Ski Resort and the fabled **Girdwood Forest Fair** (www.girdwoodforest fair.com), Girdwood is a dog-and-kid kind of town with excellent hiking, fine restaurants and a feel-good vibe that will have you staying longer than anticipated.

⊙ Sights

Crow Creek Mine MINE
(www.crowcreekmine.com; Mile 3.5 Crow Creek Rd;
adult/child $10/free; ⊙9am-6pm; 🅿) Girdwood
was named for James Girdwood, who staked
the first claim on Crow Creek in 1896. Two
years later the Crow Creek Mine was built
and today you can still see some original
buildings and sluices at this working mine.
You can even learn how to pan for gold
and then give it a try yourself (adult/child
$20/10) or pitch the tent and spend the
night ($10). It's a peaceful little place and
worth a visit just to walk around.

**FREE Girdwood Center for
Visual Arts** GALLERY
(www.gcvaonline.org; Olympic Circle; ⊙10am-6pm)
In town this center serves as an artisan cooperative during the summer and is filled with
the work of those locals who get inspired by
the majestic scenery that surrounds them.

Alyeska Resort Tram CABLE CAR
(☎754-2275; www.alyeskaresort.com; adult/child
$20/10; ⊙9:30am-9:30pm; 🅿) The Alyeska Ski
Resort Tram offers the easiest route to the
alpine area during the summer. The resort
offers a Tram & Lunch Combo (adult/child
$30/16) that lets you wander the alpine ter-
rain and then grab a bite at the Glacier Express Restaurant located in the Upper Tram
Terminal.

🏃 Activities

Hiking

Take the Alyeska Resort Tram to the easy,
1-mile **Alyeska Glacier View Trail**, in an
alpine area with views of the tiny Alyeska
Glacier. You can continue up the ridge to
climb the so-called summit of Mt Alyeska,
a high point of 3939ft. The true summit lies
further to the south, but is not a climb for
casual hikers.

Winner Creek Gorge is an easy, pleasant
hike that winds 5.5 miles through lush forest, ending in the gorge itself, where Winner
Creek becomes a series of cascades. The first
half of the trail is a boardwalk superhighway,
but toward the end it can get quite muddy.
From the gorge you can connect to the **Iditarod National Historic Trail** for a 7.7-mile
loop. Either way, you'll cross the gorge on an
ultrafun hand-tram. The most popular trailhead is near Arlberg Rd: walk along the bike
path past the Alyeska Prince Hotel, toward
the bottom of the tram. Look for the footpath
heading into the forest.

The highly recommended **Crow Pass
Trail** is a short but beautiful alpine hike that
has gold-mining relics and an alpine lake,
and often there are Dall sheep on the slopes
above. It's 4 miles to Raven Glacier, the traditional turnaround point of the trail, and 3
miles to a **USFS cabin** (☎877-444-6777, 518-
885-3639; www.recreation.gov; cabins $35). Or
you can continue on the three-day, 26-mile
route along the Iditarod National Historic
Trail to the Eagle River Nature Center. The
trailhead is 5.8 miles north of Alyeska Hwy
on Crow Creek Rd.

Cycling

The Indian–Girdwood Trail – a paved path
that leads out of the valley and along the
Seward Hwy above Turnagain Arm, dubbed
Bird-to-Gird – is the most scenic ride here.
The fabulous route extends to Mile 103 of the
highway, linking Alyeska Resort with Indian
Creek, 17 miles away. **Girdwood Ski & Cy-
clery** (☎783-2453; www.girdwoodskicyclery.com;

CATCHING THE BORE TIDE

One attraction along the Turnagain Arm stretch of the Seward Hwy is unique among
sights already original: the bore tide. The bore tide is a neat trick of geography that requires a combination of narrow, shallow waters and rapidly rising tides. Swooping as a
wave sometimes 6ft in height (and satisfyingly loud), the tide fills the arm in one go. It
travels at speeds of up to 15mph, and every now and then you'll catch a brave surfer or
kayaker riding it into the arm.

So, how to catch this dramatic rush?

First, consult a tide table, or grab a schedule, available at any Anchorage visitors center. The most extreme bore tides occur during days with minus tides between -2ft and
-5.5ft, but if your timing doesn't hit a huge minus, aim for a new or full moon period. Once
you've determined your day, pick your spot. The most popular is Beluga Point (Mile 110),
and a wise choice. If you miss the tide, you can always drive further up the arm and catch
it at Bird Point (Mile 96).

bicycles per 3hr/day $15/30; ⊙10am-7pm) will rent you the bikes to enjoy it.

Alyeska Resort has been installing elevated tread single-tracks for mountain bikers, suitable for beginners as well as adrenaline addicts. The tram and chairs 4 and 6 will carry cyclists and their wheels all the way up to Glacier Bowl if they choose and then a variety of intermediate and advance trails lead them downhill. Easier trails depart from the resort itself. A day pass for the lifts is $40. You can purchase it or rent downhill bikes with pads and helmet at **Alyeska Daylodge Rental Shop** (☑754-2553; per day $100).

☞ Tours

Alpine Air   SCENIC FLIGHTS
(☑783-2360; www.alpineairalaska.com; Girdwood airport) Has a 30-minute glacier tour ($225) and an hour-long tour in which the helicopter lands on the ice ($335).

Ascending Path   HIKING
(☑783-0505; www.theascendingpath.com) This climbing-guide service has a three-hour glacier hike on Alyeska Glacier ($139), and a midnight-sun glacier trek from mid-June to mid-July that begins at 8pm. The company also offers a three-hour rock-climbing outing designed for beginners ($129).

Chugach Express   DOGSLED
(☑783-2266; www.chugachexpress.com; Arlberg Ave; adult/child $59/29; ⊙9am, 11am, 3pm & 5pm) Offers a tour of Dario Martinez's kennel, a nine-time participant of the Iditarod Sled Dog Race. Along with cuddling puppies and hearing Iditarod Tales you also get a dogsled ride. Pick up the Chugach Express van at the Alyeska Tram.

Hotel Alyeska   BOUTIQUE TOURS
(☑754-2111, www.alyeskaresort.com; 1000 Arlberg Ave) Whether you want to golf, paraglide, photograph brown bears or do a yoga session in the alpine, this resort has the (expensive) tour for you.

Spencer Whistle Stop Train   GLACIER
(☑265-2494, 800-544-0552; www.akrr.com) You can ride the Alaska Railroad to Spencer Glacier, where you can hike a 3.4-mile trail to the face of the glacier or join a guided walk with a USFS Ranger. Whistle Stop hikers have from 1:45pm to 4:30pm to complete the hike and meet the train for the return. Or you can camp overnight at a group campsite. The round-trip fares from Girdwood

and Anchorage include transport (adult/child $103/52); save money by catching the train directly at the Portage station (adult/child $64/32).

🛏 Sleeping

At the Alyeska Ski Area, **Alyeska Accommodations** (☑783-2000, 888-783-2001; www.alyeskaaccommodations.com; r $120-450) sublets massive, privately owned (and decorated) condos, many with full kitchens, hot tubs and saunas. If you need something smaller, it also rents out rooms and cabins.

B&Bs make up the bulk of Girdwood's lodging and are the only midrange option. The **Alyeska/Girdwood Accommodations Association** (☑222-4858; www.agaa.biz) can find last-minute rooms. Girdwood has a 12% bed tax.

┌─────┐
│ TOP │ **Alyeska Hostel**   HOSTEL $
│CHOICE│
└─────┘
(☑783-2222; www.alyeskahostel.com; 227 Alta Dr; dm/s/d $20/45/56; ⊛) A cozy, no smoking, no shoes guesthouse with a private cabin ($75), private room, eight bunks and killer mountain views. The one dorm room sleeps eight; make sure you book ahead.

Hotel Alyeska   RESORT $$$
(☑754-2111, www.alyeskaresort.com; 1000 Arlberg Ave; d $229-249, ste $349; ⊛🛜@🏊) This place earned four stars from AAA because it deserved them – from the whirlpool with a view to bathrobes and slippers in every room, this place is swanky. For something less swanky you can park your RV in the day lodge for $10 a night and then ride the resort shuttle to use the pool or take a shower.

Carriage House B&B   B&B $$
(☑783-9464, 888-961-9464; www.thecarriage houseandb.com; Mile 0.3 Crow Creek Rd; r $125-150; ⊛🛜) A stunning cedar house within walking distance of the town center. Breakfast is made with eggs from the chickens clucking around outside and is served in a vaulted-ceiling common room that overlooks the mountains.

Glacier View B&B   B&B $$
(☑783-1160, 350-0674; www.glacierviewbnb.com; Alpina Way; r $130-180; ⊛🛜) The most upscale B&B in the area with four guest rooms along with an extra-large hot tub and a common area where you can view the mountains and see six glaciers. Rooms come with full breakfast.

Bud & Carol's B&B

B&B **$**

(☑783-3182; www.budandcarolsbandb.com; 211 Brighton Rd; r $85; ☎🖰) Located at the base of the ski hill, this B&B offers two rooms with private bath and a fully equipped kitchen stocked with all you need for a hearty continental breakfast.

✖ Eating

For such a tiny place, Girdwood has an amazing selection of restaurants that often pull their patrons in from Anchorage. Since it's part of the municipality of Anchorage, all restaurants and bars are refreshingly smoke-free.

TOP CHOICE | Maxine's Glacier City Bistro

MEDITERRANEAN **$$**

(☑783-1234; Crow Creek Rd; lunch $10-13, dinner $13-26; ☯lunch Wed-Mon, dinner daily; 🖰) Maxine's is a Mediterranean bistro with a Girdwood feel (friendly dogs congregate outside while their owners eat). Share the meze or rosemary lamb, as they're huge, but keep the wonton tacos for yourself. Live music livens up the already colorful place on Friday and Saturday nights while Wednesday is reserved for open mic.

Double Musky Inn

CAJUN **$$$**

(www.doublemuskyinn.com; Crow Creek Rd; dinner $22-45; ☯dinner Tue-Sun) Folks drive down from Anchorage for the French pepper steak – New York strip encrusted in cracked pepper and covered with a spicy burgundy sauce – the reason you have to wait (reservations are not accepted) two hours on weekends. The cuisine is Cajun accented, hence the masks and mardi-gras beads hanging from the ceiling. The desserts are divine.

Bake Shop

BAKERY **$**

(www.thebakeshop.com; Olympic Circle; breakfast $6-10, lunch $7-8; ☯breakfast, lunch & dinner) Always busy, this bright and art-filled place serves wholesome omelets with fresh-baked breads, all of which you can enjoy at one of the large wooden tables. One of the giant cinnamon rolls is big enough to share with a friend – or not.

Jack Sprat

MODERN AMERICAN **$$$**

(☑783-5225; www.jacksprat.com; Olympic Circle Dr; brunch $9-13, dinner $19-32; ☯brunch Sat & Sun, dinner daily; 🖰) Creative fresh cuisine at the base of the ski hill. Many dishes are vegetarian-friendly and made from organically grown ingredients such as grilled vegetable pasta with homemade gnocchi and

toasted walnut pesto. Remodeled in 2011, the restaurant is larger and now has outdoor sitting but reservations are recommended.

Seven Glaciers Restaurant

SEAFOOD **$$$**

(☑754-2237; dinner $32-52; ☯dinner) Sitting on top of Mt Alyeska, 2300ft above sea level, is the best of Alyeska Resort's six restaurants and bars. The hotel tram will take you to an evening of gourmet dining and absolutely stunning views that include Turnagain Arm and, yes, seven glaciers. The menu is dominated by seafood; even the meat mains are offered with a side of king crab.

🖋 Casa Del Sol

MEXICAN **$**

(158 Holmgren Pl; mains $6-12; ☯lunch & dinner) Attached to the Girdwood Laundromall, this small joint serves up fresh Mexican food and homemade salsa. Or just relax at one of its outdoor tables and enjoy a beer while your laundry spins.

Chair 5 Restaurant

PIZZA **$$**

(www.chairfive.com; 5 Lindblad Ave; medium pizza $13-17, dinner $17-28; ☯lunch & dinner) The kind of bar and restaurant skiers love after a long day on the slopes. It features more than 60 beers, including a dozen on tap, 15 types of gourmet pizzas, big burgers and a lot of blackened halibut.

Crow Creek Mercantile

MARKET **$**

(Nightower Rd; ☯7am-midnight Mon-Fri, from 8am Sat & Sun) Girdwood's tiny grocery store also has some ready-to-eat items.

ⓘ Information

There are ATMs at the Tesoro Station, Alyeska Resort and Crow Creek Mercantile.

Girdwood Chamber of Commerce (www.girdwoodalaska.com) No visitors center but a great website for pretrip planning.

Girdwood Clinic (☑783-1355; Hightower Rd; ☯10am-6pm Tue-Sat) Offers basic medical care.

Girdwood Laundromall (☑317-0512; 158 Holmgren Pl; ☯7am-9pm; @🖰) Voted the number one Laundromat in the US by *American Coin-Op Magazine*, this place also has themed coin-op showers complete with nature sounds, plus internet access (per minute 15¢, free wireless) and an ATM.

Grind (☑783-2020; Hightower Rd; ☯7am-6pm Mon-Fri, 9am-5pm Sat & Sun; 🖰) The Grind serves up free wireless with your latte, and has a secondhand bookstore in back.

Scott & Wesley Gerrish Library (☑343-4024; 250 Egloff Dr; ☯1-6pm Tue & Thu, 1-8pm Wed,

10am-6pm Fri & Sat; @🛜) Girdwood's library has 10 terminals for free internet access, as well as wireless.

USFS Glacier Ranger Station (☎783-3242; Ranger Station Rd; ☉8am-5pm Mon-Fri) Has topo maps, a viewing scope, and information on area hikes, campgrounds and public-use cabins.

❶ Getting There & Around

Alaska Railroad (☎265-2494, 800-544-0552; www.akrr.com) Although the fare is steep, you could hop on the Alaska Railroad in Anchorage for a day trip to Girdwood (one way adult/child $59/30). On its way to Seward, the *Coastal Classic* train arrives at Girdwood at 8am daily during the summer and again at 9pm for the return journey to Anchorage.

Glacier Valley Transit (☎382-9908; www.glaciervalleytransit.com) Girdwood's bus service operates from Alyeska Resort to the Seward Hwy at $1 a ride.

Magic Bus (☎230-6773; www.themagicbus.com) An accommodating charter-bus service that leaves Anchorage at 7:45am and departs from Girdwood for the return trip at 6:30pm (one way/round-trip $30/50).

Seward Bus Lines (☎563-0800, 888-420-7788; www.sewardbuslines.net) Can arrange transport to Seward and Anchorage from Girdwood.

South of Girdwood

Seward Hwy continues southeast past Girdwood and a few nifty tourist attractions to what's left of Portage, which was destroyed by the 1964 Good Friday Earthquake and is basically a few structures sinking into the nearby mud flats.

The Wetland Observation Platform (Mile 81) features interpretive plaques on the ducks, arctic terns, bald eagles and other wildlife inhabiting the area.

Alaska Wildlife Conservation Center (☎783-2025; www.alaskawildlife.org; Mile 79; adult/child $10/7.50; ☉8am-8pm) is a nonprofit wildlife center where injured and rescued animals are on display. If you haven't seen a bear or moose on your trip yet, swing through.

Portage Glacier

Portage Glacier Access Rd leaves Seward Hwy at Mile 79, continuing 5.4 miles to the **Begich-Boggs Visitors Center** (☎783-2326; adult/child $5/free; ☉9am-6pm; 👶) en route to Whittier, on the other side of the Anton Memorial Tunnel.

The building, with its observation decks and telescopes, was designed to provide great views of Portage Glacier. But ironically (and to the dismay of thousands of tourists) the glacier has retreated so fast you can no longer see it from the center. Still, inside are neat high-tech wildlife displays and the excellent movie, *Voices from the Ice*.

Most people view the glacier through **Gray Line** (☎277-5581; www.graylinealaska.com), whose cruise boat MV *Ptarmigan* departs from a dock near the Begich-Boggs Center five times daily from June to September for a trip to the glacier face. It's a costly one-hour cruise; adult/child $29/14.50 or $79/39 with transportation from Anchorage. If you have a pair of hiking boots, Portage Pass Trail, a mile-long trek to the pass, will provide a good view of Portage Glacier. The trail begins near the tunnel on the Whittier side, so it's a $12-per-car fare to drive through and then return.

The multi-use **Trail of Blue Ice** parallels Portage Glacier Access Rd and meanders through forest on a wide gravel (and occasionally boardwalk) trail, connecting Portage Lake to the Seward Hwy. Another interesting hike is **Byron Glacier View Trail**, a single, flat mile to an unusually ice-worm-infested snowfield and grand glacier views.

There are two USFS campgrounds. **Black Bear Campground** (Mile 3.7 Portage Glacier Access Rd; campsites $14) is beautiful and woodsy – and caters more to tent campers – while **Williwaw Campground** (Mile 4.3 Portage Glacier Access Rd; campsites $18-28) is stunningly located beneath Explorer Glacier and receives more of an RV crowd. Both campgrounds are extremely popular, although sites at Williwaw can be reserved in advance through **National Recreation Reservation Service** (☎877-444-6777, 518-885-3639; www.recreation.gov).

NORTH OF ANCHORAGE

As you drive out of Anchorage, you'll soon parallel Knik Arm, while the Chugach Mountains stay to your right. Small communities dot either side of the road, but Eagle River and Eklutna offer the best access to the mountains. Both communities are worthy of a day trip from Anchorage, but to escape the hustle of the city, you can use these small towns as a base for exploring both Anchorage and the wilds around it.

Glenn Highway

In Anchorage, 5th Ave becomes Glenn Hwy, running 189 miles through Palmer, where it makes a junction with the George Parks Hwy, to Glennallen and the Richardson Hwy. Milepost distances are measured from Anchorage.

At Mile 11.5 of Glenn Hwy is Eagle River Campground (Hiland Rd exit; campsites $15), with beautiful walk-in sites. The river runs closest to the shady sites in the 'Rapids' section. Keep in mind this is one of the most popular campsites in the state and half the sites can be reserved up to a year in advance through Lifetime Adventures (☎764-4644, 800-952-8624; www.lifetimeadventures.net).

EAGLE RIVER
POP 30,000

At Mile 13.4 of Glenn Hwy is the exit to Old Glenn Hwy, which takes you through the bedroom communities of Eagle River and Chugiak. Eagle River has something of a city center; the Eagle River Town Square off Business Blvd, and just about every business you'll need. The Bear Paw Festival, held here in July, is worth the trip just for the 'Slippery Salmon Olympics,' which involves racing with a hula hoop, serving tray and, of course, a large dead fish. Most people, however, come here for the drive down Eagle River Rd.

Sights & Activities

Eagle River Road   DRIVING TOUR
This stunning sidetrip into the heart of the Chugach Mountains follows the Eagle River for 13 miles. The road is paved and winding, and at Mile 7.4 there is a put-in for rafts to float the Class I and II section of the river. The road ends at the Eagle River Nature Center (☎694-2108; www.ernc.org; 32750 Eagle River Rd; admission per vehicle $5; ⊙10am-5pm; 🚻). The log-cabin center offers wildlife displays, telescopes for finding Dall sheep, guided hikes on most Saturday and Sundays, and heaps of programs for kids.

Rodak Nature Trail   HIKING
Several trails depart from the Eagle River Nature Center, with Rodak Nature Trail being the easiest. Children will love the mile-long interpretive path, as it swings by an impressive overlook straddling a salmon stream and a huge beaver dam. Albert Loop Trail is a slightly more challenging 3-mile hike through boreal forest and along Eagle River.

Iditarod National Historic Trail   HIKING
The National Historic Iditarod Trail is a 26-mile trek used by gold miners and sled-dog teams until 1918, when the Alaska Railroad was finished. It's a three-day hike through superb mountain scenery to Girdwood, and the region's best backpack adventure. For details, see p58.

For a shorter outing you can turn around at the Perch, a very large rock in the middle of wonderland, then backtrack to the Dew Mound Trail at Echo Bend and loop back to the Nature Center, making this a scenic 8-mile trip. Pitch a tent at Rapids Camp (Mile 1.7) or Echo Bend (Mile 3), or rent one of two yurts ($65 per night) close by.

Thunderbird Falls   WATERFALL
Thunderbird Falls, closer to Eklutna, is a rewarding 2-mile walk with a gorgeous little waterfall for the grand finale. Anchorage's People Mover bus 102 stops at the trailhead, off the Thunderbird Falls exit of Glenn Hwy.

🛏 Sleeping & Eating

Eagle River has a 12% bed tax, and all restaurants are smoke-free.

Alaska Chalet B&B   B&B $$
(☎694-1528, 877-694-1528; www.alaskachaletbb.com; 11031 Gulkana Cr; r/ste $105/135; ⊛@) In a small neighborhood within walking distance of downtown Eagle River, this is a European-style B&B. The clean guest quarters are separate from the main house and include kitchenettes, and the host speaks German.

Eagle River Motel   MOTEL $
(☎694-5000, 866-256-6835; www.eaglerivermotel.com; 11111 Old Eagle River Rd; s/d $89/99) Rooms are equipped with microwaves and refrigerators, and it's a better deal than you'd find in Anchorage.

Haute Quarter Grill   AMERICAN $$$
(☎622-4745; http://hautequartergrill.com; 11221 Old Glenn Hwy; dinner $19-30; ⊙dinner Tue-Sat) A highly recommended splurge, its menu offers a lot of gourmet for your dollar. You can skip the main all together and feast on an outstanding blackened halibut Caesar salad.

Jitters   COFFEE HOUSE $
(www.jitterseagleriver.com; 11401 Old Glenn Hwy; quick eats $5-10; ⊙5:30am-9pm Mon-Fri, 6am-7pm Sat, 7am-7pm Sun; 🛜) The best place to stop after a rainy hike. It serves up soup, sandwiches and pastries in a warm environment; live music is often playing throughout the day.

SARAH PALIN'S WASILLA

For years Wasilla (pop 7831) was a quick stop for most visitors to either pick up supplies at the state's largest Wal-Mart before heading to Denali National Park or to visit the town's main attractions: Iditarod Trail Headquarters (www.iditarod.com; Mile 2.2 Knik Rd; admission free; ⊙8am-7pm) or the Dorothy Page Museum (www.cityofwasilla.com/museum; 323 Main St; adult/child $3/free; ⊙9am-5pm Mon-Sat).

Then the nation discovered Sarah Palin during the 2008 presidential campaign and this town, or Alaska for that matter, hasn't been the same since.

Palin was only three when her father, a science teacher, moved his family from Idaho to Alaska in 1964 to accept a teaching position. Eventually he relocated to Wasilla, where senior point-guard Palin led her high-school girls' basketball team to the Alaska state championship. Over the next few years, Palin finished third in the 1984 Miss Alaska pageant, worked as a sports reporter for an Anchorage TV station and married her high school sweetheart.

Then, in 1992, the self-described 'hockey mom' won a seat on the Wasilla City Council and four years later, at 32, she was elected Wasilla's mayor. But the turning point for Palin was in 2004 when she resigned as the head of the Alaska Oil and Gas Conservation Commission over ethical violations by another commissioner. Two years later, when Palin ran for governor, promising 'transparency and trust' in Alaska politics, she struck a chord with many residents disillusioned with the career politicians, corruption and cronyism. The results were stunning. In the Republican primary she crushed incumbent Governor Frank Murkowski by more than 30 percentage points. In the general election, she handily beat former Democratic Governor Tony Knowles to not only become Alaska's first female governor but also, at age 42, its youngest.

Two years later Republican presidential candidate John McCain tapped Palin as his running mate, making her the first Alaskan and only the second woman to run on a major US party ticket. The national campaign was rough for Palin: there was the announcement of her unwed teenage daughter's pregnancy and an interview with CBS News anchor Katie Couric in which she stumbled badly over foreign policy questions. But Palin's pro-life views on abortion, strong advocacy of gun ownership and conservative fiscal beliefs excited the right wing of the Republican party, while her trademark 'you betcha' phrase became a rallying cry for the so-called Joe Six-Packs of America.

Even though the Republicans lost the presidential campaign, Palin became a Tea Party favorite. She shocked the political world in 2009 by resigning as Alaska governor and then the literary world when her first book, *Going Rogue: An American Life*, became one of only four political memoirs to sell more than a million copies in its first two weeks. Almost immediately a movement was organized to position Palin for the Republican nomination in 2012, but in October 2011 she announced that she would not run.

Today Palin is recognized more as a national political celebrity than she is as an Alaskan, evident in her purchasing a second home in Arizona in 2011. Still, in Alaska nobody has more full-size cutouts gracing the doors of gift shops and restaurants. And a day doesn't go by in Wasilla without a tourist asking a local, 'Where's Sarah Palin?'

ℹ Information

Acute Family Medicine Clinic (☑622-4325; 11470 Business Blvd; ⊙9am-7pm Mon-Fri, 9am-5pm Sat & Sun) Offers walk-in service.

Chugiak-Eagle River Chamber of Commerce (☑694-4702; www.cer.org; 12001 Business Blvd; ⊙9am-4pm Mon-Fri)

Chugiak-Eagle River Library (⊙noon-7pm Tue-Thu, 10am-6pm Fri & Sat; @) In the Chugiak-Eagle River Town Center.

Key Bank (10928 Eagle River Rd) Also has an ATM.

Laundry Basket (12110 Business Blvd) Located in the Regional Park Plaza.

EKLUTNA
POP 335

This 350-year-old Alaska Native village is just west of the Eklutna Lake Rd exit, Mile 26.5 of Glenn Hwy. One of the most interesting anthropological sites in the region is preserved at Eklutna Village Historical Park (☑688-6026; tour adult/child $5/2.50; ⊙10am-4pm), where the uneasy marriage of the Athabascan and Russian Orthodox cultures is enshrined. The interior of St Nicholas Church is modeled after Noah's ark while outside, outdoor altars abound, including a heartfelt lean-to for St Herman, patron saint of Alaska. The most revealing structures, however, are the 80 brightly colored spirit boxes in the nearby Denáina Athabascan cemetery. Invest your time in one of the half-hour tours.

🏃 Activities

Eklutna Lake is 10 long, bumpy miles east on Eklutna Lake Rd. It's worth every minute once the sky suddenly opens, unveiling a stunning valley with glacier-and-peak-ringed Eklutna Lake, the largest body of water in Chugach State Park, at its center. This slice of Chugach State Park is a recreational paradise with more than 27 miles of hiking and mountain-biking trails.

Lakeside Trail   MOUNTAIN BIKING, HIKING
This trail is a flat 13-miles to the other end of the lake, passing two excellent and free backcountry camping areas: Eklutna Alex Campground (Mile 9) and Kanchee Campground (Mile 11). East Fork Trail diverts from the main trail at Mile 10.5 and it runs another 5.5 miles to a great view of Mt Bashful, the tallest mountain (8005ft) in the park. Keep going an easy 1 mile past the Lakeside Trail terminus to view the receding Eklutna Glacier. ATVs can use the trails Sunday through Wednesday, hikers and cyclists anytime.

Bold Ridge Trail   HIKING
To reach the alpine, hike this steep 3.5-mile trail that begins 5 miles along the Lakeshore Trail and continues to a saddle below Bold Peak (7522ft), where there are views of the valley, Eklutna Glacier and even Knik Arm. People with the energy can scramble up nearby ridges. Plan on two hours to climb the trail and an hour for the return. To actually climb Bold Peak requires serious equipment.

Twin Peaks Trail   HIKING
This route to the mountains is shorter (3.5 miles from the parking lot), but just as steep. It takes you through lush forest into alpine meadows presided over by the imposing eponymous peaks. Berries, wildlife and great lake views make scrambling toward the top downright enjoyable.

Eklutna Lake   KAYAKING
This 7-mile long lake makes for great paddling. Lifetime Adventures (☑746-4644, 800-952-8624; www.lifetimeadventures.net; Eklutna Lake State Recreation Area; ⊙10am-6pm) rents kayaks (single/double $40/45 half-day, $60/65 full day) and mountain bikes (half-/

full day $25/35). It also offers a fun Paddle & Pedal rental where you kayak down the lake and then ride a mountain bike back ($75 per person).

🛌 Sleeping

Eklutna Lake State Recreation Area   CAMPGROUND $
(campsites $10) Has a rustic campground at the west end of the lake and is a beautiful place to spend a night. But even with 50 sites it's often filled.

Alaska Wilderness Cabins   CABIN $
(☑688-6201, 800-764-6201; www.goalaskan.com; Eklutna Lake Rd; cabin/r $50/70) Offers accommodations ranging from its cozy Eklutna room with a view of the lake to a pair of cabins without electricity or running water.

Palmer

POP 5937
Filled with old farming-related buildings, Palmer at times feels more like the Midwest than Alaska, except that it's ringed by mountains. Many downtown venues exude 1930s ambience, with antique furniture and wood floors. Sure, Palmer is subjected to the same suburban sprawl as anywhere else, but its charm lies in its unique history and living agricultural community. For those who want to skip the city hassles and high prices of Anchorage, Palmer is an excellent option with just enough choices in lodging, restaurants and sights to keep you satisfied for a day or two.

From Eklutna Lake Rd, Glenn Hwy continues north, crossing Knik and Matanuska Rivers at the northern end of Cook Inlet, and at Mile 35.3 reaching a major junction with the George Parks Hwy. At this point, Glenn Hwy curves sharply to the east and heads into Palmer, 7 miles away. If you're driving, a much more scenic way to reach Palmer is to leave Glenn Hwy just before it crosses Knik River and follow Old Glenn Hwy into town.

History

Born during President Roosevelt's New Deal, Palmer was one of the great social experiments in an era when human nature was believed infinitely flexible. The mission was to transplant 200 farming families, who were refugees from the Depression-era dustbowl (the worst agricultural disaster in US history), to Alaska, where they would cultivate a new agricultural economy.

Trainloads of Midwesterners and their Sears & Roebuck furniture were deposited in the Matanuska and Susitna valleys, both deemed suitable by the government for such endeavors. Nearly everything was imported, from building materials (and plans) to teachers. Soil rich by Alaskan standards enjoyed a growing season just long enough for cool-weather grains and certain vegetables. There was little margin for error, however, and any unexpected frost could destroy an entire year of seed and sweat.

Original buildings stand throughout Palmer, many of which have been refurbished and maintain their hearty wooden farm feel. Descendents of the original colonists, who refer to themselves as Colony children or grandchildren, still inhabit Palmer and have wonderful stories to tell.

◎ Sights & Activities

FREE Palmer Museum of History & Art   MUSEUM
(723 S Valley Way; ◐9am-6pm) The log cabin that used to be just a visitor center is now more museum than brochures with local art and interesting displays on Palmer's agricultural past.

FREE Matanuska Valley Agricultural Showcase   GARDENS
(723 S Valley Way; ◐8am-7pm Jun-Aug) Outside the visitor center is Matanuska Valley Agricultural Showcase, a garden featuring flowers and the area's famous oversized vegetables. But you have to be passing through in August if you want to see a cabbage bigger than a basketball. Every Friday during summer is Friday Fling (◐11am-6pm Jun-Aug), an open-air market with local produce, art, crafts, food and live music.

Colony House Museum   MUSEUM
(☎745-1935; 316 E Elmwood Ave; adult/child $2/1; ◐10am-4pm Tue-Sat) This friendly museum is run by Colony children, and their enthusiasm for Palmer's history is evident. Take the time for a guided tour, and you'll leave with an appreciation of the enormity of the colonizing project. The museum itself was a 'Colony Farm House' built during the original settlement of Palmer, and its eight rooms are still furnished with artifacts and stories from that era. To bring the living-room piano to Alaska, members of one pioneer family left behind their luggage and stuffed

their clothes in it, the only way to make their weight allotment.

Knik Glacier   GLACIER
Trekkies take note: Knik Glacier is best known as the setting where a portion of *Star Trek VI* was filmed. You can get a partial view of the ice floe at Mile 7 of Knik River Rd off Old Glenn Hwy but the best way to experience it is on an airboat ride up the Knik River. Knik Glacier Tours (☎746-1577; www.knikglacier.com; adult/child $100/50) has four-hour tours departing at 10am and 2pm daily.

Farms
If you have a vehicle, cruise through Palmer's back roads past original Colony farms. Go northeast 9 miles on Glenn Hwy and hop on Farm Loop Rd; look for vegetable stands if you're passing through here from mid- to late summer.

Pyrah's Pioneer Peak Farm   FARM
(www.pppfarm.net; Mile 2.8 Bodenberg Loop Rd; ◐9am-5pm Mon, to 9pm Tue-Sat) South of Palmer, Pyrah's Pioneer Peak Farm is the largest pick-your-own-vegetables place in the Mat-Su Valley, with would-be farmers in the fields from July to early October picking everything from peas and potatoes to carrots and cabbages.

Reindeer Farm   FARM
(www.reindeerfarm.com; Mile 11.5 Old Glenn Hwy; adult/child $7/5; ◐10am-6pm) The Reindeer Farm is one of the original Colony farms and a great place to bring the kids. Here they will be able to pet and feed the reindeer, and are encouraged to think the reindeer are connected to Santa. There's also elk, moose and bison to take photos of. Rubber boots are provided.

Musk Ox Farm   FARM
(☎745-4151; www.muskoxfarm.org; Mile 50 Glenn Hwy; adult/child $9/5; ◐10am-6pm) The Musk Ox Farm is the only domestic herd of these big, shaggy beasts in the world. These ice-age critters are intelligent enough to have evolved a complex social structure that allows survival under incredibly harsh conditions. Yes, you'll probably get to pet them, too. Qiviut (pronounced 'kiv-ee-oot'), the incredibly warm, soft and pricey ($40 per ounce) material made from the musk ox's soft undercoat, is harvested here; fine sweaters and hats are for sale in the gift shop. Tours are given every 45 minutes.

HATCHER PASS

A sidetrip from Palmer (or even a base) is the photogenic Hatcher Pass. This alpine passage cuts through the Talkeetna Mountains and leads to meadows, ridges and glaciers. Gold was the first treasure people found here; today it's footpaths, abandoned mines and popular climbs that outshine the precious metal.

The main attraction of Hatcher Pass is 272-acre Independence Mine State Historical Park (Mile 18 Hatcher Pass Rd; admission per vehicle $5), a huge, abandoned gold mine sprawled out in an alpine valley. The 1930s facility, built by the Alaska-Pacific Mining Company (APC), was for 10 years the second-most-productive hardrock gold mine in Alaska. At its peak, in 1941, APC employed 204 workers here, blasted almost 12 miles of tunnels and recovered 34,416oz of gold, today worth almost $18 million. The mine was finally abandoned in 1955.

Today you can explore the structures, hike several trails and take in the stunning views at Hatcher Pass. The visitors center (☎745-2827; ◷11am-7pm) has a map of the park, a simulated mining tunnel, displays on the ways to mine gold (panning, placer mining and hardrock) and guided tours (adult/child $6/3) at 1pm and 3pm. From the center, follow Hardrock Trail past the dilapidated buildings, which include bunkhouses and a mill complex that is built into the side of the mountain and looks like an avalanche of falling timber. Make an effort to climb up the trail to the water tunnel portal, where there is a great view of the entire complex and a blast of cold air pouring out of the mountain.

Hatcher Pass also offers some of the best alpine hiking in the Mat-Su areas. The easy, beautiful Gold Mint Trail begins at a parking lot across from Motherlode Lodge, at Mile 14 Fishhook–Willow Rd. The trail follows the Little Susitna River into a gently sloping mountain valley and within 3 miles you spot the ruins of Lonesome Mine. Keep hiking and you'll eventually reach Mint Glacier.

With two alpine lakes, lots of waterfalls, glaciers and towering walls of granite, the 7-mile Reed Lakes Trail (9 miles to the upper lake) is worth the climb, which includes some serious scrambling. Once you reach upper Reed Lake, continue for a mile to Bomber Glacier, where the ruin of a B-29 bomber lies in memorial to six men who perished there in a 1957 crash. A mile past Motherlode Lodge, a road to Archangel Valley splits off from Fishhook–Willow Rd and leads to the Reed Lakes trailhead, a wide road. If you've got a 4WD, you can (theoretically) drive the first 3 miles of the Craigie Creek Trail, posted along the Fishhook–Willow Rd just west of Hatcher Pass. It's better, however, to walk the gently climbing old road up a valley and past several abandoned mining operations to the head of the creek. It then becomes a very steep trail for 3 miles to Dogsled Pass, where you can access several wilderness trails into the Talkeetna Mountains.

If the weather is nice and you have the funds it's hard to pass up spending the night at the pass. Hatcher Pass Lodge (☎745-5897; www.hatcherpasslodge.com; Mile 17.5 Hatcher Pass Rd; r/cabins $95/165; ☻), inside the state park, is a highly recommended splurge. Aside from spectacular views at 3000ft, the lodge has seven cabins, three rooms, a (pricey) restaurant and bar, and a sauna built over a rushing mountain stream.

Hiking

There is some great hiking in the Mat-Su area and a more complete list is available from the Mat-Su Trails & Parks Foundation (www.matsutrails.org).

Lazy Mountain Trail   HIKING

The best hike near Palmer is the berry-lined climb to the top of 3720ft Lazy Mountain. The 2.5-mile trail is steep at times, but makes for a pleasant trek that ends in an alpine setting with good views of Matanuska Valley farms. Take Old Glenn Hwy across the Matanuska River, turn left onto Clark-Wolverine Rd and then right onto Huntley Rd; follow it to the Equestrian Center parking lot and trailhead, marked 'Foot Trail.' Plan on three to five hours for the round-trip.

Matanuska Peak Trail   HIKING

The 8-mile Matanuska Peak Trail is also often steep. It traverses the south slope of Lazy Mountain, above the McRoberts Creek Valley. As you ascend Matanuska Peak, you'll climb 5670ft in 4 miles – be prepared for a long day. You'll be richly rewarded for your hard work, however, by the views of the Knik and Matanuska Rivers, as well as Cook Inlet. To reach the trailhead, take Old Glenn Hwy from Palmer toward Butte and turn left onto Smith Rd at Mile 15.5. Follow Smith Rd for 1.4 miles, until it ends at the trailhead parking lot.

Pioneer Ridge Trail
HIKING

Pioneer Ridge Trail is a 5.7-mile route from Knik River Rd that climbs the main ridge extending southeast from Pioneer Peaks (6400ft). You'll climb through forest until you reach the alpine tundra at 3200ft. Once on the ridge, South Pioneer Peak is a mile to the northwest, and North Pioneer Peak is 2 miles. Don't try to scale any peaks without rock-climbing experience and equipment. To the southeast, the ridge leads toward Bold Peak, the Hunter Creek drainage and eventually Eklutna Lake. To reach the trailhead, turn onto Knik River Rd, just before crossing the river on Old Glenn Hwy, and follow it for almost 3.8 miles to a posted trailhead on the right.

✺ Festivals & Events

Palmer becomes the state's hottest ticket during the **Alaska State Fair** (www.alaskastatefair.org; per day adult/child $10/6), a rollicking 12-day event that ends on Labor Day, the first Monday in September. The fair features live music and prized livestock from the surrounding area, as well as horse shows, a rodeo, a carnival and, of course, the giant cabbage weigh-off to see who grew the biggest one in the valley (the 2010 winner was the largest ever: 127lb!). If greased pigs, Spam-sponsored recipe contests and the Great Alaskan Husband Holler contest aren't enough to get you here, try this: berry pie cook-offs.

The fairground is also home to the **Mat-Su Miners** (☎745-6401; www.matsuminers.org; adult/child $4/2), another semipro team of the Alaska Baseball League that plays against clubs like Fairbanks Goldpanners and the Anchorage Bucs. Until 1980 the Palmer players were the Valley Green Giants but changed their name for obvious reasons.

Celebrate the first farmers arriving in Palmer at **Colony Days** (www.palmerchamber.org) with a bed race down Main St, a dunk tank with the mayor, and a good old hometown parade. There's also lots of yummy food, naturally.

🛏 Sleeping

If you arrive late, the Palmer Visitor Center has a courtesy phone outside with direct lines connected to area accommodations. There is also the **Mat-Su B&B Association** (www.alaskabnbhosts.com) that lists almost 30 B&Bs in the area, including 10 in Palmer. Add 8% tax to the prices here.

TOP CHOICE Colony Inn
HISTORIC HOTEL **$$**

(☎745-3330; 325 E Elmwood Ave; s/d $100/130; ☺@) What was constructed in 1935 as the Matanuska Colony Teacher's Dorm is now Palmer's nicest lodge. The 12 rooms are spacious, especially the corner rooms, well kept and equipped with TVs, pedestal sinks and whirlpool tubs. There's an inviting parlor for reading, furnished with antiques. Register at the Valley Hotel.

Hatcher Pass B&B
CABIN **$$**

(☎745-6788; www.hatcherpassbb.com; Mile 6.6 Palmer-Fishhook Rd; cabin s/d $109/149; ☺🐾) If you have wheels you can rent a cabin at several places on the way to Hatcher Pass. This B&B, 6 miles from Palmer, offers five button-cute log cabins with kitchenettes and fridges stocked with everything you need to make breakfast.

River Crest Manor
B&B **$**

(☎746-6214; www.rivercrestmanor.com; 2655 Old Glenn Hwy; r $100-110, cabin $120; ☺🐾) A beautiful, expansive home that provides three guest rooms and a cabin across the road from the Matanuska River. It's 1.5 miles from downtown Palmer.

Matanuska River Park
CAMPGROUND **$**

(☎745-9631; Mile 17.5 Old Glenn Hwy; tentsites/RV sites $10/15) A delightful and very affordable campground less than a half-mile east of town. Some of the 80 sites are wooded, while winding around ponds and the Matanuska River are a series of short foot trails.

Pioneer Motel
MOTEL **$**

(☎745-3425; www.thepioneermotel.com; 124 W Arctic Ave; s/d $79/94; 🐾) Your best budget option. The rooms are nicer than the outside appearance indicates and come with microwaves, coffeemakers and refrigerators. Quilt-like comforters brighten the rooms.

Valley Hotel
HOTEL **$**

(☎745-3330, Alaska only 800-478-7666; 606 S Alaska St; r $85; ☺🐾) This longtime hotel received a badly needed facelift in 2011 and now its small rooms are much more palatable. On the 1st floor its Caboose Lounge is a friendly pub to end a day while the 24-hour cafe is a great place to start one.

✗ Eating

Hearty cuisine, often utilizing locally grown produce, makes Palmer's expanding restaurant scene unique in Alaska.

TOP CHOICE Turkey Red   FUSION $$
(www.turkeyred.com; 550 S Alaska St; lunch $8-12, dinner $14-28; ☉breakfast, lunch & dinner Mon-Sat; ☑) Palmer's classiest restaurant is a bright and colorful cafe serving fresh dishes made from scratch including wonderful fresh-baked breads and desserts. Vegetarians won't go hungry here, and much of the produce is organic and locally grown.

Vagabond Blues   COFFEE HOUSE $
(www.vagblues.com; 642 S Alaska St; light meals $4-7; ☉7am-9pm Mon-Sat, 8am-6pm Sun; ☎) The cultural heartbeat of Palmer is this cozy coffee shop, with local art on the walls and often live music at night. It has healthy sandwiches, soups and salads.

Rusty's   AMERICAN $$
(320 E Dahlia St; mains $17-30; ☉lunch & dinner Tue-Sat) Housed in the renovated Palmer Trading Post whose walls are adorned with historic photos, this restaurant also has a delightful outdoor area where every seat has a view of the mountains. The portions are huge and the homemade desserts heavenly, especially Rusty's bread pudding with whiskey sauce.

Inn Café   CAFE $$
(325 E Elmwood Ave; sandwiches $9-10, brunch $16; ☉lunch Mon-Fri, brunch Sun) This former teacher's dorm now houses a pleasant restaurant with the kind of creaky wood-floored ambience expected in Palmer. Sandwiches and salads are served on weekdays, and brunch is on Sunday.

Colony Kitchen   BREAKFAST $$
(1890 Glenn Hwy; breakfast $7-13, dinner $12-22; ☉breakfast, lunch & dinner) If you like your breakfast big, you'll be stoked: not only is your most important meal huge, but it's served all day. You'll eat beneath stuffed birds suspended from the ceiling (hence its other name, the Noisy Goose Café).

ℹ Information

Alaskana Bookstore (564 S Denali St; ☉noon-5:30pm Fri-Sun) Huge selection of used and rare, state-related tomes.

Fireside Books (720 S Alaska St; ☎) New and used books, many locally oriented, and a good selection of maps.

Mat-Su Regional Hospital (☑861-6000; 2500 S Woodworth Loop) Gleaming and new, near the intersection of the Parks and Glenn Hwys.

Palmer Library (655 S Valley Way; ☉noon-6pm Mon-Fri, 10am-2pm Sat; @) An excellent library with free internet access.

Palmer Visitor Center (☑745-2880; www.palmerchamber.org; 723 S Valley Way; ☉9am-6pm) Within the Palmer Museum of History & Art; has a booking phone outside and pamphlets, books, maps and free coffee inside.

Post office (cnr S Cobb St & W Cedar Ave)

Wash Day Too (127 S Alaska St; @) Shower ($5 per 20 minutes) or access the internet ($4 per 30 minutes) while you launder.

Wells Fargo (705 S Bailey St) Lets you drain that account.

ℹ Getting There & Around

The Mat-Su Community Transit system, **Mascot** (☑376-5006; www.matsutransit.com; single ride/day pass $2.50/6), makes six trips daily between Wasilla and Palmer, and three commuter runs from the Valley to the Transit Center in Anchorage. If staying in Anchorage you can use the bus for a cheap day trip to Palmer, or vice versa. All buses stop at Carrs.

   Alaska Cab (☑746-2727) and **Mat-Su Taxi** (☑373-5861) both provide service around town, as well as to Wasilla ($30 to $40) and Anchorage ($70 to $80).

Prince William Sound

Best Places to Eat

» Saffron Project (p200)

» Baja Taco (p206)

» Harborside Pizza (p206)

Best Places to Stay

» Copper River Watershed Project (p205)

» Robe Lake Lodge (p197)

Why Go?

Enclosed in a jagged-edged circle and infused with fjords and glaciers, Prince William Sound is a stunner. With only three cities, the 15,000 sq mile region is mostly wilderness packed with quiet coves and rainy islands.

Despite sharing a similar environment, Prince William Sound's three cities couldn't be more different. Each arose from a different need and blossomed in a different manner. Valdez is dominated by slopes: the North Slope, from which the Trans-Alaska Pipeline originates, and the near vertical crags that surround it.

Earthy Cordova is isolated from roads, cruise ships and oil money. The salmon-rich ocean fuels the economy, and when locals need to hit the open road they head out to the Copper River Hwy.

Whittier is a living relic of WWII: a small town created solely as a military hideout and practically overshadowed by the mountains that kept it safe during the war.

Take your pick.

When to Go

Valdez

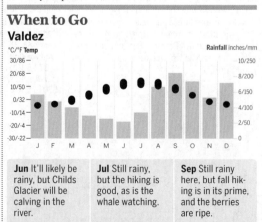

Jun It'll likely be rainy, but Childs Glacier will be calving in the river.

Jul Still rainy, but the hiking is good, as is the whale watching.

Sep Still rainy here, but fall hiking is in its prime, and the berries are ripe.

History

Prince William Sound was long a crossroads of Alaska Native cultures; the region has been inhabited at various times by coastal Chugach Inuit people, Athabascans originally from the Interior, and Tlingits who traveled up from Alaska's panhandle. The first European to arrive was Vitus Bering, a Dan-ish navigator sailing for the tsar of Russia, who anchored his ship near Kayak Island, east of Copper River, in 1741.

The Sound's three major towns have rather divergent modern histories. Valdez was settled in 1897, when 4000 gold prospectors took what had been billed as the 'All-American Route' to the Klondike goldfields.

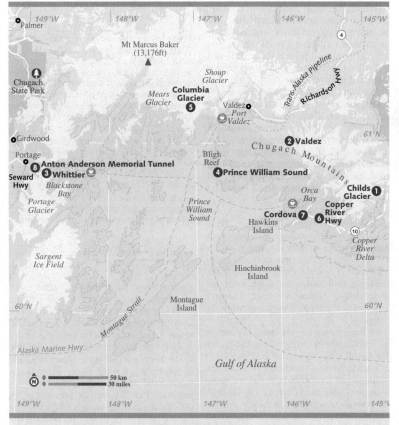

Prince William Sound Highlights

1 Listening, from your tent, to the apocalyptic thunder of **Childs Glacier** calving (p201)

2 Taking a helicopter ride above and around **Valdez' vertical peaks** (p196)

3 Spending an afternoon wandering the **Buckner building** in Whittier (p210)

4 **Spotting Dall porpoises** in the Sound (p212)

5 Watching icebergs from **Columbia Glacier** glow on the horizon as you glide by on the Alaska state ferry (p201)

6 Road-tripping down the **Copper River Highway** and marveling at the open land of the Copper River Delta

7 Chatting with friendly locals, decked in rubber boots, on the deck of the **Reluctant Fisherman Inn** in Cordova (p205)

8 Driving down the **Anton Anderson Memorial Tunnel** (p208), the longest combined railroad–vehicle tunnel in the US

It turned out to be one of the most dangerous trails, with hundreds of poorly provisioned dreamers dying on the trek across two glaciers and through the uncharted Chugach Mountains.

Over the next 60 years the community largely languished until catastrophe struck again, in the form of the 1964 Good Friday Earthquake, which killed over 30 locals and forced the wholesale relocation of the town. However, Valdez' fortunes turned in the 1970s when it was selected as the terminus of the Trans-Alaska Pipeline. The $9 billion project was a windfall beyond those early miners' wildest dreams; the population grew by 320% and the town never looked back.

Cordova's past is somewhat less fraught with catastrophe. A cannery village since the late 1800s, it was chosen a century ago as the port for a railway from the Kennecott copper mines near McCarthy. By 1916 it was a boomtown, with millions of dollars worth of ore passing through its docks. The railroad and town prospered until 1938, when the mine closed and the railroad ceased operations. Cordova then turned to fishing, its main economic base today.

The Sound's third community, Whittier, is of more recent origin, having been built as a secret military installation during WWII, when the Japanese were assaulting the Aleutian Islands. The army maintained the town until 1968, after which, as in Cordova, fishing became the main industry. Tourism now puts food on many residents' plates.

In recent decades, the most monumental event in the Sound has been the *Exxon Valdez* oil spill, which dumped at least 11 million gallons of petroleum into the sea, killing countless birds and marine mammals, and devastating the fishing industry for several years. Though fishing – and the environment – has largely rebounded, oil is still easy to find beneath the surface of beaches, and certain species are not expected to recover.

Dangers & Annoyances

By definition, glaciers move at a glacial pace, so you'd think they'd be harmless. In glacier-strewn Prince William Sound, however, they can be a real hazard. Not only have trekkers and mountaineers been killed when they've plunged into crevasses in the ice, but glaciers can also wreak havoc when they calve. Massive chunks often crack free from Childs Glacier, outside Cordova, and occasionally they're big enough to create mini tsunamis in the river. In recent years, Columbia Glacier has been retreating rapidly (the source of all those icebergs glowing on the horizon) and giant underwater bergs have broken free only to pop to the surface in a random location. Use caution if you're in a kayak.

ℹ️ Getting There & Around

Prince William Sound is all about the sea, and by far the best way to get around is on water. The **Alaska Marine Highway ferry** (☎800-642-0066; www.ferryalaska.com) provides a fairly convenient, fairly affordable service, linking Valdez and Cordova daily and making three runs per week between Valdez, Cordova and Whittier. But the ferry is more than just transport: it's an experience. There's something transcendent about bundling up on deck and watching the mountain-riddled, fjord-riven, watery world unfold.

Both Valdez and Whittier are highway accessible; the former is the beginning of the Richardson Hwy and the latter is connected to the Seward Hwy via the continent's longest automobile–rail tunnel.

Finally, planes are an option in Cordova and Valdez, where daily scheduled flights provide service to Anchorage and other major centers.

VALDEZ

POP 3792

Despite its natural attractions, Valdez is not primarily a tourist mecca. Nor, despite its proximity to the Sound, is it mainly a fishing village. On August 1, 1977, when the first tanker of oil issued forth from the Trans-Alaska Pipeline Terminal across the bay, Valdez became an oil town. Though it's hard to ignore the vertical slopes surrounding Valdez (and why would you want to?), it's just as difficult to ignore the presence of Big Oil. Massive storage tanks squat across the harbor, and the drive into town along the Richardson Hwy overlooks the pipeline as it snakes its way from the northern oil fields to this (in)famous port.

Valdez is still one of Alaska's prettiest spots, with glaciers galore, wildlife running amok and a Norman Rockwell–style harbor cradled by some of the highest coastal mountains (topping 7000ft) in the world. The city offers excellent paddling, hiking and other outdoor adventures, plus some quality restaurants, accommodations and museums, as befits a city blessed by the biggest boom Alaska has ever known.

◉ Sights

Valdez Museum
MUSEUM

(☏835-2764; www.valdezmuseum.org; 217 Egan Dr; adult/child $7/free; ⊙9am-5pm) This gargantuan museum includes an ornate, steam-powered antique fire engine, a 19th-century saloon bar and the ceremonial first barrel of oil to flow from the Trans-Alaska Pipeline. There are arresting photos of the six minutes when Valdez was shaken to pieces by the 1964 Good Friday Earthquake, and an exhibit featuring correspondence from stampeders attempting the grueling All-American Route from Valdez to the inland goldfields. A new oil spill exhibit shows the daily oil usage around the world, and a compelling video about those affected by the spill.

'Remembering Old Valdez' annex
MUSEUM

(☏835-5407; 436 Hazelet Ave; admission $4, free with Valdez Museum ticket; ⊙9am-5pm) Operated by the Valdez Museum, this annex is dominated by a scale model of the Old Valdez township. Each home destroyed in the Good Friday Earthquake has been restored in miniature, with the family's name in front. Other exhibits on the earthquake and subsequent tsunamis and fires are moving, but none are as heart-wrenching as the recordings of ham-radio operators communicating across the Sound as the quake wore on. A new earthquake and tsunami exhibit includes a theater where you can see the award-winning film *Between the Glacier and the Sea*, a collection of first-hand accounts of the 1964 earthquake.

FREE Maxine & Jesse Whitney Museum
MUSEUM

(☏834-1690; 303 Lowe St; admission free; ⊙9am-7pm; 🛗) This high-quality museum is devoted to Alaska Native culture and Alaskan wildlife, and features ivory and baleen artwork, moose-antler furniture, and natural-history displays, including some very creative taxidermy. Kid-delighting exhibits include fossils and arrowheads in cool pull-out drawers.

Small-Boat Harbor
HARBOR

Valdez' harbor is a classic: raucous with gulls and eagles, reeking of fish guts and sea salt and creosote, and home to all manner of vessels. The benches and long boardwalk are ideal for watching lucky anglers weighing in 100lb or 200lb halibut, and for taking in the fairy-tale mountainscape in the background. Nearby is the civic center (Fidalgo Dr), which has more picnic tables and panoramic vistas.

Old Valdez
HISTORIC SITE

Valdez has been unduly blessed by nature, but at 5:46pm on March 27, 1964 came payback time. Some 45 miles west of town and roughly 14 miles under the ground, a fault ruptured, triggering a magnitude 9.2 earthquake – the most powerful ever in American history. The land rippled as though it was water as Valdez slid into the harbor; tsunamis destroyed what was left. More than 30 people died.

After the quake, survivors labored to relocate and rebuild Valdez at its present site. But if you drive out on the Richardson Hwy you can see the ghostly and overgrown foundations of Old Valdez. The Earthquake Memorial, listing the names of the dead, is reached by turning off the highway onto the unsigned gravel road just south of Mark's Repair. On the day of the quake, Valdez' post office was here; in mere moments the ground sank so far that nowadays high tides reach the spot.

Trans-Alaska Pipeline Terminal
LANDMARK

Across the inlet from town, Valdez' ever-pumping heart once welcomed visitors, but since September 11, 2001 stricter security protocols have closed it to the public. From the end of Dayville Rd you can still get a peek at the facility, including the storage tanks holding nine million barrels of oil apiece. But heed the dire warnings: plenty of septuagenarian RVers have been pulled over and interrogated for getting too close. Those truly interested in the terminal can learn more about it at the Maxine & Jesse Whitney Museum (p193), which offers a pipeline 'video tour,' featuring great photography and a narrative that amounts to little more than Big Oil hype, and the Valdez Museum (p193), which has a newer pipeline exhibit.

🏃 Activities

Hiking

Valdez has a number of scenic and historic trails to get you away from town and up into the surrounding slopes. For a winter trails map, head to the civic center on Fidalgo Dr.

Dock Point Trail
HIKING

Not so much a hike as an enjoyable stroll through Dock Point Park beside the small-boat harbor, this 1-mile loop offers views of the peaks and the port, proximity to eagle nests, as well as salmonberry and blueberry picking.

Valdez

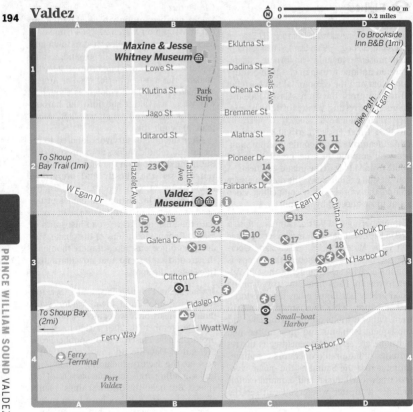

Mineral Creek Trail HIKING

A great walk away from town is the trek to the old Smith Stamping Mill. Built by WL Smith in 1913, the mill required only two men to operate it and used mercury to remove the gold from the ore.

To reach the trailhead, turn onto Mineral Creek Rd from Hanagita St. The marginal road bumps along for 5.5 miles and then turns into a mile-long trail to the old mill. Bears and mountain goats are often visible on this hike.

Shoup Bay Trail HIKING

This verdant stunner has views of Port Valdez, Shoup Glacier and the impressive Gold Creek delta. Turn around when you reach Gold Creek Bridge at Mile 3.5 to make this a somewhat challenging day, or go another seven steep, difficult and not always perfectly maintained miles along the water (and sometimes through it), bearing right to follow Shoup Bay to its tidewater glacier.

A free campsite and two reservable public-use cabins (in Soldotna ☐262-5581; www.alaskastateparks.org; $65), Kittiwake and Moraine, are at the end of the trail, near a noisy kittiwake rookery. McAllister Creek Cabin ($65) is accessible by boat only. The trailhead is at a parking lot at the western terminus of Egan Dr.

Solomon Gulch Trail HIKING

A mile past the Solomon Gulch Fish Hatchery on Dayville Rd, this 1.7-mile trail is a steep uphill hike that quickly leads to splendid views of Port Valdez and the city below. It ends at Solomon Lake, which is the source of 80% of Valdez' power.

Goat Trail HIKING

The oldest hike in the area is the Goat Trail, originally an Alaska Native trade route and later used by Captain Abercrombie in his search for safe passage to the Interior. Today, you can pick up the posted trailhead at Mile

Valdez

13.5 of the Richardson Hwy, just past Horsetail Falls in Keystone Canyon. A few spots have been washed out; don't try to cross any rushing streams.

Paddling

This is a kayaker's paradise, though folks sticking to the bay will be rewarded with views of seagulls fighting over cannery offal for the first hour or so. Independent kayakers should be aware of no-go zones around the pipeline terminal and moving tankers; contact the **US Coast Guard** (☏835-7222; 105 Clifton Dr) for current regulations.

TOP CHOICE **Anadyr Adventures**   KAYAKING
(☏835-2814, 800-865-2925; www.anadyradventures. com; 225 N Harbor Dr) Rents kayaks to (very) experienced paddlers (single/double $45/65, discounts for multiple days) and offers guided trips, ranging from a day at Columbia Glacier ($229) to several days on the water aboard a 'mothership' (two days $1050). A new, unique and very popular tour is of the Valdez Glacier ice caves, which includes both hiking and kayaking on and in the magnificent blue ice of this freshwater glacier ($110).

Unbeaten Path   KAYAKING
(☏255-7245; www.unbeatenpathseakayaking.com) A newcomer on the scene, Unbeaten Path specializes in longer, custom trips using top-end equipment: guides and customers use the same gear. All trips, including overnight camping, 'mothership', and lodge-based ones, are beginner- and advanced-kayaker friendly. A two-day trip to Shoup Bay costs $200 per day, plus the cost of a water taxi.

Pangaea Adventures   KAYAKING
(☏835-8442, 800-660-9637; www.alaskasummer. com; 107 N Harbor Dr) Pangaea Adventures has guided tours, costing from $59 for a three-hour trip on Duck Flats to $229 for a day trip to Columbia Glacier. It also does longer custom tours and rents kayaks ($45/65 per single/double).

SHOUP BAY

Protected as a state marine park, this bay off Valdez Arm makes for a great overnight kayaking trip. The bay is home to a retreating glacier, which has two tidal basins and an underwater moraine that protects harbor seals and other sea life. It's about 10 miles to the bay and another 4 miles up to the glacier. You must enter the bay two hours before the incoming tide to avoid swift tidal currents.

COLUMBIA GLACIER

A mile wide and rising 300ft from the waterline at its face, this is the largest tidewater glacier in Prince William Sound, and a

THE EXXON VALDEZ

Two decades after the *Exxon Valdez* left Valdez' Trans-Alaska Pipeline Terminal with a tippled captain, causing what was – until Deepwater Horizon – the worst environmental disaster in modern American history, the damage lingers. Not only can oil from the 1989 spill still be collected from just beneath the surface of beaches throughout the Sound, but, while certain fisheries have rebounded, herring stocks haven't recovered at all. The Dungeness crab population remains low and many pink-salmon runs have been eliminated. Loons, harlequin ducks, otters and seals still suffer the effects of the spill. And, at the time of writing, the citizens whose lives were permanently changed have yet to receive any portion of the original $5 billion awarded by an Anchorage jury in 1994.

On June 26, 2008 the US Supreme Court reduced the punitive damage awards from a previous reduction of $2.5 billion to $507 million. The jury is still out on whether the plaintiffs will receive any interest on that amount.

Thankfully, other legacies of the disaster are more inspiring. Long-recommended security measures have finally been enacted at oil-processing facilities across the nation. Double-hulled tankers, once a pipe dream of environmentalists, will be a pipeline requirement by 2015; some are already in service. Tugs must once again escort tankers passing through Prince William Sound. And the *Exxon Valdez* itself, now renamed the *SeaRiver Mediterranean,* has been banned from ever returning to Valdez.

spectacular spot to spend a few days kayaking and watching seals and other wildlife. In recent years the glacier has been in 'catastrophic retreat,' filling its fjord with so many calved bergs that it's difficult to get within miles of the face. Only experienced paddlers should attempt to paddle the open water from Valdez Arm to the glacier, a multiday trip. Others should arrange for a drop-off and pickup; Anadyr Adventures (p195) is a good one to call.

LOWE RIVER

This glacial river, 12 miles from Valdez, cuts through impressive Keystone Canyon. The popular float features Class III rapids, sheer canyon walls and cascading waterfalls. The highlight is Bridal Veil Falls, which drops 900ft from the canyon walls. No tour operators were running trips down the river when we visited, but it's worth contacting the Valdez Visitor Information Center (p201) to see if anyone is guiding.

☞ Tours

Columbia Glacier is the second-largest tidewater glacier in North America, spilling forth from the Chugach Mountains and ending with a face as high as a football field. Several tour companies can take you into Columbia Bay, west of Port Valdez, but it's difficult for any boat to get close to the face as the water is too clogged with ice. You're more likely to see calving further west in Unakwik Inlet, where the more accessible

Mears Glacier, a smaller ice-tongue, dumps bergs from a snout just half the height of Columbia's.

TOP CHOICE Lu-Lu Belle Glacier Wildlife Cruises BOAT
(☑835-5141, 800-411-0090; www.lulubelletours.com; Kobuk Dr) The dainty and ornately appointed MV *Lu-Lu Belle* is all polished wood, leather and oriental rugs. Cruise into Columbia Bay where, unless winds have cleared away the ice, wildlife is more the attraction than glacier-calving. The tour departs at 1pm daily, costing $105.

TOP CHOICE Vertical Solutions SCENIC FLIGHTS
(☑831-0643, 831-1619, 831-0699; verticalsolutions@live.com) An awesome way to see the glaciers and peaks around Valdez is on a helicopter. A half-hour tour is $330 for three people or less and well worth every penny: you'll be up close to wildlife (including bears and goats), glaciers and historic mines. Custom and aerial photography trips are also available.

Stan Stephens Glacier & Wildlife Cruises BOAT
(☑835-4731, 866-867-1297; www.stanstephenscruises.com; 112 N Harbor Dr) The biggest tour operator in town runs large vessels on seven-hour journeys to Columbia Glacier ($115) and nine-hour trips ($150) to both Columbia and Mears Glaciers. Lunch and lots of tummy-warming tea are included.

✿ Festivals & Events

Gold Rush Days   CULTURAL

A five-day festival in mid-August that includes a parade, bed races, dances, a free
fish feed and a portable jailhouse that's
pulled throughout town by locals, who
arrest people without beards and other
innocent bystanders.

🛏 Sleeping

As Valdez doesn't have a hostel, devout bud-
geteers will have to settle for a campsite. The
visitor center (p201) has a 24-hour hotline
outside, where you can book last-minute
rooms. Valdez' 6% bed tax is not included in
the rates quoted here.

Robe Lake Lodge   LODGE $$

(☎831-2339, 835-9118; www.robelakelodge.com;
Mile 6 Richardson Hwy; s/d $159/169; ⊜🖥) Brand
new and immaculate, this large home has
six rooms (all with shared bath) available.
The place is built out of full scribe logs, with
massive beams crossing the vaulted ceilings.
The hot tub has a view of the absurdly pretty
Robe Lake – as does the wraparound balco-
ny – but you can also warm up in the sauna.
Continental breakfast is served in the great
room, and if you rent the whole place out
($850) you have access to the full kitchen.
There are also trails to the lake, and a canoe
for paddling around.

Valdez Glacier Campground   CAMPGROUND $

(☎835-2282; Airport Rd; campsites/RV sites
$15/20) Located 6 miles out of town, this
spot has 101 pleasant wooded sites and a nice

waterfall. Though it's privately owned, it has
a noncommercial feel. Recently added hot
showers (free for campers) are a huge bonus.

Brookside Inn B&B   B&B $$

(☎835-9130, 866-316-9130; www.brooksidein
nbb.com; 1465 Richardson Hwy; r $150; ⊜🖥) This
100-year-old home originated in Fort Lis-
cum, was moved to Old Valdez, and then
to its present location after the earthquake.
Though a recent remodel that replaced the
original floors detracts from the ambience,
it's still a clean and cozy option. Breakfast is
served on a large sun porch.

Bear Paw RV Campground   CAMPGROUND $

(☎835-2530; www.bearpawrvpark.com; 101 N Harbor Dr; campsites/RV sites $25/35) Conveniently
located right downtown, this campground
has two locations: one is for RVs, and the
other (on Wyatt Way within walking distance to the ferry) has a wooded glade just
for tents – and adults.

L&L's B&B   B&B $

(☎835-4447; www.lnlalaska.com; 533 W Hanagita
St; r with/without bath $85/75; ⊜🖥) Located in
a big, airy suburban home, this B&B has five
rooms, two bicycles at your disposal and a
continental breakfast.

Downtown B&B Inn   B&B $

(☎835-2791, 800-478-2791; www.valdezdown
towninn.com; 113 Galena Dr; r with/without bath
$110/95; ⊜🖥) This place is more hotel than
B&B, though you do get breakfast with your
clean, basic room. Some are dorm-style; one
holds a party of eight.

HELI-SKIING

To a certain set of unhinged individuals, Valdez is legendary not for its oil spill or its earthquake, but for being *the* place to strap on skis, slip from a helicopter and plunge into the
snowy abyss.

Thanks to geography and climate, nowhere else do such steep slopes get so much
sticky snow. At inland ski resorts in, say, Colorado, dry powder barely clings to 50-degree
inclines; here in the coastal Chugach Mountains, the sopping-wet flakes glue to angles of
60-plus-degrees, creating ski slopes where elsewhere there'd be cliffs. Factor in 1000in
of snow per winter and mountains that descend 7000ft from peak to sea, and you've got
a ski-bum's version of Eden.

Since extreme skiing exploded here a decade ago, numerous companies have cropped
up to capitalize. **Valdez Heli-Ski Guides** (☎835-4528; www.valdezheliskiguides.com) offers
a day of heli-skiing (usually six runs) for $925; **H2O Heli-Guides** (☎835-8418; www.alas
kahelicopterskiing.com) has three-day heli-skiing packages – including lodging – for $4614.
Alas, the ski season lasts only from February to the end of April; after that, extremists will
have to settle for H2O's mellower summer offerings – for instance, spending a day with
crampons and ice-axes, scaling a sheer blue-ice cliff on Worthington Glacier ($225).

Copper River Delta

Just outside Cordova, the mountains step back and make room for the sky. Here you'll find the 700,000-acre Copper River Delta, a wildlife-rich wilderness with amazing opportunities for hiking, fishing and birding. This 60-mile arc, formed by six glacier-fed river systems, ends with twin wonders: the improbable Million Dollar Bridge and the breathtaking Childs Glacier.

You can cross the Delta on the Copper River Hwy (p201), built on the old railroad to Kennecott mines. Millions of birds stop here during spring and fall, including seven million western sandpipers and the entire population of West Coast dunlins. Other species include Arctic terns, dusty Canada geese, trumpeter swans, great blue herons and bald eagles. Moose, brown bears, beavers and porcupines are also visible sometimes.

At the end of the highway is the massive Childs Glacier, which you're likely to hear before you see. A rarity in Alaska, Childs is advancing some 500ft a year, perpetually dumping bergs into Copper River. Heed the warnings: the glacier is a mere 1200ft away, and potentially deadly waves can reverberate quickly across the river when particularly big bergs break off the glacier.

Just beyond Childs Glacier is the Million Dollar Bridge. You can drive, bike or walk on it to take in the views. Downstream is grumbling Childs, while upstream is Miles Glacier – the source of those icebergs racing beneath you. In 1910, Miles' rapid advance threatened the newly constructed bridge, forcing workers to chisel at its face day and night. It stopped just feet from the struts. Now, it's 4 miles distant.

TOP COPPER RIVER DELTA HIKES

» Sheridan Mountain Trail (p204)
» Saddlebag Glacier Trail (p204)
» McKinley Lake Trail (p204)
» Pipeline Lakes Trail (p204)

Clockwise from top left

1. Western sandpiper 2. Nearby Prince William Sound, which can be viewed from Crater Lake Trail (p203)
3. Childs Glacier 4. Million Dollar Bridge

Totem Inn
HOTEL $$

(835-4443, 888-808-4431; www.toteminn.com; 144 E Egan Dr; r/cabins $209/219;) This large place has refrigerators and microwaves in each room. The suites are deluxe, while the older rooms are a bit small. Small cabins are in the back and aren't much bigger than the rooms.

Keystone Hotel
HOTEL $

(835-3851, 888-835-0665; www.keystonehotel. com; 401 W Egan Dr; s/d $85/95;) A modular relic of the pipeline boom years with lots of clean, cramped, prefab rooms, plus continental breakfast.

Pipeline Inn
HOTEL $

(835-4444; 112 Egan Dr; r $90-100) The rooms are aging, but many are large and good for larger groups. All come with refrigerators and microwaves.

Eagle's Rest RV Park
CAMPGROUND $

(835-2373, 800-553-7275; www.eaglesrestrv. com; 631 E Pioneer Dr; campsites $27, RV sites $37-47, cabins $135-155;) Has showers ($8) and laundry, but the tent sites are a bit open and bland.

✖ Eating

TOP CHOICE Saffron Project
INDIAN $$$

(831-1403; 310 Pioneer Dr; mains $24-32; dinner Tue-Sun) Hands down the best Indian food in all of Alaska. The menu is small, with only three dishes (usually a chicken, a lamb and a vegetarian option) that rotate weekly, but don't worry; you get to sample all three before you have to make a decision. You'll eat with your hands, except for dessert: a ramekin of hand-churned ice cream with Indian spices ($2).

Magpie's Bakery
CAFE $

(www.magpiesbakery.com; 224 Galena Dr; soup $7-9, quiche $4; breakfast & lunch) Cozy up in this historic home with a breakfast sandwich, homemade soup or hot espresso drink. It's a sweet little place to duck out of the rain.

Old Town Burgers
BURGERS $

(E Pioneer Dr; burgers $8-10; lunch & dinner) This new and super-popular joint often has a line out the door. Besides burgers, you can get homemade curly fries ($3.75) or a halibut Caesar salad ($15.50). There is lots of seating and the line moves fast.

Fat Mermaid
PIZZA $$

(143 N Harbor Dr; sandwiches $12-13, pizza $16-27; breakfast, lunch & dinner) Valdez' newest joint is trying hard. It's a bit haphazard inside, but the pizzas are good and there are at least a dozen beers on tap.

Totem Inn Restaurant
AMERICAN $$

(144 E Egan Dr; breakfast $8-13, lunch & dinner $10-20; 5am-11pm) In the morning, tourists and locals flock here for the Alaska-sized breakfasts. Lunch is all about burgers and sandwiches, while dinner has decent seafood.

Ernesto's Taqueria
MEXICAN $

(328 Egan Dr; meals $7-9; dinner) Locally loved, this place serves large portions of serviceable Mexican food on the cheap, and has a cold selection of Mexican beer.

Harbor Cafe
BURGERS $$

(835-4776; 255 N Harbor Dr; burgers $12-16; lunch & dinner) This menu has a wide selection of decent burgers and sandwiches, which you can enjoy on the bright, covered sundeck.

Other recommendations:

Fu Kung
CHINESE $

(207 Kobuk Dr; lunch $7-10, dinner $12-17; lunch & dinner Mon-Sat, dinner Sun) Fantastic Chinese food. Lunch specials include egg rolls and quality wonton soup.

Mike's Palace
ITALIAN $$

(201 N Harbor Dr; mains $10-20; lunch & dinner) This locals' favorite specializes in Italian dinners, but also has a few Mexican dishes to spice things up.

Alaska Halibut House
FAST FOOD $

(208 Meals Ave; fish $4-10; lunch & dinner) Frying up fresh local fish, this place is what every fast-food joint should be. The halibut basket is delish.

Safeway
GROCERY $

(185 Meals Ave; 4:30am-midnight) With its impressive sandwich and salad bar, this grocery store is among Valdez' best places for a bite.

🍷 Drinking & Entertainment

Pipeline Club
BAR

(112 Egan Dr) If you've ever hugged a tree in your life, this crowd may not be for you. This smoky lounge is the watering hole where Captain Hazelwood had his famous scotch-on-the-rocks before running the *Exxon Valdez* aground.

Wheelhouse Bar
BAR

(100 N Harbor Dr) Located at the Best Western, this bar has excellent harbor views in a smoke-free setting. You can also get good grub from the new THC Off the Hook (the Harbor Cafe's sister restaurant), located next door.

ℹ Information

Crooked Creek Information Site (☏835-4680; Mile 0.9 Richardson Hwy) Staffed by US Forest Service (USFS) naturalists in a brand new building, this place offers great advice about all manner of outdoorsy activities. The nearby viewing platform is an excellent place to park yourself while watching chum and pink salmon spawn in July and August.

Harbormaster's office (☏835-4981; 300 N Harbor Dr) Has showers ($4).

Post office (cnr Galena Dr & Tatitlek Ave)

Valdez Providence Medical Center (☏835-2249; 911 Meals Ave) Has an emergency room.

Valdez Consortium Library (☏835-4632; 212 Fairbanks Dr; ⊙10am-6pm Mon & Fri, 10am-8pm Tue-Thu, noon-5pm Sat, from 1pm Sun; 🛜) Head here for free internet access.

Valdez Medical Clinic (☏835-4811; 912 Meals Ave) Provides walk-in care.

Valdez Visitor Information Center (☏835-2984; www.valdezalaska.com; 104 Chenega Dr; ⊙8am-7pm Mon-Sat, noon-7pm Sun) Has free maps and a courtesy phone for booking accommodations. There's an unstaffed information booth at the airport.

Wells Fargo (☏835-4381; 337 Egan Dr) This bank can probably handle extremely large accounts considering the presence of the local oil fields.

ℹ Getting There & Around

AIR There are flight services with **ERA Alaska** (☏835-2636; www.flyera.com) three times daily between Anchorage and Valdez; one-way tickets start from around $165 to $200, depending on how early you make your reservations. The **Valdez Airport** (Airport Rd) is 3 miles from town, off the Richardson Hwy.

BICYCLE Bikes can be rented (per half/full day $15/25) through the outdoorsy folk at Anadyr Adventures (p195).

BOAT Within Prince William Sound, the **Alaska Marine Highway ferry** (☏835-4436, 800-642-0066; www.ferryalaska.com) provides daily services from Valdez to Cordova ($50) and Whittier ($89). The newer speedier ferry halves the old times, but on the older, slower ferry you are more likely to see whales and sea lions as you amble pleasantly along.

CORDOVA

POP 2240

Cut off from Alaska's road system (for now), Cordova is slightly inconvenient and somewhat expensive to get to. Perhaps that's why this picturesque outpost, spread thinly between Orca Inlet and Eyak Lake, and overshadowed by Mt Eccles, can still claim to be one of the Alaskan coast's truly endangered species: a fishing village that hasn't sold its soul to tourism. That's all the more reason to visit.

Though not set in the same sort of mountain-thronged kingdom as Valdez, Cordova is more appealing: a quaint cluster of rainforest-rotted homes climbing up a pretty hillside overlooking the busy harbor. Populating the place are folks who, you can't help thinking, exemplify what's best about Alaska: ruggedly independent freethinkers, clad in rubber boots and driving rusted-out Subarus, unconcerned with image or pretense, and friendly as hell. They seem to revel in their isolation. In recent years, pro-development politicians have proposed connecting the community to the state highway system. Judging from the ubiquity of 'No Road' bumper stickers in town, it's a prospect the locals abhor.

Visitors will be enthralled by what lies beyond the town limits. Just outside the city, along the Copper River Hwy, is one of the largest wetlands in Alaska, with more than 40 miles of trails threading through spectacular glaciers, alpine meadows and the remarkable Copper River Delta. Into that delta run some of the world's finest salmon, and fishermen here turn them into what may be the fattest and finest fillets you'll ever enjoy.

Cordova's main north–south drag is officially 1st St, but is often called Main St – the names are used interchangeably. 1st St becomes the Copper River Hwy as it leaves town, connecting Cordova to the airport at Mile 12, continuing another 40 miles to Childs Glacier and Million Dollar Bridge.

◉ Sights

Cordova Museum
MUSEUM

(622 1st St; admission by donation; ⊙10am-6pm Mon-Fri, to 5pm Sat) Adjacent to the Cordova Library, this museum is a small, grassroots collection worth seeing. Displays cover local marine life, relics from the town's early history – including a captivating lighthouse lens – and a three-seater *bidarka* (kayak) made from spruce pine and 12 sealskins.

PRINCE WILLIAM SOUND CORDOVA

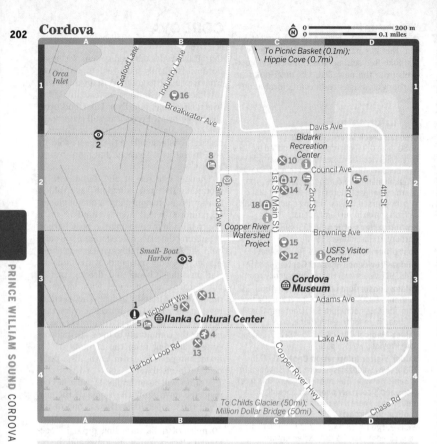

Cordova

◎ Top Sights

Cordova Museum	C3
Ilanka Cultural Center	B3

◎ Sights

1	Cordova Fisherman's Memorial	B3
2	Prince William Sound Science Center	A2
3	Small-Boat Harbor	B3

✦ Activities, Courses & Tours

4	Cordova Coastal Outfitters	B4

▭ Sleeping

5	Lighthouse Inn	B3
6	Northern Nights Inn	D2
7	Prince William Motel	C2
8	Reluctant Fisherman Inn	B2

✕ Eating

9	AC Value Center	B3
10	Ambrosia	C2
11	Baja Taco	B3
12	Coho Cafe	C3
13	Harborside Pizza	B4
14	Killer Whale Cafe	C2
	Reluctant Fisherman Restaurant	(see 8)

◉ Drinking

15	Alaskan Hotel & Bar	C3
16	Anchor Bar	B1
	Reluctant Fisherman Bar	(see 8)

⌂ Shopping

17	Copper River Fleece	C2
18	Orca Book & Sound	C2

Want your heart wrenched? Peruse the museum's coverage of the *Exxon Valdez* oil spill. The amateur photos and local newspaper headlines revive the horror more vividly than any slick documentary. Then there's the jar of oily sediment collected in 2006 – nearly 20 years after the spill.

The museum will have a new home across the street in the Cordova Center Auditorium, which is supposed to be completed by the end of 2012.

FREE **Ilanka Cultural Center** CULTURAL CENTER
(☑424-7903; 110 Nicholoff Way; admission free; ⊙10am-5pm Mon-Fri) This excellent museum operated by local Alaska Natives, has a small but high-quality collection of Alaska Native art from all over the state. Don't miss the intact killer-whale skeleton – one of only five in the world – with flippers that could give you quite a slap. Also on display is artist Mike Webber's *Shame Pole,* a totem pole that tells the grim tale of the oil spill, spitting back Exxon's then-top official Don Cornett's famous words, 'We will make you whole again.' This place also has a wonderful gift shop and offers classes on such crafty subjects as scrimshaw and spruce-root weaving. Call for a schedule.

Prince William Sound Science Center SCIENCE CENTER
(☑424-5800; www.pwssc.org; 300 Breakwater Ave; admission free; ⊙8:30am-5:30pm Mon-Fri; ⚐) This dockside **research facility** offers themed 'Discovery Packs' for kids, which include information on the birds, flora and geology of Cordova. You can call ahead to reserve a pack, or stop by to pick one up. Inside the facility there's not much for visitors save for an impressively enormous gray-whale skull suspended from the ceiling, some oil sediments and t-shirts.

Small-Boat Harbor HARBOR
In Cordova, the standard greeting among locals is 'Been fishing?' Unsurprisingly, the harbor is the community's heart, humming throughout the season as fishers frantically try to meet their quota before the runs are closed. The fishing fleet is composed primarily of seiners and gillnetters, with the method used by the fishers determining the species of salmon they pursue. The former primarily target pink salmon, while the latter, generally one-person operations, go for kings and reds early in the season and silvers later on.

Watching over the hubbub is the **Cordova Fisherman's Memorial**, a quiet place dominated by artist Joan Bugbee Jackson's sculpture *The Southeasterly* (1985), and spotted with flower bouquets.

Salmon Canneries BUILDINGS
Every summer Cordova's population swells with youths hoping to make a mint canning salmon on 30-hour shifts. Whether you're curious about the effects of sleep deprivation on adventurous teenagers or just want to see how some of the finest salmon in the world is processed, ask at the chamber of commerce about canneries offering tours. You can watch your *own* catch get processed at **Prime Select Seafoods** (☑424-7750, 888-870-7292; www.pssifish.com; 210 Seafood Lane), a smaller-scale operation that packs salmon and ships it to your home.

🏃 Activities

Hiking

More than 35 miles of trails are accessible from Cordova roads. Several of these paths lead to USFS cabins (p205). As in much of the Southeast, the hiking in this area is excellent, combining lush forest with alpine terrain, great views and glaciers.

Heney Ridge Trail HIKING
Cordova's most popular trail – as it's accessible without a car – is this scenic, fairly easy 3.7-mile route beginning at Mile 5.1 of Whitshed Rd. The first stretch winds around Hartney Bay, followed by a mellow 2-mile climb through forests and wildflowers (and, in rainy weather, lots of mud – rubber boots are recommended) to the treeline. It's another steep mile up to the ridge, where you'll enjoy a gorgeous view.

Crater Lake & Power Creek Trails HIKING
The 2.4-mile Crater Lake Trail begins on Eyak Lake across from Skater's Cabin. The trail ascends steeply but is easy to follow as it winds through lush forest. At the top it offers panoramic views of both the Copper River Delta and Prince William Sound. Plan on two to four hours for the round-trip.

Once at the lake you can continue with a 4.5-mile ridge route to Alice Smith Intertie, which descends to the Power Creek Trail. The entire 12-mile loop makes for an ideal overnight backpacking trip. Halfway along the ridge is a free-use shelter, while at Mile 4.2 of the Power Creek Trail is the **USFS Power Creek Cabin** (☑877-444-6777,

518-885-3639; www.recreation.gov; $35). Arrange to be dropped off at the Power Creek trailhead and hike all the way back into town via the Mt Eyak Trail.

McKinley Lake & Pipeline Lakes Trails
HIKING

The 2.5-mile McKinley Lake Trail begins at Mile 21.6 of the Copper River Hwy and leads to the head of the lake and the remains of the Lucky Strike gold mine. There are two USFS cabins (☎877-444-6777, 518-885-3639; www.recreation.gov; $35): McKinley Lake Cabin, just past the trailhead, and McKinley Trail Cabin, at Mile 2.4. The abandoned Lucky Strike mine is accessible via an unmaintained trail behind McKinley Trail Cabin.

Departing from the midway point of the McKinley Lake Trail is the Pipeline Lakes Trail, which loops back to the Copper River Hwy at Mile 21.4. Almost all of this marshy 2-mile trail has been boardwalked to provide easier access to several small lakes packed with grayling and cutthroat trout, but if it's rainy consider bringing rubber boots.

Sheridan Mountain Trail
HIKING

This trail starts near the picnic tables at the end of Sheridan Glacier Rd, which runs 4.3 miles from the turnoff at Mile 13 of Copper River Hwy. Most of the 2.9-mile route is a moderate climb, which passes through mature forests before breaking out into an alpine basin. From there, the view of mountains and the Sheridan and Sherman Glaciers is stunning, and it only gets better when you start climbing the surrounding rim. This trail isn't the best maintained, putting it into the 'difficult' category.

Saddlebag Glacier Trail
HIKING

You reach this trail via a firewood-cutting road at Mile 25 of Copper River Hwy. It's an easy 3-mile walk through cottonwoods and spruce, emerging at Saddlebag Lake. Outstanding views of surrounding peaks and cliffs (and maybe mountain goats) are made even more fabulous by the namesake glacier, which litters the lake with icebergs.

Cycling

Most of Cordova's trails are too muddy and steep to ride; an exception is the Saddlebag Glacier Trail. However, if you have a few days, the Copper River Hwy itself is a remarkable mountain-bike route. Plan on at least three days if you ride out to the end of the road and back, or two days if you are

dropped off at the end of the road and then ride the 48 miles back to town.

Skiing

The small but much-loved Mt Eyak ski area (☎424-7766; 6th St; ⊙mid-Nov–mid-May), just a quick walk from town, features an 800ft drop, an average of 118in of natural snow annually, and runs that accommodate everyone from novice snowboarders to world-class skiers. The most famous attraction is the vintage ski lift from Sun Valley, Idaho.

Birding

The Copper River Delta and the rich waters of Prince William Sound attract an astonishing number and variety of birds. Spring migration is the busiest, and that is when the town hosts the Copper River Delta Shorebird Festival (p205). Stop at the USFS Visitor Center (p207) for a birding checklist and advice about where to break out the binoculars.

A favorite birding area is Hartney Bay, 6 miles southwest of town along Whitshed Rd, where as many as 70,000 shorebirds congregate during spring migration. Bring rubber boots and plan to be there two hours before or after high tide for the best fall and spring viewing conditions. Sawmill Bay, at Mile 3 of Whitshed Rd, is also a prime bird-watching spot.

Another good place for bird and wildlife watching is Alaganik Slough. Turn south on Alaganik Slough Rd at Mile 17 of Copper River Hwy and travel 3 miles to the end, where a picnic area and boardwalk offer great views of dusky Canada geese, bald eagles and other feathered friends.

Paddling

The Copper River flows for 287 miles, beginning at Copper Glacier near Slana in the Interior and ending in the Gulf of Alaska, east of Cordova. Most of the river is for experienced rafters, as rapids, glaciers and narrow canyons give it a white-water rating of Class II–III much of the way. The 20-mile stretch between Million Dollar Bridge and Flag Point, at Mile 27 of the Copper River Hwy, is considerably wider and slower. Below Flag Point, the river becomes heavily braided, which inevitably means dragging your boat through shallow channels.

Cordova Coastal Outfitters
KAYAKING

(☎424-7424, 800-357-5145; www.cordovacoastal.com; Harbor Loop Rd; kayaks per day single/double $35/50) If the ocean is more to your taste,

Cordova Coastal Outfitters, in a cabin behind the AC Value Center, rents kayaks and arranges guided tours in placid, pristine Orca Inlet north of town.

Wilderness Cabins

There are nine **USFS cabins** (☎877-444-6777, 518-885-3639; www.recreation.gov; $25-45) located in the Cordova area, and they're much easier to reserve than those in other South-central Alaskan parts. Three are best accessible by boat or plane: Tideman Slough bunks six in the wilderness of the Copper River flats; Softuk Bar sleeps six on a remote beach 40 miles southeast of Cordova; and popular Martin Lake, 30 minutes east of town by floatplane, has a rowboat and sleeps six people. Two others are along the McKinley Lake Trail (p204) and a third is on the Power Creek Trail (p203). Hinchinbrook Island, 20 minutes from Cordova by plane and, at most, two hours by boat, has three more cabins: Shelter Bay, Double Bay and Hook Point.

★✦ Festivals & Events

Iceworm Festival   CULTURAL
(www.cordovachamber.com) Cordova's famous homegrown, tongue-in-cheek event is held on the second weekend of February. See p205.

Copper River Delta Shorebird Festival   CULTURAL
On the first weekend of May, this festival celebrates the largest migration in the USA, as some five million shorebirds throng the delta – the biggest continuous wetland on the Pacific coast – en route to their Arctic breeding grounds. The festival draws birders from the world over, and features presentations and workshops by international experts and field trips to the prime viewing areas. Nonbirders, don't scoff: this event fills every hotel room in town.

🛏 Sleeping

Cordova tacks on 12% in bed-and-sales tax to the rates listed here.

Copper River Watershed Project   CAMPGROUND $
(☎424-7282; Hippie Cove; tent sites $5) Several raised tent platforms set back in the woods near Hippie Cove, a half-mile north of the ferry terminal, are a good option for those leaving on an early-morning ferry. Pay at the Bidarki Recreation Center (p207). There are no showers or sinks, just an outhouse.

Skater's Cabin   CABIN $
(☎424-7282; cabin 1st/2nd/3rd night $25/35/50) In a beautiful setting on Eyak Lake, with a nice gravel beach and a woodstove, this place can be booked through the Bidarki Recreation Center (p207). The escalating prices are to deter multiday use so more people can enjoy it. Note that there are no bunks inside so you'll have to sleep on the floor (or, as one author who is afraid of mice did, on the table).

Northern Nights Inn   INN $
(☎424-5356; www.northernnightsinn.com; cnr 3rd St & Council Ave; r $85-125; ❀🖥) In a 100-year-old house painted Kennecott red, rooms range from basic to suites with kitchenettes. Some have peek-a-boo views of the bay, and all are furnished with antiques and period pieces.

CORDOVA ICEWORM FESTIVAL

They're real, and every February Cordovans celebrate them. Ice worms spend their entire lives on ice, and if they warm up too much they disintegrate (read: melt). These little critters feed on snow algae, and thread through tiny cracks in the ice. Their coloring tends to mimic glacial ice: white or blue. They're just mysterious enough that not only did they became the topic of a Robert Service poem, *Ballad of the Ice Worm Cocktail*, but they've also captured the attention of NASA, which has been studying what makes the worms such excellent survivors.

Towards the end of a Cordovan winter, it might feel as if you, too, have spent your entire life on ice, which is why, in 1961, Cordova residents got together and decided to break the monotony of the winter (and celebrate their survival of it, no doubt) with the Iceworm Festival.

This tongue-in-cheek celebration includes the crowning of a Miss Iceworm; the Survival Suit Race, in which participants don survival suits and plunge into the harbor; and a parade that culminates with a giant iceworm float. The festivities last a full week, which might be what it takes to snap out of a long winter.

Cordova Rose Lodge
INN $$

(☎424-7673; www.cordovarose.com; 1315 Whitshed Rd; r $85-145; 🖥@) This spot has a higgledy-piggledy assortment of structures, including rooms in a large barge docked – sort of – on Odiak Slough. All come with breakfast and have use of a communal living room and kitchen.

Reluctant Fisherman Inn
HOTEL $$

(☎424-3272, 800-770-3272; www.reluctantfisherman.com; cnr Railroad & Council Aves; r $135-185; 🖥🛜) As close to luxurious as Cordova gets, this place overhangs Orca Inlet and has a restaurant and lounge. Some of the tidy rooms have been remodeled; all are shipshape.

Orca Adventure Lodge
LODGE $$

(☎424-7249, 866-424-6722; www.orcaadventurelodge.com; Orca Rd; d from $140; 🖥🛜) Housed in the historic Orca Cannery 2 miles north of downtown, this waterfront lodge caters to adventurers with daily adventure-tour packages, and can include meals at the cafe.

Lighthouse Inn
INN $$

(☎424-7080; www.cordovalighthouseinn.com; 203 Nicholoff Way; r $145; 🖥🛜) This inn has brilliant views of the small-boat harbor from its small, plush rooms, all with private baths.

Prince William Motel
MOTEL $$

(☎424-3201; www.pwmotel.com; 501 2nd St; r/ste $120/140; 🛜) There are eight rooms with kitchenettes, and eight more with full kitchens at this utilitarian motel. Some of the units were remodeled recently, but be sure to ask for a non-smoking one.

Odiak Camper Park
CAMPGROUND $

(☎424-7282; Whitshed Rd; campsites/RV sites $5/22) A half-mile from town, this is basically a gravel parking lot with a rest room and a view. Make reservations at the Bidarki Recreation Center (p207).

✕ Eating

TOP CHOICE Baja Taco
MEXICAN $

(Harbor Loop Rd; fast food $6-10; ⊘7am-9pm) Graft a bus onto a cabin, add flowers, cattle skulls and nautical implements, and what do you have? The best fish-taco stand north of San Diego. It also serves beer, espressos and great Mexican-flavored breakfasts – try the *migas*.

Harborside Pizza
PIZZA $

(☎424-3730; 131 Harbor Loop Rd; 12in pizza $13-23, per slice $2.50; ⊘lunch & dinner Mon-Sat) Ask anyone where to eat in town, and this

small food cart is bound to be one of the first places listed. A wood-fired oven and hand-tossed dough ensure cheesy goodness, and if you're not into eating outside then they'll deliver to your door. Though pizza is definitely their specialty, you can also devour calzones, subs and salads.

Killer Whale Cafe
CAFE $

(1st St; breakfast $5-10, sandwiches & burgers $8-10; ⊘6:30am-3pm Mon-Sat, to 1pm Sun) Though this locally-loved cafe was still serving hearty breakfasts and fresh soups, wraps and sandwiches when we visited, it had plans to change into a deli.

Reluctant Fisherman Restaurant
SEAFOOD $$

(☎424-3272, 800-770-3272; cnr Railroad & Council Aves; meals $8-35; ⊘lunch & dinner) The white tablecloths give an aura of class, until you get close and realize that they're vinyl. No matter; the seafood is fresh and fused wonderfully into Asian dishes, plus the harbor view is stunning.

Picnic Basket
FAST FOOD $

(Railroad Ave; meals $3-9; ⊘lunch & dinner Tue-Sun) This spot does the cheapest (and best) halibut and chips in town, in addition to homemade desserts, wraps and shakes.

Other recommendations:

Coho Cafe
BREAKFAST $

(604 1st St; breakfast $7-11; ⊘breakfast & lunch) In the back of a dive bar, but popular for their greasy spoon breakfasts – especially the sourdough pancakes.

Ambrosia
ITALIAN $$

(413 1st St; dinner $12-20, pizza $15-30; ⊘lunch & dinner) Nothing pretentious here, but the Italian food comes out steaming hot. Plus, wine by the glass is only $4.

AC Value Center
SUPERMARKET $

(106 Nicholoff Way; ⊘7:30am-10pm Mon-Sat, 8am-9pm Sun) A supermarket with a deli, espresso bar, ATM and Western Union.

🍷 Drinking & Entertainment

There's not much of a formal entertainment scene in Cordova, but with scads of young cannery workers thronging the place in the summertime, there always seems to be a jam session going on somewhere.

Powder House Bar
BAR

(Mile 2, Copper River Hwy; dinner $8-20; ⊘10am-late Mon-Sat, from noon Sun; 🖥) Overlooking Eyak Lake on the site of the original Copper River

LAUREN PADAWER: FOUNDER OF ALASKA GLACIAL MUD CO

Cordova calls the birdwatcher, sea kayaker, artist, fly and deep-sea fisherman, backcountry skier/boarder, biologist and hunter. It's nestled within a slender strip of mountainous rainforest and wetlands and cloaked with glaciers, rivers and snow-capped rugged peaks. I love Cordova's fishing culture and Native Alaskan history, mountain springwater, clean air and Copper River salmon!

Copper River Delta

Check out salmon fishing, hiking, bird-watching, glacier-trekking, river rafting and berry-picking. You can drive the Copper River Hwy (p207) out to the Million Dollar Bridge, where you can camp near Childs Glacier and just downriver from Miles Glacier.

Day Hiking

The USFS Cordova Ranger District has an extensive network of hiking trails and cabin rentals – Mt Eyak/Crater Lake, Power Creek, Sheridan Mountain and Glacier, Haystack, Saddlebag, Heney Ridge, Eyak River are just some of my favorites, but there's more to choose from. Make it an overnight stay by booking one of the USFS's wilderness cabins (p205).

Eating Fresh Seafood

I love the fish tacos at Baja Taco (p206). Fresh Windy Bay Oysters are available throughout the summer at the Alaskan Hotel & Bar (p207), while the Reluctant Fisherman (p206) has a five-star menu with an outstanding view.

& Northwestern Railroad powder house, this is a fun place with live music, excellent beer, soup and sandwiches for lunch, and quality steak and seafood dinners. Friday is sushi day – it starts at noon and goes till the sushi's all gone.

Reluctant Fisherman Bar BAR
(cnr Railroad & Council Aves; ☻) The best part about this bar, besides a healthy selection of microbrews on tap, is its harborview deck. You'll be rubbing shoulders and jockeying for a table with all the locals on a sunny evening.

Alaskan Hotel & Bar BAR
(600 1st St) This raucous fishers' bar offers wine tastings 5pm to 7pm on Wednesday.

Anchor Bar BAR
(Breakwater Ave) Across from the small-boat harbor, this is your basic watering hole that's open 'as long as there are fish.'

🛍 Shopping

Fill up your backpack with a couple of unique souvenirs from Cordova.

Copper River Fleece CLOTHING
(☎424-4304; www.copperriverfleece.com; 504 1st St) You'll see folks around town sporting these high-quality, unique fleece jackets, vests and hats. Colorful trim is the company's signature, and most of the sewing is done upstairs from the shop.

Orca Book & Sound BOOKS
(☎424-5305; 507 1st St; ☉7am-5pm Mon-Sat; ☎) Besides being your best source for locally oriented literature, there's a Buddhist lending library upstairs and the owners are friendly, helpful and knowledgeable about the area. There's also espresso, outdoor clothing, wireless internet ($6 per hour) and internet terminals ($9 per hour).

ℹ Information

Bidarki Recreation Center (☎424-7282; cnr 2nd St & Council Ave; ☉9am-9:30pm Mon-Sat) For $10 you get a shower plus all-day use of the sauna and the fitness room.

Chamber of Commerce (☎424-7260; www.cordovachamber.com, www.cordovaalaska.com; 404 1st St; ☉10am-4pm Mon-Fri) If you find it open, you can get visitor info here, or just call and leave a message – the friendly folks will call you back.

Cordova Community Medical Center (☎424-8000; 602 Chase Rd) Provides emergency services.

Cordova Library (☎424-6667; 622 1st St; ☉10am-8pm Tue-Fri, to 5pm Sat, 1-5pm Sun; ☎) In the same building as the Cordova Museum (and also set to move across the street in 2012). Has the best lowdown on the town: lots of pamphlets, plus B&B listings and free city maps. Internet access is free and very popular with the cannery crew; put your name on the list and *then* check out the museum.

Harbormaster's Office (☑424-6400; Nichol-off Way) Has excellent $5 showers and a small book swap.

Post Office (cnr Railroad & Council Aves) Near the small-boat harbor.

USFS Visitor Center (☑424-7661; 612 2nd St; ☺8am-5pm Mon-Fri) This excellent office has the latest on trails, campsites and wildlife in the Copper River basin.

Wells Fargo (☑424-3258; 515 1st St) Has fresh cash in its 24hr ATM.

ⓘ Getting There & Around

Compact Cordova can be easily explored on foot, but the major problem for travelers exploring the outlying Copper River area is finding transportation. Hitchhiking along the Copper River Hwy is possible, though you might not encounter many passing motorists, even in the summer months.

AIR ERA Alaska (☑800-866-8394; www.flyera.com) flies twice daily between Anchorage and Cordova's Merle K 'Mudhole' Smith Airport; an advance-purchase ticket is $164/328 one way/round-trip. **Alaska Airlines** (☑800-252-7522; www.alaskaair.com) comes here on a milk run from Anchorage to Yakutat and Juneau once per day. To Juneau, an advance-purchase ticket is $164/352 one way/round-trip.

BOAT The **Alaska Marine Highway** (☑424-7333, 800-642-0066; www.ferryalaska.com) runs ferries daily to Valdez ($50, four hours) and Whittier ($89, 6½ hours). You can now choose to take the bright speed ferry, which halves the time of the older ferry, but both trips are scenic and pleasant. Note that several times a week the trip to Whittier routes through Valdez, making the journey an all-day affair.

BICYCLE Cordova Coastal Outfitters (p208) rents mountain bikes for $18 a day, including water bottles and a rack for gear.

CAR Chinook Auto Rentals (☑424-5279, 877-424-5279; www.chinookautorentals.com; Mile 13 Copper River Hwy) rents SUVs for visiting the glacier for $75 per day and smaller cars for $65.

WHITTIER

POP 157

You can see glaciers and brown bears, even mountains taller than Denali, without once visiting Alaska. But you will never, in a lifetime of searching, find another place quite like Whittier.

Shortly after the Japanese attack on the Aleutian Islands during WWII, the US began looking for a spot to build a secret military installation. The proposed base needed to be not only an ice-free port, but also as inaccessible as possible, lost in visibility-reducing cloud cover and surrounded by impassable mountains. They found it all right here.

And so, in this place that would be considered uninhabitable by almost any standard, surrounded by 3500ft peaks and hung with sloppy gray clouds most of the year, Whittier was built. A supply tunnel was blasted out of solid granite, one of Alaska's true engineering marvels, and more than 1000 people were housed in a single tower, the Buckner Building. It wasn't picturesque, but it was efficient.

The army maintained Whittier until 1968, leaving behind not only the Buckner Building, now abandoned, but also the 14-story-tall Begich Towers, where, it seems, some 80% of Whittiots now reside. A labyrinth of underground tunnels connects the complex with schools and businesses, which certainly cuts down on snow-shoveling time. The structure has also given rise to a unique society, where 150-odd people, though virtually isolated from the outside world, live only a few cinder blocks away from one another. It's obviously a must-see attraction for cultural anthropologists.

The rest of us, however, come to Whittier for many of the reasons the military did. The impossibly remote location provides access to an almost unspoiled wilderness of water, ice and granite. Kayaking and scuba diving are superb, and the docks are packed with cruise ships and water-taxis waiting to take you out into the wildlife-rich waters. The town itself is rarely described as adorable, but then it's never really had the luxury of such pretensions.

For years Whittier was accessible only by train or boat, despite being only 11 miles from the most traveled highway in Alaska. But in 2000, the Anton Anderson Memorial Tunnel was overhauled for auto traffic, and since then, one of the most abnormal places imaginable has been easily accessible – though normalization seems yet to happen.

Whittier was never created for vehicle traffic, so despite being compact it's a bit disorienting: it doesn't have so much a streetscape as a variety of routes through its massive parking lot and rail yard. Pedestrian tunnels stretch from the ferry dock to the Begich Towers; besides there, the energy is focused along the waterfront. Most services and businesses are located there.

🏃 Activities

Hiking

Portage Pass Trail   HIKING

Whittier's sole USFS-maintained trail is a superb afternoon hike, providing good views of Portage Glacier, Passage Canal and the surrounding mountains and glaciers. Even better, hike up in the late afternoon and spend the evening camping at Divide Lake.

The Portage Pass Trail is along an old roadbed and is easy to follow. To reach it, head west of town toward the tunnel, then follow the signs to the left onto a road crossing the railroad tracks. You'll find a parking area at the trailhead. Proceed along the right fork as it begins to climb steeply along the flank of the mountain. There's a steady ascent for a mile, finishing at a promontory (elevation 750ft) that offers views of Portage Glacier and Passage Canal to the east.

The trail then descends for a half-mile to Divide Lake and Portage Pass. At this point the trail ends, and a route through alder trees continues to descend to a beach on Portage Lake. It's a 2-mile hike one way from the trailhead to the lake, and it's well worth bashing some brush at the end. There are great views from the shores of Portage Lake and plenty of places to set up camp on the alluvial flats.

Shotgun Cove Trail   HIKING

This 0.8-mile walk along a dirt road leads to the First Salmon Run Picnic Area, so named because of the king and silver salmon runs during June and late August. The forest and mountains en route are scenic but, in true Whittier fashion, the roadsides are debris-strewn and the picnic area is in disrepair.

From the northeast corner of the Buckner Building, follow Salmon Run Rd up the mountain, staying to the right at the first fork and to the left at the second fork.

At the picnic area you can cross a bridge over the stream and continue another 3 miles to Second Salmon Run. This walk, along what is known as Shotgun Cove Rd, is exceptionally scenic, with views of Billings Glacier most of the way.

Paddling

Whittier is a prime location for sea kayakers, as it's practically surrounded by glaciated fjords and inlets. The most common overnight trip from Whittier is Blackstone Bay, which contains a pair of tidewater glaciers, Blackstone and Beloit. Many kayakers utilize charter boats to access the dramatic fjords to the north, including Harriman Fjord, College Fjord and Unakwik Inlet.

209

TOP CHOICE ⟩ Prince William Sound Kayak Center   KAYAKING

(☑472-2452, 877-472-2452; www.pwskayakcenter.com; Eastern Ave; ⊙7am-7pm) This well-known organization, established for 32 years, rents kayaks (single/double $50/80, discounted for multiple days) and runs guided tours, including three-hour paddles to the kittiwake rookery (per person $80 based on four people) and daylong excursions to Blackstone Bay (for two people $425; hefty discount if you can get six folks together). It also has escorts for multiday trips. These aren't guided tours: while escorts will suggest camping spots and routes, you're in charge of your own trip, including food and gear. It's a neat option for independent-minded folks who don't have the experience to feel comfortable spending a week on the water solo. The company will also let customers 'camp' and use the climbing wall inside its cavernous (but waterproof) facility.

Lazy Otter Charters   KAYAKING

(☑694-6887, 800-587-6887; www.lazyotter.com; Harbor View Rd; ⊙6:30am-7pm) Offers escorted day trips to Blackstone Bay (per person $195) for a minimum of four people. It also runs a water-taxi and rents out fiberglass kayaks (per day singles/doubles $45/85).

Alaska Sea Kayakers   KAYAKING

(☑472-2534, 877-472-2534; www.alaskaseakayakers.com; The Triangle; ⊙7am-7pm) Rents out kayaks ($40 to $75 per day), arranges water-taxis and takes multiday tours to places like Harriman Fjord, Nellie Juan Glacier and Whale Bay. It has two booking offices (the second at Lot 11, Harbor View Rd) and both will set you up with whatever you need.

Epic Charters   KAYAKING

(☑242-4339; www.epicchartersalaska.com; Harbor Loop Rd; kayak per day single/double $45/55; ⊙8am-6pm) Rents out kayaks and also offers guided kayak charters and glacier viewing from $195 total, whether you have one or two people.

Wilderness Cabins

There are six USFS cabins (☑877-444-6777, 518-885-3639; www.recreation.gov; $35) accessible by boat from Whittier. Pigot Bay and Paulson Bay are the closest, with excellent

WANDERING THROUGH WHITTIER

Whittier's dystopian townscape is perversely intriguing, and thus well worth a stroll. Start at Begich Towers, visible from anywhere in town, where the 1st, 14th and 15th floors are open to nonresidents. Watching children playing in the cinder-block corridors, you can't help contemplating how much of your private business would be common knowledge if you'd grown up here.

From the southwest corner of Begich Towers, you can look west to Whittier Creek, while above it, falling from the ridge of a glacial cirque, is picturesque Horsetail Falls. Locals use the cascade to gauge the weather: if the tail is whipping upwards, it's too windy to go out in a boat. There are also great views of dozens of other waterfalls streaking from the snowfields to the Sound.

Heading back toward the waterfront along Eastern Ave, you'll come to the rather extravagantly named Prince William Sound Museum (100 Whittier St; adult/child $3/1.50; ☉variable), which occupies an ill-lit room beside the Anchor Inn Grocery Store. The space has lots of tidy displays about Whittier's military history, but the most striking exhibit is about the man who engineered the town's tunnel, Anton Anderson. A Swedish-Australian immigrant, Anderson discovered he had a knack for carving holes through mountains, and then found he had a knack for politics, eventually becoming the mayor of Anchorage.

Climbing Blackstone Rd from the museum, the Buckner Building dominates the otherwise picture-postcard view. Once the largest structure in Alaska, the 'city under one roof' looms dismal and abandoned above town; the use of asbestos in the structure has complicated attempts to remodel or tear down the eerie edifice.

From here, walk along the Shotgun Cove Trail (p209), which winds through blueberry and salmonberry thickets to First Salmon Run Picnic Area, and then head a quarter mile down the road to your right (northeast) to get to Smitty's Cove. At low tide you can comb the beach westward, following the water's edge past the ferry terminal to the Triangle.

This clutter of restaurants, tour outfits and quirkier-than-average gift shops is fun; don't miss Log Cabin Gifts (☏472-2501; The Triangle; ☉11am-6pm), Whittier's best stab at adorable. The knickknacks, including lots of high-quality leatherwork, are handmade by owner Brenda Tolman, but the live reindeer outside are the real crowd pleasers. If it's wet out, though, they'll be back in their pen in front of the Begich Towers. Apparently, they don't like rain – which makes it tough to live in Whittier.

Continue along the water to the small-boat harbor, where you'll find local commercial fishing boats and a whole lot of pleasure vessels owned by Anchorage-based weekenders. After checking out the fleet, finish up your tour with a meal at any of the good, inexpensive eateries lining the water.

salmon fishing and good views; Harrison Lagoon has the best access for mobility-impaired folks, plus some great tide pools; Shrode Lake comes with a boat; Coghill Lake is a scenic spot with good fishing and berry-picking; and South Culross Passage is on a picturesque cove on Culross Island.

Diving

Whittier is a top spot for (involuntary shiver) Alaskan scuba diving – it's one of the wildest places easily accessible to human beings. The best time to dive is March through June.

Popular dive sites include the Dutch Group islands, known for high visibility offshore and for the kittiwake rookery. In this spot, a combination of steep cliffs and fresh fertilizer from the birds above has created a gently swaying rainbow of nudibranchs. Good places to view giant Pacific octopuses, wolf eels and crabs the size of manhole covers can be found in Esther and Culross Passages, close to South Culross Passage cabin (☏877-444-6777, 518-885-3639; www.recreation.gov; $45). Divers also often head to Smitty's Cove, which is east of the ferry terminal and is the only dive spot accessible by foot.

Lazy Otter Charters (p209) can provide water-taxi service to the best underwater locations. It charges a minimum of $185 for the boat plus additional fees that are based on mileage.

☞ Tours

Various tour boats sail from the small-boat harbor into a rugged, icy world that's unbelievably rich in wildlife. On the way to Harriman Fjord, ships pass so close to a kittiwake rookery that you can see the eggs in the nests of the black-legged birds.

Lazy Otter Charters (p209) offers a custom half-day tour of Blackstone Bay (per person $185), with a four-person minimum. A custom full-day, eight- to nine-hour tour of Prince William Sound is $235 per person, also with a four-person minimum.

Major Marine Tours   BOAT TOUR
(☎800-764-7300, 472-2573; www.majormarine. com; Harbor Loop Rd) Has a USFS ranger on every cruise. It does a five-hour tour of glacier-riddled Blackstone Bay for $107/53.50 (plus tax) per adult/child.

Phillips Tours   BOAT TOUR
(☎276-8023, 800-544-0529; www.26glaciers. com; Harbor View Rd) Packs in 26 glaciers on a speedy boat ride for $139/79 per adult/child. Don't blink.

Prince William Sound Cruises & Tours   BOAT TOUR
(☎472-2410, 800-992-1297; www.princewilliam sound.com; 1 Harbor Pier) Offers 'quality time' with the very active Surprise Glacier on its six-hour tour of Esther Passage (per adult/child $144/72).

🛏 Sleeping

Those wishing to stay overnight in Whittier face unappealing options: camping in puddles, flopping at a dive of a hotel or paying through the nose for something nicer. Ask around and locals will point you to informal (and free) camping spots along Salmon Run Rd. Also note that a 5% sales tax will be added to the prices listed here.

Inn at Whittier   HOTEL $$$
(☎472-3200; www.innatwhittier.com; Harbor Loop Rd; r $169-299; ☻⑲) Rooms are bland but the view isn't – make sure you spend the $20 extra for a water view. Besides double rooms, you can also rent a two-story townhouse suite. Rates are considerably less from mid-April to mid-May. Attached is a high-end restaurant and Whittier's best stab at a swank bar.

June's B&B   B&B $$
(☎472-6001, 888-472-2396; www.whittiersuiteson line.com; Lot 7, Harbor View Rd; condos $145-450;

☻) This business offers an insight into the local lifestyle, putting you up in comfortable, homey suites atop Begich Towers. Occasionally owner June rents out an economy suite on the ground floor.

Anchor Inn   MOTEL $$
(☎472-2354; www.anchorinnwhittier.com; 100 Whittier St; s/d $105/131; ☻⑲) This multipurpose venue has cinder-block walls, and overlooks a junkyard on one side and the rail yard on the other, but it'll do in a pinch. There's an attached restaurant, bar, laundry and grocery store.

Creekside Campground   CAMPGROUND $
(Glacier St; campsites $10) There's only one official campground in Whittier: the horrid Creekside Campground, which is basically a mud-soaked, clear-cut gravel quarry.

🍴 Eating

Cafe Orca   CAFE $
(www.alaskacafeorca.com; The Triangle; light meals $8-12; ⊙11am-7pm) Gourmet sandwiches, some of the best chowder on the Sound, and a great little waterfront deck are the perfect combination for the best lunch in town. If it's raining, sit inside with a hot espresso.

Varly's Swiftwater Seafood Cafe   CAFE $$
(www.swiftwaterseafoodcafe.com; The Triangle; mains $6-14; ⊙lunch & dinner) The fish and chips hit the spot when it's raining horizontally outside. You can peruse the photos of famous Alaskan shipwrecks over your rhubarb crisp ($4.50).

China Sea   CHINESE $$
(☎472-3663; The Triangle; lunch $8-10, dinner $10-19; ⊙lunch & dinner) Serving up Chinese and Korean food, this place has an $11 lunch buffet featuring fresh 'halibut à la Peking.'

Restaurant at the Inn at Whittier   STEAKHOUSE $$$
(☎472-3200; Harbor Loop Rd; breakfast & lunch $8-18, dinner $23-30; ⊙breakfast, lunch & dinner) This dining room has glorious views of the Sound and cooks up steaks and seafood. Have a martini at the posh lounge attached to the restaurant.

Harbor Store   SUPERMARKET $
(Harbor View Rd; ⊙8am-8pm) This store has groceries and snacks for your hike.

Anchor Inn Grocery Store   SUPERMARKET $
(100 Whittier St; ⊙9am-10pm) A bigger grocery store across town.

❶ Information

The post office is in Begich Towers, along with the police and fire stations, a medical clinic – even a church.

Anchor Inn (☑472-2354; 100 Whittier St; www.anchorinnwhittier.com; ❂9am-10pm; ☎) Has an ATM, wireless internet, a coin-op laundry and showers.

Harbormaster's Office (Harbor View Rd) Has pay phones and showers.

Harbor Store (☑472-2277; Harbor View Rd; ❂8am-8pm) Has an ATM and sells phone cards.

USFS Information Yurt (Harbor View Rd) Was closed due to lack of funding in 2011, but may be open in the future. Contact the headquarters in Girdwood for more information on hiking, camping, paddling and cabins in the area (☑783-3242).

❶ Getting There & Around

Whittier is one of those places where getting there is half the fun. Sometimes, leaving can be even better.

BOAT The **Alaska Marine Highway ferry** (☑800-642-0066; www.ferryalaska.com) sails three times per week direct to Valdez ($89, 3½ to seven hours), and another three times per week direct to Cordova for the same price. Both trips are super-scenic – think Dall porpoises, Stellar sea lions and a kittiwake rookery. Twice per month a ferry departs from Whittier, crosses the Gulf of Alaska and docks in Juneau ($221, 39 hours). The ferry terminal is beside the Triangle.

BUS Magic Bus (☑230-6773; www.themagic bus.com) has a daily bus between Anchorage and Whittier (one way/round trip $40/50, 1½ hours), which leaves Anchorage at 9:30am and departs Whittier for the return trip at 5:30pm. You'll have plenty of time to catch the 12:45 ferry. **Whittier Shuttle** (☑350-6010, 1-888-257-8527; www.whittiershuttle.com) coordinates with the cruise ships' schedules, running shuttles from Whittier to Anchorage at 8:30am, and returning from Anchorage at 12:30pm (one-way $29). **Prince William Sound Cruises & Tours** (☑472-2410, 877-777-2805; www. princewilliamsound.com) can book independent travelers on the shuttle between Anchorage and Whittier ($69 either one-way or round-trip, 2½ hours). The bus leaves downtown Anchorage around 8:30am, and makes the return drive from Whittier at 5pm.

CAR Whittier Access Rd, also known as Portage Glacier Access Rd, leaves the Seward Hwy at Mile 79, continuing to Whittier through the claustrophobic Anton Anderson Memorial Tunnel (www.dot.state.ak.us/creg/whittiertunnel/ index.shtml), which at 2.7 miles long is the longest 'railroad-highway' tunnel in North America. Negotiating the damp one-lane shaft as you skid across the train tracks is almost worth the steep price of admission (per car/RV $12/20) which is charged only if you're entering Whittier; if you bring your car into town on the Alaska Marine Hwy you can exit through the tunnel for free. Eastbound and westbound traffic alternate every 30 minutes, with interruptions for the Alaska Railroad. Bring a magazine.

TRAIN The **Alaska Railroad** (☑265-2494, 800-544-0552; www.akrr.com) operates the *Glacier Discovery* train between Anchorage and Whittier (one way/round trip $65/80, two hours) daily May through September. It departs Anchorage at 10am and Whittier at 6:45pm.

Kenai Peninsula

Best Places to Eat

» Cosmic Kitchen (p246)

» Smoke Shack (p223)

» Samovar Café (p239)

» Bowman's Bear Creek
Lodge (p216)

» Two Sisters Bakery (p246)

Best Places to Stay

» Alaska Paddle Inn (p222)

» Eagle Watch (p238)

» Old Town B&B (p244)

» Across the Bay Tent &
Breakfast (p250)

Why Go?

Set enticingly across Turnagain Arm from Anchorage, the Kenai Peninsula is a veritable jungle gym for Anchorage residents and tourists alike. With two main roads splintering across an area the size of Belgium, the peninsula is an accessible wilderness, allowing visitors to edge as far away from civilization as they feel comfortable.

The Kenai Mountains form the eastern two-thirds of the peninsula, and there are more hiking trails and alpine lakes here than you can explore in a summer. Glaciers are crammed into every cranny, and the comparatively flat western side of the peninsula is pocked with trout-filled lakes excellent for canoeing. The peninsula's towns are as varied as the topography, with fishing towns, an arts capital and Russian Old Believer villages. And then there's the marine world: the peninsula's jagged coastline makes for some of the best kayaking you'll find, with waters full of marine mammals, birds and fish.

When to Go

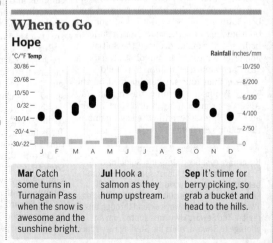

Hope

Mar Catch some turns in Turnagain Pass when the snow is awesome and the sunshine bright.

Jul Hook a salmon as they hump upstream.

Sep It's time for berry picking, so grab a bucket and head to the hills.

History

For millennia, Dena'ina Indians made the Kenai Peninsula their home, as did Alutiiqs in the south and Chugaches in the east. They largely subsisted as many modern residents do: by pulling fish from the area's bountiful waterways. In 1741 Vitus Bering, a Dane sailing for the Russians, was the first European to lay eyes on the peninsula; in 1778 British explorer Captain James Cook sailed up the inlet that would bear his name, landing north of the present-day city of Kenai and claiming the area for England. Despite that, the first white settlement on the peninsula was Russian – St Nicholas Redoubt, founded at the mouth of the Kenai River as a fur trading post in 1791. Orthodox missionaries arrived soon thereafter, and many of the local Alaska Natives were converted to that faith.

When Alaska came under American rule in 1867, the US established Fort Kenay near where the redoubt had stood. The surrounding settlement endured as a commercial fishing village until 1957, when the nearby Swanson River became the site of the state's first major oil strike. Kenai has been an oil town ever since.

The Alaska Railroad made its start in Seward in 1903, where Resurrection Bay was the closest ice-free port. The Kenai Peninsula was officially on the map as the main thoroughfare for goods to Anchorage, and eventually for coal leaving the state.

The 1964 Good Friday Earthquake hit the peninsula really hard. After the earth finally stopped churning, oil tanks exploded and tsunamis rolled through Seward, ravaging the town. With the bridges, railroad and boat harbor gone, Seward was suddenly cut off from the rest of the state. Homer suffered badly too: the quake dropped the Spit by 6ft and leveled most of the buildings. It took six years and almost $7 million to rebuild.

Since then tourism has boomed on the Kenai Peninsula, turning the region into Alaska's premier playground for visitors and locals, and becoming a key engine of the region's economy.

ⓘ Getting There & Around

If you have ever been stuck in a Soldotna traffic jam or inhaled the fumes spewing out from behind a string of Seward-bound RVs, you'll know: the Kenai Peninsula is a place of vehicles. Two busy, paved highways extend through this region. The Seward Hwy runs south from Anchorage to Seward, while the Sterling Hwy spurs westward off the Seward Hwy to Soldotna, then drops down to Homer. If you don't have your own wheels, you could rent some in Anchorage. Alternatively, hop aboard a long-haul bus. **Homer Stage Line** (☑868-3914; www.stagelinein homer.com) operates daily between Anchorage, Homer and Seward.

Another (excellent) transport possibility is rail; the southern terminus of the **Alaska Railroad** (☑265-2494, 800-544-0552; www.akrr.com) is at Seward, which is visited daily by trains from Anchorage.

Finally, as with everywhere in Alaska, there's always flying. Homer and the city of Kenai are served by **ERA Alaska** (☑266-8394, 800-866-8394; www.flyera.com); many of the peninsula's other towns also have airstrips and scheduled flights.

SEWARD HIGHWAY

The Seward Hwy is a road-trip-lover's delight, with smooth, winding turns through mountains that have you craning your neck around every corner. The 127 miles of highway is all Scenic Byway, and there are plenty of turnoffs for gawking and snapping photos. Keep in mind that the mileposts along the highway show distances from Seward (Mile 0) to Anchorage (Mile 127). The first section of this road – from Anchorage to Portage Glacier (Mile 79) – is covered in the Anchorage chapter (p178).

Turnagain Pass & Around

After it leaves Turnagain Arm, Seward Hwy heads for the hills. Near Mile 68 it begins climbing into the alpine region of Turnagain Pass, where there's a roadside stop with garbage cans and toilets. In early summer, this area is a kaleidoscope of wildflowers.

Bertha Creek Campground (Mile 65, Seward Hwy; campsites $10), just across the Bertha Creek Bridge, is understandably popular – site No 6 even has a waterfall view. You can spend a day climbing the alpine slopes of the pass here, or head to Mile 64 and the northern trailhead of both the 23-mile Johnson Pass Trail and the paved Sixmile Bike Trail, which runs 8 miles – not six – along the highway.

Granite Creek Campground (Mile 63, Seward Hwy; campsites $10) is reminiscent of Yosemite Valley: wildflower meadows, dramatic mountains...the works. Sites fill up fast.

The Seward Hwy heads south of this junction to Upper Summit Lake, surrounded by neck-craning peaks. The lakeside Tenderfoot

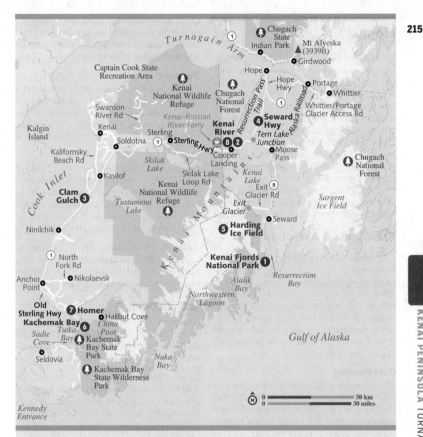

Kenai Peninsula Highlights

1 Watching whales breach as you sit in a kayak in **Kenai Fjords National Park** (p225)

2 Rubbing shoulders with hundreds of other anglers during the height of the **salmon season** (p229)

3 Digging for Alaska-sized **razor clams** (p237)

4 Rolling down the **Seward Highway** (p214), one of the most scenic highways in the state

5 Hiking up to one of the last remnants of the ice age, the **Harding Ice Field** (p221)

6 Escaping across **Kachemak Bay** for berry picking and mountain biking (p253)

7 Feasting on the culinary spread in **Homer** (p246) after perusing its many art galleries

8 Rafting down the **Kenai River** (p228) on a sunny day

Creek Campground (Mile 46, Seward Hwy; sites $14) has 27 sites that are open enough to catch the view but wooded enough for privacy.

Within walking distance of the campground is **Summit Lake Lodge** (244-2031; www.summitlakelodge.com; Mile 45.8, Seward Hwy; d $90;), with basic rooms, newer cabins, an espresso/gift shop and a bustling **restaurant** (lunch $7-14, dinner $11-23; 8am-11pm).

The **Devil's Pass Trail** (Mile 39.4 Seward Hwy) is a very well signed, difficult 10-mile hike over a 2400ft gap to the Resurrection Pass Trail (p61).

At **Tern Lake Junction** (Mile 37 Seward Hwy) – also known as 'The Y' – is the turnoff for the Sterling Hwy, which runs another 143 miles to Homer.

Hope

POP 147

Hope has beautiful views of Turnagain Arm, a quaint and historic downtown, wonderful restaurants and gold rush-era relics, and incredible camping and hiking opportunities. With all this great stuff to distract you, it might take a minute to figure out what's missing. Give up? Here's a hint: just try to find one lame tourist trap.

Somehow, the moose-nugget jewelry purveyors have passed this place by, perhaps missing the turnoff at Mile 56.7 of the Seward Hwy, or failing to follow the winding Hope Hwy the 16.5 miles necessary to reach this rustic hamlet. Don't make the same mistake.

◎ Sights & Activities

FREE Hope-Sunrise Mining Museum   MUSEUM
(✆782-3740; Old Hope Rd; ◷noon-4pm) This small log cabin preserves relics from early miners and homesteaders with a great deal of respect. Creaky buildings give a feel for life at the turn of the 20th century; a quick guided tour is worth the tip for history buffs and anyone with a little extra time.

Gold Panning

There are about 125 mining claims throughout the Chugach National Forest. Some of the more serious prospectors actually make money, but most are happy to take home a bottle with a few flakes of gold in it.

The Hope area provides numerous opportunities for the amateur panner, including a 20-acre claim that the US Forest Service (USFS) has set aside near the Resurrection Pass trailhead for recreational mining.

Hiking

The northern trailhead of the legendary 39-mile Resurrection Pass Trail (p61) is near the end of Resurrection Creek Rd. From Porcupine Campground, two fine trails lead to scenic points overlooking Turnagain Arm.

The Gull Rock Trail is a flat 5-mile (one way), four- to six-hour walk to Gull Rock, a rocky point 140ft above the Turnagain shoreline. The trail follows an old wagon road built at the turn of the 19th century, and along the way you can explore the remains of a cabin and sawmill.

Hope Point is steep and a bit more difficult, following an alpine ridge 5 miles for incredible views of Turnagain Arm. Begin at an unmarked trail along the right-hand side of the small Porcupine Creek. Except for an early-summer snowfield, you'll find no water after Porcupine Creek.

Paddling

Sixmile Creek is serious white water, with thrilling – and dangerous – rapids through deep gorges that survivors describe as 'the best roller coaster in Alaska.' The first two canyons are rated Class IV; the third canyon is a big, bad Class V.

Chugach Outdoor Center   RAFTING
(✆277-7238; www.chugachoutdoorcenter.com; Mile 7.5, Hope Hwy) Guided trips down Sixmile twice daily during summer. The two-canyon run is $99 per person; to defy death on all three canyons it's $149 per person.

Nova River Runners   RAFTING
(✆800-746-5753; www.novalaska.com) Also does twice-daily trips down the river, at $95 for the Class III–IV canyons, and $139 for the Class V.

⌂ Sleeping

Near the end of Resurrection Creek Rd, just before and just after the Resurrection Pass trailhead, are many underdeveloped camping spots beneath a verdant canopy.

Coeur d'Alene Campground   CAMPGROUND $
(Mile 6.4, Palmer Rd; campsites free) A gorgeous informal campground at the end of a narrow, winding back road in an alpine valley.

Porcupine Campground   CAMPGROUND $
(Mile 17.8, Hope Hwy; campsites $14) Popular for a reason: it's the trailhead for Hope Point and Gull Rock, and has transcendent views (especially from sites 4, 6, 8 and 10) of Turnagain Arm. It's highly recommended.

Bowman's Bear Creek Lodge   CABIN $$$
(✆782-3141; www.bowmansbearcreeklodge.com; Mile 15.9, Hope Hwy; campsites $210; ☺) This place has five hand-hewn log cabins (with shared baths) surrounding a beautiful pond and burbling creek. Room rates include a four-course meal at the excellent restaurant.

✗ Eating

TOP CHOICE Bowman's Bear Creek Lodge   AMERICAN $$
(✆782-3141; Mile 15.9, Hope Hwy; dinner $10-24; ◷dinner) A fabulous menu that changes daily, with homemade desserts, seafood specials and a friendly, intimate dining room. Two seatings per night; reservations required.

Tito's Discovery Cafe CAFE $$
(Mile 16.5, Hope Hwy; breakfast $6-10, wraps $11-12, dinners $12-16; ⊙breakfast, lunch & dinner) This is a very popular eatery that serves homemade soups, seafood wraps and local gossip. It's best for breakfast – go for the triple-berry pancakes.

Seaview Cafe CAFE $$
(B St; mains $10-20; ⊙lunch & dinner) Serves up good beer and chowder with views of the Arm. There's always live music on weekends.

ℹ️ Information

Alaska Dacha (☑782-3223; Mile 15.8, Hope Hwy; ⊙9am-9pm) Has sundries, showers, internet and laundry.

Chamber of Commerce (www.hopealaska.info) A good site for pretrip planning.

Hope Library (☑782-3121; Old Hope Rd; donation appreciated; ⊙when the neon sign says 'open'; 📶) In a one-room 1938 schoolhouse. Don't miss its gift shop next door, which sells locally made crafts to help support this grassroots facility.

Post office (Palmer Rd)

ℹ️ Getting There & Away

Hope remains idyllic in part because of its isolation. Though the **Seward Bus Line** (☑224-3608) and **Homer Stage Line** (☑224-3608; www.stagelineinhomer.com) will drop you off at the junction of the Hope and Seward Hwys, the only way to get to the town proper is by driving, hitching, pedaling or plodding.

Moose Pass & Around

POP 201

Four miles south of Tern Lake Junction on the Seward Hwy is the trailhead for the Carter Lake Trail (Mile 33 Seward Hwy), a steep 1.9-mile 4WD track providing quick access to subalpine terrain and Carter Lake, where you can continue another mile to some excellent campsites and Crescent Lake. Sturdy hikers can press on another 4 miles to Crescent Lake Cabin (☑877-444-6777; www.recreation.gov; cabins $45). If you're not driving, Seward-bound buses can drop you off here.

At Mile 29.4 the village of Moose Pass relaxes along the banks of Upper Trail Lake. Founded during the Hope-Sunrise gold rush of the late 19th century, Moose Pass (which was named by a mail carrier who couldn't get past one of the critters) came into its own when the original Iditar-

od National Historic [...] the lake in 1910-11. Tod[...] is known for its lively Su[...] **Festival**.

Just South of Moose Pass are a [...] ing options close enough to Seward [...] as a base, but far enough out to escape [...] crowds.

Renfro's Lakeside Retreat (☑288-5059; www.renfroslakesideretreat.com; 27177 Seward Hwy; RV sites from $25, cabins from $125; ⊜) has mediocre RV sites but fabulous lakeside cabins, with fire pits and lofts with views.

Nearby, the **Trail River Campground** (www.recreation.gov; Mile 24, Seward Hwy; campsites $18) is run by the USFS and has 91 lovely sites among tall spruce trees along Kenai Lake and Lower Trail River.

After departing Moose Pass, the highway winds through national forest. At Mile 23, the **Ptarmigan Creek Trail** leads 3.5 miles from the campground to Ptarmigan Lake. Here you'll find turquoise, trout-filled waters that reflect the mountains that cradle it. A 4-mile trail continues around the north side of the lake, which is brushy in places and wet in others; plan on five hours for the round-trip. The **Ptarmigan Creek Campground** (campsites $14) has 16 sites that were once shady but now resemble a clear-cut in places due to the spruce beetle.

The **Victor Creek Trail** (Mile 19.7, Seward Hwy), on the east side of the highway, is a fairly steep path that ascends 3 miles to good views of the surrounding mountains.

If everywhere else is full, head to **Primrose Landing Campground** (Mile 17.2, Seward Hwy; sites $10), a quiet and wooded spot with wonderful views of Kenai Lake, plus a rushing creek. It's also where the Primrose Trail begins. This trail leads south to Lost Lake, and traverses to Mile 5 of the Seward Hwy. About 2 miles up the path is an unmarked side trail to the right, which leads to a magnificent waterfall – the source of that roaring you can hear as you hike. See p220 for more info on the Lost Lake hike.

The **Grayling Lake Trail**, which is accessed from a parking lot at Mile 13.2, leads walkers for two pleasant miles to Grayling Lake, a beautiful spot with views of Snow River and (surprise surprise!) excellent fishing for grayling. Side trails connect Grayling Lake with Meridian and Leech Lakes. This makes for an excellent hiking trail to take the kids on.

Trail was cut around
by the small town
mer Solstice
ew sleep-
to use
the

217

em, rewarding
arm and phe-
ntains and sea.
oth the Alaska
Hwy, and a final
own is easily ac-
ts Fourth of July
eing the biggest –
and wildest . Seward's shops, small-boat harbor and 360-degree views offer plenty to entertain you for days, but can also serve as a base for excursions into the marine and mountainous playgrounds. Travelers flock to kayak, hike, fish, whale-watch and glacier-view.

The body of the city is divided into two centers: the newer, touristy harbor and the historic downtown. Lowell Point stretches to the south of town, and other amenities can be found just north along the Seward Hwy.

History

Seward got its start in 1903, when settlers arrived plotting construction of a northbound rail line. Once the Alaska Railroad was completed two decades later, this ice-free port would become the most important shipping terminal on the Kenai Peninsula. The city also served as the start of the 1200-mile Iditarod National Historic Trail to Nome, along a major dogsled thoroughfare via the Interior and Bush. In WWII the town got another boost when the US Army built Fort McGilvray at Caines Head, just south of town.

⊙ Sights

Alaska SeaLife Center AQUARIUM
(☑224-6300, 800-224-2525; www.alaskasealife.org; 301 Railway Ave; adult/child $20/10; ◷10am-5pm) A fitting legacy of the *Exxon Valdez* oil spill settlement, this $56-million marine research center is more than just one of Alaska's finest attractions. As the only coldwater marine-science facility in the Western Hemisphere, it serves as a research and educational center and provides rehabilitation for injured marine animals. For $15 more you can take a Behind-the-Scenes tour of labs and habitats. Kids will love the tidepool touch tank, where they can hold sea anemones and starfish.

Without a doubt the highlight, however, is a series of two story-deep, glass-sided tanks: upstairs you get the above-water view of seabird rookeries and recuperating harbor

Seward

Seward

seals, while below deck you'll be eyeball-to-eyeball with prowling sea lions and puffins diving for dinner. An outdoor observation platform offers a fabulous view of the mountains ringing Resurrection Bay and a chance to watch salmon thrash their way up a fish ladder. Plan to spend the better part of one of your best afternoons here.

It's worth it to include an Encounter tour ($79): you'll get face to face with the creatures you normally only see behind the glass.

Benny Benson Memorial   MONUMENT
This humble monument at the corner of the Seward Hwy and Dairy Hill Lane honors Seward's favorite son, Benny Benson. In 1926 the orphaned 13-year-old Alaska Native boy submitted his design for the Alaska state flag, arguably the loveliest in the Union. His stellar design (you can see one of his first at the library) includes the North Star, symbolizing the northernmost state, the Great Bear constellation for strength, and a blue background for both the sky and the forget-me-not, Alaska's state flower. Seward will never forget.

Seward Museum   MUSEUM
(☑224-3902; 336 3rd Ave; adult/child $3/50¢; ☉10am-5pm) This eclectic, if a bit dusty, museum has an excellent Iditarod exhibit; a rare 49-star US flag; and relics of Seward's Russian era, the 1964 Good Friday Earthquake and the 1989 oil spill. There are also lots of amusing antiques, including an ancient electric hair-curling machine and a 'cow raincoat' designed for the oft-drenched cattle at the now-defunct Seward dairy. The staff are enthusiastic and knowledgeable, and worth engaging. The museum has plans to move to a new site next to the library in 2013.

Small-Boat Harbor   HARBOR
The small-boat harbor, at the northern end of 4th Ave, hums during the summer with fishing boats, charter vessels, cruise ships and a number of sailboats. At its heart is the **harbormaster's office** (☑224-3138; ☉8am-5pm). Look for the huge anchors outside. Radiating outward from the docks are seasonal restaurants, espresso bars, tourist offices, hotels and almost any other service the visitor might want.

🏃 Activities
Hiking
Mt Marathon Trail   HIKING
According to local legend, grocer Gus Borgan wagered $100 in 1909 that no one could run Mt Marathon in an hour, and the race was on. Winner James Walters clocked in at 62 minutes, losing the bet but becoming a legend. The 3.1-mile suffer-fest quickly became a celebrated Fourth of July event and today is Alaska's most famous footrace, pitting runners from all over the world against the 3022ft-high peak. In 1981 Bill Spencer set the record at 43 minutes, 23 seconds. Many runners take twice as long, and each year several end up with bloody knees or broken bones after tumbling during the hell-bent descent.

You can trek to the top several ways. At the end of Monroe St, the so-called Jeep Trail provides easier (though not drivable) access to the peak and a heavenly bowl behind the mountain. At the west end of Jefferson St, you can access either a trailhead with switchbacks to mellow the ascent, or the official route, which begins at a nearby cliff face behind the water tanks. Be careful: the runner's trail is painful – think Stairmaster with a view – and every summer several tourists who didn't know what they were in for are rescued.

Iditarod National Historic Trail   HIKING

Though the celebrated Iditarod Race to Nome currently departs from Anchorage, the legendary trail actually begins in Seward. In 1995 Mitch Seavey mushed from Seward along this well-worn path into Anchorage, where he continued with the regularly scheduled Iditarod; he finished 20th. At the foot of Ballaine Blvd, a new memorial marks Mile 0 and a paved bike path heads 2 miles north along the beach.

A far more interesting segment of the trail for hikers, however, can be reached by heading east 2 miles on Nash Rd, which intersects the Seward Hwy at Mile 3.2. From here you can follow the Iditarod National Historic Trail through woods and thick brush for a 4-mile hike to Bear Lake. Nearby is the unmarked trailhead for the Mt Alice Trail, a fairly difficult and highly recommended 2.5-mile climb to the alpine summit. Bald eagles, blueberries and stunning views can be had elsewhere, but it's the solitude – this trail is relatively unused – and afternoon light that make Mt Alice great. Back at Bear Lake, you can either backtrack to town or forge on another 11 miles to rejoin the Seward Hwy.

Two Lakes Trail   HIKING

This easy 1-mile loop circumnavigates pleasant Two Lakes Park (cnr 2nd Ave & C St), through woods and picnic grounds, across a creek and around the two promised lakes at the base of Mt Marathon. Unsatisfied hikers can access the Jeep Trail nearby, which climbs Mt Marathon, for a much more intense climb.

Lost Lake Trail   HIKING

This challenging 7-mile trail to an alpine lake is one of the most scenic hikes the Kenai Peninsula has to offer in midsummer. The trailhead is in Lost Lake subdivision, at Mile 5.3 of the Seward Hwy. At 4.5 miles up the trail is the Clemens Memorial Cabin, which has amazing views of Resurrection Bay and is also a good winter destination. The final 2 miles are above the treeline, making the shores of Lost Lake a wondrous place to pitch a tent.

If you'd rather not return the same way, continue around the east side of Lost Lake to the Primrose Trail, an 8-mile alpine trek ending at Primrose Landing Campground at Mile 17.2 of the Seward Hwy. Plan on seven to 10 hours for the round-trip to Lost Lake, and bring a camp stove, as wood is hard to come by.

Caines Head State Recreation Area   HIKING

This 6000-acre preserve, 5.5 miles south of Seward on Resurrection Bay, contains WWII military facilities (bring a flashlight for exploring), a 650ft headland, the Coastal Trail and two public-use cabins. There's a $5 day-use fee for the recreation area, paid at the trailhead. If you're not up for an overnight backpacking excursion, the hike to Tonsina Point is an easy 3-mile round-trip. In 2006, however, floods washed out the Tonsina Creek bridge, making it necessary for hikers to trek along the creek to the shore and cross the stream where it braids. Beyond that you will need to time your passage with low tide.

Glacier Trekking

TOP
CHOICE **Exit Glacier Guides**   ICE-HIKING

(☎224-5569; www.exitglacierguides.com) Exit Glacier Guides gives you the chance to tread upon Seward's backyard glacier. Its five-hour ice-hiking trip costs $125 per person, gears you up with ice axes and crampons, ascends part-way up the Harding Ice Field Trail and then heads out onto the glacier for crevasse exploration and interpretive glaciology. It also offers helicopter trips to an isolated glacier in the national forest ($275 to $350).

Mountain Biking

Popular with hikers, the Lost Lake Trail makes for sometimes steep and technical, but highly rewarding, single-track riding. Local cyclists say the Iditarod National Historic Trail and the Resurrection River Trail are also good rides.

Seward Adventure Company   MOUNTAIN BIKING

(☎362-7433; www.sewardbiketours.com) Run by cycling aficionado Karl, Seward Adventure Company offers guided day trips ($80 to $145) to Devil's Pass and the Iditarod Trail, to name a few. Bikes are provided, and multiday custom trips can include meals and

EXIT GLACIER

The marquee attraction of Kenai Fjords National Park is Exit Glacier, named by explorers crossing the Harding Ice Field who found the glacier a suitable way to 'exit' the ice and mountains.

From the Exit Glacier Nature Center, the Outwash Plain Trail is an easy half-mile walk to the glacier's alluvial plain – a flat expanse of pulverized silt and gravel, cut through by braids of gray meltwater. The Overlook Loop Trail leaves the first loop and climbs steeply to an overlook at the side of the glacier before returning; don't skip the short spur to Falls Overlook, a scenic cascade off the upper trail. Both trails make for a short hike, not much more than a mile in length; you can return along the half-mile nature trail through cottonwood forest, alder thickets and old glacial moraines before emerging at the ranger station. Note how the land becomes more vegetated the further you get from the ice – the result of having had more time to recover from its glacial scouring.

For a long, steep hike and a view the likes of which you may never see elsewhere, hike up the Harding Ice Field Trail. Pack food and water, because it's a long and steep walk, but gazing across the vast expanse of ice – one of the last remnants of the ice age – is an experience that can't be replicated.

lodging. Winter tours on fat-tire snow bikes are also available.

Paddling

Though the best and most impressive paddling in the region is within Kenai Fjords National Park, getting there requires a costly water-taxi. If you're looking to save money and don't mind foregoing the park's tidewater glaciers and more ample wildlife, kayaking right outside Seward in Resurrection Bay can still make for a stunning day on the water. Both Sunny Cove Sea Kayaking (☏800-770-9119; www.sunnycove.com; small-boat harbor) and Kayak Adventures Worldwide (☏224-3960; www.kayakak.com; 328 3rd Ave) guide half- and full-day trips in the bay. The latter, as well as Adventure 60 North (☏224-2600; www.adventure60.com; Mile 3, Seward Hwy) and Miller's Landing (☏224-5739, 866-541-5739; www.millerslandingak.com; cnr Lowell Rd & Beach St), also rents out kayaks.

Dogsledding

Hey, this is where the Iditarod started. Why not meet the dogs?

IdidaRide   DOGSLED TOURS
(☏800-478-3139; www.ididaride.com; Exit Glacier Rd; adult/child $69/34.50) IdidaRide is cheesy, but it's more like Stilton than Velveeta: after touring Iditarod veteran Mitch Seavey's kennels and hearing junior mushers discuss their experiences with subzero sleep deprivation, delicate doggy feet and cutthroat competition, you'll be treated to a 2-mile

training run guided by Iditarod veterans in a cart hitched behind a team of huskies.

Godwin Glacier Dog Sled Tours   DOGSLED TOURS
(☏888-989-8239; www.alaskadogsled.com; per person $300) This company goes one better, transporting you by helicopter to an alpine glacier, where you'll be met by lots of dogs and a genuine snow-sledding adventure, even in July.

Wilderness Cabins

You can paddle, fly or hike to a remote, rustic lodging administered by the Alaska Division of Parks, USFS or even the National Park Service, as Kenai Fjords National Park has several boat-accessible public-use cabins.

Orca Island Cabins   YURTS
(☏491-1988; www.orcaislandcabins.com; yurts per person $199) In Humpy Cove, 9 miles southeast of Seward, this privately owned place has three onshore yurts with private baths and kitchens. All have propane-powered ranges and water-heaters but no electricity. These are a great choice for those who want to rough it without roughing it *too* much. The price includes water-taxi and kayak rentals.

Clemens Memorial Cabin   CABIN
(☏877-444-6777, 518-885-3639; www.recreation.gov; cabins $45) Located 4.5 miles up the Lost Lake Trail, this renovated public-use cabin sleeps eight and is located at the treeline, providing spectacular views of Resurrection Bay.

Derby Cove Cabin
CABIN

(www.alaskastateparks.org; cabins $65) Just off the tidal trail between Tonsina Point and North Beach in Caines Head State Recreation Area, 4 miles from the Lowell Point trailhead. This public-use cabin can be accessed on foot at low tide, or by kayak any time.

Callisto Canyon Cabin
CABIN

(www.alaskastateparks.org; cabins $65) A public-use cabin located just off the tidal trail, a half-mile before you reach Derby Cove. It can be reached on foot or by kayak.

Resurrection River Cabin
CABIN

(☎877-444-6777, 518-885-3639; www.recreation.gov; cabins $35) This public-use cabin is 6.5 miles from the southern trailhead of the Resurrection River Trail.

★☆ Festivals & Events

Seward knows how to party, and these are just a few of the more popular events.

Polar Bear Jumpoff Festival
CULTURAL

A favorite of costumed masochists who plunge into frigid Resurrection Bay with a smile in mid-January, all to raise money for cancer.

Mt Marathon Race
CULTURAL

This Fourth of July race attracts runners who like to test themselves by running up a near vertical peak, and fans who like to drink beer and yell.

Silver Salmon Derby
CULTURAL

An event held in mid-August that gets even bigger crowds, all vying for prizes in excess of $150,000.

Seward Music & Arts Festival
MUSIC

Held the last weekend in September, this summer's-end celebration brings together an eclectic mix of local artists and musicians, and is particularly kid-friendly, with circus training and mural-painting.

🛏 Sleeping

Above and beyond the listed rates you have to add 11% in Seward sales and bed taxes. Near Exit Glacier, Kenai Fjords National Park maintains one free, drive-up campground. There are lots of informal campsites along Exit Glacier Rd.

Among Seward's midrange places, dozens are B&Bs; you can book through **Alaska's Point of View** (☎224-2323, 800-844-2424), even at the last minute.

TOP CHOICE Alaska Paddle Inn
B&B $$$

(☎362-2628; www.alaskapaddleinn.com; 13745 Beach Dr; r from $209; ⊜⊚) Two custom-built rooms overlook a private beach and Resurrection Bay on Lowell Point. Arched ceilings, walk-in tiled showers and gas fireplaces make this place both one of the coziest and classiest in Seward. Discounts for stays of multiple days.

Waterfront Campground
CAMPGROUND $

(☎224-3331; Ballaine Blvd; sites $10, RV camp-sites $15-30) Perfectly situated between the city center and boat harbor, with stunning views. There's also a compact skateboard park, a massive playground and a paved bicycle path running through. Hot showers are only $2.

Moby Dick Hostel
HOSTEL $

(☎224-7072; www.mobydickhostel.com; 430 3rd Ave; dm/r $22/75; ⊜⊚) Friendly, well located and popular with a new quiet annex across the street. It costs $3 to rent linen, and you can't use your sleeping bag. You can book tours here for a 10% discount.

Snow River Hostel
HOSTEL $

(☎440-1907; www.snowriverhostelseward.org; Mile 16 Seward Hwy; dm/d/cabins $20/50/50; ⊜) Nestled beside the forest and a burbling creek, this cordwood place is some distance from town, but worth the trip for the idyllic atmosphere and easy access to challenging Lost Lake Trail. The kitchen comes stocked with pancake mix.

Kayaker's Cove
HOSTEL $

(☎224-8662; www.kayakerscove.net; dm/cabins $20/60; ⊜) Located 12 miles southeast of Seward near Fox Island in a lush little cove, this place is accessible by kayak or water-taxi only. There's a shared kitchen, and you'll need to bring your own food. It rents out single/double kayaks for $20/30.

Ballaine House B&B
B&B $

(☎224-2362; www.superpage.com/ballaine; 437 3rd Ave; s $50, d $65-82; ⊜) One of the original Seward homes, the Ballaine House caters to outdoor-oriented folks, does cook-to-order breakfasts and offers a wealth of advice on what to do around town. It's an excellent bargain.

Stoney Creek Inn
B&B $$

(☎224-3940; www.stoneycreekinn.net; Stoney Creek Ave; d $139-154; ⊜⊚) This secluded place has five rooms sharing a common

KARI ANDERSON: SEWARD HARBORMASTER

There are fantastic opportunities here to experience the marine environment: whale watching, charter fishing and sailing, to name a few. I grew up in Seward and started working on boats when I was 16. I've never missed a summer here, and I'm proud to call it home.

Kayak a Tidewater Glacier

This is one of the few places in the world where you can get up close and personal with glaciers as they meet the ocean. The perspective from a kayak is unbeatable. The crackling berg bits, the seals swimming around you...I can only describe it as epic.

Alaska SeaLife Center

The SeaLife Center is one of the northern-most marine research facilities in the world, with beautiful public exhibits. Meet the staff and listen to their stories of rehabilitating injured marine mammals, and conducting scientific research.

Seward Small-Boat Harbor

An evening stroll in the harbor is one of my favorite activities when I have company in town. Seward has a rich maritime history and there's a variety of vessels that home-port here. It's great spot to take photos of fishermen cleaning their catch, and playful otters swimming between the boats.

area, and comes with a fantastic sauna and hot tub next to a deliciously icy-cold salmon stream. The barbecue area is a great place to grill up your catch. Continental breakfast included.

Van Gilder Hotel HISTORIC HOTEL **$$**
(☎800-478-0460; www.vangilderhotel.com; 307 Adams St; d $119-229; ☎) Gossips say poltergeists plague the 1st floor of this landmark, which dates from 1916. If you dare to spend the night, however, you'll find elegant suites with antique furnishings, plus some affordable European pensions without baths.

Hotel Seward HISTORIC HOTEL **$$**
(☎224-8001, 800-440-2444; www.hotelsewardalaska.com; 221 5th Ave; r $99-450; ☎☎) The 'historic' side has been remodeled and has affordable shared-bath rooms; the new wing makes for an excellent splurge with grand views of Resurrection Bay. An old-time saloon serves up appetizers, but the lobby is definitely overdoing it in the taxidermy department.

Forest Acres Campground CAMPGROUND **$**
(☎224-4055; cnr Hemlock St & Seward Hwy; tent sites $10, RV sites $15-30) Located 2 miles north of town just off the Seward Hwy on Hemlock St; has quiet sites shaded by towering spruce.

Murphy's Motel MOTEL **$$**
(☎224-8090; www.murphysmotel.com; 911 4th Ave; s/d $129/149; ☎) You'll find nice harbor

views from private decks at this clean and professional place. There are some smaller rooms without views and deluxe kitchen units ($169).

Miller's Landing CAMPGROUND **$**
(☎224-5739, 866-541-5739; www.millerslandingak.com; cnr Lowell Rd & Beach St; tent sites/RV sites $26/36, cabins $50-150) This touristplex – offering everything from campsites to kayak rentals to fishing charters – isn't very clean or organized, but the waterfront location is hard to beat.

Breeze Inn MOTEL **$$**
(☎224-5283; www.breezeinn.com; 1306 Seward Hwy; r $139-279; ☎☎☎) This harbor center place lacks charm or soul, but is conveniently located.

✕ Eating

TOP CHOICE Smoke Shack BARBECUE **$**
(411 Port Ave; breakfast & lunch $6-11, dinner $10-16; ☉6am-8pm) Housed in a rail car, this joint oozes blue-collar atmosphere. It has the best breakfast in town (biscuits and gravy made from scratch) and pulled pork for dinner.

Railway Cantina MEXICAN **$**
(light meals $6-12; ☉lunch & dinner) Near the small-boat harbor, this spot offers unorthodox quesadillas, burritos and tacos. Try the blackened halibut burrito, with your choice of salsa (we like the pineapple-ginger).

Exit Glacier Salmon Bake
SEAFOOD $$

(Exit Glacier Rd; lunch $6-10, dinner $18-22; ☺lunch & dinner) Its motto – 'cheap beer and lousy food' – is wrong on the second count. Locals like the salmon sandwich, which you can adorn with pickles from a barrel.

Resurrection Roadhouse
PIZZA $$

(www.sewardwindsong.com; Exit Glacier Rd; breakfast & lunch $9-14, dinner $18-46; ☺breakfast, lunch & dinner) This local favorite is home to the 'Buddha Belly' pizza, sweet-potato fries that are well worth traveling for, and the best deck in town. It also has a vast range of on-tap brews, and the bar is open until midnight.

Ranting Raven
BAKERY $

(238 4th Ave; light meals $3-6; ☺breakfast & lunch) Excellent pastries and cookies (seriously, you have to try the lemon shortbread) and equally awesome soups at lunchtime. Everything is made in-house, and the gift shop at the front is a great place to pick up local art.

Ray's Waterfront
SEAFOOD $$

(✆224-5606; lunch $10-16, dinner $19-31; ☺lunch & dinner) Hands down, this is Seward's culinary high point, with attentive service, picture-postcard views and the finest seafood above water.

Bakery Cafe at the Harbor
BAKERY $

(1210 4th Ave; breakfast & lunch $3-8, dinner $5-12; ☺5am-7pm) This busy joint is a bargain: breakfast is delish and dinner includes half-pound burgers on homemade buns. Also sells box lunches for those going out on the bay for the day.

Christo's Palace
PIZZA $$

(133 4th Ave; dinner $19-25; ☺11am-midnight) Has a huge dining room dominated by a 1950s Brunswick bar (featuring a great selection of beer on tap). The pizza gets raves.

Resurrect Art Coffee House Gallery
CAFE $

(320 3rd Ave; ☺7am-7pm) Located in an old high-ceilinged church, this place serves espressos, Italian sodas and bagels, displays great local art and hosts live jazz on Tuesday nights. The best place to read the paper and check out the view is from the airy choir loft.

Sea Bean Cafe
CAFE $

(225 4th Ave; light meals $2-7; ☺7am-8pm; ☎) Serves hot paninis, wraps, Belgian waffles, ice cream, smoothies and espressos.

Safeway
SUPERMARKET $

(Mile 1.5, Seward Hwy; ☺5am-midnight) Has sushi, espressos, a sandwich bar and all the groceries you need.

Drinking & Entertainment

Seward has no shortage of welcoming watering holes, most featuring a mix of young and old, locals and tourists. Almost all the bars are downtown, and most are smoke-filled.

Seward Alehouse
BAR

(215 4th Ave; ☺) This fun pub is the only smoke-free bar in town. There's a good selection of beers on tap and a dance party-starting jukebox.

Thorn's Showcase Lounge
LOUNGE

(208 4th St; mains $14-18) This saloon serves the strongest drinks in town – try its white Russians. The Jim Beam collection is valued at thousands of dollars; can you spot the pipeline bottle?

Yukon Bar
BAR

(201 4th Ave) There are hundreds of dollars pinned to this bar's ceiling and almost nightly live music in the summer. It's festive.

Pit Bar
BAR

(Mile 3.5, Seward Hwy; ☺to 5am) Just past Exit Glacier Rd; this is where the crowd heads when the bars close in town.

Liberty Theatre
THEATER

(✆224-5418; 304 4th Ave; admission $7) A delightful little WWII-era cinema showing first-run flicks daily.

Information

First National Bank of Anchorage (✆224-4200; 303 4th Ave; ☺10am-5pm Mon-Thu, 9am-6pm Fri) One of two banks in town. There are ATMs in Safeway and the Yukon Bar.

Post office (cnr 5th Ave & Madison St) The informal community gathering place.

Providence Seward Medical Center (✆224-5205; 417 1st Ave) At the west end of Jefferson St.

Sea Bean Cafe (225 4th Ave; free wireless, internet access per 15min/1hr $2/7; ☺7am-9pm; ☎) On the main drag.

Seward Library (238 5th Ave; internet access free; ☺10am-9pm Mon-Fri, to 7pm Sat; ☎) Sells used books and displays what it claims is Benny Benson's first signed flag.

Suds N' Swirl (335 3rd Ave; laundry per wash $3.25; ☺7am-8:30pm) Attached to a wonderful cafe, the Sip-N-Spin.

TOURIST INFORMATION Chamber of Commerce (✆224-8051; www.sewardak.org; 2001

Seward Hwy/3rd Ave; ⊙9am-6pm Mon-Sat, to 4pm Sun) At the entrance to town, this helpful place provides everything from trail maps to local menus, plus lots of good advice.

Harbormaster's Office (☑224-3138; small-boat harbor; ⊙8am-5pm) Has showers for $2 (24 hours).

Kenai Fjords National Park Visitor Center (⊙8:30am-7pm) Beside the small-boat harbor.

Seward Parks and Recreation (☑224-4054; 519 4th Ave; adult/child $4/2; ⊙10am-9pm Mon-Fri) Has a gym and sauna as well as showers. Locals call it the 'AVTEC gym,' for the school that shares the building.

USFS Ranger Station (☑224-3374; 334 4th Ave; ⊙8am-5pm Mon-Fri) Has maps and information about Seward's outstanding selection of trails, cabins and campgrounds.

ℹ Getting There & Around

BICYCLE Seward Bike Shop (☑224-2448; 411 Port Ave; per half/full-day cruisers $14/23, mountain bikes $21/38; ⊙9:30am-6:30pm Mon-Sat, 11am-4pm Sun) Rents out bikes and has the latest details on local biking trails.

BUS Seward Bus Line (☑224-3608; www.sewardbuslines.net) Departs at 9:30am daily en route to Anchorage ($50).

Homer Stage Line (☑422-7037; www.stagelineinhomer.com) Runs daily from Seward to Homer ($87).

Park Connection (☑800-266-8625; www.alaskacoach.com) Has a daily service from Seward to Denali Park (one way $145) via Anchorage (one way $55 to $65). A visit to the Anchorage Museum is included.

SHUTTLE Seward Shuttle When cruise ships are in town, the free shuttle runs between the ferry terminal and downtown every 15 to 20 minutes.

TRAIN Alaska Railroad (☑265-2494, 800-544-0552; www.akrr.com; 408 Port Ave; one way/round-trip $75/119) Offers a daily run to Anchorage from May to September. It's more than just public transportation; it's one of the most famous rides in Alaska, complete with glaciers, steep gorges and rugged mountain scenery.

Kenai Fjords National Park

Seward is the gateway to Kenai Fjords National Park, created in 1980 to protect 587,000 acres of Alaska's most awesome, impenetrable wilderness. Crowning the park is the massive Harding Ice Field; from it, countless tidewater glaciers pour down, carving the coast into dizzying fjords.

With such a landscape – and an abundance of marine wildlife to boot – the park is a major tourist attraction. Unfortunately, it's also an expensive one. That is why road-accessible Exit Glacier is its highlight attraction, drawing more than 100,000 tourists each summer. Hardier souls can ascend to the Harding Ice Field from the same trailhead, but only experienced mountaineers equipped with skis, ice axes and crampons can investigate the 900 sq miles of ice.

The vast majority of visitors either take a quick trip to Exit Glacier's face or splurge on a tour-boat cruise along the coast. For those who want to spend more time in the park, the coastal fjords are a blue-water kayaker's dream; to reach the area, though, you either have to paddle the sections exposed to the Gulf of Alaska or pay for a drop-off service.

⚡ Activities

Hiking

Ranger-Led Hikes   HIKING

At 10am, 2pm and 4pm daily, rangers at the Exit Glacier Nature Center lead free one-hour hikes to the face of the glacier, providing information on the wildlife and natural history of the area. For a more strenuous outing, show up at the nature center on a Saturday at 9am for the guided ascent of the Harding Ice Field Trail. The trek lasts eight hours; pack a lunch and rain gear.

Harding Ice Field Trail   HIKING

This strenuous and yet extremely popular 4-mile trail follows Exit Glacier up to Harding Ice Field. The 936-sq-mile expanse remained undiscovered until the early 1900s, when a map-surveying team discovered that eight coastal glaciers flowed from the exact same system.

Today you can rediscover it via a steep, roughly cut and sometimes slippery ascent to 3500ft; for reasonably fit trekkers, that's a good three- or four-hour trip. Beware of bears; they're common here.

The trek is well worth it for those with the stamina, as it provides spectacular views of not only the ice field but Exit Glacier and the valley below. The upper section of the route is snow-covered for much of the year; bring a jacket and watch for crevasses, which may be hidden under a thin and unstable bridge of snow. Camping up here is a great idea, but the free, tiny public-use cabin at the top is for emergencies only.

Resurrection River Trail   HIKING

This 16-mile trail accesses a 72-mile trail system connecting Seward and Hope. The continuous trail is broken only by the Sterling Hwy and provides a wonderful wilderness adventure through streams, rivers, lakes, wooded lowlands and alpine areas. It's difficult and expensive to maintain, so expect to encounter natural hassles like downed trees; boggy patches and washed-out sections are common. Resurrection River Cabin is 7 miles from the trailhead.

The southern trailhead is at Mile 8 of Exit Glacier Rd. The northern trailhead joins the Russian Lakes Trail 5 miles from Cooper Lake or 16 miles from the Russian River Campground off the Sterling Hwy. The hike from the Seward Hwy to the Sterling Hwy is a 40-mile trip, including Exit Glacier.

Paddling

Bluewater paddles out of Resurrection Bay along the coastline of the park are for experienced kayakers only; others should invest in a drop-off service. You'll be rewarded, however, with wildlife encounters and close-up views of the glaciers from a unique perspective.

With several glaciers to visit, Aialik Bay is a popular arm for kayakers. Many people hire water-taxis to drop them near Aialik Glacier, then take three or four days to paddle south past Pedersen Glacier and into Holgate Arm, where they're picked up. The high point of the trip is Holgate Glacier, an active tidewater glacier that's the main feature of all the boat tours.

Northwestern Lagoon is more expensive to reach but much more isolated, with not nearly as many tour boats. The wildlife is excellent, especially the seabirds and sea otters, and more than a half-dozen glaciers can be seen. Plan on three to four days if you're being dropped inside the lagoon.

Most companies can arrange drop-off and pickup; it's about $250 for the round-trip to Aialik Bay and $275 to $300 for the more remote Northwestern Lagoon.

TOP CHOICE Kayak Adventures Worldwide   KAYAKING

(☏224-3960; www.kayakak.com) A highly respected, eco-oriented operation that guides educationally based half- and full-day trips ($70 to $130). It also arranges a two-day adventure with Exit Glacier Guides (see p220) for a day of kayaking and a day of glacier hiking.

Sunny Cove Sea Kayaking   KAYAKING

(☏224-8810, 800-770-9119; www.sunnycove.com) It doesn't rent out kayaks, but does arrange a multitude of different trips, including $65 three-hour paddles in Resurrection Bay, $399 full-day journeys in Aialik Bay, and excursions that combine a half-day of paddling with a salmon-bake lunch on Fox Island and a Kenai Fjords cruise ($129 to $179).

Miller's Landing   KAYAKING

(☏224-5739, 866-541-5739; www.millerslandingak.com) Rents out kayaks (single/double $45/50) and equipment, and also provides a water-taxi service as far as Aialik Bay, as does Alaska Saltwater Lodge (☏224-5271; www.alaskasaltwaterlodge.com).

☞ Tours

The easiest and most popular way to view the park's dramatic fjords, glaciers and abundant wildlife is from a cruise ship. Several companies offer the same basic tours: wildlife cruises (three to five hours) take in Resurrection Bay without really entering the park. Don't bother. Much better tours (eight to 10 hours) explore Holgate Arm or Northwestern Lagoon. Some offer a buffet lunch on beautiful Fox Island, which basically means spending an hour picking at trays of overcooked salmon when you could instead be whale watching. Eat on the boat.

Kenai Fjords Tours   BOAT

(☏224-8068, 877-777-2805; www.kenaifjords.com) With an office base at the small-boat harbor in Seward, Kenai Fjords Tours goes the furthest into the park (Northwestern Fjord; per adult/child $175/87) and offers the widest variety of options, including an all-inclusive overnight on Fox Island at the Kenai Fjords Wilderness Lodge (per person $404 based on double occupancy). Smaller vessels are available for more intimate tours, often adapted to the interests of the group. It also does package deals that include rail travel from Anchorage.

Major Marine Tours   BOAT

(☏224-8030, 800-764-7300; www.majormarine.com) Major Marine Tours includes a national park ranger on every boat. It has a half-day Resurrection Bay tour (per adult/child $79/39) and a full-day viewing Holgate Arm ($149/74). The latter tour is a local favorite. With both tours, you can add a prime rib and salmon buffet feast for $15. it has an office base at the small-boat harbor in Seward.

Kayak Adventures Worldwide KAYAKING
(224-3960; www.kayakak.com) Offers several
joined sailing and kayaking tours, where you
can paddle all day and return to a snug bed
on the water.

Scenic Mountain Air SCENIC FLIGHTS
(224-6607; www.sewardair.com) For flightseeing trips, contact Scenic Mountain Air at
Seward airport for flights over the fjords.
Prices start at $189 for an hour and rise to
$264 for 1½ hours. It's also possible to char-
ter a plane for $330 per hour (seats three).

🛏 Sleeping

Kenai Fjords Glacier Lodge CABIN $$$
(783-2928, 800-334-8730; www.kenaifjordsgla
cierlodge.com; cabins per person from $650) On
gorgeous Pedersen Lagoon, this new lodge
has 16 rustic-chic cabins (with private baths
and electricity) connected by a network of
boardwalks. The all-inclusive price is a bet-
ter deal for longer stays and includes trans-
portation from Seward, gourmet meals, gla-
cier cruises and guided kayaking.

Exit Glacier Campground CAMPGROUND $
(Exit Glacier Rd; tent sites free) The only formal
campground in the park. It has great walk-
in sites for tents only and a bear-proof food-
storage area. Other campsites are dotted
along Exit Glacier Rd – look for small turn-
offs in the alders.

Public-use Cabins CABIN $
(224-3175; www.nps.gov/kefj/planyourvisit/pu
blicusecabins_summer.htm; cabins $50) There
are three cabins along the fjords, in addi-
tion to countless other informal campsites
that line the kayak-accessible beaches of
Aialik Bay and Northwestern Lagoon. **Aialik
Cabin** is on a beach that's perfect for hik-
ing, beachcombing and whale watching;
Holgate Arm Cabin has a spectacular view
of Holgate Glacier; and **North Arm Cabin** is
actually much closer to Homer. You'll want
to reserve these well in advance through the
Alaska Public Lands Information Center
(271-2742).

ℹ Information

Exit Glacier Nature Center (⊙9am-8pm)
At the Exit Glacier trailhead; has interpretive
displays, sells postcards and field guides, and
is the starting point for ranger-guided hikes.
Kenai Fjords National Park Visitor Center
(1212 4th Ave, Seward; ⊙8:30am-7pm) In
Seward's small-boat harbor; has information on

hiking and camping, and issues free backcoun-
try permits.

ℹ Getting There & Around

To reach the coastal fjords, you'll need to take a
tour or catch a water-taxi with **Miller's Landing**
(224-5739, 866-541-5739; www.millersland
ingak.com) or **Alaska Saltwater Lodge** (224-
5271; www.alaskasaltwaterlodge.com).

Getting to Exit Glacier is a bit easier. If you
don't have a car, **Exit Glacier Guides** (224-
5569) runs an hourly shuttle to the glacier in its
recycled-vegetable-oil van between 8:30am and
4:30pm. The van departs from the Holiday Inn
Express at the small-boat harbor and costs $10
round-trip. Otherwise, there are cabs: **Glacier
Taxi** (224-5678) charges $50 for as many
people as you can squeeze in.

STERLING HIGHWAY

At Tern Lake Junction, the paved Sterling
Hwy turns off from the Seward Hwy, head-
ing westward through the forests and moun-
tains to Soldotna and then bending south
along Cook Inlet toward Homer.

Tern Lake Junction to Cooper Landing

From **Tern Lake Junction** (Mile 37, Seward
Hwy) it's only 58 miles to Soldotna, not much
more than an hour's drive. Yet this stretch
contains so many hiking, camping and ca-
noeing opportunities that it would take you
a month to enjoy them all. Surrounded by
the Chugach National Forest and Kenai Na-
tional Wildlife Refuge, the Sterling Hwy and
its side roads pass a dozen trails, 20 camp-
grounds and an almost endless number of
lakes, rivers and streams. Mileposts along
the highway show distances from Seward,
with Tern Lake Junction at Mile 37 the start-
ing point of the Sterling Hwy.

During July and August, be prepared to
stop at a handful of campgrounds before
finding an available site.

For good, basic rooms, there's **Sunrise
Inn & Cafe** (595-1222; Mile 45 Sterling Hwy;
RV sites/r $25/125, meals $8-15; ⊙7am-10pm),
which has RV spaces but no campsites. It's
a grand place to stop for affordable and
outstanding dishes like the vegetarian 4:20
Love Burger or the Hippie Girl breakfast. Be-
ware, however, the Pig Vomit Omelet.

Just past Sunrise Inn, **Quartz Creek
Campground** (Mile 0.3, Quartz Creek Rd; tent

sites/RV sites $18/28) on the shores of Kenai Lake is crazily popular with RVs and anglers during salmon runs. The campground is so developed that the sites are paved.

The Crescent Creek Trail, about half a mile beyond the Crescent Creek Campground, leads 6.5 miles to the outlet of Crescent Lake and the USFS's Crescent Saddle Cabin (☎877-444-6777; www.recreation.gov; cabins $45). It's an easy walk or bike ride and has spectacular autumn colors in September. Anglers can fish for Arctic grayling in the lake during the summer. The Carter Lake Trail connects the east end of the lake to the Seward Hwy, with a rough path along the south side of the lake between the two trails.

Cooper Landing & Around

POP 395

After skirting the north end of Kenai Lake, you enter scenic Cooper Landing (Mile 48.4). The picturesque outpost, named for Joseph Cooper, a miner who worked the area in the 1880s, is best known for its rich and brutal combat salmon fishing along the Russian and Kenai Rivers. While rustic log-cabin lodges featuring giant fish freezers are still the lifeblood of this town, the trails and white-water rafting opportunities attract a very different sort of tourist.

◉ Sights & Activities

FREE K'Beq Interpretive Site   ARCHAEOLOGICAL SITE
(☎398-8867; Mile 52.6, Sterling Hwy; ⊙11:30am-5pm) This riverfront site, run by the local Kenaitzie tribe, is a refreshing reminder of what this area was like before the flood of sport fishermen. A quarter-mile boardwalk winds past an ancient house pit and other archaeological relics, while interpretive panels address berry picking, steam bathbuilding and more traditional methods of catching fish on the Kenai. Several guided tours depart throughout the day.

Fishing

Most of the fishing on the Upper Kenai is for rainbow trout, Dolly Varden, and silver and sockeye salmon. Expect to pay at least $150 for a half-day on the water and more than $200 for a full day.

Alaska River Adventures   FISHING
(☎595-2000, 888-836-9027; www.alaskariveradventures.com; Mile 47.9, Sterling Hwy)

Alaska Rivers Company   FISHING
(☎595-1226; www.alaskariverscompany.com; Mile 49.9, Sterling Hwy)

Hiking

Cooper Landing is the starting point for two of the Kenai Peninsula's loveliest multiday trails: the 39-mile Resurrection Pass Trail to Hope; and the 21-mile Russian Lakes Trail, a favorite of fishers and families.

Other Activities

TOP CHOICE Alaska Horseman Trail Adventures   HORSEBACK RIDING
(☎595-1806; www.alaskahorsemen.com; Mile 45, Sterling Hwy) This is the place to feel like a cowboy or girl. It offers horseback rides along Quartz and Crescent Creeks (per half-/full day $130/175) and pricier guided overnight trips that include rafting (called the 'Saddle Paddle') and/or flightseeing or custom fishing trips. The guest ranch includes squawking peacocks, a hot tub and sauna, and a wall-tent cabin (per night $150).

Alaska River Adventures   RAFTING
(☎595-2000, 888-836-9027; www.alaskariveradventures.com; Mile 48, Sterling Hwy) Runs scenic three-hour floats on the Kenai (per person $54). The coolest trip, however, is the Paddle Saddle ($199), which combines a float trip with gold panning and a two-hour horseback ride.

Alaska Rivers Company   RAFTING
(☎595-1226, 888-595-1226; www.alaskariverscompany.com; Mile 49.9, Sterling Hwy) Runs guided raft trips down the Kenai River (per half-/full day $49/142), with the longer trip bumping over some Class III rapids.

Kenai Lake Sea Kayak Adventures   KAYAKING
(☎595-3441; www.kenailake.com; Mile 0.3, Quartz Creek Rd) Has guided three-hour sea-kayak trips on Kenai Lake ($73) that are a good introduction to paddling, in a stunning setting to boot.

🛏 Sleeping

Drifters Lodge   CABIN $$
(☎595-5555; www.drifterslodge.com; Mile 48.3, Sterling Hwy; cabins $335-375, r $100-230) Six tidy and fresh cabins come with memory-foam mattresses, river views and kitchenettes, while five smaller rooms share bathrooms and leafy views. A brook babbles next to the sauna, and there's a nightly campfire for ghost stories. Drifters also

In a place that's mostly natural and wild, there are few sights more unnatural than what happens each summer wherever Alaska's best salmon rivers meet a busy road. When the fish are running, the banks become a human frenzy – a ceaseless string of men, women and children hip-to-hip, hundreds of fishing rods whipping to and fro, the air filled with curses and cries of joy, the waters rippling with dozens of fish dancing on taut and sometimes tangled lines. The banks are a jumble of coolers and tackle boxes and catches-of-the-day. Rub your eyes all you want: the scene is for real. This is combat fishing.

As with any form of combat, there are subtle rules that guide the chaos. Among them: don't wade out in front of other anglers, or snap up their spot on the bank if they briefly step away. (On the other hand, don't let the glares of the earlier arrivals dissuade you from taking your proper place in the fray.) Try to give your neighbor space – and whatever you do, don't foul your line with theirs. Most importantly, if you get a bite, shout, 'Fish on!' so others can reel in their lines and give you room to wrestle your catch. In combat fishing, you don't 'play' a fish; you land it fast, so others can rejoin the fight.

takes folks out on the river – a two-hour float costs $50.

Cooper Creek Campground CAMPGROUND $
(Mile 50.7, Sterling Hwy; sites $18-28) This campground has 29 sites on both sides of the highway, including some right on the Kenai River. Good luck hooking one of those.

Russian River Campground CAMPGROUND $
(www.recreation.gov; Mile 52.6, Sterling Hwy; s/d sites $18/28) Located where the Russian and Kenai Rivers merge, this place is beautiful and incredibly popular when red salmon are spawning; you'll want to reserve one of the 83 sites. It costs $11 just to park there.

Kenai Riverside Campground & RV Park CAMPGROUND $
(☑595-1406, 888-536-2478; www.kenairiverside campground.com; 16918 Sterling Hwy; tent sites/ RV sites/r $18/35/69) Has wooded campsites along the river and six shared-bath rooms that are clean and bright, if a bit small. Cabins are available for $179 with breakfast.

Hutch B&B B&B $
(☑598-1270; www.arctic.net/~hutch; Mile 48.5, Sterling Hwy; incl breakfast r $80-99, cabins $225; ☺☺@) In a three-story, balcony-ringed lodge, the big, simple, clean rooms are the best deal in town, and its mini mess hall the cutest. Nightly campfires add a social angle.

✕ Eating

Sackett's Kenai Grill CAFE $$
(16201 Sterling Hwy; sandwiches $6-10, pizza $12-18; ☺breakfast, lunch & dinner Tue-Sun) Everything here is made from scratch: from the buns to the barbecued pork and the pizza

dough. It's a local favorite and a great place to stop before and after a day on the river.

Kingfisher Roadhouse SEAFOOD $$
(Mile 47.4, Sterling Hwy; mains $15-25; ☺dinner) Overlooking Kenai Lake, this steak and seafood place has the best atmosphere in town. If you've had enough fish, try the organic Kingfisher Bleus burger; it's the perfect replenishment after a long hike.

Cooper Landing Grocery GROCERY $
Mile 48.2, Sterling Hwy; ☺10am-8pm) Has scads of snacks and souvenirs.

ⓘ Information

Chamber of Commerce (☑595-8888; www. cooperlandingchamber.com; 19194 Sterling Hwy) The doors are unlocked if volunteer staff aren't around; you'll find a few brochures but the website is actually more informative.

Cooper Landing Library (☑595-1241; Bean Creek Rd; ☺Mon-Sat; @) Close to Mile 47.7, Sterling Hwy; offers free internet access after you purchase a $5 library card. It's worth it just to enjoy the wood stove. Open late mornings and afternoons.

Wildman's (☑595-1456, 866-595-1456; www. wildmans.org; Mile 47.5, Sterling Hwy; ☺6am-11pm) Your basic backcountry superstore, with snacks, booze, espresso beverages, an ATM, laundry and showers ($4).

ⓘ Getting There & Around

If you're without wheels, your best option for reaching Cooper Landing is **Homer Stage Line** (☑868-3914; www.stagelineinhomer.com), which runs daily buses through here from both Anchorage and Homer. From either end, it's $54 per person one way.

Kenai Peninsula Highlights

Jutting into Cook Inlet is a land mass the size of a small European country. With mountains, glaciers, an ice field, fjords, rivers and lakes, there are at least a summer's worth of recreational opportunities. Here are a few of our favorite sights and activities.

Road Tripping

1 A 126-mile road trip that could last all day – or all week! Driving the Seward Hwy (p214) gives you the chance to spot Dall sheep, beluga whales, moose, glacial streams and even a bore tide.

Drive-in Glacier

2 Witness calving tidewater glaciers, breaching whales and a small river of ice dripping down from Harding Ice Field's Exit Glacier (p221). You can take a boat tour or drive on up to the glacier in Kenai Fjords National Park. What's your fancy?

Arctic Art

3 The arts capital of Alaska (p238) basks in a special light on the shores of Kachemak Bay. Spend time here filling your belly in its array of dining options, peruse the art galleries and kayak to the mountains across the bay.

Mountain Masochists

4 The Mt Marathon Race (p219) is a 3022ft pain fest held on the Fourth of July in Seward. You'll get a kink in your neck watching runners go from sea level to summit and back in under an hour.

Clockwise from top left
1. Seward Hwy **2.** Exit Glacier and Harding Ice Field
3. Salty Dawg Saloon (p247), Homer Spit **4.** View from atop Mt Marathon

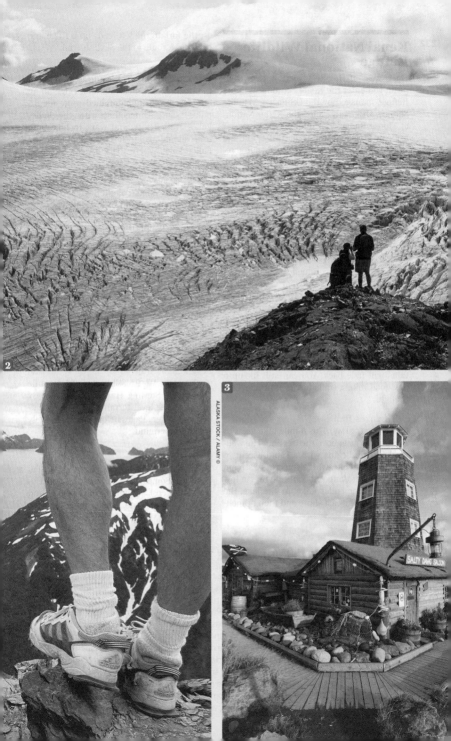

SALTY DAWG SALOON

Kenai National Wildlife Refuge

Once west of the Resurrection Pass trailhead, you enter the Kenai National Wildlife Refuge, managed by the US Fish & Wildlife Service. Originally called the Kenai National Moose Range, 1.73 million acres was set aside by President Roosevelt in 1941 and the 1980 Alaska Lands Act increased that acreage to the almost 2 million acres that it now encompasses. It supports impressive populations of Dall sheep, moose, caribou and bear, and has attracted hunters from around the world since the early 1900s.

◉ Sights & Activities

Russian River Ferry   FERRY
(Mile 55, Sterling Hwy; per passenger $10.25) This ferry, west of the confluence of the Kenai and Russian Rivers, transports more than 30,000 anglers across the water every summer to some of the finest fishing anywhere. It costs $11.25 just to park there; the ferry fee is in addition to that.

Hiking
As the highway heads southwest, the mountains will fade back. You can still hit up a few good hiking trails before that happens, though.

Fuller Lakes Trail   HIKING
(Mile 57, Sterling Hwy) This 3-mile hike leads to Fuller Lake just above the treeline. The well-marked trail begins with a rapid ascent to Lower Fuller Lake, where you cross a stream over a beaver dam and continue over a low pass to Upper Fuller Lake. At the lake, the trail follows the east shore and then branch-

es; the fork to the left leads up a ridge and becomes a route to the Skyline Trail.

Skyline Trail   HIKING
(Mile 61, Sterling Hwy) This route ascends above the treeline and then follows a ridge on an unmarked and unmaintained route for 6.5 miles before connecting with the Fuller Lakes Trail. Those who want to hike both trails should plan to stay overnight at Upper Fuller Lake, where there are several good campsites.

SKILAK LAKE ROAD
Drive along Skilak Lake Rd, which makes a scenic 19-mile loop off the Sterling Hwy and provides access to an assortment of popular recreational opportunities.

Kenai River Trail   HIKING
(Mile 0.6, Skilak Lake Rd) A half-mile down this trail are wonderful views of the Kenai River Canyon.

Skilak Lookout Trail   HIKING
(Mile 5.5, Skilak Lake Rd) Ascends 2.6 miles to a knob (elevation 1450ft) that has a panoramic view of the mountains and lakes. Plan on four to five hours for the round-trip.

Seven Lakes Trail   HIKING
(Engineer Lake, Mile 9.5, Skilak Lake Rd) A 4.4-mile hike to the Sterling Hwy. The trail is easy walking over level terrain and passes Hidden and Hikers Lakes before ending at Kelly Lake Campground.

🛏 Sleeping

There are five campgrounds along Skilak Lake Rd. Some, like Hidden Lake and Upper Skilak, cost $10 a night for a vehicle and $5 for a walk-in site, while others are free.

EXPLORING THE REFUGE CANOE TRAIL SYSTEM

One of only two wilderness canoe systems established in the US (the other is the Boundary Waters, Minnesota), the Kenai National Wildlife Refuge Canoe Trail System (www.fws.gov) offers yet another unique experience for the Alaskan visitor. Divided into two areas, the Swan Lake and the Swanson River routes, the system connects 120 miles of lakes and water trails in an undulating landscape.

Swan Lake is the more popular area, covering 60 miles and 30 lakes, and connecting to the Moose River. The Swanson River route requires longer portages and isn't as well marked as Swan Lake, but you'll be rewarded for effort with solitude and excellent trout fishing. This route covers 80 miles, 40 lakes and 46 miles of the Swanson River.

Several outfitters can rent you canoes and paddles: try Alaska Canoe & Campground (☎262-2331; www.alaskacanoetrips.com; 35292 Sterling Hwy; per 12/24hr $37.50/52.50, 3 days or more per night $42.50), which also rents out rafts and kayaks.

The campgrounds are well marked, running from east to west:

CAMPGROUND	SITES	LOCATION
Hidden Lake	44	Mile 3.6
Upper Skilak Lake	25	Mile 8.4
Lower Ohmer Lake	3	Mile 8.6
Engineer Lake	4	Mile 9.7
Lower Skilak Lake	14	Mile 14

If you choose to stay on the Sterling Hwy past the Skilak Lake Rd junction, a side road at Mile 69 leads south to the Peterson Lake Campground (campsites free) and Kelly Lake Campground (campsites free), near one end of the Seven Lakes Trail. Watson Lake Campground (Mile 71.3 Sterling Hwy; campsites free) has three sites. Four miles down the highway is the west junction with Skilak Lake Rd.

At Mile 81, the Sterling Hwy divides into a four-lane road, and you soon arrive in the small town of Sterling (pop 1800), where the Moose River empties into the Kenai.

Izaak Walton Recreation Site (Mile 82, Sterling Hwy; campsites $13), at the confluence of the Kenai and Moose Rivers, is popular among anglers during the salmon runs and with paddlers ending their Swan Lake route canoe trip at the Moose River Bridge.

Swanson River Road, at Mile 85 of the Sterling Hwy, heads north for 18 miles, with Swan Lake Rd heading east for 12 miles at the end of Swanson River Rd. The roads offer access to the Swanson River and Swan Lake canoe routes, and three campgrounds: Dolly Varden Lake Campground (Mile 14, Swanson River Rd; sites free), Rainbow Lake Campground (Mile 16 Swanson River Rd; campsites free) and Swanson River Campground (campsites free) at the very end of the road. Even without a canoe, you'll enjoy exploring the trails that connect prized fishing holes.

Across the Sterling Hwy from Swanson River Rd is the entrance to Scout Lake Rd, where you'll find the Scout Lake Campground (campsites $10) and Morgans Landing State Recreation Area (campsites $13). This is a particularly scenic area on the bluffs overlooking the Kenai River, a 3.5-mile drive from the Sterling Hwy.

ℹ Information

Kenai National Wildlife Refuge Visitor Contact Station (Mile 58, Sterling Hwy; ⊘10am-4pm), near the junction of Skilak Lake Rd, has up-to-date information on camping, hiking, canoeing and fishing throughout the refuge.

City of Kenai & Around

POP 7945

At first blush, Kenai is a sorry sight – an object lesson in poor city planning. It's not convenient – 10 miles northwest of Soldotna and the Sterling Hwy – or especially picturesque, existing primarily as a support community for the drilling operations at Cook Inlet.

It's long been a rare bird: a major Alaskan city with minimal tourism. Lately, though, this faded boomtown has taken some hesitant steps toward wooing visitors – especially those tantalized by the excellent salmon fishing that takes place at the mouth of the Kenai River.

The first Russian Orthodox Church on mainland Alaska today presides over a replica of the 1867 fort, which hasn't fully realized its potential as adorable tourist magnet. And then there's the view: Mt Redoubt (the volcano that erupted steam and ash in December 1989) to the southwest, Mt Iliamna at the head of the Aleutian Range and the Alaska Range to the northwest. Nice.

North of town, around Mile 19 of the Kenai Spur Hwy, is Alaska's largest concentration of oil infrastructure outside Prudhoe Bay: 15 oil platforms.

⊙ Sights & Activities

Kenai Visitors & Cultural Center   CULTURAL CENTER
(☑283-1991; www.visitkenai.com; 11471 Kenai Spur Hwy; adult/child $5/free; ⊘10am-6pm Mon-Sat, noon-5pm Sun) This excellent visitors center is among Kenai's main attractions. The museum features historical exhibits on the city's Russian heritage, offshore drilling and a room full of stuffed wildlife staring down from the rafters. It also has quality Alaska Native art from around the state. Free movies about the city's strange history are screened, and docents offer summer interpretive programs.

Old Town Kenai   HISTORIC SITE
From the visitors center, follow Overland Ave west to what locals refer to as 'Old Town' – an odd amalgam of historic structures and low-rent apartments, all stupendously situated high above the mouth of the Kenai River. You can pick up a free *Walking Tour* pamphlet at the visitors center. Near Cook Inlet, the US military established Fort Kenay in 1867 and stationed more than 100 men here. What stands today is a replica

constructed as part of the Alaska Centennial in 1967. It's not open to the public.

Across Mission St from the fort is the ornate **Russian Orthodox Church**, a white-clapboard structure topped with baby blue onion domes. Built in 1895, it's the oldest Orthodox church on mainland Alaska and was renovated in 2009. Staff at the visitor center can call to check the hours for you. West of the church overlooking the water is **St Nicholas Chapel**, built in 1906 on the burial site of Father Igumen Nicolai, Kenai's first resident priest.

Head southeast on Mission St, and you'll be traveling along the **Bluff**, a good vantage point to view the mouth of the Kenai River or the mountainous terrain on the west side of Cook Inlet. Look for belugas in the late spring and early summer.

Kenai Beach
BEACH

Down below the bluffs is an oddity in Alaska: a sweeping, sandy beach, ideal for picnicking, Frisbee-chucking and other waterfront fun. There are stellar views of the volcanoes across the inlet, and from July 10 to 31 you can watch hundreds of frantic fishermen dip-net for sockeye salmon at the mouth of the Kenai River. (Sadly, unless you've lived in Alaska for the past year, you can't participate.)

Captain Cook State Recreation Area
PARK

By following the Kenai Spur Hwy north for 36 miles, you'll first pass the trailer parks and chemical plants of the North Kenai industrial district before reaching this uncrowded state recreation area that encompasses 4000 acres of forests, lakes, rivers and beaches along Cook Inlet. The area offers swimming, camping and the beauty of the inlet in a setting that is unaffected by the stampede for salmon to the south.

The Kenai Spur Hwy ends in the park after first passing Stormy Lake, where you'll find a bathhouse and a swimming area along the water's edge. **Discovery Campground** (campsites $10) has 53 sites on the bluff overlooking Cook Inlet, where some of the world's greatest tides ebb and flow. The fishing in Swanson River is great, and this is a fine place to end the Swan Lake canoe route.

🛏 Sleeping

Finding last-minute rooms during summer's king salmon runs can be more challenging than hauling in a 70-pounder, but for help log onto the website of **Kenai Peninsula B&B Association** (www.kenaipeninsulabba.com). If you're on a tight budget, head north along the Kenai Spur Hwy, where several motels cater to oil workers and offer lower rates. Kenai adds 10% in bed-and-sales tax.

Harborside Cottages B&B
B&B $$

(☑283-6162, 888-283-6162; www.harborsidecottages.com; cnr Main St & Riverview Ave; cottages $150-195; ☺🐕) This place has five small-but-immaculate whitewashed cottages, each equipped with kitchenettes. The views here are spectacular; you can step outside your cottage and right to the edge of the bluff.

Beluga Lookout Lodge & RV Park
CAMPGROUND $

(☑283-5999; www.belugalookout.com; 929 Mission St; tent sites $30, RV sites $40-50, r $75-129; 🐕) This campground expanded into a 'lodge' in 2009 and now has super-clean (if a bit small) rooms that have either ocean or river views. The campground is little more than a parking lot with a nice view. There's also a gift shop, as well as laundry and showers and a nice covered sitting area for gazing at the ocean.

Uptown Motel
MOTEL $$

(☑283-3660; www.uptownmotel.com; 47 Spur View Dr; r $169-179; @) The rooms here are clean and the very cool lobby is full of antiques, including an old barber's chair and cash register.

🍴 Eating & Drinking

Veronica's Coffee House
CAFE $

(604 Peterson Way; light meals $3-8; ☺breakfast & lunch) In an Old Town log building dating from 1918, Veronica's serves espressos and healthy sandwiches and hosts open mics, folk jams and live bands. There's a warm wooden sun porch filled with flowers – the best place in town to relax with a sandwich.

Louie's Restaurant
STEAKHOUSE $$$

(☑283-3660; 47 Spur View Dr; dinner $19-29; ☺5am-11pm) Under stuffed moose and elk heads in the Uptown Motel, Louie's serves the best surf-and-turf in the city.

Charlotte's Restaurant
CAFE $

(115 Willow St; ☺breakfast & lunch Mon-Sat) Grab sandwiches or just some fresh-baked goodies for your beach picnic.

Safeway
GROCERY $

(10576 Kenai Spur Hwy; ☺24hr) Offers the usual groceries, plus it has a deli and salad bar.

ℹ Information

Alaska USA Bank (☑800-525-9094; 230 Kenai Spur Hwy; ⊙10am-6pm Mon-Sat) Has a 24-hour ATM.

Central Peninsula General Hospital (☑262-4404; Marydale Dr) Just west of the Kenai Spur Hwy.

Kenai Community Library (☑283-4378; 163 Main St Loop; ⊙10am-8pm Mon-Thu, to 5pm Fri & Sat; 🛜) Has free internet access; bring an ID.

Kenai Visitors & Cultural Center (☑283-1991; www.visitkenai.com; 11471 Kenai Spur Hwy; ⊙9am-7pm Mon-Fri, 10am-6pm Sat & Sun; 🛜) Has all the usual pamphlets and can get last-minute rooms in the area's B&Bs.

Post office (140 Bidarka St) Just north of the Kenai Spur Hwy.

Wash-n-Dry (☑283-8473; 502 Lake St; ⊙8am-10pm) Has a laundry and showers ($5.30).

ℹ Getting There & Around

Kenai has the main airport on the peninsula and is served by **ERA Alaska** (☑283-3168, 800-866-8394; www.flyera.com), which offers 17 daily flights between Anchorage and Kenai. The round-trip fare is between $170 and $210.

   Homer Stage Line (☑868-3914; www.stage lineinhomer.com) buses make daily trips departing from Kenai to Seward ($50).

   For taxis, **Alaska Cabs** (☑283-6000) serves Kenai and Soldotna.

Soldotna

POP 4515

Blink hard and you still won't miss Soldotna, try as you might. A town whose clot of stoplights inspired the local nickname 'Slowdotna' would be just another ugly, overcommercialized roadside-service center, interchangeable with a zillion other American towns, save for one thing: a river runs through it, filled to bursting with the biggest salmon on the planet. Indeed, the world's largest sport-caught king salmon was reeled in right here – a 97.2lb behemoth, hooked by local resident Les Anderson in 1985. Biologists believe genetics and the fact that Kenai River salmon often spend an extra year at sea account for their gargantuan size. A trophy salmon elsewhere in Alaska is a 50lb fish, while here, anglers don't get too excited until a king salmon tops 75lb.

   Situated where the Sterling Hwy crosses the Kenai River, Soldotna sprawls in every direction, including practically to the city of Kenai, some 12 miles northwest along

the Kenai Spur Hwy. The intersection of the Spur Hwy and the Sterling Hwy is referred to as the 'Y.'

◉ Sights

Soldotna Homestead Museum   MUSEUM
(☑262-3832; 44790 Sterling Hwy; entry by donation; ⊙10am-4pm Tue-Sat, from noon Sun) This museum includes a wonderful collection of homesteaders' cabins spread through six wooded acres in Centennial Park. There's also a one-room schoolhouse, a torture-chamber collection of early dental tools, an excellent natural history display with archaeological finds, and a replica of the $7.2-million check the US paid Russia for Alaska. Free guided tours.

Kenai National Wildlife Refuge Headquarters   PARK
Opposite Kalifornsky Beach Rd near the Kenai River is the junction with Funny River Rd. Turn left (east) here and turn right (south) immediately onto Ski Hill Rd, following it for a mile to reach this excellent, kid-friendly **information center** (☑262-7021; admission free; ⊙8am-4:30pm Mon-Fri, from 9am Sat & Sun). It features displays on the life cycles of salmon, daily wildlife films and naturalist-led outdoor programs. Several short loop trails begin at the visitors center and wind into the nearby woods or to a viewing platform on Headquarters Lake. Ask for a map; it's a great area for birding.

ᚷ Activities

Fishing

From mid-May through September, runs of red, silver and king salmon make the lower Kenai River among the hottest sportfishing spots in Alaska. If you're green to the scene but want to wet a line, first drop by the visitors center where staff members will assist you in determining where to fish and what to fish for. They can also hook you up with a guide, who'll charge you up to $300 a day but vastly improve your chances of catching dinner – and of not violating the river's fairly Kafkaesque regulations.

   Rather go it alone? From the shore, you've still got a shot at catching reds (from mid-July to early August) and silvers (late July through August). Try casting from the 'fish-walk' below the visitors center, or from city campgrounds. If you don't have your own rod, you can pick up inexpensive gear from **Trustworthy Hardware** (☑262-4655; 44370 Sterling Hwy; ⊙8am-8pm Mon-Fri, 9am-6pm Sat,

10am-6pm Sun), right across the highway from Sal's Klondike Diner.

🛏 Sleeping

Spending the night in Soldotna is a catch-22: outside fishing season there's no reason to stay here; in season, there's nowhere to stay – just about every campsite and room is taken. What's left will cost you dearly. Make reservations. The chamber of commerce can locate last-minute rooms, or call **Accommodations on the Kenai** (☎1-866-417-3518), a referral service for area B&Bs, lodges and fish camps. The **Kenai Peninsula B&B Association** (www.kenaipeninsulabba.com) has listings for the entire peninsula.

Diamond M Ranch   RESORT $
(☎283-9424, 866-283-9424; www.diamond mranch.com; Mile 16.5, Kalifornsky Beach Rd; campsites $30-40, r $70-149, cabins $99-159; ☻🛜) Fifteen years ago, this was just the Martin family farm – but with fishermen constantly asking to camp in their field, the Martins converted it to a tourist megaplex, complete with kids' programs, walking tours, movie nights and horse rides. If you get up early enough, you can help milk the cows that share the 80 acres with an extensive campground, cabins and full B&B.

Kenai River Lodge   HOTEL $$
(☎262-4292; www.kenairiverlodge.com; 393 River side Dr; r $120-200, ste $400; ☻🛜) Has a private fishing hole right outside and delicious river views. All rooms come with coffee, microwave and fridge. It's worth it to splurge for the river-facing rooms.

Soldotna B&B Lodge   B&B $$
(☎262-4779, 877-262-4779; www.soldotnalodge. com; 399 Lovers Lane; r $99-357; ☻🛜) This is the luxury place, drawing blue-chip anglers and honeymooners. It has plush rooms, custom adventure and fishing packages, and some rooms without baths. There's breakfast in a riverfront sunroom and a private fishing hole for reds.

Centennial Park Campground   CAMPGROUND $
(☎262-5299; www.ci.soldotna.ak.us; cnr Sterling Hwy & Kalifornsky Beach Rd; campsites $17) Maintained by the city, this 176-site campground has boardwalked fishing access to the Kenai River. The day-use fee is $6.

Swiftwater Park Campground   CAMPGROUND $
(☎262-5299; www.ci.soldotna.ak.us; cnr E Redoubt Ave & Rinehart St; campsites $17) Also run by the

city; it doesn't have a boardwalk but is still a good place for pulling in prized salmon. If you just want to fish, it's $6 to park for the day.

🍴 Eating & Drinking

TOP CHOICE Fine Thyme Cafe   CAFE $
(43977 Sterling Hwy; lunch $6-10; ☻breakfast & lunch Mon-Sat, lunch Sun) Eat inside surrounded by books, or enjoy the sun on a garden patio surrounded by flowers. Geared towards lunch, this darling place is attached to River City Books and serves homemade soups, wraps, salads and sandwiches.

St Elias Brewing Company   PIZZERIA $$
(434 Sharkathmi Ave; dinner $8-14; ☻dinner) Stone-fired 11in pizzas and sandwiches served in an echoing brewery. Delicious. Beer-lovers should order the sampler.

Moose is Loose   CAFE $
(44278 Sterling Hwy; snacks $2-7; ☻breakfast & lunch Tue-Sun) This Moose comes with coffee and goodies galore, including a huge array of fresh doughnuts.

Mykel's   SEAFOOD $$$
(☎262-4305; www.mykels.com; dinner $18-34; ☻lunch & dinner) This is Soldotna's fanciest place, with high-backed leather booths and dishes like walnut-crusted salmon with a raspberry buerre blanc ($27).

Odie's Deli   DELI $
(44315 Sterling Hwy; sandwiches $9-11; ☻breakfast & lunch) Try whimsical cupcakes (try the Breakfast in Bed: maple and bacon) and build-your-own-sandwiches on homemade bread.

Sal's Klondike Diner   DINER $
(44619 Sterling Hwy; breakfast & lunch $5-9, dinner $9-14; ☻24hr) Soldotna's best stab at a tourist trap, this diner is jammed with weary travelers, gabbing locals and frantic waitresses. The meals aren't as tasty as they are ample.

Fred Meyer   GROCERY $
(43843 Sterling Hwy) This supermarket has a deli, salad bar, bakery, espresso and any camping gear that you forgot.

ℹ Information

Central Peninsula General Hospital (☎262-4404; Marydale Dr) Just west of the Kenai Spur Hwy.

Joyce Carver Memorial Library (235 S Binkley St; ☻9am-8pm Mon-Thu, noon-6pm Fri, from

Almost all of the beaches on the west side of the Kenai Peninsula (Clam Gulch, Deep Creek, Ninilchik and Whiskey Gulch) have a good supply of razor clams, considered by mollusk connoisseurs to be a true delicacy. Not only do razors have the best flavor, but they're also among the largest of the mollusks. The average razor clam is 3.5in long.

To clam, you first have to purchase a sportfishing license (a one-day visitor's license is $20, and a seven-day license is $55). The daily bag limit is 60 clams, but remember – that's an awful lot of clams to clean and eat. Two dozen per person are more than enough for a meal. While the clamming's good from April to August, the best time is July, right before spawning. And though you can dig for clams any time the tide is out, the best clamming is during extra-low, 'minus,' tides. Consult a tide book – and count on hundreds of other clammers to do the same.

» For equipment, you'll need a narrow-bladed clam shovel that can either be purchased or rented at many lodges and stores near the clamming areas. You'll also want rubber boots, rubber gloves, a bucket and a pair of pants to which you're not terribly attached.

» Once on the beach, you have to play detective. Look for the clam's 'footprint,' a dimple mark left behind when it withdraws its neck. That's your clue to the clam's whereabouts, but don't dig directly below the imprint or you'll break its shell. You have to be quick, as a razor clam can bury itself and be gone in seconds.

» Once you're successful, leave the clams in a bucket of seawater or, better yet, beer, for several hours to allow them to 'clean themselves.' Many locals say a handful of cornmeal helps this process. The best way to cook clams is right on the beach over an open fire while you're taking in the mountain scenery. Use a large covered pot and steam the clams in saltwater or, for more flavor, in white wine with a clove of garlic.

Here's where to go:

» **Clam Gulch** This is the most popular and, many say, most productive spot by far. The Clam Gulch State Recreation Area is a half-mile from Mile 118 of the Sterling Hwy, where there's a short access road to the beach from the campground.

» **Ninilchik** The best bet is to camp at Ninilchik View State Campground, located above the old village of Ninilchik. From there, you can walk to beaches for clamming.

» **Deep Creek** Just south of Ninilchik is the Deep Creek State Recreation Site, where there's camping and plenty of parking along the beach.

» **Whiskey Gulch** Look for the turnoff at about Mile 154 of the Sterling Hwy. Unless you have a 4WD vehicle, park at the elbow-turn above the beach.

» **Mud Bay** On the east side of the Homer Spit is Mud Bay, a stretch abundant with eastern soft-shells, cockles and blue mussels. Some surf clams (rednecks) and razor clams can also be found on the Cook Inlet side of the Spit.

9am Sat; 🖳) Near the post office; has free internet access with an ID.

Post office (175 S Binkley St) Just west of the Kenai Spur Hwy and north of the Soldotna 'Y.'

Soldotna Chamber of Commerce & Visitors Center (📠262-1337; www.visitsoldotna.com; 44790 Sterling Hwy; ⏰9am-7pm; 🖳) Has internet plus up-to-date fishing reports and a nice boardwalk along the river.

Wash & Dry (1221 Smith Way; ⏰24hr summer; 🖳) Near the intersection of the Kenai Spur and Sterling Hwys at the Soldotna 'Y'; has showers ($5), laundry and free wireless internet.

Wells Fargo (44552 Sterling Hwy) Has cash and an eclectic collection of historical exhibits.

ℹ Getting There & Around

Homer Stage Line (📠868-3914; www.stage lineinhomer.com) buses pass through daily en route to Anchorage ($70) and Homer ($50).

South to Homer

After you pass Soldotna, traffic thins out as the Sterling Hwy rambles south, hugging the coastline and opening up to grand views of Cook Inlet. This stretch is 78 miles long and it passes through a handful of small villages near some great clamming areas, ending at the charming town of Homer. Take your time in this area; the coastline and Homer are worth every day you decide to spend there.

NINILCHIK
POP 827

This appealing little village is well worth spending a night, either at its stellar hostel, its affordable hotels or one of its numerous campsites boasting volcano views.

The community is among the oldest on the Kenai Peninsula, having been settled in the 1820s by employees of the Russian-American Company. Many stayed even after imperial Russia sold Alaska to the US, and their descendants form the heart of the present community.

◉ Sights & Activities

The main event in Ninilchik is the Kenai Peninsula State Fair, the 'biggest little fair in Alaska,' which takes place annually in mid-August.

Old Ninilchik Village   HISTORIC SITE
The site of the original community, this is a postcard scene of faded log cabins in tall grass and beached fishing boats against the spectacular backdrop of Mt Redoubt.

Old Russian Church   CHURCH
Reached via a posted footpath behind the Village Cache Gift Shop, the historic bluff-top structure was built in 1901, sports five golden onion domes, and commands an unbelievable view of Cook Inlet and the volcanoes on the other side. Adjoining it is a prim Russian Orthodox cemetery of white-picket cribs.

Clamming
Clamming is Ninilchik's No 1 summer pastime. At low tide, go to either Ninchilik Beach State Recreation Site, across the river from the old village, or Deep Creek State Recreation Site. It costs $5 to park at the state recreation areas. You can either purchase a shovel ($16) and bucket ($5) at the Ninilchik General Store or rent them from the Village Cache.

⊨ Sleeping & Eating

TOP CHOICE Eagle Watch   HOSTEL $
(☑567-3905; www.theeaglewatchhostel.com; Mile 3, Oilwell Rd; dm/r $13/35) This hostel, situated on an outrageously scenic and peaceful bluff high above the Ninilchik River, really lives up to its name: eagles throng here, feeding on spawned-out salmon in the

waters below. The facilities are charmingly rough-hewn but immaculate, and you're free to use the friendly owners' clam shovels and buckets. There is a lockout from 10am through to 5pm.

Ninilchik View State Campground   CAMPGROUND $
(Mile 135.5 Sterling Hwy; campsites $10) By far the best of Ninilchik's public campgrounds, it's set atop a wooded bluff with a view of the old village and Cook Inlet. A stairway leads down to the beach.

Ninilchik River Campground   CAMPGROUND $
(Mile 134.9 Sterling Hwy; campsites $10) Across the Sterling Hwy from Coal St; this campground has great river access and some pleasant trails.

Alaskan Angler RV Resort   CABIN $$
(☑800-347-4114; www.afishhunt.com; Kingsley Rd; tent sites/RV sites $15/42, cabins $129-169) A privately owned place with on-site fish processing. There is also a tenting area back in the trees, and guests who are traveling without their own gear onboard are able to rent rods and reels ($10), hip boots ($5) and clam shovels ($5).

Roscoe's Pizza   PIZZA $$
(15915 Sterling Hwy; pizza $12-25; ⊘lunch & dinner) Hand-tossed dough made from scratch makes this a perfect place to fill up after a day of clam slamming.

ⓘ Information

Alaskan Angler RV Resort (☑800-347-4114; Kingsley Rd) For a shower ($2) or laundry facilities.

Ninilchik General Store (☑567-3378; Mile 135.7, Sterling Hwy; ⊘9am-10pm) Has an ATM, lots of fishing and camping gear, and you will find a few tourist-oriented brochures posted out the front of the store.

Homer
POP 4231

Lucky is the visitor who drives into Homer on a clear day. As the Sterling Hwy descends into town, a panorama of mountains sweeps across the horizon in front of you. The Homer Spit slowly comes into view, jutting into a glittering Kachemak Bay, and just when you think the view might unwind forever, it ends with the dramatic Grewingk Glacier.

Hearing travelers' tales of Homer, you half expect to find lotus-eaters and mermaids lounging about. At first blush,

NIKOLAEVSK

Tucked inconspicuously down a winding road from Anchor Point sits one of several Russian Old Believer Villages on the Kenai Peninsula. The Old Believers are members of a sect that split from mainstream Russian Orthodoxy in the 1650s, defending their 'old beliefs' in the face of what they considered heretical reforms. Long considered outcasts in Russia, they fled communism in 1917, ending up in Brazil, then Oregon, and then – in 1968 – Alaska, where they finally felt they could enjoy religious freedom while avoiding the corruptive influences of modernity.

Alaska's Old Believers are hardcore traditionalists, speaking mainly Russian, marrying in their teens, raising substantial broods of children, and living simply. The men – usually farmers or fishermen – are forbidden from trimming their beards; the women typically cover their hair and are garbed in long dresses. The Old Believers tend to keep to themselves, inhabiting a handful of isolated villages on the Kenai Peninsula, of which Nikolaevsk is the most prominent.

To get there, head 10 miles east on North Fork Rd, which departs from the Sterling Hwy in the heart of Anchor Point and winds through hillbilly homesteads and open, rolling forest. Right before the pavement ends, hang a left at Nikolaevsk Rd. Two miles later, you'll enter the village.

To really get into the heart of Nikolaevsk, you must follow the signs to the **Samovar Café & B&B** (235-6867; www.russiangiftsnina.com; mains $5-12; 10am-10pm Mon-Fri, to 8pm Sat), which has more than simply the best Russian food on the peninsula, and more than a wonderful collection of cheap and colorful (and pretty basic) **accommodations** (tent sites/RV sites $15/29, r $39-79). This small restaurant is a wacky welcome mat into the world of the Old Believers. Nina, the proprietor, is an electrical engineer, writer and force of nature. She'll offer you two dining choices: in the sunroom, where she'll simply serve your meal through a window; or inside, where you can 'dine in Russia.' This choice (which requires a reservation) gets you an inside seat, borscht, cream puffs and delicious *pelmeni* (Siberian dumplings), Nina's stories and a photo session where she'll dress you up in traditional Orthodox gear. The experience is well worth the purchase. You'll stumble out of the cafe feeling like you visited another country, in another time.

though, Homer's appeal might not be evident. The city isn't overhung with mountains like Seward, nor does it have the quaint townscape of Cordova. It sprawls a bit, it's choked with tourists, isn't lushly forested, lacks legendary hikes, and has a windswept waterfront that makes kayaking a bitch. And then there's the Homer Spit – a tourist trap you may love to hate.

Stick around for a bit, however, and Homer will make you a believer. For one thing, there's the panorama, and the promise that it holds. Across Kachemak Bay, glaciers and peaks and fjords beckon – a trekkers' and paddlers' playground to which Homer is the portal.

And then there's the vibe: the town is a magnet for radicals, artists and folks disillusioned with mainstream society, who've formed a critical mass here, dreaming up a sort of utopian vision for their city, and striving – with grins on their faces – to enact it. Because of that, this is the arts capital of Southcentral Alaska, with great galleries, museums, theater and music.

Homer lies at the end of the Sterling Hwy, 233 road miles from Anchorage. For tourists, there are two distinct sections of town. The 'downtown' area, built on a hill between high bluffs to the north and Kachemak Bay to the south, lies along – or near – busy Pioneer Ave. Heading eastward, Pioneer Ave becomes rural East End Rd, with a number of other lodging and eating options. The second section of Homer, and certainly the most notorious, is the Homer Spit, a skinny tongue of sand licking halfway across Kachemak Bay.

History

Homer was founded, and picked up its name, when Homer Pennock, an adventurer from Michigan, landed on the Spit with a crew of gold-seekers in 1896, convinced that Kachemak Bay was the key to their riches. It wasn't, and Pennock was soon lured to the Klondike, where he also failed to find gold. Three years later the Cook Inlet Coal Field Company established the first of a succession of coalmines in the area. It was fishing,

Homer

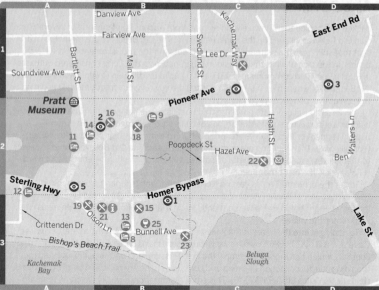

Homer

though, that would come to dominate the town's economy for most of the 1900s.

◎ Sights

Homer Spit   NEIGHBORHOOD
(Map p244) Generally known as 'the Spit', this long needle of land – a 4.5-mile sand bar stretching into Kachemak Bay – is viewed by some folks as the most fun place in Alaska. Others wish another earthquake would come along and sink the thing. Regardless, the Spit throbs all summer with tourists who mass here in unimaginable density, gobbling fish-and-chips, quaffing specialty

0 500 m
0 0.25 miles

by, rents out rods ($10 to $20) as well as rakes and shovels (each $5) for clamming.

TOP CHOICE **Pratt Museum** MUSEUM
(Map p240; ☑235-8635; www.prattmuseum.org; 3779 Bartlett St; adult/child $8/4; ☺10am-6pm) This museum is fantastic – so much so, it has loaned exhibits to the Smithsonian. There's lots of local art and Alaska Native artifacts, but a more impressive feature is the interactive displays on the area's wildlife, designed to mesmerize both kids and ex-kids. More sobering is the Storm Warning Theater, with harrowing tales about fishing on Kachemak Bay, where making a living can end your life. A box of tissues is provided for those brought to tears. And then there's the 'Darkened Waters' exhibit, a stunning and emotional look at the Exxon oil spill.

More light-hearted and whimsical, and perhaps the coolest aspect of the museum, is the Forest Ecology Trail, where artists can contribute to the 'Facing the Elements' exhibit. Paths wind through the trees, and you'll stumble upon small exhibits, be they mirrors, rocks or pottery. A must-do.

The Pratt also offers 1½-hour harbor tours ($5) throughout summer at 3pm Friday and Saturday, leaving from the Salty Dawg Saloon.

FREE **Alaska Islands & Ocean Visitor Center** VISITOR CENTER
(Map p240; www.islandsandocean.org; 95 Sterling Hwy; ☺9am-6pm) More a research facility and museum than a visitors center, this impressive place has numerous cool interactive exhibits, perhaps the best of which is a room that's a replica seabird colony, complete with cacophonous bird calls and surround-view flocking. There's also a decent film about ship-based marine research, a hands-on discovery lab, a pole that shows Homer's tides in real time, and a slate of daily educational programs and guided walks. It's operated jointly by the Kachemak Bay Research Reserve and the Alaska Maritime National Wildlife Refuge, which, though headquartered in Homer, mainly takes in the distant Aleutian Islands.

FREE **Center for Alaskan Coastal Studies** CULTURAL CENTER
(Map p240; ☑235-6667; www.akcoastalstudies.org; 708 Smokey Way; ☺9am-5pm Mon-Fri) This nonprofit organization devoted to promoting appreciation of Kachemak Bay's ecosystem,

coffees, purchasing alpaca sweaters, arranging bear-watching trips, watching theatrical performances and – oh yeah – going fishing in search of 300lb halibut. The hub of all this activity is the small-boat harbor, one of the best facilities in Southcentral Alaska and home to more than 700 boats. Close by is the Seafarer's Memorial, which, amid all the Spit's hubbub, is a solemn monument to residents lost at sea.

Beachcombing, bald-eagle watching (they seem as common here as pigeons in New York City) and observing recently docked fishermen angling for cute tourist chicks at the Salty Dawg Saloon are all favorite activities. You can also go clamming at Mud Bay, on the east side of the Spit. Blue mussels, an excellent shellfish overlooked by many people, are the most abundant.

If you'd rather catch your dinner than shovel or buy it, try your luck at the Fishing Hole, just before the Pier One Theater. The small lagoon is the site of a 'terminal fishery,' in which salmon are planted by the state and return three or four years later to a place where they can't spawn. Kings can be caught here from mid-May to the end of June, while silvers run in August. Sportsman's Supply & Rental (Map p244; ☑235-2617; 1114 Freight Dock Rd; ☺6am-midnight), close

KENAI PENINSULA HOMER

runs the Carl E Wynn Nature Center and the Peterson Bay Field Station, both of which offer guided hikes and educational programs throughout the summer. Drop by to learn more about their offerings, and to get maps and info about Kachemak Bay State Park. It also operates the **Yurt on the Spit** (Map p244; Homer Spit Rd; ⊙noon-5pm), right behind Mako's Water-Taxi, which does a daily 'Creatures of the Dock' tour at 1pm and 4pm ($5).

Carl E Wynn Nature Center NATURE RESERVE
(off Map p244; Skyline Dr; adult/child $7/5; ⊙10am-6pm) Situated on the bluffs above Homer, this moose-ridden 140-acre reserve is highly recommended for families and anyone interested in the area's ethnobotany. With a few short interpretive nature trails, one of them boardwalked and wheelchair accessible, this is a grand place to learn which plants can be used to heal a cut, condition your hair or munch for lunch. Naturalist-led hikes leave at 10am and 2pm daily in summer. It also has a slate of lectures and other programs; call the center for a schedule.

🏃 Activities

Hiking

For all its natural beauty, Homer has few good public trails. For a map of short hiking routes around town, pick up the *Walking Guide to the Homer Area* at the visitor center.

Bishop's Beach Trail HIKING
This hike (Map p244) is a leisurely waterfront trek from Homer. The views of Kachemak Bay and the Kenai Mountains are superb, while the marine life that scurries along the sand at low tide is fascinating.

Grab a scone from Two Sisters Bakery and take a wander down the beach.

Diamond Creek Trail HIKING
This trailhead is opposite Diamond Ridge Rd, 5 miles north along the Sterling Hwy. The trail begins by descending along Diamond Creek, then hits the beach. Check a tide book, and leave before low tide and return before high tide. High tides cover most of the sand, forcing you to scramble onto the base of the nearby cliffs. Walk the 7 miles into town; eventually you meet up with Bishop's Beach Trail.

Homestead Trail HIKING
This 6.7-mile trek (Map p244) from Rogers Loop Rd to the City Reservoir, just off Skyline Dr on Crossman Ridge Rd, is a 2.5-mile walk to Rucksack Dr, which crosses Diamond Ridge Rd. Along the way you pass through open meadows, with panoramic views of Kachemak Bay, and Mt Iliamna and Mt Redoubt on the other side of Cook Inlet. There's an old homestead cabin and a nice bench for taking in the view along the way. The trek continues another 4.2 miles, following Rucksack Dr and Crossman Ridge Rd to the reservoir. Cars are banned from both dirt roads.

To reach the trail, head out of town on the Sterling Hwy and turn right on Rogers Loop Rd across from the Bay View Inn. The trailhead is a half-mile further, on your right.

Halibut Fishing

There are more than two dozen charter captains working out of the Spit, and they charge anywhere from $200 to $400 for a halibut trip. A good option to go with is **Rainbow Tours** (Map p244; ☎235-7272, Homer Spit Rd), but peruse the board beside the Halibut Derby Office (Map p244); it lists the biggest fish caught that summer, along with who captained the boat. Other than that, the biggest distinction between the charter operations is vessel size: bigger boats bounce around less when the waves kick, meaning greater comfort and less *mal de mer*. Make sure you buy a derby ticket (see p243).

Cycling & Mountain Biking

Though Homer lacks formal mountain-biking trails, the dirt roads in the hills above town lend themselves to some great rides, especially along Diamond Ridge Rd and Skyline Dr. For an easy tour, head out E End Rd, which extends 20 miles east to the head of Kachemak Bay. There's also good biking to be had in Seldovia, an easy day or overnight trip from Homer by water-taxi.

Paddling

Though, theoretically, you could spend a wavy day paddling in the vicinity of the Spit, you'll find infinitely better scenery, more varied wildlife and far more sheltered waters across the bay in the Kachemak Bay State Park. Due to fast currents and massive waves, attempting the wide-open crossing is a poor idea; you're better off taking your kayak across on a water-taxi or renting one from the various companies that maintain fleets of kayaks on the far side.

Bear Viewing

Due largely to the density of tourists visiting Homer, the town has become a major

The cold, dark season of unemployment has inspired a saying in these parts: 'If you're starving, you might as well be an artist.' Just browsing these great galleries is a treat, and on the first Friday of the month, many break out the wine and cheese, and stay open late for a series of openings all over town. This is just the tip of the iceberg – grab a free *Downtown Homer Art Galleries* flyer at the visitors center with many more gallery listings, or stop by the **Homer Council of the Arts** (Map p240; ☑235-4288; www.homerart. org; 355 W Pioneer Ave; ☺9am-6pm Mon-Fri), with its own awesome gallery and information on various tours.

» **Art Shop Gallery** (Map p240; ☑235-7076; 202 W Pioneer Ave; ☺10am-7pm Mon-Sat, 11am-5pm Sun)

» **Bunnell Street Gallery** (Map p240; ☑235-2662; www.bunnellstreetgallery.org; 106 W Bunnell Ave; ☺10am-6pm Mon-Sat, noon-4pm Sun)

» **Fireweed Gallery** (Map p240; ☑235-3411; 475 E Pioneer Ave; ☺10am-6pm Mon-Sat, 11am-5pm Sun)

» **Ptarmigan Arts** (Map p240; ☑235-5345; 471 E Pioneer Ave; ☺10am-7pm Mon-Sat, 10am-6pm Sun)

departure point for bear-watching trips to the famed bruin haven of Katmai National Park, located on the Alaska Peninsula 100-plus miles southwest by floatplane. Due to the distances involved, these trips cost a pretty penny: expect to pay between $500 and $600 per person for a day trip. However, that may be a small price to pay for the iconic Alaskan photo: a slavering brown bear, perched atop a waterfall, snapping its fangs on an airborne salmon.

Bald Mountain Air BEAR VIEWING
(Map p244; ☑235-7969; www.baldmountainair. com; Homer Spit Rd; per person $615) Runs trips to the park headquarters at Brooks Camp, where countless bears converge to snag salmon ascending Brooks River – and where countless tourists converge to watch them. Also flies 'where no-one else goes' in June and August to spot bears when they aren't at Brooks Camp.

Emerald Air Service BEAR VIEWING
(☑235-6993; www.emeraldairservice.com; 1320 Lake Shore Dr; per person $675) Run by respected naturalists this offers a more wilderness-oriented experience, bypassing Brooks Camp and seeking out bears along isolated Katmai beaches and salmon streams.

☆ Festivals & Events

There's always something happening in Homer, especially in May – check to see what's on at the visitors center.

Homer Jackpot Halibut Derby CULTURAL
(www.homerhalibutderby.com) May 1 marks the beginning of the five-month, $200,000-plus contest to catch the biggest fish (in 2010, it was a 354.6-pounder). Tickets cost $10, are good for one day of fishing, and can be bought at numerous places in Homer, including the derby office on the Spit. If you're going on a halibut charter, you may as well buy a ticket. Many a traveler has missed out on the jackpot because they didn't have a ticket.

Kachemak Bay Shorebird Festival CULTURAL
(www.homeralaska.org/shorebird) Brings hundreds of birders and 100,000 shorebirds to Mud Bay in early May, making it the largest bird migration site along the Alaskan road system. The tidal flats of Homer become the staging area for thousands of birds, including one-third of the world's surfbirds.

Kachemak Bay Wooden Boat Festival CULTURAL
(www.kbwbs.org) Back in 2010, this gathering switched from spring to September. It celebrates the craft, design and history of wooden boat-building, and is rounded out by tall tales of drama on the high seas.

🛏 Sleeping

Homer has B&Bs galore. There are two reservation services with many more listings than we can include here: **Cabins & Cottages Network** (☑235-0191; www.cabinsinhomer.com) and **Homer's Finest Bed & Breakfast Network**

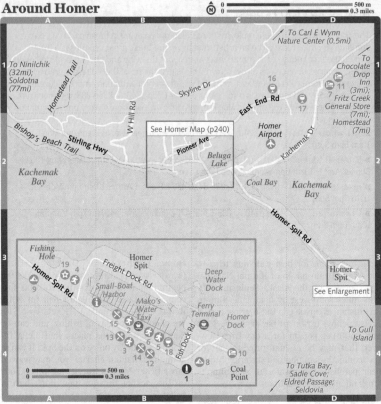

(☎235-4983; www.homeraccommodations.com). Homer adds a 7.5% sales tax to lodging.

TOP CHOICE Old Town B&B   B&B **$$**

(Map p240; ☎235-7558; www.oldtownbedand breakfast.com; 106 W Bunnell Ave; d $110-130; ⊜🛜) There are beautiful rooms with wood floors, great views, fresh flowers and cookies, and lots of antiques scattered through this atmospheric place. Breakfast is served in a lovely little sitting room. Since it's above the Bunnell Street Gallery, there's usually something cool going on downstairs.

🌿Homer Hostel   HOSTEL **$**

(Map p240; ☎235-1463; www.homerhostel.com; 304 W Pioneer Ave; dm/s/d $25/51/63; ⊜🛜) This hostel is perfectly located downtown in a funky old house. There are discounts for stays of more than one night, and you can rent bikes and store your backpacks for $1 per day. Say hi to the chickens out back.

Karen Hornaday Memorial Campground   CAMPGROUND **$**

(tent sites/RV sites $8/15) Below the bluffs just north of downtown, this is the best camping option in Homer. It has private, wooded sites with impressive views and is probably a better choice for families with small children than the campgrounds on the Spit: unlike those, it has a playground instead of the Salty Dawg Saloon.

Room at the Harbor   B&B **$$**

(Map p244; ☎299-7748; Homer Spit Rd; r $120; ⊜) This establishment has one beautiful room upstairs from Spit Sisters; cozy up with a scone and a book. Though the shower is in the room, one of the beds is in its own nook overlooking the boat harbor.

Pioneer Inn   MOTEL **$$**

(Map p240; ☎235-5670, 800-782-9655; www. pioneerinnhomerak.com; 244 W Pioneer Ave; r $99-129; ⊜🛜) Has a couple of smaller (and

Around Homer

thus cheaper) rooms, along with a number of near-luxurious larger suites with kitchenettes. The owners are super-friendly and the location is central. The suites are a good bargain.

Seaside Farm   HOSTEL $
(Map p244; ☎235-7850; www.seasidealaska.com; E End Rd; sites/dm/r/cabins $10/20/65/75) Located 5 miles from the city center, this is more like Burning Man than a regulation youth hostel. Run by Mossy Kilcher, pop star Jewel Kilcher's aunt, Seaside Farm has a meadow campground with views of Grewingk Glacier, somewhat dingy dorms and basic cabins. The outdoor cooking pavilion is patrolled by roosters and impromptu jam sessions often spark up around the campfire.

Ocean Shores Motel   MOTEL $$
(Map p240; ☎235-7775, 800-770-7775; www.oceanshoresalaska.com; 451 Sterling Hwy; d $119-199; ☻🅟) This has clean and spacious rooms, most with pleasant decks and awe-

some views. Those down by the ocean cost the most; the cheaper ones are up on the hill and lack good views. The owner is a serious kayak buff and worth talking to if you're planning to paddle.

Beluga Lake Lodge   HOTEL $$
(Map p240; ☎235-5995; www.belugalakelodging.com; 204 Ocean Dr Loop; d $135-375; ☻🅟) This lodge overlooks its namesake lake and is pleasant and clean; the smallest rooms are cozy while the biggest ones sleep eight and have full kitchens. A nice bar often hosts live music.

Bear Creek Lodging   B&B $$$
(☎235-8484; www.bearcreekwineryalaska.com; Bear Creek Dr; ste $245; ☻) On a hillside at the Bear Creek Winery, this place has two suites (each with a kitchenette), a hot tub overlooking the fruit vineyard and koi pond, and a complimentary bottle of vino beside each bed.

Homer Spit Campground   CAMPGROUND $
(Map p244; ☎235-8206; Homer Spit Rd; tent sites/RV sites $30/48; 🅟) Catering more to the RV crowd, this Spit-end place has coin-operated laundry facilities, showers ($5) and about 150 bald eagles.

Driftwood Inn   MOTEL $$
(Map p240; ☎235-8019, 800-478-8019; www.thedriftwoodinn.com; 135 W Bunnell Ave; RV sites $34-49, r $75-180, cottage $275; ☻🅟) This joint has a hodge-podge of accommodations, including European-style rooms with or without baths, snug, cedar-finished 'ships quarters,' a house with a deck affording some stunning oceanfront views, and RV sites.

Homer Spit Public Camping   CAMPGROUND $
(Map p244; Homer Spit Rd; tent sites/RV sites $8/15) On the west beach of Homer Spit a catch-as-catch-can tent city springs up every night of the summer. It's a beautiful spot, though often windy (make sure you add weight to your tent if you leave), crowded and sometimes rowdy. The self-registration stand is right across the road from Sportsman's Supply.

Glacier View Cabins   CABIN $$
(Map p244; ☎235-1915; www.glacierviewcabins.com; 59565 E End Rd; cabins $110-150; ☻🅟) These log cabins sit in a sort of suburban utopia: a wide expanse of lawn has views of Kachemak Bay over neighborhood rooftops. The less expensive cabins have kitchenettes while the others have full kitchens. Fire

pits and barbecues on the decks add to the homey feel.

Homer Floatplane Lodge LODGE $$
(Map p240; ☑877-235-9600, 235-4160; www.float planelodge.com; 2144 Lakeshore Dr; r from $125; ☺☙) There are three slips for floatplanes and a variety of all-inclusive packages on offer, such as a three-night stay covering lodging, meals, beer and wine, and halibut fishing for $1500 (plus 7.5% tax). Cabins and rooms come with kitchenettes and are cozy as can be.

Land's End Resort HOTEL $$
(Map p244; ☑800-478-0400; www.lands-end -resort.com; r $149-270; ☺☙⊛) Located at the end of the Spit, it's considered a luxury hotel for its grand views and storied ambience, but only the pricier rooms really fit that description. There's a spa, hot tub and swimming pool. New privately owned 'lodges' (luxury condos) crowd the Spit's beach like a city skyline; you can rent a room in one for $200 to $250 or an entire place for $375 to $500.

Heritage Hotel HOTEL $$
(Map p240; ☑235-7787, 800-380-7787; 147 E Pioneer Ave; r $119-165; ☺☙) Housed in a 1948 log cabin, it has an older section with small, rustically decorated rooms, plus a newer wing with rooms that are larger but less charming.

🍴 Eating

Loosen your belt, because bite for bite, no place in Alaska has the culinary variety of Homer. Though there are some good options on the Spit, you'll pay substantially more than for dining in town. Note that most places close by 9pm.

TOP CHOICE Cosmic Kitchen MEXICAN $
(Map p240; 510 E Pioneer Ave; burritos & sandwiches $6-11; ☺9am-8pm Mon-Sat, to 3pm Sun; ☙) With excellent burritos, burgers and a salsa bar, this joint is the place to go for a filling meal on the cheap; it's probably the best bargain in town. It also serves breakfast until 3pm and has a deck for sunny evenings.

TOP CHOICE Two Sisters Bakery BAKERY $
(Map p240; www.twosistersbakery.net; 233 E Bunnell Ave; light meals $3-8, dinner mains $15-18; ☺breakfast, lunch & dinner) A beloved Homer institution with espresso and great fresh-baked bread, plus quiche, soups, salads and

pizza by the slice. It's now serving a rotating dinner menu with creative dishes such as sweet potato falafel lettuce wraps ($10) or a steaming bowl of Vietnamese pho ($8).

Maura's Cafe DELI $$
(Map p240; www.maurascafe.com; 248 W Pioneer Ave; sandwiches $13; ☺lunch & dinner) Homerites consistently recommend this place, which serves up hearty – yet civilized – sandwiches and salads. Get some imported meat and cheese for a picnic on Bishop's Beach. If animal products aren't your thing, don't despair – in true Homer fashion, Maura's is vegan friendly.

Fritz Creek General Store DELI $
(off Map p244; Mile 8.2, E End Rd; snacks $3-8; ☺7am-9pm Mon-Sat, 10am-6pm Sun) What is an excellent deli doing all the way out on East End Rd? This place serves some of the best take-out food in Homer – it's worth the drive for the veggie burritos alone, but you shouldn't leave without dessert. It also does pizza, tamales, hoagies (sandwiches) and espresso.

Cafe Cups FUSION $$
(Map p240; ☑235-8330; 162 W Pioneer Ave; dinner $11-30; ☺dinner Tue-Sat) In a charming little building (you'll know it by the cups outside) with a changing menu that includes excellent curries and fresh fish. Though the food is delicious, the service can be quite harried.

Finn's Pizza PIZZA $$
(Map p244; Homer Spit Rd; pizza $10-20) Finn's wood-fired pizzas are best enjoyed with a pint of ale in the sunny upstairs solarium. Is there anything better than an excellent pizza and unobstructed views of the bay? We don't think so. You can also get soup, salad and polenta.

Fat Olives ITALIAN $$
(Map p240; www.fatolivesrestaurant.com; 276 Olson Lane; dinner $16-29; ☺11am-9:30pm) Housed in the old 'bus barn,' this chic and hyper-popular pizza joint/wine bar serves affordable appetizers like prosciutto-wrapped Alaskan scallops and delicious mains like wood oven-roasted rack of lamb. Almost everything is fresh and homemade. You can also grab a huge slice of pizza to go ($5).

🍴 Mermaid Cafe FUSION $$
(Map p240; ☑235-7649; 3487 Main St; tapas $8-15, mains $18-26; ☺lunch & dinner) Homer's newest restaurant is getting rave reviews for tapas,

such as stuffed dates, and daily rotating dinner mains. As much as possible is locally grown and harvested, including meats. For lunch there's pizza ($14) and sandwiches ($13). Stays open a bit later than most restaurants.

Fresh Sourdough Express ORGANIC $
(Map p240; 1316 Ocean Dr; breakfast $6-10, lunch & dinner $6-11; ⏰breakfast, lunch & dinner) This is the first official 'green' restaurant in Alaska, and you can taste it. Almost everything is organic and as much as possible locally raised or grown. Come here for breakfast – you'll be served a small bakery sweet while you wait for your 'howling hotcakes.' Box lunches are also available.

Spit Sisters BAKERY $
(Map p244; www.spitsisterscafe.com; Homer Spit Rd; pastries $2-5; ⏰7am-7pm) There's a great view overlooking the small-boat harbor, and delicacies to enjoy – apricot scones, blackberry muffins, sticky buns – made by the revered Two Sisters Bakery in town. Gourmet boxed lunches are perfect for a day on the water.

Homestead FUSION $$$
(off Map p244; ☎235-8723; www.thehomesteadrestaurant.net; Mile 8.2, E End Rd; dinner $26-32; ⏰dinner) One of Homer's oldest and priciest restaurants, with mains such as the Chelsea Duck ($28) and the Seafood Duet ($29) – wild shrimp and Alaskan scallops. Though the waiters wear black ties, patrons can come as they are (hey, this is Homer, after all).

Duncan House Diner CAFE $
(Map p240; 125 E Pioneer Ave; breakfast & lunch $6-11; ⏰6am-3pm) This busy downtown place fries up home-style breakfast among home-style decor.

Aloha Drive-In HAWAIIAN $
(Map p240; 3522 Main St; burgers $6-8; ⏰lunch & dinner) One of the few independent restaurants in Homer to be open past 9pm (you can order until 11pm!), the Aloha does rice bowls, pork sandwiches and teriyaki chicken.

Captain Pattie's SEAFOOD $$
(Map p244; Homer Spit Rd; lunch $11-18, dinner $20-29; ⏰lunch & dinner) This oceanfront eatery has become a Spit institution by selling overpriced seafood to a constant stream of landlubbers. It claims its halibut is Alaska's

best, but those in the know always order crab.

Boardwalk SEAFOOD $$
(Map p244; Homer Spit Rd; fast food $5-15; ⏰lunch & dinner) Widely viewed as the best place on the Spit for halibut – tempura-battered, fried and served kabob-style (its motto is 'Where the fish comes on a stick').

Safeway GROCERY $
(Map p240; Mile 90, Sterling Hwy; ⏰5am-midnight) On the way to the Spit, this is the best place in town for groceries, fresh-baked breads, deli sandwiches and salads.

🍷 Drinking & Entertainment

The bumper sticker says it all: 'Homer, Alaska: A quaint drinking village with a fishing problem.'

Salty Dawg Saloon BAR
(Map p244; Homer Spit Rd) Maybe the most storied bar on the Kenai Peninsula, the Salty Dawg is one of those places that's famous for being famous. In the evenings every square foot of its wood-shaving-laden floor is packed with tourists singing along to sea shanties and rubbing elbows with the occasional fisherman. The lighthouse tower atop the whole party, visible from anywhere in town, stays lit during opening hours.

Ring of Fire Meadery BREWERY
(Map p240; 178 E Bunnell Ave; ⏰noon-6pm) This isn't a bar, but there's a tasting room where you can sample the award-winning mead, made with locally grown berries and fruit. You can choose from 20 flavors, which are fermented in high-end bourbon barrels. It's unique and highly recommended.

Homer Brewing Company BREWERY
(Map p240; www.homerbrew.com; 1411 Lakeshore Dr; ⏰noon-7pm Mon-Sat, to 6pm Sun) Like the Meadery, this isn't a bar, but it does offer 'tours' with free samples of fresh beer – try the broken birch bitter ale, and then grab a growler to go.

Bear Creek Winery WINE BAR
(Map p244; www.bearcreekwineryalaska.com; Bear Creek Dr; ⏰10am-6pm) Wineries are scarcer than vineyards in Alaska, but this impressive family-run operation bottles some fine berry-based wines, plus fireweed mead and rhubarb vino. It conducts tours and complimentary tastings daily in the summer, and sells its product on-site.

Down East Saloon BAR

(Map p244; 3125 E End Rd) This spacious bar is where locals head to listen to live music. The view is killer, but you'll likely be paying more attention to whichever Homer talent is on stage.

Pier One Theatre THEATER

(Map p244; 235-7333; www.pieronetheatre.org; Homer Spit Rd) Live drama and comedy are performed in a 'come-as-you-are' warehouse next to the Fishing Hole on the Spit. Shows start at 8:15pm Friday and Saturday, and 7:30pm Sunday during summer.

ℹ️ Information

INTERNET ACCESS Homer Public Library (500 Hazel Ave; 10am-8pm Tue & Thu, to 6pm Mon, Wed, Fri & Sat) Homer's excellent library is arty and airy, with a decidedly Homer-esque selection of magazines. Internet access is free, and it even has laptop cubicles with a view of Kachemak Bay.

K-Bay Caffé (www.kbaycaffe.com; 59415 E End Rd; 6:30am-7pm Mon-Sat, 7:30am-6pm Sun;) Has free internet access (donations appreciated) on one computer, plus wi-fi. The locally roasted coffee is the best in town, and you can enjoy a 'cup of love' in the sunroom.

LAUNDRY East End Laundry (Mile 2.9, E End Rd; 10am-8pm Mon-Sat) Convenient to Seaside Farm.

Sportsman's Supply & Rental (1114 Freight Dock Rd; 6am-midnight) Offers showers ($7) and laundry right on the Spit.

Washboard Laundromat The showers ($6) come with towels and last as long as you want.

MEDICAL SERVICES Homer Medical Clinic (235-8586; 4136 Bartlett St) Next door to South Peninsula Hospital; for walk-in service.

South Peninsula Hospital (235-8101, 866-235-0369; Bartlett St) North of the Pratt Museum.

MONEY Wells Fargo (88 Sterling Hwy) For cash, this is as good a bank as any.

POST Post office (Map p240; 3658 Heath St) Send your stunning Homer postcards from here.

TOURIST INFORMATION Halibut Derby Office (235-7740; www.homerhalibutderby. com; Homer Spit Rd; 5:30am-8am & 3-7pm) Has a few pamphlets and is the official weigh-in station for the Homer Halibut Derby.

Homer Visitor Center & Chamber of Commerce (235-7740; www.homeralaska.org; 201 Sterling Hwy; 9am-6pm Mon-Fri, from 10am Sat & Sun) Has countless brochures and a funky mosaic on the floor. It's operated by the chamber of commerce, however, and only provides info on members.

ℹ️ Getting There & Around

AIR The contract carrier for Alaska Airlines, **ERA Alaska** (266-8394, 800-866-8394; www.flyera.com) provides daily flights between Homer and Anchorage from Homer's airport, 1.7 miles east of town on Kachemak Dr. The advance-purchase fare runs at about $140 one way, or $250 for the round-trip. **Smokey Bay Air** (235-1511; www.smokeybayair.com; 2100 Kachemak Dr) offers flights to Seldovia for $50 each way.

BICYCLE Homer Saw & Cycle (235-8406; 1532 Ocean Dr; 9am-5:30pm Mon-Fri, 11am-5pm Sat) Rents out mountain bikes and hybrids ($25 per day).

Cycle Logical (226-2925; www.cyclelogi calhomer.com; 3585 E End Rd; 9am-6pm Tue-Sat, by appt Mon) Has disc-brake-equiped mountain bikes for $20/30 per half-/full day.

BOAT The Alaska Marine Highway provides a thrice-weekly service from Homer to Seldovia (each way $33, 1½ hours) and Kodiak ($74, 9½ hours), with a connecting service to the Aleutians. The **ferry terminal** (235-8449; www. ferryalaska.com) is found at the end of Homer Spit. **Rainbow Tours** (235-7272; Homer Spit Rd; one way/round-trip $30/45) offers the inexpensive Rainbow Connection shuttle from Homer to Seldovia. It departs at 9am, gets to Seldovia an hour later, and then returns to take you back to Homer at 5pm. It'll transport your bike for $5 and your kayak for $10. The new **Seldovia Ferry** (435-3299; www.seldovi abayferry.com; Lot 21, Freight Dock Rd; one way/round-trip $32/64) takes passengers to Seldovia three times per day, with departures from Homer at 9:45am, 2:15pm and 4:15pm. The first two include a tour of Eldridge Passage.

Many water-taxi operations shuttle campers and kayakers between Homer and points across Kachemak Bay. Though the companies are good and work closely together, the most respected by far is **Mako's Water-Taxi** (235-9055; www. makoswatertaxi.com; Homer Spit Rd). It usually charges $75 (includes state park fee) per person round-trip with a two-person minimum.

BUS Homer Stage Line (868-3914; www. stagelineinhomer.com) Runs daily from Homer to Anchorage (one way/round-trip $87/174), Seward ($97/187) and all points in between.

CAR Polar Car Rental (235-5998; airport) To obtain an affordable rental car, this small dealer has subcompacts for $67 a day.

TAXI Kostas Taxi (399-8008, 399-8115) and **Kachecab** (235-1950) are fierce rivals, and can get you anywhere around town for a reasonable fare.

Seldovia

POP 319

If the tourist-thronged towns of the Kenai Peninsula have left you frazzled, catch a boat to Seldovia, about 15 miles from Homer on the far side of Kachemak Bay and in a world of its own. Living up to the nickname 'City of Secluded Charm,' the community has managed to retain much of its old Alaskan character, and can be a restful (and inexpensive) day or overnight trip from Homer. It's a compact town, easily toured in about an hour, and the airport is a mere half-mile from 'downtown.'

History

One of the oldest settlements on Cook Inlet, Russians founded the town in the late 18th century and named it after their word *selde-voy,* meaning 'herring bay.' By the 1890s Seldovia had become an important shipping and supply center for the region, and the town boomed right into the 1920s with salmon canning, fur farming and, of course, a (short-lived) herring industry.

But then the highway came, stretching only as far as the tip of the Homer Spit. After it was completed in the 1950s, Seldovia's importance as a supply center began to dwindle. Today it relies primarily on fishing but is making its best stab at becoming a tourist destination. It's a process that's happening in fits and starts: the hiking and biking possibilities here are excellent and the accommodations are plush, but the culinary offerings are limited and the galleries feel a bit like desperate rummage sales. All in all you'll find a village with quaintness to spare, but little tourist infrastructure, which may be the best thing about the place.

◉ Sights

Seldovia Village Tribe Visitor Center
VISITOR CENTER

(☎234-7898; www.svt.org; cnr Airport Ave & Main St; ☉7am-5pm) This visitors center, opened in 2005, showcases Seldovia's Alaska Native heritage – a unique blend of Alutiiq (Eskimo) and Tanaina (Indian) cultures. The small, tidy museum covers the history of Alaska Natives in the area, and its subsistence display is informative and interesting. This is also the place to buy souvenirs.

Alaska Tribal Cache
CULTURAL CENTER

(☎234-7898; www.svt.org; 234 Main St; ☉10am-6pm Mon-Sat, noon-5pm Sun) Run by the Seldovia Native Association, the Alaska Tribal Cache across town sells jams and jellies, all made on-site with fresh wild berries picked by local kids – and shoestring travelers.

St Nicholas Orthodox Church
CHURCH

(tinetteh@ptialaska.net; ☉services 6pm Sat, 10am Sun) Seldovia's most popular attraction is this onion-domed church, which overlooks the town from a hill just off Main St. Built in 1891 and restored in the 1970s, the church is open only during services and by appointment. Note the chandelier, made from old barrel staves. Though there is no resident clergyman, occasionally the priest from Nanwalek travels here to conduct services.

Outside Beach
BEACH

This beach is an excellent place for wildlife sightings and a little beachcombing. To reach it, follow Anderson Way (Jakolof Bay Rd) out of town for a mile, then head left at the first fork to reach the picnic area at Outside Beach Park. You stand a good chance of spotting eagles, seabirds and possibly even otters here. At low tide, you can explore the sea life among the rocks, and on a clear day the views of Mt Redoubt and Mt Iliamna are stunning.

🏃 Activities

Berry Picking

Seldovia is known best for its blueberries, which grow so thick just outside town that from late August to mid-September you often can rake your fingers through the bushes and fill a two-quart bucket in minutes. You'll also come across plenty of low-bush cranberries and salmonberries, a species not found around Homer. Be aware, however, that many of the best berry areas are on tribal land; before setting out, stop at the Seldovia Village Tribe (☎234-7898; www.svt. org; 234 Main St), which will sell you a berry-picking permit for a nominal fee. If you're feeling light in the wallet, you may even be able to sell your harvest to the Alaska Tribal Cache for about $2 per pound.

Hiking

The Otterbahn Trail was famously created by local high school students, who dubbed it the 'we-worked-hard-so-you-better-like-it trail.' The trailhead lies behind Susan B English School, off Winfred Ave. Lined with salmonberries and affording great views of Graduation Peak, it skirts the coastline most of the way and reaches Outside Beach in 1.5

miles. Make sure you hike it at tides below 17ft, as the last stretch runs across a slough that is only legally passable when the water is out. (Property above 17ft is private.)

Two trails start from Jakolof Bay Rd. You can either hike down the beach toward the head of Seldovia Bay at low tide, or you can follow a 4.5-mile logging road to reach several secluded coves. There is also the Tutka/Jakolof Trail, a 2.5-mile trail to a campsite on the Tutka Lagoon, the site of a state salmon-rearing facility. The posted trail departs from Jakolof Bay Rd about 10.5 miles east of town.

The town's newest hike is the rigorous Rocky Ridge Trail, where 800ft of climbing will be rewarded with remarkable views of the bay, the town and Mt Iliamna. The trail starts (or ends) on Rocky St and loops back to the road near the airport, covering about 3 miles.

Cycling

Seldovia's nearly carless streets and outlying gravel roads make for ideal biking; mountain bikes can be brought over from Homer. Those looking for a fairly leisurely ride can pedal the 10-mile Jakolof Bay Rd, which winds along the coast nearly to the head of Jakolof Bay. For a more rigorous experience, continue on another 6 miles beyond the end of the maintained road, climbing 1200ft into the alpine country at the base of Red Mountain.

In the past, fit cyclists could also depart from Jakolof Bay Rd for an epic 30-mile round-trip ride along the rough Rocky River Rd, which cuts across the tip of the Kenai Peninsula to Windy Bay. In recent years washouts have made the road largely impassable; inquire about current conditions.

Paddling

There are some excellent kayaking opportunities in the Seldovia area. Just north, Eldred Passage and the three islands (Cohen, Yukon and Hesketh) that mark its entrance are prime spots for viewing otters, sea lions and seals, while the northern shore of Yukon Island features caves and tunnels that can be explored at high tide. Even closer are Sadie Cove, and Tutka and Jakolof Bays, where you can paddle in protected water amid interesting geological features, and near numerous camping areas along the beaches.

Kayak'Atak KAYAKING
(☏234-7425; www.alaska.net/~kayaks; kayaks 1st day single/double $50/80, subsequent days $35/50) Rents out kayaks and can help arrange transportation throughout the bay. It also offers various guided tours starting from $80, some including a 'gourmet lunch.' Make reservations in advance.

☞ Tours

Smokey Bay Air AIR
(☏235-1511; www.smokeybayair.com; 2100 Kachemak Dr; one way $50) Offers a scenic 12-minute flight from Homer, over the Kenai Mountains and Kachemak Bay to Seldovia.

Mako's Water-Taxi BOAT & AIR
(☏235-9055; www.makoswatertaxi.com; drop-off at Homer Spit Rd; round-trip $135) Has an excellent tour that takes you by boat, car and plane. Mako's drops you off at Jakolof Bay, from which you'll be driven to Seldovia. You return to Homer via a short flightseeing trip.

Central Charters BOAT
(☏235-7847, 800-478-7847; www.centralcharter.com; drop-off at Homer Spit Rd, one way/round-trip $30/48) Does a daily six-hour tour from Homer, leaving at 11am, circling Gull Island, and deboarding you in Seldovia to enjoy the village for the afternoon.

🛏 Sleeping

You won't have problems finding a good room in this town.

TOP CHOICE **Across the Bay Tent & Breakfast** CABIN $$
(☏summer 235-3633, winter 345-2571; www.tentandbreakfastalaska.com; tent cabins per person $75; ⊜🐾) Located 8 miles from town on Jakolof Bay, this is something a little different. Its cabinlike tents include a full breakfast, and for $110 per day you can get a package that includes all your meals – dinner could consist of fresh oysters, beach-grilled salmon or halibut stew with a side of garden-grown greens. The offbeat resort also rents out mountain bikes for $25 per day and organizes guided kayak trips (per half-day with lunch $85). Bring your sleeping bag.

Seldovia Rowing Club B&B B&B $$
(☏234-7614; www.seldoviarowingclub.net; 343 Bay St; r $135) Located on the Old Boardwalk, this place (the first B&B in Southcentral Alaska) has homey suites decorated with quilts, antiques and owner Susan Mumma's outstanding watercolors. She serves big breakfasts and often hosts in-house music concerts.

Seldovia Wilderness RV Park CAMPGROUND $
(☏234-7643; tent sites/RV sites $5/10) About a mile out of town, this is a city-maintained

campground on spectacular Outside Beach. You can pay for your site at the ferry terminal or harbormaster's office.

Sea Parrot Inn INN $$
(☎632-6135, 234-7829; www.seaparrotinn.com; 226 Main St; d $165; ☺☎) Harbor views, a nice deck, wood floors, continental breakfast and a social atmosphere (thanks to a shared great room) make this a nice town-center spot. Laundry and showers are also available for campers.

Bridgekeeper's Inn B&B B&B $$
(☎234-7535; www.thebridgekeepersinn.com; 223 Kachemak Dr; r $140-150; ☺) A cozy place with private baths and full breakfasts; one room has a balcony overlooking the salmon-filled slough.

Boardwalk Hotel HOTEL $
(☎234-7816, 800-238-7862; www.theseldoviaboardwalkhotel.com; 234 Main St; r $70-115; ☺) Has big, beautiful rooms and a family-style atmosphere. Pricier rooms have huge windows overlooking the bay and small-boat harbor.

Dancing Eagles CABIN $$$
(☎360-6363; www.dancingeagles.com; cabins $175) Great for groups or families: has one queen bedroom with kitchen and bath, and a sleeping loft that sleeps four.

Seldovia Bayview Suites APARTMENTS $$
(☎234-7631, 800-478-7898; www.bayviewsuites.com; 381 Main St; r without/with view $129/179) Though the apartment-style rooms here are sterile and charmless, they're spacious and blessed with beautiful views; enjoy them from the waterside hot tub. The $299 suite will sleep eight comfortably, plus 30 on the floor.

✗ Eating

Perhaps the most frustrating thing about Seldovia is that it can sleep far more people than it can feed. If you're just visiting for the day, make a beeline for one of the establishments below when the ferry gets in, or just wait an hour until the boat crowd fills up and wanders off.

TOP CHOICE Fenske's Warehouse Books & Coffee CAFE $
(230 Kachemak St; snacks $2-5; ☺9am-5pm) This incredibly cozy place is tucked in the forest above the slough like a juicy secret. Stacks of books fill the small space, and you can get coffee, hot chocolate and birdhouse

cookies to nibble on while you read away a rainy day. Should you get lucky with a sunny afternoon, a spacious deck lounges over the water; relax and watch the tide do its thing.

Tidepool Cafe CAFE $$
(☎260-6766; 267 Main St; breakfast $6-11, lunch $9-16, dinner $16-30; ☺7am-3pm daily, 5:30-9pm Wed-Sun) In a sunny space overlooking the harbor, this eclectic eatery serves great wraps, sandwiches and espressos, and has offerings like a Thai codwich ($13) and a pumpkin ginger waffle ($7). You'll need reservations for dinner.

Mad Fish SEAFOOD $$
(☎234-7676; 221 Main St; lunch $9-11, dinner $13-29; ☺11:30am-9pm) This venue is a bit overpriced but serves adequate croissant sandwiches and chowder. Its bread is fresh-baked.

Linwood Bar & Grill BAR $$
(257 Main St; burgers $11-13, pizzas $13-25; ☺grill 6-10pm) A dark harborfront saloon which has plenty of cigarette smoke to go with your meal.

ℹ Information

The post office is on the corner of Main St and Seldovia St. There's an ATM at Linwood Bar & Grill but no banks in town.

Harbormaster's Office (☎234-7886; ☺8am-9pm) Has toilets and pamphlets.

Information stand (Main St) Close to the small-boat harbor, with a few flyers tacked up; several more flyers are available in the Harbormaster's Office.

Library (☎234-7662; 250 Seldovia St; ☺afternoon Tue, Thu & Sat; @☎) Has one terminal for internet access as well as wi-fi.

Sea Parrot Inn (226 Main St; ☺9am-9pm) Offers showers (10 minutes $7.50) with soap and towel, as well as laundry (wash and dry $10.50).

Seldovia Chamber of Commerce (www.seldoviachamber.org) Its website is great for pre-trip planning.

Seldovia Medical Clinic (☎234-7825; 250 Seldovia St; ☺Mon, Wed & Fri 9am-noon & 1-4pm) Also by appointment.

Seldovia Village Tribe Visitor Center (☎234-7898; www.svt.org; cnr Airport Ave & Main St; ☺7am-5pm) Where to book the Seldovia Bay Ferry.

ℹ Getting There & Around

AIR Homer Air (☎235-8591; www.homerair.com; one way/round-trip $52.50/105) Flies to Seldovia hourly.

ACROSS THE BAY

Opposite Homer but outside Kachemak Bay State Park is a handful of compelling destinations easily accessible by water-taxi.

Gull Island

Halfway between the Spit and Halibut Cove, the 40ft-high Gull Island attracts some 16,000 nesting seabirds: puffins, kittiwakes, murres, cormorants and many more species. If you can cope with the stench, you'll enjoy photographing the birds up close, even if you don't have a 300mm lens.

Mako's Water-Taxi (☎235-9055; www.makoswatertaxi.com; Homer Spit Rd, Homer Spit) has a one-hour island tour (per person $40, three-person minimum) and a two-hour tour that includes adorable sea otters (per person $75, four-person minimum). Several other companies do Gull Island tours as well.

Halibut Cove

Halibut Cove is an absurdly quaint village of 30 permanent residents. In the early 1920s the cove had 42 herring salteries and more than 1000 residents. Today it's home to the noted Saltry restaurant, several art galleries and a warren of boardwalks – but no roads.

The Danny J (☎226-2424, 296-2223) travels to the cove twice daily. It departs from Homer at noon, swings past Gull Island and arrives at 1:30pm. There, you have 2½ hours to explore and have lunch. The ferry returns to the Spit by 5pm and then makes an evening run to the cove for dinner, returning to Homer at 10pm. The noon tour costs $50 per person, while the evening trip costs $30.

For many couples, dining at the Saltry (☎296-2223; lunch $11-22, dinner $14-25) makes for the ultimate date, with an outdoor deck over the aquamarine inlet and excellent seafood and vegetarian cuisine. Its lunch seatings are at 1:30pm and 3pm; for dinner it's 6pm or 7:30pm. After eating, check out the galleries.

North of Seldovia

In Tutka Bay, Sadie Cove and Eldred Passage are a selection of quality lodges accessed only by water-taxi.

Located on Eldred Passage, Otter Cove Resort (☎235-6212, 800-426-6212; www.ottercoveresort.com; cabins $80) has affordable camping-style cabins (but with electricity) near the Sadie Knob Trail, rents out kayaks (per single/double $40/70) and guides single- and multiday paddling trips. Round-trip transportation is $70.

Tutka Bay Wilderness Lodge (☎274-2710; www.withinthewild.com; r per person from $900) is an all-inclusive resort with chalets, cottages and rooms surrounding the lodge house, where guests enjoy meals with a sweeping view of the inlet and Jakolof Mountain. The accommodations are very comfortable, the food is excellent and the amenities include a sauna, deepwater dock, boathouse and hiking trails. Activities range from clamming to sea kayaking to a maritime cuisine cooking school.

Sadie Cove Wilderness Lodge (☎888-283-7234, 235-2350; www.sadiecove.com; r per person $450) is just to the north of Tutka Bay in Sadie Cove. This wilderness lodge offers similar amenities – cabins, sauna, outdoor hot tub, Alaskan seafood dinners – but it's not quite as elegant or pricey.

BICYCLE There are no bicycle rentals in town, despite the area being a great mountain-bike destination. Rent a bike in Homer and bring it on the ferry.

BOAT Alaska Marine Highway ferries provide twice-weekly service between Homer and Seldovia ($33, 1½ hours) with connecting service throughout the peninsula and the Aleutians. The Seldovia ferry terminal (☎234-7886, www.ferryalaska.com) is at the north end of Main St.

Rainbow Tours (☎235-7272; drop-off at Homer Spit Rd; one way/round-trip $30/45) Offers the inexpensive Rainbow Connection shuttle from Homer to Seldovia. It departs at 10:30am, gets to Seldovia about two hours later, and then returns to take you back to

Homer at 5pm. It'll transport your bike for $5 and your kayak for $10.

Seldovia Bay Ferry (☑435-3299; www.seldo viabayferry.com; cnr Airport Ave & Main St; one way/round-trip $32/64) The newest addition to ferry services, with three departures per day: from Seldovia at 8am, 12:30pm and 4:30pm. The two earlier departures include a tour of Gull Island and Eldridge Passage.

TAXI For rides out to Jakolof Bay Rd or to the airport, try **Seldovia Cab & Limousine** (☑399-0469).

Kachemak Bay State Park

Stand on Homer Spit and look south, and an alluring wonderland sprawls before you: a luxuriantly green coastline, sliced by fjords and topped by sparkling glaciers and rugged peaks. This is Kachemak Bay State Park, which, along with Kachemak Bay State Wilderness Park to the south, includes 350,000 acres of idyllic wilderness accessible only by bush plane or boat. It was Alaska's first state park; according to locals, it remains the best.

The most popular attraction is Grewingk Glacier, which can be seen across the bay from Homer. Viewing the glacier at closer range means a boat trip to the park and a very popular one-way hike of 3.5 miles. Outside the glacier, however, you can easily escape into the wilds by either hiking or kayaking. With more than 40 miles of trails, plenty of sheltered waterways, numerous campsites and a few enclosed accommodation options, this is a highly recommended outing for a day or three.

◉ Sights & Activities

Peterson Bay Field Station   NATURE RESERVE
(☑235-2778) Though technically it's outside the park, this field station operated by the Center for Alaskan Coastal Studies provides an excellent introduction to the ecology and natural history of the area. In summer, staff members lead day-long educational tours of the coastal forest and waterfront tidepools; the best intertidal beasties are seen during extremely low, or 'minus,' tides. Inside the station, too, you can get up close and personal with a touch tank full of squishy sea creatures. It costs $105, which includes the boat ride over from the Spit. For $155 you can combine a morning natural history tour with an afternoon of guided paddling in Peterson and China Poot Bays. If you want to overnight here, the station has bunks and yurts.

Hiking

Glacier Lake Trail   HIKING
The most popular hike in Kachemak Bay State Park is this 3.5-mile, one-way trail that begins at the Glacier Spit trailhead, near the small Rusty Lagoon Campground. The level, easy-to-follow trek proceeds across the glacial outwash and ends at a lake with superb views of Grewingk Glacier. Camping on the lake is spectacular, and often the shoreline is littered with icebergs (and day-trippers). At Mile 1.4 you can connect to the 6.5-mile Grewingk Glacier Trail, with a hand-tram and access to the face of the glacier. If you don't have time for the entire hike, there are excellent views less than a mile from the tram.

Saddle Trail   HIKING
A mile-long trail starting in Halibut Cove; it connects to the Glacier Lake Trail for a nice loop.

Alpine Ridge Trail   HIKING
At the high point of the Saddle Trail you will reach the posted junction for this 2-mile climb to an alpine ridge above the glacier. The climb can be steep at times but manageable for most hikers with day packs. On a nice day, the views of the ice and Kachemak Bay are stunning.

Lagoon Trail   HIKING
Also departing from the Saddle Trail is this 5.5-mile route that leads to the ranger station at the head of Halibut Cove Lagoon. Along the way it passes the Goat Rope Spur Trail, a steep 1-mile climb to the alpine tundra. You also pass the posted junction of Halibut Creek Trail. If Grewingk Glacier is too crowded for you, follow this trail a half-mile to Halibut Creek to spend the night in a beautiful, but much more remote, valley.

The Lagoon Trail is considered a difficult hike and involves fording Halibut Creek, which should be done at low tide. At the ranger station, more trails extend south to several lakes, as well as Poot Peak and the Wosnesenski River.

Poot Peak   HIKING
Poot Peak is a difficult, slick, rocky ascent of 2600ft. The trailhead begins at the Halibut Cove Lagoon, where a moderate 2.6-mile climb along the China Poot Lake Trail takes you to a campsite on the lake. From there, the trail to the peak diverges after the Wosnesenski River Trail junction. For a little over a mile you'll clamber upward through thinning forest until you reach the Summit Spur, where

the route climbs even more precipitously to the mountain's lower summit, 2100ft in elevation. From here, reaching the very top involves scaling a shifting wall of scree, a feat that should be attempted only by those who have some rock-climbing experience. In wet weather, it should be avoided altogether. Getting from the lake to the summit and back will likely take the better part of a day.

Grace Ridge Trail   HIKING
This is a 7-mile trail that stretches from a campsite at Kayak Beach trailhead to deep inside Tutka Bay in the state park. Much of the hike runs above the treeline along the crest of Grace Ridge, where, needless to say, the views are stunning. There's also access from the Sea Star Cove public-use cabin. You could hike the trail in a day, but it makes a great two-day trek with an overnight camp.

Emerald Lake Trail   HIKING
This steep, difficult 6.4-mile trail begins at Grewingk Glacial Lake and leads to Portlock Plateau. You'll witness firsthand the reclamation of the wasted forest (due to spruce bark beetle damage) by brushy alder and birch, considered delicacies by local wildlife. At Mile 2.1 a spur trail reaches the scenic Emerald Lake, and there are great views of the bay from the plateau. In spring, stream crossings can be challenging.

Paddling
You can spend three or four days paddling the many fjords of the park, departing from Homer and making overnight stops at Glacier Spit or Halibut Cove. Think twice before crossing Kachemak Bay from the Spit, however; the currents and tides are powerful and can cause serious problems for inexperienced paddlers.

Seaside Adventures   KAYAKING
(235-6672; www.seasideadventure.com; trips incl water-taxi half-/full day $110/150) A tiny family-run outfit, Seaside Adventures will show you the bay on kayak complete with running commentary about local flora and fauna.

St Augustine Charters   KAYAKING
(299-1894; www.homerkayaking.com; paddles incl water-taxi half-/full-day $100/140) Offers many guided tours from its Petersen Bay office, including multiday paddling and trekking trips through state parks, camping at seaside sites. 'Paddle Hike Dine' ($195) is a popular day of kayaking and hiking, ending with dinner at Saltry restaurant in Halibut Cove (p252).

True North Kayak Adventures   KAYAKING
(235-0708; www.truenorthkayak.com) Based on Yukon Island and with an office on Homer Spit, True North Kayak Adventures runs half-day paddles amid the otters, with eagles overhead, for $105 (water-taxi included). Once you've spent all that time crossing the bay, however, it makes more sense to spring for the full-day paddle ($150), or at least the three-quarter-day ($130). There are also several multiday options that cross Eldred Passage into Tutka Bay or Sadie Cove. For experienced kayakers, it rents rigid single/double kayaks for $45/65 per day.

🛏 Sleeping
Camping is permitted throughout Kachemak Bay State Park. Moreover, numerous free, primitive camping areas have been developed, usually at waterfront trailheads or along trails. Consult the Alaska Division of Parks for the locations and facilities.

Center for Alaskan Coastal Studies YURTS $
(235-6667; www.akcoastalstudies.org; Heath St; 9am-5pm Mon-Fri) This organization reserves bunks ($25) or yurts ($80) close to its Peterson Bay Field Station, just outside the park. Lodgers can use the kitchen at the field station.

Public-use Cabins   CABIN $
(269-8400; 262-5581; www.alaskastateparks. org; cabins $65) There are six cabins that can be reserved in the park. Three are in Halibut Cove: Lagoon Overlook, with a pair of bunk-beds; Lagoon East Cabin, which has disabled access; and Lagoon West Cabin, a half-mile west of the public dock. China Poot Lake Cabin is a 2.4-mile hike from Halibut Cove on the shore of what's also called Leisure Lake. Moose Valley Cabin is about 2.5 miles from the Halibut Cove Lagoon Ranger Station and only sleeps two ($35). Sea Star Cove Cabin, on the south shore of Tutka Bay, is convenient to the Tutka Lake Trail. China Poot Cabin is accessible by kayak or water-taxi. Make reservations for any of them months in advance.

Yurts   YURTS $
(235-0132; www.alaskanyurtrentals.com; yurts $75.25) There are eight of these for rent in the park, maintained by a private operator. All are near the ocean and equipped with bunks and woodstoves. They're located at the mouth of Humpy Creek, at the mouth of Halibut Cove, in China Poot Bay, near the

North Eldred Passage Trailhead, near the northwest and southeast Grace Ridge Trailheads, in Tutka Bay and on Quarry Beach at the mouth of Sadie Cove.

ℹ️ Information

Center for Alaskan Coastal Studies (☎235-6667; www.akcoastalstudies.org) Has maps and information about the park, both at its downtown Homer headquarters off Lake St and at its yurt on the Spit behind Mako's Water-Taxi. National Geographic's *Trails Illustrated* map of the park is an excellent resource, depicting hiking routes, public-use cabins, docks and campsites, and it's available here. The Center also operates the Peterson Bay Field Station across the bay.

Mako's Water-Taxi (☎235-9055; www.mako swatertaxi.com) Can give you the lowdown on possible hikes and paddles in the park – and about the logistics of getting over and back.

ℹ️ Getting There & Around

A number of water-taxis offer drop-off and pickup service (round-trip $50 to $80). Because boat access to some of the trailheads is tidally dependent, you'll need to work with them to establish a precise rendezvous time and location – and then be sure to stick to it.

Ashore Water Taxi (☎235-2341; www.ashore watertaxi.com) Charges $75 per person with a two-person minimum to any place in the park.

Mako's Water-Taxi (☎235-9055; www. makoswatertaxi.com) The most respected of Homer's water-taxi services, famed for making timely pickups even in foul weather – and for dropping off beer to unsuspecting campers. For most cross-bay destinations from Homer Spit it charges $75 with a two-person minimum. To Seldovia, the boat costs $250 one way, so grab all your friends and fill 'er up.

Denali & the Interior

Best Places to Eat

» 229 Parks (p272)

» Talkeetna Alaskan Lodge (p280)

» McCarthy Lodge (p319)

» Prospectors Pizzeria & Ale House (p272)

» Pump House Restaurant (p295)

Best Places to Stay

» Wonder Lake Campground (p268)

» Ma Johnson's Hotel (p318)

» Denali Hwy Cabins (p286)

» Ah, Rose Marie B&B (p293)

» Talkeetna Roadhouse (p279)

Why Go?

Adventures are served up raw in this part of the state, or barbecued with a pint of handcrafted beer. It's your choice. The best of the Interior can be found forging a trail alone down a braided riverbed, but once-in-a-lifetime encounters with natural wonders can also be had from the seat of a rumbling park bus.

The big name in this region is Denali National Park, blessed with the continent's mightiest mountain, abundant megafauna and easy access. But don't miss the small towns, with their clapboard facades, quirky museums and tales from the days of working some of the biggest mineral finds in history.

Compared to most places in the developed world, the Interior is a trackless hinterland; for Alaska, however, it's got roads galore. With most routes so scenic they've become destinations in themselves, it's best to have an open schedule when you head out.

When to Go

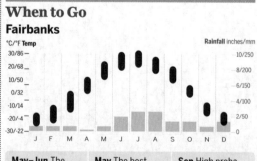

Fairbanks

May–Jun The tundra comes alive with millions of migratory birds.

May The best month to visit Denali National Park for clear views of Mt McKinley.

Sep High probability of seeing the northern lights in Fairbanks.

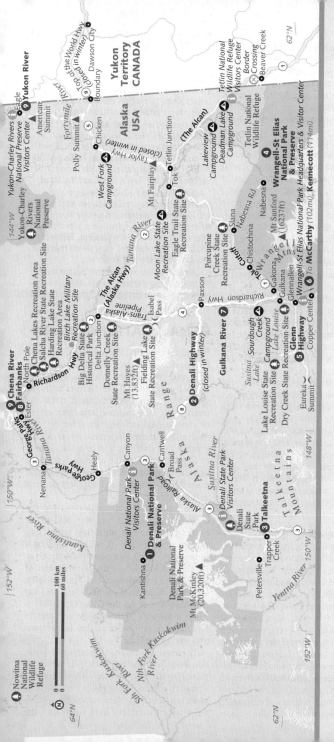

Denali & the Interior Highlights

1 Viewing wildlife on the **Park Road** (p260)

2 Hiking, canoeing or birdwatching off the lonely, scenic **Denali Highway** (p284)

3 Circling the highest mountain in North America on a **flightseeing tour** (p277) out of Talkeetna

4 Stepping into the great expanse of untouched wilderness in **Wrangell-St Elias National Park** (p316)

5 Cruising the **Glenn Highway** (p311)

6 Exploring mountains, glaciers and massive copper mine remains around **Kennecott** (p320) and **McCarthy** (p318)

7 **Fishing** some of Alaska's best salmon streams

8 Beholding the **northern lights** (p294) from Fairbanks

9 Paddling the gentle **Chena River** (p290) or the remote, untamed **Yukon** (p310)

History

If archaeologists are correct, Interior Alaska was the corridor through which the rest of the continent was peopled, as waves of hunter-gatherers migrated across the Bering land bridge to points south. Ancestors of the region's present Native group, the Athabascans, are thought to have been here at least 6000 years.

It wasn't until the 1800s that the first white people began to trickle in. The newcomers were mainly traders: Russians, who established posts along the lower Yukon and Kuskokwim Rivers, and Britons, who began trading at Fort Yukon, on the upper Yukon River, in the 1840s. Later came prospectors, whose discoveries transformed this region, beginning with the first major gold rush in the Fortymile district in the 1880s. Similar rushes, for gold and also copper, subsequently gave rise to many Interior communities.

Transportation projects brought the next wave of growth. In 1914 Congress agreed to fund the building of the USA's northernmost railroad, from Seward to Fairbanks. At the peak of construction, 4500 workers labored along the route, and their base camps became boomtowns.

Two decades later, during WWII, the building of the Alcan had the same effect on the eastern Interior: both Tok and Delta Junction got their start as highway construction camps, while Fairbanks saw a second boom in its economy and population. Another three decades after *that* came the biggest undertaking the Interior has ever seen: the laying of the $8 billion Trans-Alaska Pipeline, which transects Alaska, running from Valdez to the Arctic Ocean at Prudhoe Bay.

Dangers & Annoyances

Getting lost in the backcountry is a real possibility, as national and state parks, national forest and Bureau of Land Management (BLM) areas have few marked trails. Come prepared with a compass, topographic map, GPS (optional), enough food and water to get you by for a few extra days, and most importantly the skills to use your equipment properly. Long sleeves and light pants will help fend off mosquitoes, while our bear tips (p414) should prevent any unpleasant encounters with these creatures. Glacier travel and mountaineering are dangerous endeavors. If you don't know how to self-arrest and perform a crevasse rescue (or don't know what these things are), you should go with a qualified guide.

ⓘ Getting There & Around

With scenic highways such as George Parks, the Alcan, Richardson, Glenn, Denali and Taylor crisscrossing this region, consider renting a vehicle to get around at your own pace.

Bus services are limited. **Alaska Direct Bus Line** (☑800-770-6652; www.alaskadirect busline.com) travels the Alcan, Tok Cutoff and Glenn Hwy, while **Alaska/Yukon Trails** (☑800-770-7275; www.alaskashuttle.com) covers George Parks and Taylor Hwys, and the Alcan.

Alaska Railroad (☑265-2494; www.alas karailroad.com) runs daily between Anchorage and Fairbanks. The train is a mellow, scenic alternative to driving, with depots at two of the Interior's most-visited destinations: Talkeetna and Denali National Park. After Denali the route lacks dramatic scenery, however.

For much of Alaska's heartland, bush plane is the only way to get around. Even small Interior villages usually have airstrips and scheduled flights.

DENALI NATIONAL PARK

For many travelers, Denali National Park & Preserve (www.nps.gov/dena) is the beginning and end of their Alaskan adventure. And why shouldn't it be? Here is probably your best chance in the Interior (if not in the entire state) of seeing a grizzly bear, moose or caribou, and maybe even a fox or wolf. And unlike most wilderness areas in the country, you don't have to be a backpacker to view this wildlife. The window of the park bus will do just fine for a close look at these magnificent creatures roaming free in their natural habitat.

For those with a bit more time and the desire to get further into the wild, there are vast expanses of untracked country to explore – more than six million acres of it to be exact. That's more landmass than the US state of Massachusetts. At the center of it all is the icy behemoth of Mt McKinley, known to most Alaskans as Denali and native Athabascans as the Great One. This is North America's highest peak and rightly celebrated as an icon of all that is awesome and wild in the state.

There's only one road through the park: the 92-mile unpaved Park Rd, which is closed to private vehicles after Mile 14. The park entrance area (Map p260), where most visitors congregate, extends a scant 4 miles up Park Rd. It's here you'll find the park headquarters, visitor center and main campground, as well as the Wilderness Access Center (WAC) where you pay your park entrance fee and arrange campground and shuttle bus bookings to take you further into the park. In a trailer across the lot from the WAC sits the Backcountry Information Center (BIC), where backpackers get backcountry permits and bear-proof food containers.

There are few places to stay within the park, excluding campgrounds, and only one restaurant. The majority of visitors base themselves in the nearby communities of Canyon, McKinley Village, Carlo Creek and Healy.

History

The Athabascan people used what is now called Denali National Park as hunting grounds, but it wasn't until gold was found near Kantishna in 1905 that the area really began to see development. With the gold stampede came the big-game hunters, and things weren't looking very good for this amazing stretch of wilderness until a noted hunter and naturalist, Charles Sheldon, came to town.

Sheldon, stunned by the destruction, mounted a campaign to protect the region. From this, Mt McKinley National Park was born. Later, as a result of the 1980 Alaska National Interest Lands Conservation Act, the park was enlarged by 4 million acres, and renamed Denali National Park & Preserve.

In 1923, when the railroad arrived, 36 visitors enjoyed the splendor of the new park. Nowadays some 400,000 visitors are received annually. A number of unique visitor-management strategies have been created to deal with the masses, and generally they've been successful. The Denali National Park of today is still the great wilderness it was decades ago.

Dangers & Annoyances

Do not approach moose; they can be extremely dangerous animals, especially females with their young. Be bear conscious, but remember that in the park's history, no visitor has ever been killed by a bear. Rather,

---

DENALI PLANNING GUIDE

Consider making reservations at least six months in advance for a park campsite during the height of summer, and at least three months for accommodation outside the park. The park entrance fee is $10 per person, good for seven days. Vehicles are charged another $20.

When to Come

From May 15 to June 1, park services are just starting up and access to the backcountry is limited. Visitor numbers are low but shuttle buses only run as far as Toklat River. From June 1 to 8, access increases and the shuttle buses run as far as Eielson Visitor Center. After June 8, the park is in full swing till late August.

Shuttle buses stop running in the second week of September. After a few days in which lottery-winning Alaska residents are allowed to take their private vehicles past Mile 14, Park Rd closes to all traffic until the following May.

While most area lodges close, Riley Creek Campground stays open in winter and camping is free, though the water and sewage facilities don't operate. If you have the equipment, you can use the unplowed Park Rd and the rest of the park for cross-country skiing, snowshoeing or dogsledding.

What to Bring

Bring all your own gear if you're camping, as supplies are limited. Basic groceries and dehydrated meals can be purchased; enough for a few days camping in the backcountry, for example.

The park tends to be cool, cloudy and drizzly most of the summer. Don't forget your rain gear.

Reservations

From December 1 you can reserve campsites and shuttle buses online through the Denali National Park Reservation Service (272-7275; www.reservedenali.com).

Note that sites in the Sanctuary River and Igloo Creek campgrounds can only be reserved in person at the WAC two days in advance, and backcountry permits one day in advance.

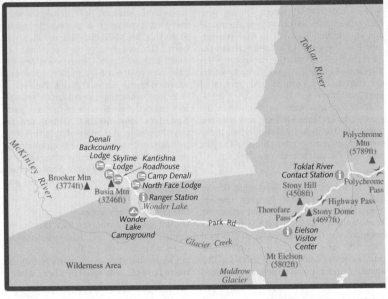

most tourist fatalities here are at the hands of frigid, snowmelt-swollen waterways: learn the techniques for safe river crossings if you plan on hiking in the backcountry.

⊙ Sights & Activities

PARK ROAD

The Park Rd begins at George Parks Hwy and winds 92 miles through the heart of the park, ending at Kantishna, an old mining settlement and the site of several wilderness lodges. Early on, park officials envisaged the onset of bumper-to-bumper traffic jams along this road and wisely closed almost all of it to private vehicles. With few exceptions, motorists can drive only to a parking area along the Savage River at Mile 14, a mile beyond the Savage River Campground. To venture further along the road you must walk, cycle, be part of a tour or, most popularly, take a park shuttle or camper bus.

If you're planning to spend the day riding the buses (it's an eight-hour round-trip to the Eielson Visitor Center, the most popular day trip in the park), pack plenty of food and drink. It can be a long, dusty ride, and in the park there are only limited services at the Toklat River Contact Station and Eielson Visitor Center. Carry a park map so you know where you are and can scope out

ridges or riverbeds that appeal to you for hiking.

Mt McKinley   MOUNTAIN

At 20,320ft, McKinley is almost 4 miles high. What makes it notable as one of the world's great scenic mountains, however, is the sheer independent rise of its bulk. McKinley begins at a base of just 2000ft, which means that on a clear day you will be transfixed by over 18,000 feet of ascending rock, ice and snow. Mt Everest, no slouch itself when it comes to memorable vistas, by contrast only rises 12,000 feet from its base on the Tibetan Plateau.

Despite its lofty heights, the mountain is not visible from the park entrance or the nearby campgrounds and hotel. Your first glimpse of it comes between Mile 9 and Mile 11 of Park Rd, if you're blessed with a clear day. The rule of thumb stressed by the National Park Service (NPS) rangers is that Mt McKinley is hidden two out of every three days, but that's a random example – it could be clear for a week and then hidden for the next month. While the 'Great One' might not be visible for most of the first 15 miles, this is the best stretch to spot moose because of the proliferation of spruce and especially willow, the animal's favorite food. The open flats before Savage River (Map

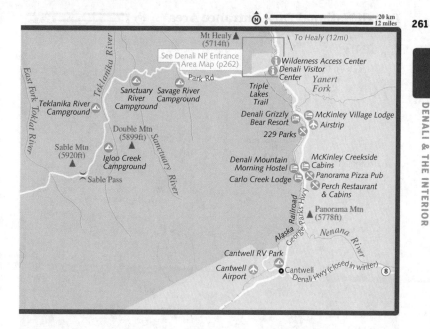

p260; Mile 15) are good for spotting caribou and sometimes brown bears.

SAVAGE RIVER TO EIELSON VISITOR CENTER

From Savage River, the road dips into the Sanctuary and Teklanika River valleys, and Mt McKinley disappears behind the foothills. Igloo Creek Campground (Map p260; Mile 34) is the unofficial beginning of 'bear country.'

After passing through the canyon formed by the Igloo and Cathedral Mountains, the road ascends to 3880ft Sable Pass (Map p260; Mile 38.5). The canyon and surrounding mountains are excellent places to view Dall sheep, while the pass is known as a prime habitat for Toklat brown bears.

Given the prevalence of big brown bears and other wildlife, the area around Sable Pass is permanently closed to hikers and backpackers. From here, the road drops to the bridge over the East Fork Toklat River (Map p260; Mile 44). Hikers can trek from the bridge along the riverbanks both north and south.

Polychrome Pass Overlook (Map p260; Mile 47) is a rest stop for the shuttle buses. This scenic area, at 3500ft, has views of the Toklat River to the south.

Folks on the shuttle bus normally stop at the Toklat River Contact Station (Map p260; Mile 53; ☺9am-7pm) on the way back.

There are a few displays and some books for sale, as well as scopes to check out Dall sheep on the neighboring hills.

Eielson Visitor Center (Map p260; Mile 66; ☺9am-7pm), on the far side of Thorofare Pass (3900ft), is the most common turning-around point for day-trippers taking the shuttle or tour buses into the park. This remote outpost is built directly into the tundra slopes and Mt McKinley seems to almost loom over you from the observation decks. Inside there's a massive panorama to give you an idea of the mountain's topography, as well as more utilitarian features such as toilets and potable water. Note that there is no food at all available here.

Two ranger-led hikes are offered daily in summer: a two-hour 'tough' hike starting at noon and heading up the ridge behind the facilities; and an easier one-hour hike down to the river starting at 1pm.

EIELSON TO KANTISHNA

Past Eielson, Park Rd drops to the valley below, passing a sign for Muldrow Glacier (Map p260; Mile 74.4). At this point, the glacier lies about a mile to the south, and the terminus of the 32-mile ice floe is clearly visible, though you might not recognize it because the ice is covered with a mat of plant life. If the weather is cloudy and Mt McKinley and

Denali National Park Entrance Area

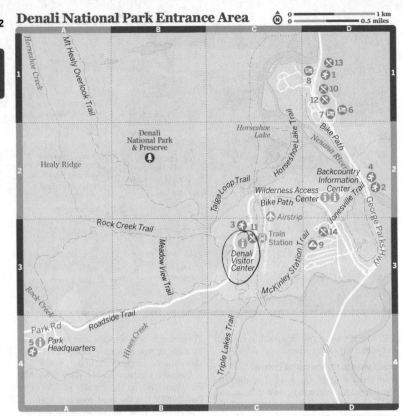

Denali National Park Entrance Area

the surrounding peaks are hidden, the final 20 miles of the bus trip are still an enjoyable ride through rolling tundra and past small glacier-made lakes known as kettle ponds. Study the pools of water carefully to spot beavers or waterfowl.

Wonder Lake Campground (Map p260; Mile 84), only 26 miles from Mt McKinley, sees the beauty of the mountain doubled on a clear day as the peak reflects off the lake's surface. Sadly, the heavy demand for the 28 campsites and the numerous overcast days caused by Mt McKinley itself prevent the majority of visitors from ever seeing this remarkable panorama. If you do experience the reddish sunset on the summit reflecting off the still waters of the lake, cherish the moment.

The campground is on a low rise above the lake's southern end. The famous McKinley-reflected-in-the-lake photos are taken along the northeast shore, 2 miles beyond the campground.

Kantishna (Map p260; Mile 90) is mainly a destination for people staying in the area's private lodges. The buses turn around here after a 40-minute rest, and begin the long trip back to the WAC.

Wildlife Watching
Because hunting has never been allowed in the park, professional photographers refer to animals in Denali as 'approachable wildlife.' That means bear, moose, Dall sheep and caribou aren't as skittish here as in other regions of the state. For this reason, and because Park Rd was built to maximize the chances of seeing wildlife by traversing high open ground, the national park is an excellent place to view a variety of animals.

On board the park shuttle buses, your fellow passengers will be armed with binoculars and cameras to help scour the terrain for animals, most of which are so accustomed to the rambling buses that they rarely run and hide. When someone spots something and yells 'Stop!', the driver will pull over for viewing and picture taking. The best wildlife watching is on the first morning bus.

BEARS
In the area of the park that most people visit (north of the Alaska Range), there are an estimated 350 grizzly bears and an unknown number of black bears. Grizzlies tend to inhabit tundra areas, while black bears stick to the forests. With most of Denali's streams fed by glaciers, the fishing is poor and bears must rely on vegetation for 85% of their diet. As a result, most male grizzlies here range from only 300lb to 600lb, while their cousins on the salmon-rich coasts can easily top 1000lb.

There is no guarantee of seeing a grizzly in the park, but most park bus drivers say

» **May** Wildlife becoming active; vegetation greening up; clear skies and high visibility; tourist and mosquito numbers low; migrant birds arriving

» **June** Caribou, moose and Dall sheep calving; alpine-zone wildflowers blooming

» **July** Bit of everything; everywhere is accessible

» **August** Autumn foliage; blueberries and cranberries are out

» **September** Moose rutting; brilliant autumn foliage; northern lights visible; clear skies and high visibility; tourist and mosquito numbers down again; migrating birds passing through

they spot around five to eight per day along the road.

MOOSE
Anywhere between 2000 and 2500 moose roam the park, and they are almost always found in stands of spruce and willow shrubs (their favorite food). Backpackers should be wary when plowing blindly through areas of thick groundcover, especially in early September, when the bulls clash over breeding rights to the cows.

CARIBOU
All the park's caribou belong to the Denali herd – one of 32 herds in Alaska – which presently numbers around 2000 animals. The best time to spot caribou in large groups is in late summer, when the animals begin to band in anticipation of the fall migration. They are often spotted in earlier summer in small bands on the hillsides. Look for unusual patches of white that just don't seem to belong there.

WOLVES
Consider yourself lucky if you spot a wolf in the park. Denali is home to a fluctuating population, with approximately 70 wolves living in the 10 packs currently being monitored. 'In summer, wolf packs are less likely to travel in a large group because they center their activity around a den or rendezvous site, with one or more adults often remaining there with the pups,' says Park Wildlife Biologist Tom Meier. Your best shot at sighting a wolf is along the Park Rd, or near Igloo Creek Campground.

In addition to moose, caribou, wolves and bears, Denali is home to 33 other species of mammal – from wolverines to mice – as well as 159 varieties of bird (including the golden eagle, tundra swan, rock ptarmigan, jaeger and great horned owl), 10 types of fish and a lone amphibian, the wood frog.

Ranger-Led Activities

If you're hesitant about venturing into the wilds on your own, or merely looking to kill some time until your desired backcountry unit opens, Denali offers a daily slate of worthwhile free ranger-led hikes and presentations.

Sled-Dog Demonstrations   DOGSLEDDING

(Map p262; Park Headquarters; ⊘10am, 2pm & 4pm) Denali is the only US national park where rangers conduct winter patrols via dog team. In summer the huskies serve a different purpose: amusing and educating the legions of tourists who sign up for the park's free daily tours of the sled-dog kennels, and dog demonstrations. The 40-minute show takes place at Park Headquarters; free buses head there from the visitor center, departing 40 minutes before each starting time.

Campground Programs   GUIDED TOURS

At the Riley Creek, Savage River, Teklanika and Wonder Lake campgrounds, rangers present 45-minute talks on Denali's wildlife and natural history or whatever topic they want to expound upon. Talks begin at 7:30pm daily and you're welcome to show up even if you're not camping.

Entrance-Area Hikes   WALKING TOURS

(Map p262) To join a ranger on an easy, guided stroll (ranging from 30 minutes to 2½ hours) along the park's entrance area trails, check out the schedule at the visitor center.

Discovery Hikes   HIKING

These are moderate-to-strenuous, three- to five-hour hikes departing from Park Rd. The location varies from day to day; you can find out the schedule at the visitor center. Sign up there one or two days in advance and then go to the WAC to reserve a shuttle ticket ($31.50). Shuttles leave at 8am. Note that hiking is off-trail so be sure to have sturdy footwear, and to pack rain gear, food and water.

Day Hiking

Even for those who have neither the desire nor the equipment for an overnight trek, hiking is still the best way to enjoy the park and to see the land and its wildlife. You can hike virtually anywhere here that hasn't been closed to prevent an impact on wildlife.

But the park has few established trails outside the entrance area; most hiking is cross-country over open terrain. Nature trails exist at some of the rest stops along Park Rd, and while you won't get lost following these trails, neither will you experience the primal thrill of making your own route across the landscape. A good compromise for those unsure of entering the backcountry on their own is to take a ranger-led Discovery Hike.

For a day hike (which doesn't require a permit), just ride the shuttle bus and get off at any valley, riverbed or ridge that grabs your fancy. Check in at the BIC for suggestions.

Park Entrance Area   HIKING

(Map p262) A few short, well-maintained trails web the park entrance area. The Horseshoe Lake Trail, accessed at Mile 1.2 of Park Rd by the railroad crossing, is a leisurely 1½-mile walk through the woods to the lake overlook, followed by a steep trail to the water's edge and beaver dam at the end. The Taiga Loop Trail, also commencing from the railroad tracks, turns west from the Horseshoe Lake Trail and leads to both Mt Healy Overlook Trail and Rock Creek Trail.

The moderate 2.3-mile Rock Creek Trail leads west to the park headquarters and dog kennels. It's far easier hiking this trail downhill from the headquarters end, where the trail begins just before Park Rd. From here it crosses Rock Creek but doesn't stay with the stream. Instead, it climbs a gentle slope of mixed aspen and spruce forest, breaks out along a ridge with scenic views of Mt Healy and George Parks Hwy, and then begins a rapid descent to its end at the Taiga Trail.

The Roadside Trail parallels Park Rd and takes you 1.5 miles from the visitor center to Park Headquarters. The 1.6-mile McKinley Station Trail takes you from the visitor center to the WAC and also connects with the Jonesville Trail to Canyon.

Triple Lakes Trail   HIKING

(Map p262) When it opened in 2011, this 8.6 mile-long trail (six to eight hours) quickly gained a reputation as the entrance area's best day hike. The terrain and vegetation are more varied than on other trails, and there is a palpable feeling along the way that you have truly entered the wilds. From the McKinley Station Trail the path begins after

The Athabascans called it Denali or the 'Great One.' Their brethren to the south in the Susitna Valley called it Doleika, the 'Big Mountain.' The Aleuts meanwhile referred to it as Traleika. The first European to spot the peak, George Vancouver, didn't bother to call it anything, while Ferdinand von Wrangell, a prominent Russian administrator in the 19th century, wrote Tenada on his maps. So why do we largely know North America's highest peak by the name McKinley?

During the gold rush days, the mountain underwent yet another name change, this time to Densmore's Mountain in honor of a local prospector. But soon afterwards it was dubbed Mt McKinley, after William McKinley, an Ohioan who would soon become president of the United States. And that name seemed to have stuck, at least officially.

But the name 'Denali' slowly began creeping back into people's minds, and finally made the maps in 1980 when the park was redesignated as Denali National Park & Preserve and the Alaskan Geographic Board officially renamed the mountain Denali. Despite these statewide changes, US mapmakers still refer to Denali as McKinley. While it serves as an easy way to differentiate between park and mountain (the reason we left it in this book), it's mainly one stalwart congressman from Ohio, Ralph Regula, who keeps the name from changing. Every time Denali – we mean, um, McKinley – comes up for a name change, the congressman blocks it. But the blocking won't go on for long. Across the US – and the world for that matter – many colonial and European names are being replaced by their original, aboriginal equivalents. Given that William McKinley never even visited Alaska, it seems likely the mountain will one day return to the name it had for centuries before there was such a place as Ohio, or even the USA.

a bridge crossing of Hines Creek. The trail is flat at first and the forest cover unusually lush. In about a mile you begin to climb up switchbacks until eventually reaching a ridgetop affording yodel-inspiring views of the Alaska Range and the valleys formed by Hines Creek and the Nenana River.

After a long run along the ridgeline, the path begins to descend, first to the Triple Lakes and then to George Parks Hwy. After crossing the highway bridge it's a short walk to McKinley Village Lodge, where you can catch a shuttle ($5) back to the visitor center.

Mt Healy Overlook Trail HIKING
(Map p262) The combination good workout and rewarding views over the Nenana River valley, Healy Ridge and other ridgelines makes this another highly popular day hike in the entrance area. The trail veers off the Taiga Loop Trail and makes a steep climb up Mt Healy, ascending 1700ft in 2.5 miles. While you begin in a forest of spruce, alder and aspen, higher up you enter alpine tundra: a world of moss, lichen, wildflowers and incredible views. Keep an eye out for the large hoary marmots (a northern cousin of the groundhog), and the pika, a small relative of the rabbit. Plan on three to four hours for the return hike.

From the overlook (3425ft), hardy hikers can climb another mile to the high point of Healy Ridge (4217ft), or another 2 miles to the summit of Mt Healy (5714ft).

Savage River Loop Trail HIKING
You can get to this trailhead by car (Mile 14), but you are better off taking the free Savage River Shuttle Bus as the small parking lot here often fills up. The 2-mile loop is wheelchair accessible for the first half-mile and runs north from the Park Rd on either side of the river. People looking for a longer hike can continue past the bridge that marks the 'official' turn-around point along an informal trail paralleling the river's west bank.

Mountain Vista to Savage River Trail HIKING
Expected to be completed in 2012, this 5- to 6-mile trail will begin at Mountain Vista (Mile 13) – a new day-use area marking a historic camp – run up the alpine ridgeline to the north and then head west to Savage River.

Backpacking
The park is divided into 87 backcountry units, and for 41 of these only a regulated number of backpackers (usually four to six) are allowed in at a time. You may spend a maximum of seven nights in any one unit, and a maximum of 30 consecutive nights in the backcountry. For more information download *A Denali*

Backpacking Guide from the national park's website (www.nps.gov/dena).

Permits are needed if you want to overnight and you can obtain these at the BIC, where you'll also find wall maps with the unit outlines and a quota board indicating the number of vacancies in each. Permits are issued only a day in advance, and the most popular units fill up fast. It pays to be flexible: decide what areas you're aiming for, and be prepared to take any zone that's open. If you're picky, you might have to wait several days.

After you have decided where to go, the next step is to watch the required backcountry orientation video, followed by a brief safety talk that covers, among other things, proper use of the bear-resistant food containers (BRFCs) you'll receive free of charge with your permit. The containers are bulky, but they work – they've reduced bear encounters dramatically since 1986. It's also worth noting that you're required to pack-out dirty toilet paper (you bury your waste), so be sure to carry at least a dozen ziplock bags. Finally, after receiving your permit, buy the topographic maps ($8) for your unit and then head over to the WAC to purchase a ticket on a camper bus ($29.25) to get you out to the starting point of your hike.

For an overview of the different units in the park, check out the park's website again for the brilliant *Backcountry Camping and Hiking Guide,* which includes unit-by-unit descriptions including access points, possible hiking corridors, dangers and, maybe best of all, pictures from the area. At the BIC office you can also peruse the *Backcountry Companion for Denali National Park* by Jon Nierenberg (Alaska National History Association), which is now out of print.

It's important to realize that Denali's backcountry is a trailless wilderness and you are literally required to blaze your own path. The key to successful backcountry travel is being able to use a compass and read a topographic map. Riverbeds are easy to follow and make excellent avenues for the backpacker. Formed by glaciers during the last ice age, the valleys never fill though individual braids can get dangerously high and fast, and must be forded with caution.

Ridges are also good routes to hike along if the weather isn't foul. The treeline in Denali is at 2700ft, and above that you'll usually find tussock or moist tundra – humps of watery grass that make for sloppy hiking. In extensive stretches of tussock, the hiking has been best described as 'walking on basketballs.' Above 3400ft you'll encounter alpine or dry tundra, which generally makes for excellent trekking. Note that cross-country hikers should not walk in a line; rather, rangers recommend that you fan out to avoid creating trails.

Regardless of where you're headed, remember that 5 miles is a full-day trip for the average backpacker in Denali's backcountry.

The mandate of the BIC is self-discovery, and their rigid restrictions ensure that you (and those after you) will always be able to trek and camp in a piece of untrammeled nature.

Cycling

No special permit is needed to cycle on Park Rd, but cycling off-road is prohibited. Camper buses and some shuttle buses will carry bicycles, but only two at a time and only if you have a reservation. Many cyclists ride the bus in and cycle back out, carrying their gear and staying at campsites they've reserved along the way. It's also possible to take an early-morning bus in, ride for several hours and catch a bus back the same day. The highest point on the road is Highway Pass (3980ft). The entrance area is 1585ft.

Denali Outdoor Center   BICYCLE RENTAL
(Map p262; www.denalioutdoorcenter.com; Mile 238.9, George Parks Hwy) You can rent bicycles at this Canyon fixture for $7 per hour (minimum two-hour rental) or $40 for a full day. Rates include a helmet, water bottle, tools and lock.

Park Mart Store   BICYCLE RENTAL
(Map p262; Mile 238.4, George Parks Hwy) Also in Canyon. Rents out mountain bikes for $30 a day.

☞ Tours

The park shuttle buses are the most common 'tours' along Park Rd, but there are others. The following Park Rd tours include narration by a certified guide; the Natural History tour is probably the most popular. See www.nps.gov/dena for more and www.reservedenali.com for reservations.

Natural History Tour   GUIDED TOUR
Get your fill of all things Denali on this four-to five-hour trip ($64) out to Primrose Ridge (Mile 17).

Tundra Wilderness Tour GUIDED TOUR

This seven- to eight-hour tour ($107.50) to Toklat River (Mile 53) focuses on wildlife viewing.

Kantishna Experience GUIDED TOUR

The longest tour (12 hours, $159), this one goes to the end of the road to the old mining area of Kantishna (Mile 92).

ATVs

Denali ATV Adventures ADVENTURE SPORTS
(Map p262; ☑683-4288; www.denaliatv.com; Mile 247, George Parks Hwy) Offers two- and four-hour butt-busting rides for $95 to $275. Note that you will not be riding in the park.

Flightseeing

Most flightseeing around Denali leaves from Talkeetna, but some companies also operate out of the park area.

Denali Air SCENIC FLIGHTS
(☑683-2261; www.denaliair.com) Charges $250 to $350 for narrated flights of about an hour around the mountain. Flights leave from the company's airstrip at Mile 229.5 of George Parks Hwy.

Era Helicopters SCENIC FLIGHTS
(Map p262; ☑683-2574; www.eraflightseeing. com; Mile 238, George Parks Hwy) Will take you up on a 50-minute Denali tour ($335) or a 75-minute flight that includes a glacier landing ($415). Heli-hiking trips are also available. The helipad is on the northern side of the Nenana River Bridge, at the southern end of Canyon.

Kantishna Air Taxi SCENIC FLIGHTS
(☑683-1223; www.katair.com) Based at Skyline Lodge, flies out of Kantishna, the park entrance and Healy. Hour-long flightseeing excursions around Mt McKinley are $225 per person from Kantishna.

River Rafting

Thanks to Denali Park tourists, the Nenana River is the most popular white-water rafting area in Alaska. The river's main whitewater stretch begins near the park entrance and ends 10 miles north, near Healy. It's rated Class III and IV, and involves standing waves, rapids and holes with names such as 'Coffee Grinder' in sheer-sided canyons. South of the park entrance the river is much milder, but to many it's just as interesting as it veers away from both the highway and the railroad, increasing your chances of sighting wildlife.

Raft companies offer similar guided trips on both stretches in which either the guide does all the work or you help paddle. Advanced reservations (no deposit) are accepted, and all trips include dry suits and shuttle pickups. The canyon and the easier 'wilderness' paddles go for between $75 and $85, and last around two hours.

Denali Outdoor Center RAFTING
(Map p262; ☑683-1925; www.denalioutdoorcenter. com; Mile 238.9, George Parks Hwy) Considered one of the finest rafting outfits, with good equipment, a safety-first philosophy and friendly guides. Also offers half-day excursions and inflatable kayak tours.

Raft Denali RAFTING
(Map p262; ☑800-789-7238; www.raftdenali.com; Mile 238, George Parks Hwy) Also offers trips for families with children as young as five.

Too-loó-uk River Guides RAFTING
(Map p262; ☑683-1542; www.akrivers.com; Mile 239 George Parks Hwy) Affiliated with Denali Mountain Works and runs guided multiday wilderness raft trips across the state. The trips range from five to 10 days and start at $2200 per person.

Courses

Murie Science & Learning Center COURSES
(Map p262; Mile 1.5, Park Rd; www.muriesc.org; ☺9:30am-5pm) Representing eight of Alaska's arctic and subarctic parks, the center is *the* place to come for information on research taking place within the park and around the state. During the summer there are presentations and half-day 'Denaliology' courses, as well as multiday field seminars (coordinated with Alaska Geographic), teacher training and youth camps.

Denali Education Center ADVENTURE TOURS
(☑683-2597; www.denali.org) Offers day and extended educational/backpacking programs, including a number specifically designed for seniors and youth.

Sleeping

You definitely want something reserved in midsummer – even if it's just a campsite – before you show up. Note the Denali Borough charges a 7% accommodations tax on top of the following prices listed (except for campsites).

DENALI FOR CHILDREN

The average age of visitors to Denali National Park is 62, so there is understandably not a heavy focus on programs, talks and activities for kids. The park does sponsor a Junior Ranger program, however, in which children receive a badge after completely a number of challenges. Better are the free Discovery Packs, which include a binder filled with scientific activities and also the tools needed to carry out experiments. Among other fun things, kids can test the water quality of nearby streams and make plaster casts of animal tracks.

The **Murie Science & Learning Center** (Map p262) has a number of hands-on exhibits suitable for children, and a few of the 'Denali-ology' day courses are specifically designed for families with younger children. **Denali Education Center** also has day and multiday youth programs ranging from 'bug camps' (for budding entomologists) to extended backpacking trips.

Note that children 14 and under can ride the park buses free, while 15- to 17-year-olds can purchase a ticket for half-price.

WITHIN THE PARK

Kantishna excepted, lodgings are not available inside park boundaries, so if you want overnight shelter within the park you'll need a tent or RV. The following campgrounds are listed in order along Park Rd.

Riley Creek Campground CAMPGROUND $
(Map p262; Mile 0.2, Park Rd; tent sites $14, campsites $22-28) At the park's main entrance and within earshot of George Parks Hwy, this is Denali's largest and most developed campground. The campground is open year-round and has 146 sites for tents and RVs, piped-in water, flush toilets and evening interpretive programs. Walk-ins have their own section in C lot. The location is convenient for access to Riley Creek Mercantile, the WAC, visitor center and many hikes.

Savage River Campground CAMPGROUND $
(Map p260; Mile 13, Park Rd; campsites $22-28) Despite its name, this is a mile short of the actual river, and close to the new Mountain Vista rest area. It's one of only two campgrounds with a view of Mt McKinley. The 33 sites can accommodate both RVs and tents, with such amenities as flush toilets, piped-in water and evening presentations.

Sanctuary River Campground CAMPGROUND $
(Map p260; Mile 23, Park Rd; tent sites $9) This is the next campground down the road from Savage River and nicely set on the banks of a large glacial river. The seven sites can't be reserved in advance, however, and there's no piped-in water. The area is great for day hiking, though. Head south to trek along the river or climb Mt Wright or Primrose Ridge

to the north for an opportunity to photograph Dall sheep.

Teklanika River Campground CAMPGROUND $
(Map p260; Mile 29, Park Rd; campsites $16) There are 53 sites, flush toilets, piped-in water and evening programs at this campground, popular with tenters, RVers and the occasional wolf or two. You can drive to this campground but you must stay a minimum of three days if you do, and you can't use your vehicle until you're ready to return to the park entrance.

Igloo Creek Campground CAMPGROUND $
(Map p260; Mile 34, Park Rd; tent sites $9) This small, waterless, seven-site camping area marks the beginning of true bear country. The day hiking around here is excellent, especially the numerous ridges around Igloo Mountain and Cathedral that provide routes into alpine areas.

Wonder Lake Campground CAMPGROUND $
(Map p260; Mile 85, Park Rd; tent sites $16) This is the jewel of Denali campgrounds, thanks to its eye-popping views of Mt McKinley. The facility has 28 sites for tents only but does offer flush toilets and piped-in water. If you're lucky enough to reserve a site, book it for three nights and then pray that the mountain appears during one of the days you're there. Also, pack plenty of insect repellent and maybe even a headnet: the bugs are vicious in midsummer.

KANTISHNA

The Park Rd ends at this privately owned island of land, an old gold-mining enclave that was outside the park's original boundary but was enveloped by additions in 1980. Kantishna provides the ultimate lodging location. Many options include meals and round-trip transportation from the park entrance.

Camp Denali
LODGE $$$

(Map p260; 683-2290; www.campdenali.com; s/d cabins without bath per minimum 3-night stay $1645/3090) Verging on legendary, Camp Denali has been the gold standard among Kantishna lodges for the last half-century. Widely spread across the ridgeline, the camp's simple, comfortable cabins elegantly complement the backcountry experience while minimizing impact on the natural world. Think of it as luxury camping, with gourmet meals, guided hikes, free bicycle and canoe rentals, killer views of the mountain, and staff so devoted to Denali that you'll come away feeling like the beneficiary of a precious gift. You can only arrive or depart on Mondays or Fridays, so you'll need to plan accordingly.

North Face Lodge
LODGE $$$

(Map p260; 683-2290; www.campdenali.com; s/d per minimum 3-night stay $1645/3090) Affiliated with Camp Denali and just down the hill, this is a more traditionally appointed lodge complete with bath en suites, cozy lounge with fireplace and library. You gain amenities here, but you lose that extra intimacy with the land that Camp Denali provides. Like Camp Denali, you can only get here or leave on Mondays and Fridays.

Denali Backcountry Lodge
LODGE $$$

(Map p260; 376-1992, 877-233-6254; www.denalilodge.com; s/d incl meals $515/930) The last lodge on the road, this is a great-looking place on the banks of Moose Creek with comfortable modern cabins and common areas. Transport, meals and guided activities are included.

Skyline Lodge
LODGE $$$

(Map p260; 683-1223; www.katair.com; d without bath $235) This four room, solar-powered lodge serves as Kantishna Air Taxi's base of operations. Guests have use of a common area, dining room, bath and shower block, and decks overlooking the Kantishna Valley. Add $40 per person for meals.

Kantishna Roadhouse
LODGE $$$

(Map p260; 800-942-7420; www.kantishnaroadhouse.com; s/d incl meals $535/870) Owned by park concessionaire Doyon, Kantishna Roadhouse has clean modern cabins, a beautiful dining room, bar and guided activities. Room rates include round-trip transport from the park entrance and various guided activities. Note there is a two-day minimum stay.

CANYON

Canyon (Mile 238.5) is certainly a convenient place to stay. The park entrance is just a mile down the road, and there are plenty of places to eat, drink, shop and arrange tours. However, the area (it's not even a town) is in essence a rather characterless sprawl down both sides of the highway.

McKinley Chalet Resort
RESORT $$$

(Map p262; 800-276-7234; www.denaliparkresorts.com; Mile 238.5, George Parks Hwy; r $259-329;) This 42-acre complex is considered the top high-end lodging in the Canyon area, and while it mostly caters to the cruise ship crowd, there is a quiet area down by the river reserved for independent travelers. With multiple food and beverage outlets, an outdoor activity center offering rafting (with its own launch area), cycling and guided hiking, all your life support systems are pretty much in one place. In 2010 the Chalet won a national park eco award for its numerous green initiatives, including water-saving and energy-efficiency programs, and a recycling program for the entire Canyon area.

Crow's Nest
CABIN $$$

(Map p262; 683-2723, 888-917-8130; www.denalicrowsnest.com; Mile 238.5, George Parks Hwy; cabins $202;) Rustic but proud might describe the feel of the Nest rooms, arranged in terraced rows that afford better and better views the higher up you go. Old pictures add a welcome touch to the room design and the top terrace hot tub is a nice treat on those summer nights when it never gets dark. The lodge runs a free shuttle bus into the park from 5am to 10pm.

Denali Park Salmon Bake
Restaurant & Cabins
CABIN $$

(Map p262; 683-7283; www.thebakerocks.com; Mile 238.5, George Parks Hwy; cabins without/with bath $69/145;) Standard cabins come with TVs, heaters and baths, and are on the dingy side of clean. The economy rooms have shared bath and a shingle exterior with a white tarpaulin roof cover, giving the place a bit of a work-camp atmosphere. There's a free 24-hour shuttle to and from the park for guests.

MCKINLEY VILLAGE

Six miles south of the park entrance, McKinley Village (Mile 229–231) sits at a cozy bend of the Nenana River. The area is far less commercialized than Canyon and is served by a courtesy bus ($5) running from 6am to 10pm between McKinley Village Lodge, Canyon, the visitor center and the WAC. If you need to withdraw money, the McKinley Village Lodge has an ATM in the lobby.

Denali Grizzly Bear Resort
CABIN **$**

(Map p260; ✆683-2696; www.denaligrizzlybear.com; Mile 231.1, George Parks Hwy; campsites $24, tent cabins from $30, cabins $65-260; 🛜) This place offers wooded campsites by the Nenana River, platform tent cabins and 23 well-spaced cabins in various configurations. Some cabins are modern and come with private bath, river views and kitchens, while other are genuine historical structures with tons of Alaskan character (including one log cabin that was dismantled and brought in from Fairbanks). There's also a 72-room hotel with river-facing rooms and cabin-like interiors. Communal amenities include hot showers and laundry facilities. The only downside is that the young staff here can be a bit cold.

Denali River Cabins
CABIN **$$**

(✆800-230-7275; www.seedenali.com; Mile 231, George Parks Hwy; cabins incl breakfast $139-215; 🛜) They really pack 'em in here, though the riverfront cabins retain a surprisingly secluded feel and a homey interior that Mom might have designed herself. The veritable rabbit warren that is the site of the main cluster of cabins is likely going to be hit and miss for a good night's sleep depending on your neighbors.

The on-site **restaurant** (⊙lunch & dinner; mains $12-22) serves some mighty fine comfort foods like ribs and pasta.

McKinley Village Lodge
LODGE **$$$**

(Map p260; ✆683 8900; www.denaliparkresorts.com; Mile 231 George Parks Hwy; r $189-254; 🛜) Large grounds set on the banks of the Nenana River and a gorgeous wooden deck for enjoying a drink in the evening are the highlights of this log-cabin-style complex. Rooms sport a liberal use of wood, but overall this is a generic-looking place with online deals making it much more attractive at times. The lodge runs a courtesy shuttle to the Denali Visitor Center, WAC and Canyon. It's free for guests and $5 for everyone else.

CARLO CREEK

Located 12 miles south of the park entrance (Mile 224), this is one of the best places to stay near Denali Park, especially for independent travelers looking for a chilled-out experience that includes a gorgeous mountain backdrop. Most of the businesses here are family run, with some now seeing the second or third generations taking over.

There's good hiking nearby (stop in at the youth hostel to get the lowdown on area tromps), and both the Denali Mountain Morning Hostel and Panorama Pizza Pub offer shuttle service to the park. It's definitely nice to have wheels, though, if you decide to stay here.

Denali Mountain Morning Hostel
HOSTEL **$**

(Map p260; ✆683-7503; www.hostelalaska.com; Mile 224.1, George Parks Hwy; dm/d $32/80, cabins $75-160; 🛜) Perched beside the gurgling Carlo Creek, this is the area's only true hostel. Only open during the summer months, the hostel features a hotchpotch of tent-cabins, log cabins and platform tents. Of course there's a fire pit, and visitors can cook meals and swap tales in the 'octagon' – the hostel's common area. Laundry facilities are available and the hostel offers free shuttle service to/from the WAC four times a day.

⬆TOP CHOICE Carlo Creek Lodge
CABIN **$$**

(Map p260; ✆683-2576; www.denaliparklodging.com; cabins without bath $84-90, with bath $120-145; 🛜@) The 32-acre grounds are treed, the views are grand and the hand-hewn log cabins filled with genuine old Alaskan charm. Now in the hands of the grandson of the original homesteaders who settled this scenic little plot by the creek, the lodge has a fresh feel but still a healthy respect for tradition (Tucker is not replacing those flower print bedspreads for anything.) Communal amenities include a laundry room, spiffy shower block, barbecue and cooking areas.

McKinley Creekside Cabins
CABIN **$$**

(Map p260; ✆683-2277; www.mckinleycabins.com; cabins $139-199; 🛜) This is a friendly, well-run place with the most modern cabins in Carlo Creek. Given that the grounds aren't well treed, it's best to get a creekside cabin so you can enjoy the warble of the water and the wide-open views from your porch. The popular **cafe** (⊙6am-10pm; breakfast $10-12) at the front of the premises serves some tasty home fare, including breakfasts.

KRIS FISTER: PARK RANGER & INTERPRETER

My job is to communicate the park's messages to a broad range of audiences. I have lived in Alaska year-round for over 10 years, and spent an additional six summers as a seasonal park ranger here. I have worked for the National Park Service (NPS) for more than 27 years, most of that time as a park ranger-interpreter.

Don't Miss

No absolutes. If your schedule allows, just get out into the park as far as you can and enjoy the landscape and its inhabitants. I recommend visitors go at least as far as the Eielson Visitor Center at Mile 66. Don't have your heart set on seeing Denali/Mt McKinley – it's the icing on the cake if you do.

Spotting Wildlife

Early or late in the day may be more productive (because it may be too warm for much of the wildlife during the main part of the day). Look for movement, and for colors or shapes that are different from their surroundings (ie that don't fit in). Binoculars are a must – not everything is next to the road.

Top Day Hikes

My favorite hikes vary, depending on the season and my mood. I enjoy hiking the Triple Lakes Trail (all or only partway), along Primrose Ridge, and to various places in Highway and Thorofare passes.

Park Trivia

Denali is known for its charismatic wildlife, but it's perhaps not as well known that thousands of trace fossils (tracks, footprints or body prints) of dinosaurs and other animals who roamed this area 65 to 100 million years ago have been found since the first discovery of a track in 2005.

Best Thing About Working in DNP

I am amazed at what I can see on any given day out along the Park Rd.

Perch Restaurant & Cabins CABIN **$$**
(Map p260; ☑683-2523; www.denaliperchresort.com; cabins without/with bath incl breakfast buffet $85/125; ☞) The best cabins here sit creekside, in particular the stylish A-frame No 3. Shared-bath cabins look to be on slightly too friendly (close) terms with each other. Note that Perch runs a free shuttle bus to/from the park.

HEALY

Healy (Mile 249.5), a pleasant decentralized community about 12 miles north of the park entrance, has a range of lodging options but you'll need your own vehicle if you plan to stay here.

TOP CHOICE EarthSong Lodge CABIN **$$**
(☑683-2863; www.earthsonglodge.com; Mile 4, Stampede Rd; cabins $155-215) North of Healy, off Mile 251, George Parks Hwy, this spotlessly clean lodge is pretty much on its own in green fields above the treeline. The

private-bath cabins have an appealing at-home styling with decorative touches such as sprays of wildflowers and hand-carved ornaments. Breakfast and dinner are available in an adjacent cafe and there are sled-dog demos, a nightly slide show, berry picking in the nearby fields in July and August, and dogsled adventure tours in winter. The lodge is just a short climb away from stunning views of Mt McKinley, and just in case you wanted to know more about that mountain, there's proprietor Jon Nierenberg, a former Denali ranger, who quite literally wrote the book on hiking in the park's backcountry.

Denali Dome Home B&B B&B **$$$**
(☑683-1239, 800-983-1239; www.denalidomehome.com; Mile 0.5, Healy Spur Rd; r with breakfast $190; ☞) This is not a yurt but a huge, intriguing geodesic house on a 5-acre lot offering one of the best B&B experiences in Alaska. There are seven modern rooms (with

partial antique furnishings), an open common area with fireplace, and a small business area. The owners are absolute oracles of wisdom when it comes to Denali Park, and do a bang-up job with breakfast. They also offer car rental.

Otto Lake Cabins & Camping CAMPGROUND $
(☑888-303-1925; Mile.5, Otto Lake Rd; campsites per person $8) This well-treed campground offers lakeside and ridgetop sites, as well as a few walk-ins. There are beautiful views of the lake and surrounding hill country, a clean shower block ($4), canoe and bicycle rentals (per hour $8), and a resident moose who may just stick his head in your tent for a visit during the night. To get here, turn west at Mile 247, George Parks Hwy onto Otto Lake Rd and look for the Denali Outdoor Center sign.

✖ Eating & Drinking

Groceries are limited and expensive in the Denali Park area, so stock up in Fairbanks, Anchorage or Wasilla before coming here. Inside the park itself there are no restaurants except the Morino Grill. Luckily, the neighboring towns are not far apart, so there's a good variety of eating and drinking options to choose from.

WITHIN THE PARK
Morino Grill BURGERS $$
(Map p262; Mile 1.5, Park Rd; mains $8-11; ⊙11am-6pm; 🗟) This cafeteria-style establishment is the only eatery within the park. It has burgers, paninis and veggie chili, as well as seafood chowder and reindeer stew. There's a cafe and to-go section at the front but the sandwiches are pricier than at the Mercantile.

Riley Creek Mercantile DELI $
(Map p262, Mile 0.2, Park Rd; ⊙7am-11pm; 🗟) Next to the Riley Creek Campground, the mercantile has a decent selection of groceries, as well as fresh coffee, deli sandwiches and wraps. There's also a small selection of camping supplies such as gas, headnets and trail mix.

Wilderness Access Center SNACK SHOP $
(Map p262; Mile 0.5, Park Rd; ⊙5am-7pm; 🗟) The center has a limited array of backpacker-oriented foods and snacks.

CANYON
Prospectors Pizzeria & Ale House PIZZERIA $$
(Map p262; http://prospectorspizza.com; Mile 238.9, George Parks Hwy; ⊙11am-11pm, bar to 1am; pizza $16-28, sandwiches $12-14) Set in the Old Northern Lights Theatre building, this cavernous alehouse-cum-pizza parlor has quickly become one of the most popular eating establishments in the park area; if Canyon seems empty, check here. In addition to a menu with two-dozen oven-baked pizza choices there are some 50 beers available on tap from almost all of Alaska's small breweries.

Black Bear Coffee House CAFE $
(Map p262; Mile 238.5, George Parks Hwy; sandwiches $10; 🗟) Under the direction of the new ownership, the Bear now stresses 'organic coffee and free wireless.' This funky place also has deli sandwiches, soups and some really nice pastries (made on-site).

Overlook Bar & Grill BURGERS $$
(Map p262; ☑683-2723; www.denalicrowsnest.com; Mile 238.5, George Parks Hwy; mains $23-35; 🗟) Situated across from the Crow's Nest cabins, there is an appealing roughhewn vibe to this place. Burgers (from $13) are the specialty but anything tastes good when matched with those valley views. If you're looking for a party, come here after midnight when the bar is taken over by seasonal workers and locals. There's a free shuttle bus from 5am to 10pm.

Denali Salmon Bake ALASKAN $$
(Map p262; ☑683-7283; www.thebakerocks.com; Mile 238.5, George Parks Hwy; burgers $16, mains $19-29; ⊙7am-11pm) The Bake offers some quirky starters like Yak-a-dilla (locally raised yak quesadilla) and a well-regarded halibut and chips. The bar is open 24/7 and there's a free 24-hour shuttle.

Park Mart Store SELF-CATERING $
(Map p262; Mile 238.4, George Parks Hwy; ⊙7am-10pm) This gas-station-cum-convenience-store-cum-liquor-store has a decent range of groceries. There's a farmers market on Wednesday and Saturday, daily bicycle rentals ($30 per day) and an ATM.

MCKINLEY VILLAGE
TOP CHOICE 229 Parks ORGANIC $$$
(Map p260; ☑683-2567; www.229parks.com; Mile 229, George Parks Hwy; dinner $24-34; ⊙8-11am & 5-10pm Tue-Sun) South of McKinley Village, this stylish timber-frame hideaway is quintessentially modern Alaskan: locally owned, organic and fervently committed to both the community and environment. Everything is made on-site including the bread and butter, and the menu changes daily, though it

usually features local game dishes and a veritable cornucopia of vegetarian options. And don't worry if you can't finish every mouthful: scraps go to feed local sled dogs. Reservations are definitely recommended here.

CARLO CREEK

Perch Restaurant & Cabins   AMERICAN $$

(Map p260; 683-2523; www.denaliperchresort.com; breakfast $8-9, dinner mains $14-26; breakfast & dinner) It's called the Perch for a reason, as the restaurant sits high on a moraine above Carlo Creek, with an almost eye-level view of the surrounding peaks. It's just a quick jaunt from the highway, however, and on a sunny day a meal or drink on the deck should be mandatory. Perch serves great steaks and salmon dishes, and has a decent wine and Alaskan beer selection. There's a free shuttle to and from the park.

Panorama Pizza Pub   PIZZERIA $$

(Map p260; Mile 224, George Parks Hwy; 12in pizzas $16-18; 3pm-midnight) This Carlo Creek eatery was once the family's gift shop but now offers good beer, burgers and pizza pies, with midsummer salads coming from a Healy-based organic grower. Later at night the place becomes more 'pub' than 'pizzeria' with locals, travelers and seasonal workers congregating for live music, open mike and pub quizzes. Panorama shares a free shuttle with Perch Restaurant so you can get here even if you aren't staying in Carlo Creek. If he's around, ask Josh why he opens at the odd hour of 3pm.

HEALY

Rose's Café   DINER $$

(Mile 249.5, George Parks Hwy; mains $10-15; 6:30am-10pm;) This classic breakfast, burger-and-pie joint is your best bet in town. The covered outdoor seating area out the back and authentic diner-style counter seating adds to its *Nighthawks*-meets-*Easy Rider* appeal.

Miner's Market & Deli   DELI $

(Mile 248.4, George Parks Hwy; 24hr) A surprisingly good selection of groceries (including fresh produce) can be purchased at this market attached to a gas station. The deli (6am-3pm) even sells breakfast, sandwiches and Prospectors Pizzeria slices.

☆ Entertainment

Many of the area's restaurants double up as bars and feature live music, open mikes, karaoke nights and the like during the week.

Check out the Denali Salmon Bake, Prospectors Pizzeria & Ale House, and Panorama Pizza Pub.

49th State Brewing Company   BREWERY

(www.49statebrewing.com; Mile 248.4, George Parks Hwy; 3pm-late) One of the latest breweries to hit the Alaskan handcrafted scene, Healy-based 49th State holds nightly events in its attached restaurant/bar and twice a month large outdoor concerts on its front grounds. Although the brewery advertises that it displays the famous *Into the Wild* bus, it's the one from the Sean Penn–directed movie not the real one Chris McCandless died in.

🖉 Charles Sheldon Center   CULTURAL CENTER

(www.denali.org; 9am-6pm) At the back of the McKinley Village Lodge in McKinley Village, this community center holds local talks and speeches, art shows and theatrical and musical performances, all designed to 'inspire personal connections to Denali.'

🛍 Shopping

Denali Bookstore   BOOKS

(Mile 1.5, Park Rd; 9am-7pm) Across from the Denali Visitor Center. It has field guides, topographic maps, coffee-table books and Alaskan literature.

Denali Mountain Works   OUTDOOR EQUIPMENT

(Mile 239, George Parks Hwy; 9am-9pm) This jam-packed Canyon store sells camping gear, clothing and pretty much anything you'd need for a few days in the backcountry. It also rents out tents, stoves and other outdoor gear, and has dehydrated meals.

ℹ Information

INTERNET ACCESS Wireless is widely available in restaurants and lodgings. Riley Creek Mercantile has strong wireless and outlets outside for plugging in laptops. If you sit in the laundry room you can avoid the mosquitoes.

LAUNDRY Riley Creek Mercantile (683-9246; Mile 0.2, Park Rd; 7am-11pm) Showers ($4) and coin-op laundry facilities.

MEDICAL SERVICES Canyon Clinic (683-4433; Mile 238.8, George Parks Hwy; 9am-6pm) Only open during summer months but on call 24 hours.

Healy Clinic (683-2211; Healy Spur Rd) In the Tri-Valley Community Center, 13 miles north of the park and a half-mile east of George Parks Hwy.

MONEY There are ATMs in McKinley Chalet and Denali Salmon Bake. The closest full-service bank is in Healy.

Park Mart Store (⊙7am-10pm) In the heart of Canyon, this gas-station-cum-grocery-store-cum-liquor-store has an ATM.

TELEPHONE You can get cell phone reception up to Mile 5 on the Park Rd.

TOURIST INFORMATION Backcountry Information Center (BIC; Mile 0.5, Park Rd; ⊙9am-6pm) If you want to overnight in Denali's backcountry, you'll need to come to the BIC, just across the parking lot from the WAC.

Denali Visitor Center (www.nps.gov/dena; Mile 1.5, Park Rd; ⊙8am-6pm) The place to come for an executive summary of Denali National Park, with quality displays on the area's natural and human history. Every half-hour in the theater the beautifully photographed, unnarrated film *Heartbeats of Denali* provides a peek at the park's wildlife and scenery. You can also pick up a selection of park literature here, including the NPS' indispensable *Alpenglow* booklet, which functions as a user's manual to Denali.

Wilderness Access Center (WAC; Mile 0.5, Park Rd; ⊙5am-7pm) There's a general-purpose info desk, cafe, snack and gear shop, but the WAC's main function is as the park's transport hub and campground-reservation center. Pay your park-entrance fee here (except interagency, handicapped and senior passes, which are purchased at the visitor center).

ⓘ Getting Around

You'll find the area between Canyon and McKinley Village well served by public transport. North or south of there you may need your own car, though Denali Mountain Morning Hostel in Carlo Creek now provides limited transport to the WAC, as does Panorama Pizza Pub. Within the park itself is a good system of free and paid shuttle buses.

Within the Park

SHUTTLE BUSES Shuttle buses are big, clunky school-bus-style affairs aimed at wildlife watchers and day hikers, with the occasional bus also carrying bicycles in. The drivers are concessionaire employees, not NPS naturalists, but most provide unofficial natural history information en route. Day hikers don't need a backcountry permit and can get off anywhere (and multiple times) along Park Rd. After hiking, flag down the next bus that comes along and produce your bus-ticket stub. Due to space considerations, you might have to wait a bus or two during peak season. The bus to Wonder Lake heads into the park as early as 5:45am but the usual ones to Toklat or Eielson start running around 7am. The last return bus (from Eielson) leaves around 6:30pm; check carefully when the last bus from your destination returns. Also note the exact schedule changes

every year. It's wise to reserve a seat as far in advance as possible. The cost varies, and there are three-for-two passes, allowing three days of travel for the price of two. Sample fares include Savage River (Mile 14; free), Polychrome Pass (Mile 47; $24.50), Toklat River (Mile 53; $24.50), Eielson Visitor Center (Mile 66; $31.50), Wonder Lake (Mile 85; $43.25) and Kantishna ($47.25).

CAMPER BUSES Camper buses ferry overnight campers, backpackers and cyclists, offering ample space to stow gear. To take these buses you must have a campsite or backcountry unit reserved along Park Rd, or be toting a bicycle. If you don't have a campground booking, you can't ride *in* on the camper bus, but you can probably hitch a ride *back* on one. The buses cost $31.50 to anywhere along the road. As with shuttle buses, it's good to reserve as far ahead as possible.

COURTESY BUSES & SHUTTLES The free **Riley Creek Loop Bus** makes a circuit through the park entrance area, picking up at the visitor center every half-hour and stopping at the Murie Science & Learning Center, Horseshoe Lake trailhead, WAC, Park Headquarters and Riley Creek Campground. The park also has a free Dog Sled Demo Bus, which departs the visitor center en route to the Park Headquarters 40 minutes before each show.

Outside the Park

Many restaurants and lodges run their own shuttle buses, which means you can get about reasonably well without your own vehicle. Some charge $5 while others are free if you are staying or eating (or if the driver can't be bothered to charge you). Some also have regular pickups, while others will come for any potential customer at any time. Check the listings in Sleeping and Eating & Drinking for shuttles to your destination and also inquire at the WAC.

TAXI If you need one, try **Caribou Cab** (⌨683-5000) based in Healy.

ⓘ Getting There & Away

Located on George Parks Hwy, about four hours north of Anchorage and two hours south of Fairbanks, Denali is easy to access without your own vehicle.

BUS Both northbound and southbound bus services are available from Denali National Park. **Alaska Bus Guy** (⌨720 6541; www.alaskabusguy.com) departs Denali at 1pm for both Anchorage ($75, 4½ hours) and Fairbanks ($75, 2½ hours), and will make a stop anywhere along the Glenn Parks Hwy. **Alaska/Yukon Trails** (⌨800-770-7275; www.alaskashuttle.com) offers southbound buses that pick up in major Canyon hotels, the visitor center and WAC around noon, reaching Anchorage ($75) by 6:30pm. There are drops at several locales in Anchorage, including the youth hostels and airport (for $7 more). Northbound buses leave Denali around noon and arrive in Fairbanks ($55, $7 extra to airport) at 4pm. **Denali Transportation** ([✆]683-4765) offers shuttle service in and around Denali. **Park Connection** ([✆]800-266-8625; www.alaskacoach.com) runs two buses a day from major Canyon hotels to Anchorage ($80/90, 7:30am/2pm) and one a day to Seward ($145, 7:45am). From Anchorage, buses leave at 7am and 3pm for Denali.

TRAIN The most enjoyable way to arrive or depart from the park is aboard the **Alaska Railroad** ([✆]265-2494; www.alaskarailroad. com), with its viewing-dome cars that provide sweeping views of Mt McKinley and the Susitna and Nenana River valleys along the way. All trains arrive at the depot beside the visitor center, only staying long enough for passengers to board. The northbound train departs from Denali at 3.55pm and reaches Fairbanks at 8pm. The southbound train departs Denali at 12:25pm and gets into Anchorage at 8pm. The one-way fare to/from Anchorage starts at $146; to/from Fairbanks is $64. Note that the trip between Denali and Fairbanks is mostly flat and uninspiring.

GEORGE PARKS HIGHWAY

This ribbon of highway, drizzled ever so lovingly over vast stretches of wilderness, offers up one of Alaska's top road journeys. From a beginning at the junction with Glenn Hwy (35 miles north of Anchorage), the Parks Hwy runs 327 miles to Fairbanks, Alaska's second largest city. Along the way it's a veritable Denali Alley with a state park, national park and highway all named after the Great One. And while there's no doubt what everyone's final destination is, the rest is no mere sideshow. There are views that won't be outdone later, a half-dozen local favorite hikes and paddles, and one spunky former boomtown that's now most everyone's idea of a good time.

Mileposts along the highway indicate distances from Anchorage. Wasilla, at Mile 42.2, is covered in the Anchorage & Around chapter (p184).

Nancy Lake State Recreation Area

Located along the Nancy Lake Parkway, jutting off George Parks Hwy at Mile 67.3, this state recreation area (www.dnr.alaska.

gov/parks; day-use $5) is one of Alaska's few flat, lake-studded parks, offering camping, fishing, canoeing and hiking. Although it lacks the dramatic scenery of the country to the north, the 22,685-acre area can be peaceful on weekdays – and thronging with Anchorage and Mat-Su residents on weekends. Download a map of the park from the website as the area can be confusing.

🏃 Activities

Paddling

Lynx Lake Loop   CANOEING

The Lynx Lake Loop is the most popular canoe trail in the park. This two-day, 16-mile trip takes you to 14 lakes and over an equal number of portages. The route begins and ends at the posted trailhead for the Tanaina Lake Canoe Trail at Mile 4.5 of the parkway. The portages are well marked, and many of them are planked where they cross wet sections. The route includes 12 backcountry campsites, accessible only by canoe, but bring a camp stove because campfires are prohibited in the backcountry.

Rent canoes through the long-established Tippecanoe Rentals ([✆]495-6688; www.paddlealaska.com), which has a rental shed at South Rolly Lake Campground and also has canoes right at the start of the Lynx Lake paddle and Red Shirt Lake. Rates begin at $20 for an eight-hour day, and go up to $75 for a four to seven day rental. Note that the park adds a $12 fee to each rental.

Hiking

Red Shirt Lake Trail   HIKING

(Mile 6.5 Nancy Lake Pkwy) The park's main hiking route is the Red Shirt Lake Trail, which begins at the entrance of the South Rolly Lake Campground at the end of the parkway. It leads 3 miles south, primarily on high ground, and along the way you'll pass Red Shirt Overlook, offering scenic views of the surrounding lake country and the Chugach Mountains on the horizon.

The trail ends at Red Shirt Lake's northern end. There are backcountry campsites along the lake and Tippecanoe Rentals keeps boats here (reserve at South Rolly Lake Campground).

🛏 Sleeping

The recreation area offers two campgrounds accessible by road, many backcountry campsites and 13 public-use cabins (per night $45 to $60) spread around the park. Reserve the latter through the Alaska Division of Parks

(☎745-3975; www.dnr.alaska.gov/parks/cabins/matsu.htm; Mile 0.7, Bogard Rd), online or in person at its Wasilla office.

South Rolly Lake Campground
CAMPGROUND $

(campsites $10) This drive-in campground has 98 secluded sites and is large enough that you stand a good chance of finding an open site, even on the weekend.

Nancy Lake State Recreation Site
CAMPGROUND $

(campsites $10) Just off George Parks Hwy south of the entrance to the parkway, this is the only other vehicle-accessible campground. There's little privacy between the 30 sites, however, and there's no pretty lake view.

Talkeetna

POP 1062

This peppery little town at the end of the road was once the quintessential off-the-grid Alaskan community. Today it's the most visited town on the road from Anchorage to Fairbanks, with the biggest draw its proximity to that other star local attraction, Mt McKinley. Among alpinists, Talkeetna is famed as the staging area for ascents of the 'Great One.' For everyone else, it's a place to get into the wilds without breaking a sweat: Talkeetna offers some of Alaska's best flightseeing and fishing, as well as fun rafting, cycling and hiking. Finally, a bevy of interesting characters are usually around at night to share a growler with in the clapboard-fronted watering holes on Main St.

Despite the tourism numbers, Talkeetna retains a palpable community spirit, evident in the careful preservation of historical buildings, and in the desire to keep the town's cultural life abuzz with frequent music concerts and live theater. So drop by, stay the night and dive into the syncopated cultural landscape that still makes the town unique.

Talkeetna is reached by turning at Mile 98.7 of George Parks Hwy onto the Talkeetna Spur Rd. This 14-mile paved road ends at the junction with Main St. The train station depot is off a side road about a half-mile south of town and the airport is almost due east off 2nd St. While there are a few visitor services dotting the spur road, almost everything you'll need is within a stone's throw of Main St, which begins with a 'Welcome to Beautiful Downtown Talkeetna' sign at the park and ends a few blocks later at the riverbank.

History

Though famed for its proximity to the mountains, Talkeetna sits in flat, lushly wooded country near the confluence of the Susitna, Talkeetna and Chulitna Rivers (the town gets its name from a Tanaina word meaning 'river of plenty').

Talkeetna began as a supply center for gold miners working the Susitna River region at the turn of the 20th century. It boomed during the building of the railroad from Seward to Fairbanks. In 1914 Congress agreed to fund the building of the USA's northernmost railroad, and at the peak of construction, 4500 workers labored along the route. Their base camps, such as Talkeetna, became boomtowns. Much of this legacy is still visible in the town center, with its collection of log cabins and two-story buildings with clapboard facades.

Talkeetna's population declined after the railway was finished, and dwindled once again after the nearby ores were mined to near depletion. New life was injected after the construction of the Talkeetna Spur Rd, which brought a flood of climbers and tourists that shows no sign of ever slowing down.

◎ Sights & Activities

Talkeetna Historical Society Museum
MUSEUM

(admission $3; ⊙10am-6pm) A block south of Main St, look for this small complex of restored buildings that includes the town's 1936 schoolhouse, a fully furnished trapper's cabin and train depot. There are exhibits devoted to Don Sheldon (the bush pilot who pioneered landing climbers on Mt McKinley to cut down on hiking time), as well as trapping and mining artifacts.

Pick up the museum brochure *Talkeetna's Historic Walking Tour* if you want to head out on your own and explore more old buildings around town.

Mountaineering Ranger Station
VISITOR CENTER

(☎733-2231; cnr 1st & B Sts; ⊙8am-5:30pm) Whether you're intrigued by high-altitude alpinism or boggled by it, this ranger station provides an excellent window into that rarefied world. In addition to coordinating the numerous expeditions to Mt McKinley during the spring and summer, the station functions as a visitor center, with maps, books, photos and video presentations about the Alaska Range. Ranger-led activities begin daily at 1:30am and 1pm.

Hurricane Turn Train TRAIN

Sometimes called the 'Local' or the 'Bud Car,' this flagstop train (one of the last still running in America) provides a local rural service from Thursday through Sunday (and some major holidays) in the summertime. Departure from Talkeetna is at 12:15pm for the trip north to Hurricane Gulch, where the train turns around and heads back the same day. This 'milk run' takes you within view of Mt McKinley and into some remote areas, and because the train goes slower and is less noisy than the *Denali Star,* your chances of spotting wildlife are greater. You also have a better opportunity to mingle with local residents. The round-trip adult fare for the 5½-hour (100-mile) journey is $96.

Hiking & Cycling

One of the easiest but most scenic walks in the area begins at the end of Main St on the sandy banks of the Talkeetna River. There are stunning views across the waterway of Mt McKinley on a clear day.

Just south of town, a cycling/walking route parallels the Talkeetna Spur Rd almost 14 miles back to the Glenn Parks Hwy. At Mile 12 (2 miles south of town), the road begins to climb and behind you McKinley suddenly fills up half the sky.

Just a little further is the turn for Comsat Rd, which quickly leads to the Talkeetna Lakes Park Day-Use Area offering short hikes around X and Y Lakes.

From the lakes you can either retrace your route back to town or continue up Comsat Rd and take the first left at Christiansen Lake Rd. In a short while, you'll pass Christiansen Lake (where you can swim) and then reach a dead end with a lookout over the river flats and, if you're lucky, McKinley in the distance.

The trail past the stop sign leads to Beaver Rd, which eventually runs into F St. You can follow this road back to the Talkeetna Spur Rd just south of town. Pick up a copy of *Talkeetna Town & Trail Map* for a rough map of this and other routes.

Tours

Flightseeing

When in Talkeetna, it is pretty much mandatory to go flightseeing around nearby Mt McKinley, both because it is an intrinsically exhilarating experience and because flights are actually cheaper when taken from here than they can be found from within Denali National Park. There are four local operations, all well established, all similar with regards to safety, professionalism and price, and all recipients of fawning reviews from their customers.

Decide what sort of trip works best for you and ask the right questions before you sign up. Plan on spending anywhere from around $195 to $360 per person for a flight, depending on the length (usually between one and two hours) and whether you want to land on a glacier or circle the summit. For fly fishing and wildlife tours, contact Alaska Bush & Float Plane (☎733 1693; Mile 9, Spur Rd).

The following companies all have their offices near the airstrip, a short jaunt across the railroad tracks from downtown, and also on Main St toward the end near the river.

K2 Aviation SCENIC FLIGHTS
(☎733-2291; www.flyk2.com)

Talkeetna Aero Services SCENIC FLIGHTS
(☎733-2899; www.talkeetnaaero.com)

Talkeetna Air Taxi SCENIC FLIGHTS
(☎733-2218; www.talkeetnaair.com)

Sheldon Air Service SCENIC FLIGHTS
(☎733-2321; www.sheldonairservice.com)

Fishing

Fishing around Talkeetna is amazing, with runs of every species of Pacific salmon plus grayling, rainbow trout and Dolly Varden.

Phantom Salmon Charters FISHING
(☎733-2328; phantomsalmon@mtaonline.net) Contact Rhett Nealis.

Denali Southside Fishing Guides FISHING
(☎733-7238; www.denaliriverguides.com) Contact Pauly about fishing for rainbow trout and grayling.

Nature & River Tours

Talkeetna River Guides RAFTING
(☎733-2677; www.talkeetnariverguides.com; Main St) To get out onto Talkeetna's many nearby waterways, sign up with Talkeetna River Guides, who'll put you in a raft for a placid two-hour float on the Talkeetna River ($79) or a four-hour float on the Chulitna River, through Denali State Park ($115).

SCALING THE MOUNTAIN

So, has gazing at lordly Mt McKinley from the seat of an aircraft infected you with summit fever?

If so, you're suffering from a century-old sickness. James Wickersham, the US district judge in Alaska, made the first documented attempt to scale Denali, reaching the 7500ft mark of the 20,320ft peak in 1903. His effort inspired a rash of ensuing bids, including Dr Frederick Cook's 1906 effort (which he falsely claimed was a success) and the 1910 Sourdough Expedition, where four Fairbanks miners, carrying only hot chocolate, doughnuts and a 14ft spruce pole, topped out on the North Peak only to realize it was 850ft lower than the true, more southerly summit.

Success finally came in 1913 when Hudson Stuck, Henry Karstens, Robert Tatum and Walter Harper reached the top on June 7. From there they saw the spruce pole on the North Peak to verify the claims of the Sourdough Expedition.

The most important date for many climbers, however, is 1951. That year, Bradford Washburn arrived and pioneered the West Buttress route, by far the preferred avenue to the top. Not long after, Talkeetna's two most famous characters – Ray 'the Pirate' Genet and Don Sheldon – began to have an impact on the climbing world. Genet was an Alaskan mountaineer who made a record 25 climbs up Mt McKinley, while Sheldon was a legendary glacier pilot. The two worked closely in guiding climbers to the top and, more importantly, rescuing those who failed. Sadly, the town lost both in quick succession, with Sheldon dying of cancer in 1975 and Genet freezing to death on Mt Everest four years later.

Nowadays, Denali's storied mountaineering history adds considerably to the mythic business of scaling the peak. Between 1200 and 1300 climbers attempt it each year, spending an average of three weeks on the slopes. About 80% use the West Buttress route, which involves flying in a ski plane from Talkeetna to the 7200ft Kahiltna Glacier and from there climbing for the South Peak, passing a medical/rescue camp maintained by mountaineering clubs and the NPS at 14,220ft.

In a good season (April through July), when storms are not constantly sweeping across the range, more than 50% will be successful. In a bad year that rate falls below 40%, and several climbers may die. Particularly grim was the *annus horribilis* of 1991, when 11 lives were lost.

The most solemn way to appreciate the effect of the mountain is to visit the cemetery in Talkeetna, a restful spot set among tall trees on 2nd St, just off Talkeetna Spur Rd near the airport. Don Sheldon's grave is the most prominent, with the epitaph 'He wagered with the wind and won.' The Mt McKinley Climber's Memorial includes a stone for Ray Genet, despite the fact that his body was never removed from the slopes of Mt Everest. The most touching sight, however, is a memorial with the names and ages of all the climbers who've died on Mt McKinley and neighboring peaks.

If you're a seasoned alpinist you can mount an expedition yourself, or be among the 25% of Mt McKinley climbers who are part of guided ascents. If you're looking for a local guiding company, contact **Alaska Mountaineering School** (www.climbalaska.org), which charges $6300 to lead you up the mountain.

Folks without high-altitude credentials would be better off opting for one of the company's one-, two- or three-day glacier treks on the shoulders of the mountain – a fine way to get a taste of what the mountaineers endure, but at an altitude that isn't life-threatening. These excursions cost from $1090, which covers the glacier flight and all the gear you'll need for the experience of a lifetime. The school also offers mountaineering and glacier-travel courses ranging from $375 for a two-day glacier-travel seminar at Matanuska Glacier to $2800 for an intensive 12-day course.

Alaska Nature Guides GUIDED TOURS
(☑733-1237; www.alaskanatureguides.com) Offers nature walking tours around Talkeetna ($59), and can arrange for custom trips, focusing mainly on hiking and birding.

🛏 Sleeping

The Matanuska-Susitna Borough charges a 5% accommodations tax on top of the following prices.

Meandering Moose Lodge · LODGE $$

(☑733-1000; www.meandering-moose-lodging.com; 14677 E Cabin Spike Ave; cabins with breakfast $80-160; B&B r with breakfast $80-145; 🛜) Sitting a couple of miles northeast from the center of town, this collection of cabins nicely balances rustic charm and creature comforts. Private log cabins can hold up to 10 people (there's lots of extra space in funky hideaway lofts), and feature full kitchens and bathrooms (except the lowest priced ones which share). The B&B cabin features modern rooms, a shared living space and kitchen, and an interior design that wouldn't be out of place in a high-end suburb.

The lodge has bicycles for rent (and is just minutes away from an extensive trail system), and across the street is a private pond that guests can use for swimming. It's a bit tricky to get here the first time so ask the owners to pick you up or meet in town.

Talkeetna Roadhouse · HISTORIC HOTEL $

(☑733-1351; www.talkeetnaroadhouse.com; Main St; dm/d/tr $21/65/95, 4-person cabins $125; 🛜) The real Alaskan deal, this roadhouse dates from 1917 and maintains seven small private rooms, a bunkroom and a couple of rustic cabins out back. In keeping with the old-time setting, it's shared bath all the way, though the antique-strewn sitting room does offer free wi-fi. In early summer expect to see scores of climbers coming in and out the doors.

The Roadhouse also operates the fully equipped **Trapper John's Cabin** ($137) down the road.

Talkeetna Hostel International · HOSTEL $

(☑733-4678; www.talkeetnahostel.com; I St; tent sites/dm/s/d/cabin $12/22/50/65/50; @🛜) Popular with climbers and backpackers alike, this well-loved hostel has a converted VW van ($35) you can sleep in as well as a busy dorm, private rooms and makeshift campground on the back lawn. There's a large common area and kitchen, laundry, free internet, and the occasional fire for swapping tales and fighting the mozzies.

To get here, take 2nd St (the airport road) off Talkeetna Spur Rd; you'll pass I St on the way to the runway at the end of the road. The hostel is just up the road on the right.

Talkeetna Alaskan Lodge · LODGE $$$

(☑733-9500; www.talkeetnalodge.com; Mile 12.5, Talkeetna Spur Rd; r $279-409) This high-end Alaska Native Corporation–owned lodge has a hillside setting that could hardly offer more perfect views of the Alaska Range. Rooms are spacious and quietly stylish, and cruise-ship and noncruise-ship guests are housed in different buildings (for the quiet and comfort of the individual traveler). This is a place to enjoy good service and fine surroundings, but in an atmosphere as relaxed as a roadside diner.

The lodge can arrange almost any activity you care for in Talkeetna, from flightseeing to dogsled tours. Check the website for frequent room deals.

River Park Campground · CAMPGROUND $

(tent sites $10) This informal place (with self check-in) at the end of Main St is a bit shrouded campground, but close to the river and the action. No RVs.

Talkeetna Boat Launch & Campgrounds · CAMPGROUND $

(☑733-2604; campsites $20) East of the tracks at the north end of F St, this tree-shrouded campground offers sites near the Talkeetna River and has restrooms, showers ($4) and a small store. It's best to have your own vehicle if you want to stay here.

Fairview Inn · HISTORIC HOTEL $

(☑733-2423; Main St; r without bath $55) Above the bar, the tiny but brightly painted flophouse rooms are first come, first served.

Latitude 62 Lodge/Motel · HOTEL $

(☑733-2262; Mile 13.5, Talkeetna Spur Rd; s/d $75/85.50) The restaurant and bar may have hunting-lodge decor but the rooms are small and characterless. Better is the cabin for two ($130) in the center of town.

🍴 Eating

You won't go hungry for food or choice in Talkeetna, and just to make it easy, almost everything is crowded onto a few blocks off Main St.

Talkeetna Roadhouse · BREAKFAST $

(Main St; breakfast $9-14, dishes $5-7; ⊘breakfast, lunch, dinner; 🛜) This venerable, colorful establishment has the best breakfast in town. Half-orders are adequate; full orders are mountain-sized. The restaurant also doubles as a bakery, cooking up giant cinnamon rolls in the morning, and lasagna, pasties and salads during the day. The long table seating is great for meeting other guests and travelers.

Talkeetna Alaskan Lodge
SEAFOOD $$

(Mile 12.5, Talkeetna Spur Rd; burgers & sandwiches $10-15, dinner mains $22-35; ⏱lunch & dinner) With prices comparable to most eateries in town, but with a jaw-dropping view of McKinley and the Alaska Range from the elevated deck, it's well worth taking the shuttle or walking out here for a meal. The restaurant offers both fine dining (centered on fresh fish) and casual roadhouse fare, a good selection of fine wines and handcrafted beer, and live music on the deck once a week.

Mountain High Pizza Pie
PIZZERIA $

(www.mhpp.biz; Main St; pizza slices from $3.50, sandwiches $5.50-10.50; ⏱11am-10pm; 🛜♿) Casual and quirky (Buddhist-inspired tie-dye hangings and knotted wood sculptures adorn the walls), this pizzeria-cum-diner delivers the melted-cheese goods. The outdoor seating area seems a bit of an afterthought, but it's popular with those looking to down some Alaskan microbrews with their grub.

West Rib Pub & Grill
BURGERS $$

(Main St; burgers & sandwiches $9.95-15.95; ⏱noon-2am) Located at the back of Nagley's Store, this is a really terrific place to soak in Talkeetna's chilled out live-and-let-live vibe, rubbing shoulders with visitors and locals alike. It's got burgers, salmon and halibut, plenty of craft brews and, if it's sunny, outdoor seating.

Wildflower Café
SANDWICHES $$

(Main St; sandwiches $16, mains $29-35; ⏱11am-9pm) Yummy burgers, grilled salmon sandwiches, large wholesome mains and a deck facing Main St are just a few reasons this place is constantly abuzz with diners. There's also a good salad menu selection if you need to fill up on greens.

Nagley's Store
SELF-CATERING $

(Main St; ⏱7am-10pm) In a historic building across from the park at the start of Main St. Groceries are pricey but there are daily lunchtime fresh burritos, coffee, soup and salads. A well-stocked beer and spirit shop is attached.

Cubby's Marketplace
SUPERMARKET $

(⏱10am-10pm Mon-Sat, to 8pm Sun) At the junction of George Parks Hwy and Talkeetna Spur Rd, this is a genuine supermarket with fresh produce and a deli. You can take the Sunshine Transit bus here.

🍺 Drinking

Pretty much every joint in town will serve you a beer, and most of them have fine outdoor perches for people watching. The Fairbanks Inn also has a beer garden out back in summer.

Denali Brewing Company
BREWERY

(Main St; www.denalibrewingcompany.com; ⏱11am-8pm) Beer from this popular local brewery, which opened up in 2009, has already found its way right across the state. Fortunately it's also available in Talkeetna: for $2 you can sample a 5oz taster, or if you splash out $35 you can purchase yourself a 2.25-gallon party pig. There is an outdoor garden facing Main St, where you can relax and enjoy whatever tipple you choose.

☆ Entertainment

There's live music or some kind of performance at least a few nights a week at the Fairview Inn, the Twister Creek Restaurant (www.denalibrewingcompany.com; Main St; ⏱9am-10pm) beside the Denali Brewing Company, and at Talkeetna Roadhouse.

The Denali Arts Council, based in the Sheldon Community Arts Hangar (D St;

THE FAIRVIEW INN

Though not an official museum, the **Fairview Inn** (Main St; ⏱noon-late) might as well be. Founded in 1923 to serve as the overnight stop between Seward and Fairbanks on the newly constructed Alaska Railroad, the inn is listed on the National Register of Historic Places. Its old plank-floored saloon is classic Alaska: its walls are covered with racks of antlers, various furry critters and lots of local memorabilia. One corner holds Talkeetna's only slot machine; another is devoted to President Warren G Harding. When the railroad was finished in 1923, Harding arrived in Alaska and rode the rails to the Nenana River, where he hammered in the golden spike. Talkeetna locals swear (with grins on their faces) that he stopped at the Fairview Inn on the way home, was poisoned, and wound up dying in San Francisco less than a week later. Ever since, the Fairview has remained a fine place to be poisoned.

www.denaliartscouncil.org) across from the museum, runs theatrical performances and an arts program throughout the summer. It also sponsors a family-friendly live outdoor music show in the Village Park (corner of Main St and Talkeetna Spur Rd) on Friday evenings.

Shopping

Not surprisingly, Talkeetna has a range of gift shops, selling all manner of kitsch and collectibles.

Artisans Open Air Market ARTS & CRAFTS
(⊙10am-6:30pm Fri-Mon) Located outside the Sheldon Community Arts Hangar, this weekend arts fare offers a smorgasbord of local and native crafts, clothing, storybooks, jewelry and more.

Information

There are fickle ATMs in Nagley's and Twister Creek Restaurant. Almost all eating and drinking establishments have free wireless. The **library** (Mile 13.5, Talkeetna Spur Rd; ⊙11am-6pm) has wireless and free computer use.

Talkeetna-Denali Visitor Center (⊙9am-7pm) is 14 miles from town at the junction of the George Parks Hwy. You will pass it if you drive into Talkeetna.

Getting There & Away

Check the notice board outside the post office (behind Sheldon Arts Hangar) for information on shared rides.

BUS Alaska Bus Guy (☑720-6541; www.alaskabusguy.com) runs vans to Anchorage ($60) leaving at 3:30pm, and to Denali National Park ($60) at 9:30pm. **Alaska/Yukon Trails** (☑479-2277; www.alaskashuttle.com) Has buses departing from Talkeetna Roadhouse daily at 10:15am heading for Denali Park ($59, three hours), continuing on to Fairbanks ($92, 6½ hours). They also leave at 4:15pm for Anchorage ($59, 2½ hours). **Denali Overland Transportation** (☑733-2384; www.denalioverland.com; Denali Dry Goods Store, Main St) runs shuttles to and from Anchorage and less often to and from Denali ($85 per person, based on four-person minimum). The schedule is very loose.

TRAIN From mid-May to mid-September, Alaska Railroad's **Denali Star** (www.akrr.com) stops daily in Talkeetna on its run between Anchorage (one way $89) and Fairbanks. Talkeetna to Denali costs $85 and Talkeetna to Fairbanks is $124.

Getting Around

Sunshine Transit (☑354-3885) This community shuttle (per ride $3) runs from town out to the George Parks Hwy, making stops anywhere riders request. Buses run about every 30 minutes from 7:15am to 4:45pm. You can catch the bus at the Roadhouse, and also find the full schedule there.

Talkeetna Taxi (☑355-8294; www.talkeetnataxi.com) Offers service within town and also charters during the climbing season.

Denali State Park

At 325,240 acres, Denali State Park is the fourth-largest state park in Alaska and is roughly half the size of Rhode Island. The park covers the transition zone between the coastal region and the spine of the Alaska Range, and among the dense forests you can look forward to distant shots of towering peaks, including Mt McKinley and the glaciers on its southern slopes. Some say that on a clear day the panorama here that includes Mt McKinley is the most spectacular mountain view in North America.

The park is largely undeveloped but does offer a handful of turnoffs, trails, rental cabins and campgrounds that can be reached from George Parks Hwy, which runs through the park. In general, though, you need to be better prepared for any hiking and backpacking adventures than at the same-named national park to the north. But this may be the state park's blessing, for it means it lacks the crowds and there are no long waits or tight regulations.

At the height of the summer season, experienced backpackers may want to consider this park as a hassle-free and cheaper alternative. The entrance to the park is at Mile 132.2 of George Parks Hwy.

Activities

The excellent hiking trails and alpine routes crossing the park are popular with locals. Keep in mind that in the backcountry, open fires are allowed only on the gravel bars of major rivers. Pack a stove if you plan to camp overnight.

The Chulitna River runs through the park. Floats can be arranged in Talkeetna.

Byers Lake Loop Trail HIKING
If you only have a few hours, but want to get away from it all, head out on this easy 4.8-mile trek around the lake. The path begins at Byers Lake Campground (Mile 147, George Parks

Hwy), passes six hike-in campsites on the other side, and then returns to the original campground after a bridge crossing. If you want to go for a paddle across the lake, you can rent canoes or kayaks ($15 per hour, $45 full day) at the Byers Lake Campground through Southside River Guides (☎733-7238).

Little Coal Creek Trail   HIKING
This trail departs from Mile 163.9 of George Parks Hwy, ascending to the alpine areas of Kesugi Ridge. From there you can continue to the summit of Indian Mountain, an ascent of about 3300ft, or continue along the ridge to either Byers Lake or Troublesome Creek. It's a 9-mile round-trip to Indian Peak and 27.4 miles to Byers Lake.

Kesugi Ridge Traverse   HIKING
For a moderate to difficult three- to four-day (24.7-mile) hike above the treeline with superb views of McKinley and the Alaska Range, try this popular hike connecting the Little Coal Creek Trail with the Byers Lake Trail. You can begin from either end but most hikers start at the Little Coal Creek Trailhead as the switchback ascent to the ridgeline is easier. Once on the Kesugi Ridge (a Tanainan Indian word for 'ancient one'), head south along the cairn- and flag-marked route until you connect with the Byers Lake Trail. From here the trail leads to the Byers Lake Campground at Mile 147 of George Parks Hwy.

For a shorter hike (17.2 miles), exit via the Ermine Hill Trail.

Troublesome Creek Trail   HIKING
Scheduled to fully reopen for summer 2012, the route begins at a posted trailhead in the parking area at Mile 137.6 of George Parks Hwy and ascends alongside the creek until it reaches the treeline. From here you enter an open territory of alpine lakes and big country views, where the route is marked only by rock cairns as it heads north to Byers Lake.

The 15-mile backpacking trip to Byers Lake Campground is of moderate difficulty, but if you're more adventurous you can continue to Little Coal Creek Trail, a 36-mile trek above the treeline. Views from the ridges are spectacular.

Ermine Hill Trail   HIKING
This wonderful short day-hike (3 miles one way) up to Kesugi Ridge begins at Mile 156.5, George Parks Hwy. You'll see McKinley quite quickly on the way up the switchbacks and also be rewarded with views of Ermine Lake

and some intriguing rock formations along the ridgetop.

🛏 Sleeping

Denali Viewpoint South Campground   CAMPGROUND $
(Mile 135.2, George Parks Hwy; campsites $10) While the campground is little more than a parking lot with toilets and small patches of grass for setting up a tent, you overlook the broad Chulitna River valley while Mt McKinley and adjacent peaks of the Alaska Range overwhelm you from above. Interpretive displays and a spotting scope help you enjoy the panorama.

Denali Viewpoint North Campground   CAMPGROUND $
(Mile 162.7, George Parks Hwy; campsites $10) A similar setup with the South Campground, and with rival views, North has 20 sites around a parking lot and a few walk-in sites in a level glade up a slope.

Byers Lake Campground   CAMPGROUND $
(Mile 147, George Parks Hwy; campsites $10) In addition to 73 sites, this campground offers walk-in sites along the loop trail around the lake, and state park's Byers Lake cabins 1, 2 and 3. You can drive to cabin 1; cabin 2 is a half-mile hike from there, while cabin 3 is a further 70 yards beyond that. Cabins are $60 a night and can be reserved in advance online at the Alaska Division of Parks (☎745-3975; www.alaskastateparks.org).

Lower Troublesome Creek Campground   CAMPGROUND $
(Mile 137.2, George Parks Hwy; tent sites $10) A treed and rather primitive little campground with toilets, drinking water and 20 walk-in sites just yards from the parking lot.

ⓘ Information

Denali State Park Visitors Center (www.dnr.alaska.gov/parks/unit/denali1.htm; Mile 147, George Parks Hwy; ⊙9am-6pm) is at the Alaska Veterans Memorial, just north of Byers Lake Campground. Volunteer staff are usually well informed about the area, and maps and brochures are available for sale. A full account of the park, including trail information and maps, can be found on the website.

Cantwell & Broad Pass

The northern boundary of Denali State Park is at Mile 168.5, George Parks Hwy. Situated at Mile 203.6, Broad Pass (2300ft) is a dividing line: rivers to the south drain into Cook Inlet, while waters to the north flow to the Yukon River. The area is at the treeline and worth a stop for some hiking. The mountain valley, surrounded by tall white peaks, is unquestionably one of the most beautiful spots along George Parks Hwy or the Alaska Railroad – both use the low gap to cross the Alaska Range.

North from the pass, George Parks Hwy descends 6 miles to Cantwell (pop 211), at the junction with Denali Hwy. At the junction you'll find gas and convenience stores. The 'town' itself is 2 miles west of here on the extension of the Denali Hwy. If you need to stay, there are a few places around including Cantwell RV Park (768-2210; www.alaskaone.com/cantwellrv; campsites $15;), which has showers and laundry. The RV park is half a mile west of the George Parks Hwy on the road into town.

Nenana

POP 341

The only significant town encountered between Denali National Park and Fairbanks is Nenana (nee-na-nuh, like 'banana'), which lies at the confluence of the Nenana and Tanana (tan-uh-naw, not like 'banana') Rivers. Though the big industry here is barging freight downstream, for visitors and northerners alike the community is most famous for the Nenana Ice Classic, an eminently Alaskan game of chance in which prognosticators attempt to profit by guessing when the ice will break up on the Nenana River.

Historically, Nenana (Mile 305 of George Parks Hwy) was little more than a roadhouse until it was chosen as the base for building the northern portion of the Alaska Railroad in 1916. The construction camp quickly became a boomtown that made history on July 15, 1923, when President Warren G Harding arrived to hammer in the golden spike on the northern side of the Tanana. The sickly Harding, the first president ever to visit Alaska, missed the golden spike the first two times, or so the story goes, but finally drove it in to complete the railroad.

Most shops and businesses can be found off A St, which runs four blocks from the very helpful Nenana Visitor Center (832-5435; www.nenana.org; 8am-6pm), at the entrance to town, to the train station beside the river.

◉ Sights

Nenana Train Station HISTORIC BUILDING
In preparation for the president's arrival the following year, the Nenana train station was built in 1922 at the north end of A St. Extensively restored in 1988, it's now on the National Register of Historic Places. The building includes the jumbled Alaska Railroad Museum (9:30am-6pm), which displays not just railroad memorabilia but local artifacts ranging from ice tongs to animal traps. East of the station, a monument commemorates Harding's visit.

BREAKING THE ICE IN NENANA

For stir-crazy Alaskans, nothing heralds the end of winter like the breakup of ice on the nearest river. It's a subject of much anticipation everywhere in the state – but nowhere more than in Nenana, where this seasonal guessing game has become the state's pre-eminent gamble.

The Nenana Ice Classic (www.nenanaakiceclassic.com) began in 1917 when cabin-feverish Alaska Railroad surveyors pooled $800 and bet on when the ice would disintegrate on the frozen Tanana River. Eight decades later the wager is the same, but the stakes are much higher: the 2011 jackpot reached $338,062.

Anyone can play: just shell out $2.50 and register your guess, down to the month, day, hour and minute. Come the following spring, the first movement of the ice will be determined by a 'tripod' which stands guard on the Tanana, 300ft from shore. Any surge will dislodge the tripod, which tugs on a cord, in turn stopping a clock onshore.

And when will it happen? Your prediction is as good as anybody's. The vast majority of breakups have been between April 29 and May 12, and for what it's worth, almost never between midnight and 9am.

But don't get too excited: no matter what time you guess, many others will likely guess the same. If you win, your payout will likely be just a fraction of the total jackpot.

St Mark's Episcopal Church   CHURCH
(cnr Front & Market Sts) Within eyeshot of the train station, this handsome church dates from 1905. The interior has a few lovely handcrafted features including an altar with traditional Athabascan beadwork.

Alfred Starr Nenana Cultural Center   CULTURAL CENTER
(☉9am-6pm) This riverfront center informs visitors about local culture and history.

Taku Chief   HISTORIC BOAT
The *Taku Chief* river tug once pushed barges along the Tanana River and now spruces up the grounds outside the visitor center.

🛏 Sleeping & Eating

Nenana RV Park & Campground   CAMPGROUND $
(☏832-5230; nenanarv@gmail.com; cnr 4th & B Sts; campsites $10, RV sites $15-28) This pleasant, well-run campground has an area for tenters in a grassy patch by a covered picnic area that can also be used as a shelter if it rains. Resembling a hostel setup more than campground, the main building offers a small common area with free coffee, free showers and cheap laundry ($2).

Rough Woods Inn & Café   INN $$
(☏832-5299; www.roughwoodsinn.biz; 623 A St; r $95-145; 🖥) Right on A St, between the visitor center and train station, this inn is more noted for food, especially breakfasts ($6 to $10), though some of the rooms have kitchenettes which may be of use to travelers.

Moocher's Bar   BAR
(A St) The locals' favorite, across from the Railroad Museum.

DENALI HIGHWAY

Considered one of Alaska's most stunning drives, this 135-mile route was opened in 1957 as the only road to the national park. It became a secondary route after George Parks Hwy was completed in 1972, and now from mid-May to October sees a light but steady flow of hikers, hunters, mountain bikers, anglers and birdwatchers. A highway in only the titular sense, Denali is basically a gravel road from Cantwell, just south of Denali National Park on George Parks Hwy, to Paxson on Richardson Hwy.

Most of the highway is at or near the treeline, running along the foothills of the Alaska Range and through glacial valleys where you can see stretches of alpine tundra, enormous glaciers and braided rivers. All that scenery is a blessing, because the road itself, though perfectly passable in a standard auto, is slow going. Expect to average just 35mph, taking six hours from end to end.

There are no established communities along the way, but the roadhouses provide food, beds and sometimes gas. Most of the development is at the Paxson end of the highway. If you're driving, fill up with gas at Paxson or Cantwell. The following descriptions follow the route from west to east.

Cantwell to Tangle Lakes

Within 3 miles from the turnoff at Cantwell, the pavement ends, rough gravel takes over, and the road ascends into the sort of big-sky territory that will dominate it for the duration.

There are stellar views of Mt McKinley starting at Mile 124. At Mile 85, climb a small hill for a spellbinding panorama of the Alaska Range including Mt Debora and Mount Hess. From a lookout at Mile 37, you'll have no trouble identifying the MacLaren Glacier to the north. This is also where the highway peaks out at 4068ft.

◉ Sights & Activities

Eskers   GLACIER
The Denali area abounds in fascinating geological features, from majestic glaciers to the easy-to-overlook thin ridges of silt, sand and gravel known as eskers. These deposits, once contained by glacier walls, remain as elongated mounds after the ice melts and around Mile 59 the highway actually runs on top of one.

🐾 Crazy Dog Kennels   DOGSLEDDING
(☏388-6039; www.denalihighwaytours.com; kennel tour $15) On the MacLaren River's far side is the summer operation of two-time Yukon Quest champ John Schandelmeier and his wife, Zoya DeNure, an Iditarod finisher. Impassioned about their pups, they run the only dog yard in Alaska that rescues unwanted sled dogs and turns them into racers. In August and September, overnight trips are available on a husky-pulled wheeled cart for $200 per person (two person minimum).

Hiking

Several potential hiking trails, none sign-posted, branch off the highway in the dozen or so miles after Gracious House Lodge, a roadhouse at Mile 82. Use topographical maps and ask at lodges for clear directions and the latest on conditions. Note that many trails are only really suitable for motorized vehicles. For clearer paths, see the Tangle Lakes to Paxson section (p286).

Paddling

At Mile 118, pull in to begin a float down the silt-choked Nenana River. The river can be paddled in Class I to II conditions from here to George Parks Hwy, 18 river miles distant. Novices should pull out at that point, as after the highway it gets way hairier.

🛏 Sleeping & Eating

The Denali Hwy between Cantwell and Tangle Lakes features scores of pull-offs that are ideal for informal camping.

Crazy Dog Cabins   CABIN $
(☑347-9013; www.denalihighwaytours.com; Mile 42, Denali Hwy; cabins with shared bath $50-85) Run by the hospitable owners of the Crazy Dog Kennels, the comfortable hand-hewn log cabins offer cooking facilities, wood stoves for heat, and all the quiet time you could ask for.

MacLaren River Lodge   LODGE $$
(☑822-5444; www.maclarenlodge.com; Mile 42, Denali Hwy; dm/r with shared bath $25/60, cabins $150; 🐾) The lodge sits on the edge of the MacLaren River and features a bar and restaurant open for breakfast, lunch and dinner. The dorm is set inside Whitney's Cabin, the oldest cabin on the Denali Hwy, while the rooms are remodeled Atco units.

Brushkana Creek
Campground   CAMPGROUND $
(Mile 104.3, Denali Hwy; campsites $8) If you can't find your own little hideaway tent spot off the highway, this campground offers 22 not-very-private sites, a picnic shelter, drinking water and a meat rack for the hunters who invade the area in late summer and fall.

Tangle Lakes to Paxson

After several miles of lonely road, the Denali Hwy suddenly gets busier and better maintained as it descends into the Tangle Lakes Archeological District, a magnet for birders, anglers and paddlers. Pavement begins around Mile 21. Most of the lakes – as many as 40 in springtime – can be seen from the Wrangell Mountain Viewpoint at Mile 13.

🏃 Activities

Paddling

If you just want to paddle around pretty Round Tangle Lake for a few hours, you can rent a canoe from Tangle River Inn (☑822-3970; www.tangleriverinn.com; Mile 20, Denali Hwy; per hour/day $5/35).

Delta River Canoe Route   CANOEING
This 35-mile paddle starts at Tangle Lakes Campground and ends a few hundred yards from Mile 212.5 of the Richardson Hwy. After crossing Round Tangle Lake, the route continues to Lower Tangle Lake, where you must make a portage around a waterfall. Below the falls is a set of Class III rapids that you must either line for 2 miles or paddle if you have an experienced hand. Be warned though that every year canoeists damage their boats beyond repair on these rapids and have to hike 15 miles back out to the Denali Hwy. After the rapids, the remainder of the route is a much milder trip though there are still Class II sections.

For a more thorough overview and map, download or pick up *The Delta National Wild and Scenic River* brochure from the BLM (www.blm.gov/ak) website.

Upper Tangle Lakes Canoe Route   CANOEING
Though an easier and shorter paddle than the Delta River Route, this one does require four portages (unmarked but easy to work out in the low-bush tundra). The route starts at the Delta Wayside at Mile 21.7 of the Denali Hwy, and then passes through Upper Tangle Lake before ending at Dickey Lake, 9 miles to the south. There is a 1.2-mile portage into Dickey Lake.

From here, experienced paddlers can continue by following Dickey Lake's outlet to the southeast into the Middle Fork of the Gulkana River. For the first 3 miles the river is shallow and mild, but then it plunges into a steep canyon where canoeists have to contend with Class III and IV rapids. Most canoeists choose to line their boats, though some make a portage. Allow seven days for the 76-mile trip from Tangle Lakes to Sourdough Creek Campground on the Gulkana River off the Richardson Hwy.

All paddlers trying this route must have topo maps. The useful BLM (www.blm.com/ak) brochure *Gulkana National Wild River Floater's Guide* can be downloaded from the website.

Hiking

Pick up a map of the TLAD (Tangle Lakes Archeological District) Trails Brochure at the highway lodges or download from the BLM (www.blm.gov/ak) website for an overview of the system.

Osar Lake Trail Hiking   HIKING
(Mile 37) On the southern side of the highway, this easy 7.2-mile trail leads to Osar Lake and wide views of the MacLaren River valley. In August and September you'll be sharing the path with hunters.

MacLaren Summit Trail   HIKING
(Mile 37) Starting across the road from the Osar Lake Trail, this 3-mile mostly dry route runs north across the tundra to MacLaren Summit.

Landmark Gap Trail   HIKING
(Mile 24.6) This 3-mile trail leads north to Landmark Gap Lake, at an elevation of 3217ft. You can't see the lake from the highway, but you can spot the noticeable gap between the Amphitheater Mountains.

Glacier Lake Trail   HIKING
(Mile 30) A new and drier route to the lake is now opened and a further path to Sevenmile Lake, several miles to the north, is in the works.

Swede Lake Trail   HIKING
(Mile 16.2) From a trailhead on the southern side of the highway, this path (mostly used by motorized vehicles and mountain bikers) runs south about 10 miles to the Middle Fork of the Gulkana River. From here there is access to the Alphabet Hills and Dickey Lake.

🛏 Sleeping

TOP CHOICE Denali Highway Cabins   CABIN $$
(☎822 5972; www.denalihwy.com; Denali Hwy; cabins with breakfast $150-170; 🛜) A couple of hundred feet up the Denali Hwy, this place is pure Alaskan gold. It's got pedigree (it's the oldest running lodge on the highway), authority (it's run by naturalist Dr Audubon Bakewell, coauthor of the *Birding in Alaska* guide) and fine accommodation. The modern log cabins, each with a private balcony, sit along the Gulkana River, and feature real flush toilets among other civilized comforts. There are also surprisingly cozy prefab tents ($150, shared bath) and a simpler four-bed dorm ($25, no reservations accepted). A full kitchen is open to all guests, as well as kayak ($40 to $50) and bicycle rentals ($35 to $45), highly regarded birding tours ($50) and evening float trips ($50).

Tangle River Inn   LODGE $
(☎822-3970; www.tangleriverinn.com; Mile 20 Denali Hwy; r without/with bath $74/99, cabins $149; 🛜) Though it may appear at first like a truck stop, or a tidy depot, this is in fact a well-run lodge with a good range of sleeping options. There are private cabins, family rooms and a bunkhouse (groups only) spread across the gravel hilltop. The restaurant serves tasty home-style meals with tranquil views of Sugarloaf Mountain and the Tangle Lakes thrown in for free. The lodge is popular with anglers but come June birdwatchers flock from all corners of the world to set their binoculars on Arctic warblers, wheateaters and golden plovers, among many other winged worthies.

Tangle Lakes Campground   CAMPGROUND $
(Mile 21.5, Denali Hwy; campsites free) On the shores of Round Tangle Lake, this 22-site campground is still free despite its popularity. Walk the short Tangle Ridge Hiking Trail for first-rate views of the Tangle Lakes and Alaska Range.

FAIRBANKS

POP 35,252

A spread-out maze of strip malls and snaking rivers, Fairbanks is also the major transport hub for the Interior. It's not an attractive city by any means, but don't just rush through here on the way to somewhere else. Fairbanks has some of Alaska's best museums, including a new native culture center and a knockout antique auto collection, a host of excellent paddles and a full summer schedule of festivals. In the fall and winter there's no better place to catch the aurora.

The relaxed pace of the city, and its function as a center for so many booms and busts, makes it a great place to meet the full range of Alaskan archetypes: from homesteaders and dog mushers to conservationists, prospectors, oil rig workers, native artists and the university students who somehow manage to keep their focus on the books when the daylight hours are few and the temperatures off the scale.

Most of what you'll want to see is concentrated in the small downtown area, the hilltop campus of the University of Alaska Fairbanks (UAF), the large nature reserve to the north and the grassy parks along the shores of the meandering Chena River. Given that these are all divided by miles and miles of fairly dreary sprawl, having a vehicle will make your stay far more enjoyable.

History

The city was founded in 1901, as a result of a journey ET Barnette undertook up the Tanana River on the SS *Lavelle Young*. Barnette was hauling supplies to the Tanacross goldfields but a detour up the shallow Chena River stranded him at what is now the corner of 1st Ave and Cushman St. Barnette could have been just another failed trading-post merchant in the Great White North, but local miners convinced him to set up shop. The following year the Italian prospector Felix Pedro (who had incidentally been one of Barnette's first customers) struck gold 12 miles north of here.

A large boomtown sprang to life amid the hordes of miners stampeding into the area, and by 1908 more than 18,000 people resided in the Fairbanks Mining District. In the ensuing decade, other gold rushes largely drained the population, but ironically the city's gold-mining industry was to outlast any other in the state.

While WWII and the construction of the Alcan and military bases produced the next boom in the city's economy, nothing affected Fairbanks quite like the Trans-Alaska Pipeline. From 1973 to 1977, when construction of the pipeline was at its height, the town was bursting at its seams as the principal gateway to the North Slope.

The aftermath of the pipeline construction was just as extreme. The city's population shrank and unemployment crept toward 25%.

By the late 1990s, however, the city was on the rebound – thanks to tourism and, once again, gold. Just north of town is the Fort Knox Gold Mine – Alaska's largest. In 2010 Fort Knox produced 349,729oz of gold and employed more than 400 workers.

Maps

Nearly every touristy joint in Fairbanks gives out the free *Fairbanks Yellow Map for Campers & Independent Travelers,* which does a good job of simplifying the town's knotty streetscape.

◉ Sights

University of Alaska Museum of the North
MUSEUM

(Map p288; www.uaf.edu/museum; 907 Yukon Dr; admission $10; ⊙9am-9pm) In an architecturally abstract igloo-and-aurora-inspired edifice sits one of Alaska's finest museums, with artifact-rich exhibits on the geology, history, culture and trivia of each region of the state. The most famous display covers the life and death of Blue Babe with all the precision and detail of a *CSI* episode. Babe, a 36,000-year-old bison, was found preserved in the permafrost by Fairbanks-area miners. But just how and why and by whom did this beast meet his end?

The museum theatre runs three films several times daily (admission $5): *Dynamic Aurora* is a multimedia look at the northern lights; *Winter* talks about, you guessed it, winter; and *You are Here* discusses the museum itself. Upstairs, the Rose Berry Alaska Art Gallery covers 2000 years of northern works, ranging from ancient ivory carvings to wood masks to contemporary photographs.

TOP CHOICE Fountainhead Antique Auto Museum
MUSEUM

(Map p288; www.fountainheadmuseum.com; 212 Wedgewood Dr; admission $8; ⊙11am-10pm Sun-Thu, to 6pm Fri & Sat) This world-class collection of 70 working antique vehicles highlights both the evolution of the automobile from the late 19th century, and also motor vehicle history in Alaska: there are one-of-a-kind items such as the 1898 Hay Motor Carriage and also Alaska's first 'car,' an ungainly wagon-wheeled contraption built by Bobby Sheldon to win the heart of a local lass (sadly, he failed). Great lighting, informative write-ups, a superb collection of old Alaskan photos and displays of vintage clothing over an eight-decade period make this museum an almost embarrassment of riches.

To get here, head east down College Rd and turn left on Margaret Ave. Then follow the signs into the Wedgewood Resort.

Creamer's Field Migratory Waterfowl Refuge
NATURE RESERVE

(Map p288) Birds have been migrating through this idyllic little stretch of farmland for millennia, and when the local dairy finally shut its doors, the community rallied to preserve the land. More than 100 species can now be seen in the summer months,

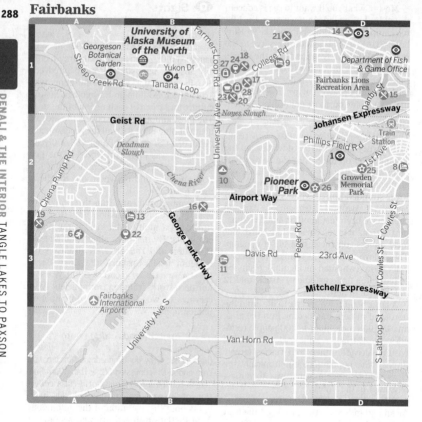

including sandhill cranes, which appear in the thousands during August.

The **Farmhouse Visitor Center** (☺9:30am-5pm) has a handbook to help you get the most out of the short trails through the nearby boreal forest and wetlands (bring bug spray). Volunteers also lead one-hour nature walks at 7pm Monday through Friday.

Large Animal Research Station   WILDLIFE RESERVE
(☎474-5724; www.uaf.edu/lars) If you can't make a trip to the Arctic for a little wildlife observation, consider a visit to this research station that tends herds of musk oxen, reindeer and caribou. The station studies the animals' unique adaptations to a sub-Arctic climate, and viewing areas outside the fenced pastures allow a free look at the herds any time. The facility itself, however, can only be entered on guided walks ($10) on Tuesday, Thursday and Friday at 10am, noon and 2pm. To reach the station, head north from the university campus on Farmers Loop Rd, bear left onto Ballaine Rd, and then turn left again on Yankovich Rd. The center is a further 1.2 miles up on the right.

FREE **Pioneer Park**   HISTORIC SITE
(Map p288; Airport Way at Peger Rd; ☺stores & museums noon-8pm, park 24hr) The most prominent sight in this rather dowdy 44-acre theme park is the **SS Nenana**, a hulking stern-wheeler that once plied the Yukon River.

Despite the cartoonish name, **Gold Rush Town** is a block of genuine relocated historic cabins and clapboard-fronted shops. Some of the interiors are walk-in museums inside, and the Palace Theatre & Saloon offers nightly entertainment. This is a good location for photographs.

Across the park, the geodesic **Pioneer Air Transportation Museum** (admission $3) is chock-full of exhibits on the state's ground-

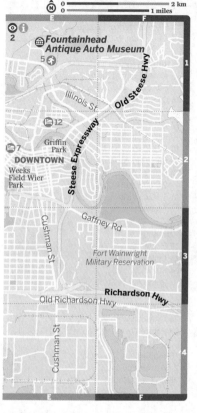

Fairbanks Convention & Visitor Center

Located near the front of the complex, this section is stocked full of brochures, pamphlets and friendly knowledgeable staff. There's also free wireless and computer use.

Tanana Chiefs Conference Cultural Programs

(www.tananachiefs.org) The programs, under the title 'Cultural Connections,' are designed to both share native culture with the wider world, and also ensure it survives to the next generation. There are one-hour **cultural performances** (admission $10; ⊙1pm, 3pm & 6:30pm), live **craft-making demonstrations** (⊙1-6pm Mon-Fri), and the opportunity to make your own crafts under the guidance of native artists.

For families, there's a **portrait studio** (⊙11am-6pm Mon-Fri) to get your snapshots in traditional Athabascan garb (per family $65). These are absolutely gorgeous pieces of clothing, handmade by some very talented native women. The chief's jacket, for example, was made by Dixie Alexander, who has a similar piece displayed in the Smithsonian Institute.

Alaska Public Lands Information Center (www.alaskacenters.gov/fairbanks.cfm; ⊙8am-6pm) An excellent resource if you're planning on visiting any state or national parks and reserves in the region. The center has topo maps ($8 to $9), informative brochures on highways such as the Dalton, and handouts on paddling routes, hiking and cycling paths, recreational gold mining, berry picking and much more.

FREE **Fairbanks Community & Dog Mushing Museum** MUSEUM (Map p292; 410 Cushman St; ⊙10am-8pm Mon-Sat, 11am-4pm Sun) This homespun place traces the city's history through old photos, newspaper clippings and historical artifacts from daily life. A new wing covers sled-dog culture and history.

Historic Buildings CHURCHES Heading west along 1st Ave, you'll find half a dozen old log cabins and several historic buildings, including **St Matthew's Episcopal Church**, a beautiful log structure built in 1905 and rebuilt in 1948 after a fire. **Immaculate Conception Church** (Map p292), just across the Chena River Bridge from Golden Heart Plaza, was built in 1904 and moved to its present location in 1911. It's a

breaking aviation history – there's even an experimental gyroplane and a 'flying saucer.' A miniature train, the **Crooked Creek & Whiskey Island Railroad**, gives rides ($2) around the park for a global overview.

To get to Pioneer Park, take the MACS Blue or Red Line bus.

DOWNTOWN FAIRBANKS

Morris Thompson Cultural & Visitors Center CULTURAL CENTER (Map p292; www.morristhompsoncenter.org; 101 Dunkel St; ⊙8am-9pm; @ 🛜) Make this center – a union of three different agencies – your first stop in Fairbanks, not just to get the lowdown on what's happening, but to see some of that happening stuff, too. Inside are exhibits on Alaskan history and native culture, as well as daily movies and cultural performances. Outside on the grounds check out the historic cabin and funky moose antler arch.

Fairbanks

national historic monument and features beautiful painted-glass windows.

🏃 Activities

Fairbanks has plenty to keep outdoor enthusiasts enthusiastic. Much of the best trekking and paddling, however, is well out of town. In winter the rivers freeze up, making ideal ski-touring trails.

Hiking

Unlike Anchorage or Juneau, Fairbanks doesn't have outstanding hiking on its doorstep. The best trail for an extended hiking trip is the impressive Pinnell Mountain Trail (p67) at Mile 85.5 and Mile 107.3 of the Steese Hwy. For a variety of long and short hikes, you'll need to head to the Chena River State Recreation Area. For more options, stop in at the visitor center.

Cycling

Fairbanks has a network of cycle routes in and around the city, and cycling is a decent way to get around if you don't have a car. One of the more popular and scenic rides (about 17 miles long) is to head north on Illinois St from downtown, and then loop around on College Rd and Farmers Loop Rd/University Ave. Pick up a free *Bikeways* map at the Morris Thompson Culture & Visitors Center.

Alaska Outdoor Rentals & Guides   BICYCLE RENTAL
(Map p288; www.2paddle1.com; Pioneer Park; ⊙11am-7pm) Located on the river behind Pioneer Park, it rents out mountain bikes (per three hours $19, per day $27).

Go North Hostel   BICYCLE RENTAL
(Map p288; www.gonorthalaska.com; 3500 Davis Rd) Also has mountain bikes for $25 to $35 per day.

Paddling

The Fairbanks area offers a wide variety of canoeing and kayaking opportunities, from leisurely day to overnight trips into the surrounding area; for extended backcountry expeditions, see Beaver Creek (p68) or head over to the visitor center for suggestions.

Several local places rent out boats and run shuttles to put-ins and take-outs: **Alaska Outdoor Rentals & Guides** (Map p288; www.2paddle1.com; Pioneer Park; ⊙11am-7pm) will set you up with a canoe for $52 per day and, for another $19, pick you up at downstream locations.

Go North Hostel (Map p288; www.gonorthalaska.com; 3500 Davis Rd) has canoes for $20 to $48 per day, can help with trip planning and can also transport you to and from rivers throughout the Interior if you give advance notice.

Great Fairbanks Pub Paddle   CANOEING
A pleasant afternoon can be spent paddling the mild Chena River, especially when combined with stops for drinks, pub grub, horseshoes and other games at Pike's Landing, the Pump House and other bars and restaurants along the way. To take part in this beloved pub paddle, head to Alaska Outdoor Rentals & Guides in Pioneer Park where you can rent a canoe and also arrange a pickup at the end. Of course, it's dangerous to paddle while inebriated, so exercise restraint and caution.

Chena & Tanana Rivers   CANOEING
Those looking for an overnight – or even longer – paddle, should try a float down the Chena River from Chena Hot Springs Rd, east of Fairbanks, or a pleasant two-day trip down the Tanana River. The popular 60-mile Tanana trip usually begins from the end of Chena Pump Rd and finishes in the town of Nenana, where you can return with your canoe to Fairbanks on the Alaska Railroad.

Chatanika River   CANOEING
For a one- or two-day trip, paddle the Chatanika River, 28 miles southwest from Cripple Creek BLM Campground (Mile 60, Steese Hwy). The route parallels the road until the take-out at Upper Chatanika River State Campground (Mile 39, Steese Hwy). For an extended trip you can continue another 17 miles to a bridge at Mile 11 of the Elliot Hwy.

Gold Panning
If you've been bitten by the gold bug, Fairbanks is an ideal area to try your hand at panning. Start at **Alaskan Prospectors & Geologists Supply** (Map p288; 504 College Rd; ⊙10:30am-5pm Tue-Fri, from 12:30pm Sat), which sells all the necessary equipment for recreational prospecting.

The next stop should be the Alaska Public Lands Information Center in the visitor center for handouts and up-to-date information. Popular places in the area include the **Discovery Claim** on Pedro Creek off the Steese Hwy (across from the Felix Pedro Monument), and several other locations further up the Steese Hwy.

FAIRBANKS MIDNIGHT SPORTS

Tourists aren't the only folks who are made manic by Alaska's endless summer days. Fairbanksans, all too aware that darkness and cold are just around the corner, play outdoors at all hours of the night.

The most revered of the city's wee-hour athletic activities is the **Midnight Sun Baseball Game**, held every solstice since 1906, without artificial light and, thus far, never canceled due to darkness (but postponed in 2011 for rain). For the past four decades the game has pitted the local Goldpanners against an Alaska Baseball League rival. The contest is invariably the most popular of the season, and when the first pitch is hurled, at 10:30pm, the sun is still well above the horizon. By midnight – when play pauses for the traditional singing of the 'Alaska's Flag' song – the sun is low, and at the end of nine innings it's gone. Its glow, however, lights the sky until sunrise, two hours later.

If you're more a fan of links than diamonds, Fairbanks also has a couple of golf courses where you can tee up well past your normal bedtime. **North Star Golf Club** (www.northstargolf.com; 330 Golf Club Dr; 18 holes $35) is an 18-hole course where visitors can start a round as late as 10pm. Also in the area is the venerable nine-hole **Fairbanks Golf & Country Club** (479-6555; 1735 Farmers Loop Rd; 9 holes $19, after midnight $10). Hazards at the courses include moose, marmot and sandhill crane.

Downtown Fairbanks

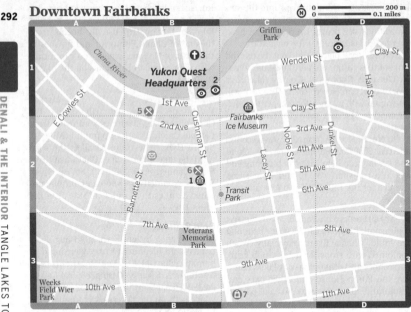

Downtown Fairbanks

☞ Tours

Northern Alaska Tour Co   SCENIC FLIGHTS
(☎474-8600; www.northernalaska.com) The Arctic Circle may be an imaginary line, but it's become one of Fairbanks' biggest draws, with small air-charter companies doing booming business flying travelers on sightseeing excursions across it. This company's tours fly to Coldfoot and return by bus along the Dalton Hwy for $379.

Gold Dredge No 8   GOLD PANNING
(www.golddredgeno8.com; 1755 Old Steese Hwy N; admission incl lunch $14.95) The arrival of the Alaska Railroad in 1923 prompted major mining companies to bring their money and their three-story-high mechanized dredges to the region. The behemoths worked nonstop, making mincemeat of the terrain. The most famous of these, Gold Dredge No 8, a five-deck, 250ft dredge, ran from 1928 to 1959 and recovered 7.5 million oz of gold. Eventually it was listed as a national historic site, and today is probably the most-viewed dredge in the state. Despite the official address, it's off the Old Steese Hwy at Mile 10, Goldstream Rd.

Note that individual travelers must join a scheduled tour to enter. Call for times.

El Dorado Gold Mine   GOLD PANNING
(☎479-6673; www.eldoradogoldmine.com; Mile 1.3, Elliot Hwy; admission $34.95) The two-hour train tour (9:45am and 3pm Sunday to Friday, 3pm Saturday), on a mile-long narrow-gauge track, winds through a reconstructed mining camp and culminates with visitors panning gold-laden dirt. Make reservations before heading out.

Alaska Tails of the Trail   DOG SLEDDING
(☑455-6469; www.maryshields.com; adult/child $35/25) Well-known musher and writer Mary Shields (she was the first woman to complete the Iditarod) offers an intimate two-hour glimpse into the life of a dog team and the Alaskans who raise and love them. Tours start at 10am and 7:30pm, and you're asked to call first to confirm space and then make an online reservation. The kennels are just north of the Large Animal Research Center on the UAF campus. Transportation is available for $20 for the round-trip.

Riverboat Discovery   BOAT
(Map p288; ☑479-6673; www.riverboatdiscovery. com; 1975 Discovery Dr, Mile 4.5, Airport Way; adult/child $54/37.95) Departing at 8:45am and 2pm daily, this 3½-hour tour navigates the Chena River via a historic stern-wheeler, stopping at a replica of an Athabascan village as well as the riverfront home and kennels of Susan Butcher, four-time winner of the Iditarod.

✸✸ Festivals & Events

Summer Solstice Celebrations   CULTURAL
(www.downtownfairbanks.com) Festivities take place on or around June 21, when the sun shines for almost 23 hours, and include footraces, arts and crafts booths, and the Midnight Sun Festival and Midnight Sun Baseball Game.

Fairbanks Summer Arts Festival   CULTURAL
(www.fsaf.org) In the last two weeks of July, numerous concerts and workshops in the performing and visual arts are held on the UAF campus as part of this yearly event.

Golden Days   CULTURAL
Fairbanks' largest summer happening, staged in the third week of July, commem-

orates the city's golden past, with beer, sourdough pancakes, and events ranging from rubber-ducky races to horse-and-rider shootouts.

World Eskimo-Indian Olympics   CULTURAL
(Map p288; www.weio.org, Carlson Center, 2010 2nd Ave) Held on the second-to-last weekend in July at the Carlson Center, this four-day event attracts indigenous people from across the Far North, who display their athletic prowess in contests like the Alaska High Kick and test their pain thresholds in games such as the Knuckle Hop. There's also dancing, cultural performances and plenty of traditional regalia.

Tanana Valley State Fair   CULTURAL
(Map p288; www.tananavalleyfair.org, Tanana Valley Fairgrounds, College Rd) Held in early to mid-August at the Tanana Valley Fairgrounds, Alaska's oldest fair has sideshows, entertainment and livestock contests.

🛏 Sleeping

Fairbanks offers all manner of lodging options, from tents to tony resorts. Most of the campgrounds are along Airport Way, University Ave and College Rd, while hostels are scattered throughout the city. There are more than 100 B&Bs, many of which are in the downtown area; visit the visitor center for brochures. Remember, Fairbanks has an 8% bed tax.

Ah, Rose Marie B&B   B&B $
TOP CHOICE
(Map p288; ☑456-2040; www.akpub.com/akbbrv/ahrose.html; 302 Cowles St; s/d $65/90; 🛜) This long-running and very well regarded B&B is now split into two units: the original 80-year-old Dutch-built cottage with its charming heritage atmosphere, and a next door

---

THE YUKON QUEST: ALASKA'S 'TOUGH' DOG RACE

Like a handful of other Alaskan towns, Fairbanks bills itself as the dog-mushing capital of the world. The town's claim to fame is the **Yukon Quest**, which takes place each February and covers 1023 miles between here and Whitehorse along many of the early trails used by trappers, miners and the postal service. Though less famous than the Iditarod, mushers will attest that the Quest is tougher. One female musher described it to us as being like childbirth: unbelievably painful at the time but worth it afterwards.

Over the course of the race, teams climb four mountains more than 3000ft high and run along hundreds of miles of the frozen Yukon River. While the Iditarod has 25 rest stops, the Quest has only six. The Yukon Quest has its new **headquarters** (Map p292; ⏲10am-6pm Mon-Fri, 11-4pm Sat & Sun) in the old Log Cabin Visitor Center on the corner of 1st Ave and Cushman St. There's a small exhibit on the grueling race and a gift shop where proceeds go towards the organization of the race. Mushers are usually on hand with dogs from 11am to 4pm to talk and answer questions.

annex (single/double/triple $75/99/129) with a stylish modern interior. A super-friendly father-and-son team run the units, and while the son is a font of information on outdoor activities (he's cycled the Dalton Hwy in winter), the father prides himself (among other things) on his breakfasts.

Go North Hostel HOSTEL **$**
(Map p288; ✆479-7271; www.gonorthalaska.com; 3500 Davis Rd; tent sites $6 plus per person $6, tepee dm $18, dm $25; @🖥) Fairbanks' best hostel houses backpackers in wall tents, a tepee with two beds (that makes for a great semiprivate room) and a chilled-out camping area. There's nearly everything you could imagine here: bicycle, car and canoe rental, guided backcountry trips, book exchange, internet, foosball and a common kitchen area. It's a long walk from town or from the nearest bus stop (at Fred Meyer), but **Go North Taxi** (✆452-9999) has fixed rates for guests (to/from train station/airport $8/10).

Minnie Street B&B Inn B&B **$$**
(Map p288; ✆456-1802; www.minniestreetbandb. com; 345 Minnie St; r without/with bath $139/169, ste $199-239; 🖥) North of downtown and across the river, this spacious B&B literally occupies a square block of turf. Near matching-sized breakfasts are served by the friendly owners, as well as bountiful advice on what to do around Fairbanks. Four suites come with their own full kitchens and bathrooms, and for the ultimate in privacy and space you can rent an entire house with space for six ($219). All guests have access to an outside deck and barbecue.

Alaska Heritage House B&B B&B **$$**
(Map p288; ✆456-4100; www.alaskaheritagehouse. com; 410 Cowles St; r $159-199; 🖥) Probably the fanciest B&B in town, Heritage House was built in 1916 by Arthur Williams as a way to lure his future wife up to the Great White North to marry him. The home is on the national historic register, and each room has its own flair.

Pike's Waterfront Lodge LODGE **$$$**
(Map p288; ✆456-4500; www.pikeslodge.com; 1850 Hoselton Rd; r from $235, cabins $279; @🖥) This upscale lodge has an enviable position on the green banks of the Chena River. Room decor tilts toward the matronly, but there's also a row of spiffy log cabins with their own grass lawn. Service here is quick and friendly, local artwork adorns the public spaces, and amenities include a steam room, sauna, exercise facilities and the popular **Pike's Landing** (burgers $10-14, dinner mains $25-33) with its Alaskan-sized deck facing the river. It's good to reserve for both the lodge and restaurant. Online room rates for the weekends can be half the published rate.

THE NORTHERN LIGHTS

Fairbanks' best attraction is also its furthest-flung: the aurora borealis, better known as the northern lights, which take place 50 to 200 miles above Earth. As solar winds flow across the upper atmosphere, they hit gas molecules, which light up much like the high-vacuum electrical discharge of a neon sign. The result is a solar-powered lightshow of ghostly, undulating colors streaming across the sky. In the dead of winter, the aurora can be visible for hours. Other evenings 'the event,' as many call it, lasts less than 10 minutes, with the aurora often spinning into a giant green ball and then fading. Milky green and white are the most common colors of the lights; red is rare. In 1958 the northern sky was so 'bloody' with brilliant red auroras that fire trucks rushed out to the hills surrounding Fairbanks, expecting to find massive forest fires.

This polar phenomenon has been seen as far south as Mexico, but Fairbanks is the undisputed aurora capital. Somebody in northern Minnesota might witness fewer than 20 'events' a year and in Anchorage around 150, but in Fairbanks you can see the lights an average of 240 nights a year. North of Fairbanks, the number begins to decrease, and at the North Pole the lights are visible for fewer than 100 nights a year.

Regrettably, from May to mid-August there's too much daylight in Alaska to see an 'event,' but generally in late summer the aurora begins to appear in the Interior and can be enjoyed if you're willing to be awake at 2am. By mid-September the lights are dazzling, and people are already asking, 'Did you see the lights last night?'

The best viewing in Fairbanks is in the outlying hills, away from city lights, or at the University of Alaska Fairbanks.

Billie's Backpackers Hostel
HOSTEL $

(Map p288; ☎479-2034; www.alaskahostel.com; 2895 Mack Blvd; tent sites/dm/r $15/33/99; @ 🖘) Billie's was undergoing a needed update at the time of writing, with a new front deck going in, and general interior improvements to walls and furnishings. Unlikely to change is the easy-breezy international scene that makes this place regularly full in summer. Billie's has typical hostel amenities such as showers, laundry and kitchen, but it also offers nice touches such as a mosquito-netted communal tent for campers, and free use of bicycles.

The hostel is off the MACS Red Line and not far from the university. From College Rd turn right on Westwood Ave and walk one block south.

Chena River State Recreation Site
CAMPGROUND $

(Map p288; walk-in/drive-up sites $10/17; RV sites $28; 🖘) This lushly wooded campground has 61 sites, tables, toilets, fireplaces, water and a boat launch. It's served by the MACS Red, Yellow and Blue lines.

Tanana Valley Campground
CAMPGROUND $

(Map p288; ☎456-7956; 1800 College Rd; campsites/RV sites $16/20) Another well-treed campground with showers and laundry facilities.

✗ Eating

DOWNTOWN

The downtown area has a handful of restaurants in close proximity, representing a range of ethnic cuisines including Thai, Greek and Italian.

Gambardella's Pasta Bella
ITALIAN $$

(Map p292; www.gambardellas.com; 706 2nd Ave; mains $17-28; ⊙11am-10pm) *The* place for Italian food in Fairbanks, with luscious pasta dishes, gourmet subs, pizzas and homemade bread. There's an outdoor area that's a delight during Fairbanks' long summer days.

McCafferty's Coffee House
CAFE $

(Map p292; 408 Cushman St; ⊙7am-8pm Mon-Thu, to 11pm Fri, 9am-11pm Sat, 9am-5pm Sun) This upbeat espresso emporium also serves good daily soups and baked goods. Live music adds atmosphere on Friday and Saturday nights.

🖋 A Taste of Alaska
ALASKAN $$$

(Map p292; 101 Dunkel St) The Tenana Chiefs Conference at the Morris Thompson Cultural & Visitors Center offers traditional

Athabascan dining for private groups of five or more. Contact Dixie Alexander for more (velmaalexander@tananachiefs.org).

UNIVERSITY AREA

Second Story Café
CAFE $

(Map p288; 3525 College Rd; wraps & sandwiches $7; ⊙9am-7pm Mon-Sat, 11am-4pm Sun; @ 🖘) Above Gulliver's Books is this great little hangout with potent espressos, chai and smoothies, as well as killer wraps and sandwiches.

Pita Place
FALAFEL $

(Map p288; www.pitasite.com; 3300 College Rd; full/half pita $4.75/8; ⊙11am-6pm Wed-Sat) The stand is humble, the pita divine and made entirely from scratch.

Sam's Sourdough Café
DINER $$

(Map p288; University Ave at Cameron St; breakfast $6.95-11.95, dinner mains $11.95) Considered by many to be the town's best diner, this place serves up sourdough pancakes all day long, as well as burgers, fish-and-chips, steaks and creamy mashed potatoes.

Bun on the Run
BAKERY $

(Map p288; 3480 College Rd; pastries from $3; ⊙6:30am-4pm Mon-Fri, 9am-2pm Sat) In a pink trailer in the Beaver Sports parking lot, 'the Bun' cranks out delicious pastries and sandwiches, and has quite a following.

Hot Licks
ICE CREAM $

(Map p288; www.hotlicks.net; 3453 College Rd; cones $3.50, sundaes $5-7; ⊙noon-10pm) On warm days, the line for the homemade ice cream here is insane. Find out why with a double-scoop cone of the fresh daily specials.

Tanana Valley Farmers Market
MARKET $

(Map p288; www.tvfmarket.com; College Rd at Caribou Dr; ⊙11am-4pm Wed, from 9am Sat) The market sells fresh produce, baked goods and local handicrafts. Come in late August and you can buy a 20lb cabbage. It's occasionally open on Sundays.

AIRPORT WAY & AROUND

Pump House Restaurant
STEAKHOUSE $$$

(Map p288; ☎479-8452; www.pumphouse.com; Mile 1.3; Chena Pump Rd; dinner $18-36; ⊙lunch & dinner) Located 4 miles from downtown, this national historic site was once a pump house during the gold-mining era. It's loaded with character and collectibles, but the food is undistinguished and the dining area takes itself a bit too seriously. Fortunately the guests don't, which still makes this a great place to turn dinner into an evening, or to enjoy a Sunday brunch out on the deck overlooking the Chena River. The MACS Yellow Line goes by here.

Cookie Jar
BREAKFAST $

(Map p288; www.cookiejarfairbanks.com; 1006 Cadillac Ct; breakfast $7.95-9.95; ☺6:30am-8pm Mon-Thu, to 9pm Fri & Sat, 8am-4pm Sun; 🛜🚼) Though bizarrely situated behind a pair of car dealerships off Danby St, Cookie Jar lives up to its name as one of Fairbanks' top spots to indulge a sweet tooth. But this is also a great little breakfast and lunch shop with filling specials and an endless cup of coffee. There's a kid's menu available.

Alaska Salmon Bake
SALMON BAKE $$$

(Map p288; www.akvisit.com; adult/child $31/15; ☺5-9pm; 🚼) Hungry souls should take in the touristy, tasty, tongue-in-cheek salmon bake at Pioneer Park, which serves all-you-can-eat grilled salmon, halibut, cod, prime rib and countless sides. A $6 shuttle bus is available from major hotels.

Fred Meyer
SUPERMARKET $

(Map p288; ✆474-1400; cnr Old Airport Rd & Airport Way; ☺7am-11pm) This airplane hangar–sized store has every grocery imaginable, plus bulk foods, an extensive salad bar and all sorts of ready-to-eat fare.

AROUND FAIRBANKS

Some of the most locally recommended places to eat in town are actually just outside town. The following are both found in Fox, reached by heading north on Steese Hwy and turning onto the Old Steese Hwy at Fox. The brewery is practically right at the intersection with the two highways, while Turtle Club is 1 mile further down.

Turtle Club
RIBS $$

(✆457-3883; Mile 10, Old Steese Hwy; dinner $22.95-36.95; ☺dinner) Not a club but more of a roadhouse reputed for its prime ribs. Reservations are recommended.

Silver Gulch Brewery
BURGERS $$

(Mile 11, Old Steese Hwy; burgers $11, mains $15-34; ☺4-10pm Mon-Fri, from 11am Sat & Sun) This cavernous, slightly overdone brewpub makes the best beer in the region but plenty of people come here just for the pub grub.

🍷 Drinking & Entertainment

As Alaska's second-biggest city, Fairbanks always has something on the go. For the lowdown on live music, movies and such,

check the listings in 'Latitude 65,' printed each Friday in the *Fairbanks Daily News-Miner.*

Pump House Saloon
PUB

(Map p288; Mile 1.3, Chena Pump Rd) Enjoys the riverfront ambience of the Pump House Restaurant but with a bar menu that won't break the bank.

Palace Theatre & Saloon
THEATER

(Map p288; ✆452-7274; www.akvisit.com; adult/child $18/9) Pioneer Park comes alive at night in this historical theater with honky-tonk piano, cancan dancers and other acts in the 'Golden Heart Revue.' Showtime is 8:15pm nightly. Dinner at the park's nearby Alaska Salmon Bake takes place before the show.

College Coffeehouse
CAFE

(Map p288; 3677 College Rd; coffee $2-4.25; ☺7am-midnight Mon-Fri, from 8am Sat & Sun; @🛜) In the Campus Corner Mall, this is one of the best spots in Fairbanks to pick up on the city's off-beat vibe. There's frequent live music.

Marlin
BAR

(Map p288; 3412 College Rd) A subterranean dive hosting Fairbanks' edgiest musical acts most nights of the week.

AROUND FAIRBANKS

Blue Loon
LIVE MUSIC

(www.theblueloon.com; Mile 352.5, George Parks Hwy) One of the Fairbanks area's most popular nightspots, the Loon features live bands and DJs, dancing, food and lots of good beer. A couple times a summer it may even pull in an older big-name act like the Violent Femmes or the Bare Naked Ladies. To get here, head out of town a few miles on George Parks Hwy.

🛍 Shopping

At the time of writing, the Morris Thompson Cultural & Visitors Center was just getting a gift shop going that would sell genuine and unique pieces of native art from all over Alaska.

Alaska House Art Gallery
ARTS & CRAFTS

(Map p292; cnr 10th Ave & Cushman St; ☺11am-7pm Mon-Sat) In a log building at the southern end of downtown, the gallery specializes in indigenous and native-themed creations. Artists can often be found on the premises demonstrating their talents or telling stories.

There's a fair bit of controversy about whether rental companies can legally prohibit you from taking an ordinary compact vehicle on gravel highways (and whether insurance would cover you in case of accident). For the time being, it's best to comply for the toughest of roads like the Dalton or Taylor Hwys and get a rough-road-worthy vehicle. Expect to pay $200 to $250 a day (mileage may be extra, depending on how many days you rent) when everything is added up. Note that rental taxes are very high, at 18%, and so are gas prices: do inquire about the vehicle's mileage as it can mean hundreds of dollars in the difference. The two main companies to contact in Fairbanks for SUV and truck rental are **Dalton Highway Auto Rentals** (474-3530; www.arctic-outfitters.com; 3820 University Ave, east ramp of Fairbanks International Airport) and **Go North Car & RV Rental** (479-7272; www.gonorthalaska.com; 3713 S Lathrop St). Both can provide insurance if you need it.

Gulliver's Books
BOOKS

(Map p288; www.gullivers-books.com; 3525 College Rd; 9am-9pm Mon-Fri, to 8pm Sat, 11am-6pm Sun;) Next to Campus Corner Mall, near UAF, this is by far the best bookstore in town, selling new and used books and plenty of Alaskan titles.

Beaver Sports
SPORTS

(Map p288; www.beaversports.com; 3480 College Rd; 10am-8pm Mon-Fri, to 7pm Sat, 11am-5pm Sun) Sells mountain bikes and mountains of every species of wilderness equipment. There's also a handy message board for exchanging info with fellow adventurers or securing used gear.

ℹ Information

Wireless is common around town and there are free computers at the visitor center.

B&C Laundromat (Campus Corner Mall; 7am-9:30pm) Has coin-operated laundry ($3.25 per load) and showers ($4.50).

Fairbanks Memorial Hospital (452-8181; 1650 W Cowles St) Emergency care; south of Airport Way.

Key Bank of Alaska (100 Cushman St) Has an ATM. Most strip mall areas also have a bank and ATM.

ℹ Getting There & Away

AIR Alaska Airlines (800-252-7522; www.alaskaair.com) flies direct to Anchorage (where there are connections to the rest of Alaska, the Lower 48 and overseas), Barrow and Seattle. Round-trip advance-purchase fare to Anchorage is around $230 to $330; to Seattle it's upwards of $700. **Air North** (800-661-0407; www.flyairnorth.com) flies to Whitehorse and Dawson City. For travel into the Bush, try **Era Alaska** (266-8394; www.flyera.com), **Warbelow's Air Ventures** (474-0518; www.warbelows.

com) or **Wright Air Service** (474-0502; www.wrightair.net).

BUS Alaska Bus Guy (720 6541; www.alaskabusguy.com) departs Fairbanks at 7am for Denali ($70, three hours) and on to Anchorage ($145, 10½ hours), and will make stops anywhere along Glenn Parks Hwy. **Alaska Direct Bus Line** (800-770-6652; www.alaskadirectbusline.com) buses leave at 9:30am from the downtown Transit Park for Whitehorse ($220, 14 hours) on Sunday, Wednesday and Friday. Along the way they stop at Delta Junction ($60, two hours), Tok ($95, 5½ hours), Beaver Creek ($125, eight hours) and Haines Junction ($185, 10 hours). At Tok, you can transfer to a bus for Glennallen and Anchorage. At Whitehorse you can catch the company's bus to Skagway. **Alaska/Yukon Trails** (800-770-7275; www.alaskashuttle.com) buses leave daily around 9am from various points in Fairbanks (including the hostels) and travel down the George Parks Hwy to Denali National Park (one way $55, three hours), Talkeetna ($92, seven hours) and Anchorage ($99, 10 hours). The company also has a service to Dawson City, Yukon Territory, via the Taylor Hwy, leaving at 8:30am ($169, nine hours).

CAR & MOTORCYCLE If you're driving to Fairbanks from Canada, you'll likely be coming up the Alcan. It's a good 12 hours from Whitehorse to Fairbanks, with little en route, save for Tok and a few other highway service communities. From Anchorage, it's six hours to Fairbanks up George Parks Hwy.

TRAIN Alaska Railroad (458-6025; www.alaskarailroad.com) leaves Fairbanks daily at 8:15am from mid-May to mid-September. The train gets to Denali National Park at noon and Anchorage at 8pm. The **station** (6:30am-3pm) is at the southern end of Danby St. One-way fare to Denali National Park is $64, and $210 to Anchorage. The MACS Red Line runs buses to and from the station.

ℹ Getting Around

TO/FROM THE AIRPORT Fairbanks International Airport (www.dot.state.ak.us/faiiap) is at the west end of Airport Way, 4 miles from town and beyond walking distance of anywhere you'll want to get to. **MACS Yellow Line** (www.co.fairbanks.ak.us/transportation) bus swings by here seven times a day Monday to Friday (three times on Saturday) between 7:30am and 7:15pm, charging $1.50 and taking you past some Airport Way motels and the Go North Hostel en route to the Transit Park. **Airlink Shuttle Service** (☑ 452 3337) runs a shuttle service from the airport for small groups ($10.50 for the first three people). Baggage and more people are extra. A taxi will cost around $15 to $20 depending on where you are going in town.

CAR Considering Fairbanks' noncentralized streetscape, as well as the worthwhile drives beyond town, you'll likely want a vehicle while you're here. All the national rental agencies (Avis, National, Budget, Payless, Hertz) have counters at the airport. Remember that car rentals get dinged with an 18% tax. **Arctic Rent-A-Car** (☑ 561-2990; www.arcticrentacar.com; 1130 W International Airport Rd) near the airport is one of the cheapest options if you plan only to drive within the Fairbanks area.

PUBLIC TRANSPORTATION The **Metropolitan Area Commuter Service** (MACS; www.co.fairbanks.ak.us/transportation) is of limited use for travelers. Buses run sporadically from around 6:15am to 8:15pm Monday to Friday, with even more limited service on Saturday and none on Sunday. The **Transit Park** (cnr Cushman St & 5th Ave) is the system's central hub – all six of the colored route buses stop here. The fare on all routes is $1.50, or you can purchase an unlimited day pass for $3. Schedules are posted on bus stops and also online.

TAXI Cabs charge around $3 per mile, with a $1 flag fall. Try **Alaska Cab** (☑ 455-7777) or **Yellow Cab** (☑ 455-5555). **Go North Taxi** (☑ 452 9999) has flat rates if you are staying at the hostel.

AROUND FAIRBANKS

There are a number of day trips and longer adventures to be had in the outlying areas. Along the Steese and Elliot Hwys you'll find plenty of good hiking and paddling.

Chena Hot Springs Road

This fireweed-lined, forest-flanked corridor parallels the languid Chena River 56 miles to the Chena Hot Springs Resort, the closest hot springs to Fairbanks and also the most developed. The road is paved and in good condition. From Mile 26 to Mile 51 it passes through Chena River State Recreation Area, a 397-sq-mile preserve encompassing the river valley and nearby alpine areas. Some of the Fairbanks area's best hiking, canoeing and fishing can be found here, usually just steps away from the road.

🏃 Activities

Trail maps are sometimes available at the start of hiking trails but it's best to drop by the Morris Thompson Cultural & Visitors Center in Fairbanks beforehand as it is always stocked.

Chena River CANOEING

With no whitewater and comparatively few other hazards, the peaceful Chena River offers a variety of day and multiday canoeing possibilities, with access points all along Chena Hot Springs Rd.

Granite Tors Trail Loop HIKING

The 15-mile Granite Tors Trail Loop – accessed from the Tors Trail State Campground, at Mile 39.5 – ascends into an alpine area with unusual tors, isolated pinnacles of granite rising out of the tundra. The first set is 6 miles from the trailhead but the best group lies 2 miles further along the trail. In total this is an eight- to 10-hour trek that gains 2700ft in elevation. There's a free-use shelter midway.

Angel Rocks Trail HIKING

Angel Rocks is a moderate two- to three-hour, 3.5-mile loop trail that leads to Angel Rocks, large granite outcroppings near the north boundary of the recreation area. The elevation gain is a modest 900ft.

The trail is also the first leg of the Angel Rocks–Chena Hot Springs Traverse, a more difficult 8.3-mile trek that ends at the Chena Hot Springs Resort. Roughly halfway along the traverse is a free-use shelter.

The posted trailhead for Angel Rocks is just south of a rest area at Mile 49. The lower trailhead for the Chena Dome Trail is practically across the street.

Chena Dome Trail HIKING

The upper trailhead for the most popular hike in the area, Chena Dome Trail (p66), is at Mile 50.5. The trail follows the ridge for almost 30 miles in a loop around the Angel Creek drainage area. The first 3 miles to the treeline make an excellent day hike.

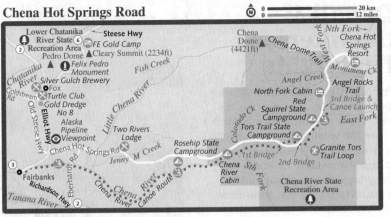

Chena Hot Springs   SPRINGS

The burbling Chena Hot Springs were discovered by gold miners in 1905, and quickly became the area's premier soaking spot. At the heart of a 40-sq-mile geothermal area, the springs produce a steady stream of water that, at 156°F, must be cooled before you can even think about bathing in it. You can only enjoy the waters at the Chena Hot Springs Resort (admission $10; ⊙7am-midnight) which has aging indoor facilities (with chlorinated waters) and a large outdoor boulder-ringed pool with pure hot spring water for adults only.

Other activities at the resort include mountain biking, hiking, horseback riding and fishing the local streams for grayling. The cavernous Ice Museum (admission $15) has tours every two hours from 11am to 7pm, and features work from carver Steve Brice that includes life-size jousting knights, chandeliers and a bar where martinis are served in ice glasses. Just remember the ice loo is only for show.

The entire museum (which has bedrooms and ice beds) can be rented for $600 a night.

🛏 Sleeping & Eating

There are a number of sleeping options in the area, including three popular state-run campgrounds and seven public-use cabins. Two of the cabins are on the road, while the rest are accessible via short but often very wet hikes. The cabins vary in size, sleeping between four and nine people, and can be reserved via the Alaska Division of Parks and Outdoor Recreation (☎451-2695; www. alaskastateparks.org).

Chena River Cabin   CABIN $

(Mile 32.2, Chena Hot Springs Rd; per night $40) A newer, road-accessible cabin in a stand of spruce and birch overlooking the river.

North Fork Cabin   CABIN $

(Mile 47.7, Chena Hot Springs Rd; per night $40) Further down the road, it also has access to the river.

Rosehip State Campground   CAMPGROUND $

(Mile 27, Chena Hot Springs Rd; campsites $10) Has a nature trail and 36 treed, well-spaced sites, some right on the riverbank.

Tors Trail State Campground   CAMPGROUND $

(Mile 39.5, Chena Hot Springs Rd; campsites $10) Twenty-four sites in a stand of spruce, with a canoe launch on the Chena River. Across the highway is Granite Tors Trail Loop trailhead.

Red Squirrel State
Campground   CAMPGROUND $

(Mile 42.8, Chena Hot Springs Rd; campsites $10) There are no designated sites here, but when it's not busy the grassy area bordering the pond makes for a charming camping spot.

🍃 Chena Hot Springs Resort   RESORT $$$

(☎451-8104; www.chenahotsprings.com; Mile 56.6, Chena Hot Springs Rd; campsites $20, r $189-249, yurts with outhouse $65) This come-as-you-are complex is at its best in winter when snow covers the ground and the aurora lights up the sky. Otherwise the rooms are a bit overpriced in summer, especially the older wing, which is getting a bit tatty. The resort's restaurant (lunch mains $10-15, dinner mains $16-25) whips up decent meals, and the adjacent

Denali & the Interior Highlights

Visitors often come to the Interior for Mt McKinley, but stay for the rest. There are few places in Alaska where the wildlife is so commonly spotted, where pure wilderness is so easily accessed, or where so many legendary highways criss-cross, offering unique adventure after adventure to the willing.

Wilderness Park

1 There's more untracked wilderness and wildlife at Wrangell-St Elias National Park (p316) than at Denali National Park, and only a fraction of the visitors. A junction of several mountain ranges, the park is an adventure playground with world-class glacier trekking, backcountry hiking and paddling.

Legendary Wildlife

2 Having a close encounter with Alaska's wildlife is on the bucket list of every visitor. Whether it's a grizzly bear or moose, a Dall sheep or one of hundreds of bird species you're wanting to see, this region won't disappoint.

Rough Riding

3 It's a bouncy ride along the dirt of the 135-mile Denali Hwy (p284) – a marvelous landscape of glaciers, braided river valleys, chain lakes and panoramas of the Alaska Range – but that just keeps down the number of vehicles you'll be sharing it with.

The Great One

4 The tallest mountain in North America, Mt McKinley (p260) sets the stage for one of the world's toughest climbs and most stunning alpine landscapes. Take in views of the mountain from stops along the Park Rd or splash out on a bush-plane flight around the summit.

Clockwise from top left
1. Hiking towards Root Glacier to go ice climbing **2.** Caribou on alert **3.** Denali Highway **4.** Summiting Mt McKinley

bar area doesn't quite overpower you with Yukon Quest memorabilia.

Two Rivers Lodge   PUB $$

(Mile 16, Chena Hot Springs Rd; burgers $11-17, dinner $24-36; ☺5-10pm Mon-Fri, from 3pm Sat & Sun) Steak, seafood and poultry are the focus at this rustic lodge, complete with hunting trophies, but good roadhouse meals (burgers, ribs, sandwiches) are found in the lounge.

ℹ Getting There & Away

Chena Hot Springs Resort (☎451-8104) runs a shuttle-van service from Fairbanks ($125 roundtrip with a two-person minimum) but you'd be better off renting a car. Hitchhiking is not the grand effort it is on the Elliot Hwy, because of the heavy summer usage of the recreation area.

Steese Highway

The scenic but severely lonely Steese Hwy follows an old miners' trail 162 miles from Fairbanks to the Athabascan village of Circle on the Yukon River. This hilly and winding road is paved for the first 53 miles, and then has a good gravel base to the mining settlement of Central. In the final 30 miles it narrows and becomes considerably rougher and more twisty. While an interesting drive, the route's main attraction – Circle Hot Springs – has been closed for several years.

A short drive up the highway may be worthwhile to see the Felix Pedro Monument (Mile 16.6, Steese Hwy), which commemorates the miner whose gold strike gave birth to Fairbanks. The stream across the highway – now known as Pedro Creek – is where it all happened.

Beyond this is the FE Gold Camp (Mile 27.9), a national historic site. The camp was built in 1925 for the dredging that went on from 1927 to 1957 and removed an estimated $70 million in gold (at yesterday's prices).

A few miles beyond, the landscape opens up, revealing expansive vistas as well as evidence of forest-fire activity. There are several state campgrounds including Cripple Creek BLM Campground (Mile 60; campsites $6), which is the uppermost access point to the Chatanika River canoe route.

Access points for the Pinnell Mountain Trail are at Mile 85.6 and Mile 107.3. The first trailhead is Twelvemile Summit, which offers remarkable alpine views and is often snowy well into June. Even if you have no desire to undertake the three-day trek, the first 2 miles is an easy climb past unusual rock formations.

The Birch Creek Canoe Route (www.blm.gov/ak) begins at Mile 94, where a short road leads down to a canoe launch on the creek. The wilderness trip is a seven- to 10-day, 110-mile paddle to the exit point, at Mile 140.5 or 147.2 of the highway. The overall rating of the river is Class II, but there are some Class III and possibly Class IV parts that require lining your canoe.

Eagle Summit (elevation 3624ft) at Mile 107 has a parking area for the second trailhead of the Pinnell Mountain Trail. A climb of less than a mile leads to the mountaintop, the highest point along the Steese Hwy and a place where the midnight sun can be observed skimming the horizon around the summer solstice. On a clear day, summiting here can feel like ascending to heaven. The peak is also near a caribou migration route.

NORTH POLE, ALASKA

Well, it *seemed* like a good idea: back in the 1940s, a development corporation bought up a sleepy homestead southeast of Fairbanks and, in a bid to attract toy manufacturers, named it North Pole. Though the Fortune 500 companies never came knocking, a steady stream of smirking tourists and their starry-eyed kids have been wandering through ever since.

Today this community of 2200 souls, 15 minutes (12 miles) south of Fairbanks, would be a forgettable clutch of churches and fast-food franchises if it weren't for its name and year-round devotion to the Yuletide. Streetlamps are decorated with candy cane stripes, local businesses work a Santa into their name no matter how, and streets bear such festive monikers as Mistletoe Lane. At the North Pole Post Office (325 S Santa Claus Lane), hundreds of thousands of letters arrive annually, simply addressed to 'Santa Claus, North Pole, Alaska.'

The town's biggest attraction is Santa Claus House (www.santaclaushouse.com; 101 St Nicholas Dr, off Richardson Hwy; ☺8am-8pm), between the North Pole exits. The sprawling barnlike store holds endless aisles of Christmas ornaments and toys, a live Santa to listen to your Christmas wishes, a giant statue of Santa and the 'North Pole' – a candy-striped post.

Twenty miles later the highway passes through Central (Mile 127.5), a former supply stop on the trail from Circle City, and finally to Circle itself (Mile 162, Steese Hwy), once a bustling town of 1200 with theaters, dance halls and 28 saloons. Circle was known as the 'largest log-cabin city in the world' until the Klondike Gold Rush (1897–98) reduced its population and the river gobbled up much of the original townscape.

Elliot Highway

From the crossroad with the Steese Hwy at Fox, just north of Fairbanks, the Elliot Hwy extends 154 miles north and then west to Manley Hot Springs, a small settlement near the Tanana River. Along the way are a number of free campgrounds as well as public-use cabins (per cabin $25) that need to be reserved through the BLM (📞474-2251) in Fairbanks.

The first half of the highway is paved, the rest is gravel, and there's no gas and few services until you reach the end. Diversions along the way are comparatively few, but the leisurely, scenic drive, coupled with the disarming charms of Manley Hot Springs, makes it a worthwhile one- or two-day road trip.

At Mile 11 is the Lower Chatanika River State Recreation Area, a 400-acre unmaintained park offering fishing, boating and informal camping opportunities along the Chatanika River.

At Mile 28, look for the Wickersham Dome Trailhead parking lot and an information box. From here, trails lead to two public-use cabins. Lee's Cabin is a 7-mile hike in and overlooks the White Mountains. Borealis-Le Fevre Cabin is a 20-mile hike over the White Mountains Summit Trail.

A bridge crosses the Tolovana River at Mile 57 and nearby is an old unmaintained BLM campground. The fishing here is good for grayling and northern pike, though the mosquitoes are of legendary proportions. Before the bridge is the start of the Colorado Creek Trail to the public-use Windy Gap Cabin, but this is not recommended for summer use as the trail is exceptionally boggy.

Ten miles before the junction with the Dalton Hwy, at Mile 62, a 500yd spur road on the right leads to the public-use Fred Blixt Cabin.

Livengood (lye-ven-good), 2 miles east of the highway at Mile 71, has no services and is little more than a maintenance station with a scattering of log shanties. Here, the Elliot Hwy swings west and in 2 miles, at the junction of the Dalton Hwy, the pavement ends and the road becomes a rutted, rocky lane. Traffic evaporates and until Manley Hot Springs you may not see another vehicle.

In short order the Elliot Hwy ascends to a high subalpine ridge, which it follows for miles, and on clear days affords views of Mt McKinley to the south. In some areas, the open country invites off-road hiking, and the breeze is often strong enough to keep mosquitoes at bay.

The rustic, privately managed Tolovana Hot Springs (📞455-6706; www.tolovanahotsprings.com; 2-/4-/6-person cabins $50/75/100) can be accessed via a taxing 11-mile overland hike south from Mile 93. Facilities consist of outdoor wood tubs bubbling with 125°F to 145°F water, outhouses, a drinking water barrel and three cabins that must be reserved in advance. The trailhead isn't signposted, so contact the managers for directions.

At Mile 110, a paved side road runs 11 miles to the small Athabascan village of Minto (pop 180), which isn't known for welcoming strangers.

Beyond Minto, the Elliot Hwy briefly becomes winding and hilly, and then suddenly, at Mile 120, there's chip-sealing for the next 17 miles. Hutlinana Creek is reached at Mile 129, and a quarter mile east of the bridge (on the right) is the start of an 8-mile creekside trail to Hutlinana Warm Springs, an undeveloped thermal area with a rock-wall pool. The springs are visited mainly in winter; in summer, the buggy bushwhack seems uninviting.

From the bridge it's another 23 miles southwest to Manley Hot Springs.

MANLEY HOT SPRINGS
POP 72

The town of Manley Hot Springs (http://fairbanks-alaska.com/manley-hot-springs.htm) may be one of the loveliest discoveries you'll make around the Fairbanks area. At the end of a long, lonely road, this well-kept town is full of friendly folks, tidy log homes and luxuriant gardens. Located between Hot Springs Slough and the Tanana River, the community was first homesteaded in 1902 by JF Karshner, just as the US Army Signal Corps arrived to put in a telegraph station. A few years later, as the place boomed with miners from the nearby Eureka and Tofty districts, Frank Manley arrived and built a four-story hotel. Most of the miners are gone now, but Manley's name – and the spirit of an earlier era – remains. In modern times the town has been a hotbed of high-level dog-mushing: champs like Charlie Boulding, Joe Redington Jr and four-time Iditarod champ Susan Butcher have all lived here.

◎ Sights & Activities

Hot Springs   SPRINGS
(☑672-3231; admission per hr $5; ⊙24hr) Just before crossing the slough, you pass the town's namesake hot springs, privately owned by famously hospitable Chuck and Gladys Dart. Bathing takes place within a huge, thermal-heated greenhouse that brings to mind a veritable Babylonian garden of grapes, Asian pears and hibiscus flowers.

Deep in this jungle are three spring-fed concrete tubs, each burbling at different temperatures. Pay your money (which gives you sole access to the springs for an hour), hose yourself down and soak away in this deliriously un-Alaskan setting. Heed the signs to not pick the fruit but do call ahead to reserve a time slot.

Manley Boat Charters   BOAT TOURS
(☑672-3271; boat rental per hr $75) Across the slough and 3 miles beyond the village is the broad Tanana River, just upstream from its confluence with the Yukon. Frank Gurtler of Manley Boat Charters can take you fishing or just show you the sights along the waterway.

Iditarod Kennels   DOG SLEDDING
(☑672 3412; www.joeredington.com; tours $25) Run by famed dog sled–racer Joe Redington Jr, these 1½-hour kennel tours delve into the history of dog mushing and racing, as well as Manley itself and the ways and means of rural living. Reservations are preferred to drop-ins.

🛏 Sleeping & Eating

Manley Roadhouse   HISTORIC HOTEL $$
(☑672-3161; www.manleyroadhouse.com; r without bath $80, with bath $120-140) Facing the slough, this antique-strewn, century-old establishment has clean, uncomplicated rooms and is the social center of town. The bar boasts an impressive array of liquor and beer choices, while the restaurant (sandwiches & burgers $9-15; dinner mains $17-25; ⊙8am-8pm) offers home-style cooking in the adjacent sitting room. Aside from the historical rooms, very basic cabins ($130) are available across a grassy field.

Public Campground   CAMPGROUND $
(campsites $5) The slough-facing campground is just past the bridge. Pay at the roadhouse. Showers are available for $5.

Manley Trading Post   SELF-CATERING $
(⊙10am-5pm) For groceries, expensive gas, liquor and postal services.

❶ Getting There & Away
With so little traffic on Elliot Hwy, hitching is ill-advised – though if someone does come along, they'll likely take pity on you. You can rent a vehicle in Fairbanks, however, or contact **Warbelow's Air Ventures** (☑474-0518; www.warbelows.com), in Fairbanks, which has three flights a week to Manley Hot Springs for $170 per round-trip.

THE ALCAN/ALASKA HIGHWAY

One of the most impressive engineering feats of the 20th century, the Alcan stretches 1390 miles from Dawson Creek, British Columbia, to Delta Junction, Alaska. A drive up (or down) the Alaska Hwy is one of those once-in-a-lifetime road trips that many folks dream of and very few actually go and accomplish.

The highway was famously punched through the wilderness in a mere eight months in 1942, as part of a WWII effort to protect Alaska from expansionist Japan. Commonly known as the Alcan, short for 'Alaska–Canada Military Hwy', it remains the only year-round overland route that links the 49th state to the Lower 48.

Approximately 300 of its miles, paved and well maintained, are within Alaska, between Fairbanks and the Yukon Territory border. The 98-mile stretch from Delta Junction to Fairbanks is 'technically' the Richardson Hwy, but most figure this to be the final leg of the Alcan and we, too, treat it as such.

Fairbanks to Delta Junction
From Fairbanks, Richardson Hwy runs 98 relatively unscenic miles to Delta Junction, with little of interest save a few campsites and recreation areas for boating and fishing. From Delta Junction, the Richardson continues to the south via Glennallen to Valdez, while the Alcan branches off and passes through Tok en route to Canada.

Chena Lakes Recreation Area (Mile 346.7, Richardson Hwy; campsites $10-12, day-use parking $5) was the last phase of an Army Corps of Engineers flood-control project prompted by the Chena River's flooding of Fairbanks in 1967.

Two separate parks make up the area, offering nature paths, paved trails and swimming, plus canoe, sailboat and paddleboat rentals. Three campground loops provide access to about 80 sites. Note that the entrance to the recreation area is 2 miles off the Richardson Hwy. Follow the signs after you exit.

Salcha River State Recreation Site (Mile 323.3, Richardson Hwy; campsites $10) offers access to the Salcha and Tanana Rivers for fishing and boating ($10 boat launch). It has a basic camping area on a gravel bar, plus the reservable Salcha River Public-Use Cabin (✉451-2705; www.dnr.state.ak.us/parks/cabins; per night $25) right by the boat dock. To reach the state recreation site, turn in at the Salcha Marine boat dealership.

Harding Lake State Recreation Area (Mile 321.5, Richardson Hwy; campsites $10, day-use parking $5, boat launch $10) is 43 miles from Fairbanks and 1.5 miles northeast of the Alcan. The 90-site wooded campground features more amenities than most in the area, with a ranger office, picnic shelters, horseshoes, volleyball, swimming, canoeing, and fishing (char and pike) in the natural lake. Five group walk-in sites are on the water.

Birch Lake Military Recreation Site (Mile 305.5, Richardson Hwy; campsites $10, day-use parking $5; boat launch $10) is jam-packed on weekends, so save this charming lakefront campsite for quieter times.

Not far from the sprawl of Delta Junction is the turnoff at Mile 293.7 for Tenderfoot Pottery (www.tenderfootpottery.com; pieces $25-65; ⊙9am-9pm), a small studio run by a local ceramicist.

Delta Junction

POP 949

For most visitors, Delta Junction is notable for a technicality: it proclaims itself the end of the Alcan, as the famous highway joins Richardson Hwy here to complete the route to Fairbanks. The town began as a construction camp and picked up its name as it lies at the junction between the two highways. Most travelers use the town as a fuel and grocery stop, with a quick visit to the historic Sullivan's Roadhouse, and Rika's Road-

house and Landing. The big Deltana Fair (www.deltanafair.com), with giant vegetables, livestock shows, parades and live music, is on the last weekend of July.

◉ Sights

FREE Big Delta State Historical Park   PARK (✉895-4201; www.rikas.com; Mile 274.5, Richardson Hwy; sites $5; ⊙8am-8pm) A few miles north of town is the area's best attraction. The 10-acre historical park on the Tanana River preserves Rika's Roadhouse and Landing, an important crossroads for travelers, miners and soldiers on the Fairbanks–Valdez Trail from 1909 to 1947. You can easily spend a couple of hours here wandering the pretty grounds, and exploring buildings stocked with displays of turn-of-the-century farming and roadhouse life.

FREE Sullivan Roadhouse   HISTORIC BUILDING (⊙9am-6pm) Across the parking lot from the visitor center, this classic log structure (on the National Register of Historic Places) was built in 1906 to serve travelers along the Fairbanks–Valdez Trail. In 1997 the cabin was moved, log by log, from Fort Greely to its present location and now serves as a museum with a collection of exhibits dedicated to travel in Alaska in the early 1900s, the roadhouse era.

🛏 Sleeping & Eating

Delta Junction is blessed with scads of nearby campgrounds and no bed tax. Eating options in town are limited.

Big Delta State Historical Park   CAMPGROUND $ (✉895-4201; www.rikas.com; Mile 274.5, Richardson Hwy; campsites $5; ⊙8am-8pm) Just off the parking lot is a small wooded campground. Within the park, look for the à la carte Packhouse Pavilion Restaurant (sandwiches $7.50; ⊙9am-5pm), which sells tasty sandwiches and baked goods, and is probably the best place for a meal in the area.

Delta State Recreation Site   CAMPGROUND $ (Mile 267, Richardson Hwy; campsites $10) A mile north of the visitor center, this is the closest public campground to town. It has 24 sites, some overlooking the local airstrip.

Clearwater State Recreation Site   CAMPGROUND $ (campsites $10) With 16 wooded and well-spaced sites, most overlooking the peaceful

Clearwater Creek, this is a lovely little spot to spend a night. The site is 13 miles northeast of town. To get there, first follow Richardson Hwy and then turn right on Jack Warren Rd, 2.4 miles north of the visitor center. Head 10.5 miles east and look for signs to the campground. Clearwater Creek has good grayling fishing and some paddling options.

Quartz Lake State Recreation Area
CAMPGROUND **$**

(Mile 277.8, Richardson Hwy; campsites $10) Covering 600 acres north of town (3 miles from the Richardson Hwy), this area has two camping areas: one by Lost Lake and another closer to the entrance. Both are accessible by road, and there is additional primitive camping at Bluff Point, accessible by a 3-mile trail starting near the lake. Also starting near the lake is a rugged 1.7 mile trail (one way) to Bert Mountain (1820ft).

The public-use **cabins** (http://dnr.alaska.gov/parks/cabins; per night $25) are other sleeping options.

Kelly's Alaska Country Inn
MOTEL **$$**

(☏895-4667; www.kellysalaskacountryinn.com; 1616 Richardson Hwy; s/d $129/139; ☏) Two blocks north of the visitor center, Kelly's has spacious, clean rooms, some with kitchenettes.

IGA Food Cache
SUPERMARKET **$**

(Mile 266, Richardson Hwy; ☺6:30am-10pm Mon-Sat, 8am-9pm Sun) A half-mile north of the visitor center, this grocery store features a bakery, deli and espresso cart, and also sells homemade soup and other ready-to-eat items to go.

❶ Information

Delta Community Library (2291 Deborah St; ☺10am-6pm Mon-Fri, to 5pm Sat, noon-5pm Sun; @☏) The best place in town to check your email.

Delta Junction Visitor Center (www.deltachamber.org; Mile 1422, the Alcan; ☺8am-8pm) More of a gift shop than a visitor center, this place is usually jammed with RVers clamoring to purchase 'End-of-the-Alaska-Highway' certificates ($1).

❶ Getting There & Away

Alaska Direct Bus Line (☏800-770-6652; www.alaskadirectbusline.com) stops in Delta Junction on Sunday, Wednesday and Friday on its run between Fairbanks ($60) and Tok. From Tok you can continue to Whitehorse, Glennallen or Anchorage.

Tok
POP 1546

Tok, 92 miles up the Alcan from the Canadian border, is the first Alaskan town motorists on multiweek pilgrimages from the Lower 48 will encounter. Thus, this hodgepodge of gas stations, motels and RV parks is viewed with a strange, out-of-proportion reverence, like a sort of pearly gates opening onto heavenly Alaska. The town was born in 1942 as a construction camp for the highway, and was originally called Tokyo Camp until anti-Japanese sentiment caused locals to shorten it to Tok. From here, the rest of the state beckons: the Alcan heads 206 miles northwest to Fairbanks; the Tok Cutoff/Glenn Hwy reaches 328 miles southwest to Anchorage; and the Taylor Hwy curls back 161 miles to Eagle.

🛏 Sleeping

There is no bed tax in Tok.

Mooseberry Inn
B&B **$$**

(☏883-5496; www.amooseberryinn.com; Mile 1316, the Alcan; r $129-149; ☏) Just 2.5 miles west of Tok, this B&B has cute and comfy rooms, private balconies and a big breakfast in a homey family atmosphere, making it one of the best options outside of town. The friendly owner speaks German. To get here, head south of the Alcan at Mile 1316 on Scooby Rd, then take a quick right on Maes Way.

Thompson's Eagle Claw
CABINS, CAMPGROUND **$**

(☏940 5558; www.thompsonseaglesclaw.com; Borealis & West C St; tent sites/cabins $10/40) Though the motorcycling enthusiasts who opened this campground have a soft spot for the two-wheeled traveler, anyone and everyone is welcome to stay. Carved out of a thick spruce forest, the expansive grounds offer a steamhouse, cabins, primitive campsites, teepees ($20), a four-person bunkhouse (per person $10) and even the chance to sleep in an old ambulance ($20, sleeps two). The site is completely off the electric grid but has well water.

Tok River State Recreation Site
CAMPGROUND **$**

(Mile 1309, the Alcan; campsites $15) On the Tok River's east bank, 4.5 miles east of Tok, this pleasant 27-site campground has a boat launch and picnic shelter.

Moon Lake State Recreation Site

CAMPGROUND $

(Mile 1331.5, the Alcan; campsites $15) Fourteen sites sit next to placid Moon Lake, 17 miles west of Tok on the Alcan.

 Eating & Drinking

Fast Eddy's
DINER $$

(Mile 1313.3, the Alcan; burgers $8-12, pizza $14-22; ⊘6am-11pm; 🛜🍴) Perhaps the most famous eatery on the Alcan, Eddy's delivers decent diner food with surprisingly less attitude than you'd expect from such a place.

Three Bears Grocery
SUPERMARKET $

(1314 the Alcan; ⊘7am-10pm) Across the Alcan from the Alaska Public Lands Information Center, there's a decent selection of groceries and a few baked goods.

ℹ Information

Tok Mainstreet Visitors Center (⊘8am-7pm Mon-Sat, from 9am Sun) Near the corner of the Tok Cutoff and the Alcan.

Tundra Lodge & RV Park (Mile 1315, the Alcan) Showers ($4) are available here, just west of the visitor center.

ℹ Getting There & Away

BUS Alaska Direct Bus Line (📞800-770-6652; www.alaskadirectbusline.com) Passes through Tok on Sunday, Wednesday and Friday, stopping at the village of Texaco. From there, buses head northwest to Fairbanks ($95, four hours), southwest to Anchorage ($120, eight hours) and southeast to Whitehorse ($150, nine hours), where you can transfer to a bus to Skagway.

Alaska/Yukon Trails (📞800-770-7275; www.alaskashuttle.com) Runs vans on Sunday, Tuesday and Friday from Fairbanks to Dawson City and will stop in Tok only if they already have at least two people starting from Fairbanks. The fare from Tok is $125.

HITCHHIKING Check the message board at the Tok Mainstreet Visitors Center if you're trying to hitch a ride through Canada. Note that the Canadian customs post has developed a tough reputation and hitchhikers, especially Americans, may be turned back for having insufficient funds.

Tok to Canada

The journey from Tok (Mile 1314) to the Canadian border comprises 92 miles of the paved but often frost-heaved Alcan as it weaves through low-slung mountains and vast wetlands. Thirteen miles east of Tok sits Tetlin Junction, where Taylor Hwy branches off toward Eagle, with connections via the Top of the World Hwy to Dawson City.

Shortly after the junction you'll reach the 932,000-acre **Tetlin National Wildlife Refuge** (http://tetlin.fws.gov), which skirts the highway's south side all the way to the border. Waterlogged by countless lakes, marshes, streams and rivers, the refuge is a home or migratory pit stop for 180 species of bird. The best viewing is typically from April to early June, when swans, geese, ducks, sandhill cranes and raptors are on their way through.

Two USFWS campgrounds are available just off the highway, and backcountry camping is permitted throughout the refuge. **Lakeview Campground** (Mile 1256.7; campsites free) features 11 sites on a hillside overlooking beautiful Yager Lake, where you can see the St Elias Range to the south on a nice day. **Deadman Lake Campground** (Mile 1249.3; campsites free) has 15 sites, a boat ramp and a short nature trail. Presentations by rangers are held weekdays at 7pm.

The **Tetlin National Wildlife Refuge Visitor Center** (Mile 1229; ⊘8am-4:30pm), a sod-covered log cabin with a huge viewing deck, overlooks the Scotty and Desper Creek drainage areas. The Mentasta and Nutsotin Mountains loom in the distance. Inside, the cabin is packed with interpretive displays on wildlife, mountains and Athabascan craftwork; beading demonstrations take place regularly.

Ten miles on, you'll reach the Canadian border. The spot is marked by an observation deck and plaque; another 18 miles beyond is the Canadian customs post, just outside Beaver Creek, Yukon.

TAYLOR HIGHWAY

The Taylor Hwy runs 161 miles north from Tetlin Junction (13 miles east of Tok on the Alcan) through the lovable tourist trap of Chicken to the sleepy, historic community of Eagle on the Yukon River. Wildfires in 2004 and 2005 scarred many sections of the scenic drive, including around Mt Fairplay, Polly Summit and American Summit. But the large swaths of burnt spruce forest create an interesting 'Seussical' landscape, scenic in its own way. The route was once infamously rough, but these days the only white-knuckle stretch is the last 65 miles from Jack Wade Junction to Eagle. The highway closes in winter (generally from October to May), when you can still get to Eagle by plane, snow machine or dog sled.

The highway takes paddlers to both the Fortymile River and the Yukon-Charley Rivers National Preserve, and also offers much off-road hiking. As on the Denali Hwy, many of the trailheads are unmarked, so it's necessary to have good topographic maps. Many trails are off-road-vehicle tracks that hunters use heavily in late summer and fall.

By Alaskan standards summer traffic is light to moderate until Jack Wade Junction, where the majority of vehicles continue east to Dawson City, Yukon, via the Top of the World Hwy. Hitchhikers aiming for Eagle from the junction will need patience. Leave Tok or Dawson with a full tank of gasoline, as roadside services are limited.

The first section of the Taylor, from Tetlin Junction (Mile 0) to just shy of Chicken, is now paved. Within 9 miles of Tetlin Junction you'll begin to climb Mt Fairplay (5541ft). At Mile 35 a lookout near the summit is marked by an interpretive sign describing the history of Taylor Hwy. From here you should see superb views of Mt Fairplay and the valleys and forks of Fortymile River to the north. The surrounding alpine area offers good hiking for those wanting to stretch their legs.

The first state campground is the 25-site West Fork Campground (Mile 49; campsites $10) but there are informal camping spots all along the road. Travelers packing gold pans can try their luck in West Fork River, which is also the first access point for a canoe trip down Fortymile River.

Chicken

POP 9

After crossing a bridge over Fortymile River's Mosquito Fork at Mile 64.4, Taylor Hwy enters dusty Chicken, once a thriving mining center and now more of a punchline than an actual community. The town's name allegedly originated at a meeting of resident miners in the late 1800s. As the story goes, the men voted to dub their new tent-city 'Ptarmigan,' since that chickenlike bird (now the Alaskan state bird) was rampant in the area. Trouble is, no-one could spell it. The town's name has been Chicken ever since and, lest you forget, a colossal horror-flick-inspired mascot sits high above town on a knoll near Pedro Dredge.

In retrospect, the naming was a savvy move. Nowadays, folks flock here for 'Go peckers!' coffee mugs, 'I got laid in Chicken' caps and pictures of themselves in front of the Chicken Poop outhouses. In the third weekend of June, check out the increasingly popular Chickenstock Music Concert (see its Facebook page for more).

◉ Sights & Activities

Chicken's work-camp appearance is no act and an old pile of rusting pipes is as likely to be labeled a tourist attraction as some pun on chickens.

Mining History & Goldpanning

Dominating the town's skyline (after Monster Chicken, of course) is the Pedro Gold Dredge, which worked creeks in the area from 1959 to 1967. Chicken Gold Camp (www.chickengold.com) runs tours ($8) and is currently at work on a mining museum.

The camp also offers gold panning ($10) near the dredge, and more advanced recreational mining down the road at a working claim where you can sluice (per day $25 to $60) your way to riches. It's not unheard of for visitors to come away with an ounce of gold after a day's work.

Just north of Chicken is Chicken Creek Bridge, built on tailing piles from the mining era. The creek, and most other tributaries of the Fortymile River, are covered from one end to the other by active mining claims.

Kayaking

The nearby Fortymile River is a popular recreational kayak route. Chicken Gold Camp (www.chickengold.com) rents out kayaks for $35 for a half-day float. Shuttle services are also available for $45. The bridge over South Fork (Mile 75.3) marks the most popular access point for the Fortymile River canoe route.

🛌 Sleeping & Eating

There's no bed tax in Chicken.

Chicken Gold Camp   CABINS, CAMPGROUND $
(www.chickengold.com; campsites/RV sites $14/28, cabins $90-115; 🐾) On a spur road to the right as you enter Chicken, the camp offers Chicken's toniest setting with work-a-day cabins and a gravel lot camping area. It's a friendly family-run place, however, and the cafe (sandwiches $11; ⏰7:30am-7:30pm) in the Chicken Creek Outpost is a good hangout.

Goldpanner   CABINS, CAMPGROUND $
(www.townofchicken.com; Mile 66.8 Taylor Hwy; campsites $15, RV sites $26-36, cabins $99-119; ⏰8am-10pm) On Taylor Hwy, just before

Chicken Creek, is another gravel lot featuring cabins, rooms, a gift shop and the only flush toilets in Chicken. Goldpanner also offers 'hostel' rooms, though these are really just bare singles and doubles for $45 and $55.

Chicken Creek Café, Liquor Store & Mercantile Emporium   DINER $
(www.chickenalaska.com; breakfast $5-10, lunch & dinner $10-16; ⊙7:30am-7pm) Profiting the most from chicken kitsch seems to be this row of clapboard buildings across from Chicken Gold Camp. The gift shop is extensive, the saloon has hats from every corner of the world, and the cafe, unsurprisingly, features lots of chicken on the menu.

Fortymile River

Historic Fortymile River, designated as Fortymile National Wild River, offers an excellent escape into scenic wilderness for paddlers experienced in lining their canoes around rapids. It's also a step back into Alaska's gold-rush era; the river passes abandoned communities, including Franklin, Steele Creek and Fortymile, as well as some present-day mining operations. The best place to start paddling is at the South Fork Bridge Wayside (Mile 75, Taylor Hwy), as the access points south of here on Taylor Hwy are often a little too shallow for an enjoyable trip.

Many canoeists paddle the 40 miles from South Fork Bridge to the Fortymile Bridge Wayside (Mile 112, Taylor Hwy), home of the

Forty-Mile Riverboat Tours (larryjune@starband.net; Mile 113.2, Taylor Hwy) complex. This two- to three-day trip involves three sets of Class III rapids. For a greater adventure, continue and paddle the Fortymile into the Yukon River; from here, head north to Eagle at the end of the Taylor Hwy. This trip is 140 miles long, takes seven to 10 days, and requires lining your canoe past several sets of rapids in Fortymile River.

See the *Fortymile Wild and Scenic River* pages on the BLM (www.blm.gov/ak) website for route planning, maps and more.

Eagle Canoe Rentals (🖉547-2203; www.eaglecanoerentals), in Eagle, is the closest place to get an expedition-worthy canoe or raft.

Eagle

POP 129

From Jack Wade Junction, the Taylor Hwy continues north 58 miles on one of the worst (though highly scenic) stretches of highway in Alaska to Eagle (pop 129). This quaint hamlet of log cabins and clapboard houses is one of the better-preserved boomtowns of the Alaskan mining era. The original settlement, today called Eagle Village, was established by the Athabascans long before Francois Mercier arrived in the early 1880s and built a trading post in the area. A permanent community of miners took up residence in 1898, and in 1900 President Theodore Roosevelt issued a charter that made Eagle the first incorporated city of the Interior.

TOP OF THE WORLD HIGHWAY TO DAWSON CITY

Northeast of Chicken at Jack Wade Junction (Mile 95.7, Taylor Hwy), the Taylor meets the Top of the World Hwy, gateway to Dawson City. This grail of the Klondike Gold Rush is now one of the Far North's most intriguing, fun-drunk towns. It's also just 79 miles away (downhill mostly) with a stop at the international border. Be forewarned, though: Canadian customs is open only from 8am to 6pm Alaska time (call the Tok Visitor Center on 🖉883-5775 to confirm). Arrive too late and you'll be camping in the parking lot until morning. Also remember that these days even US citizens will be required to show a passport.

Beyond the border, the highway – mainly paved now, but with lots of gravel patches under repair – lives up to its name, twisting along high-country ridgetops with flabbergasting views and all sorts of off-road hiking options. There's significant wildfire damage around this area, but you'll still get some lovely panoramas. After 66 miles of this you wind your way down to the Yukon River, where a car ferry conveys you across the water to Dawson City.

If you're without wheels, you can ride along the Top of the World Hwy with Alaska/Yukon Trails (🖉800-770-7275; www.alaskashuttle.com), whose buses come this way each day in summer from Fairbanks ($149 one way, minimum two passengers). For more on Dawson City, consult Lonely Planet's *British Columbia*, which covers the Yukon Territory.

The gold strikes of the early 1900s, most notably at Fairbanks, began drawing residents away from Eagle. At one point, it is said, the population of Eagle dipped to nine residents, seven of whom served on the city council. When the Taylor Hwy was completed in the 1950s, however, the town's population increased to its present level.

In 2010, floods wiped out most of Front St in Eagle and so badly damaged the highway that tour buses, and even the passenger tour boat between Dawson City and Eagle, the Yukon Queen II (www.hollandamerica.com), were not running a year later. As a result, Eagle's restaurants also remained closed, though the Eagle Campground (☑883-5121; campsites $10), north of Fort Egbert, and Falcon Inn B&B (☑547-2254; http://falconinn.mystarband.net; 220 Front St; s/d $125/145) were still operating. Hopefully, the situation will improve.

◉ Sights & Activities

Historical Buildings

Residents say Eagle has the state's largest 'museum system,' boasting five restored turn-of-the-20th-century buildings. If you're spending a day here, the best way to see the buildings and learn the town's history is to take the Eagle Historical Society (www.eagleak.org; tour $7) two-hour town walking tour. The tours start daily at 9am, and in addition to Eagle City Hall and the Log Church, the tour takes you into the restored Fort Egbert, originally built in 1999 by the US Army as part of its effort to maintain law and order in the Alaskan Interior.

Paddling

During its heyday, Eagle was an important riverboat landing for traffic moving up and down the Yukon. Today it's a departure point for the many paddlers who float along the river through the Yukon-Charley Rivers National Preserve. The 150-mile trip extends from Eagle to Circle, at the end of the Steese Hwy northeast of Fairbanks; most paddlers take six to 10 days, though some require as few as three.

It's not a difficult paddle, but it must be planned carefully. Kayakers and canoeists should come prepared for insects, but can usually camp either in public-use cabins or on open beaches and river bars, where winds keep the bugs at bay. They also need to be prepared for extremes in weather; freezing nights can be followed by daytime temperatures of 90°F.

Contact Eagle Canoe Rentals (☑547-2203; www.eaglecanoerentals.com) for boat rentals and information. The Yukon-Charley Rivers National Preserve Visitor Center (www.nps.gov/yuch; ◷8am-5pm) in Eagle is also worth contacting. The center is off 1st St near the river and airstrip.

ⓘ Getting There & Around

There are no buses to Eagle. If driving, check in at the Tok Visitor Center for the latest road conditions. Everts Air Alaska (☑450-2300; www.evertsair.com, one way $170) flies to Eagle most days of the week from Fairbanks.

TOK CUTOFF & GLENN HIGHWAY

The quickest path from the Alcan to Anchorage, the paved Tok Cutoff/Glenn Hwy offers some of the best hiking, boating and gawkworthy scenery in the state. The rugged 328-mile route is graced by both the Wrangell and Chugach Mountains. Glennallen and Palmer are significant-sized communities along the way.

Tok Cutoff

Narrow and forest-flanked, the Tok Cutoff runs 125 miles from Tok to Gakona Junction. There it meets the Richardson Hwy, which heads 14 miles south to Glennallen, the eastern terminus of the Glenn Hwy. There are glorious views of towering Mt Sanford and the Wrangell Mountains on a clear day.

The first of only two public campgrounds on Tok Cutoff pops up at Mile 109.5 as you drive south from Tok. Eagle Trail State Recreation Site (campsites $15), near Clearwater Creek, has 35 sites, drinking water and toilets. The historic Old Slana Cutoff Hwy, which at one time extended from Tok to Valdez, now provides a leisurely 20-minute nature walk in the vicinity of the campground. Look for the posted trailhead near the covered picnic shelters.

Another 45 miles southwest along the highway, just north of the Nabesna Rd junction, is the 240-acre Porcupine Creek State Recreation Site (Mile 64.2, Tok Cutoff; campsites $15), offering 12 wooded sites in a scenic spot along the creek. A mile north along the highway you'll find a historical marker and the first views of Mt Sanford (16,237ft), a dormant volcano.

Officially, the Tok Cutoff ends at Gakona Junction, 125 miles southwest of Tok, where it merges with the Richardson Hwy. Nearby is Gakona Lodge (✆822-3482; www.gakonalodge.com; Mile 2, Tok Cutoff; r with shared bath $95, cabins with bath $115-150, tepee $35; ☎), a lovely log roadhouse dating from 1905 and listed on the National Register of Historic Places. Even if you aren't staying the night, the friendly owners will let you snoop around. Rooms are small, in keeping with the old-time atmosphere, and the warped floorboards in the hallways are a source of both amusement and pride. In addition to accommodation, the roadhouse has a dining room (◷5-10pm), Trapper's Den Tavern (a former US Army Corp of Engineers supply room) and, according to some, a resident ghost. Fishing tours are offered on the Klutina and Gulkana Rivers, which offer some of Alaska's best salmon fishing.

From Gakona Junction, follow the Richardson Hwy 14 miles south to the Glenn Hwy junction.

Glenn Highway

Among Alaska's most jaw-dropping drives, the Glenn runs 189 miles from the Richardson Hwy at Glennallen through the Chugach Range to Anchorage, merging with the George Parks Hwy just after Palmer. Appropriately, most of this corridor was declared a National Scenic Byway. Along the route, outdoor opportunities abound: there's great alpine hiking around Eureka Summit, easy access to the humbling Matanuska Glacier, and some of the state's best white water in the nearby Matanuska River. Note there is a 5% bed tax in this area.

GLENNALLEN
POP 554

Glennallen is referred to by its civic fathers as 'the hub' of Alaska's road system, which is appropriate, because despite the impressive vistas, most travelers will find little to do here but leave. Located at the axis of the Glenn and Richardson Hwys, the town is a supply center for those going to Wrangell-St Elias National Park.

Within town, the Copper River Valley Visitor Center (◷9am-7pm), at the exact junction of the highways, is useful if you need a stack of brochures. West of here along the Glenn Hwy you'll find the region's only full-service bank, a Wells Fargo (Mile 187.5, Glenn Hwy), which has an ATM.

🛏 Sleeping & Eating

Dry Creek State Recreation
Site   CAMPGROUND $
(Mile 117.5, Richardson Hwy; campsites $15) For camping, your best bet is this very peaceful, spruce-shrouded site, 5 miles northeast of town on the Richardson Hwy.

Northern Nights Campground CAMPGROUND $
(✆822-3199; www.northernnightscampground. com; Mile 188.7, Glenn Hwy; campsites/RV sites $12/20; ◷8am-8pm; ☎) Sites don't have much privacy but this is a clean, well-run campground, and centrally located. Showers are $4 and the wi-fi is free.

Tok Thai Food   THAI $$
(dishes $10-14) There are a few diners in town, but undeniably the best food is served straight from the window of a purple bus in the lot at the junction of the Glenn and Richardson Hwys. The spring rolls are superb.

Omni Park's Place   SUPERMARKET $
(Mile 187, Glenn Hwy; ◷7am-10pm Mon-Fri, 8am-9pm Sat, 9am-9pm Sun) Has a large well-stocked grocery selection and deli.

❶ Getting There & Around

For hitchhikers, Glennallen is notorious as a place for getting stuck when trying to thumb a ride north to the Alcan. Luckily, buses are available. Alaska Direct Bus Lines (✆800-770-6652; www.alaskadirectbusline.com) passes through town every Sunday, Wednesday and Friday en route to and from Anchorage ($55, five hours) and Tok ($65, three hours). Call for departure times and pick-up locations.

The vans of Kennicott Shuttle (✆822-5292; www.kennicottshuttle.com) run to and from McCarthy in Wrangell-St Elias National Park daily in summer (round-trip same day/different day $99/139). The trip takes about four hours each way and leaves Glennallen at 7am. You'll need to make a reservation.

TOLSONA CREEK TO MATANUSKA GLACIER

West of Glennallen, the Glenn Hwy slowly ascends through woodland into wide-open high country, affording drop-dead views of the Chugach and Talkeetna Mountains, and limitless hiking opportunities. If you're driving, anticipate plenty of stops to get out and coo over the scenery.

From Little Nelchina River at around the 140 Mile mark, the Glenn Hwy begins to ascend, and Gunsight Mountain comes into view (you have to look hard to see the origin of its name). From Eureka Summit, the highway's highest point (3222ft, Mile 129.3), you can see both Gunsight Mountain and the Chugach Mountains to the south. The Nelchina Glacier spills down in the middle here and the Talkeetna Mountains strut to the northwest. The open view extends to the west, where the highway drops into the river valley that separates the two mountain chains.

From here the Glenn Hwy begins to descend, and the surrounding scenery fires up the imagination as the Talkeetna Mountains loom in the distance and you pass the Sphinx-like rock formation known as the Lion's Head at Mile 114. A half-mile further, the highway reaches the first viewpoint of Matanuska Glacier. To the north is Sheep Mountain, aptly named as you can often spot Dall sheep on its slopes.

◉ Sights & Activities

HIKING

Chickaloon-Knik Nelchina Trail System   HIKING

Once a gold miner's route used before the Glenn Hwy was built, today this network of dirt roads and rough trails extends to Palmer and beyond, and is popular with backpackers and off-road vehicles alike. The system is not maintained regularly, and hikers attempting any part of it should have extensive outdoor experience and the appropriate topographic maps. The main access point is at Mile 118.5 in a large parking lot off the highway.

There are five main hikes, ranging from two to three hours (8.5 miles) for the trail to Knob Lake, to three to four days (32 miles) for the Belanger Pass & Syncline Mountain Trail. The latter can also be mountain biked in one long day. A basic overview map of the area hikes, including distance and times, is provided at the trailhead.

The trailhead rest area is also a popular vantage point for birdwatchers. With a bit of patience you might be able to get the fixed spotting scopes to reveal a variety of raptors resting in the trees in the wide valley below. In particular, be on the lookout for the hawk owl, which is visible during the day.

Sheep Mountain Lodge Trails   HIKING

The lodge (Mile 113.3, Glenn Hwy) maintains a network of easy to follow trails in the overlooking hills. The paths are open to all, and outstanding views and the chance to see Dall sheep are among the highlights. Non-guests can park in the lodge's gravel lot or at the nearby airstrip.

Mae West Lake Trail   HIKING

A pullout at Mile 169.3 marks the start of this mile-long trail to a long, narrow lake fed by Little Woods Creek.

Lost Cabin Lake Trail   HIKING

This trail winds 2 miles to the lake and is a berry-picker's delight from late summer to early fall. Look for the trailhead at a pullout on the southern side of the Glenn hwy at Mile 165.8.

☞ Tours

If you want to get into, over or onto the mountains, contact Blue Ice Aviation (☑354-6040; www.blueiceaviation.com; Mile 115, Glenn Hwy), which runs standard flightseeing and backpacking tours and more extreme custom trips such as glacier cycling.

🛏 Sleeping & Eating

🖊 Sheep Mountain Lodge   LODGE $$

(☑745-5121; www.sheepmountain.com; Mile 113.5, Glenn Hwy; dm $15, cabins $159-189; 🐾) Among the finest and most scenically situated lodges along the highway, Sheep Mountain features a cafe, bar, sauna (free for cabin guests), comfortable log cabins and a bunkhouse dorm with free showers. The lodge also maintains a lovely network of easy trails in the surrounding hills. The restaurant (dinner mains $23-28) serves the area's best meals.

Tundra Rose Guest Cottages   CABIN $$

(☑745-5865; www.tundrarosebnb.com; Mile 109.5, Glenn Hwy; 2-/4-person cottages $138/148) In a glacier-view setting that's as pretty as the name implies, this family-run place has a more cozy and personal atmosphere than Sheep Mountain Lodge. The owners also run the Grand View Cafe (Mile 109.75, Glenn Hwy; sandwiches $8-11; ⊘8am-9pm; 🐾) just down the road. You can shower ($2.75) at the adjacent RV park.

Lake Louise State Recreation Area   CAMPGROUND $

(campsites $15) At Mile 160, a 19-mile spur road runs north to this scenic recreation site popular among Alaskans keen on swimming, boating and angling for grayling and trout. There are 52 campsites in two campgrounds, and a few lodges and numerous private cabins around the lake as well.

Tolsona Wilderness Campground   CAMPGROUND $

(☑822-3865; www.tolsona.com; Mile 173, Glenn Hwy; campsites $25, RV sites $35-40) The first campground west of Glennallen, this private facility has more than 80 sites bordering Tolsona Creek. In addition to coin-operated showers, there are laundry facilities, and wireless in the main office.

MATANUSKA GLACIER TO PALMER

One of Alaska's most accessible ice tongues, Matanuska Glacier nearly licks the Glenn Hwy as it stretches 27 miles from its source in the Chugach Mountains. Beyond the glacier and almost 12 miles beyond Sutton is the junction with the Fishhook-Willow Rd, which provides access to Independence Mine State Historical Park. The highway then descends into the agricultural center of Palmer.

From Palmer, the Glenn Hwy merges with the George Parks Hwy and continues south to Anchorage, 43 miles away.

◉ Sights & Activities

Matanuska Glacier   GLACIER
Some 18,000 years ago the glacier covered the entire area where the city of Palmer sits today. It must have appeared a supernatural force back then, whereas these days it's *merely* a grand spectacle and open geological classroom.

Entry to Matanuska is via Glacier Park Resort (Mile 102, Glenn Hwy), which charges $20 to follow its private road to a parking lot at the terminal moraine. From there, a self-guided trail will take you a couple of hundred yards onto the gravel-laced ice, carved and braided with translucent blue streams and pitted with deep ponds.

To go further, duck into the office of MICA Guides (☑351-7587; www.micaguides.com; Mile 102.5, Glenn Hwy), where you'll be outfitted with a helmet, crampons and trekking poles, and led on a 1½-hour glacier tour ($45), a three-hour trek ($70) or a six-hour ice-climbing excursion ($130).

Purinton Creek Trail   HIKING
The trail starts at Mile 91 (look for the signpost) and continues 12 miles to the foot of Boulder Creek. Most of the final 7-mile trek runs along the river's gravel bars. The accompanying Chugach Mountains scenery is excellent, and you'll find good camping spots along Boulder Creek.

FREE **Alpine Historical Park**   HISTORICAL BUILDINGS
(Mile 61, Glenn Hwy; ⊙9am-6pm) A picnic or photo-opp stop, the park preserves several buildings, including the Chickaloon Bunk-house and the original Sutton post office, which now houses a museum.

☞ Tours

Nova   RAFTING
(☑800-746-5753; www.novalaska.com; Mile 76.5, Glenn Hwy, Chickaloon; ♿) Almost across the highway from the King Mountain State Recreation Site sits the headquarters of one of Alaska's pioneering rafting companies. Nova offers daily runs of the Matanuska River, including a mild three-hour float (adult/child $60/40) suitable for kids aged five and up. Wilder half-day trips feature Class IV rapids around Lion's Head ($85 to $90 per person).

From early June to mid-July there's also the extremely popular evening Lion's Head run, departing at 7pm and including a riverside cookout. Nova can also guide you along glacier hikes (from $65) and extended river trips on the Matanuska, Talkeetna, Copper, Chickaloon and Tana Rivers for anywhere from $350 to $3000.

🛏 Sleeping

Matanuska Glacier State Recreation Site   CAMPGROUND $
(Mile 101, Glenn Hwy; campsites $15) Just steps away from outrageous glacier vistas in the rest area parking lot sits this campground with 12 tree-shrouded sites. At the far edge of the lot is the mile-long interpretative Edge Nature Trail.

King Mountain State Recreation Site   CAMPGROUND $
(Mile 76, Glenn Hwy; campsites $15) This 22-site campground on the banks of the Matanuska River has excellent views of King Mountain to the southeast.

RICHARDSON HIGHWAY

This is about as postcard perfect as you can get without leaving the cozy confines of your vehicle. Sprinkles of wildflowers shimmer in the wind along the roadside, while off in the distance the sheltering shoulders of the Alaska and Chugach Mountains stand guard. To the south, you get access to the vast wilderness of Wrangell-St Elias National Park. And on every step of the way there are chances to hike, cycle (many cyclists go ahead and do the entire route) and stop for photos.

Alaska's first highway, the Richardson runs 266 miles from Fairbanks to Valdez.

However, the 98-mile stretch between Fairbanks and Delta Junction is popularly considered part of the Alcan, and our coverage of the Richardson thus begins at Delta Junction, where the Alcan branches away to the east. Because the mile markers on the Richardson start in Valdez, drivers traveling from north to south will find the numbers descending.

The Richardson was originally scouted in 1919 by US Army Captain WR Abercrombie, who was looking for a way to link the gold town of Eagle with the warm-water port of Valdez. At first it was a telegraph line and footpath, but it quickly turned into a wagon trail following the turn-of-the-20th-century gold strikes at Fairbanks. Along the way it passes waterfalls, glaciers, five major rivers and the Trans-Alaska Pipeline, which parallels the road most of the way.

Delta Junction to Glennallen

Richardson Hwy runs 151 relatively untrafficked miles from Delta Junction to Glennallen. The route has plenty of curves, hills and frost heaves, but is otherwise in fine condition.

DONNELLY CREEK & AROUND

After departing Delta Junction's 'Triangle,' where the Alcan merges with Richardson Hwy at Mile 266, the highway soon passes Fort Greely (Mile 261) and, a few minutes later, the Alaska Pipeline's Pump Station No 9.

A turnoff at Mile 243.5 offers one of the best views you'll get of the pipeline, as it plunges beneath the highway. Interpretive signage provides an overview of the pipeline's history and engineering, including a fascinating explanation of how 'thermal siphons' protect the permafrost by sucking heat from areas where the pipeline is buried. There are also spectacular panoramas to the southwest of three of the highest peaks in the Alaska Range. From south to west, you can see Mt Deborah (12,339ft), Hess Mountain (11,940ft) and Mt Hayes (13,832ft).

Another interesting turnoff, at Mile 241.3, overlooks the calving grounds of the Delta buffalo herd to the west. In 1928, 23 bison were relocated here from Montana for the pleasure of sportsmen and today they number more than 400. The animals have established a migratory pattern that includes summering and calving along the Delta River. If you have binoculars you may be able to spot dozens of the beasts.

The first public campground between Delta Junction and Glennallen is just after Mile 238, where a short loop road leads west of the highway to Donnelly Creek State Recreation Site (campsites $10), which has 12 sites. This is a great place to camp, as it's seldom crowded and is extremely scenic, with good views of the towering Alaska Range. Occasionally the Delta bison herd can be seen from the campground.

At Mile 225.4 you'll find a viewpoint with picnic tables and a historical marker pointing out what little ice remains of Black Rapids Glacier to the west. Once known as the 'Galloping Glacier,' this ice river advanced 3 miles in the winter of 1936 to almost engulf the highway.

From here, the highway ascends into alpine country and the scenery turns gonzo, with the road snaking under sweeping, scree-sided peaks. At Mile 200.5, a gravel spur leads 2 miles west to Fielding Lake State Recreation Site (campsites free), where a willow-riddled 17-site campground sits in a lovely area above the treeline at 2973ft. The state's Fielding Lake Cabin (www.dnr.state.ak.us/parks/cabins; per night $35) is also available here by online reservation.

In another 3 miles the highway crests its highest point, Isabel Pass (3000ft). The pass is marked by a historical sign dedicated to Captain Wilds Richardson, after whom the highway is named. From this point you can view Gulkana Glacier to the northeast and the Isabel Pass pipeline camp below it.

For much of the next 12 miles the highway parallels the frothing headwaters of the Gulkana River as it pours toward Paxson.

PAXSON & AROUND

At Mile 185.5 of the Richardson Hwy, the junction with the Denali Hwy, you'll find the small service center of Paxson (population 43).

You can gas up and even grab a surprisingly good burger ($11 to $13) at the rundown-looking Paxson Lodge (cnr Richardson & Denali Hwys). A far superior place to spend the night is at the Denali Highway Cabins (p286), a couple of hundred feet up the Denali Hwy.

Ten miles south on the Richardson Hwy, a gravel spur leads 1.5 miles west to Paxson Lake BLM Campground (Mile 175.5, Richardson Hwy; campsites $6-12). With 50 sites around the lakeshore, this is the best public campsite on the highway.

The Richardson Hwy bypasses Copper Center, but don't you do the same. This quaint village of 335 residents, reached by detouring a few miles down Old Richardson Hwy, is prettily situated on the sockeye-salmon-rich Klutina River and offers a handful of worthwhile sights, including the mining, trapping and Alcan Hwy development exhibits at the George Ashby Museum (Mile 101, Old Richardson Hwy; admission by donation; ⊙10am-5pm Mon-Sat, from 11am Sun). The staff are trained historians and more than happy to answer questions. Just across the road is the Copper Center Lodge (☎822-3245; www.coppercenterlodge.com; Mile 101, Old Richardson Hwy; r $125; 🛜), established in 1896 and run by the same family since the late 1940s. Basic roadhouse food (burgers and sandwiches $9 to $16) is available in the ground-floor restaurant.

Rounding out the area are a few local artist shops and the nearby Chapel on the Hill, a stately-looking log structure built in 1942 and for now waiting for relocation closer to the museum and lodge area.

Over the next 20 miles, the Richardson Hwy descends from the Alaska Range, presenting sweeping views of the Wrangell Mountains to the southeast and the Chugach Mountains to the southwest.

🏃 Activities

Paxson to Sourdough Float　　CANOEING

For experienced boaters, the Paxson BLM Campground is also a popular put-in for white-water trips on the main branch of the Gulkana River to Sourdough Creek Campground. This is a 45-mile journey involving several challenging rapids, including the Class IV Canyon Rapids. Although there's a short portage around these rapids, rough Class III waters follow. If you're interested in the route, the BLM (www.blm.gov/ak) offers the super-informative 17-page *Gulkana River Users Guide for Paxson to Sourdough Float* for download from its website.

Gulkana River　　CANOEING

At Mile 147.5 of the Richardson Hwy, the BLM's 42-site Sourdough Creek Campground (campsites $12) provides canoeists and rafters another access to the popular Gulkana River. Located in scrubby forestland that bugs seem to love, the campground has a boat launch, a fishing deck and trails leading to a river observation shelter.

From here, you can take a river float down 35 placid miles to the highway bridge at Gulkana (Mile 126.8), making for a pleasant one- or two-day paddle. All the land from Sourdough Creek Campground south belongs to the Ahtna Native Corporation, which charges boaters to camp. The exceptions – three single-acre sites – are signposted along the riverbanks and have short trails leading back to the highway. From the take-out at the Gulkana River Bridge you are 3 miles south of Gakona Junction, where Tok Cutoff heads northeast to Tok; and 11 miles north of Glennallen, where the Richardson Hwy intersects with the Glenn Hwy.

Raft rentals and shuttle services for many of the area's rivers, including the Gulkana, can be arranged through River Wrangellers (☎822-3967; www.alaskariverwrangellers.com).

Glennallen to Valdez

One of Alaska's most spectacular drives, the 115 miles of the Richardson Hwy between Glennallen and Valdez lead through a paradise of snowy summits, panoramic passes and gorgeous gorges.

Nine miles south of Glennallen is a turn-off to the Wrangell-St Elias National Park Visitor Center. Just south of the visitor center, at Mile 106, Old Richardson Hwy loops off the main highway, offering access to Copper Center. Old Richardson Hwy rejoins the Richardson Hwy at Mile 100.2.

You'll reach a lookout over Willow Lake at Mile 87.6. The lake can be stunning on a clear day, with the water reflecting the Wrangell Mountains, a 100-mile chain that includes 11 peaks over 10,000ft. The two most prominent peaks visible from the lookout are Mt Drum, 28 miles to the northeast, and Mt Wrangell, Alaska's largest active volcano, to the east. Mt Wrangell is 14,163ft, and on some days you can see a plume of steam rising from its crater.

Squirrel Creek State Campground (Mile 79.6; campsites $15) is a scenic 25-site camping area on the banks of the creek. You can fish for grayling and rainbow trout here.

Fourteen miles further along, you'll reach what used to be the Little Tonsina River State Recreation Site. Though it's closed, a path leads down to the water, where anglers can fish for Dolly Varden most of the summer.

At Mile 28.6, the turnoff to Worthington Glacier State Recreation Site leads you to the glacier's face via a short access road. The recreation area includes outhouses, picnic tables and a large, covered viewing area. The mile-long unmaintained Worthington Glacier Ridge Trail begins at the parking lot and follows the crest of the moraine. It's a scenic hike and follows the edge of the glacier, but exercise caution: never hike on the glacier itself due to its unstable crevasses.

As the highway ascends toward Thompson Pass (Mile 26, 2678ft) it climbs above the treeline, and the weather can be windy and foul. On the other side, several scenic turnoffs with short trails descending the ridgelines allow lucky early summer visitors to ooh and aah at a riot of wildflowers. Blueberry Lake State Recreation Site (Mile 24.1; campsites $15) offers 15 sites and several covered picnic shelters in a beautiful alpine setting surrounded by lofty peaks. There's good fishing for rainbow trout in the nearby lakes.

At Mile 14.8, you'll reach the northern end of narrow Keystone Canyon. Tucked away in a little bend is an abandoned hand-drilled tunnel that residents of Valdez began but never finished when they were competing with Cordova for the railroad to the Kennecott copper mines. A historical marker at the entrance briefly describes how nine companies fought to develop the short route from the coast to the mines, leading to the 'shootout in Keystone Canyon.'

For the next 2 miles you'll pass through the dark-walled canyon and, like everyone else, make a stop at two high, full-throated waterfalls: Bridal Veil Falls and, half a mile further, Horsetail Falls. Large turnouts at both allow you to get out and fill your lungs with the pure ionized air.

Leaving the canyon at Mile 12.8, the road begins a long, gradual descent into Valdez.

WRANGELL-ST ELIAS NATIONAL PARK

One of the world's few remaining stands of 'absolute wilderness,' Wrangell-St Elias National Park is the closest you're going to get to 'the wild as God imagined it' in all of Alaska.

Formed in 1980, this is the United States' largest national park, stretching north 170 miles from the Gulf of Alaska and encompassing 13.2 million acres of mountains, foothills and river valleys. Together with Canada's Kluane National Park, Wrangell-St Elias forms a 20-million-acre protected region. The continent's second- and third-highest peaks are here as well as nine of the 16 highest peaks in the US.

In fact the area is a veritable crossroads of mountain ranges. To the north are the Wrangell Mountains; to the south, the Chugach; and thrusting from the Gulf of Alaska and clashing with the Wrangell Mountains are the St Elias. Spilling out from the peaks are extensive ice fields and more than 100 major glaciers, including some of the world's largest and most active. The Bagley Ice Field, near the coast, is 127 miles long, making it the largest subpolar mass of ice in North America. The Malaspina Glacier, which pours out of the St Elias Mountains between Icy Bay and Yakutat Bay, is larger than Rhode Island. Unfortunately, many of these glaciers are retreating at an alarming rate, and actually changing the geography, leaving new fjords, terminal moraines and ponds in their wake.

Wildlife, which includes moose, black and brown bear, Dall sheep, mountain goat, wolf, wolverine, beaver and three of Alaska's 32 caribou herds, is more diverse and plentiful here than in any other Alaskan park. It's not as easily seen, however, as on the Park Rd through Denali.

McCarthy Road

Edgerton Hwy and McCarthy Rd combine to form a 92-mile route into the heart of Wrangell-St Elias National Park. The 32-mile Edgerton Hwy, fully paved, begins at Mile 82.6 of the Richardson Hwy. If you want to camp before reaching the park, the best bet is lovely Liberty Falls State Recreation Site (Mile 24, Edgerton Hwy; campsites $10), where the eponymous cascade sends its waters rushing past several tent platforms.

The end of Edgerton Hwy is 10 miles beyond, at little Chitina. The McCarthy Rd (and hence Wrangell-St Elias National Park) then begins, auspiciously enough, after you pass through a single-lane notch blasted through a granite outcrop. The dirt route is a rump-shaker but even a regular car can make it if you go slow (35mph max) and stay in the center to avoid running over old rail spikes. (Contact Ma Johnson's Hotel in McCarthy about car rental companies that will let you take their vehicles on the road.)

From here for 60 miles eastward you trace the abandoned Copper River & Northwest Railroad bed that was used to transport copper from the mines to Cordova. The first few miles offer spectacular views of the Chugach Mountains, the east–west range that separates the Chitina Valley lowlands from the Gulf of Alaska. Peaks average 7000ft to 8000ft. Below is the mighty Copper River, one of the world's greatest waterways for king and red salmon.

At Mile 14.5 the access road to the trailheads for the Dixie Pass (p65), Nugget and Kotsina Trails begin across from the Strelna airstrip.

Just a couple of miles further up, at Mile 17, the one-lane, 525ft-long Kuskulana River Bridge spans a steep-sided gorge a vertigo-inducing 238ft above the riverbed. Built in 1910, the historic railway span has long been known as 'the biggest thrill on the road to McCarthy.'

Another 43 miles along the road ends at the Kennicott River. To get into McCarthy or Kennecott, cross the river on the narrow footbridge. On the other side, a shuttle (☑554-4411; one way $5; ☺9am-8:30pm) can take you to McCarthy (half a mile) or Kennecott (4.5 miles), or you can walk or cycle the distance. There's parking for private vehicles by the bridge for $10 a day.

CHITINA
POP 113

For most travelers, Chitina is noteworthy as the last place you can purchase gas but this tiny lakeside hamlet nested among high ridgelines is a worthwhile destination on its own. The scenery is pretty, there's good hiking and wildlife-viewing opportunities, and this is one of the few places you can easily watch fish wheels at work. The wheels, which look much like a paddle wheel with baskets, sit just offshore and turn with the river's current. When a fish is caught in a basket, it's lifted up and then deposited into a trough. A slow day might see no salmon caught, while a great day could see a dozen.

To see the fish wheels, head out to the airport and follow the side road down toward the runway. Keep left and shortly you'll be within view of the Copper River and the wheels. To watch dip-netters in action, head down O'Brien Creek Rd, which is just past Gilpatrick's Hotel Chitina. There are some

WRANGELL-ST ELIAS PLANNING GUIDE

Access

Only two rough dirt roads penetrate the interior. The Nabesna Rd cuts into the park's northern reaches, but the more popular access is the rough, dirt McCarthy Rd, which ends at the historic mining towns of McCarthy and Kennecott. With few visitors, you can come here even in the height of summer and still have some alone time. The winters see a lot of snow – the road is still open, though most of the hotels are closed.

Food, Lodging & Tours

McCarthy and Kennecott offer lodging, food, tour companies and other services. There are few places to buy groceries in the area, however, so bring your own supplies if camping.

Information

Wrangell-St Elias National Park Headquarters & Visitor Center (www.nps.gov/wrst; Mile 106.8, Richardson Hwy; ☺8am-4:30pm) Ten miles south of the Glenn Hwy–Richardson Hwy junction, this is the best place for info and trip suggestions. You can also pick up topographic maps, view displays and videos on the park, and leave your backpacking itinerary.

Kennecott Visitor Center (☺9am-5:30pm) On the main road in Kennecott.

Slana Ranger Station (Mile 0.2, Nabesna Rd; ☺8am-5pm) For visitors heading down the Nabesna Rd.

Yakutat Ranger Station (☺8am-5pm Mon-Fri) If you're exploring the park's southeastern coastal regions, stop by here.

fantastic views along the way of the Copper River Valley.

Chitina has a grocery store, a laundry with showers, ranger station, and restaurant and saloon in the Gilpatrick's Hotel Chitina (www.hotelchitina.com; Mile 33, Edgerton Hwy). You can camp for free along the road to O'Brien Creek or at the lakes outside town. The best place to stay in town is Chitina Guest Cabins (☑823-2266; www.pawandfeathers.com; Mile 33.2, Edgerton Hwy; dm $45, cabins with breakfast $150) in a bit of forested land just off the highway, though only kids aged 12 and up can stay here. Although the well-made and comfortably furnished cabins have no showers or toilets, the outhouses are spotless (and dare we say even stylish?), and a shower block was in the works at the time of writing. Bicycles and canoes are available for free for cabin guests, while hostel guests have access to a kitchen and outdoor eating area under a giant mosquito net.

McCarthy

A funky mountain hamlet just half a mile past the end of the road, McCarthy (year-round population around 40) exudes the spirit of the Alaskan frontier like few can. Facing the Kennicott Glacier's terminal moraine and just a stone's throw from the river, the tiny community is a car-free idyll, where the handful of gravel roads wind past rotting cabins and lovingly restored boomtown-era buildings.

While nearby Kennecott was a company town, self-contained and serious, McCarthy was created in the early 1900s for miners as a place of 'wine, women and song.' In other words, it had several saloons, restaurants and a red-light district. The spirit remains lively today, and McCarthy is definitely the best spot to stay for indie travelers, though most of the area's attractions are closer to Kennecott.

Once you've crossed the Kennicott River on the footbridge, follow the road across another footbridge and continue half a mile further to the McCarthy-Kennecott Historical Museum (⊙2-7pm). This old railroad depot is worth a quick drop-in to view the historical photographs, mining artifacts and model of McCarthy in its heyday. The road splits at the museum, with one lane bending back 500ft to downtown (such as it is) McCarthy, and the other continuing toward Kennecott, 4.5 miles up the road.

At the end of downtown McCarthy, check out the Wrangell Mountain Center (www.wrangells.org), an environmental NGO/community center with summer field courses for university students, arts and science programs for children, writing workshops and interpretative walks. The center sits in The Old Hardware Store and is always open.

🛏 Sleeping

There are camping and lodging options on either side of the Kennicott River. There's also good camping at the foot of the Root Glacier. It's important to camp away from the road and be bear savvy, as many human-habituated bears have been reported in the area.

By the summer of 2012 the town should have wireless internet available.

TOP CHOICE Ma Johnson's Hotel HISTORIC HOTEL $$
(☑554-5402; www.mccarthylodge.com; s/d/tr without bath $129/169/179) This is simply one of the most charming and authentic character hotels you'll find in the state of Alaska. So dedicated are the owners to preserving the 1920s boarding-house atmosphere that rooms do not have electrical outlets, nor en suite bathrooms, nor particularly thick walls. What they do have are quaint antique furnishings either from McCarthy itself or the same era, handmade quilts, and a number of little pampering niceties like good soaps and bathrobes. The downstairs parlor is movie-set perfect and genuinely gets everyone out socializing and mingling (one more reason why the rooms are kept small). This place obviously isn't for everyone, but then again, neither are pearls.

Glacier View Campground CAMPGROUND $
(☑554-4490; www.glacierviewcampground.com; sites/cabins without bath $24/95) A half-mile back from the river at the road's end, this very friendly place has stony sites with just enough scrub and space to maintain your privacy, hot showers ($10) and mountain bikes (full day $25). The on-site restaurant (burgers $15; ⊙10am-10pm) enjoys a good local reputation for its burgers, and is blessed with views of Root Glacier from the deck.

Kennicott River Lodge & Hostel CABINS, HOSTEL $$
(☑554-4441; www.kennicottriverlodge.com; dm $30, cabins without bath $100-150) A short walk back from the road's end is this handsome two-story log lodge with private and dorm

For connoisseurs of roads less traveled, Alaska offers few lonelier motorways than the Nabesna Rd, jutting 42 miles south from the Tok Cutoff into the northern reaches of Wrangell-St Elias National Park.

Turning onto the Nabesna Rd from the cutoff, you'll find yourself in a place the signs call Slana (pop 124). Somewhere back through the trees there's an Alaska Native settlement on the northern banks of the Slana River, where fish wheels still scoop salmon during the summer run. Also in the area are more recent settlers: in the early 1980s this was one of the last places in the USA to be opened to homesteading.

Before continuing, stop in at the NPS **Slana Ranger Station** (Mile 0.2, Nabesna Rd; ⊙8am-5pm), where you can get info about road conditions and hikes, purchase USGS maps, peruse displays and collect the free *The K'elt'aeni*, the official guide to Wrangell–St Elias National Park & Preserve, which has a *Nabesna Road Guide* section.

In the 4 miles between the ranger station and the park entrance you'll pass a handful of accommodations. Offbeat and friendly as the all outdoors is **Huck Hobbit's Homestead** (☑822-3196; campsites per person $5, cabins per person $25, breakfast $15, dinner $20), a wind-and-solar-powered 87-acre wilderness retreat. Cabins are rustic, but include a cooking area and shower block. Stay an extra day here if you can. The scenery is beautiful and you can rent canoes for a half-day float down the gentle Slana River ($60 per canoe, includes shuttle).

Upon entering the park proper, the Nabesna Rd turns to gravel. It's manageable in a 2WD vehicle for the first 29 miles, but after that several streams flow over it, making it impassable in high water (call the ranger station for the latest on road conditions). Although there are no formal campgrounds along the road, primitive sites, often with picnic tables and outhouses, exist at several waysides. Maintenance ends at Mile 42, though a rough track continues 4 miles to the private Nabesna Gold Mine, a National Historic Site.

For a comparatively easy hike, try the 4-mile **Caribou Creek Trail** (Mile 19.2, Nabesna Rd), which ascends 800ft from the road to a dilapidated cabin with unbeatable views of the surrounding peaks. A tougher day trek is the 5-mile **Skookum Volcano Trail** (Mile 36.2 Nabesna Rd), which climbs 2800ft through a deeply eroded volcanic system, ending at a high alpine pass frequented by Dall sheep. From there you can either retrace your steps or follow the rocky streambed another 3 miles back down to the road.

cabins. Amenities include a great communal kitchen and common room, a bright outhouse and a Finnish sauna. Views include mountains, forests, tundra and glaciers.

✐ Currant Ridge Cabins · CABINS $$
(☑554-4424; www.currantridgecabins.com; Mile 56.7, McCarthy Rd; cabins $189) On a mountainside not far from the 'end of the road,' these well-designed log cabins feature bathrooms (including bathtubs), full kitchens and large decks for taking in the outrageous mountain views. During the summer season, all power is provided by photovoltaic panels.

Lancaster's Hotel · HOTEL $
(☑554-4402; www.mccarthylodge.com; McCarthy Main St; s/d/q without bath $68/98/148) Run by the same folks as Ma Johnson's Hotel, the Lancaster is a no-frills option for those who want to soak in the Main St vibe but are on a tighter budget. There's no kitchen here but a reading room is available and you can store your bags when you head out into the wilds.

✕ Eating & Drinking

McCarthy (and nearby Kennecott, too) offers some great food not just for where you are, but for anywhere.

McCarthy Lodge · INTERNATIONAL $
(☑554-4402; www.mccarthylodge.com; McCarthy Main St; ⊙dinner) With a New York–trained chef at the helm, the Lodge kitchen has been setting a spell over the taste buds of visitors for a few years now, and getting some prestigious recognition by food and wine experts in the process. Every evening there is a set four-course meal (per person $40) that may include local salmon, duck and greenhouse veggies, while Wednesdays,

Fridays and Sundays you can sit down to a grand multicourse tasting feast for $125 per person.

Roadside Potatohead   TEX-MEX $

(breakfast $8-11, burritos $10; ⊙9am-7pm Mon-Fri, from 8am Sat & Sun) Deck out your own Mr Potatohead doll as you dine in this screened-in snack shack just off McCarthy's Main St. No dish is a miss and the chicken fajita pita could well be the perfect post-hike recovery food.

Golden Saloon   BAR, BREAKFAST

(McCarthy Main St) Connected to the McCarthy Lodge, this is the area's only true bar, with pool, frequent live music and an always intriguing cast of drinkers. There's breakfast in the morning when the bar is closed, and a casual bar menu from 5pm to 10pm.

Kennecott

Workaday serious, Kennecott was once the Bert to McCarthy's Ernie. But with a wealth of old wood structures, including the Potala-like Concentration Mill, and a backdrop of glaciers and rugged peaks filled with fun (or challenging) hikes, mountain bike rides and rafting, Kennecott is now the area's adventure playground.

◉ Sights & Activities

Kennecott Visitor Center   VISITOR CENTER

(⊙9am-5:30pm) The center, which sits in the town's former post office and general store, has loads of information on the area, including a short film on the copper boom. There are also five 15-minute ranger-led walks around town every day that begin here.

Kennicott Glacier   GLACIER

'Oh no, they destroyed this valley!' If you're like 99% of visitors, that's exactly what you'll think as you reach Kennecott and look across the valley at a rolling landscape of dirt and rubble. But no, that isn't a dump of mine tailings from the copper boom days but the Kennicott Glacier moraine. Listen carefully and you can hear rocks shifting and buried ice cracking.

The glacier is thinning terribly and has dropped in height 175ft over the past eight decades. As one interpretation sign notes, in the 1930s some locals didn't even realize that they lived in a valley, so high was the ice field.

Kennecott Mill Town   HISTORIC SITE

Pretty much all of Kennecott comprises the mill town and there are dozens of old wood and log buildings that have been restored, stabilized or purposely left in a state of decrepitude. The most interesting collection is toward the end of town and includes the 14-story Concentration Mill & Leaching Plant (tour $25), which used to process the copper ore through a multistage process. You can only enter the mill on a two-hour tour led by St Elias Alpine Guides (three tours daily), but this is highly recommended both for the stunning views from the top floors and the chance to get up close and personal with the hulking machinery.

Hiking & Backpacking

There are a few excellent hikes around town, and an endless range if you are able to backpack or fly by bush plane deeper into the park. Unlike Denali, you don't need a backcountry permit, but you are encouraged to leave an itinerary at any of the ranger stations, where you can also get advice and pick up a bear canister for your trip. There's a refundable deposit required for the canister.

You can also drop by the visitor center in Kennecott for maps and ideas for both day and overnight hikes. There are literally two full folders of options. Popular overnight hikes include Donoho Peak, Erie Lake and McCarthy Creek.

Root Glacier Trail   HIKING

Beginning at the far edge of town past the Concentration Mill, the Root Glacier Trail is an easy 4- or 8-mile round-trip route out to the sparkling white-and-blue ice. Signposts mark the route and the path itself is clear and well used as far as the primitive Jumbo Creek Campsites. From here you can head left to the glacier or continue straight another 2 miles along a rougher track. At the end the Erie Mine Bunkhouse will be visible on the slopes above you. Check at the visitor center for the latest on the conditions of the climb up. Most of this trail can also be ridden on a mountain bike.

Bonanza Mine Trail   HIKING

Another excellent hike from Kennecott follows this alpine trail, a round-trip of almost 9 miles. Begin on the path to the Root Glacier Trail and then turn off to the right at

In 1900 miners 'Tarantula Jack' Smith and Clarence Warner reconnoitered Kennicott Glacier's east side until they arrived at a creek and found traces of copper. They named the creek Bonanza, and was it ever – the entire mountainside turned out to hold some of the richest copper deposits ever uncovered.

Eventually, a group of investors bought the existing stakes and formed the Kennecott Copper Corporation, named when a clerical worker misspelled Kennicott (which is why, nowadays, the town is spelled with an 'e' while the river, glacier and other natural features get an 'i'). First the syndicate built its railroad: 196 miles of track through the wilderness, including the leg that's now McCarthy Rd and Cordova's famous Million Dollar Bridge. The line cost $23 million before it even reached the mines in 1911.

From 1911 until 1938 the mines operated around the clock and reported a net profit of more than $100 million. By 1938 most of the rich ore had been exhausted, and in November that year the mine was closed permanently. With the exception of a steam turbine and two large diesel engines, everything was left behind, and Kennecott became a perfectly preserved slice of US mining history.

Unfortunately, when the railroad bed was converted to a road in 1974, Kennecott also became the country's biggest help-yourself hardware store. Locals were taking windows, doors and wiring, while tourists were picking the town clean of tools, railroad spikes and anything else they could haul away as souvenirs.

In 1998 the NPS purchased the mill, power plant and many of the buildings from private owners as the first step to restoring them. At the time of writing, the old mill town was undergoing extensive renovations.

the clearly marked junction. This is a steep uphill walk with 3800ft of elevation gain. Once above the treeline, the views over the Kennicott and Chitina Valleys are stunning.

Expect three to five hours for this hike up if the weather is good and half that time to return. Water is available at the top, but carry at least a quart (1L) if the day is hot.

☞ Tours

St Elias Alpine Guides   ADVENTURE TOUR
(☏345-9048; www.steliasguides.com) In addition to the Concentration Mill tours, the company can equip you with crampons for half-day hikes on Root Glacier ($70) or take you on a full-day alpine hike to the mining ruins at the base of Castle Mountain ($95). Also offers multiday fly-in hiking and rafting.

Kennicott Wilderness Guides ADVENTURE TOUR
(☏554-4444; www.kennicottguides.com) The other local guiding firm, also extremely experienced, offering small group ice-climbing and glacier excursions from $60, and a wide variety of multiday hiking trips.

Copper Oar   ADVENTURE TOUR
(☏554-4453; www.copperoar.com) Offers a popular full-day float along the Kennicott, Nizina and Chitina Rivers, with a return to McCarthy by bush plane. The high point is

going through the vertical-walled Nizina Canyon. This trip costs $285 per person (two person minimum). The company also offers multiday paddles, glacier and alpine hikes.

Flightseeing

Wrangell Mountain Air   SCENIC FLIGHTS
(☏554-4400; www.wrangellmountainair.com; McCarthy Main St) Has a fantastic reputation and can do a backcountry drop or a wide range of scenic flights from $100 (35 minutes) to $230 (90 minutes) per person with a two-person minimum.

🛏 Sleeping

Kennicott Glacier Lodge   HOTEL **$$**
(☏258-2350; www.kennicottlodge.com; s/d from $165/175; ☎) Built in 1987, this sprawling hotel has a bit of a 'Grande Dame' feel though the service is warm and relaxed. The original wing rooms all have shared bath, while the annex rooms are en suite. Both wings offer glacier-view rooms and complete meal plans.

✗ Eating & Drinking

Kennicott Glacier Lodge   AMERICAN **$$**
(☏258-2350; www.kennicottlodge.com; lunch $9-13, dinner $33-36) You'll need a reservation for the well-regarded family-style dinners, and there's only one seating: at 7pm.

Tailor Made Pizza PIZZERIA $

(slice $6, pizzas $16-32; ⊙11:30am-6pm) Delicious, filling slices and whole pizzas are served straight from a bus window just off the main road on a glacier-view flat.

❶ Getting There & Around

AIR Copper Valley Air (☑866-570-4200; www.coppervalleyair.com) has packages from Anchorage or Glennallen that include a stay at Ma Johnson's Hotel. **Wrangell Mountain Air** (☑554-4411; www.wrangellmountainair.com)

offers daily scheduled flights between McCarthy and Chitina ($124 one way).

BICYCLE You can rent mountain bikes at Glacier View Campground.

BUS Kennicott Shuttle (☑822-5292; www.kennicottshuttle.com) Vans leave Glennallen daily at 7am for McCarthy (round-trip same day/different day $99/139) and depart at 4:30pm for the return trip. It's about four hours each way and you'll need to make a reservation.

Kodiak, Katmai & Southwest Alaska

Best Places to Eat

» Old Powerhouse (p332)

» Chart Room (p347)

» Donut Hole (p342)

Best Places to Stay

» Channel View B&B (p331)

» Brooks Camp (p342)

Why Go?

Southwest Alaska stretches 1500 miles into oblivion, and is about as remote as you can get in a state that prides itself on hard-to-reach places.

It boasts the world's largest bears, on Kodiak Island; Alaska's richest salmon runs, in Bristol Bay; and the largest gathering of nesting seabirds in the world, on the tiny Pribilof Islands.

It is mostly an island-studded region with stormy weather and violent volcanoes. This is the northern rim of the Ring of Fire. Along the Alaska Peninsula and the Aleutian Islands are 46 active volcanoes – the greatest concentration in North America.

But you can't drive to Southwest Alaska, making the region hard to reach, expensive to visit and easy to bypass. However, the adventurous do find their way here, because even in Alaska there are few experiences quite like riding a ferry across the North Pacific or watching 1000lb bears gorge themselves on salmon.

When to Go

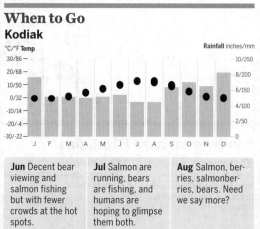

Kodiak

Jun Decent bear viewing and salmon fishing but with fewer crowds at the hot spots.

Jul Salmon are running, bears are fishing, and humans are hoping to glimpse them both.

Aug Salmon, berries, salmonberries, bears. Need we say more?

Southwest Alaska Highlights

1 Photographing brown bears as they snap salmon from **Brooks Falls** (p339) in Katmai National Park & Preserve

2 Feasting on king crab in **Unalaska** (p347), where it's as fresh as can be

3 Riding the **MV Tustumena** (p336) out the long arm of the Aleutian chain

162°W
160°W
158°W
156°W

Bethel

Kuskokwin River

Kuskokwim Mountains

Togiak
National
Wildlife Refuge

5 **Wood-Tikchik**
State Park

Lake
Aleknagik

Goodnews
Bay

Dillingham

Cape
Newenham

Round
Island

Naknek

Hagemeister
Island

Walrus Islands
State Game
Sanctuary

Bristol
Bay

King
Salmon

Brooks
Camp

McNeil River
State Game
Sanctuary

Kamishak
Bay

Fourpeaked
Mtn (6903ft)

Shuyak
Island
State Park

1 **Katmai**
National
Park &
Preserve

4

Valley of
10,000
Smokes

Becharof National
Wildlife Refuge

Becharof
Lake

Ugashik

Alaska Peninsula
National
Wildlife Refuge

Aniakchak
National Monument
& Preserve

Aleutian Islands

3

Pavlof
(8250ft)

Pavlof's Sister
(7028ft)

Cold
Bay

King
Cove

Sand
Point

Mt Veniaminof
(7075ft)

Chignik

Alaska
Peninsula
National
Wildlife Refuge

Shumagin
Islands

Chirikof
Island

PACIFIC
OCEAN

162°W
160°W
158°W
156°W
154°W

Lake Clark
National Park
& Preserve

Mt Redoubt
(10,197ft)

Lake
Clark

Port
Alsworth

Iliamna

Iliamna
Lake

Mt Iliamna
(10,016ft)

Kenai
Soldotna

Sterling

Skilak
Lake

60°N

Ninilchik

Homer

Seldovia

Kachemak
Bay
State
Park

Kennedy
Entrance

Afognak Island
State Park

58°N

Shelikof Strait

Port Lions

Kodiak

Pasagshak State
Recreation Site **6**

Kodiak
Launch
Complex

Kodiak
National
Wildlife
Refuge

Kodiak
Island

Trinity
Islands

56°N

54°N

4 Hiking the surreal
landscape of the **Valley of**
10,000 Smokes (p340)
in Katmai National Park &
Preserve

5 Floating the rivers in
Wood-Tikchik State Park
(p340)

6 Watching surfers brave
the cold waters at **Pasagshak**
River State Recreation Site
(p336)

Climate

With little to protect it from the high winds and storms that sweep across the North Pacific, Southwest is home to the worst weather in Alaska. Kodiak is greatly affected by the turbulent Gulf of Alaska and receives 80in of rain per year, along with regular blankets of pea-soup fog and occasional blustery winds. On the northern edge of the Pacific, Unalaska and the Alaskan Peninsula receive less rain (annual precipitation ranges from 60in to 70in), but are renowned for unpredictable and stormy weather. Rain, fog and high winds are common. Summer temperatures range from 45°F to 65°F, with the clearest weather often occurring in early summer and fall.

History

More than any other region of the state, Southwest Alaska has the most turbulent history, marked by massacres, violent eruptions and WWII bombings.

When Stepan Glotov and his Russian fur-trading party landed at present-day Dutch Harbor in 1759, there were more than 30,000 Aleuts living on Unalaska and Amaknak Islands. After the Aleuts destroyed four ships and killed 175 fur hunters in 1763, the Russians returned and began a systematic elimination of Aleuts, massacring or enslaving them. It's estimated that by 1830 only 200 to 400 Aleuts were living on Unalaska.

The Russians first landed on Kodiak Island in 1763 and returned 20 years later when Siberian fur trader Gregorii Shelikof established a settlement at Three Saints Bay. Shelikof's attempts to 'subdue' the indigenous people resulted in another bloodbath where more than 1000 Alutiiqs were massacred, or drowned during their efforts to escape.

The czar recalled Shelikof and in 1791 sent Aleksandr Baranov to manage the Russian-American Company. After an earthquake nearly destroyed the settlement at Three Saints Bay, Baranov moved his operations to more stable ground at present-day Kodiak. It became a bustling port and was the capital of Russian America until 1804, when Baranov moved again, this time to Sitka.

Some violence in Southwest Alaska was caused by nature. In 1912 Mt Katmai on the nearby Alaska Peninsula erupted, blotting out the sun for three days and blanketing Kodiak with 18in of ash. Kodiak's 400 residents escaped to sea on a ship but soon returned to find buildings collapsed, ash drifts

several feet high and spawning salmon choking in ash-filled streams.

The town was a struggling fishing port until WWII when it became the major staging area for the North Pacific operations. At one point Kodiak's population topped 25,000, with a submarine base at Women's Bay, an army outpost at Buskin River and gun emplacements protecting Fort Abercrombie.

Kodiak was spared from attack during WWII, but the Japanese bombed Unalaska only six months after bombing Pearl Harbor and then invaded Attu and Kiska Islands. More hardship followed: the Good Friday Earthquake of 1964 leveled downtown Kodiak and wiped out its fishing fleet; the king-crab fishery crashed in the early 1980s; and the *Exxon Valdez* oil spill soiled the coastline at the end of the decade. But this region rebounded after each disaster, and today Unalaska and Kodiak are among the top three fishing ports in the country.

ℹ Getting There & Away

Alaska Airlines (☎800-252-7522; www.alaskaair.com) and **PenAir** (☎800-448-4226; www.penair.com) service the region and one or the other provides daily flights to Kodiak, King Salmon, Unalaska, Dillingham and Bethel. **Era Alaska** (☎800-866-8394; www.eraaviation.com) also flies to Kodiak from a number of destinations throughout Alaska.

The most affordable way to reach the region is via the **Alaska Marine Highway** (☎800-642-0066; www.ferryalaska.com), which has stops at Kodiak, Unalaska and a handful of small villages in between.

KODIAK ISLAND

The only thing bigger than a Kodiak brown bear is the island itself. Stretching across 3670 sq miles and more than 100 miles long, Kodiak is Alaska's largest island and the US's second largest, after the Big Island of Hawaii. It's fitting then that its most famous residents are the world's largest terrestrial carnivores. Fattened by the island's legendary, abundant salmon runs, Kodiak brown bears grow to gargantuan proportions – males can weigh up to 1500lb – and an estimated 3000 of them live in the Kodiak Archipelago.

There are also people on the island – roughly 14,000 – but for the most part they're tucked away in the northeast corner. The vast majority of this island is a green and jagged wilderness that was so deeply carved by glaciers, no point on land is more than 15 miles from the ocean. A few roads will lead you out of the city to isolated spots along the coast, but throughout most of the Kodiak Archipelago, towns and roads are nonexistent.

Kodiak

POP 13,049

Kodiak is a workers' town. Unlike many ports in the southeast, tourism in Kodiak is nice, but not necessary. Hence, there are no campgrounds near the city, nobody running a shuttle service to the airport, and the town's one hostel is filled with cannery workers.

Everybody is too busy working, primarily at sea. Kodiak sits at the crossroads of some of the most productive fishing grounds in the world and is home to Alaska's largest fishing fleet – 650 boats, including the state's largest trawl, longline and crab vessels. The fleet and the 12 shore-based processors, including the *Star of Kodiak,* a WWII vessel converted into a fish plant downtown, account for more than 50% of employment on the island.

Kodiak works hard. It's consistently one of the top three fishing ports in the country and second only to Dutch Harbor for value of product and tonnage processed. Since the king-crab moratorium in 1983, Kodiak has diversified to catch everything from salmon, pollock and cod to sea cucumbers. In 1995 Kodiak set a record when 49 million lb of salmon crossed its docks.

It is also home to the largest US coastguard station, while at Cape Narrow, at the south end of the island, is the Kodiak Launch Complex (KLC), a $38 million low-earth orbit launch facility.

You'll find residents friendly: lively at night in the bars, and often stopping to offer you a lift even without a thumb being extended. But in the morning they go to work. This is the real Alaska: unaltered, unassuming and not inundated by tourism. Arrive for the scenery, stay to enjoy outdoor adventures that range from kayaking to photographing a 1000lb bear. But most of all, come to Kodiak to meet people who struggle at sea to earn a living on the stormy edge of the Pacific Ocean. This is a lesson in life worth the price of an airline ticket from Anchorage.

The town of Kodiak is on the east side of the island, with three main roads splintering from the city center.

◉ Sights

Baranov Museum MUSEUM
(☏486-5920; 101 Marine Way; adult/child $5/free; ☺10am-4pm Mon-Sat) Housed in the oldest Russian structure in Alaska, across the street from the visitor center, the Baranov Museum fills the Erskine House, which the Russians built in 1808 as a storehouse for precious sea-otter pelts. Today it holds many items from the Russian period of Kodiak's history, along with fine examples of Alutiiq basketry and carvings. A set of notebooks covers Katmai's historical events, including the 1964 tsunami, volcanic eruptions and both World Wars. The gift shop is particularly interesting, offering a wide selection of *matreshkas* (nesting dolls), brass samovars and other Russian crafts. The museum also opens when cruise ships are in town.

Holy Resurrection Cathedral CHURCH
(☏486-5532; 385 Kashevarof St) Near the Alutiiq Museum on Mission Rd, Holy Resurrection Church serves the oldest Russian Orthodox parish in the New World, established in 1794. The present church, marked by its beautiful blue onion domes, was built in 1945 and is the third one to occupy this site. You are free to join tours that are staged when a cruise ship is in. The adjacent small gift shop is stocked with *matreshkas,* religious books and icons, and also keeps hours according to cruise ship schedules.

Kodiak National Wildlife Refuge Visitor Center VISITOR CENTER
(☏487-2626; 402 Center St; ☺9am-5pm) This excellent visitor center focuses on the Kodiak brown bear, the most famous resident of the refuge, with an exhibit room that's especially well suited for children, a short film on the bears and a bookstore. A variety of kids' programs are offered, with the schedule posted on the front door. Interested in seeing a big bruin? Stop here first.

Alutiiq Museum & Archaeological Repository MUSEUM
(☏486-7004; www.alutiiqmuseum.org; 215 Mission Rd; adult/child $5/free; ☺9am-5pm Mon-Fri, to 3pm Sat & Sun) Preserving the 7500-year heritage of Kodiak's indigenous Alutiiq people is the Alutiiq Museum & Archaeological Repository. The exhibits display one of the largest collections of Alutiiq artifacts in the state, ranging from a kayaker in his waterproof parka of seal gut to a 19th-century spruce-root hat and the corner of a sod house. Take time to

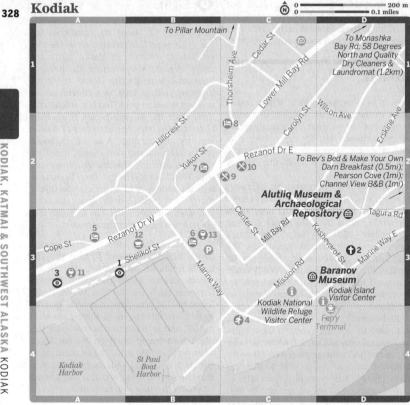

explore 'Sharing Words,' an intriguing interactive computer program that uses village
elders to teach Alutiiq words and songs in
an attempt to save the indigenous language.

St Paul Boat Harbor   HARBOR
The pulse of this city can be found in its boat
harbors. St Paul Boat Harbor is downtown,
and the larger of the two. Begin with the
Harbor Walkway (Shelikof St), where a series
of interesting interpretive displays line the
boardwalk above the docks. Then descend to
the rows of vessels, where you can talk to the
crews or even look for a job.

**Fort Abercrombie State
Historical Park**   PARK
This military fort, 4.5 miles northeast of Kodiak, off Monashka Bay Rd, was built by the
US Army during WWII for a Japanese invasion that never came. In the end, Kodiak's
lousy weather kept the Japanese bombers
away from the island. The fort is now a 186-

acre state historical park, sitting majestically
on the cliffs above scenic Monashka Bay.
Between its pair of 8in guns is Ready Ammunition Bunker, which stored 400 rounds
of ammunition during the war. Today it
contains the small Kodiak Military History
Museum (☑486-7015; adult/child $3/free; ☺1-
4pm Sat-Mon).

Just as interesting as the gun emplacements are the tidal pools found along the
park's rocky shorelines, where an afternoon of
searching for sea creatures can be spent. Park
naturalists lead exploration walks when there
are significant low tides and tidepool snoop-
ing is at its best. Call the Alaska Division of
Parks (☑486-6339) for exact days and times.

Pillar Mountain   MOUNTAIN
From the top of this 1270ft mountain behind
the city you'll have excellent views of the surrounding mountains, ocean, beaches and
islands. One side seems to plunge directly
down to the harbor below, and the other

Kodiak

KODIAK, KATMAI & SOUTHWEST ALASKA KODIAK

not always marked. Windfall can make following the track difficult, or even totally conceal it. Still, hiking trails are the best avenues to the natural beauty of Kodiak Island.

The best source of hiking information is the Alaska Division of Parks (☑486-6339) or the excellent *Kodiak Audubon's Hiking & Birding Guide* (sold at various places around town, including the Kodiak National Wildlife Refuge Visitor Center, for $13), a large waterproof topographical map with notes on the trails and birds.

For transportation and company on the trail, the local Audubon Society offers group hikes almost every Saturday and Sunday from May to October, meeting at 9:30am at the ferry terminal. You can get a list of the hikes and the contact person from the Kodiak Island Visitor Center or the Kodiak National Wildlife Refuge Visitor Center.

Barometer Mountain   HIKING
This popular hiking trail is a steep climb and a 4-mile round-trip to the 2452ft summit. To reach the trailhead, follow Chiniak Rd south of Buskin River State Recreation Site and turn right on Burma Rd, the first road immediately after passing the end of the airport's runway. Look for a well-worn trail on the left. The trek, which begins in thick alder before climbing the hogback ridge of the mountain, provides spectacular views of Kodiak and the bays south of the city.

Termination Point   HIKING
This 5-mile loop starts at the end of Monashka Bay Rd and branches into several trails near Termination Point, a spectacular peninsula that juts out into Narrow Strait. Most hiking is done in a lush Sitka spruce forest. If you're nervous about your navigational skills, simply hike the coastal half of the loop and then backtrack.

North Sister Mountain   HIKING
Starting 150ft up a creek bed a mile before the end of Monashka Bay Rd, this trail (find it on the left side of the creek bed) first leads up steeply through dense brush, but then levels off on alpine tundra. The summit of North Sister (2100ft) is the first peak seen (to your left), about a mile from the trailhead. The other two Sisters are also accessible from here.

Pyramid Mountain   HIKING
Two trails, both of which start on Anton Larsen Bay Rd, lead to the top of Pyramid Mountain (2401ft). Avoid the easternmost trail, accessed off the golf course, which is

overlooks the green interior of Kodiak Island. Pick up the bumpy dirt road to the top by walking or driving north up Thorsheim Ave and turning left on Maple Ave, which runs into Pillar Mountain Rd. You'll end up where the giant wind turbines slice through the fog.

Kodiak Island Brewing Co   BREWERY
(☑486-2537; 338 Shelikof St; ⓢnoon-7pm) This is another of Alaska's great one-man breweries. Behind the counter, pouring the suds, is brewmaster/owner/tour guide Ben Millstein. He'll be more than happy to give you a short tour (it's only a one-room operation) or simply let you taste the five beers he brews. A small tasting room is a great refuge from the rain, and you can purchase up to two pints. The Liquid Sunshine is so good you might walk out with a half-gallon growler or even a case-sized party pig.

🖈 Activities

Hiking
The Kodiak area has dozens of hiking trails, but few are maintained and trailheads are

brush-choked and hard going. Instead, continue west to Anton Larsen Pass, where the other trail begins in the parking area on the right. It's a steep but easy-to-follow 2-mile climb to the top.

Anton Larsen Pass   HIKING

This 5-mile loop is a scenic ridge walk and a far easier alpine hike than Barometer Mountain. The trail begins just north of the gravel parking lot, at the pass on the left side of Anton Larsen Bay Rd. A well-defined trail leads you through meadows; at a fork, the trail heads right to cross a bridge and climbs to a broad alpine ridge. Once on top, use the rolling ridge to skirt a distinctive, glacial valley before descending back to the fork in the trail.

Cycling

Mountain bikers will find Kodiak's gravel roads interesting to ride on, especially 12-mile Anton Larsen Bay Rd. Leading northwest from near Buskin River State Recreation Site, the road crosses a mountain pass and leads to the island's west side, where you will find quiet coves and shorelines to explore. Plan on two hours for the ride to Anton Larsen Bay. Another favorite is Burma Rd, picked up near the airport (see the Barometer Mountain hike, p329). It can be combined with a stretch of Chiniak Rd for a 12-mile, two- to three-hour loop.

58 Degrees North   BICYCLE RENTAL

(☑486-6249; 1231 Mill Bay Rd; per 24hr $25; ☺11am-6pm Mon-Sat) An outdoor shop that rents out mountain bikes. If you are planning to do a lot of bike exploration, purchase the *Kodiak Island Mountain Bike Guide* for $9.

Paddling

With its many bays and protected inlets, scenic coastline and offshore rookeries, Kodiak is a kayaker's dream. Unfortunately, there is nowhere in Kodiak to rent a kayak.

Alaska Wilderness Adventures   KAYAKING

(☑487-2397; www.kodiakswildside.com; full day $145-160) Specializes in whale watching and photography tours, along with seeing other marine wildlife like sea otters and puffins, from kayaks. Destinations depend on where the wildlife is.

Kodiak for Children

If the kids are tagging along in Kodiak, cross the Zharoff Memorial Bridge to Near Island, where you'll find several attractions well suited to families. Best of all, they're free.

FREE **Kodiak Fisheries Research Center**   AQUARIUM

(☑481-1800; www.kodiakak.us; Trident Way; ☺8am-4:30pm Mon-Fri) Opened in 1998 to house the fisheries research being conducted by various agencies, the center has an interesting lobby that includes displays, touch tanks, a large aquarium and a 19ft Cuvier's beaked whale skeleton.

FREE **North End Park**   PARK

(Trident Way) Reached as soon as you cross the bridge, the small park is laced with forested trails that converge at a stairway to the shoreline. At low tide you can search the tidepools here for starfish, sea anemones and other marine life.

FREE **St Herman Harbor**   HARBOR

(Dog Bay Rd) A great place to look for sea lions, which often use the Dog Bay Breakwall as a haul-out, while eagles are usually perched in the trees onshore.

🖝 Tours

Several companies provide either a city tour of Kodiak or a daylong scenery-viewing tour that includes Baranov Museum, Pillar Mountain and Fort Abercrombie State Historical Park. But Kodiak is one place where you should skip the ground tour and hit the water.

TOP CHOICE **Galley Gourmet**   BOAT

(☑486-5079; www.galleygourmet.biz; dinner cruise $150) Along with whale-watching and harbor cruises, Marty and Marion Owen offer a delightful dinner cruise onboard their 42ft yacht. Marty navigates the boat while Marion whips up meals – such as halibut with mango and mint salsa or poundcake infused with wild rose petals – and serves them on white table linen with views of coastal scenery and wildlife. The nightly dinner cruise is 3½ hours; brunch is a two-hour cruise and is offered only on the weekends ($100).

Kodiak Adventures Unlimited   TOURS

(☑486-8766; www.kodiakadventuresunlimited.com; 105 Marine Way; ☺8am-5pm Mon-Fri, to 3pm Sat & Sun) A clearinghouse of sorts for private tours and charters, the very friendly Kodiak Adventures Unlimited can book you bear-viewing tours as well as halibut and guided river fishing excursions. Staff will also help you find free stuff, sending you off with marked-up maps.

There is a wide variety of wildlife in Kodiak National Wildlife Refuge but almost everybody arrives hoping to catch a glimpse of just one animal – the Kodiak bear. This subspecies of the brown bear, *Ursus arctos middendorffi*, is the largest land carnivore in the world. Males normally weigh in at more than 800lb but have been known to exceed 1500lb. Females usually weigh in at 400lb to 600lb. Biologists estimate there are over 3000 brown bears living in the archipelago, or one bear per 1.5 sq miles, with more than 2300 on Kodiak Island itself. That's three times the number of brown bears in the rest of the USA. From mid-July to mid-September, the bears congregate at streams to gorge themselves on spawning salmon. The runs are so heavy that the bears often become selective, and many feast only on females and then eat only the belly portion containing the eggs.

That's the best time to see the bears, and the most common way to do it is with a bear-sighting flight. Just about every air-charter company in town offers a bear-watching flight. The average tour is a four-hour trip that includes two hours on the ground photographing bears, and costs $450 to $550 per person.

Among the many air services offering bear tours are **Andrew Airways** (487-2566; www.andrewairways.com), **Harvey Flying Service** (487-2621; www.harveyflyingservice.com), **Kingfisher Aviation** (486-5155, 866-486-5155; www.kingfisheraviation.com) and **Sea Hawk Air** (486-8282, 800-770-4295; www.seahawkair.com).

A much more adventurous way of seeing the bears is through **Kodiak Treks** (487-2122; www.kodiaktreks.com), which offers low-impact, small-group bear-watching trips from its remote lodge on an island in Uyak Bay. Harry Dodge, a noted bear biologist, leads guests from the lodge, by boat and boot, to various viewing spots to view up to two dozen bears. The cost is $300 per person per day and covers lodging, meals and equipment but not your charter flight to Uyak Bay.

Helios Sea Tours   BOAT
(486-5310; www.kodiakrivercamps.com; 5hr tours $160-290) Offers three-, five- and seven-hour marine and whale-watching tours on a smaller 27ft vessel.

Kodiak Tours   BUS
(486-3920; www.kodiaktours.com; half-/full day $55/100) The best operator of tours on land: they've been in business for over 20 years. Uses a minibus and can arrange bear viewing.

★ Festivals & Events

Kodiak Crab Festival   CULTURAL
(www.kodiak.org) The town's best event, it was first held in 1958 to celebrate the end of crabbing season. Today the week-long event in late May features parades, a blessing of the fleet, foot and kayak races, fishing-skills contests (such as a survival-suit race) and a lot of cooked king crab.

Bear Country Music Festival   MUSIC
Features country, bluegrass and Alaskan music in mid-July.

State Fair & Rodeo   CULTURAL
(www.kodiakrodeoandstatefair.com) Held on Labor Day weekend at the Kodiak Fairgrounds. Grab your lasso.

🛏 Sleeping

Lodging is expensive in Kodiak and there's an 11% sales and bed tax on top of all tariffs. The most current list of B&Bs is on the website of the **visitor center** (www.kodiak.org).

Channel View B&B   B&B **$$**
TOP CHOICE
(486-2470; www.kodiakchannelview.com; 1010 Steller Way; r/ste $125/135; 🕙🛜) Run by a couple of world travelers, history buffs and art collectors, Channel View offers a a range of subtle delights: historic Kodiak photos, fossils collected from the island and arranged in a rainy rock garden, and original artwork from travels abroad. Room options include a single or queen, a studio apartment or a one-bedroom apartment. As the name implies, there are views of the channel below through fir trees and from a spacious deck. Host Mary is a fifth-generation islander, and serves full gourmet breakfasts.

Fort Abercrombie State Historical Park   CAMPGROUND **$**
(Mile 4, E Rezanof Dr; campsites $10) Four and a half miles northeast of Kodiak, this park has 13 wooded sites in a delightfully mossy forest. A few are walk-in, and feel very secluded. Trails meander around the bluffs,

beach and small lake, and it's a great place to wander.

Pearson Cove Bed & Breakfast
B&B $$

(☑486-5301; www.pearsoncove.com; 900 Mission St; r $115; ☺☎) One of the best deals in town; for $115 you pretty much get the lower two stories of a house that spills down a hillside to the boatyard. Choose between two bedrooms and then relax in the large sitting room that overlooks Pearson Cove. A small kitchenette is available, but owner Jan will whip you up breakfast.

Bev's Bed & Make Your Own Darn Breakfast
B&B $$

(☑486-8217; www.bevsbedandbreakfast.com; 1510 Mission Rd; r $85-110; ☺☎) Bev no longer runs this B&B, but the host often brings down muffins and fresh-baked breads for breakfast. And you still can't beat the price for what you get: four comfortable bedrooms with queen-size beds, a fully stocked kitchen that you can use any time, laundry and cable TV, all within a 15-minute walk of downtown.

Annie's by the Sea B&B
B&B $$$

(☑539-1473; www.anniesbythesea.com; 2990 Spruce Cape Rd; r $159; ☺☎) An airy private accommodation with a giant kitchen and lofty windows overlooking the ocean, Annie's is a good choice for those looking for a bit more privacy and space than most B&Bs offer.

Buskin River State Recreation Site
CAMPGROUND $

(Mile 4.5, W Rezanof Dr; campsites $10) Four miles southwest of the city, this 168-acre park includes a 15-site rustic campground, the closest to the city, along with a self-guided nature trail and good salmon fishing in the Buskin River.

Russian Heritage Inn
HOTEL $$

(☑486-5657; www.russianheritageinn.com; 119 Yukon St; r $80-90, ste $120-140; ☎) You pick this motel for location and price. All rooms have microwaves, coffeemakers and small refrigerators. The suites were recently updated, and management plans to do a round on the aging rooms.

Shelikof Lodge
HOTEL $$

(☑486-4141; www.shelikoflodgealaska.com; 211 Thorsheim Ave; s/d $100/111; ☺☎) Nicest rooms downtown for what you pay, plus a good restaurant and a lounge that's not the smokiest in town. A bonus is the airport shuttle service, which is rare in Kodiak.

Best Western Kodiak Inn
HOTEL $$$

(☑486-5712, 888-563-4254; www.kodiakinn.com; 236 W Rezanof Dr; r $169-184; ☺☎) Kodiak's largest and most upscale motel is downtown and has 81 rooms along with a fine restaurant, outdoor hot tub and airport-shuttle service. Suites run to $259 and are quite large.

Kodiak Island Hostel
HOSTEL $

(☑481-3100; http://kodiakislandhostel.com; 508 W Marine Way; dm $30; ☺☎) Kodiak's single hostel has a great location around the block from the ferry terminal. It offers weekly and monthly rates, which means that you'll be sharing space with a lot of (male) cannery workers who are there for the summer. The biggest dorm sleeps 26, but feels much smaller thanks to privacy screens. You can also pop in for a shower ($6.50) or laundry ($3.50 wash). Unfortunately, there's no real kitchen space and only one shower.

🍴 Eating

TOP CHOICE Old Powerhouse
JAPANESE $$

(☑481-1088; 516 Marine Way; lunch special $8-10, dinner $15-22; ☺lunch & dinner Mon-Sat, dinner Sun; ☺) Kodiak's best dining experience, this historic power plant has been beautifully renovated into a Japanese seafood restaurant. The waterfront location places you on an outdoor deck, or in a solarium, watching fishing boats glide right past, while feasting on almost all-local sushi and seafood or excellent *udon, soba* and *yakisoba* noodles.

Java Flats
CAFE $

(Bell's Flats; breakfast $6-9, lunch $10-12; ☺breakfast & lunch Tue-Sun; ☺) Located outside of town a bit, Java Flats throws together wholesome goodness with hearty burritos, salads and sandwiches. Wash them down with a steamy espresso drink and you'll be set for hours. Both vegetarians and carnivores are welcome.

Mill Bay Coffee & Pastries
CAFE $

(www.millbaycoffee.com; 3833 E Rezanof Dr; breakfast $5-7, lunch $10-14; ☺7am-6pm Mon-Sat, 8am-5pm Sun; ☺☎) What's a French chef doing in Kodiak? Joel Chenet's love of hunting is the reason this city is blessed with the best pastries in Alaska, hands down. Get there early: the case is empty of tortes, éclairs and apple pies by mid-afternoon.

Monk's Rock Coffeehouse & Bookstore
CAFE $

(202 W Rezanof Dr; sandwiches $5-7; ☺10am-6pm Mon-Fri, to 5pm Sat; ☺) A relaxing place with

lots of Alaskan titles, Russian Orthodox books and icons, and comfortable sofas. The lattes are potent and the soups and sandwiches very affordable.

El Chicano
MEXICAN $$

(103 Center St; lunch $8-11, dinner $11-17; ☺lunch & dinner) A sprawling restaurant and bar that serves big portions of Mexican food and 'grande' margaritas. It might not be the most authentic Mexican in Alaska but it has the local beer on tap and there is an outdoor deck for the three days in summer the sun's out.

Safeway
GROCERY $

(2685 Mill Bay Rd; ☺6am-midnight) Kodiak's largest and best grocery store has ready-to-eat items, an espresso counter and a seating area.

Drinking & Entertainment

Clustered around the city waterfront and small-boat harbor are a handful of bars that cater to Kodiak's fishing industry. If you visit these at night you'll find them interesting places, overflowing with skippers, deckhands and cannery workers drinking hard and talking lively.

Henry's Great Alaskan
PUB

(512 Marine Way; ☺11:25am-10pm Mon-Thu, to 10:30pm Fri & Sat, noon-9:30pm Sun) Henry's bills itself as a restaurant but is really more of a bar. Located on the mall in front of the small-boat harbor, it's hopping with fishermen and their friends. It's less smoky than other venues and has a decent pub menu.

Harborside Coffee & Goods
CAFE

(216 Shelikof St; ☺6:30am-7pm Mon-Sat, from 7am Sun; ☺☎) An espresso bar overlooking the harbor, with a bulletin board listing deckhand jobs.

Chart Room Lounge
LOUNGE

(236 W Rezanof Dr) Situated in the Kodiak Inn, the 2nd-floor location here allows you to sip a glass of wine with a nice view of the harbor and mountains. An acoustic guitar player on Fridays makes the setting even mellower.

B'n'B Bar
BAR

(326 Shelikof St) Across from the harbor, B'n'B claims to be Alaska's oldest bar, having served its first beer in 1899. It's a fishermen's bar with a giant king crab on the wall, and the most level pool table in a town that feels an earthquake now and then.

Rendezvous
BAR

(11653 Chiniak Hwy) This bar and restaurant is a 15-minute drive out of town, past the Coast Guard base, but its atmosphere is worth the gas (even at $5 a gallon). It hosts the best live music in Kodiak, with singers taking the stage several times a month.

ℹ Information

A Holmes Johnson Memorial Library (☑486-8686; 319 Lower Mill Bay Rd; ☺10am-9pm Mon-Fri, to 5pm Sat, 1-5pm Sun; ☎) Offers free internet access on 10 computers and is a great place to hole up and read. If you don't have a laptop, sign up for a terminal and then peruse the books.

Alaska Division of Parks (☑486-6339; 1400 Abercrombie Dr; ☺8am-4:30pm Mon-Fri, hr vary Sat & Sun) Maintains an office at Fort Abercrombie State Historical Park, 4.5 miles northeast of the city off Monashka Bay Rd, and is the place for information on trails, campgrounds and recreational cabins.

Kodiak Island Ambulatory Care Clinic (☑486-6188; ste 102, 1202 Center St; ☺8am-6pm Mon-Fri, 9am-3pm Sat) For emergency and walk-in medical care.

Kodiak Island Visitor Center (☑486-4782, 800-789-4782; www.kodiak.org; 100 Marine Way; ☺8am-5pm Mon-Fri) Next to the ferry terminal, with brochures and maps of the city. Hours tend to vary during summer.

Kodiak National Wildlife Refuge Visitor Center (☑487-2626; http://kodiak.fws.gov; 402 Center St; ☺9am-5pm) This new visitor center is downtown and loaded with information.

Post office (419 Lower Mill Bay Rd) The main post office is just northeast of the library.

Quality Dry Cleaners & Laundromat (☑486-2638; Ole Johnson Ave & Mill Bay Rd; ☺8am-8pm) Also has showers for $5 (soap and towel included).

Wells Fargo (☑486-3126; 202 Marine Way) Has an ATM and a king-crab display in its lobby.

ℹ Getting There & Away

Both **Alaska Airlines** (☑487-4363, 800-252-7522; www.alaskaair.com) and its contract carrier **ERA Alaska** (☑487-4363; www.eraaviation.com) fly to Kodiak daily. Fares range between $300 and $350. The airport is 5 miles south of Kodiak on Chiniak Rd. Other than the offerings from a few motels, there is no shuttle service into town. **A&B Taxi** (☑486-4343) charges $20 for the ride.

Alaska Marine Highway's MV *Tustumena* stops at **Kodiak Ferry Terminal** (☑486-3800; www.alaskaferry.org; 100 Marine Way) several times a week, coming from Homer (one way $74, 9½ hours), and stopping twice a week at Port Lions,

1. Cape Chiniak
Fireweed sets the landscape aflame on the flanks of an overlook in Cape Chiniak, Kodiak Island (p337).

2. Sea Otter, Glacier Bay National Park
Other marine life that can be seen at Glacier Bay (p131) are seals, porpoises and killer whales.

3. Unalaska Lobster Fisherman

Dutch Harbor (p343) shot into the limelight in 2007, when Discovery Channel's *Deadliest Catch* emerged as a popular reality TV show.

4. Kodiak Island

Jagged snow-capped cliffs dominate the skyline above Kodiak Island (326).

5. Red Fox, Katmai National Park

As well as at Katmai (p339), red foxes can be seen at Wood-Tikchik State Park (p340).

3

MICHAEL MELFORD / GETTY ©

The easiest way to see 'Bush Alaska' without flying is to hop onto the Alaska Marine Highway ferry when it runs to the eastern end of the Aleutian Islands. The MV *Tustumena*, a 290ft vessel that holds 220 passengers, is one of only two ferries in the Alaska Marine Highway fleet rated as an oceangoing ship; hence its nickname, the 'Trusty *Tusty*.' It is also one of the oldest vessels in the fleet, thus its other nickname the 'Rusty *Tusty*.'

Riding the *Tusty* is truly one of the best bargains in public transportation. The scenery and wildlife are spectacular. You'll pass the perfect cones of several volcanoes, the treeless but lush green mountains of the Aleutians, and distinctive rock formations and cliffs. Whales, sea lions, otters and porpoises are commonly sighted, and bird life abounds. More than 250 species of birds migrate through the Aleutians and if you don't know a puffin from a kittiwake, you can attend daily presentations by naturalists from the US Fish & Wildlife Service (USFWS).

Viewing wildlife and scenery depends, however, on the weather. It can be an extremely rough trip at times, deserving its title 'the cruise through the cradle of the storms.' The smoothest runs are from June to August, while in the fall 40ft waves and 80-knot winds are the norm. That's the reason for barf bags near the cabins and Dramamine in the vending machines, right above the Reese's Peanut Butter Cups. Its tiny bar – three stools, two tables – is called the Pitch and Roll Cocktail Lounge.

Cabins are available and are a worthwhile expense if you can manage to reserve well in advance (double $311 each way). The trip is long, and the *Tusty*'s solarium isn't as comfortable as most of the Southeast ferries for sleeping. Bring a good sleeping pad, and loads of Cup-of-Noodles, instant oatmeal and tea (there's free hot water) if you want to avoid the restaurant onboard. Also bring a good book. On days when the fog surrounds the boat, there is little to look at but the waves lapping along the side.

a nearby village on Kodiak Island. Twice a month the 'Trusty *Tusty*' continues west to Unalaska and Dutch Harbor ($293 one way from Kodiak). Several times a month the MV *Kennicott* sails to Kodiak from Homer and Whittier (one way $91, 10 hours).

ⓘ Getting Around

The cheapest car rental available in Kodiak is **Rent-A-Heap** (☑487-4001; airport terminal) which offers used, two-door compacts for $37 a day, plus 37¢ per mile. However, if you're planning to drive around the island, that mileage rate will quickly drain your funds. **Budget Rent-A-Car** (☑487-2220; airport terminal) offers compacts for $60 a day with unlimited mileage. You can rent either in town at **Port of Kodiak Gift Shop** (☑486-8550; 428 Marine Way). Book ahead to make sure you get the car you are after.

Around Kodiak

More than 100 miles of paved and gravel roads head from the city into the wilderness that surrounds Kodiak. Some of the roads are rough tracks, manageable only by 4WD vehicles, but others can be driven or hitched along to reach isolated stretches of beach, which make great fishing spots and superb coastal landscapes. These scenic areas, not the city, are the true attractions of Kodiak Island.

South of Kodiak, Chiniak Rd winds for 48 miles to Cape Greville, following the edge of three splendid bays. The road provides access to some of Alaska's best coastal scenery and there are plenty of opportunities to view sea lions and puffins offshore, especially at Cape Chiniak near the road's southern end.

Just past Mile 30 of Chiniak Rd is the junction with Pasagshak Bay Rd, which continues another 16.5 miles due south. Along its way it passes Pasagshak River State Recreation Site (Mile 8.7, Pasagshak River Rd), which has 12 free campsites near a beautiful stretch of rugged coastline, 45 miles from town. This small riverside campground is famous for its silver- and king-salmon fishing and for a river that reverses its flow four times a day with the tides.

At the end of the road is Fossil Beach, where you'll find not only the namesake fossils emerging from the cliffs, but also a few surfers braving the cold to catch the perfect wave.

KODIAK NATIONAL WILDLIFE REFUGE

This 2812-sq-mile preserve, which covers the southern two-thirds of Kodiak Island, all of Ban and Uganik Islands and a small section of Afognak Island, is the chief stronghold of the Alaska brown bear. An estimated 3500 bears reside in the refuge and the surrounding area, which is known worldwide for brown-bear hunting and to a lesser degree for salmon and steelhead fishing. Bird life is plentiful: more than 200 species have been recorded, and there are 600 breeding pairs of eagles that nest within the refuge. Flowing out of the steep fjords and deep glacial valleys and into the sea are 117 salmon-bearing streams that account for 65% of the total commercial salmon harvest in Kodiak.

The refuge's diverse habitat ranges from rugged mountains and alpine meadows to wetlands, spruce forest and grassland. No roads enter the refuge, and no maintained trails lie within it. Access into the park is by charter plane or boat out of Kodiak, and most of the refuge lies at least 25 air miles away.

Like most wilderness areas in Alaska, an extensive trip into the refuge is something that requires advance planning and some money. Begin before you arrive in Alaska by contacting the Kodiak National Wildlife Refuge Headquarters (☑487-2600; http://kodiak.fws.gov; 1390 Buskin River Rd, Kodiak, AK 99615).

If you're looking for somewhere to sleep, the Kodiak office of the US Fish & Wildlife Service (USFWS) administers nine cabins in the refuge, none accessible by road. The closest to Kodiak are Uganik Lake Cabin and Veikoda Bay Cabin. Go to www.reserveusa.com to book them; each is $45 per night. Contact the refuge visitor center (☑487-2626; http://kodiak.fws.gov; 402 Center St, Kodiak; ☺9am-5pm) for more information.

AFOGNAK ISLAND STATE PARK

Afognak Island lies just north of Kodiak Island in the archipelago. Some 75,000 acres of Afognak are protected in the pristine Afognak Island State Park, which has two public-use cabins: Laura Lake Cabin and Pillar Lake Cabin. The cabin at Pillar Lake is a short walk from a beautiful mile-long beach. Both cabins are accessed by floatplane, cost $35 a night, and are reserved through Alaska Division of Parks (☑486-6339; www.alaskastateparks.org). You can check the cabin availability and make reservations online six months in advance.

SHUYAK ISLAND STATE PARK

The northernmost island in the Kodiak Archipelago, remote and undeveloped Shuyak is 54 air miles north of Kodiak. It's only 12 miles long and 11 miles wide, but almost all of the island's 47,000 acres are taken up by Shuyak Island State Park, featuring forests of virgin Sitka spruce and a rugged shoreline dotted with secluded beaches. Otters, sea lions and Dall porpoises inhabit offshore waters, while black-tailed deer and a modest population of the famous Kodiak brown bear roam the interior.

Kayakers enjoy superb paddling in the numerous sheltered inlets, coves and channels – the area boasts more protected waterways than anywhere else in the archipelago. Most of the kayaking takes place in and around Big Bay, the heart of the state park. From the bay you can paddle and portage to four public cabins and other protected bays.

The park's four cabins are on Big Bay, Neketa Bay and Carry Inlet. The cabins ($75 per night) are cedar structures with bunks for eight, woodstoves, propane lights and cooking stoves but no running water. Shuyak Island cabins are also reserved through Alaska Division of Parks & Outdoor Recreation (☑486-6339; www.alaskastateparks.org), and can be reserved six months in advance online.

ALASKA PENINSULA

The Alaska Range doesn't suddenly stop at Mt McKinley. It keeps marching southwest to merge with the Aleutian Range and form the vertebrae of the Alaska Peninsula, Alaska's rugged arm that reaches out for the Aleutian Islands. This volcanic peninsula stretches some 550 miles from Cook Inlet to the tip at Isanotski Strait, and it includes Alaska's largest lakes – Lake Clark, Iliamna Lake and Becharof Lake – and some of the state's most active volcanoes, with Mt Redoubt and Mt Iliamna topping more than 10,000ft in height. Wildlife abounds; communities do not.

The peninsula's most popular attraction, Katmai National Park & Preserve, has turned King Salmon into the main access point. Two other preserves – McNeil River State Game Area and Lake Clark National Park & Preserve – also attract travelers, while the Alaska Marine Highway stops at four small communities along the peninsula on its way to the Aleutians.

LAKE CLARK NATIONAL PARK & PRESERVE

Only 100 miles southwest of Anchorage, Lake Clark National Park & Preserve features spectacular scenery that is a composite of Alaska: an awesome array of tundra-covered hills, mountains, glaciers, coastline, the largest lakes in the state and two active volcanoes. The centerpiece of the park is spectacular Lake Clark, a 42-mile-long turquoise body of water ringed by mountains. But the park is also where the Alaska Range merges into the Aleutian Range to form the Chigmit Mountains, and is home to two volcanoes: Mt Iliamna and Mt Redoubt. Despite its overwhelming scenery and close proximity to Alaska's largest city, less than 5000 visitors a year make it to this 5625-sq-mile preserve. So close, yet so far away.

Hiking is phenomenal, but Lake Clark is best suited to the experienced backpacker. For any pretrip planning, contact the NPS Park Headquarters (☎644-3626; www.nps. gov/lacl; 240 West 5th Ave, Ste 236, Anchorage; ☺8am-5pm Mon-Fri), in Anchorage. Port Alsworth, the main entry point for the park, has a ranger station (☎781-2117; ☺8am-5pm Mon-Fri, 9am-6pm Sat & Sun) with displays and videos on the park. There you'll find information on both the 50-mile historic Telaquana Trail as well as Twin Lakes, where dry tundra slopes provide easy travel to ridges and great views.

Float trips down any of the three designated wild rivers (the Chilikadrotna, Tlikakila and Mulchatna) are spectacular and exciting, with waterways rated from Class III to Class IV. The best way to handle a boat rental is through Alaska Raft & Kayak (☎561-7238, 800-606-5950; www.alaskaraftandkayak.com; 401 W Tudor Rd, Anchorage; ☺10am-6pm Mon-Sat), which rents out inflatable sea kayaks and canoes (per day $75) and 14ft to 16ft rafts (per day $100) in Anchorage. The shop will also deliver the boat to Lake Clark Air (☎781-2208, 888-440-2281; www.lakeclarkair.com) in Anchorage for your flight into the national park and pick it up when you return.

To reach the park in the first place, you will need to arrange with an Anchorage charter pilot for drop-off at the start of your adventure; consider Lake Clark Air (☎781-2208, 888-440-2281; www.lakeclarkair.com) which flies daily to Port Alsworth for a round-trip fare of $450.

King Salmon

POP 426

A former WWII airbase, King Salmon is now a service center with a healthy percentage of government and transportation employees living on the banks of the beautiful Naknek River.

Just under 300 air miles from Anchorage, King Salmon is the air-transport hub for Katmai National Park & Preserve. Most visitors see little more than the airport terminal and the float dock where they catch a flight into the park.

Best to avoid spending the night here if you can, by planning your trip – including having prebooked accommodations in Katmai – so that you fly out the day you arrive. There is a 10% bed tax.

On either side of the river is Dave's World/R&G Boat Rental (☎469-0012, 246-8651; Municipal Dock 1; campsites $10, 4-person cabins $100), a 160-acre spread you can camp on. It's a $5 skiff ride across the Na-

knek River. Within yelling distance of the airport is Antlers Inn (☎246-8525, 888-735-8525; www.antlersinnak.com; r/ste $190/240; ☞☎), a friendly, family-run inn with share bathrooms; suites have kitchenettes and private baths. Amazingly, it's free to camp outside.

Adjacent to the airport, King Ko Inn (☎246-3377; www.kingko.com; 100 Airport Rd; cabins s/d $195/215; ☎) has 16 cabins with private bath; eight of them also have kitchenettes. It's also home to the liveliest bar in town plus a full service restaurant. You can also try eating at Eddie's Fireplace Inn (Airport Rd; breakfast $11-14, dinner $20-32; ☺8am-9pm; ☎) across the street, with an atmospheric bar and a kitchen that is open all day.

The Katmai National Park Headquarters (☎246-3305; ☺8am-4:30pm Mon-Fri) is one block to the right from the airport in King Salmon Mall. The King Salmon Visitor Center (☎246-4250; ☺8am-5pm) is right next door to the airport and is managed by the USFS and co-run by the National Park Service and two area boroughs.

Alaska Airlines (☎800-252-7522; www.alaskaair.com) flies up to six times daily between Anchorage and King Salmon during the summer for around $500 for the round-trip.

Katmai National Park & Preserve

Katmai was the site of an earth-shattering volcanic eruption in 1912, which created the Valley of 10,000 Smokes. Today the fumaroles no longer smoke and hiss, and Katmai National Park & Preserve (☎246-3305; www.nps.gov/katm; King Salmon) is best known for bears. In July, at the peak of bear viewing, throngs of visitors arrive to watch brown bears snagging salmon in midair, just 30yd away.

Katmai is not a place to visit on a whim. Because of the cost of reaching the park, it's best to spend at least four days or more here to justify the expense. Those who can plan months in advance can arrive during July's peak bear-viewing season and stay in an affordable campground. Those who can't, often end up taking expensive day trips into the park. Neither is cheap but, no matter what the costs, for many people the bears and fishing at Katmai end up being the highlight of their Alaskan trip.

The park's summer headquarters is Brooks Camp, on the shores of Naknek Lake, 35 miles from King Salmon. The camp is best known for Brooks Falls, which thousands of bright-red sockeye salmon attempt to jump each July, much to the interest of bears and tourists. In the middle of the wilderness, this place crawls with visitors (and bears) during July, when as many as 300 people will be in Brooks Camp and the surrounding area in a single day.

When you reach the camp on a floatplane, take a good look; bears are usually seen lumbering along the beach between the lodge and the planes pulled up on the sand. If the coast is clear, you're directed to go to the NPS Visitor Center, where you are enrolled in the 'Brooks Camp School of Bear Etiquette,' a mandatory 20-minute bear orientation. Among the things you learn is that bears have the right-of-way here; if a brownie lies down right on the trail and takes a nap, no visitors use the trail until it wakes up and moves on. These 'bear jams' have been known to last hours.

Rangers at the center also answer questions, help you fill out backcountry permits, stage a variety of interpretive programs, and sell books and maps.

Most visitors come in July, when the salmon and brown bears are at their peak. Unfortunately, mosquitoes, always heavy in this area, are also at their peak. The best time for hiking and backpacking trips is from mid-August to early September, when the fall colors are brilliant, the berries ripe and juicy, and the insects scarce. Be prepared for frequent storms. In fact, be ready for rain and foul weather at any time in Katmai, and always pack warm clothing.

History

In June 1912 Novarupta Volcano erupted violently and, with the preceding earthquakes, rocked the area now known as Katmai National Park & Preserve. The wilderness was turned into a dynamic landscape of smoking valleys, ash-covered mountains and small holes and cracks fuming with steam and gas. Only one other eruption in documented historic times, on the Greek island of Santorini in 1500 BC, displaced more ash and pumice.

If the eruption had happened in New York City, people living in Chicago would have heard the explosion; the force of the eruption was 10 times greater than the 1980 eruption of Mt St Helens, in the state of Washington. For two days, people in Kodiak could not see a lantern held at arm's length, and the pumice, which reached half the world, lowered the average temperature in the northern hemisphere that year by 2°F. In history books, 1912 is remembered as the year without a summer, but the most amazing aspect of this eruption, the most dramatic natural event in the 20th century, was that no-one was killed. Katmai is that remote.

In 1916 the National Geographic Society sent Robert Grigg to explore the locality. Standing at Katmai Pass, the explorer saw for the first time the valley floor with its thousands of steam vents. He named it the Valley of 10,000 Smokes, and the name stuck. Grigg's adventures revealed the eruption's spectacular results to the world, and two years later the area was turned into a national monument. In 1980 the monument was enlarged to 4.2 million acres, and designated a national park and preserve.

Activities

Bear Viewing

Katmai has the world's largest population of protected brown bears (more than 2000). At Brooks Camp they congregate around

WOOD-TIKCHIK STATE PARK

At 2500 sq miles, Wood-Tikchik State Park (☑Anchorage year-round 269-8698, Dillingham late May-late Sep 842-2641; http://dnr.alaska.gov/parks/units/woodtik.htm) is the country's largest state park. Thirty miles north of Dillingham, on Bristol Bay, the park preserves two large systems of interconnecting lakes that are important spawning grounds for salmon. Wildlife in the park includes brown and black bears, beavers, moose, foxes and wolves. The fishing for arctic char, rainbow trout, Dolly Varden, grayling, salmon and northern pike is excellent.

With the exception of expensive fishing lodges in or just outside the park, Wood-Tikchik is almost totally undeveloped. Even the park's ranger station is outside the park, at Lake Aleknagik.

The park is an ideal place for a wilderness canoe or kayak trip. Fresh Water Adventures (☑842-5060; www.freshwateradventure.com) rents out catarafts for $100 a day.

Wood River Lakes, in the park's southern half, are connected by shallow, swiftly moving rivers. For that reason, most parties are flown in and paddle out, returning to Dillingham via the Wood River. This route eliminates the need for a pick-up flight and is an easy paddle for most intermediate canoeists.

In the park's northern half, and much more remote than the Wood River Lakes, are Tikchik Lakes, a chain of six lakes. Flat-water kayaking is popular here, and those interested in river floating can get dropped off on Nishlik or Upnuk Lake and travel along the Tikchik River into Tikchik Lake or even down the Nuyakuk and Nushagak Rivers to one of several Alaska Native villages, where air-charter flights are available back to Dillingham.

The upper lakes are more challenging and more costly to experience. But the scenery – mountains, pinnacle peaks and hanging valleys surrounding the lakes – is impressive.

The paddling season is from mid-June until early October. Be prepared for cool and rainy weather, and pack plenty of mosquito repellent. Be cautious: sudden winds on the open lakes can create whitecap conditions, and white water may exist on many of the connecting streams.

To reach Wood-Tikchik State Park, contact any of the floatplane charter companies in Dillingham, including Fresh Water Adventures (☑842-5060; www.freshwateradventure.com), based at the Dillingham Airport.

Brooks River to benefit from the easy fishing for sockeye salmon. Most of this occurs from late June through July, when 40 to 60 bears gather along a half-mile stretch of the Brooks River. In that period it is near impossible to get a campsite, a cabin or even a spot on the observation decks, without planning months in advance. The bear activity then tapers off in late July and August, when the animals follow the salmon up into the streams feeding into Brooks Lake. It increases again in September as the bears return to the lower rivers to feed on spawned-out fish. That said, a few brown bears can be seen in the Brooks Camp area during summer; a couple of younger ones always seem to be hanging around.

Brooks Camp has three established viewing areas. From the lodge, a dirt road leads to a floating bridge over the river and the first observation deck – a large platform dubbed 'Fort Stevens' by rangers, for the Alaskan senator who secured the funding for it. From here you can see the bears feeding in the mouth of the river or swimming in the bay.

Continue on the road to the Valley of 10,000 Smokes, and in half a mile a marked trail winds to Brooks Falls. Two more viewing platforms lie along this half-mile trail. The first sits above some riffles that occasionally draw sows trying to keep their cubs away from aggressive males at the falls.

The last deck, at the falls, is the prime viewing area, where you can photograph the salmon making spectacular leaps or a big brownie at the top of the cascade waiting with open jaws to catch a fish. At the peak of the salmon run, there might be eight to 12 bears here, two or three of them atop the falls themselves. The observation deck holds 40 people, and in early to mid-July it will be crammed with photographers, forcing rangers to rotate people on and off.

Hiking

Hiking and backpacking are the best ways to see the park's unusual backcountry. Like Denali National Park, in Alaska's Interior, Katmai has few formal trails; backpackers follow river bars, lake shores, gravel ridges and other natural routes. Many hiking trips begin with a ride on the park bus along the dirt road to Three Forks Overlook, in the Valley of 10,000 Smokes. The bus will also drop off and pick up hikers and backpackers along the road. The one-way fare is $51.

The only developed trail from Brooks Camp is a half-day trek to the top of Dumpling Mountain (2520ft). The trail leaves the ranger station and heads north past the campground, climbing 1.5 miles to a scenic overlook. It then continues another 2 miles to the mountain's summit, where there are superb views of the surrounding lakes.

Paddling

The area has some excellent paddling, including the Savonoski Loop, a five- to seven-day adventure; see p69 for details. Other popular trips include a 30-mile paddle from Brooks Camp to the Bay of Islands and a 10-mile paddle to Margot Creek, which has good fishing and lots of bears.

Kayaks are the overwhelming choice for most paddlers due to high winds blowing across big lakes, and possible rough water. Accomplished paddlers should have no problem, but the conditions can sometimes get dicey for novices.

Lifetime Adventures　　　KAYAKING
(☑746-4644, 800-952-8624; www.lifetimead ventures.net; folding kayaks daily single/double $55/65, weekly $265/300) Located in King Salmon or Anchorage, Lifetime Adventures rents out folding kayaks.

☞ Tours

Independent Tours

The only road in Katmai is 23 miles long. It's a scenic traverse of the park that leads from the lodge, past wildlife-inhabited meadows and river valleys and ends at Three Forks Overlook, which has a sweeping view of the Valley of 10,000 Smokes. Katmailand (☑243-5448, 800-544-0551; www. katmailand.com) runs the lodge at Brooks Camp. It has a daily bus to Three Forks Overlook and back, which leaves at 9am, with three hours at the cabin, and returns to the lodge at 4:30pm.

Each bus carries a ranger who talks during the bus trip and leads a short hike from the cabin into the valley below. Views from the cabin include almost 12 miles of barren, moonlike valley where the lava once oozed

down, with snowcapped peaks beyond. It's an amazing sight.

The fare for the tour is a steep $88 per person (with a packed lunch $96), but if the weather isn't too bad most people feel it's money well spent. Sign up for the tour at the Katmailand office across from the lodge as soon as you arrive at Brooks Camp. The bus is filled most of the summer, and you often can't get a seat without making a reservation a day or two in advance.

Brooks Lodge also offers an hour-long flightseeing tour around the park for $150 per person (two people minimum).

Package Tours

Because of the logistics of getting there and the need to plan and reserve so much in advance, many visitors arrive in Katmai as part of a one-call-does-it-all package tour. A shockingly large number are part of a one-day visit, spending large sums of money for what is basically an hour or two of bear watching. At the height of the season, in July, there can easily be 20 floatplanes or more lined up on the beach at Brooks Camp.

TOP CHOICE Hallo Bay Bear Camp　　　BEAR VIEWING
(☑235-2237, 888-535-2237; www.hallobay.com) This ecofriendly camp is on the outside coast of Katmai National Park and is designed exclusively for bear viewing. The cabins are simple but comfortable, and the camp can handle only 12 guests at a time. In such an intimate setting, the bear watching can be surreal at times. Packages include lodging, meals and guides, and begin at $1200 per person for two nights.

Katmailand　　　BEAR VIEWING
(☑243-5448, 800-544-0551; www.katmailand. com) Offers packages that are geared for either anglers or bear watchers. Its one-day tour to see the bears of Brooks Falls is $589 per person. A three-night angler's package – which includes all transportation, lodging and meals – is $1542 to $1849 per person based on double-occupancy.

Lifetime Adventures　　　CAMPING
(☑746-4644, 800-952-8624; www.lifetimeadven tures.net) If you have the time, this outfit offers a seven-day camping adventure that includes hiking in the Valley of 10,000 Smokes and kayaking near Margot River. The cost is $2750 per person and includes the flight from Anchorage, charters into the park, all equipment and guides.

🍴 Sleeping & Eating

If you plan to stay at Brooks Camp, either at the lodge or in the campground, you must make reservations. No walk-ins are accepted, so if you don't have reservations, you're limited to staying in King Salmon and visiting the park on day trips.

Campground　　　　　　　CAMPGROUND **$**

(☑reservations 877-444-6777, 518-885-3639; www. recreation.gov; campsites $8) Reservations for the campground are accepted from the first Monday of January, for that year. It might be easier to win the New York lottery than to obtain a campground reservation for prime bear-watching in July, as often the campsites are completely booked before the end of the first week of January. If you don't have a reservation, you don't get a site.

Important: the campground holds a maximum of 60 people, and reservations are made by person. If you don't provide the names of everyone in your party when you make your reservation, space will be held for just one person. Woe to the reservation-maker who gave only his or her name, then found on arrival that the campground had no room for the other members of the party. It's happened.

Brooks Lodge　　　　　　　LODGE **$$$**

(Katmailand; ☑243-5448, 800-544-0551; www.kat mailand.com) The lodge has 16 basic, but modernized, cabin-style rooms, each with two bunk beds and a private bath with shower. Cabins are rented as part of package tours that include transportation from Anchorage, and in July there is a three-night maximum stay. A three-night package is $1497 per person; a three-night stay outside of the prime bear-viewing period is $920 to $1190.

A store at Brooks Camp sells limited supplies of freeze-dried food, white gas (for camp stoves), fishing equipment, flies, and other essentials...such as beer. You can also sign up for all-you-can-eat meals at Brooks Lodge without renting a cabin (renters pay too): for adults/children, breakfasts are $15/10, lunches $19/14 and dinners $32/23. Also in the lodge is a lounge with a huge stone fireplace, soft chairs and bar service in the evening (the cocktails are the best deal). Campers can take hot showers ($8).

🌟❶ Getting There & Away

Most visitors to Katmai fly into King Salmon on **Alaska Airlines** (☑800-252-7522; www.alas kaair.com). Once you're in King Salmon, a number of air-taxi companies offer the 20-minute floatplane flight out to Brooks Camp. **Katmai Air** (☑243-5448, 800-544-0551; www.katmailand. com/air-services), the Katmailand-affiliated company, charges $176 for a round-trip.

The Lower Peninsula

Most visitors to the little fishing villages on the western peninsula arrive on the Alaska Marine Highway's MV *Tustumena,* which sails from Kodiak to Unalaska and Dutch Harbor. The ferry usually stops for two hours: long enough to get out and walk from one end of the village to the other, and for most people, that's ample. If you decide to stay over at any village, you'll be able to find food and shelter, and then return to Anchorage through **PenAir** (☑800-448-4226; www.penair.com). A one-way flight from the peninsula communities to Anchorage ranges from $475 to $525.

The first stop after departing Kodiak is **Chignik** (☑749-2280), where everybody piles off the *Tusty.* Passengers follow the boardwalk to the **Donut Hole** to indulge in blueberry-filled doughnuts, cinnamon rolls and other sweet treats, and often bring boxes of them back to the ship. It's the only time this tiny bakery has a line of people out the door – and it's well worth the wait.

The next port is on the northwest coast of Popof Island, **Sand Point** (☑383-2696; www. cityofsandpointalaska.org), the largest commercial fishing base in the Aleutians, with a population of 992. It was founded in 1898 by a San Francisco fishing company as a trading post and cod-fishing station, but also bears traces of Aleut, Scandinavian and Russian heritage. The town's **St Nicholas Chapel,** a Russian Orthodox church, was built in 1933 and is now on the National Register of Historical Places. Catch a cab during your brief stop in port for a beer at the **Sand Point Tavern,** a lively place filled with locals and summer workers.

At the Alaska Peninsula's western end, near the entrance to Cold Bay, is **King Cove** (☑497-2340; www.kingcoveview.com), founded in 1911, when a salmon cannery was built. Today, with a population of 756, it is a commercial fishing base and home to Peter Pan Seafoods, whose salmon cannery is the largest operation under one roof in Alaska.

On the west shore of the same bay is **Cold Bay** (☑532-2401; www.coldbay.org), with a population of 72. A huge airstrip was built here during WWII – today it's the third-longest in the state, making Cold Bay the transport center for the entire Aleutian chain. You can still see Quonset huts and other remains from the WWII military buildup and, if you're lucky, visit Izembek National Wildlife Refuge.

ALEUTIAN ISLANDS

Where the Alaska Peninsula ends, the Aleutian Islands begin: a jagged 1100-mile arc that stretches across the north Pacific to within 500 miles of Russia's Kamchatka Peninsula. This is a barren, windswept and violent place, as 27 of the 46 most active volcanoes in the US form islands here.

For most visitors, the Aleutians is limited to three stops aboard the Alaska Marine Highway's MV *Tustumena*. The first is a two-hour stop at False Pass (☎548-2319; http://home.gci.net/~cityoffalsepass). That is more than enough time to wander the length of this small, but picturesque, fishing village (pop 46) on the tip of Unimak Island, looking across a narrow passage at the Alaska Peninsula. The second is a very brief stop at Akutan (pop 859), another village that the ferry reaches at 5:30am before continuing on to Unalaska.

Unalaska & Dutch Harbor

POP 3580

On the road from the ferry terminal to Unalaska and Dutch Harbor, two things catch your eye: concrete pillboxes and crab pots. In a nutshell, that's the story of these twin towns on Unalaska and Amaknak Islands: the pillboxes are a violent WWII reminder of the past, while the crab pots acknowledge

the important role of commercial fishing in the towns' future.

Located at the confluence of the Pacific Ocean and the Bering Sea, one of the world's richest fisheries, Dutch Harbor is the only natural deepwater port in the Aleutians. More than 400 vessels call here each year from as many as 14 countries. From this industrialized port of canneries and fish-processing plants, the newly rebuilt Bridge to the Other Side arches over to the residential community of Unalaska.

The area, and Dutch Harbor in particular, shot into the limelight in 2007, when Discovery Channel's *The Deadliest Catch* emerged as a popular reality show on TV. Each week viewers tune in to watch crab boats and their crews battle four-story-high waves, icy temperatures and paralyzing fatigue, to fill their holds with a gold mine of king crab, before heading back to Dutch Harbor.

Ironically, since the dramatic crash of the king crab fishery in 1982, it has been pollock, an unglamorous bottom fish, that has been the backbone of Unalaska and Dutch Harbor's economy. Pollock accounts for more than 80% of all seafood processed, and is the reason the towns have been the country's number one commercial fishing port for the past 20 years. In 2006 Dutch Harbor set a record when 911 million lb of seafood, at an export value of $165 million, crossed its docks. The impact of so much fish is an influx of cannery workers, who arrive from around the world to temporarily double the area's population as they turn pollock into fish sticks or imitation crab.

THE COLD BAY LOTTERY

The most interesting attraction during the long run of the MV *Tustumena* from Kodiak to Dutch Harbor is Izembek National Wildlife Refuge (☎532-2445, 877-836-6332; www.r7.fws.gov/nwr/izembek), just outside Cold Bay. At 417,533 acres, Izembek is the smallest Alaskan refuge but still half the size of Rhode Island. It was created in 1960 to protect 142 bird species. Almost the entire North American black brant population of 135,000 birds arrives in spring and fall during the annual migration to feed on large eelgrass beds in Izembek Lagoon. When the salmon are running, brown-bear densities in the refuge can be among Alaska's highest: as many as six bears per mile along some streams. The lagoon is also home to seals and sea otters. In other words, a wildlife paradise.

The lagoon lies 11 miles from Cold Bay and is almost impossible to visit during the typical two-hour layover of the ferry...unless you're lucky. Drop your name in the lottery for the USF&WS tour that visits the lagoon every time the ferry is in port. The USF&WS naturalist onboard the MV *Tustumena* organizes the drawing because there are only 16 seats on the bus and usually 100 passengers who want to be in one of them. If you draw a ticket you'll be treated to a narrated ride out to Grant Point Wildlife Overlook, where you'll see thousands of birds, sea otters, red foxes and possibly even brown bears. The 1½-hour tour is free and, best of all, the *Tusty* won't leave without you. Or at least, not without its naturalist.

Unalaska & Dutch Harbor

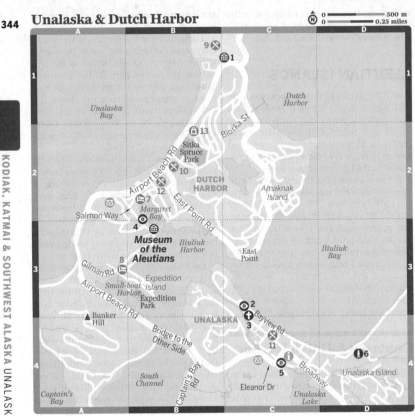

Unalaska & Dutch Harbor

◎ Top Sights
Museum of the Aleutians......................B3

◎ Sights
1 Aleutian WWII Visitor Center	C1
2 Bishop's House	C3
3 Church of the Holy Ascension	C3
4 Ounalashka Corporation	B2
5 Parks, Culture & Recreation Department	C4
6 USS Northwestern Memorial	D4

🛏 Sleeping
7 Grand Aleutian Hotel	B2
Ounalashka Corporation	(see 4)
8 UniSea Inn	A3

🍴 Eating
9 Airport Restaurant	B1
10 Amelia's	B2
Chart Room	(see 7)
11 Dutch Harbor Fast Food	C4
Harbor Sushi	(see 8)
Harbor View Bar & Grill	(see 8)
12 Safeway	B2

🍷 Drinking
Cape Cheerful Lounge...................(see 7)

🛍 Shopping
13 LFS, Inc..B2

During the 1970s Unalaska and Dutch Harbor were Alaska's version of the Wild West, with drinks, money and profanity flowing freely at every bar in town. With the crash of the king crab, the towns became more community-oriented, and with the recent drop of the pollock fishery, residents are now trying to survive another downturn in the boom-and-bust cycle of fishing.

Unfortunately, short-time visitors returning on the ferry don't have an opportunity to soak in the color and unique character of these towns. To stay longer, you need to splurge on an expensive airline ticket, something budget travelers find hard to justify. But those who do will discover a few days in Unalaska and Dutch Harbor can be a refreshing cure from an overdose of RVers, cruise ships and tour buses.

◉ Sights

TOP CHOICE **Museum of the Aleutians** MUSEUM
(☏581-5150; www.aleutians.org; 314 Salmon Way; adult/child $5/free; ⊙11am-6pm Tue-Sun) The small but impressive Museum of the Aleutians is one of the best native cultural centers in Alaska. A short walk from the Grand Aleutian Hotel, the museum relives the Aleutian story from prehistory through the Russian America period to WWII and the present. Many of the exhibits focus on the enduring relationship between the Aleuts and the Russian Orthodox Church, but, for many, the most fascinating displays are the tools, boats and grass baskets that allowed these clever and creative people to live in such a harsh environment.

Church of the Holy Ascension CHURCH
Unalaska is dominated by the Church of the Holy Ascension, the oldest Russian-built church still standing in Alaska. It was built in 1825 and then enlarged in 1894, when its floor plan was changed to a *pekov* (the shape of a crucifix). On Broadway Ave, overlooking the bay, the church and its onion domes are a photographer's delight. The church contains almost 700 pieces of art, ranging from Russian Orthodox icons and books to the largest collection of 19th-century paintings in Alaska. The best time to view the interior of the church is after services, 6:30pm on Saturday and 11am Sunday morning.

Outside the church is a small graveyard, where the largest grave marker belongs to Baron Nicholas Zass. Born in 1825 in Archangel, Russia, he eventually became bishop of the Aleutian Islands, and all of Alaska, before his death in 1882. Next door to the graveyard is the **Bishop's House**.

Aleutian WWII National Historic Area HISTORIC SITE
In 1996 Congress created this 134-acre national historic area to commemorate the bloody events of WWII that took place on the Aleutian Islands. Uniquely, the park is owned and managed by the Alaska Native Ounalashka Corporation, not the federal government.

To learn about the 'Forgotten War,' begin at the **Aleutian WWII Visitor Center** (☏581-9944; 2716 Airport Beach Rd; adult/child $4/free; ⊙10am-6pm Fri-Mon, from 1pm Tue-Thu), near the airport, in the original air control tower built in 1942. Downstairs, exhibits relive the Aleutian campaign, including the bombing of Dutch Harbor by the Japanese for two days and the Battle of Attu, the first international battle on American soil since the war of 1812. Upstairs is the re-created air control tower, and in a theater you can watch documentaries about the war effort in Alaska.

Most of the park preserves **Fort Schwatka**, on Mt Ballyhoo, the highest coastal battery ever constructed in the US. Looming nearly 1000ft above the storm-tossed waters of the Bering Sea, the Army fort encompassed more than 100 concrete observation posts, command stations and other structures built to withstand earthquakes and 100mph winds. The gun mounts here are still among the best preserved in the country, and include tunnels and bunkers that allowed gunners to cart ammunition from one side of the mountain to the other.

The 1634ft mountain of military artifacts is behind the airport and can be reached on foot or by vehicle via Ulakta Rd, picked up half a mile north of the ferry terminal, along Ballyhoo Rd. If on foot, the gravel road is an hour's climb to the top, but the views of Unalaska Island on the way up, and on top, are excellent. Pick up the free *Fort Schwatka Self-Guided Tour* brochure at the museum.

Bunker Hill HISTORIC SITE
An easier climb is Bunker Hill, also part of the national historic area. This coastal battery was known to the military as Hill 400, and was fortified with 155mm guns, ammunition magazines, water tanks, 22 Quonset huts and a concrete command post at the top. You can hike to the peak of Bunker Hill along a gravel road picked up just after crossing the bridge to Amaknak Island.

USS Northwestern Memorial MONUMENT

More war history can be found in Unalaska by following Bayview Rd to the southeast end of town. In a picturesque hillside graveyard along the bay is the USS *Northwest* memorial. Launched in 1889, the passenger and freight ship was retired in 1937, then repaired by the military in 1940 to serve as a floating bunkhouse. It was bombed during the attack on Dutch Harbor and burned for five days. In 1992, for the 50th anniversary of the event, the propeller was salvaged by divers and is now part of the memorial.

Sitka Spruce Park PARK

Within Dutch Harbor is this national historical landmark, along Biorka Dr, where the Russians planted Sitka spruce in 1805. It's the oldest recorded afforestation project in North America. Three of the gnarly spruce are said to be the originals. The park also features interpretive displays and a short trail to an edge-of-the-cliff overlook.

Expedition Park PARK

The number of bald eagles in and around Unalaska and Dutch Harbor is mindboggling. There are so many birds that locals view them as scavengers, which they are by nature, rather than the majestic symbol of the USA. And because the islands are treeless, you can see them on the roofs of houses, on streetlights and even picking through dumpsters behind stores. One of the best places (besides the dump) to photograph them up close and in a somewhat natural setting is Expedition Park, at the end of Bobby Storrs Boat Harbor, off Gilman Rd. Because the park is perched above the harbor, there are always a few birds resting in the stand of dead pines, and sometimes more than a dozen.

🏃 Activities

Hiking

Because of the treeless environment, hiking is easy here. And don't worry about bears – there aren't any.

Before hiking anywhere, even Mt Ballyhoo or Bunker Hill, you must obtain a permit (daily $6 per person and weekly $15) from the Ounalashka Corporation (☑581-1276; www.ounalashka.com; 400 Salmon Way; ☺8am-5pm Mon-Fri). Also call Unalaska's Parks, Culture & Recreation Department (PCR; ☑581-1297; 37 S 5th St; ☺6am-10pm Mon-Fri, from 8am Sat, noon-7pm Sun), which organizes hikes in summer for locals and visitors.

Uniktali Bay HIKING

There are few developed trails, but an enjoyable day can be spent hiking to Uniktali Bay, a round-trip of 8 to 10 miles. From Captain's Bay Rd, turn east on a gravel road just before Westward Cannery. Follow the road for a mile to its end; a foot trail continues along a stream. In 2 miles, the trail runs out, and you'll reach a lake in a pass between two 2000ft peaks. Continue southeast to pick up a second stream, which empties into Uniktali Bay. The bay is undeveloped, and a great place to look for glass floats washed ashore from Japanese fishing nets.

Ugadaga Bay Trail HIKING

On the southeast side of Unalaska, this pleasant hike is 2.2 miles one way along an ancient portage route. More recently, the US military ran communications lines from Unalaska all the way to Seattle, and you'll see remnants of it in eroded spots. Seal hunters were using the portage as late as the 1960s.

Paddling

The many protected harbors, bays and islets of Unalaska Island make for ideal sea-kayaking conditions. The scenery is stunning and the wildlife plentiful. It is possible to encounter Steller's sea lions, sea otters and harbor porpoises. Aleutian Adventure Sports (☑581-4489; www.aleutianadventure.com) has kayak rentals for $69 and $89 per day for single and double kayaks respectively, as well as an introductory kayak class for $75, and guided trips.

☞ Tours

If you're planning to return with the ferry, a van tour is the best way to see a lot in your short stay. But book in advance if you can; almost all tour operators have closed and the main one can get overwhelmed when the ferry pulls in.

Extra Mile Tours TOUR

(☑581-1859; www.unalaskadutchharbortour.com; 4/2hr tour $90/50) Operator Bobbie Lekanoff is very knowledgeable in indigenous and WWII history, and knows every single flower and bird.

🛏 Sleeping

Rooms are scarce here; you've only three options. It might pay to call the visitors center to see if any locals have started a B&B or are simply taking in travelers. On top of the prices listed you have to add an 8% tax.

Grand Aleutian Hotel HOTEL $$$
(☑581-3844, 866-581-3844; www.grandaleutian.com; 498 Salmon Way; s/d $164/184; 🛜) Updated rooms with memory-foam mattresses appeal to TV crews and travelers on a loose budget. The grand views from every window help make up for the slightly utilitarian – if new and clean – digs. You'll find a refrigerator and coffee maker in each room.

Ounalashka Corporation CAMPING $
(☑581-1276; www.ounalashka.com; 400 Salmon Way; permits daily/weekly per person $6/15) This native corporation owns most of the land out of town and allows camping if you obtain a permit. A flat patch shielded from the strong winds is at a premium on the island, so the best places to pitch a tent tend to be along the beach, at the foot of one of Unalaska's hills. The closest to town is on the southwest corner of Bunker Hill. Even better, but further away, is Summer Bay, 4 miles from Unalaska.

UniSea Inn MOTEL $$
(☑581-3844; 88 Salmon Way; s/d $99/110) Across the street from Dutch Harbor Mall, this 30-room inn is sandwiched between a shipyard and a fish-processing plant. Guests check in at the Grand Aleutian and are shuttled over,

but be forewarned: there's a bar downstairs and it can get loud at times.

🍴 Eating & Drinking

Chart Room SEAFOOD $$$
(☑866-581-3844; 498 Salmon Way; dinner $20-40; ⏲breakfast, lunch & dinner; 🛜) The swankiest restaurant in the Aleutian Islands, the Chart Room has more meat than seafood on its menu. But it's best known for its buffets: on the weekends, a giant brunch spread ($25) includes king crab legs, made-to-order omelets and chocolate-dipped strawberries. On Wednesday nights the seafood buffet features local halibut, salmon, shrimp and king crab, and great sushi. It's hard to imagine a $32 meal being a bargain, but for seafood lovers this one is.

Harbor View Bar & Grill PIZZA $$
(☑581-7246; 88 Salmon Way; pizza $18-29; ⏲11am-10pm) Dutch Harbor's newest restaurant, in the UniSea Inn, has pizza, salads, pasta and burgers. Attached is **Harbor Sushi** (⏲dinner Thu-Tue), the best sushi in a town that knows its seafood. The rocking bar is the best place to meet a proud extra from the early seasons of *The Deadliest Catch* (the reason for its local nickname, the 'Unisleaze').

LOCAL KNOWLEDGE

JEFF DICKRELL: HISTORY TEACHER

What has kept me in the Aleutians these past decades is the merging of the wilderness and nine millennia of history. While out walking the remote beaches one can stumble across an ancient native village, an unrecorded WWII plane wreck or walk in the footsteps of major characters in Aleutian history.

Ugadaga Bay Trail

While the natives mainly traveled by skin boat, they used a few strategic overland portages. On the far end of town, leading down to Ugadaga Bay, is one of these trails. It's an easy 2-mile hike down to the beach with wild berries growing alongside the route, a salmon stream and eagle nests. Recently, a live WWII hand grenade was found on the trail so watch your step!

Museum of the Aleutians

Come into close contact with the first inhabitants at the museum. Observe the evolution of their tools and artistry as discovered through the displays of archaeological artifacts. Make sure you open the drawers beneath the cases!

Russian Orthodox Cemetery

Research why the orthodox grave markers look the way they do if you want to understand the 'code' of the cemetery. But in between the nameless crosses (placed at the foot of the grave) you will find the graves of gold rush pioneers, early Coast Guard crewmen and rows of orphans who died of the flu in 1909.

Author of Center of the Storm: The Bombing of Dutch Harbor and the Experience of Patrol Wing Four in the Aleutians, Summer 1942

Dutch Harbor Fast Food ASIAN $

(3rd St & Broadway Ave; mains $10-12; ⊙lunch & dinner) Don't let the name fool you: this is a sit-down place serving great Asian staples such as chow mein, fried rice and pho. The pad thai comes in a pile the size of your face and is highly recommended.

Airport Restaurant ASIAN $$

(breakfast & lunch $9-14, dinner $15-27; ⊙breakfast, lunch & dinner) This restaurant is not just popular because it's located at an airport notorious for bad weather. Besides seafood and American food, there are excellent Vietnamese dishes: try the Airport Surf – a *banh mi* (Vietnamese sandwich) in disguise. If your flight is delayed, the bar is open late.

Amelia's MEXICAN $$

(Airport Beach Rd; breakfast $7-13, burgers $9-12, dinner $14-29; ⊙breakfast, lunch & dinner) This Dutch Harbor restaurant does a little of everything, from breakfast and burgers to seafood and pasta, but the majority of its menu is Mexican, including almost a dozen types of burritos. Amazingly, none of them is stuffed with crab or halibut.

Safeway GROCERY $

(2029 Airport Beach Rd; ⊙7am-11pm) Dutch Harbor's best and biggest supermarket, with fresh produce, a bakery, a hot food bar and even a seating area.

Cape Cheerful Lounge BAR $

(498 Salmon Way) The Grand Aleutian Hotel bar hops at night, and when the sun is out drinkers move to an outdoor deck. The good pub-grub menu includes sliders and barbecued meals.

🛍 Shopping

Alaska Ship Supply SOUVENIRS

(☑581-1284; www.alaskashipsupply.com; 1362 Ballyhoo Rd; ⊙7am-10pm) It's amazing how many *Deadliest Catch* buffs show up in Dutch Harbor looking for the Alaska Ship Supply hoodies that the fishing crews wear on the popular Discovery Channel show. You'll find them upstairs at Alaska Ship Supply, just past the ferry terminal.

LFS, Inc SOUVENIRS

(2315 Airport Beach Rd; ⊙8am-8pm Mon-Sat, to 4pm Sun) For an even better selection of Dutch Harbor logo clothing, raingear and other related commercial fishing gear.

ℹ Information

Iliuliuk Family & Health Clinic (☑581-1202; 34 LaVelle Ct; ⊙walk-in 8:30am-6pm Mon-Fri, to 1pm Sat) Just off Airport Beach Rd near Unalaska City Hall; has walk-in and 24-hour emergency service.

Key Bank of Alaska (☑581-1233; 100 Salmon Way) Across from the Grand Aleutian Hotel in Dutch Harbor; has a 24-hour ATM.

Post office Unalaska (82 Airport Beach Rd); Dutch Harbor (Airport Beach Rd) The Dutch Harbor post office is near the Grand Aleutian Hotel.

Unalaska/Port of Dutch Harbor Convention & Visitors Bureau (☑581-2612, 877-581-2612; www.unalaska.info; cnr 5th & Broadway, Unalaska; ⊙8am-5pm Mon-Fri, 10am-3pm Sat) Located in the Burma Street Russian Church, originally a military chapel built during WWII. Also opens when the ferry is in.

Unalaska Public Library (☑581-5060; 64 Eleanor Dr; ⊙10am-9pm Mon-Fri, noon-6pm Sat & Sun) Near the 5th St Bridge, offers free internet access on 14 computers.

ℹ Getting There & Around

Other than the twice-a-month ferry, the only way of getting out of Unalaska and Dutch Harbor is flying. The town is serviced by **PenAir** (☑800-448-4226; www.penair.com) but you book the ticket through **Alaska Airlines** (☑800-252-7522; www.alaskaair.com). There are three to four flights daily and a one-way ticket is $500 to $600.

The airport is on Amaknak Island, 3 miles from Unalaska. The ferry terminal is even further north, off Ballyhoo Rd. Cab fare to downtown Unalaska costs $10 to $12 from the airport, or $14 to $16 from the ferry. There are a zillion cabs running all over Unalaska and Dutch Harbor, including **Aleutian Taxi** (☑581-1866). There's a long list in the airport terminal.

To get out and see the island there are a couple of car rental companies, including **North Port Car Rental** (☑581-3880), which is located at the airport and has vehicles for $75 a day. A mountain bike is another way to get around as the extensive, lightly used dirt roads left over from the WWII buildup make for great riding. You can hire a mountain bike from **Aleutian Adventure Sports** (☑581-4489; www.aleutianadventuresports.com; daily/weekly $30/120).

The Bush

Best Places to Eat

» Airport Pizza (p355)

» Pepe's North of the Border (p370)

» Sam & Lee's Chinese Restaurant (p370)

» Brower's Cafe (p370)

Best Places to Stay

» Dredge No 7 Inn (p356)

» Solomon Bed & Breakfast (p354)

» Chateau de Cape Nome (p354)

» Salmon Lake Campground (p357)

» Arctic Getaway Cabin & Breakfast (p363)

Why Go?

In a state where unbounded wilderness is the norm, the Bush is like the frontier on the frontier. Towns and townly comforts are few, roads are fewer, and most of the region is accessible only by flying, floating or walking in. Yes, it takes effort to reach the ends of the earth, but the rewards are equal to the task.

In western Alaska, you can head out on extended backpacks or wilderness paddles, swagger through Nome's goldrush saloons or fly into isolated Native villages to meet the people who thrive year-round in this formidable landscape. In Arctic Alaska, explore the mythical vastness of preserves like Gates of the Arctic National Park and the Arctic National Wildlife Refuge. Here the mandate is 'self-discovery,' which may be as much about teaching us our physical limits as about our puny insignificance in the grand scale of nature.

When to Go
Nome

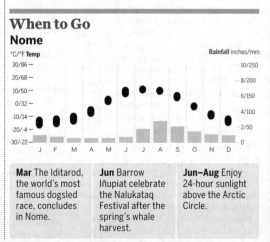

Mar The Iditarod, the world's most famous dogsled race, concludes in Nome.

Jun Barrow Iñupiat celebrate the Nalukataq Festival after the spring's whale harvest.

Jun–Aug Enjoy 24-hour sunlight above the Arctic Circle.

History

The history of the Bush is largely the history of Alaska Natives. By their own accounts, they've been here since the beginning. Archaeologists say it's not been as long as that: perhaps 6000 years for the ancestors of today's Athabascans, and about 3000 years for the Iñupiat, Yupiks and Aleuts. Either way, they've displayed remarkable ingenuity and endurance, thriving as fishers, hunters and gatherers in an environment few else could even survive in.

Europeans arrived in Alaska in the 1800s, with traders and missionaries setting up shop in numerous communities along the western coast. Whalers entered the Bering Sea around midcentury, and soon expanded into the Arctic Ocean. By 1912 they had virtually decimated the bowhead whale population.

The most climactic event in the Bush, however, was the gold rush at Nome, triggered in 1898 (just two years after the discovery of gold in the Klondike), by the 'Three Lucky Swedes' (p355). The stampede drew as many as 20,000 fortune chasers across to the Seward Peninsula, giving the region, ever so briefly, the most populous town in Alaska. Even today Nome remains the only significant non-Native community in the Bush.

Throughout the 20th century, progress in transportation, communications and social services transformed the remote region. 'Bush planes' made the area relatively accessible, and towns like Barrow, Kotzebue, Nome and Bethel became commercial hubs, in turn bringing services to the smaller villages in their orbit. Political and legal battles resulted in more schools and better health care, while the 1971 *Alaska Native Claims Settlement Act* turned villages into corporations and villagers into shareholders. Today, anywhere you go in the Bush you'll find residents engaged in a fine balancing act – coping with the challenges of the 21st century, while at the same time struggling to keep alive the values, practices and links to the land that they've passed down through countless generations and maintained for millennia.

ℹ Getting There & Around

The Bush is, almost by definition, road-less. You can drive (or be driven) up the Dalton Hwy to Deadhorse, and around Nome on an insular road network reaching out to a few surrounding destinations. Everywhere else it's fly-in only.

Alaska Airlines and Era Alaska are the main carriers, with Nome, Kotzebue and Barrow the main hubs. Regional airlines fly to smaller villages and provide air-taxi services into the wilderness.

WESTERN ALASKA

Western Alaska is home to Iñupiat, intrepid prospectors and some of the state's least-seen landscapes. Too far north (and too close to the Arctic Ocean and Bering Sea) for trees, the terrain is instead carpeted with coral-like tundra grasses and flowers, and patrolled by herds of caribou and musk ox. Highlights of the area include regional hubs like Nome and Kotzebue, and the vast tracks of little-explored wilderness in the Noatak and Bering Land Bridge National Preserves.

Nome

POP 3653

Nome is, in so many ways, an Alaskan archetype: a rough-hewn, fun-loving, undying Wild West town, thriving at the utmost edge of the planet. During its gold-rush heyday, Wyatt Earp and some 20,000 stampeders called the town home. Now with America's biggest concentration of non-Natives north of the treeline, and famed as the finishing line of that most Alaskan of races, the Iditarod, Nome is both comfortably familiar and spectacularly exotic.

Of the three major towns in the Bush – Nome, Kotzebue and Barrow – Nome is the most affordable and best set up for travelers. The streetscape is a compact, orderly, walkable grid, and most visitor-oriented businesses are concentrated on Front St, which overlooks the cold, gray Bering Sea. Nome is also among the most scenically situated of Alaska's Bush communities, and a highlight for most visitors is a road trip out to the stunning outlying coastal and interior regions.

While Nome is booked out for the Iditarod in March, the tourist season really begins in mid-May, when twitchers arrive looking for (among other species in this bird-rich environment) arctic tern, bristle-thighed curlew and Siberian bluethroat. Summer arrives very slowly, however, and if you want a chance to see green tundra and enjoy decent weather, come in late June or July. The road system outside Nome is closed from October or November to mid-May or early June.

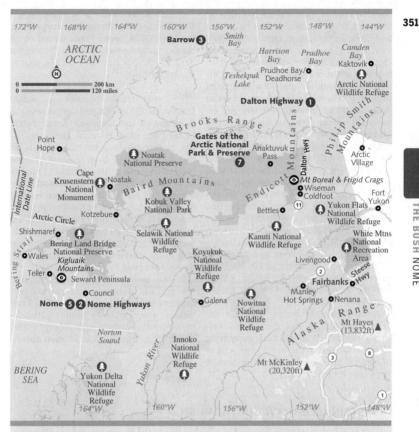

The Bush Highlights

❶ Driving the famed **Dalton Highway** (p361), aka the Haul Road, to the edge of the world

❷ Exploring the **Nome highways** (p356) for stunning Arctic scenery and endless hiking and camping opportunities

❸ Touching base with the Arctic Ocean and standing at the top of America in **Barrow** (p366)

❹ Viewing some of the world's most intriguing **wildlife**, including polar bear, musk ox and caribou

❺ Exploring the **gold rush history** of Nome (p350) and chatting with miners working active claims

❻ Learning how subsistence hunting and gathering remains at the heart of **Native culture** and communities across the Bush

❼ Entering the awesome **Gates of the Arctic National Park & Preserve** (p364) and making your own path across this unblemished wilderness

◉ Sights

Drop by the Nome Visitor Center for information on the various gold-rush-era buildings still standing in the downtown area. And, while wandering about, be on the lookout for dredge buckets. During Nome's golden heyday there were more than 100 dredges in use, each employing hundreds of buckets to scoop up gravel and dirt. Today you'll see the buckets all over town, many used as giant flowerpots.

Golden Sands Beach   GOLD PANNING
Sand zero, so to speak, of Nome's famed gold rush, the beach is still open to recreational mining and all summer long you can watch miners set up work camps along the shore.

Some will pan or open a sluice box right on the beach, while the more serious rig a sluice and dredging equipment onto a small pontoon boat and anchor it 100yd offshore. From this Rube Goldberg machine–like contraption they will spend up to four hours underwater in wet suits (pumped with hot air from the engine), essentially vacuuming the ocean floor. Miners are generally friendly, and occasionally you can even coax one to show you his gold dust and nuggets. If you catch the fever, practically every gift shop and hardware store in town sells black-plastic gold pans. As you're panning, think about the visitor who, while simply beachcombing in 1984, found a 3.5in nugget at the eastern end of the seawall that weighed 1.29oz, and remember that gold's now worth well over $1000 per ounce.

The beach stretches a mile east of town along Front St. At the height of summer, a few local children may be seen playing in the 45°F water, and on Memorial Day (in May), more than 100 masochistic residents plunge into the ice-choked waters for the annual Polar Bear Swim.

Across from the beach, just past the Tesoro Gas Station, sits a Mine Machinery Graveyard. With no roads connecting Nome to the rest of the world, once a piece of equipment makes the barge-ride here, it stays until it turns to dust.

A little further along is the Swanberg's Gold Dredge. The dredge was in operation until the 1950s, before being passed on to the city for its historic value. In the evening herds of musk ox can sometimes be seen in the nearby fields.

FREE Carrie McLain Museum   MUSEUM
(223 Front St; ☺10am-5:30pm) Currently in the basement of the Kegoayah Kozga Public Library, the small museum has some Native culture displays, but the focus is on the gold rush and Nome's history in the early 20th century. Among racks of mining equipment, historical documents and photo albums, you can see the preserved body of Fritz the sled dog, one of the leaders of the famed 1925 race to deliver diphtheria serum to Nome (the inspiration for the Iditarod). Inexpensive photo reprints of the dog team and many other moments in Alaskan history are available for sale.

If the budgeting comes through, the museum will at some point move to larger quarters and be able to display its full collection, which includes Nome's first telephone booth, saloon pianos, Native crafts, and artifacts from Alaskan aviation history.

SUSTAINABLE TRAVEL IN THE BUSH

Truly green travel is nearly impossible in Alaska's Bush. After all, you had to fly to get here, and it's likely all your heat and electricity will be provided by diesel generators. But there are ways to travel smarter and make a positive impact on both the ecosystems and cultures you will encounter along the way.

» **Keep it dry** Alcoholism and drug abuse are rampant among both whites and Natives living in the Bush. Many towns have restrictions on alcoholic consumption: they're either totally dry; damp (you can drink but not purchase alcohol); or restrictive wet (the community controls the liquor store). Respect the local laws.

» **Leave your judgments behind** Many Alaska Natives still practice subsistence hunting, heading out in sealskin boats in search of whale, seal, walrus and even polar bear. While these endangered species are protected by law, Natives can still legally hunt them. Which leads to the question:

» **To buy or not to buy?** Yes, carvings, baskets and etchings made from the ivory or baleen of hunted marine animals do make great mementos (and some are gorgeous works of art), but if you live outside the US your country likely restricts their import. If you can bring them home, consider that Natives use every part of the animal, leave nothing to waste and may well depend on the extra income to support their subsistence lifestyle. What's more, most biologists agree that this type of hunting has little or no effect on the populations of these endangered species.

» **Write to Congress** The fate of Alaska's environment may lie with the leaders of the US. Let them know what you think.

Nome

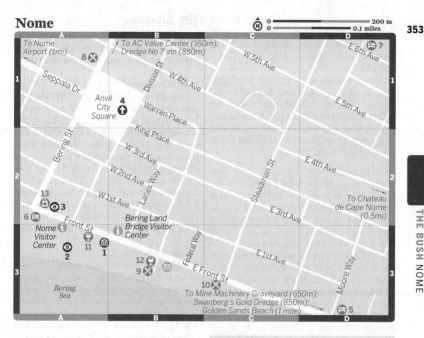

THE BUSH NOME

St Joseph Church · CHURCH

(Anvil City Sq) Built in 1901, when there were 20,000 people living in Nome, this huge church was located on Front St and used as a beacon for seamen. By the 1920s, after the population of the city had plummeted to less than 900, the Jesuits abandoned the structure. It was then used for storage by a mining company until 1996 when the city purchased the building and moved it to its present location. In the grassy square fronting the church, look for statues of the Three Lucky Swedes, dredge buckets and the 'world's largest gold pan.'

Iditarod Finish-Line Arch · LANDMARK

This imposing structure, a distinctly bent pine tree with burls, is raised over Front St every March in anticipation of the mushers and their dog sled teams ending the 1049-mile race here.

Donald Perkins Memorial Plaza · PLAZA

Next to the Nome Visitor Center is this plaza, containing a collection of old mining detritus.

🏃 Activities

If you're well prepared and the weather holds, the backcountry surrounding Nome can be hiking heaven. Though there are no

marked trails in the region, the area's three highways offer perfect access into the tundra and mountains. What's more, the lack of trees and big, rolling topography make route-finding fairly simple: just pick a point and go for it. For those who'd like a little more direction, a multipage list of suggested day hikes is available from the Nome Visitor Center.

Also providing great info on local trekking is the Bering Land Bridge Visitor Center. Every second Saturday during the summer the center leads very popular and free guided day hikes as well as birding tours in May and June. Contact the center for exact times and dates.

Anvil Mountain
HIKING

The climb up 1062ft Anvil Mountain is the closest hike to Nome and the only one that can be easily pulled off without a car. To start, follow Bering St out of town to where it changes to the Teller Hwy. About 2.5 miles down the Teller Hwy turn right on the Dexter Bypass and look for an obvious dirt road, about half a mile in, climbing up the hillside. It's about a half mile to the summit, through wonderful wildflower patches. At the top you'll find the giant parabolic antennae of the Cold War–era White Alice Communications System, plus great views of town and the ocean, as well as the Kigluaik Mountains further inland.

Tours

The Visitor Center can hook you up with operators for fishing, hunting and dogsled rides, as well as snowcat and snowmobile tours in season.

Bering Air
SCENIC FLIGHTS

(443-5464; www.beringair.com; per person $250) Offers 90-minute helicopter tours of the area (two-person minimum).

Nome Discovery Tours
TOUR

(443-2814; tours $65-185) The most intimate, highly recommended tours are run by Richard Beneville, an old song-and-dance man who decided to hang up his tap shoes to live out in the Alaska wilds. He offers everything from two-hour evening tundra exploration drives to full-day excursions to Teller, during which you'll drop in on an Iñupiat family, or to Council, with fishing along the way.

Wilderness Birding Adventures
BIRDWATCHING

(694-7442; www.wildernessbirding.com) This well-regarded Alaskan-run company offers small-group birding trips in the area. Check the website for dates and pricing.

Sleeping

Nome tacks on 11% bed and sales taxes to its accommodations. Book rooms well in advance in summer and up to a year before Iditarod.

TOP CHOICE Dredge No 7 Inn
B&B $$

(304-1270; www.dredge7inn.com; 1700 Teller Hwy; r/ste incl breakfast $125/135;) Run by an old Nome mining family, this modern inn strikes a nice balance between rustic charm and some fine Martha Stewart–inspired flourishes. Five bright private rooms share a spacious kitchen and living area decked out with leather sofas and fireplace. The Dredge Master Suite has its own kitchen. The inn is about a mile north out of town on a large lot with open views across the tundra from the back deck. Book online or there is a $10 surcharge.

Solomon Bed & Breakfast
B&B $$

(443-2403; www.solomonbnb.com; s/d with breakfast $150/160;) Is Nome not remote enough for you? Then head 34 miles down the Kougaro Rd to this new guesthouse run by the Village of Solomon, a federally recognized Native tribe. Inside a converted historic schoolhouse (built in 1939) you'll find four guest rooms, each with private bath and patio overlooking the tundra. There's also a dorm-style cabin ($75 per person) with shared bath and a communal kitchen. Meals are available at an extra cost, and canoes and kayaks by request. In June the fields of Solomon are a riot of wildflowers and migratory birds. The Last Train to Nowhere (see p357) is also just down the road and there's good fishing nearby for salmon, grayling and trout. Note that you do need your own transport to get here.

Chateau de Cape Nome
B&B $$

(443-2083; cussy@nome.net; 1105 E 4th Ave; r from $115) Overlooking the tundra and the Bering Sea on the far eastern edge of town is another excellent inn run by a descendant of gold rush–era pioneers. Owner 'Cussy' Kauer and her homestay are both troves of local history, and the B&B is just a short walk from Golden Sands Beach. Try to get a room with a view.

Nome Nugget Inn
HOTEL $$

(443-4189, www.nomenuggetinnhotel.com; 315 Front St; r $110-120;) In the thick of things downtown, the Nugget has 45 smallish rooms, about half with ocean views. The clapboard front and memorabilia-laden lobby promise more, but the rooms are compact

THREE LUCKY SWEDES

In September 1898 Jafet Lindeberg, Erik Lindblom and John Brynteson hit the jackpot in Nome. Although newcomers from Scandinavia, with only eight weeks' mining experience between them, they found gold in Anvil Creek, just a few miles outside present-day Nome. Though one of them – Lindeberg – was Norwegian, they were dubbed the 'Three Lucky Swedes.' Their discovery triggered the greatest stampede on Alaskan soil, a 'poor man's gold rush' in which digging for gold was said to be easier than stealing it.

By the following year, 'Anvil City' was a tent metropolis of 10,000 people. Among them was Wyatt Earp, the former marshal and noted gunslinger who teamed up with Doc Holliday to win the famous shoot-out at the OK Corral in Tombstone, Arizona.

Earp was actually on his way to the Klondike Gold Rush when he read about Alaska's new boomtown. He quickly switched his destination and after the spring thaw of 1899 arrived in Nome, on a steamer with his wife, Josie. Teaming up with a partner, Earp immediately built the Dexter – the first two-story wooden structure in what was basically still a tent city full of prospectors. It was Nome's largest and most luxurious saloon, with 12ft ceilings and 12 plush clubrooms upstairs, and was located only a block from 'the Stockade,' the city's red-light district.

Earp's timing was amazing. By July of that year, John Hummel, a prospector from Idaho, had discovered gold on the beaches. News of the 'golden sands' resulted in 2000 stampeders working the shoreline that summer, panning more than $1 million in gold dust. It was a banner year, with each man recovering $20 to $100 of gold per day on the edge of the Bering Sea. When the news finally reached Seattle in 1900, it set off yet another stampede of hopeful miners. By the end of that year there were 20,000 people in the town that is now called Nome, making it Alaska's largest city.

Over the ensuing century, mining slowed, the population fizzled and the township suffered numerous disasters. Fires all but destroyed Nome in 1905 and 1934, and a violent Bering Sea storm overpowered the sea walls in 1974.

As for Earp, by October 1901, having already endured two winters on the Bering Sea, he left Nome with his wife and, as legend has it, $80,000 – a fortune at that time. The Swedes came out even richer, despite some early troubles with claim jumpers and bogus lawsuits. The men formed the Pioneer Mining Company and by the early 1920s had recovered more than $20 million in gold. Lucky indeed.

and characterless. The best part of the interior is the old saloon with views of the Bering Sea. It's now an exclusive sitting room for guests, and while no alcohol is served there is good Vietnamese drip coffee available.

Aurora Inn　　　　　　　　　　HOTEL $$
(☑443-3838; www.aurorainnome.com; E Front St, at Moore Way; d $155-265; ☏) At the far edge of town, and just a short walk to Golden Sands Beach, the Aurora offers generic-style comfort in simple motel-style rooms, some with full kitchenettes.

You can camp for free on Golden Sands Beach, but do so a bit down the beach as the street sweepers dump debris here daily. Showers are available at the **Nome Recreation Center** (208 E 6th Ave; showers $5; ⊙5:30am-10pm Mon-Fri). You can reach the center by heading up Steadman St and turning right on E 6th Ave. Further from town it's unofficially permissible to camp just about anywhere: simply hike away from the road corridor, avoid private property and active mining claims, and clean up after yourself. About 40 miles north of town, on Kougarok Rd, there is also the lovely, free Salmon Lake Campground (p357), run by the Bureau of Land Management (BLM).

✖ Eating

There are almost a dozen places to eat in Nome, mostly sit-down restaurants of the pizza and American-style Chinese variety.

Airport Pizza　　　　　　　　PIZZERIA $$
(406 Bering St; pizzas $15-34; ☏🍴) The first place locals will recommend, this pizza-pub has a lively decor, friendly service and an assortment of pizza and Tex-Mex dishes that could pass muster most anywhere.

Polar Café　　　　　　　　BREAKFAST $$
(Front St; breakfast mains $10-14, lunch mains $12-16, dinner mains $19-28; ☏) This popular

waterfront eatery serves straightforward food that delivers. As a bonus it has open views of the Bering Sea (not as impressive as the Subway's, though), friendly service and a $10 salad bar.

AC Value Center   SUPERMARKET **$**
(cnr Bering St & Nome Bypass; ⊙7:30am-10pm Mon-Sat, 10am-9pm Sun) This supermarket is at the northern edge of town straight up Bering St and has a bakery, espresso counter and deli with limited ready-to-eat items.

Subway   SANDWICHES **$**
(E Front St; ⊙8am-11pm Mon-Sat, 9am-10pm Sun; sandwiches $8) At the far eastern edge of downtown, the Subway has the best sit-down views of the Bering Sea.

🍸 Drinking

Even by Alaskan standards, drinking in Nome is legendary. There are more saloons here than in the rest of Bush Alaska combined, which unfortunately means drunks wandering the streets sometimes from morning till night. Most bars are clustered around Front St.

Board of Trade Saloon   BAR
(212 Front St) Dating to 1900, the saloon claims to be the oldest on the Bering Sea and is certainly the most notorious.

Anchor Tavern   BAR
(114 Front St) Come here for a quieter hangout where you can sit and chat with locals. There's a good selection of beer on tap.

Airport Pizza   SPORTS BAR
(406 Bering St) The sports-bar of the restaurant is the tamest (or most civilized, depending on your view) spot in town for a drink. A selection of Alaskan brews is available.

🛍 Shopping

Arctic Trading Post   BOOKS
(67 Front St; ⊙7:30am-10pm) Has a good selection of books on the region and the Iditarod.

Chukotka Alaska   ARTS & CRAFTS
(514 Lomen Ave) Sells indigenous crafts and has a good book collection. The friendly owner will talk your ear off if you give him the chance. The shop is a few blocks west of Bering St.

❶ Information

Bering Land Bridge Visitor Center (www.nps.gov/bela; 179 Front St; ⊙8am-5pm Mon-Fri, 9am-3pm Sat) In the Sitnasuak Native Corporation Building, this National Park Service (NPS) center has a wealth of information on hiking, fishing, winter tours and wildlife in the area. The center is dedicated to Beringia, the 1000-mile-wide landmass that linked Alaska and Siberia until about 10,000 years ago, and has displays on mammoths, early Alaska Native culture and reindeer herding. There's a series of short videos shown on request.

Kegoayah Kozga Public Library (223 Front St; ⊙noon-8pm Mon-Thu, to 6pm Fri & Sat; @) Offers free internet access. Has also been in operation since 1902 and has a section of rare and 1st-edition books.

Nome Visitor Center (www.visitnomealaska.com; 301 Front St; ⊙8am-7pm Mon-Fri, 10am-6pm Sat & Sun) Make this your first stop in Nome: the extremely helpful staff will load you with brochures, advice and coffee. The website is also very informative on everything to do, see and consume in town.

Wells Fargo (109A Front St) In the historic Miner's and Merchant's Bank Building (dating from 1904); has a 24-hour ATM.

❶ Getting There & Around

Nome is serviced by **Alaska Airlines** (☎800-252-7522; www.alaskaair.com), which offers daily flights to Anchorage for $500 to $600 (book as far in advance as you can) as well as flights to Fairbanks ($600 to $800; daily). Most flights are just a couple of hours long but some through Kotzebue can take literally half a day with waits and transfers.

Nome's airport is a little more than a mile from town. You can walk or catch a cab for $6 per person. Try **Mr. Kab** (☎443-6000).

If renting a vehicle book well ahead of time. **Stampede Rent-A-Car** (☎443-3838; cnr Front St & Moore Way; vehicles per day $100-160) is in the Aurora Inn and offers SUVs, vans and pickups. **Dredge No 7 Inn** also rents out trucks for $100 a day. Both offer unlimited miles. When budgeting for a rental, keep in mind that gas in Nome is expensive and your vehicle likely won't get good mileage.

Hitchhiking is possible and locals are really good about picking people up. But you must be patient – and willing to sit in the back of an open pickup on very dusty roads.

Around Nome

Radiating east, north and northwest from Nome are its finest features: three gravel roads, each offering passage into a land of sweeping tundra, crystal-clear rivers and rugged mountains. Along the way you'll find

THE LAST TRAIN TO NOWHERE

In all of Bush Alaska, it's almost certainly the most-photographed landmark: a set of steam locomotives, utterly out of place and out of time, moldering on the Arctic tundra off the Nome–Council Road, hundreds of miles from the nearest functioning railway. Dubbed the Last Train to Nowhere, the three engines first plied the elevated lines of New York City in the 1880s, until Manhattan switched from steam to electric-driven trains. In 1903 the upstart Council City & Solomon River Railroad purchased the locomotives and transported them north, hoping to profit by servicing inland mines from the coast. Though the company surveyed some 50 miles of potential track, only half of that was built. By 1907 the operation went belly-up. Six years later a powerful storm sealed the Last Train's fate by destroying the Solomon River railroad bridge and stranding the engines on the tundra forever. Truly, it was the end of the line.

some of the best chances in Alaska to see waterfowl, caribou, bears and musk oxen. But be prepared: there's no gas and few other services along Nome's highways; instead, you'll encounter road-shrouding dust, rocks and narrow elevated sections of road that can easily dump you into a marsh. Going slow is key. Take twice as long as you would on pavement.

NOME–COUNCIL ROAD

This 73-mile route, which heads northeast to the old mining village of Council, is perhaps the best excursion if you have time for only one of Nome's roads. For the first 30 miles it hugs the glimmering Bering Sea coastline and passes a motley, but very photogenic, array of shacks, cabins, tepees and Quonset huts used by Nome residents as summer cottages and fishing and hunting camps. Natives have hunted and fished in this area for millennia, and the many depressions dotting the landscape are the sites of former camps.

On sunny days, the miles of beaches outside Nome beckon – but note how far inland autumn storms have tossed driftwood. At Mile 22 the road passes Safety Roadhouse, a dollar-bill-bedecked dive of a watering hole, and then crosses the birders' wonderland of Safety Sound, which once formed the eastern edge of the Bering Land Bridge. Ten miles further along is Bonanza Crossing, on the far side of which is the Last Train to Nowhere, a series of abandoned locomotives. Just to the north is the ghost town of Solomon, which was originally established in 1900 and once boasted a population of 1000 and seven saloons. The town was destroyed by a storm in 1913, relocated to higher ground and then further decimated by the 1918 flu epidemic. These days there's a B&B (p354) open in summer in the former schoolhouse.

Near Mile 40 you pass the first of two gold dredges within a couple of miles of each other. By 1912 almost 40 dredges worked the Seward Peninsula, and many are still visible from the Nome road system. The two on this road are in the best shape and are the most picturesque. Nome–Council Road begins climbing after the second dredge and reaches Stookum Pass at Mile 53. There's a parking area at the pass, so you can pull off and admire the views or take a hike on the nearby ridges.

The road ends at Mile 73 at Council. Actually, the road ends at the banks of the Niukluk River, and Council is on the other side. Most of the houses here are weekend getaways for people living in Nome, and there are currently no year-round residents. Locals drive across the river – with the water often reaching their running boards. Tourists with rental vehicles should stay put. There are no services or shops in Council, but the Niukluk is an excellent place to fish for grayling.

KOUGAROK ROAD

Also known as Nome–Taylor Rd, Kougarok Rd leads 86 miles north from Nome through the heart of the Kigluaik Mountains. There are a few artifacts from the gold-rush days, and the best mountain scenery and hiking in the Nome area, along the way. You can access the highway two ways: from its juncture off the Nome–Council Road just east of town, or via the Dexter Bypass, which spurs off the Nome–Teller Rd a few miles northeast of Nome.

The Kigluaiks spring up almost immediately, flanking the road until around Mile 40, where the free, BLM-operated Salmon Lake Campground is beautifully situated at the northern end of the large Salmon Lake. The

1. House in Barrow
The sun doesn't set for 82 days each year – from May to early August – in Barrow (p366), the northernmost city in Alaska.

2. Polar Bear Cub
Between 20,000 and 25,000 wild polar bears remain in the Arctic (p368).

2

3. Anaktuvuk Pass Cemetery
The trail-less Gates of the Arctic National Park & Preserve (p364) is one of the world's wildest areas.

4. Dried Salmon
Salmon are still traditionally dried at fish camps along the Bering Sea.

5. Iñupiat girl, Barrow
The appeal of Barrow (p366) owes as much to Iñupiat culture as it does to the city's novel latitude.

3

FLIGHT OF THE KING ISLANDERS

The King Islanders once lived 40 miles out to sea from Cape Douglas. They called their little island Ukivok and themselves the Aseuluk. They spent summers on the mainland, engaged in subsistence living and later, with the establishment of Nome, sold ivory carvings. By the 1950s, however, fewer and fewer families were making the 'commute' back and forth between seasons, and when the Bureau of Indian Affairs closed the island's school for good, the last families had no choice but to relocate.

The King Islanders of today mostly live in Nome, and some still practice a subsistence lifestyle. They head northwest of town to Cape Woolley in the summer to fish and out to sea in their sealskin *umiaks* (kayaks) in winter to hunt for whale and walrus. The Islanders continue to be renowned for their dancing and ivory carving, and if you are lucky you may see a performance while staying in Nome. It's difficult to visit King Island – though some top-end cruise ships are making the journey (p37) – but you can learn more about the people at the Nome Visitor Center or by checking in online with the King Island Native Community (www.kawerak.org/tribalHomePages/kingIsland/index.html).

facility features nine willow-girdled sites with tables, fire rings and an outhouse. The outlet for the Pilgrim River, where you can watch sockeye salmon spawn in August, is close.

Just before Mile 54 is Pilgrim River Rd, a rocky lane that heads northwest. The road climbs a pass where there's great ridge walking, then descends into a valley dotted with small tundra lakes. Less than 8 miles from Kougarok Rd, Pilgrim River Rd ends at the gate of Pilgrim Hot Springs. A roadhouse and saloon were located here during the gold rush, but they burnt down in 1908. Later there was an orphanage for children who lost their parents in the 1918 influenza epidemic. If you want to enter the hot spring area, first check in at the Nome Visitor Center as you'll need to fill out a form.

Kougarok Road crosses Pilgrim River at Mile 60, the Kuzitrin River at Mile 68 and the Kougarok Bridge at Mile 86. This is one of the best areas to look for herds of musk oxen. At all three bridges you can fish for grayling, Dolly Varden and salmon, among other species.

Beyond the Kougarok Bridge the road becomes a rough track impassable to cars. The extremely determined, however, can shoulder a pack and continue overland for a very challenging, boggy, unmarked 30-plus miles to Serpentine Hot Springs, inside the Bering Land Bridge National Preserve. A free, first-come, first served bunkhouse-style cabin there sleeps 15 to 20, and there's a bathhouse for slipping into the 140°F to 170°F waters. Almost no-one hikes both ways; consider chartering a plane in or out. Check at the Bering Land Bridge Visitor Center for flight operators and also to pick up their informative brochure on the springs.

NOME–TELLER ROAD

This road leads 73 miles (a one-way drive of at least two hours) to Teller, a year-round, subsistence Iñupiat village of 256 people. The landscape en route is vast and undulating, with steep climbs across spectacular rolling tundra. Hiking opportunities are numerous, as are chances to view musk oxen and a portion of the reindeer herd communally owned by families in Teller. The huge Alaska Gold Company dredge, which operated until the mid-1990s, lies just north of Nome on the Nome–Teller Rd.

The road also crosses a number of rivers that drain the southern side of the Kigluaik Mountains, all of them offering fishing opportunities. The Snake (spanned near Mile 8), Sinuk (Mile 26.7) and Feather rivers (Mile 37.4) are three of the more productive waterways for Arctic grayling, Dolly Varden and salmon. Ten miles from Teller you'll crest a ridge that affords sublime views of Port Clarence, with the village of Brevig Mission on the far side.

Teller lies at the westernmost end of the westernmost road in North America. This wind-wracked community overlooks the slate waters of the Bering Sea and stretches along a tapering gravel spit near the mouth of Grantley Harbor. Roald Amundsen, one of the greatest figures in polar exploration, returned to earth here after his legendary 70-hour airship flight over the North Pole on May 14, 1926. In 1985 Teller again made the headlines when Libby Riddles, then a Teller resident, became the first woman to win the Iditarod.

Though Teller is a scenic place – witness the fishnets set just offshore and the salmon hanging from racks on the beach – there's little for a visitor to do.

Still, out of respect for the residents (who are likely tired of drive-by gawkers from Nome), park your car and ask one of the village kids for directions to the tiny community store. There you can buy a snack and perhaps a handmade craft, supporting the Teller economy and facilitating interaction with the locals.

With rising sea levels and melting permafrost, there are plans to move Teller, but the move, if it happens, will take several years.

ARCTIC ALASKA

Perhaps the least-visited portion of the state, Alaska's Arctic region is tough and expensive to visit. But for those looking for moon-like dystopian towns, you might have just hit the jackpot. Of course, there's also plenty of outdoor stuff to do: paddling the numerous rivers, backpacking in little-visited national parks and preserves or driving the precarious and prodigious Dalton Hwy. Arctic Alaska has no cities, but 'hubs' like Bettles, Barrow and Coldfoot will get you started.

Dalton Highway

There are precious few adventures to be had while sitting down – but then, most road trips aren't on the legendary Dalton Hwy. Also known as Haul Road, this punishing truck route rambles 414 miles from Alaska's Interior to the North Slope, paralleling the Trans-Alaska Pipeline to its source at the Prudhoe Bay Oil Field. The highway reaches further north than any other on the continent and is the only way to motor through the stunning Brooks Range and the Arctic without a behemoth 4WD.

Fueled by crude-oil fever, the Dalton was built in a whirlwind five months in 1974. For the ensuing two decades, however, it was effectively a private driveway for the gas companies, until a bitter battle in the state legislature opened all but the last 8 miles to the Arctic Ocean (accessible now by private tours out of Deadhorse; see p364).

Though the Dalton is slowly being tamed (since 2000, around 130 miles have been paved) and thousands of ordinary tourists drive it every summer, it's still not a road that suffers fools. In summer the 28ft-wide corridor is a dusty minefield of potholes and

frost heaves, its embankments littered with blown tires. Paint scratches and window chips are inevitable, which is why most car-rental companies don't allow their vehicles here. There are few services – telephones, tire repair, fuel, restaurants – and none for the final 225 miles from Wiseman to Deadhorse.

The road is open year-round, but you should only tackle it between late May and early September, when there's virtually endless light and little snow and ice. Drive with headlights on, carry two spares, extra water and fuel, and always slow down and swing wide for oncoming trucks. Expect a 40mph average and two hard days to reach Deadhorse.

☞ Tours

Tour prices are comparable to the cost of renting (and fueling) your own vehicle and so offer a reasonable alternative to those not keen on tackling the challenges of the Dalton on their own.

Northern Alaska Tour Company SCENIC TOUR (☑474-8600; www.northernalaska.com) Offers all sorts of packages, including a three-day tour ($1089, per person based on double occupancy) that involves a drive up or down the Dalton (with a flight going the other way).

Trans Arctic Circle Treks SCENIC TOUR (☑479-5451; www.arctictreks.com) Charges $989 per person (based on double occupancy) for a similar three-day Dalton Hwy tour.

ⓘ Information

For more information on the highway, visit the Alaska Public Lands Information Center in the Morris Thompson Visitors Center in Fairbanks (see p289) and pick up a copy of the 24-page leaflet *The Dalton Highway Visitor Guide*. The guide covers history, safety, services, accommodation, points of interest and wildlife and also includes mileage charts and maps.

Also check out the website of the **BLM Central Yukon Field Office** (www.blm.gov/ak/st/en/prog/recreation/dalton_hwy.html), the agency that maintains the highway's campgrounds, rest areas and visitor center. You can download the previous year's visitor guide here.

ⓘ Getting There & Around

The vans of **Dalton Highway Express** (☑474-3555; www.daltonhighwayexpress.com) run twice a week between Fairbanks and Prudhoe Bay in summer, but only if they have bookings. Vans stop overnight at Deadhorse and give

THE ALASKA PIPELINE

Love it or loathe it, if you're driving Alaska's Richardson or Dalton Hwys, the Trans-Alaska Pipeline will be your traveling companion. The steely tube, 4ft wide and 800 miles long, parallels the highways from Prudhoe Bay on the Arctic Ocean down to Valdez, Alaska's northernmost ice-free port. En route, it spans 500-odd waterways and three mountain ranges, transporting about 600,000 barrels of crude oil per day – 12% of US domestic production – to tankers waiting in Prince William Sound. Back in its heyday, the pipeline was carrying around 2 million barrels per day. With dwindling reserves, however, they've cut down the flow and expect to continue to reduce it unless new sources, such as those in the Arctic National Wildlife Refuge (p365), are opened up for drilling.

Before construction began in 1974, the debate over the pipeline was among America's hardest-fought conservation battles. Both sides viewed themselves as defenders of the Last Frontier; boosters viewed the project as a grand act of Alaskan pioneering, and opponents called it an affront to all that's wild and wonderful about the 49th state. After the pipeline's completion – three years and $8 billion later – the late University of Alaska president William R Wood likened it to 'a silken thread, half-hidden across the palace carpet.' Many have had less kind words for it, especially in light of the numerous spills that have occurred over the years.

For about 380 of its miles, the Trans-Alaska Pipeline – like most pipelines – runs underground. Elsewhere it can't, because the 110°F to 55.6°F oil it carries would melt the permafrost. It's in those places – particularly where it crosses the highway – that you'll get your best look at the line. Especially good views can be had at Mile 243.5 of the Richardson Hwy south of Delta Junction, on the Dalton Hwy at the Yukon River crossing, and at the spur road to Wiseman. Just north of Fairbanks you can walk right up to the pipeline, stand under it, and even move in for a kiss if you are so inclined (as some are).

Be forewarned, however: elsewhere it's a bad move to get too close to the pipeline, much less to fondle, fold, bend, spindle or mutilate it. After September 11, 2001, officials identified the pipe as Alaska's number one terrorist target, ramping up security and for a while even operating a checkpoint on the Dalton Hwy. Their fears weren't entirely unfounded: in 1999, Canadian Alfred Reumayr was arrested for plotting to blow up the pipeline (apparently to make big profits on oil futures). In 2001, a drunken hunter also shot it with a .338-caliber rifle and 285,000 gallons spewed out. Officials say the pipeline has been shot – with no spillage caused – dozens of other times.

you time to take an early-morning oil-field tour before returning the next day. It's a hard-core way to travel, however, with two 16-hour riding days back-to-back. The round-trip fare to the Arctic Circle is $168, Coldfoot $212, Galbraith Lake $308 and Deadhorse $442.

Trucks and SUVs can be rented in Fairbanks (p298).

MILE 0 TO 175

Mile 0 of the Dalton is at the junction with the Elliot Hwy, 84 miles from Fairbanks. Immediately, the Haul Road announces itself: the pavement ends and loose gravel and blind curves begin. A road sign informs you that the speed limit is 50mph – for the next 416 miles!

This first section of highway carries you through scraggy boreal (taiga) forest. At Mile 56 the highway crosses the 2290ft-long, wooden-decked Yukon River Bridge – the only place where the legendary waterway is

spanned in Alaska. On the far bank is the BLM's Yukon Crossing Visitor Contact Station (www.blm.gov/ak/st/en/prog/recreation/dalton_hwy.html; ⊙9am-6pm Jun-Aug), featuring displays on the road and the terrain you're about to enter.

On the opposite side of the highway is the Yukon River Camp (☑474-3557; www.yukonrivercamp.com; r with shared bath $199), a utilitarian truck stop with work-camp-style rooms, showers, costly gas, a gift shop and restaurant (⊙9am-9pm).

The road then clambers back out of the river valley, across burned-over patches of forest (the remains of interior-wide fires in 2004 and 2005), and into an alpine area with the 40ft-high granite tor of Finger Mountain beckoning to the east. You pass the imaginary line of the Arctic Circle at Mile 115, and for good 24-7 views of the sun, continue to Gobblers Knob, a hilltop lookout at

Mile 132. From Gobbler's Knob northward, the pyramids of the Brooks Range begin to dominate the scene. In the next 50 miles you'll cross several grayling-rich streams, including Prospect Creek, which, in January 1971, experienced America's lowest-ever temperature: -80°F.

COLDFOOT

At Mile 175, in a mountain-rimmed hollow, you'll arrive in Coldfoot. Originally Slate Creek, the village was renamed when the first settlers, a group of greenhorn miners, got 'cold feet' at the thought of spending the 1898 winter in the district and headed south. Coldfoot was a ghost town by 1912, but nowadays there is an airstrip, post office and trooper detachment. There's also Coldfoot Camp (✆474-3500; www.coldfootcamp.com; r $198; ⊙24hr), a truck stop with the last gas station until Deadhorse, spartan rooms and a restaurant with passable diner-style fare. Frozen Foot Saloon is Alaska's northernmost bar if you care for a tipple.

A world apart is the Arctic Interagency Visitor Center (✆678-5209; ⊙10am-10pm Jun-Aug), on the opposite side of the highway. This impressive $5-million structure opened in 2004 and features museum-quality displays about the Arctic and its denizens. As the visitor center employees will tell you, the area's best lodging is down the highway 5 miles at Marion Creek Campground (Mile 180; campsites $10). This 27-site campground almost always has space and is in an open spruce forest with stunning views of the Brooks Range.

You can hire charter flights to Gates Of The Arctic National Park & Preserve and the Arctic National Wildlife Refuge with Coldfoot-based Coyote Air Service (✆678-5995; www.flycoyote.com).

WISEMAN

POP 18

Those seeking a bed – or wanting an antidote to Coldfoot's culture of the quick-and-dirty – should push on to Wiseman, a century-old log-cabin village accessible via a short dirt spur road at Mile 189. The only authentic town on the Dalton, Wiseman occupies an enviable spot, overhung by peaks and fronting the Middle Fork of the Koyukuk River. Its heyday was 1910, when it replaced the original Coldfoot as a hub for area gold miners.

The Wiseman Historical Museum, near the entrance to town, is only open to tour bus groups, but individual travelers might try to see if Wiseman's wise man, Jack Reakoff, is around. This engaging, urbane trapper will discourse at length about local history and wildlife. Many buildings from the gold-rush era still stand, including those of Arctic Getaway Cabin & Breakfast (✆678-4456; www.arcticgetaway.com; cabins incl breakfast $105-210), which offers a sunny two-person cabin and antique-laden four-person cabins. All come with breakfast and have kitchenettes available for making your other meals. At Boreal Lodge (✆678-4556; www.boreallodge.com; s/d

CYCLING THE HAUL ROAD

Every summer a few dozen hardy souls tackle this epic route under their own power. It's not a place to learn the ins and outs of long-distance cycling, but for the prepared and experienced it can be a trip of a lifetime.

Most riders catch the shuttle van to Deadhorse and ride back to Fairbanks, as it can be difficult to coordinate with the van's return schedule (twice a week but only if there are customers going both ways). Count on eight to 12 days to complete the route, with long days in the saddle and primitive camping at night. Water is available in streams but make sure to treat it first.

Changing weather systems can blow in quickly so be prepared for snow, icy rains and also hot temperatures (sometimes in the same day). Road conditions can also deteriorate fast. As Welshman Rob Hickman told us after he completed the route in June 2011 as part of a Pan-American Hwy ride to Tierra del Fuego, after rains, 'a decent gravel road could turn to a ready-mix slurry.' Other sections he described as like riding on 'ball bearings.'

But truck drivers were surprisingly good about giving riders like him a bit of space, and it was seldom more than 30 minutes between vehicles. With everyone aware of the dangers and hardships of the Dalton, it was never a problem to flag drivers down for backup when a bear had gotten too close, or even for a drink of water on a long stretch.

And if that makes Haul Road sound a little too tame, you can always try the ride in winter, pulling your supplies behind you on a sleigh. It's been done.

without bath $70/90, cabin $140), next door, the rooms are cheaper but more institutional. There's a full kitchen for guests.

MILE 190 TO 414

North from Wiseman the Dalton skirts the eastern edge of Gates of the Arctic National Park (p364). Dall sheep are often visible on the mountain slopes, and by Mile 194 the first views appear of the massive wall of Sukak-pak Mountain (4459ft) looming dead ahead. At Mile 235 you kiss the woods goodbye: the famed Last Spruce (now dead) stands near a turnout on the highway's east side.

Atigun Pass (Mile 242), at an elevation of 4739ft, is the highest highway pass in Alaska and marks the Continental Divide. The view from the top – with the Philip Smith Mountains to the east and the Endicotts to the west – will steal your breath away.

Once you reach the turnoff for the unde-veloped Galbraith Lake Campground at Mile 275, the Brooks Range is largely behind you. From here on down it's all rolling tundra. In this terrain, hiking and camping options are limitless, wildflowers and berries grow in profusion, and wildlife is rather easy to spot, not least because from May 10 to August 2 the sun never sets.

At the beginning and end of summer, watch for migrating waterbirds thronging roadside ponds and caribou – members of the 31,000-head Central Arctic herd – grazing nearby. Also, keep an eye out for weird polar phenomena such as pingos – protuberant hills with a frozen center – and ice-wedge polygons, which shape the tundra into bizarre geometric patterns.

DEADHORSE

You'll know the coast draws near when the weather turns dire. The gloom sets the mood for your arrival at the dystopia of Deadhorse, the world's northernmost anticlimax. Centered around Lake Colleen, this is no town – nobody lives here permanently – but a sad expanse of aluminum-clad warehouses, machinery-laden lots and workmen counting the moments until they return south.

Don't even think about camping: the tundra is a quagmire and the gravel pads are plied by speeding pickups. Having come all this way you can either turn around (after gassing up with what is, ironically, some of America's costliest petrol) or wait for the morning and take a two-hour oilfield tour run by Arctic Caribou Inn (☑866-659-2368; arcticcaribouinn@nmsusa.com; www.arcticcaribou inn.com; tours $45). Note that you must sign up at least 24 hours in advance to gain security clearance.

Prudhoe Bay Hotel (☑659-2449; www.prudhoebayhotel.com; dm with shared bath $125, s/d $150/250) and Arctic Caribou Inn (☑866-659-2368; www.arcticcaribouinn.com; d/tr $190/250), both near the airport, aren't froufrou, but the room price includes quality cafe-style meals. They're the only food service around and are open to nonguests.

Mail can be posted in Deadhorse, and souvenirs and sundries bought at the general store, located on the town's eastern edge.

Gates of the Arctic National Park & Preserve

The Gates of the Arctic National Park & Preserve is one of the world's finest wilderness areas. Covering 13,125 sq miles, the park (www.nps.gov/gaar/index.htm) straddles the ragged spine of the Brooks Range, America's northernmost chain of mountains, and sprawls 800 miles from east to west. Tundra covers the land, and animals (including grizzlies, wolves, Dall sheep, moose, caribou and wolverines) roam unfettered. There's great fishing – for grayling and arctic char in the clear streams, and for lake trout in the larger, deeper lakes.

Within the park are dozens of rivers to run, miles of valleys and tundra slopes to hike and, of course, the 'gates' themselves: Mt Boreal and Frigid Crags, which flank the north fork of the Koyukuk River. In 1929 Robert Marshall found an unobstructed path northward to the Arctic through these landmark peaks and his name for the passage has stuck ever since.

The park contains no visitor facilities, campgrounds or trails, and the NPS is intent upon maintaining its virgin quality. Rangers urge a seven-person limit on trekking parties, and they've also begun strongly encouraging visitors to get off the (literally) beaten path. They are particularly concerned about the effect that blogs, websites and even guidebooks such as this can have in increasing traffic to specific routes (and damage to the fragile Arctic environment). As one ranger put it, 'Detailed route planning is not addressed in our trip-planning packets or on our park website, because Congress set this area aside as a trail-less wilderness area specifically so that each visitor can find their own experience here.'

Unguided trekkers, paddlers and climbers entering the park should be well versed in wilderness travel; they should also check in at one of the ranger stations for a backcountry orientation and updates on river hazards and bear activity. To avoid confrontations with bears, campers are required to carry bear-proof food canisters, which can be checked out free of charge from the ranger stations.

Bettles is the main gateway to Gates of the Arctic, offering meals, lodging and air transport into the backcountry. Other visitors fly in from **Coldfoot** (p363) on the Dalton Hwy, or hike in directly from **Wiseman** (p363), just north of Coldfoot.

The remote village of **Anaktuvuk Pass**, in the far north of the park, is another access point if traveling by foot, though you'll need to fly here first. The small Native village was established in the 1950s by the last remaining group of seminomadic Nunamiut. Contact the Anaktuvuk Ranger Station for more information on visiting the park from here.

◉ Sights & Activities

Hiking

Most backpackers enter the park by way of charter air-taxi, which can land on lakes, rivers or river bars. Once on the ground they often follow the long, open valleys for extended treks or work their way to higher elevations where open tundra provides good hiking terrain.

While this appears to make planning an impossibly vague task, the landscape limits the areas that aircraft can land or pick you up, as well as where you can hike. Park staff suggest consulting flight and guide companies, as well as topographic maps, for possible routes and then running it by them to make sure the area is not overused. If it is, they can suggest alternatives.

WORTH A TRIP

ARCTIC NATIONAL WILDLIFE REFUGE

Seldom has so much furor involved a place so few have ever been. The Arctic National Wildlife Refuge (ANWR; http://arctic.fws.gov) is a 19.6-million-acre wilderness in Alaska's northeast corner, straddling the eastern Brooks Range from the treeless Arctic Coast to the taiga of the Porcupine River Valley. For years the refuge has been at the core of a white-hot debate over whether to drill beneath its coastal plain, which is thought to contain billions of barrels of crude oil and natural gas (see p399)

Beyond the bragging rights of visiting one of the most remote regions of the world, ANWR attracts with its boundless wilderness and surprisingly diverse wildlife. This 'Serengeti of the north' is home to dozens of land mammals, including grizzlies, musk ox, Dall sheep and the second largest herd of caribou in North America. Over 20 rivers cut through the region, several suitable for multiday paddles, as well as the four highest peaks in the Brooks Range. For adventurers, photographers and lovers of all things untamed and untrammeled, there are few more appealing destinations.

Visiting ANWR (an-wahr) is easier said than done. There are no visitor facilities of any sort, and even reaching the refuge can be tricky. There's only one place, for example, ANWR can be accessed by car: just north of Atigun Pass on the Dalton Hwy, where the road and the refuge briefly touch. However, this is an important wintering and lambing habitat for Dall sheep and, as elsewhere, visitors are encouraged to minimize their impact by traveling in small groups and avoiding creating trails when they walk.

To get deep into ANWR, you will need to fly. For a list of charter companies, consult the refuge's website. A few, like Coldfoot-based Coyote Air Service (☎678-5995; www. flycoyote.com), operate flightseeing trips. There are also plenty of outfitters that operate trips in the refuge. Most, including the excellent Alaska Discovery/Mountain Travel Sobek (☎888-831-7526; www.mtsobek.com), float the Kongakut, Sheenjek, Hulahula and other rivers; some, such as ABEC's Alaska Adventures (☎457-8907; www.abecalaska.com), lead multiday backpacking excursions or easier base camp explorations along the porcupine caribou migration route. From Kaktovik (p369), various guides offer polar bear sighting trips.

No matter what you choose to do in ANWR, you'd be wise to come soon. By the time you read this, drilling may already have begun.

The only treks that don't require chartering a plane are those beginning from the Dalton Hwy (near Wiseman), or from the village of Anukyuvuk Pass. For hikes from the highway, which lead into several different areas along the eastern border of the park, stop at the Arctic Interagency Visitor Center in Coldfoot for advice and assistance in trip planning. Several well-known routes in this area are showing too much wear and even beginning to affect the livelihood of subsistence hunters.

Hiking into the park from Anukyuvuk Pass is surprisingly one of the more economical options, as you only need to pay for a regular scheduled flight to the village from Fairbanks. From the airstrip it's just a few miles' hike into the northern edge of the park. You can camp for free by the airstrip if needed, but elsewhere get permission until you enter the park.

Paddling

Floatable rivers in the park include the John, Alatna, Noatak, Kobuk, Koyukuk and Tinayguk. The waterways range in difficulty from Class I to III, and you should consult the park or guide companies about possible routes.

Canoes and rafts can be rented in Bettles at the Bettles Lodge (☑692-5111; www.bettles lodge.com; per week canoe/raft $275/350).

☞ Tours

Guide and air companies must be registered and approved for business by the national park. The park website has a complete list, which includes ABEC's Alaska Adventures (☑457-8907; www.abecalaska.com) and Arctic Wild (☑479-8203; www.arcticwild.com).

⌂ Sleeping

If you need a place to stay before heading out into the wild, Bettles Lodge (☑692-5111; www.bettleslodge.com; dm $45, r $195-225) has accommodations; a variety of camping items, such as stoves, coolers, gas, bear spray, and mosquito jackets, are also for sale and rent.

ⓘ Information

For more information check out the park's website. If the Trip Planning Packet doesn't answer all your questions, contact the park directly.
Anaktuvuk Ranger Station (☑661-3520; www.nps.gov/gaar) Can help you plan your trip from Anaktuvuk.

Arctic Interagency Visitor Center In Coldfoot (p366); has info for those accessing the park from the Dalton Hwy.
Bettles Ranger Station & Visitor Center (☑692-5495; www.nps.gov/gaar; ☺8am-5pm daily Jun-Sep, 8am-5pm Mon-Fri winter) In a log building less than a quarter mile from the airstrip.

ⓘ Getting There & Away

Wright Air Service (☑474-0502; www.wrightairservice.com) flies daily from Fairbanks to Bettles ($340 round-trip) and Anuktukuk Pass ($390 round-trip). **Bettles Air Service** (☑692-5111; www.bettlesair.com) also covers the routes.

From Bettles it's necessary to charter an air-taxi to your destination within the park. Most areas can be reached in under two hours. Check with **Brooks Range Aviation** (☑692-5444; http://brooksrange.com) or Bettles Air Service for air charters.

From Coldfoot on the Dalton Hwy you can hire a charter flight with **Coyote Air Service** (☑678-5995; www.flycoyote.com).

Barrow

POP 4091

Barrow is the northernmost settlement in the USA, and the largest Iñupiat community in Alaska. Originally called Ukpeagvik, which means 'place to hunt snowy owls,' the town is situated 330 miles above the Arctic Circle. It's a flat, bleak, fogbound and strangely evocative place locked in almost perpetual winter. It's also a town of surprising contradictions.

On one hand, Barrow's wealth is famous: due to the spoils of North Slope petroleum it boasts facilities, such as its Iñupiat Heritage Center, which are unusual in a town this size. On the flip side, it's an Arctic slum packed with ramshackle structures wallowing in frozen mud.

It's also at once ancient and modern. Iñupiat have dwelled here for at least two millennia and still run the place: Barrow, as the seat of the North Slope Borough (a countylike government covering an area larger than Nebraska), is the administrative and commercial hub of Alaska's Far North. Yet locals have retained much of their traditional culture, best symbolized by the spring whale harvests and seen during the Nalukataq Festival staged in June to celebrate successful hunts.

DIXIE ALEXANDER: 'ATHABASCAN LIVING CULTURAL TREASURE'

Dixie Alexander is Director of Cultural Connections at the Morris Thompson Cultural & Visitor Centers in Fairbanks. A native Athabascan, born and raised in Fork Yukon, Dixie is recognized for her decades of work in promoting Native culture. An accomplished teacher and practitioner of many Native crafts, Dixie's work can be seen at the UAF Museum of the North and the Smithsonian Institute.

Favorite Spot

I really love being on the Yukon River in the morning. It's so very beautiful, like riding on glass, the sun coming up making everything warm and light on the water. It just makes you feel alive.

Dos & Don'ts

For travelers the most important thing is to know the difference between Eskimo and Indian. And when you go to a Native village, always say hello to the elders first. Whether you wave or shake hands, it's respectful to do this first to elders. You should ask before taking pictures of people, but there's no problem taking pictures of other things. And don't worry if people tease or poke fun at you. It's our way of showing fondness.

Best Time to Travel

I would say July. It's hot. Beautiful. We are starting to catch king salmon and pick berries. The gardens are in. Everyone is harvesting. It's an exciting time.

Barrow's appeal is as much the Iñupiat culture, served up by some of Alaska's warmest citizens, as its novel latitude. The midnight sun doesn't set here for 82 days, from May to early August.

Barrow lies along the northeasterly trending shore of the icebound Chukchi Sea, and is divided into two sections. Directly north of the airport is Barrow proper: it's home to most of the hotels and restaurants and interlaced with a warren of gravel streets, including Stevenson St, which runs along the water. Heading east along the shore takes you past Isatquaq, or Middle Lagoon, and then into Browerville. This is a more residential area but also where the heritage center, post office and grocery store are located. It's about 2 miles from one end of town to the other, making it easy enough for people to walk if the weather cooperates for long enough.

◉ Sights & Activities

The main thing to do at the 'top of the world' is bundle up, stand on the shore of the Arctic Ocean, dip something of yourself in the water, and gaze toward the North Pole.

Iñupiat Heritage Center CULTURAL CENTER
(Ahkovak St; www.nps.gov/inup; admission $10; ⊙8:30am-5pm Mon-Fri, 1-4pm Sat & Sun) This 24,000-sq-ft facility houses a museum, gift shop and a large multipurpose room where short traditional dancing-and-drumming performances take place each afternoon ($20). Local craftspeople often assemble in the lobby to sell masks, whalebone carvings and fur garments and are happy to talk about craft and technique. In the center's galleries, displays include everything from poster-size B&W portraits of local elders to a 35ft-long replica of a bowhead skeleton to a detailed (and artifact-rich) breakdown of traditional whaling culture and hunting practices.

Point Barrow LANDMARK
Follow the shore 12 miles northeast of the city and you'll come to Point Barrow, a narrow spit of land that's the northernmost extremity of the US (though not, as locals sometimes claim, North America). In the winter and spring this is where polar bears den; in the summer it's the featured stop of organized tours. You can also take a taxi out there but you'll have to walk the last section in.

Barrow Arctic Science Consortium LECTURES
(www.arcticscience.org; Beach Rd; ⊙1:30pm Sat) Hosts free scientific lectures most Saturdays. It's located at the Ilisagvik College, about 3 miles east of town on the Beach Rd. See the website for lecture details.

SAVING THE POLAR BEAR

Biologists estimate 20,000 to 25,000 polar bears live in the Arctic. That sounds like a healthy population but the bears' dependence on sea ice makes them vulnerable.

Polar bears need ice as a platform for hunting seals, their main source of food. They also need it for traveling, mating and sometimes giving birth. But for several decades now the northern ice cap has been shrinking, thinning and taking longer to form each winter. With a reduced habitat and reduced feeding season polar bears are breeding less often and building insufficient storages of fat. The lean summer months, when the bears live on land and scavenge or fast, are becoming even leaner, putting great stress on the animals' health.

There is also the problem of hunting. In most countries where polar bears roam there are restrictions on the number that can be killed, but scientists have long argued that these levels are unsustainable. In May 2008, the bears were finally listed as 'threatened' under the US Endangered Species Act, and importation of bear trophies was banned. The latter measure has proven so far quite significant, as most bear hunting by Americans actually takes place in Canada. In 2010, the Canadian government made their own move toward conservation by banning the *export* of polar bear parts, thus helping to deliver a severe double blow to the annual hunt.

Unfortunately, while these new policies have resulted in a general decrease in the numbers killed each season, the future of the bear is hardly guaranteed. The loss of polar ice has been blamed directly on global warming and there's no remedy for that disaster anywhere on the horizon.

Hiking

You can stroll the gravel roads, or gray-sand beaches, that parallel the sea to view *umiaks*, giant jawbones of bowhead whales, fish-drying racks and the jumbled Arctic pack ice that even in July spans the horizon.

On the waterfront opposite Apayauk St at the southwest end of town (turn left as you exit the airport) is Ukpiagvik, the site of an ancient Iñupiat village marked by the remains of semisubterranean sod huts. From that site, continue southwest out of town and when the road splits go left toward Freshwater Lake. After about 3 miles you'll come to a row of satellite dishes that face directly out and not up. It's an odd sight and makes for an interesting photo to drive home just how far north you are.

Birding & Wildlife-Watching

Barrow is a birder's paradise with at least 185 avian species making a stop here during the summer months. Most serious twitchers are on organized tours, but anyone with a pair of binoculars will find a few hours out of town a rewarding experience. In the absence of trees, birds nest on the ground and are easy to spot. Drop by Pepe's North of the Border for a complete list of the species found here in summer and then follow the walk, above, to Freshwater Lake. Another excellent spot is east of Bowerville along the Cakeater Rd heading toward Point Barrow.

If you want to see a polar bear, it's best to take a tour. But don't get your hopes up too high: they're tough to spot, especially in the summer months.

☞ Tours

Tundra Tours SCENIC TOUR
(☏852-3900, 800-882-8478; www.tundratoursinc.com) Barrow's major package-tour operator hauls sightseers around both town and tundra. A blanket toss and Alaska Native dance performance are included in the six-hour excursion, which costs $135 per person.

**Wilderness Birding
Adventures** BIRDWATCHING
(☏694-7442; www.wildernessbirding.com) Runs small-group birding tours to the Arctic region, including Barrow.

✹ Festivals & Events

Nalukataq Festival CULTURAL
The Nalukataq Festival is held in late June, when the spring whaling hunt has been completed. Depending on how successful the whaling captains have been, the festival lasts anywhere from a few days to more than a week. It's a rare cultural experience and worth timing your trip to Barrow around it if at all possible. One Iñupiat tradition calls for whaling crews to share their bounty with the village, and during the festival you'll see families carrying off platters and plastic

bags full of raw whale meat. Dishes served include muktuk, the pink blubbery part of the whale, which is boiled, pickled or even eaten raw with hot mustard or soy sauce.

The main event of the festival is the blanket toss, in which locals use a sealskin tarp to toss people into the air – the effect is much like bouncing on a trampoline. For the jumper, the object is to reach the highest heights (this supposedly replicates ancient efforts to spot game in the distance) and inevitably there are a number of sprains and fractures, though no-one to our knowledge has ever lost an eye.

🛏 Sleeping

Camping is ill advised around Barrow due to extreme weather and the potential for up-close encounters with curious, carnivorous polar bears. Given Barrow's compact size, it's possible to catch a morning flight in and a late evening flight out and still see just about everything you're likely to see.

Book well in advance if you do spend the night, and note that there's a 5% bed tax.

King Eider Inn INN $$
(☑852-4700; www.kingeider.net; 1752 Ahkovak St; s/d $185/194; ☺📶) With a snug log-cabin feel, wood-post beds and an inviting fireplace in the lobby, the Eider is the top choice in town unless you really need the views from the Top of the World Hotel. The inn is almost directly across from the airport exit.

Barrow Airport Inn HOTEL $$
(☑852-2525; airportinn@barrow.com; 1815 Momegana St; r incl breakfast $125; 📶) A few minutes' walk from the airport, the 15 rooms are simply furnished but do the trick for a night's stay. Some have kitchenettes, but these are usually booked far in advance by research teams.

Top of the World Hotel HOTEL $$$
(☑852-3900; www.tundratoursinc.com; 1200 Agvik St; s/d from $215/235; 📶) Barrow's most expensive hotel has no more to offer than the others save room service and, in about half the rooms, ocean views. Most package-tour visitors stay here so book well in advance.

EXPLORE MORE OF THE BUSH

Here are a few more places in the Bush that might be worth checking out. Airlines that fly into these areas include **Bering Air** (www.beringair.com) and **Warbelows** (www.warbe lows.com), which does a mail run into some very remote villages.

» **Kotzebue** Situated 26 miles above the Arctic Circle, Kotzebue is one of Alaska's northernmost hubs and a base for some of the finest river-running in Arctic Alaska along the **Kobuk National Wild River** and **Noatak National Wild River**, the latter beginning in the Gates of the Arctic National Park & Preserve. For more information, contact the **Innaigvik Education & Information Center** (☑442-3890), maintained by the NPS. This is the best visitor resource in Kotzebue, with ample info on the region's 9 million acres of parklands and on Kotzebue in general.

» **Shishmaref** On the northern edge of the Seward Peninsula, this Iñupiat community will not be there for long. It's literally falling into the ocean thanks to melting permafrost, rising sea levels and global warming. Visit the town before it's gone. You can also kick off adventures into the Bering Land Bridge National Preserve from here.

» **St Lawrence Island** Way out there in the Bering Sea this island, inhabited primarily by Alaskan and Siberian Yupik, is a good place for watching birds and sea mammals. It's also renowned for its Native ivory carvers. There are hotels in both Gamble and Savoonga, and a new road system allows for easier access to birding areas. Contact **Wilderness Birding Adventures** (www.wildernessbirdingadventures.com) for more information.

» **Brevig Mission** Intrepid travelers won't even need to fly to get to this small Native village. You can arrange a skiff from Teller.

» **Kaktovik** This Iñupiat enclave on the northern shore of Barter Island, in the Beaufort Sea east of Barrow, lies within the boundaries of ANWR. There are visitor services such as hotels and recently guides have begun to offer polar bear tours. See http://arctic.fws.gov for a list of operators and www.kaktovik.com for more on the village.

✕ Eating

Barrow has a surprisingly diverse range of eateries, with pizza, Japanese, Chinese, Mexican and Korean all on offer. Barrow is a 'damp' town, however, so don't expect to be throwing back lagers with your chimichangas or kimchi.

Sam & Lee's Chinese Restaurant CHINESE $$
(cnr Nachik & Kiogak St; breakfast mains $12-15, lunch & dinner mains $18; ⊘6am-2am) Ostensibly a Chinese restaurant, this joint has good American-style breakfasts and all-you-can-eat lunch buffets on weekdays ($14). In addition to the food, the bright diner atmosphere and lively staff make this a popular local hangout.

Pepe's North of the Border MEXICAN $$
(1204 Agvik St; mains $10-16; ⊘breakfast, lunch & dinner) Attached to the Top of the World Hotel, this 'northernmost Mexican restaurant in the world' has achieved renown thanks to the tireless Barrow-boosting efforts of owner Fran Tate. The food is decent and eclectic, with tacos (for as low as $3), burritos, chimichangas and other Tex-Mex staples.

Brower's Café BURGERS $$
(3220 Brower Hill; burgers $10-15; ⊘11am-11pm Mon-Sat, noon-10pm Sun) Named after Charles Brower, an American whaler, this beachfront structure hails from the late 19th century. There are whaling antiques inside and a whale-jawbone arch out front, but this is merely a burger and sandwich joint, with some Korean and Chinese dishes rounding out the menu.

AC Store SUPERMARKET $$
(cnr Stuaqpak & Agvik Sts; ⊘7am-10pm Mon-Sat, 9am-9pm Sun) Over in Browerville across from the Iñupiat Heritage Center this supermarket has quick eats and groceries at diet-inducing prices. Many visitors come by just to take pictures of the $10-plus gallons of milk.

ℹ Information

You can pick up a map and information guide at the airport and most restaurants and hotels. The airport has strong and free wi-fi, as do hotels.

Iñupiat Heritage Center (Ahkovak St; ⊘8:30am-5pm Mon-Fri, 1-4pm Sat & Sun; @) The library here has free internet.

Post office (cnr Eben Hobson & Tahak Sts) To send your postcards from the top of the world.

Wells Fargo (cnr Agvik & Kiogak Sts) Has a 24-hour ATM.

ℹ Getting There & Around

While you can get to Barrow in the winter by ice road, it's best to fly. **Alaska Airlines** (www.alaskaair.com) flies daily from Fairbanks ($500 to $650 round-trip) and Anchorage ($600 to $750 round-trip). Travel time can take anywhere from 1½ to 10 hours depending on connections and delays.

The airport is an easy stroll from all three hotels, and most other points of interest can also be reached by walking. However, cabs are available for a flat fee of $5. Try **Arctic Cab** (✆852-2227) or **Barrow Taxi** (✆852-2222).

Understand
Alaska

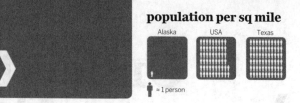

population per sq mile

Alaska   USA   Texas

≈ 1 person

Alaska Today

Environmental Issues

» Population: 676,987

» Land mass: 586,400 sq miles

» Number of Rhode Islands that could fit into Alaska: 425

In other states protests are staged to save a wetland or a woodlot or a park. In Alaska the battleground is an entire ecosystem. At almost 20 million acres, the Arctic National Wildlife Refuge (ANWR) is the size of South Carolina, encompassing 18 major rivers and the greatest variety of plant and animal life – including 36 species of land mammals – of any conservation area in the circumpolar north. The North Slope is also home to 36 trillion cubic ft of natural gas, making it one of the world's largest proven reserves.

Alaskans are acutely aware of the issues, both local and global, that they face. Few question global warming in Alaska: receding glaciers, grasshoppers appearing in the Mat-Su Valley, and Native villages slipping into the sea because of melting Arctic ice quickly end any debate about climate change in the Far North. Alaska is known for its abundance of wildlife, yet in 2008 the polar bear was listed as a threatened species by the US Department of the Interior. The number of Cook Inlet beluga whales has decreased so dramatically in recent years that they are being considered for listing under the *Endangered Species Act*, and the king salmon run was so weak up the Yukon River in 2008 that even residents with subsistence rights were restricted from filling their quotas.

Politics

Alaska was at a low point both financially and politically in 2006 when Sarah Palin, a self-described 'hockey mom' and the former mayor of Wasilla, ran for governor. At the time, three former state legislators had been arrested on public corruption charges, while in Washington, DC, longtime Senator Ted Stevens and Representative Don Young were under

Media

» **Anchorage Daily News** (www.adn.com) Alaska's largest newspaper

» **Alaska Magazine** Highlights outdoor and cultural wonders

» **Alaska Public Radio Network** (www.akradio.org) Has 18 community stations

Reality TV

» **The Deadliest Catch** (Discovery Network) Crab fishing in the Bering Sea

» **Sarah Palin's Alaska** (TLC) Palin observing nature

» **Alaska State Troopers** (Nat Geo Channel) Law enforcement in the Last Frontier

Films

» **Grizzly Man** Follows activist Timothy Treadwell's life (and death) among grizzlies

» **Alone in the Wilderness** Dick Proenneke documents himself building a cabin in the 1960s

» **Into the Wild** Adaptation of John Krakauer's book

USA in land area
(% of land area)

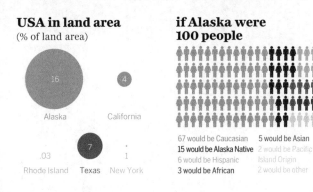

16 Alaska

4 California

.03 Rhode Island

7 Texas

1 New York

if Alaska were 100 people

67 would be Caucasian
15 would be Alaska Native
6 would be Hispanic
3 would be African

5 would be Asian
2 would be Pacific Island Origin
2 would be other

federal investigation for bribery. Palin stunned the political world when she crushed incumbent Governor Frank Murkowski in the Republican primary with almost two times the votes. She was then handed the keys to the governor's mansion in the general election. In 2008 she rocked the political world even more when presidential candidate John McCain named Palin as his running mate on the Republican ticket, vaulting her onto the national stage.

In her first year as governor, Palin worked with legislators to dramatically increase Alaska's share of royalties from oil production. When oil began its meteoric rise in price on the world markets, topping $140 a barrel in 2008, Alaska was carried along for the ride. Oil revenue pumped almost $7 billion into the state treasury that year, giving Alaska a $5 billion surplus.

But the rising price of oil was a double-edged sword for Alaska. The state has had a consistent unemployment rate near 7%, which until 2010 was one of the highest in the country (but is now one of the lowest), and the high cost of fuel is devastating to rural communities where everything must be shipped in, often by costly air freight.

In 2009 Sarah Palin resigned and was succeeded by Sean Parnell, who faces the monumental task of convincing a nation that Alaskans have a right to make a living from an economy based on removing natural resources from the country's great wilderness areas. Those opposed to drilling in the ANWR argue it will negatively affect the Porcupine herd of caribou, which use the refuge for their calving grounds. But advocates maintain that the area needed is too small to affect caribou and that the advantages outweigh the possible risks. With the skyrocketing price of gas at the pump, it might not be a hard argument to win.

» Percent of Alaska above the Arctic Circle: 30

» Highest point: Mt McKinley (20,320ft)

» Days without the sun in Barrow: 84

Books

» **Ordinary Wolves** (Seth Kantner) A tale about a boy growing up white in Bush Alaska, and his struggles to be accepted into the Native culture.

» **Two Old Women** (Velma Wallis) In this novel written by an Athabascan, two women are abandoned by their migrating tribe during a harsh winter.

» **The Way Winter Comes** (Sherry Simpson) A series of wonderful stories that chronicles life in Fairbanks from one of the best writers in the state.

Dos & Don'ts

Don't overdress Alaska is extremely casual.
Do dress warm Layers are your best bet.
Do let someone know When you head into the backcountry.
Do have a spare tire Roads can be rough.

Economy

Since the early 1980s, Alaska's economy has been fueled by oil. Nearly 90% of the state's general fund revenue comes from taxes on oil and gas production. Thanks to oil, residents do not pay state taxes on income, sales or inheritance.

But the problem with such a narrow economy based on mineral extraction is that the minerals run out. Prudhoe Bay, the largest oil field in North America, is producing less than 50% of its peak output of the mid-1980s. Approximately two-thirds of Alaskans are in favor of drilling in the ANWR and the state is pushing hard to get a gas pipeline built from the North Slope oilfields to markets in the Lower 48. Many mining projects are also in the works.

The proposed Pebble Mine in the Alaska Peninsula has upset many who are concerned about wild salmon runs and other environmental issues, but it rates as one of the top metal reserves in the world, with staggering amounts of gold, copper and molybdenum waiting to be extracted. Hard-rock mining for gold is also accelerating on the Seward Peninsula, near Nome, while in the Southeast new mines or the expansion of existing ones have been proposed from Prince of Wales Island to Juneau.

Commercial fishing, rebuilt on the bottom fishery of pollock and the marketing of wild salmon, is a renewable resource that has rebounded recently. But the industry's contribution of $100 million into the state treasury is a distant second to the oil and gas industry's almost $7 billion in 2008.

Myths

Everyone lives in igloos
Though many go without modern plumbing, no one in Alaska lives in an igloo.

Everyone drives sled dogs to work In Bush Alaska, driving a snow machine is far more common than a dog team.

There's snow year-round
Even up in Barrow the snow disappears for the summer; it sticks around on the higher mountains, though.

There are penguins in Alaska
Penguins are found only in the southern hemisphere.

Fishing Facts

52% Alaska's proportion of the USA's total catch.

90% Proportion of the country's wild salmon harvest caught in Alaska.

78,500 The number of Alaskan jobs generated by commercial fishing.

History

Alaska turned 50 in 2009, half a century after President Dwight Eisenhower officially welcomed it into the Union. It's been a long, strange road, from being labeled a frozen wasteland to the discovery of the country's largest oil reservoir; and from the persecution of Alaska Natives to the creation of Native corporations and the granting of land, money and subsistence rights that are now the envy of other indigenous peoples around the world.

Early Alaskans

It is believed that the first Alaskans migrated from Asia to North America between 15,000 and 30,000 years ago, during an ice age that lowered the sea level and created a 900-mile land bridge linking Siberia and Alaska. The nomadic groups who crossed the bridge were not bent on exploration but on following the animal herds that provided them with food and clothing.

The first major migration, which came across the land bridge from Asia, was by the Tlingits and the Haidas, who settled throughout the Southeast and British Columbia, and the Athabascans, a nomadic tribe that settled in the Interior. The other two major groups were the Iñupiat, who settled the north coast of Alaska and Canada (where they are known as Inuit), and the Yupik, who settled Southwest Alaska. The smallest group of Alaska Natives to arrive was the Aleuts of the Aleutian Islands. The Iñupiat, Yupik and Aleuts are believed to have migrated 3000 years ago and were well established by the time the Europeans arrived.

The Tlingit and Haida cultures were advanced; the tribes had permanent settlements, including large clan dwellings that housed related families. These tribes were noted for their excellent wood carving, especially carved poles, called totems, which can still be seen in Ketchikan, Sitka and many other places in the Southeast. The Tlingits were spread

TIMELINE	28,000–13,000 BC	AD 1741	1784
	The first Alaskans arrive, migrating across a 900-mile land bridge from Asia to North America and eventually settling throughout the state in tribal groups with distinct cultures.	Danish explorer Vitus Bering, employed by Peter the Great of Russia, makes his third trip to North America and becomes the first European to set foot on Alaska.	Russian Grigorii Shelikhov establishes the first permanent European settlement at Kodiak Island. Eight years later he is granted a monopoly on furs as head of the Russian-American Company.

THALATTOSAUR

across the Southeast in large numbers and occasionally went as far south as Seattle in their huge dugout canoes. Both groups had few problems gathering food, as fish and game were plentiful in the Southeast.

Life was not so easy for the Aleuts, Iñupiat and Yupik. With much colder winters and cooler summers, these people had to develop a highly effective sea-hunting culture to sustain life in the harsh regions of Alaska. This was especially true for the Iñupiat, who could not have survived the winters without their skilled ice-hunting techniques. In spring, armed only with jade-tipped harpoons, the Iñupiat, in skin-covered kayaks called *bidarkas* and *umiaks,* stalked and killed 60-ton bowhead whales. Though motorized boats replaced the kayaks and modern harpoons the jade-tipped spears, the whaling tradition lives on in places such as Barrow.

Fur Traders & Whalers Arrive

The indigenous people, despite their harsh environment, were numerous until non-Natives, particularly fur traders and whalers, brought guns, alcohol and disease that damaged the Alaska Natives' delicate relationship with nature and wiped out whole communities. At one time an estimated 20,000 Aleuts lived throughout the Aleutian Islands. In only 50 years the Russians reduced the Aleut population to less than 2000 through massacres and forced labor. The whalers who arrived at Iñupiat villages in the mid-19th century were similarly destructive, introducing alcohol, which devastated the lifestyles of entire villages. When the 50th anniversary of the Alaska Hwy was celebrated in 1992, many Alaska Natives and Canadians called the event a 'commemoration' not a 'celebration,' due to the destructive forces that the link to Canada and the rest of the USA brought, including disease, alcohol and a cash economy.

Age of Exploration

Due to the cold and stormy North Pacific, Alaska was one of the last places in the world to be mapped by Europeans.

Spanish Admiral Bartholomé de Fonte is credited by many with making the first European trip into Alaskan waters in 1640, but the first written record of the area was made by Vitus Bering, a Danish navigator sailing for the Russian tsar. In 1728 Bering's explorations demonstrated that America and Asia were two separate continents. Thirteen years later, Bering became the first European to set foot in Alaska, near Cordova. Bering and many of his crew died from scurvy during that journey, but his lieutenant returned to Europe with fur pelts and tales of fabulous seal and otter colonies, and Alaska's first boom was under way. The Aleutian Islands were quickly overtaken, with settlements at Unalaska and Kodiak Island. Chaos followed, as bands of Russian hunters robbed and

The complete skeleton of a thalattosaur, a marine reptile that lived 200 million years ago, was found in Southeast Alaska, near Kake, in 2011.

1804	1867	1878	1880
With four warships, Aleksandr Baranov defeats the Tlingit at Sitka and then establishes New Archangel as the new capital of the Russian-American Company.	Secretary of State William H Seward negotiates the US purchase of Alaska from Russia for $7.2 million. It takes six months for Congress to approve the treaty.	Ten years after a salmon saltery is opened in Klawock on Prince of Wales Island, a San Francisco company builds the first salmon cannery in Alaska.	Led by Tlingit Chief Kowee, Richard Harris and Joe Juneau discover gold in Silver Bow Basin. The next year miners change their tent city's name from Harrisburg to Juneau.

murdered each other for furs, while the Aleuts, living near the hunting grounds, were almost annihilated through massacres and forced labor. By the 1790s Russia had organized the Russian-American Company to regulate the fur trade and ease the violent competition.

The British arrived when Captain James Cook began searching the area for the Northwest Passage. Cook sailed north from Vancouver Island to Southcentral Alaska in 1778, anchoring at what is now Cook Inlet before continuing on to the Aleutian Islands, Bering Sea and Arctic Ocean. The French sent Jean-François de Galaup, comte de La Pérouse, who in 1786 made it as far as Lituya Bay, now part of Glacier Bay National Park. The wicked tides within the long, narrow bay caught the exploration party off guard, killing 21 sailors and discouraging the French from colonizing the area.

Having depleted the fur colonies in the Aleutians, Aleksandr Baranov, who headed the Russian-American Company, moved his territorial capital from Kodiak to Sitka, where he built a stunning city, dubbed 'an American Paris in Alaska.'

Seward's Folly

By the 1860s the Russians found themselves badly overextended: their involvement in Napoleon's European wars, a declining fur industry and the long lines of shipping between Sitka and the heartland of Russia were draining their national treasury. The country made several overtures to the USA to purchase Alaska, but it wasn't until 1867 that Secretary of State William H Seward signed a treaty to purchase the state for $7.2 million – less than 2¢ an acre.

By then the US public was in an uproar over the purchase of 'Seward's Ice Box' or 'Walrussia,' and on the Senate floor, the battle to ratify the treaty lasted six months. On October 18, 1867, the formal transfer of Alaska to the Americans took place in Sitka. Alaska remained a lawless, unorganized territory for the next 20 years.

This great land, remote and inaccessible to all but a few hardy settlers, stayed a dark, frozen mystery to most people, but eventually its riches were uncovered. First it was through whaling, then the phenomenal salmon runs, with the first canneries built in 1878 on Prince of Wales Island.

The Alaskan Gold Rush

What truly brought Alaska to the world's attention was gold. The promise of quick riches and frontier adventures was the most effective lure Alaska has ever had and, to some degree, still has today. Gold was discovered in the Gastineau Channel in the 1880s, and the towns of Juneau and Douglas sprang up overnight. In 1896, one of the world's most colorful

The last shot of the Civil War was fired in the Bering Sea by the CSS *Shenandoah* on June 22, 1865, 74 days after Appomattox.

View the canceled check and receipt for the 1867 purchase of Alaska from Russia at www.archives. gov/education/ lessons/alaska/ cancelled-check. html.

1882	1898	1913	1915
A US Navy cutter shells Angoon in retaliation for an uprising and then sends a landing party to loot and burn what remained of the Native village.	Klondike Gold Rush turns Skagway into Alaska's largest city, with a population of 10,000. Canadian Mounties describe the lawless town as 'little better than a hell on earth.'	Walter Harper, an Alaska Native, becomes the first person to summit Mt McKinley. He is joined by Harry Karstens, who later becomes the first superintendent of Denali National Park.	Anchorage is founded when Ship Creek is chosen as a survey camp to build the Alaska Railroad and by the end of a year is a tent city of 2000.

gold rushes took place in the Klondike region of Canada's Yukon Territory, just across the border.

Often called 'the last grand adventure,' the Klondike Gold Rush occurred when the country and much of the world was suffering a severe recession. When the banner headline of the *Seattle Post-Intelligencer* bellowed 'GOLD! GOLD! GOLD! GOLD!' on July 17, 1897, thousands of people quit their jobs and sold their homes to finance a trip to the newly created boomtown of Skagway. From this tent city almost 30,000 prospectors tackled the steep Chilkoot Trail to Lake Bennett, where they built crude rafts to float the rest of the way to the goldfields. Nearly as many people returned home along the same route, broke and disillusioned.

The number of miners who made fortunes was small, but the tales and legends that emerged were endless. The Klondike stampede, though it only lasted from 1896 to the early 1900s, was Alaska's most colorful era and earned the state the reputation of being the country's last frontier.

Within three years of the Klondike stampede Alaska's population doubled to 63,592, including more than 30,000 non-Native people. Nome, another gold boomtown, was the largest city in the territory, with 12,000 residents, while gold prompted the capital to be moved from Sitka to Juneau.

> To enter Canada on the Chilkoot Trail, miners were required to carry a year's supply of food, including 400lb of flour and 200lb of bacon.

CHILKOOT TRAIL

World War II

In June 1942, only six months after their attack on Pearl Harbor, the Japanese opened their Aleutian Islands campaign by bombing Dutch Harbor for two days and then taking Attu and Kiska Islands. Other than Guam, it was the only foreign invasion of US soil during WWII and is often dubbed 'the Forgotten War' because most Americans are unaware of what happened in Alaska. The battle to retake Attu Island was a bloody one. After 19 days and landing more than 15,000 troops, US forces recaptured the plot of barren land, but only after suffering 3929 casualties, including 549 deaths. Of the more than 2300 Japanese on Attu, fewer than 30 surrendered, with many taking their own lives.

What had quickly become apparent to both sides was the role the capricious Aleutian weather played in the campaign. Soldiers shot their own troops in the fog; unable to penetrate fog and clouds, ships were thrown against rocks and sunk in heavy seas; and pilots met the sides of mountains in low overcast skies. Bad weather literally saved Kodiak, keeping Japanese pilots at bay the night they planned to bomb it.

The Alcan & Statehood

Following the Japanese attack on the Aleutian Islands in 1942, Congress panicked and rushed to protect the rest of Alaska. Large army and air force bases were set up at Anchorage, Fairbanks, Sitka and Whittier, and

1923
President Warren G Harding comes to Alaska to celebrate the completion of the Alaska Railroad. The first president to visit Alaska dies within two weeks of his trip.

1935
The first of 200 Depression-era families from Minnesota, Wisconsin and Michigan arrive in the Matanuska Valley to begin farming as part of the New Deal experiment and Palmer is established.

ERNEST MANEWAL / LONELY PLANET IMAGES ©

» Matanuska Glacier (p313)

thousands of military personnel were stationed in Alaska. But it was the famous Alcan (also known as the Alaska Hwy) that was the single most important project of the military expansion. The road was built by the military, but Alaska's residents benefited, as the Alcan helped them access and make use of Alaska's natural resources.

In 1916 Alaska's territorial legislature submitted its first statehood bill. The effort was first quashed by the Seattle-based canned-salmon industry, which wanted to prevent local control of Alaska's resources; then the stock market crash of 1929 and WWII kept Congress occupied with more-demanding issues. But the growth that came with the Alcan, and to a lesser degree the new military bases, pushed Alaska firmly into the American culture and renewed its drive for statehood. When the US Senate passed the Alaska statehood bill on June 30, 1958, Alaska had made it into the Union and was officially proclaimed the country's 49th state by President Dwight Eisenhower the following January.

Alaska entered the 1960s full of promise, but then disaster struck: the most powerful earthquake ever recorded in North America (registering 9.2 on the Richter scale) hit Southcentral Alaska on Good Friday morning in 1964. More than 100 lives were lost, and damage was estimated at $500 million. In Anchorage, office buildings sank 10ft into the ground, and houses slid more than 1200ft off a bluff into Knik Arm. A tidal wave

BUILDING THE ALCAN

A land link between Alaska and the rest of the USA was envisioned as early as 1930, but it took WWII to turn the nation's attention north to embark on one of the greatest engineering feats of the 20th century: constructing a 1390-mile road through remote wilderness.

Deemed a military necessity and authorized by President Franklin Roosevelt only two months after the attack on Pearl Harbor, the Alcan was designed to be an overland route far enough inland to be out of range of airplanes transported on Japanese aircraft carriers. The exact route followed old winter roads, trap lines and pack trails, and by March 9, 1942, construction had begun. Within three months, more than 10,000 troops, most of them from the US Army Corps of Engineers, were in the Canadian wilderness. The soldiers felled trees, put down gravel, struggled with permafrost and built pontoon bridges, all at a breakneck pace. They endured temperatures of -30°F in April, snowfalls in June and swarms of mosquitoes and gnats for most of the summer. They worked 16-hour days, spent nights in pup tents and went weeks without hearing from commanders in base camps, much less from their families.

Given the harsh conditions, the speed with which the Alcan was built is astounding. When a final link was completed near Kluane Lake in late October, the Alcan was open, having been built in only eight months and 12 days.

1942	1959	1964	1968
Japan bombs Dutch Harbor for two days during WWII and then invades the remote Aleutian Islands of Attu and Kiska. Americans build the Alcan (Alaska Hwy).	Alaska officially becomes the 49th state when President Dwight Eisenhower signs the statehood declaration on January 3. William A Egan is sworn in as the first governor.	North America's worst earthquake, 9.2 on the Richter scale, takes place on Good Friday, devastating Anchorage and Southcentral Alaska, with 131 people losing their lives.	Oil and natural gas are discovered at Prudhoe Bay on the North Slope. The next year the state of Alaska stages a $900 million North Slope oil-lease sale.

virtually obliterated the community of Valdez. In Kodiak and Seward, 32ft of the coastline slipped into the Gulf of Alaska, and Cordova lost its entire harbor as the sea rose 16ft.

From Pump Station No 1 to Valdez, the Trans-Alaska Pipeline crosses three mountain ranges, 34 major rivers and 500 streams.

The Alaskan Black-Gold Rush

The devastating 1964 earthquake left the newborn state in a shambles, but a more pleasant gift from nature soon rushed Alaska to recovery and beyond. In 1968 Atlantic Richfield discovered massive oil deposits underneath Prudhoe Bay in the Arctic Ocean. The value of the oil doubled after the Arab oil embargo of 1973. However, it couldn't be tapped until there was a pipeline to transport it to the warm-water port of Valdez. And the pipeline couldn't be built until the US Congress, which still administered most of the land, settled the intense controversy among industry, environmentalists and Alaska Natives over historical claims to the land.

The *Alaska Native Claims Settlement Act* of 1971 was an unprecedented piece of legislation that opened the way for a consortium of oil com-

UNCLE TED

Ted Stevens was already a decorated WWII pilot and Harvard Law School graduate when in 1953, after accepting a position in Fairbanks, he moved to Alaska with his wife by driving the Alaska Hwy in the dead of winter. A mere six months later, Stevens was appointed the US Attorney for Fairbanks and was eventually elected as a state representative. In 1968 Stevens was appointed US senator for Alaska and held that position until 2009, never receiving less than 66% of the vote after his first election in 1970.

Such longevity allowed Stevens to break Strom Thurmond's record as the longest-serving Republican senator in 2007, with 38 years and three months of continual service. For the majority of Alaskans, Stevens had always been their senator – the reason many dubbed him 'senator for life.'

The senator was duly noted for his ability to bring home the 'pork': in 2008 the Feds returned $295 per Alaskan citizen in local projects (other states average only $34 per person). In 2005 Stevens was ridiculed by the national media when, in a speech from the Senate floor, he angrily opposed diverting the Bridge to Nowhere funds to help New Orleans recover from Hurricane Katrina. Congress dropped the specific allocation for the bridge, but Alaska still received the money and simply spent it elsewhere.

Stevens' legendary Senate tenure came to an end in 2009. The previous year, a jury found him guilty of federal corruption – failing to report tens of thousands of dollars in gifts and services he had received from friends – and convicted him of seven felony charges. Stevens vowed to appeal the decision, but in November Alaskans had had enough and narrowly voted him out of office in his bid for an eighth term.

In 2010 Stevens was killed in a not-unusual Alaskan accident: a small-plane crash outside of Dillingham, in Southwest Alaska.

1971	1973	1980	1985
President Richard Nixon signs the *Alaska Native Claims Settlement Act* to pave the way for the Trans-Alaska Pipeline. Alaska Natives give up claims in return for nearly $1 billion and 44 million acres.	The first Iditarod Trail Sled Dog Race is held on an old dog-team mail route blazed in 1910. The winner covers the 1150-mile race between Wasilla and Nome in 20 days.	President Jimmy Carter signs the *Alaska National Interests Lands Conservation Act* (ANILCA), preserving 79.54 million acres of wilderness and creating or enlarging 15 national parks.	Libby Riddles of Teller gambles by departing in a blizzard when no other musher would and becomes the first woman to win the Iditarod Trail Sled Dog Race.

panies to undertake the construction of the 789-mile pipeline. The Trans-Alaska Pipeline took three years to build, cost more than $8 billion – in 1977 dollars – and, at the time, was the most expensive private construction project ever undertaken. At the peak of construction, the pipeline employed 28,000 people, doing '7-12s' (seven 12-hour shifts a week).

The oil began to flow on June 20, 1977, and for a decade oil gave Alaska an economic base that was the envy of every other state, accounting for as much as 80% of state government revenue. In the explosive growth period of the mid-1980s, Alaskans enjoyed the highest per-capita income in the country. The state's budget was in the billions. Legislators in Juneau transformed Anchorage into a stunning city, with sports arenas, libraries and performing-arts centers, and provided virtually every bush town with a million-dollar school. From 1980 to 1986 this state of only half a million residents generated revenue of $26 billion.

Disaster at Valdez

For most Alaskans, the abundant oil made it hard to see beyond the gleam of the oil dollar. Reality hit hard in 1989, when the *Exxon Valdez*, a 987ft Exxon oil supertanker, rammed Bligh Reef a few hours out of the port of Valdez. The ship spilled almost 11 million gallons of North Slope crude into the bountiful waters of Prince William Sound. Alaskans and the rest of the country watched in horror as the oil spill quickly became too large for booms to contain, spreading 600 miles from the grounding site. State residents were shocked as oil began to appear from the glacier-carved cliffs of Kenai Fjords to the bird rookeries of Katmai National Park. The spill eventually contaminated 1567 miles of shoreline and killed an estimated 645,000 birds and 5000 sea otters.

Today the oil, like other resources exploited in the past, is simply running out. That pot of gold called Prudhoe Bay began its decline in 1988 and now produces less than half of its 1987 peak of two million barrels a day. The end of the Cold War and the subsequent downsizing of the US military in the early 1990s was more bad economic news for Alaska. Alaskan state revenues, once the envy of every other state governor in the country, went tumbling along with the declining oil royalties. With more than 80% of its state budget derived from oil revenue, Alaska was awash in red ink from the early 1990s until 2004, managing a balanced budget only twice.

Out of the Channel: the Exxon Valdez Oil Spill in Prince William Sound (1999), by John Keeble, is an in-depth account of Exxon's response and cover-up, which the author contends did more damage than the original spill.

1989	1994	2006	2009
The *Exxon Valdez* runs aground on Bligh Reef and spills 11 million gallons of oil into Prince William Sound, the US's biggest man-made environmental disaster until the 2010 *Deepwater Horizon* oil spill.	Alaskan Tommy Moe becomes the first American male skier to win two medals in a single Winter Olympics, capturing the gold for downhill and silver for Super G at Lillehammer, Norway.	Sarah Palin, former mayor of Wasilla, stuns the political world by beating the incumbent governor to become Alaska's first female governor, and at 42, also its youngest.	On January 3 Alaskans celebrated the 50th anniversary of their state officially being admitted to the Union, the first new state to be included since Arizona was admitted in 1912.

The Alaskan Way of Life

The state is young: Alaska just turned 50 and its residents are new, the majority having moved here from somewhere else. Yet thanks to its isolation, its spectacular scenery and, yes, its long, dark winters, Alaska has a culture that is vibrant and rich, and a northern lifestyle that is thoroughly unique.

Regional Identity

Most of Alaska may be rural, road-less areas collectively known as the Bush, but most Alaskans are urban. Almost 60% of the residents live in the three largest cities: Anchorage, Fairbanks and Juneau.

The vast majority of households in rural Alaska participate in subsistence living. Studies show that 86% use game and 95% use fish. There are also Alaskans who gather and hunt the majority of their food and live in small villages that can only be reached by boat, plane or, in the winter, snowmobile. But the majority live in urban neighborhoods, work a nine-to-five job and shop at the supermarket.

And most Alaskans are newcomers. Only 30% of the state's population was born in Alaska; the rest moved there – including all but one of its eight elected governors. Such a transient population creates a melting pot of ideas, philosophies and priorities. What they usually have in common is an interest in the great outdoors: they were lured here to either exploit it or enjoy it, and many residents do a little of both.

Thus debates in Alaska usually center on access to land, resources, and, in particular, the wilderness. There are some liberal bastions of environmentalism, Juneau and Homer being the best known, but over the years Alaskans have moved to the right, voting for Republican presidents, fighting tax increases and becoming one of the first states to pass a constitutional amendment banning same-sex marriages.

Travelers come to visit and marvel at the grand scenery. But Alaskans are here to stay, so they need to make a living in their chosen home, a land where there is little industry or farming. They regard trees, oil and fish as an opportunity to do that.

Lifestyle

In Anchorage, residents can shop at enclosed malls, spend an afternoon at one of 162 parks, go in-line skating along 122 miles of paved bike paths, or get in their car and drive to another town. By contrast, in Nunapitchuk, 400 miles west of Anchorage on the swampy tundra of the Yukon–Kuskokwim Delta, the population is 545; there are no roads to or within Nunapitchuk; homes and buildings are connected by a network of boardwalks; there is one store in town, and a health clinic.

Rural or urban, Alaskans tend to be individualistic, following few outside trends and, instead, adhering to what their harsh environment

According to a marketing research firm, Anchorage has three coffee shops per 10,000 residents, beating out even Seattle, and making it, per capita, the country's mocha mecca.

COFFEE

dictates. Mother Nature and those -30°F winter days are responsible for the Alaskan dress code, even in Anchorage's finest restaurants.

American visitors may find that most of the locals they meet in towns and cities have lifestyles similar to their own. They work, they love their weekends, they live in a variety of homes big and small, and they participate in double coupon days at supermarkets. Even in remote villages there are satellite TV dishes and internet access to the rest of the world.

But Alaska also has social ills, exacerbated on in a large measure by the environment. The isolation of small towns and the darkness of winter have contributed to Alaska being one of the top 10 states for binge and heavy drinking, and sixth overall for the amount of alcohol sold per capita. Since the 1980s, Alaska has seen some of the highest per capita use of controlled drugs in the country, and its suicide rate is twice the national average. Among Alaska Natives, it's considered an epidemic.

To survive this climate and to avoid such demons, you have to possess a passion for the land and an individualistic approach to a lifestyle that few, other than Alaskans, would choose.

Sports

The state sport of Alaska, officially adopted in 1972, is dog mushing, and the biggest spectator event is the Iditarod. But there are other spectator sports in Alaska that you don't have to bundle up to watch, including baseball. The **Alaska Baseball League** (www.alaskabaseballleague.org) features six semipro teams of good college players eyeing the major leagues. Teams include Fairbanks' **Alaska Goldpanners** (www.goldpanners.com) and the **Anchorage Bucs** (www.anchoragebucs.com), and major leaguers who have played in Alaska include sluggers Barry Bonds and Mark McGwire.

The state's most unusual sporting event is the **World Eskimo-Indian Olympics** (www.weio.org) in July, when several hundred athletes converge on Fairbanks. For four days Alaska Natives compete in greased pole walking, seal skinning, blanket toss and other events that display the skills traditionally needed for survival in a harsh environment.

THE IDITAROD

In 1948 Joe Redington Sr arrived in Alaska with just $18 in his pocket, and used $13 of it to cover a filing fee for a 101-acre homestead in Knik. By accident – some say fate – Redington's homestead was located only a few hundred feet from the historic Iditarod Trail, an old dogsled mail route from Seward to Nome. Redington was fascinated by the Iditarod Trail and the famous 'serum run' that saved the town of Nome from diphtheria in 1925, when mushers used the trail to relay medical supplies across Alaska.

Worried that snowmobiles might replace sled dogs, Redington proposed an Anchorage–Nome race along the historic trail, and then staged the first 1100-mile Iditarod in 1973. Alaska's 'Last Great Race,' the world's longest sled-dog event, was born.

The Iditarod is held in early March, when the temperatures are in the low teens and snow coverage is good. Most visitors catch the race at the start – 4th Ave and E St in Anchorage – but that is strictly ceremonial. The mushers run their teams for a few miles and then truck them up to Wasilla or Willow for a restart of the event, which sees them cross two mountain ranges, follow a frozen Yukon River for 150 miles, and pass through many native villages before arriving to cheering crowds in Nome. In 2011, veteran racer John Baker set a new record, finishing in 8 days, 18 hours, 46 minutes and 39 seconds.

The race has drawn criticism from some animal rights groups, who have protested nationally against the event, arguing that such distances are cruel. Supporters, however, contend that these sled dogs are the canine equivalents of magnificent, well-trained athletes.

If a midwinter trip to Alaska is out of range, you can still follow the famous race. Some mushers are equipped with special tracking devices on their sleds so fans can watch their progress in real time by logging on to www.iditarod.com and clicking 'Iditarod Tracker.'

IDITAROD

Women won the 1150-mile Iditarod Trail Sled Dog Race five out of six years from 1985 to 1990, and finished second the one year they didn't win it.

The War Journal of Lila Ann Smith (2007), by Irving Warner, is a moving historical novel, based on the invasion of Attu by the Japanese in WWII, and the Aleuts who became prisoners of war.

Alaska in the Popular Imagination

Alaska has a role in the collective imagination as a mysterious, often frozen, dramatically scenic land. Not surprisingly, the state's portrayal in popular media often reflects this idea.

Literature

Two of the best-known writers identified with Alaska were not native to the land nor did they spend much time there, but Jack London and Robert Service turned their Alaskan adventures into literary careers.

The first print run of Jack London's *Call of the Wild* – 10,000 books – sold out in 24 hours. London, an American, departed for the Klondike Gold Rush in 1897, hoping to get rich panning gold. Instead he produced 50 books of fiction and nonfiction in just 17 years, and became the country's highest-paid writer of the day.

Service, a Canadian bank teller, was transferred to Dawson City in 1902 and then wrote his first book of verse, *The Spell of the Yukon*. The work was an immediate success and contained his best-known ballads, 'The Shooting of Dan McGrew' and 'The Cremation of Sam McGee.' Both portray the hardship and violence of life during the gold rush.

Alaska's contemporary luminaries of literature are no less elegant in capturing the spirit of the Far North. Kotzebue author Seth Kantner followed his critically acclaimed first novel, *Ordinary Wolves*, with the equally intriguing *Shopping for Porcupine*, a series of short stories about growing up in the Alaska wilderness. One of the best Alaska Native novels is *Two Old Women* by Velma Wallis, an Athabascan born in Fort Yukon. This moving tale covers the saga of two elderly women abandoned by their migrating tribe during a harsh winter.

Other Alaskans who have captured the soul of the Far North include Nick Jans, whose *The Last Light Breaking* is considered a classic on life among the Iñupiat, and Sherry Simpson, who chronicles living in Fairbanks in the series of wonderful stories, *The Way Winter Comes*. For entertaining fiction using Alaska's commercial fishing as a stage, there's Bill McCloskey, whose three novels have characters ranging from the greenhorn fisherman to the hard-nosed cannery manager, with the plotline leaping from one to the next. His first, *Highliners*, is still his best.

Small cabins and long winter nights filled with sinister thoughts have also given rise to Alaska's share of mystery writers. Dean of the Alaskan whodunit is *New York Times* best seller Dana Stanebow, whose ex-DA investigator Kate Shugak has appeared in 15 novels, the latest being *A Deeper Sleep*. Sue Henry is equally prolific with musher-turned-crime-solver Jessie Arnold in novels such as *Murder on the Iditarod Trail* and *Cold Company*.

Cinema & TV

Hollywood and Alaska occasionally mix, especially in Hyder. This tiny, isolated town (pop 83) has been the setting for five films, most recently *Insomnia* (2002), in which Al Pacino plays a cop sent to a small Alaskan town to investigate a killer played by Robin Williams. There's also *Bear Island* (1978), loaded with stars, and *Ice Man* (1984), about scientists who find a frozen prehistoric man and bring him back to life. Alaska has also been the backdrop for TV, including the Emmy Award–winning series *Northern Exposure*, but reality TV is where it's hit the mother lode. Tough men in tough jobs star in *Tougher in Alaska*, while ordinary people must live off the land in *The Alaska Experiment*. Most popular of all is *The Deadliest Catch,* about the dangerous king crab fishery in the Bering Sea.

Recent Hollywood tax breaks have led to more films being shot in the 49th state: in 2010 Drew Barrymore and John Krasinski were on location filming *Everybody Loves Whales*, and more films are being lined up.

Native Alaska

Arts & Crafts »
Culture & Community »

Tlingit art

Arts & Crafts

Alaska Natives produce much of the state's most creative work. Not content to rest on tradition, contemporary indigenous artists push boundaries and reinterpret old forms.

Traditionally, Native artisans gathered their materials in the fall and began work in December, when cold weather forced them to remain inside. Materials varied according to what the local environment or trade routes could supply, and included wood, ivory, bone, antler, birch bark and grasses.

Production of Native crafts for a Western market began in the 18th century with Iñupiat ivory carvers and, later, Aleut basket weavers, adapting traditional forms for collectors. Today, the sale of Native art comprises a large slice of the economy in many Bush communities.

Carving

Ivory carving is practically synonymous with the Iñupiat, though they will also use wood, bone and antler. In addition to sculptures depicting hunting scenes or wild animals, scrimshaw (known as 'engraved ivory') is also produced. These incredibly detailed etchings often present a vignette of daily life on a whale bone or walrus tusk.

Yupik carvings tend to have more intricate surface detailing, and feature

LEE FOSTER / LONELY PLANET IMAGES ©

RICHARD CUMMINS/ LONELY PLANET IMAGES ©

TOP PLACES TO SEE NATIVE ART

» University of Alaska Museum of the North (p287)

» Alaska Native Medical Center (p156)

» Iñupiat Heritage Center (p367)

» Totem Heritage Center (p76) & Sitka National Historical Park (p106)

» Alaska Native Heritage Center (p175)

» Ilanka Cultural Center (p203)

» Alutiiq Museum & Archaeological Repository (p327)

Clockwise from top left
1. Traditional caribou masks in Gates of the Arctic National Park (p364) **2.** Stained-glass detail in Ketchikan (p74) **3.** Traditional carving, Alaska State Museum (p115)

stylized designs. Red clay paint is sometimes used for coloring.

Natives of the Southeast, such as the Haida and Tlingit, have a lively woodcarving tradition that's heavy on abstractions based on clan symbols. Their totem poles are known worldwide but they are also masters at wood masks and bentwood boxes.

Dolls

All Native groups share a love of dolls, and traditionally used them in ceremonies, as fertility symbols, for play, and for teaching young girls about motherhood. Modern doll-making is said to have begun in the 1940s in Kotzebue with the work of Ethel Washington, and continues today as one of the most vibrant Native art forms. Dolls can look realistic or be deliberate caricatures, such as the Chevak area 'ugly-faced' dolls with their wrinkled leather faces and humorous expressions.

Baskets

Perhaps no single form represents indigenous art better than basketry. Decorative patterns are geometric or reflect the region's animals, insects or plants. Athabascans weave baskets from alder, willow roots and birch bark; the Tlingit use cedar bark and spruce root; Yupik often decorate their baskets with sea lion whiskers and feathers and a few dye them with seal guts. Iñupiat are famous for using whale baleen, but this is in fact a 20th-century invention.

The Aleuts are perhaps the most renowned basket weavers. Using rye grass, which is tough but pliable, artists create tiny, intricately woven pieces that are highly valued.

Embroidery & Clothing

Athabascan women traditionally decorated clothing with dyed quills, but after Europeans introduced beads and embroidery techniques they quickly became masters of this decorative art. Their long, hanging baby belts are often purchased as wall hangings.

Both Haida and Yupik are renowned for *mukluks* (knee-high boots) and decorative parkas.

Culture & Community

For Alaska Natives, maintaining their culture in the face of Western influence is a great challenge.

People

About 110,000 indigenous people live in Alaska. Before 1940 they were the majority but now represent less than 15% of the population. Tribes once inhabited separate regions: the Aleuts and Alutiiqs lived from Prince William Sound to the Aleutian Islands; the Iñupiat, Yupik and Cupik occupied Alaska's northern and western coasts; the Athabascan populated the Interior; and the Tlingit, Haida, Eyak and Tsimshian lived along the southeast coasts. Urban migration has blurred lines. With 23,000 Alaska Natives, the capital is sometimes called the state's 'largest Native village'.

Village Life

Two thirds of Alaska Natives live in villages within their ancestral lands. Though outwardly modern, the heart of village life is still the practice of subsistence hunting, fishing and gathering. Though critical to rural economies, the customs and traditions associated with subsistence are also the basis of Native culture. Subsistence activities are cooperative, helping maintain community bonds, preserve traditional festivities and oral histories, facilitate a spiritual connection to the land, and provide inspiration and material for artists.

Language

Native language use varies: the last Eyak speaker died in 2008, Haida has only a handful of speakers remaining, but Yupik is still spoken by half the population. Even so, almost no children are currently learning any Native language as their mother tongue. Many factors are blamed, including satellite TV and the 'No Child Left Behind' federal education program that requires students

to demonstrate proficiency in English but not Native languages. The issue is of critical importance to Native leaders and fixes include the development of language learning software and online courses.

Challenges

There are 229 federally recognized tribes in Alaska, but no reservation system. In 1971 Alaskan Natives renounced claims to aboriginal lands in return for 44 million acres of land, $963 million and 100 shares per person in regional, urban and village corporations. While the settlement was a cause of pride, it has done little for employment and household income.

There are many other social challenges. Few issues are as serious as alcohol abuse, which has led to a high rate of fetal alcohol syndrome, domestic violence, crime and suicides. Since 1980 the state has allowed local control of alcohol and 120 villages now have some form of prohibition. Other challenges include recruiting sufficient teachers, police officers and medical professionals to the Bush, and improving the diet of Native people.

Clockwise from top left
1. Yupik dancers, Alaska Native Heritage Center (p155)
2. Tsimshian dancer, Alaska Native Heritage Center
3. Elder with traditional mask at Anaktuvuk Pass (p365)

Alaskan Landscapes

It's one thing to be told Mt McKinley is the tallest mountain in North America; it's another to see it crowning the sky in Denali National Park. It's a mountain so tall, so massive and so overwhelming, it has visitors stumbling off the park buses. As a state, Alaska is the same; a place so huge, so wild and so unpopulated, it's incomprehensible to most people until they arrive.

The Land

Dramatic mountain ranges arch across the landmass of Alaska. The Pacific Mountain System, which includes the Alaska, Aleutian and St Elias Range as well as the Chugach and Kenai Mountains, sweeps along the south before dipping into the sea southwest of Kodiak Island. Further north looms the imposing and little-visited Brooks Range, skirting the Arctic Circle.

In between the Alaska and Brooks Ranges is Interior Alaska: an immense plateau rippled by foothills, low mountains and magnificent rivers, among them the third longest in the USA, the mighty Yukon River, which runs for 2300 miles. North of the Brooks Range is the North Slope, a coastal plain of scrubby tundra that gently descends to the Arctic Ocean.

In geological terms Alaska is relatively young and still very active. The state represents the northern boundary of the chain of Pacific Ocean volcanoes known as the 'Ring of Fire' and is the most seismically active region of North America. In fact, Alaska claims 52% of the earthquakes that occur in the country and averages more than 13 each day. Most are mild shakes, but some are deadly. Three of the six largest earthquakes in the world – and seven of the 10 largest in the USA – have occurred in Alaska.

Most of the state's volcanoes lie in a 1550-mile arc from the Alaska Peninsula to the tip of the Aleutian Islands. This area contains more than 65 volcanoes, 46 of which have been active in the last 200 years. Even in the past four decades Alaska has averaged more than two eruptions per year. If you spend any time in this state, or read about its history, you will quickly recognize that belching volcanoes and trembling earthquakes (as much as glaciers and towering peaks) are defining characteristics of the last frontier.

Southeast Alaska

Southeast Alaska is a 500-mile coastal strip extending from north of Prince Rupert right across to the Gulf of Alaska. In between are the hundreds of islands of the Alexander Archipelago, and a narrow strip of coast, separated from Canada's mainland by the glacier-filled Coast Mountains. Winding through the middle of the region is the Inside

The Alaska Volcano Observatory website (www.avo.alaska.edu) has web cams and a Volcano Alert map so you can see what's shaking and where.

EARTHQUAKES

Passage waterway; it's the lifeline for isolated communities, as the rugged terrain prohibits road-building. High annual rainfall and mild temperatures have turned the Southeast into rainforest, broken up by majestic mountain ranges, glaciers and fjords that many think surpass even those in Norway.

Prince William Sound & Kenai Peninsula

Like the Southeast, much of this region (also known as Southcentral Alaska) is a jumble of rugged mountains, glaciers, steep fjords and lush forests. This mix of terrain makes Kenai Peninsula a superb recreational area for backpacking, fishing and boating, while Prince William Sound, home of Columbia Glacier, is a mecca for kayakers and other adventurers.

Geographically, the Kenai Peninsula is a grab-bag. The Chugach Range receives the most attention, but in fact mountains only cover around two-thirds of the peninsula. On the east side of the peninsula is glorious Kenai Fjords National Park, encompassing tidewater glaciers that pour down from one of the continent's largest ice fields, as well as the steep-sided fjords those glaciers have carved. Abutting the park in places, and taking in much of the most southerly part of the Kenai Peninsula, is Kachemak Bay State Park, a wondrous land of mountains, forests and fjords.

Covering much of the interior of the peninsula, the Kenai National Wildlife Refuge offers excellent canoeing and hiking routes, plus some of the world's best salmon fishing. On the west side, the land flattens out into a marshy, lake-pocked region excellent for canoeing and trout fishing.

Prince William Sound is completely enveloped by the vast Chugach National Forest, the second-largest national forest in the US.

Southwest Alaska

Stretching 1500 miles from Kodiak Island to the international date line, the Southwest is spread out over four areas: the Kodiak Archipelago including Kodiak Island, the Alaska Peninsula, the Aleutian Islands and Bristol Bay. For the most part it is an island-studded region with stormy weather and violent volcanoes. This is the northern rim of the Ring of Fire, and along the Alaska Peninsula and the Aleutian Islands are 46 active volcanoes – the greatest concentration anywhere in North America.

Southwest Alaska is home to some of the state's largest and most intriguing national parks and refuges. Katmai National Park & Preserve, on the Alaska Peninsula, and Kodiak National Wildlife Refuge are renowned for bear watching. Lake Clark National Park & Preserve, across Cook Inlet from Anchorage, is a wilderness playground for rafters, anglers and hikers.

Most of the Aleutian Islands and part of the Alaska Peninsula form the huge Alaska Maritime National Wildlife Refuge, headquartered in Homer. The refuge encompasses 3.5 million acres and more than 2500 islands, and is home to 80% of the 50 million seabirds that nest in Alaska.

Denali & the Interior

With the Alaska Range to the north, the Wrangell and Chugach Mountains to the south and the Talkeetna Mountains cutting through the middle, the Interior has a rugged appearance matching that of either Southeast or Southcentral Alaska.

Mountains are everywhere. The formidable Alaska Range creates a jagged spine through the interior's midsection, while the smaller ranges – the Chugach, Talkeetna and Wrangell to the south and the White Mountains to the north – sit on the flanks. From each of these mountain ranges run major river systems. Spruce and birch predomi-

Roadside Geology of Alaska (1988), by Cathy Connor and Daniel O'Haire, explores the geology you see from the road, covering everything from earthquakes to why there's gold on the beaches of Nome – not dull reading by any means.

Alaskan brown bear and cub at Wonder Lake, Denali National Park (p258)

nate in the lowland valleys with their tidy lakes. Higher up on the broad tundra meadows, spectacular wildflowers show their colors during summer months. Wildfire also plays its role here, wiping out vast swaths of forest nearly every summer.

Alaska's Interior holds two marquee national parks and one impressive national preserve. The big name here, of course, is Denali National Park, blessed with the continent's mightiest mountain and abundant wildlife. Wrangell-St Elias National Park, located in the region's southeast corner, is the largest national park in the US and a treasure house of glaciers and untouched wilderness. Up in the Interior's northeast is Yukon-Charley Rivers National Preserve, located at the nexus of two of the state's legendary waterways.

The Bush

This is the largest slice of Alaska and includes the Brooks Range, Arctic Alaska and western Alaska on the Bering Sea. The remote, hard-to-reach Bush is separated from the rest of the state by mountains, rivers and vast roadless distances.

The mighty Brooks Range slices this region in two. To the north, a vast plain of tundra sweeps down to the frozen wasteland of the Arctic Ocean. In the western reaches, near towns such as Nome and Kotzebue, you'll find more tundra, as well as a flat landscape of lakes and slow-moving rivers closer to the Bering Sea, and rolling coastal hills and larger mountains heading toward the interior.

The Bush has several national parks and preserves. Most famous is Gates of the Arctic National Park & Preserve, which spans the spires of the Brooks Range and offers spectacular hiking and paddling. Near Kotzebue is Kobuk Valley National Park, known for the Great Kobuk Sand Dunes and the oft-paddled Kobuk River, with the mountain-ringed Noatak National Preserve just to the north.

ANCIENT GLACIERS

The Great Kobuk Sand Dunes comprise a 25-sq-mile swath of sand, 40 miles above the Arctic Circle. Remnants of ancient glaciers, some dunes rise 100ft high.

Major Vegetation Zones of Alaska

With its vast territory extending from the frigid Arctic Ocean to the temperate Gulf of Alaska, and encompassing mountain ranges, river valleys, sweeping plains, island chains and a range of climactic conditions, Alaska harbors a diversity of ecosystems. Most of the state, however, can be categorized into three large zones: tundra, taiga and temperate forest.

Tundra

Tundra comes from the Finnish word for barren or treeless land. Of course, tundra isn't completely barren but often a bewitching landscape of grasses, herbs, mosses, lichens and, during the too short summer, blooming wildflowers. Nevertheless, tundra soil is generally poor, the diversity of plants is low and the growing season extremely short: sometimes plants have as little as one-and-a-half months a year to sprout.

Lowland tundra extends along the coastal regions of the Arctic, and the deltas of western Alaska around Nome. What's referred to as upland tundra covers the land at higher elevations above the treeline throughout the Alaska Range, as well as across the Brooks Range and all along the Aleutians.

Taiga

Taiga, also called boreal forest, runs from Interior Alaska through Canada and down past the Great Lakes. Taiga forests are low and damp,

ALASKA'S GLACIERS

Alaska is one of the few places in the world where active glaciation occurs on a grand scale, and it's surprising at first to discover that most of this occurs in the warmer southern regions of the state. There are an estimated 100,000 glaciers in Alaska, covering 29,000 sq miles, or 5% of the state, and containing three-quarters of all Alaska's fresh water. The effects of glaciation, both from current and ice age glaciers, are visible everywhere and include wide U-shaped valleys, kettle ponds, fjords and heavily silted rivers.

Glaciers are formed when the snowfall exceeds the rate of melting and the solid cap of ice that forms begins to flow like a frozen river. The rate of flow, or retreat, can be anything but 'glacial,' and sometime reaches tens of meters per day.

Glaciers are impressive-looking formations, and because ice absorbs all the colors of the spectrum except blue, they often give off a distinct blue tinge. The more overcast the day, the bluer glacial ice appears. The exceptions are glaciers that are covered with layers of rock and silt (the glacier's moraine) and appear more like mounds of dirt. A good example is the Kennicott Glacier in Wrangell-St Elias National Park, which is often confused for a vast dump of old mine tailings.

The largest glacier in Alaska is the Bering Glacier, which stretches 118 miles from the St Elias Range to the Gulf of Alaska. If you include the Bagley Ice Field, where the Bering Glacier begins, this glacial complex covers 2250 sq miles, making it larger than Delaware.

Tidewater glaciers, a perennial favorite with visitors, extend from a land base into the sea (or a lake) and calve icebergs in massive explosions of water. Active tidewater glaciers can be viewed from tour boats in Glacier Bay National Park, Kenai Fjords National Park or Prince William Sound, which has the largest collection in the state.

For a comprehensive look at these rivers of ice, from the Mendenhall in the Southeast to glaciers in the Brooks Range, check out *Glaciers of Alaska* (2001), by Alaska Geographic Society.

often broken up with lakes and bogs. The most common species of trees are white spruce, black spruce, birch and aspen. Unless they are growing beside a river, trees tend to be short and scraggly, and grow in thickets.

Most of Interior Alaska (at lower elevations) is covered in taiga. It's great moose habitat, so keep your eyes peeled when driving through such areas.

Between the taiga and tundra is a transitional area in which species from either zone may be found. On the ride up the Dalton Hwy, a famous 'Last Spruce' is a curious testament to the fact that while transitions rarely have exact boundaries, they do have to end somewhere.

Coastal Temperate Forest

Alaska's temperate forests are found, no surprise, in southeastern Alaska, along the Gulf of Alaska, as well as the eastern edge of the Kenai Peninsula. They form part of the system of coastal rainforests that runs north from the Pacific Northwest and are dominated by Sitka spruce and other softwoods. Precipitation is high in this region, the winters mild, and as a result trees can grow to be giants over 70m tall. It's no surprise that Alaska Natives from this region are masters at woodcarving, and created the splendid totem pole culture that is now famous around the world.

Climate

Oceans surround 75% of Alaska, the terrain is mountainous and the sun shines at a low angle. All this gives the state an extremely variable climate, and daily weather that is infamous for its unpredictability.

For visitors, the most spectacular part of Alaska's climate is its long days. At Point Barrow, Alaska's northernmost point, the sun doesn't set for 2½ months from May to August. In other Alaskan regions, the longest day is on June 21 (the summer solstice), when the sun sets for only two hours in Fairbanks and for five hours in the Southeast. Even after sunset in late June, however, there is still no real darkness, just a long twilight with good visibility.

Southeast Alaska

The Southeast has a temperate maritime climate; much like Seattle only wetter. Juneau averages 57in of precipitation (rain or snow) annually, and Ketchikan gets 154in a year, most of which is rain as the temperatures are mild, even in winter.

Prince William Sound & Kenai Peninsula

Precipitation is the norm in Prince William Sound. In summer, Valdez is the driest of the towns; Whittier is by far the wettest. In all communities, average July daytime temperatures are barely above 60°F. So no matter what your travel plans are, pack your fleece and some bombproof wet-weather gear.

Weather-wise, the Kenai Peninsula is a compromise: drier than Prince William Sound, warmer than the Bush, wetter and cooler (in summer) than the Interior. Especially on the coast, extremes of heat and cold are unusual. Seward's normal daily high in July is 62°F. Rainfall is quite high on the eastern coasts of the peninsula around Seward and Kenai Fjords National Park; moderate in the south near Homer and Seldovia; and somewhat less frequent on the west coast and inland around Soldotna and Cooper Landing.

Anchorage

Shielded from the dark fury of Southcentral Alaska's worst weather by the Kenai Mountains, the Anchorage Bowl receives only 14in of rain annually and enjoys a relatively mild climate: January averages 13°F and July about 58°F. Technically a sub-Arctic desert, Anchorage does have more than its fair share of overcast days, however, especially in early and late summer.

Southwest Alaska

With little to protect it from the high winds and storms that sweep across the North Pacific, the Southwest is home to the very worst weather in Alaska. Kodiak is greatly affected by the turbulent Gulf of Alaska and receives 80in of rain per year, along with regular blankets of pea-soup fog and occasional blustery winds. On the northern edge of the Pacific, Unalaska and the Alaskan Peninsula receive less rain (annual precipitation ranges from 60in to 70in), but are renowned for unpredictable and stormy bouts of weather. Southwest summer temperatures range from 45°F to 65°F. For the clearest weather, try visiting in early summer or fall.

Denali & the Interior

In this region of mountains and spacious valleys, the climate varies greatly and the weather can change on a dime. In January temperatures can sink to -60°F for days at a time, while in July they often soar to above 90°F. The norm for the summer is long days with temperatures of 60°F to 70°F. However, it is common for Denali National Park to experience at least one dump of snowfall in the lowlands between June and August.

Here, more than anywhere else in the state, it's important to have warm clothes while still being able to strip down to a T-shirt and hiking shorts. Most of the area's 10in to 15in of annual precipitation comes in the form of summer showers, with cloudy conditions common, especially north of Mt McKinley. In Denali National Park, Mt McKinley tends to be hidden by clouds more often than not.

In the Interior and up around Fairbanks, precipitation is light, but temperatures can fluctuate by more than 100°F during the year. Fort Yukon holds the record for the state's highest temperature, at 100°F in June 1915, yet it once recorded a temperature of -78°F in winter. Fairbanks has the odd summer's day that hits 90°F and always has nights during winter that drop below -60°F.

The Bush

Due to its geographical diversity, the Bush is a land of many climates. In inland areas, winter holds sway from mid-September to early May, with ceaseless weeks of clear skies, negligible humidity and temperatures colder than anywhere else in America. Alaska's all-time low, -80°F, was recorded at Prospect Creek Camp, just off the Dalton Hwy. Closer to the ocean winter lingers even longer than inland, but it is incrementally less chilly.

During the brief summer, visitors to the Bush should be prepared for anything. Barrow and Prudhoe Bay may demand a parka: July highs there often don't hit 40°F. Along the Dalton Hwy and around Nome, the weather is famously variable. Intense heat (stoked by the unsetting sun) can be as much a concern as cold.

MT MCKINLEY

Want to see if Mt McKinley is clouded over before you visit? Check out Denali National Park's webcam for the latest conditions (www.nps.gov/dena/photos-multimedia/webcams.htm).

National, State & Regional Parks

One of the main attractions of Alaska is public land, where you can play and roam freely over an area of 384,000 sq miles, more than twice the size of California. The agency in charge of the most territory is the **Bureau of Land Management** (BLM; www.blm.gov/ak; 133,594 sq miles), followed by the **US Fish & Wildlife Service** (USFWS; www.fws.gov; 120,312 sq miles) and the **National Park Service** (www.nps.gov; 84,375 sq miles).

Alaska's national parks are the crown jewels as far as most travelers are concerned, and attract more than two million visitors a year. The most popular units are Klondike Gold Rush National Historical Park, which draws 860,000 visitors a year, and Denali National Park, home of Mt McKinley, which sees around half that number. Other busy units are Glacier Bay National Park, a highlight of every cruise-ship itinerary in the Southeast, and Kenai Fjords National Park in Seward.

Alaska State Parks (www.alaskastateparks.org) oversees 119 units that are not nearly as renowned as most national parks, and thus far less crowded at trailheads and in campgrounds. The largest is the 1.6-million-acre Wood-Tikchik State Park, a roadless wilderness north of Dillingham. The most popular is Chugach State Park, the 495,000-acre unit that is Anchorage's after-work playground.

Both the BLM and the USFWS oversee many refuges and preserves that are remote, hard to reach and not set up with visitor facilities such as campgrounds and trails. The major exception is the Kenai National Wildlife Refuge, an easy drive from Anchorage, and a popular weekend destination for locals and tourists alike.

For more pretrip information, contact the **Alaska Public Lands Information Center** (www.alaskacenters.gov).

The heaviest recorded annual snowfall in Alaska was 974.5in at Thompson Pass, north of Valdez, in the winter of 1952–53.

ALASKAN LANDSCAPES NATIONAL, STATE & REGIONAL PARKS

CLIMATE CHANGE AND ALASKA

Alaska's temperatures are rising, causing permafrost to melt, coastlines to erode, forests to die (or push north into new territory), and Arctic sea ice and glaciers to melt at alarming rates. Some scientists now predict the Arctic Ocean will be entirely ice-free in summer by 2040, or even sooner. Meanwhile, Portage Glacier has retreated so fast it can no longer be viewed from its visitor center, and famed Mendenhall Glacier is expected to retreat totally on to land and cease being a tidewater glacier within five years.

Northern Alaska is ground zero when it comes to global warming, and with the vast majority of the land sitting on permafrost – and aboriginal traditions and whole ecosystems inextricably tied to the frozen earth and sea – the very balance of nature has been thrown into disaccord. At Shishmaref, a barrier island village on the Seward Peninsula, residents have watched with horror as homes have literally slipped into the Bering Sea due to the loss of protective sea ice that buffers them against storms. And Shishmaref is just one of 160 rural communities the US Army Corps of Engineers has identified as being threatened by erosion. Relocation plans have already begun for several of these.

Paradoxically, in Juneau sea levels are dropping as billions of tons of ice have melted away, literally springing the land to new heights. In some areas the land is rising 3in a year, the highest rate in North America. As a result, water tables are dropping, wetlands are drying up and property lines are having to be redrawn.

Beyond the disaster for humans, the changes to the Alaskan landscape and climate will have dramatic effects on the highly adapted organisms that call this place home. In Juneau, the rising land has already caused channels that once facilitated salmon runs to silt up and grass over. In the far north, melting summer sea ice is expected to put such pressure on the polar bear that in 2008 the animal was listed as a 'threatened' species.

Alaska is and always will be wild and big, but these days it doesn't seem as mighty as it once was.

Major Parks of Alaska

PARK	FEATURES	ACTIVITIES	PAGE
Admiralty Island National Monument	wilderness island, chain of lakes, brown bears, marine wildlife	bear viewing, kayaking, canoeing, cabin rentals	p130
Chena River State Recreation Area	Chena River, alpine areas, granite tors, campgrounds, cabin rentals	backpacking, canoeing, hiking	p298
Chugach State Park	Chugach Mountains, alpine trails, Eklutna Lake	backpacking, mountain biking, paddling, hiking, campgrounds	p159
Denali National Park	Mt McKinley, brown bears, caribou, Wonder Lake, campground	wildlife viewing, backpacking, hiking, park bus tours	p258
Denali State Park	alpine scenery, trails, views of Mt McKinley, campgrounds	backpacking, hiking, camping	p281
Gates of the Arctic National Park & Preserve	Brooks Range, Noatak River, treeless tundra, caribou	rafting, canoeing, backpacking, fishing	p364
Glacier Bay National Park & Preserve	tidewater glaciers, whales, Fairweather Mountains	kayaking, camping, whale watching, lodge, boat cruises	p131
Independence Mine State Historical Park	Talkeetna Mountains, alpine scenery, gold mine ruins, visitor center	mine tours, hiking	p187
Kachemak Bay State Park	glaciers, protected coves, alpine areas, cabin rentals	kayaking, backpacking, boat cruises	p253
Katmai National Park & Preserve	Valley of 10,000 Smokes, volcanoes, brown bears, lodge	fishing, bear viewing, backpacking, kayaking	p339
Kenai Fjords National Park	tidewater glaciers, whales, marine wildlife, steep fjords, cabin rental	boat cruises, kayaking, hiking	p225
Kenai National Wildlife Refuge	chain of lakes, Russian River, moose, campgrounds	fishing, canoeing, wildlife watching, hiking	p232
Kodiak National Wildlife Refuge	giant bears, rich salmon runs, wilderness lodges, cabin rentals	bear viewing, flightseeing, cabin rentals	p337
Misty Fiords National Monument	steep fjords, 3000ft sea cliffs, lush rainforest	boat cruises, kayaking, cabin rentals, flightseeing	p86
Tracy Arm-Fords Terror Wilderness Area	glaciers, steep fjords, a parade of icebergs, marine wildlife	boat cruises, kayaking, wildlife watching	p122
Wrangell-St Elias National Park	mountainous terrain, Kennecott mine ruins, glaciers	backpacking, flightseeing, rafting, biking, mine tours	p316

Environmental Issues

With its vast tracts of pristine land and beloved status as America's last wild frontier, Alaska's environmental issues are, more often than not, national debates. These days the focus of those debates (and a fair amount of action) centers on the effects of global warming and resource management, especially the push for mining and drilling in reserve lands.

Land

The proposed Pebble Mine development in Bristol Bay has been one of the most contentious environmental issues of the past decade. The stakes are huge for all sides. Pebble is potentially the second-largest ore deposit of its type in the world, with copper and gold deposits estimated to be worth a staggering $500 billion. The catch is the minerals would be extracted from near the headwaters of Bristol Bay and require a manmade 2-mile-wide open pit that would likely pollute streams that support the world's largest run of wild salmon. That has an unlikely alliance of environmentalists, commercial fishers and Alaska Natives up in arms.

Oil exploration in the Arctic National Wildlife Refuge (ANWR) is another unresolved issue, despite a political battle that has raged in the Lower 48 since the earliest days of President Reagan. The refuge is often labeled by environmentalists as America's Serengeti, an unspoiled wilderness inhabited by 45 species of mammals, including grizzly bears, polar bears and wolves. Millions of migratory birds use the refuge to nest, and every spring the country's second-largest caribou herd, 150,000 strong, gives birth to 40,000 calves there.

Though estimates of the amount of recoverable oil have dropped considerably in the past few years, industry is still eager to jump in, and politicians continue to argue that ANWR can help the country achieve energy independence. Currently a majority of Americans are in favor of drilling (including a majority of Alaskans) with President Obama personally opposed. Native tribes who live in and around ANWR are split over the issue.

Fisheries

The problems of resource exploitation are not restricted to oil, gas and minerals. After the king crab fishery collapsed in 1982, the commercial fishing industry was rebuilt on pollack, whose mild flavor made it the choice for imitation crab, and fish sandwiches served at fast-food restaurants. Pollack has been called 'the world's largest fishery,' but since 2006, when a record 730 million lb were processed at Dutch Harbor, the fishery has been slipping backwards. Fishing quotas have been reduced these past few years, however, and the stock may make a comeback if all goes well.

But pollack is not alone. At least four times since 1997 the salmon runs of Bristol Bay and Kuskokwim River have been declared economic disasters, and in 2008 the king salmon run up the Yukon River was so poor that even subsistence gatherers were restricted from catching them. However, in 2011, the Alaska Department of Fish and Game estimated that 203 million fish would be caught, one of the largest hauls since statehood. The department credited sound management of the fisheries as well as good conditions for the abundance.

Wrangell-St Elias, Kluane and Glacier Bay National parks as well as Tatshenshini-Alsek Provincial Park collectively form one of the largest World Heritage Sites at 24.34 million acres.

Village Voices (www.ruralcap.com) is an informative quarterly magazine focusing on the issues facing rural Native Alaskans, including the high costs of energy, homelessness, the legacy of Head Start and poor nutrition.

ALASKAN LANDSCAPES ENVIRONMENTAL ISSUES

Rural Issues

Waste management is a hot issue in Alaska's rural communities, many of which are unconnected to the rest of the state by convenient transportation routes. Though burning garbage is still a common way of reducing trash, as is dumping, more and more communities have begun to build recycling centers, practice composting, and haul back to Anchorage whatever they can. A free program called Flying Cans now takes bundled aluminum cans from rural communities to recycling plants in Anchorage via scheduled cargo flights. Energy-saving education programs are also making their way across the state, as are greenhouses. The latter are expected to have a positive impact on both nutrition and the amount of fuel used to supply rural villages with fresh produce.

For more information on environmental issues, contact these conservation organizations:

» **Alaska Sierra Club** (www.alaska.sierraclub.org)

» **No Dirty Gold** (www.nodirtygold.org) A campaign opposing abusive gold mining around the world, including the proposed Pebble Mine.

» **Southeast Alaska Conservation Council** (www.seacc.org)

» **Wilderness Society** (www.wilderness.org)

Alaskan Wildlife

Bears, Moose & Caribou »
More Land Animals »
Fish & Marine Mammals »
Birds »

Lynx (p404)

Bears, Moose & Caribou

Alaska boasts one of the Earth's great concentrations of wildlife and some species that are threatened or endangered elsewhere – brown bears, for example – thrive in the 49th state.

Bears

There are three species of bear in Alaska: brown, black and polar. Of these, you're most likely to see brown bears, as they have the greatest range.

Brown and grizzly bears are now listed as the same species *(Ursus arctos)* but there are differences. Browns live along the coast, where abundant salmon runs help them reach weights exceeding 800lb, or 1500lb in the case of the famed Kodiak. Grizzlies are browns found inland and subsist largely on grass. Normally a male weighs from 500lb to 700lb, and females half that. The most common way to identify any brown bear is by the prominent shoulder hump, easily seen behind the neck when the animal is on all fours.

Alaska has an estimated 30,000 brown bears, or more than 98% of the US population. In July and August you can see the bears fishing alongside rivers. In early fall they move into tundra regions and open meadows to feed on berries.

Though black bears *(Ursus americanus)*, which may also be colored brown or cinnamon, are the USA's most widely distributed bruin, their range is limited in Alaska. They live in most forested areas of the state, but not north of the Brooks Range, on the Seward Peninsula, or on many large islands, such as Kodiak and Admiralty. The average male black weighs from 180lb to 250lb.

Polar bears *(Ursus maritimus)* dwell only in the far north and their adaptation to a life on sea ice has given them a white, water-repellent coat, dense underfur, specialized teeth for a carnivorous diet

MARK NEWMAN / LONELY PLANET IMAGES ©

MARK NEWMAN / LONELY PLANET IMAGES ©

Clockwise from top left
1. Moose 2. Male caribou 3. Brown bear cub

DARRELL GULIN / CORBIS ©

2

(primarily seals), and hair that almost completely covers the bottom of their feet. A male polar bear weighs between 600lb and 1200lb. Plan on stopping at the zoo in Anchorage (p160), or taking a lengthy side trip to Barrow (p366) or Kaktovik (p369), if you want to see one.

Moose

Moose are long-legged in the extreme, but short-bodied despite sporting huge racks of antlers. They're the world's largest members of the deer family, and the Alaskan species is the largest of all. A newborn weighs 35lb and can grow to more than 300lb in five months; cows weigh 800lb to 1200lb; and bulls 1000lb to more than 1600lb, with antlers up to 70in wide.

The moose population ranges from an estimated 120,000 to 160,000, and historically the animal has been the most important game species in Alaska. Some 20,000 are officially hunted each year.

Caribou

Although more than a million caribou live in Alaska across 32 herds, they are relatively difficult to view as they inhabit the Interior north up to the Arctic Sea. This is a shame as the migration of the Western Arctic herd, the largest in North America with almost 500,000 animals, is one of the great wildlife events left on Earth. The herd uses the North Slope for its calving area, and in late August many of the animals cross the Noatak River and journey southward.

Caribou range in weight from 150lb to more than 400lb. The animals are crucial to the Iñupiat and other Alaska Natives, who hunt more than 30,000 a year to support their subsistence lifestyle.

The best place for visitors to see caribou is Denali National Park (p258).

More Land Animals

Wolves

While gray wolves are struggling throughout most of the USA, in Alaska their numbers are strong despite predator control programs. In total, about 8000 wolves live in Alaska, spread throughout almost every region of the state. Adult males average 85lb to 115lb, and their pelts can be gray, black, off-white, brown or yellow, with some tinges approaching red. Wolves travel, hunt, feed and operate in the social unit of a pack. In the Southeast their principal food is deer, in the Interior it's moose and in Arctic Alaska it's caribou.

Mountain Goats & Dall Sheep

Often confused with Dall sheep, mountain goats have longer hair, short black horns and deep chests. They range throughout the Southeast, fanning out north and west into the coastal mountains of Cook Inlet, as well as the Chugach and Wrangell Mountains. Good locations to see them include Glacier Bay (p131) and Wrangell-St Elias National Park (p316).

Dall Sheep are more numerous and widespread, numbering close to 80,000, and live in the Alaska, Wrangell, Chugach and Kenai mountain ranges. They are often seen

STEVEN KAZLOWSKI / SCIENCE FACTION / CORBIS ©

at Windy Corner, on the Seward Hwy, and in Denali National Park (p258).

The best time to catch rams in a horn-clashing battle for social dominance is right before the mating period, which begins in November.

Lynx

This intriguing-looking feline has unusually large paws to help it move swiftly over snowpack as it hunts snowshoe hare, its primary food source. Lynx inhabit most forested areas of Alaska, but your chances of seeing one depends on the hare population, which fluctuates over an eight-to-11-year cycle.

Beavers & River Otters

Around lakes and rivers you stand a good chance of seeing river otters and beavers or, at the very least, beaver lodges and dams. Both animals live throughout the state, with the exception of the North Slope. Often larger than their relatives further south, otters range from 15lb to 35lb, while beavers weigh between 40lb and 70lb, although 100lb beavers have been recorded in Alaska.

TOP PLACES TO SEE...

» **Brown Bears** Katmai National Park & Preserve (p339), Anan Creek Wildlife Observatory (p92)

» **Moose** Kenai National Wildlife Refuge (p232), Denali National Park (p258)

» **Seals** Tracy Arm (p122), Prince William Sound (p190)

» **Humpback Whales** Glacier Bay National Park (p131), Sitka (p103)

» **Puffins** St Lazaria Island National Wildlife Refuge (p109), Gull Island (p252)

Clockwise from top left
1. Gray wolf 2. Dall sheep 3. River otters

Fish & Marine Mammals

Whales

The three most common whales seen in coastal waters are the 50ft-long humpback, the smaller bowhead whale and the gray whale. The humpback is by far the most frequently seen by visitors on cruise ships and on the state ferries, as they often lift their flukes (tail) out of the water to begin a dive, or blow every few seconds when resting near the surface. Biologists estimate 1000 humpbacks migrate to the Southeast and more than 100 head to Prince William Sound each year.

At one time Glacier Bay was synonymous with whale watching. But today tour boats head out of almost every Southeast Alaska port, loaded with whale-watching passengers. You can also join such trips in Kenai Fjords National Park (p226), near Seward, and in Kodiak (p330).

At the Sitka WhaleFest! (p110), in early November, visitors and locals gather to listen to world-renowned biologists talk about whales, and then hop on boats to go look for them.

Dolphins & Porpoises

Dolphins and harbor porpoises are commonly seen in Alaskan waters, even from the decks of public ferries. Occasionally, passengers will also spot a pod of orcas (killer whales), and sometimes belugas, both large members of the dolphin family. Orcas, which can be more than 20ft long, are easily identified by their high black-and-white dorsal fins. The white-colored beluga ranges in length from 11ft to 16ft and weighs more than 3000lb. The 50,000 belugas that live off Alaskan shores travel in herds of more than 100. They are easily spotted in Turnagain Arm, along the Seward Hwy (p178).

ARTHUR MORRIS/CORBIS ©

W. PERRY CONWAY / CORBIS ©

Clockwise from top left
1. Harbor seal **2.** Humpback whale **3.** Walrus

Salmon

Five kinds of wild salmon can be found in Alaska: sockeye (also referred to as red salmon), king (or chinook), pink (or humpie), coho (or silver) and chum. For sheer wonders of nature it's hard to beat a run of thousands of salmon swimming upstream to spawn. From late July to mid-September, many coastal streams are so choked with the fish that at times individuals have to wait their turn to swim through narrow gaps of shallow water.

In the heart of Anchorage, Ship Creek supports runs of king, coho and pink. From a viewing platform (p153) you can watch the fish spawning upriver and also the locals trying to catch one for dinner. In downtown Ketchikan, you can watch salmon in Ketchikan Creek (p80).

Seals

The most commonly seen marine mammal, seals are often found basking in the sun on ice floes. Six species exist in Alaska, but most visitors will encounter the harbor seal, whose range includes the Southeast, Prince William Sound and the entire Gulf of Alaska. The average male weighs 200lb, reached by a diet of herring, flounder, salmon, squid and small crabs.

The ringed and bearded seals inhabit the northern Bering, Chukchi and Beaufort Seas, where sea ice forms during winter.

Walruses

Like the seal, the Pacific walrus is a pinniped (fin-footed animal) but this much larger creature is less commonly spotted. Walruses summer in the far northern Chukchi Sea and though they may number over 200,000, most visitors are likely only to encounter the tusks of these creatures in the carving of a native artist.

Birds

Alaska's vast open spaces and diversity of habitat make it unusually rich in bird life. Over 445 species have been identified statewide.

Bald Eagles

While elsewhere in America the bald eagle (a magnificent bird with a wingspan of over 8ft) is on the endangered species list, in Alaska it's commonly sighted in the Southeast, Prince William Sound and Dutch Harbor in the Aleutian Islands.

Ptarmigan

The state bird is a cousin of the prairie grouse. Three species can be found throughout Alaska in high, treeless country.

Seabirds & Waterfowl

Alaskan seabirds include the crowd-pleasing horned and tufted puffins, six species of auklet, and three species of albatross (which boast a wingspan of up to 7ft). The optimum way to see these is on a wildlife cruise to coastal breeding islands such as St Lazaria Island (p109), home to 1500 pairs of breeding tufted puffins.

An amazing variety of waterfowl migrate to Alaska each summer, including trumpeter swans, Canada geese, eider, the colorful harlequin duck and five species of loon.

Tundra Species

Tundra birds such as wheateaters, Smith's longspurs, Arctic warblers, bluethroats, and snowy owls are big draws for amateur twitchers. Prime viewing areas include Nome (p350), Barrow (p366), and the Dalton and Denali Hwys.

Bald eagle

Survival Guide

Directory A–Z

Accommodations

Alaska offers typical US accommodations, along with many atypical options such as a cabin in the mountains or a lodge in the middle of the wilderness. This guide includes recommendations for all types and budgets but it emphasizes midrange accommodations. In the regional chapters the accommodations are listed according to author preference, with a price range symbol:

» $ (budget, under $100 a night)
» $$ (midrange, $100 to $200)
» $$$ (top end, $200 and up).

Advance bookings are wise as the Alaskan tourist season is short, and rooms fill quickly in such places as Juneau, Skagway and Denali National Park. You will receive better accommodation rates during the shoulder seasons of April through May and September through October.

The rates listed in this book are for high season: June through August. The listed rates do not include local taxes, which are covered for each town at the start of the Sleeping sections. In most towns you will be hit with a local sales tax *and* a bed tax, with the combination ranging from 5% to 12% for cities such as Anchorage and Juneau.

The most affordable accommodations are hostels, campsites (bring your tent!) and campground cabins. Motels, both individually owned and national chains, are well scattered in cities and most towns. Even small rural hamlets will have a motel. The larger centers will also have a number of B&Bs housing the peak-of-summer tourists, which will range from basic rooms to plush accommodations.

As to be expected, Alaska is the land of wilderness lodges. Many of these are geared toward anglers and remote fishing opportunities, must be booked well in advance, and require floatplane transport to reach. Tribal companies and the cruise ship industry (for the land portions of their tours) are also responsible for a growing number of luxury hotels popping up across the state.

B&Bs

For travelers who want nothing to do with a tent, B&Bs can be an acceptable compromise between sleeping on the ground and sleeping in high-priced lodges. Some B&Bs are bargains, and most are cheaper than major hotels, but plan on spending $70 to $120 per night for a double room.

Many visitor centers have sections devoted to the B&Bs in their area, and courtesy booking phones. Details about specific B&Bs can be found in the regional chapters. You can also contact the following B&B reservation services to book rooms before your trip:

Alaska Private Lodgings (☏235-2148; www.alaskabandb.com) Statewide.

Anchorage Alaska Bed & Breakfast Association (☏272-5909, 888-584-5147; www.anchorage-bnb.com)

Bed and Breakfast Association of Alaska (www.alaskabba.com) Statewide.

Fairbanks Association of Bed & Breakfasts (www.ptialaska.net/~fabb)

Homer Bed & Breakfast Association (☏226-1114, 877-296-1114; www.homerbedbreakfast.com)

Kenai Peninsula Bed & Breakfast Association (☏776-8883, 866-436-2266; www.kenaipeninsulabba.com)

Ketchikan Reservation Service (☏247-5337, 800-

BOOK YOUR STAY ONLINE

For more reviews of accommodations by Lonely Planet authors, check out hotels.lonelyplanet.com/Alaska. You'll find independent reviews, as well as recommendations on the best places to stay. Best of all, you can book online.

987-5337; www.ketchikan
-lodging.com)

**Mat-Su Bed & Breakfast
Association** (www.alaskabn
bhosts.com)

Camping & Caravan Parks

Camping is king in Alaska and with a tent you'll always have cheap accommodations in the Far North. There are state, federal and private campgrounds from Ketchikan to Fairbanks. Nightly fees range from free to $15 for rustic public campgrounds and from $30 to $55 to park your recreation vehicle in a deluxe private campground with a full hook-up and heated restrooms with showers. Many towns that cater to tourists operate a municipal campground. For commercial campgrounds there's the **Alaska Campground Owner's Association** (☑866-339-9082; www.alaskacampgrounds.net).

Hostels

Thanks to an influx of backpackers and foreign travelers each summer, the number of hostels offering budget accommodations in Alaska increases almost annually. There are now more than 40, with eight in Anchorage, eight in the Southeast and even one in tiny McCarthy.

Alaska's hostels offer budget bunkrooms and kitchen facilities that range in nightly fees that range from $10 at Juneau International Hostel to $35 for the Anchorage Guest House. Most are around $25 a night. The best statewide hostel organization is the **Alaska Hostel Association** (www.alaskahostelassociation.org).

Hotels & Motels

Hotels and motels are often the most expensive lodgings you can book. Although there are bargains, the average double room in a budget hotel costs $70 to $90, a midrange motel is $100 to $200,

and a top-end hotel costs $200 and above a night.

The drawback with hotels and motels is that they tend to be full during summer. Without being part of a tour or having advance reservations, you may have trouble finding a bed available in some towns.

Resorts

Resorts – upscale hotels that have rooms, restaurants, pools and on-site activities – are not as common in Alaska as elsewhere in the USA but are increasing due to the patronage of large companies, such as Princess Tours. The finest is Girdwood's Alyeska Resort, with a four-star hotel at the base of its ski runs. If you're near Fairbanks, head to Chena Hot Springs Rd to spend some time at the Chena Hot Springs Resort for good food, log cabins and a soak in an outdoor hot tub.

Activities

Outdoor activities such as hiking, paddling, mountain biking, fishing, mountaineering and even surfing can be found in the Outdoor Activities & Adventures chapter (p30). Within the Alaska's Best Hikes & Paddles chapter, 14 of Alaska's best paddling and backpacking adventures are covered. For details on companies that offer activity tours, see p51.

Business Hours

Throughout this book, we don't list opening and closing times unless they vary significantly from the hours listed here.

Banks Monday to Friday, 9am until 4pm or 5pm. Saturday, main branches open 9am to 1pm. Sunday closed.

Bars & Clubs In cities, bars open until 2am or later, especially at weekends. Clubs stay open to 2am or beyond.

Museums & Sights Large museums and sights usually open virtually every day of the year. Smaller places open daily in the summer, open weekends only or can be completely closed in low season.

Post Offices Monday to Friday, 9am to 5pm. Saturday, noon to 3pm; main branches open longer. Sunday closed.

Restaurants Breakfast at cafes and coffee shops is served from 7am or earlier. Some restaurants open only for lunch (about noon to 3pm) or dinner (about 4pm to 10pm or later in cities). Asian restaurants often have split hours, 11am to 2pm and from 4pm.

Stores Monday to Saturday from 10am to 8pm for larger stores, to 6pm for smaller stores. Saturday from 9am to 5pm. Sunday, larger stores open 10am to 5pm.

Customs Regulations

For a complete list of US customs regulations, visit the official portal for **US Customs & Border Protection** (www.cbp.gov). Click on 'Travel' and then 'Know Before You Go' for the basics.

Travelers are allowed to bring all personal goods (including camping and hiking equipment) into the USA and Canada free of duty, along with food for two days and up to 100 cigars, 200 cigarettes and 1L of liquor or wine.

There are no forms to fill out if you are a foreign visitor bringing a vehicle into Alaska, whether it is a bicycle, motorcycle or car, nor are there forms for hunting rifles or fishing gear. Hunting rifles – handguns and automatic weapons are prohibited – must be registered in your own country, and you should bring proof of registration. There is no limit to the amount of money you can bring into Alaska, but anything over $10,000 must be registered with customs officials.

Keep in mind that endangered-species laws prohibit transporting products made of bone, skin, fur, ivory etc through Canada without a permit. Importing and exporting such items into the USA is also prohibited. If you have any doubt about a gift or item you want to purchase, call the **US Fish & Wildlife Service** (USFWS; ☑271-6198; www.fws.gov) in Anchorage or check the website.

Hunters and anglers who want to ship home their salmon, halibut or rack of caribou can do so easily. Most outfitters and guides will make the arrangements for you, including properly packaging the game. In the case of fish, most towns have a storage company that will hold your salmon or halibut in a freezer until you are ready to leave Alaska. When frozen, seafood can usually make the trip to any city in the Lower 48 without thawing.

Discount Cards

Most museums, parks and major attractions will offer reduced rates to seniors and students, but most accommodations, restaurants and small tour companies will not.

» Best seniors card for US travelers to carry is issued by the **American Association of Retired Persons** (AARP; ☑888-687-2277; www.aarp.org).

» For students, an **International Student Identity Card** (www.isic.org) will often result in discounts for attractions in cities and major towns.

» There are no Hostelling International chapters in Alaska so the HI card is of little use in the Far North.

Electricity

120V/60Hz

120V/60Hz

Embassies & Consulates

International travelers needing to locate the US embassy in their home country should visit the **US Department of State** (http://usembassy.

state.gov), which has links to all of them.

There are no embassies in Alaska, but there are a handful of foreign consulates in Anchorage to assist overseas travelers with unusual problems:

Canada (☑264-6734; Ste 220, 310 K St)

Denmark (☑279-7611; Ste 100, 3111 C St)

France (☑561-3280; Ste 100, 716 W 4th Ave)

Germany (☑274-6537; Ste 650, 425 G St)

Japan (☑562-8424; Ste 1300, 3601 C St)

Norway (☑279-6942; 8210 Sundi Dr)

UK (☑786-4848; UAA, 3211 Providence Dr.)

Food

Many travelers are surprised that food prices in a Fairbanks or Anchorage supermarket are not that much higher than what they're paying at home. Then they visit their first restaurant and a glance at the menu sends them into a two-day fast. Alaskan restaurants are more expensive than most other places in the country because of the short tourist season and the high labor costs for waiters and chefs.

In this book, restaurant prices usually refer to an average main dish at dinner and do not include drinks, appetizers, dessert or tips. Restaurants can be divided into budget, midrange and upscale. Dinner is an under-$10 affair in a budget cafe, $10 to $27 in a midrange restaurant, and usually $27 and higher at an upscale place.

The mainstay of Alaskan restaurants, particularly in small towns, is the mainstreet cafe. It opens early in the morning serving eggs, bacon, pancakes and oatmeal, and continues with hamburgers, French fries and grilled sandwiches for lunch.

There is almost always halibut and salmon on the dinner menu. Most small towns also have a hamburger hut, a small shack or trailer with picnic tables outside, serving burgers, hot dogs, wraps or fried fish.

While places catering to vegans are rare throughout Alaska, you will find at least one health food store in most midsize towns and cities, as well as a number of restaurants advertising 'vegetarian options.' Alternatively, search out Chinese and other Asian restaurants for the best selection of meatless dishes. Also keep in mind that Carrs, Safeway and other large supermarkets often have well-stocked salad bars, self-serve affairs at $6 per pound.

Gay & Lesbian Travelers

The gay community in Alaska is far smaller and much less open than in major US cities, and Alaskans in general are not as tolerant to diversity. In 1998 Alaska passed a constitutional amendment banning same-sex marriages.

In Anchorage, the only city in Alaska of any real size, you have **Identity Inc** (☎929-4528; www.identityinc.org), which has a gay and lesbian helpline, a handful of openly gay clubs and bars, and a weeklong **PrideFest** (http://alaskapride.org) in mid-June. The **Southeast Alaska Gay & Lesbian Alliance** (www.seagla.org) is based in Juneau and offers links and travel lists geared to gay visitors. The list is short, however, because most towns do not have an openly active gay community. In rural Alaska, same-sex couples should exercise discretion.

Health

There is a high level of hygiene found in Alaska, so most common infectious diseases will not be a significant concern for travelers. Superb medical care and rapid evacuation to major hospitals are both available.

» The cost of health care in the USA and Alaska is extremely high. It's essential to purchase travel health insurance if your regular policy doesn't cover you when you're abroad.

» No special vaccines are required or recommended for travel to Alaska.

» In recent years, paralytic shellfish poisoning (PSP) from eating mussels and clams has become a problem in Alaska. For a list of beaches safe to clam, check with the **Alaska Division of Environmental Health** (www.dec.state.ak.us/eh/fss/seafood/psp/psp.htm).

» Tap water in Alaska is safe to drink, but you should purify surface water taken from lakes and streams that is to be used for cooking and drinking. The simplest ways to purify water is to boil it thoroughly or use a high-quality filter.

» The most dangerous health threat outdoors is hypothermia. Dress in layers topped with a well-made, waterproof outer layer and always pack wool mittens and a hat.

» Due to Alaska's long summer days, sunburn and windburn are a primary concern for anyone trekking or paddling. Use a good sunscreen on exposed skin, even on cloudy days, and a hat

PRACTICALITIES

» Alaska has more than 30 daily, weekly and trade newspapers, with the *Anchorage Daily News* being the largest and the closest thing to a statewide newspaper.

» The largest cities have local TV stations, while radio stations are found all over Alaska.

» Voltage in Alaska is 120V – the same as everywhere else in the USA.

» There is no national sales tax in the USA and no state sales tax in Alaska, but towns have a city sales tax plus a bed tax.

» Almost every town in Alaska has a laundromat, the place to go to clean your clothes ($3 per load) or take a shower ($3 to $5).

» US distances are in feet, yards and miles. Dry weights are in ounces (oz), pounds (lb) and tons, and liquids are in pints, quarts and gallons (4 quarts).

» The US gallon is about 20% less than the imperial gallon. See the conversion chart on the inside front cover of this book.

» NTSC is the standard video system (not compatible with PAL or SECAM).

» There is no statewide smoking ban in Alaska but Anchorage and Juneau have a city ban on smoking in bars, restaurants and clubs.

BEARS IN ALASKA

Too often travelers decide to skip a wilderness trip because they hear too many bear stories. Your own equipment and outdoor experience should determine whether you take a trek into the woods, not the possibility of meeting a bear on the trail. The **Alaska Department of Fish & Game** (www.adfg.state.ak.us) emphasizes that the probability of being injured by a bear is 1/50th the chance of being injured in a car accident on any Alaskan highway.

The best way to avoid bears is to follow a few commonsense rules. Bears charge only when they feel trapped, when a hiker comes between a sow and her cubs or when enticed by food. Sing or clap when traveling through thick bush, and don't camp near bear food sources or in the middle of an obvious bear path. Stay away from thick berry patches, streams choked with salmon or beaches littered with bear droppings.

Set up the spot where you will cook and eat at least 30yd to 50yd away from your tent. In coastal areas, many backpackers eat in the tidal zone, knowing that when the high tide comes in, all evidence of food will be washed away.

At night try to place your food sacks 10ft or more off the ground by hanging them in a tree. Or consider investing in a lightweight bear-resistant container. A bear usually finds a food bag using its great sense of smell. Avoid odorous foods, such as bacon or sardines, in areas with high concentrations of bears. Avoid wearing scented cosmetics, including deodorant, as the smell attracts bears.

And please, don't take food into the tent at night. Don't even take toothpaste, hand lotion, suntan oils or anything with a smell. If a bear smells a human, it will leave; anything else might encourage it to investigate.

Encountering a Bear

If you do meet a bear on the trail, *do not* turn and run, as it will outrun you. Stop, make no sudden moves and begin talking calmly to the animal. Speaking to a bear helps it understand that you are there. If it doesn't take off right away, back up slowly before turning around and leaving the area. A bear standing on its hind legs is not on the verge of charging; it's only trying to see you better. When a bear turns sideways or begins making a series of woofing sounds, it is only challenging you for space – just back away slowly and leave. If the animal follows you, *stop* and hold your ground.

Most bear charges are bluffs, with the animal veering off at the last minute. Experienced backpackers handle a charge in different ways. Some people throw their packs 3ft in front of them, which will often distract the bear long enough for the person to back away. Many backpackers are carry defensive aerosol sprays that contain red pepper extract. These sprays cost $50 each and are effective at a ranges of 6yd to 8yd, but must be discharged downwind. Some people carry guns to fend off bear charges, but firearms should never be used as an alternative to commonsense approaches to bear encounters. You must drop the bear with one or two shots, as a wounded bear is extremely dangerous.

If an encounter is imminent, drop into a fetal position, place your hands behind your neck and play dead. If a bear continues biting you after you have assumed a defensive posture, then you must fight back vigorously.

---

and sunglasses for additional protection.

» Alaska is notorious for its biting insects, including mosquitoes, black flies, no-see-ums and deer flies. Wear long-sleeved shirts, pants that can be tucked into socks and a snug cap. Use a high-potency insect repellent and head nets in areas where there are excessive insects.

Insurance

A travel insurance policy to cover theft, loss and medical problems is a smart investment. Coverage depends on your insurance and type of ticket but should cover delays by striking employees or company actions, or a cancellation of a trip. Such

coverage may seem expensive but it's nowhere near the price of a trip to Alaska or the cost of a medical emergency in the USA.

Some policies offer lower and higher medical-expense options; the higher ones are chiefly for countries such as the USA, which have extremely high medical costs. There is a wide variety of medical and emergency repatriation policies and it's important to talk to your healthcare provider for recommendations.

For insurance on car rentals see p423.

Worldwide travel insurance is available through the **Lonely Planet** (www.lonelyplanet.com/travel_services) website. You can buy, extend and claim online any time – even if you're already on the road.

The following companies also offer travel insurance:

Access America (☎800-284-8300; www.accessamerica.com)

Insuremytrip.com (☎800-487-4722; www.insuremytrip.com)

Travel Guard (☎800-826-4919; www.travelguard.com)

Internet Access

It's easy to surf the net, make online reservations or retrieve email in Alaska. Most towns, even the smallest ones, have internet access at libraries, hotels and internet cafes. Access ranges from free at the library to $5 to $10 an hour at internet cafes. If you are hauling around a laptop, wi-fi is common in Alaska at bookstores, motels, coffee shops, airport terminals and even bars. This guide uses the internet icon (@) when accommodations or other businesses have an internet terminal for guests' use. and a wi-fi icon (🛜) for anywhere that has wireless internet access. If you're not from the US, remember you will need an AC adapter and a plug adapter for US sockets.

For the best websites for travelers headed for Alaska, see the Need to Know chapter (p17).

Legal Matters

Despite the history of marijuana in Alaska – it was once legal for personal use – possession of small amounts is now a misdemeanor punishable by up to 90 days in jail and a $1000 fine. The use of other drugs is also against the law and results in severe penalties, especially for cocaine, which is heavily abused in Alaska.

The minimum drinking age in Alaska is 21 and a government-issued photo ID (passport or driver's license) will be needed if a bartender questions your age. Alcohol abuse is also a problem in Alaska, and it's a serious offence if you are caught driving under the influence of alcohol (DUI). The blood alcohol limit in Alaska is 0.08% and the penalty for DUI is a three-month driver's license revocation, at least three days in jail and a $1500 fine.

If you are stopped by the police for any reason while driving, remember there is no system of paying on-the-spot fines and bribery is not something that works in Alaska. For traffic violations, the officer will explain your options to you and many violations can often be handled through the mail with a credit card.

The age of consent in Alaska is 16 years and travelers should note that they can be prosecuted under the law of their home country regarding age of consent, even when abroad.

Maps

Unlike many places in the world, Alaska has no shortage of accurate maps. There are detailed US Geological Survey (USGS) topographical maps to almost every corner of the state, even though most of it is still wilderness, while every visitor center has free city and road maps that are more than adequate to get from one town to the next. For free downloadable maps and driving directions

For trekking in the backcountry and in wilderness areas, the USGS topographic maps are worth the $6-per-quad cost. USGS topo maps come in a variety of scales, but hikers prefer the smallest scale of 1:63,360, with each inch equal to a mile. Canoeists and other river runners can get away with the 1:250,000 map.

In Anchorage the **USGS Earth Science Information Center** (☎786-7011; Grace Bldg, Alaska Pacific University; ⏰8:30am-4:30pm Mon-Fri) has topo maps for the entire state. You can also order maps in advance directly from **USGS** (☎888-275-8747; www.usgs.gov) or you can view and order custom topo maps from cartography websites such as **Mytopo** (☎877-587-9004; www.mytopo.com). GPS units and accompanying mapping software that includes Alaska are available from **Garmin** (www.garmin.com) and **DeLorme** (www.delorme.com).

Money

All prices quoted in this book are in US dollars unless otherwise stated. US coins come in denominations of 1¢ (penny), 5¢ (nickel), 10¢ (dime), 25¢ (quarter) and the seldom seen 50¢ (half-dollar). Quarters are the most commonly used coins in vending machines and parking meters, so it's handy to have a stash of them. Notes, commonly called bills, come in $1, $2, $5, $10, $20, $50 and $100 denominations. Keep in mind that the Canadian system is also dollars and cents but is a separate currency. For exchange rates, see the inside front cover.

ATMs

In Alaska ATMs are everywhere: banks, gas stations, supermarkets, airports and even some visitor centers.

At most ATMs you can use a credit card (Visa, MasterCard etc), a debit card or an ATM card that is linked to the Plus or Cirrus ATM networks. There is generally a fee ($1 to $3) for withdrawing cash from an ATM, but the exchange rate on transactions is usually as good if not better than what you'll get from anywhere else.

Cash

Hard cash still works. It may not be the safest way to carry funds, but nobody will hassle you when you purchase something with US dollars. Most businesses along the Alcan in Canada will also take US dollars.

Credit Cards

Like in the rest of the USA, Alaskan merchants are ready and willing to accept just about all major credit cards. Visa and MasterCard are the most widely accepted cards, but American Express and Discovery are also widely used.

Places that accept Visa and MasterCard are also likely to accept debit cards. If you are an overseas visitor, check with your bank at home to confirm that your debit card will be accepted in the USA.

Moneychangers

Banks are the best place to exchange foreign currencies as the exchange counters at the airports typically have poorer rates. **Wells Fargo** (☎800-956-4442; www.wells fargo.com), the nation's sixth-largest bank, is the dominant player in Alaska with more than 400 branches, eight in Anchorage alone. Wells Fargo can meet the needs of most visitors, including changing currency and offering 24-hour ATMs.

Tipping

Tipping in Alaska, like in the rest of the USA, is expected. The going rate for restaurants, hotels and taxis is about 15%. It is also common for visitors to tip guides, including on bus tours. If you forget, don't worry: they'll remind you.

Bars If you order food at the table and your meal is brought to you, tipping is the same as at a restaurant, 15%. If you are simply having a drink or appetizer at the bar, it's 10%.

Restaurants From 15% for cafes and chain eateries to 20% for upscale restaurants.

Taxis 15%.

Tour guides 10% for a bus tour guide, $15% to 20% for wilderness guides leading you on a glacier trek or white-water raft trip.

Traveler's Checks

Although slowly becoming obsolete thanks to ATMs, the other way to carry your funds is the time-honored method of traveler's checks. The popular brands of US traveler's checks are American Express and Visa, but keep in mind most banks won't cash them unless you have an account with them and that stores or motels will only cash denominations of $100 or less.

Post

The **US Postal Service** (☎800-275-8777; www.usps.com) is one of the world's busiest and most reliable, but even it needs another day or two to get letters and postcards to and from Alaska. With an abundance of internet cafes and the availability of internet at libraries and hostels and hotels, think email for quick notes to friends and family. For packages, especially heavy ones, it's faster to use private carriers in Alaska such as **United Parcel Service** (☎800-742-5877; www.ups.com) or **Federal Express** (☎800-463-3339; www.fedex.com).

Public Holidays

Public holidays for Alaskan residents may involve state and federal offices being closed, bus services curtailed, and shop and store hours reduced.

New Year's Day January 1

Martin Luther King Day Third Monday in January

Presidents' Day Third Monday in February

Seward's Day Last Monday in March

Easter Sunday Late March or early April

Memorial Day Last Monday in May

Independence Day (aka Fourth of July) July 4

Labor Day First Monday in September

Columbus Day Second Monday in October

Alaska Day October 18

Veterans' Day November 11

Thanksgiving Day Fourth Thursday in November

Christmas Day December 25

Telephone
Cell Phones

Cell phones work in Alaska and Alaskans love them as much as anywhere else in the USA. When calling home or locally in cities and towns, reception is excellent but overall, in a state this large, cell phone coverage can be unpredictable and sporadic at times. The culprits in most cases are mountains.

Most travelers still find their cell phones to be very useful. Before you head north, however, check your cell phone provider's roaming agreements and blackout areas. It may be possible for international travelers to purchase a prepaid SIM card that can be used in their mobile phones for local calls and voicemail. You can also purchase inexpensive cell phones from AT&T for $10 along with prepaid cards for calls at 10¢ a minute or $2 a day.

Phone Codes

Telephone area codes are simple in Alaska: the entire state shares 907, except Hyder, which uses 250. In this guidebook, the area code is always 907, unless a different one is listed before the phone number. Phone numbers that begin with 800, 877 and 866 are toll-free numbers and there is no charge for using one to call a hotel or tour operator. If you're calling from abroad, the country code for the USA is ☑1.

Phonecards

The best way to make international calls is to first purchase a phonecard. There's a wide range of phonecards sold in amounts of $5, $10 and $20, available at airports and in many convenience stores and internet cafes. Most towns and villages in Alaska have public pay phones that you can use to call home if you have a phonecard or credit card.

Time

With the exception of several Aleutian Island communities and Hyder, a small community on the Alaskan–British Columbian border, the entire state shares the same time zone, Alaska Time, which is one hour earlier than Pacific Standard Time – the zone in which Seattle, Washington, falls. When it is noon in Anchorage, it is 4pm in New York, 9pm in London and 7am the following day in Melbourne, Australia. Although there is a movement to abolish it, Alaska still has Daylight Saving Time when, like most of the country, the state sets clocks back one hour in November and forward one hour in March.

Tourist Information

The first place to contact when planning your adventure is the **Alaska Travel Industry Association** (ATIA; ☑929-2200; www.travelalaska. com), the state's tourism marketing arm. From the ATIA you can request a copy of the *Alaska Vacation Planner*, an annually updated magazine; a state highway map; and schedules for the Alaska Marine Highway ferry service.

Travel information is easy to obtain once you are on the road, as almost every city, town and village has a tourist contact center, whether it is a visitor center, a chamber of commerce or a hut near the ferry dock. These places are good sources of free maps, information on local accommodations and directions to the nearest campground or hiking trail.

Most trips to Alaska pass through one of the state's three largest cities. All have large visitors bureaus that will send out city guides in advance:

Anchorage Convention & Visitors Bureau (☑276-4118; www.anchorage.net)

Fairbanks Convention & Visitors Bureau (☑456-5774, 800-327-5774; www.explorefairbanks.com)

Juneau Convention & Visitors Bureau (☑586-1737, 800-587-2201; www.traveljuneau.com)

Travelers with Disabilities

Thanks to the American Disabilities Act, many state and federal parks have installed wheelchair-accessible sites and restrooms in their campgrounds. You can call the **Alaska Public Lands Information Center** (☑271-2599) to receive a map and campground guide to such

facilities. The Alaska Marine Highway ferries, the Alaska Railroad and many bus services and cruise ships are also equipped with wheelchair lifts and ramps to make their facilities easier to access. Chain motels and large hotels in cities and towns often have rooms set up for disabled guests, while some wilderness guiding companies are experienced in handling wheelchair-bound clients on rafting and kayaking expeditions.

The following organizations may be useful when planning your trip:

Access Alaska (☑248-4777; www.accessalaska.org) Includes statewide tourist information on accessible services and sites.

Access-Able Travel Source (www.access-able. com) A national organization with an excellent website featuring travel information and links.

Challenge Alaska (☑344-7399; www.challengealaska. org) A nonprofit organization dedicated to providing recreation opportunities for those with disabilities.

Flying Wheels Travel (☑877-451-5006; www.flying wheelstravel.com) A full-service travel agency specializing in disabled travel.

Society for Accessible Travel & Hospitality (☑212-447-7284; www.sath. org) Lobbies for better facilities and publishes *Open World* magazine.

Visas

Since September 11, the US has continually fine-tuned its national security guidelines and entry requirements. Double-check current visa and passport regulations before arriving in the USA, and apply for visas early to avoid delays. Overseas travelers may need one visa, possibly two. For citizens of many countries a US visa is required, while if you're taking the Alcan or the Alaska Marine Highway ferry from Prince Rupert in British Columbia, you may also need a Canadian visa. The Alcan begins in Canada, requiring travelers to pass from the USA into Canada and back into the USA again.

Canadians entering the USA must have proof of Canadian citizenship, such as a passport; visitors from countries in the Visa Waiver Program (see p418) may not need a visa. Visitors from all other countries need to have a US visa and a valid passport. On the website of the **US State Department** (www.travel.state.gov) there is a 'Temporary Visitors to the US' page with tips on how and where to apply for a visa and what to do if you're denied.

Note that overseas travelers should be aware of the process to re-enter the USA. Sometimes visitors get stuck in Canada due to their single-entry visa into the USA, used up when passing through the Lower 48. Canadian immigration officers often caution people whom they feel might have difficulty returning to the USA. More information about visa and other requirements for entering Canada is available on the website of the **Canada Border Services Agency** (www.cbsa-asfc.gc.ca).

Visa Application

Apart from Canadians and those entering under the Visa Waiver Program, foreign visitors need to obtain a visa from a US consulate or embassy. Most applicants must now schedule a personal interview, to which you need to bring all your documentation and proof of fee payment. Wait times for interviews vary, but afterward, barring problems, visa issuance takes from a few days to a few weeks. If concerned about a delay, check the US State Department website,

which provides a list of wait times calculated by country.

Your passport must be valid for at least six months longer than your intended stay in the USA. You'll need a recent photo (2in by 2in) and you must pay a $100 processing fee, plus in a few cases an additional visa issuance fee (check the State Department website for details). In addition to the main nonimmigration visa application form (DS-156), all men aged 16 to 45 must complete an additional form (DS-157) that details their travel plans.

Visa applicants are required to show documentation of financial stability, a round-trip or onward ticket and 'binding obligations' that will ensure their return home, such as family ties, a home or a job.

Visa Waiver Program

The Visa Waiver Program (VWP) lets citizens of some countries enter the USA for tourism purposes for up to 90 days without having a US visa. Currently there are 36 participating countries in the VWP, including Austria, Australia, Belgium, Denmark, Finland, France, Germany, Iceland, Ireland, Italy, Japan, the Netherlands, New Zealand, Norway, Spain, Sweden, Switzerland and the UK.

Under the program you *must* have a round-trip or onward ticket that is nonrefundable in the USA, a machine-readable passport (with two lines of letters, numbers and <<< along the bottom of the passport information page) and be able to show evidence of financial solvency.

As of 2009, citizens of VWP countries must register online prior to their trip with the **Electronic System for Travel Authorization** (ESTA; http://esta.cbp.dhs.gov), an automated system used to determine the eligibility of visitors traveling to the US.

Volunteering

For many travelers the only way to enjoy Alaska is to volunteer. You won't get paid, but you're often given room, board and work in a spectacular setting. Most volunteer roles are with federal or state agencies and range from trail crew workers and campground hosts to volunteering at the Arctic Interagency Visitor's Center in Coldfoot and collecting botanical inventories.

Alaska State Parks (☎269-8708; www.alaskastateparks.org)

Bureau of Land Management (BLM; ☎271-5960; www.ak.blm.gov)

Chugach National Forest (☎743-9500; www.fs.fed.us/r10/chugach)

Student Conservation Association (☎543-1700; www.thesca.org)

Tongass National Forest (☎225-3101; www.fs.fed.us/r10/tongass)

Women Travelers

While most violent crime rates are lower here than elsewhere in the USA, women should be careful at night in unfamiliar neighborhoods in cities like Anchorage and Fairbanks or when hitching alone. Use common sense; don't be afraid to say no to lifts. If camping alone, have pepper spray and know how to use it.

Alaska Women's Network (www.alaskawomensnetwork.org) Has listings of women-owned B&Bs and travel agencies across the state.

Anchorage Planned Parenthood Clinic (☎563-2229; 4001 Lake Otis Pkwy) Offers contraceptives, medical advice and services.

Women's Flyfishing (www.womensflyfishing.net) Alaska's premier outfitter for women-only fly fishing trips and a great web resource for women arriving in Alaska with a fly rod.

Transportation

GETTING THERE & AWAY

Whether you're from the US or overseas, traveling to Alaska is like traveling to a foreign country. By sea it takes almost a week on the Alaska Marine Highway ferry to reach Whittier in Prince William Sound from the Lower 48. By land a motorist in the Midwest needs 10 days to drive straight to Fairbanks.

If you're coming from the US mainland, the quickest, and least expensive, way to reach Alaska is to fly nonstop from a number of cities. If you're coming from Asia or Europe, it's almost impossible to fly directly to Alaska as few international airlines maintain a direct service to Anchorage. Today most international travelers come through the gateway cities of Seattle, Los Angeles, Minneapolis and Vancouver to Alaska.

Entering the Country

Since the September 11 terrorist attacks, air travel in the USA has permanently changed and you can now expect vigilant baggage screening procedures and personal searches. In short, you're going to have to take your shoes off. Non-US citizens should be prepared for an exhaustive questioning process at immigration.

Crossing the border into Alaska from Canada used to be a relaxed process – US citizens often passed across with just a driver's license. Now this process has also become more complicated, and all travelers should have a passport and expect more substantial questioning and possible vehicle searches.

Passport

If you are traveling to Alaska from overseas, you need a passport. Even Canadian citizens should carry one, as a driver's license alone may not be enough to satisfy customs officials. If you are a US resident passing through Canada, you will need a passport to re-enter the USA. Make sure your passport does not expire during the trip, and if you are entering the USA through the Visa Waiver Program (VWP) you *must* have a machine-readable passport. For more on VWP or visas see p417. If you are traveling with children, it's best to bring a photocopy of their birth certificates.

Air

Airports & Airlines

The vast majority of visitors to Alaska, and almost all international services, fly into **Ted Stevens Anchorage International Airport** (ANC; ☎266-2526; www.dot.state.ak.us/anc). International flights arrive at the north terminal; domestic flights arrive at the south terminal

---

CLIMATE CHANGE & TRAVEL

Every form of transport that relies on carbon-based fuel generates CO_2, the main cause of human-induced climate change. Modern travel is dependent on airplanes, which might use less fuel per mile per person than most cars but travel much greater distances. The altitude at which aircraft emit gases (including CO_2) and particles also contributes to their climate change impact. Many websites offer 'carbon calculators' that allow people to estimate the carbon emissions generated by their journey and, for those who wish to do so, to offset the impact of the greenhouse gases emitted with contributions to portfolios of climate-friendly initiatives throughout the world. Lonely Planet offsets the carbon footprint of all staff and author travel.

and a complimentary shuttle service runs between the two every 15 minutes. You'll find bus services, taxis and car-rental companies at both terminals. The airport has the usual services, including baggage storage, pay phones, ATMs, currency exchange and free wi-fi.

In recent years rising fuel costs and airline mergers have greatly reduced the number of airlines that serve Alaska:

Alaska Airlines (AS; ☑800-426-0333; www.alaskaair.com)

American Airlines (AA; ☑800-443-7300; www.aa.com)

Condor Airlines (DE; ☑800-524-6975; www.condor.de, www7.condor.com)

Continental Airlines (CO; ☑800-525-0280; www.continental.com)

Delta Air Lines (DL; ☑800-221-1212; www.delta.com)

ERA Aviation (7H; ☑800-866-8394; www.flyera.com)

Frontier Airlines (2F; ☑800-432-1159; www.frontierairlines.com)

JetBlue Airways (B6; ☑800-538-2583; www.jetblue.com)

PenAir (KS; ☑800-448-4226; www.penair.com)

Sun Country Airlines (SY; ☑800-359-6786; www.suncountry.com)

US Airways (US; ☑800-428-4322; www.usairways.com)

Tickets

Due to its lack of direct and international flights, Anchorage, and thus Alaska, is not the most competitive place for airfares. Begin any ticket search by first checking travel websites and then compare the prices against the websites of airlines that service Alaska, particularly **Alaska Airlines** (www.alaskaair.com), as it often has internet specials offered nowhere else. For a good overview of online ticket agencies and lists of travel agents worldwide, visit **Airinfo** (www.airinfo.aero).

Seattle serves as the major hub for flights into Alaska. Alaska Airlines owns the lion's share of the market, with 20 flights per day to Anchorage as well as direct flights to Ketchikan, Juneau and Fairbanks.

You can also book a nonstop flight to Anchorage from a number of other US cities. Delta flies in from Minneapolis, Phoenix and Salt Lake City. Continental flies nonstop from Houston, Chicago, Denver and San Francisco. American Airlines arrives in Anchorage from Chicago and Dallas; US Airways from Phoenix; Jet Blue from Long Beach; Frontier from Denver; and Sun Country from Minneapolis. Alaska Airlines, naturally, flies nonstop from numerous cities including Los Angeles, Denver, Chicago and Portland.

Land

What began as the Alaska-Canada Military Hwy is today the Alcan (the Alaska Hwy). This amazing 1390-mile road starts at Dawson Creek in British Columbia, ends at Delta Junction and in between winds through the vast wilderness of northwest Canada and Alaska. For those with the time, the Alcan is a unique journey north. There are several ways of traveling the Alcan: bus, car or a combination of Alaska Marine Highway ferry and bus.

Bus

A combination of buses will take you from Seattle via the Alcan to Anchorage, Fairbanks or Skagway, but service is limited, the ride is a very long one and a round-trip on a bus from Seattle to Anchorage is not cheaper than flying. From Seattle, **Greyhound Canada** (☑800-661-8747; www.greyhound.ca) goes to Whitehorse, a 60-hour-plus ride. A one-way ticket is $330 but advance purchase discounts can

lower the price significantly. From Whitehorse, **Alaska Direct** (☑800-770-6652; www.alaskadirectbusline.com) leaves three days a week for Anchorage for $240.

Car & Motorcycle

Without a doubt, driving your own car to Alaska allows you the most freedom. You can leave when you want, stop where you feel like it and plan your itinerary as you go along. It's not cheap driving to Alaska, and that's not even considering the wear and tear from the thousands of miles you'll put on your vehicle.

The Alcan is now entirely paved and, although sections of jarring potholes, frost heaves (the rippling effect of the pavement caused by freezing and thawing) and loose gravel still exist, the infamous rough conditions of 30 years ago no longer prevail. Food, gas and lodging can be found almost every 20 to 50 miles along the highway, with 100 miles being the longest stretch between fuel stops.

On the Canadian side, you'll find kilometer posts (as opposed to the mileposts found in Alaska), which are placed every 5km after the zero point in Dawson Creek. Most Alcan veterans say 300 miles a day is a good pace – one that will allow for plenty of stops to see the scenery or wildlife.

Along the way, **Tourism Yukon** (☑800-661-0494; www.travelyukon.com) operates a number of visitor centers stocked with brochures and maps:

Beaver Creek (☑867-862-7321; Mile 1202, Alcan)

Haines Junction (☑867-634-2345; Kluane National Park Headquarters)

Watson Lake (☑867-536-7469; Alcan & Campbell St)

Whitehorse (☑867-667-3084; 2nd St & Hanson Ave)

Hitchhiking

Hitchhiking is probably more common in Alaska than it is in the rest of the USA, and even more so on rural dirt roads such as the McCarthy Rd and the Denali Hwy than it is on the major paved routes. Hitchhiking is never entirely safe in any country and we don't recommend it. That said, if you're properly prepared and have sufficient time, thumbing your way along the Alcan can be an easy way to see the country while meeting local people and saving money.

The Alcan seems to inspire the pioneer spirit in travelers who drive along it. Drivers are good about picking up hitchhikers, much better than those across the Lower 48; the only problem is that there aren't really enough of them. Any part of the Alcan can be slow, but some sections are notoriously bad. The worst is probably Haines Junction, the crossroads in the Yukon where southbound hitchhikers often get stranded trying to thumb a ride to Haines in Southeast Alaska.

If you'd rather not hitchhike the entire Alcan, take the Alaska Marine Highway ferry from Bellingham, WA, to Haines, stick your thumb out and start hitchhiking from there; you'll cut the journey in half but still travel along the highway's most spectacular parts.

Sea

As an alternative to the Alcan, you can travel the Southeast's Inside Passage. From that maze of a waterway, the **Alaska Marine Highway** (☑465-3941, 800-642-0066; www.ferryalaska.com) and cruise ships then cut across the Gulf of Alaska to towns in Prince William Sound. For more on cruising the Far North and selecting a ship, see the Cruising in Alaska chapter (p37).

Tours

Package tours can often be the most affordable way to see a large chunk of Alaska, if your needs include the better hotels in each town and a full breakfast every morning. But they move quickly, leaving little time for an all-day hike or other activities.

Companies offering Alaska packages:

Alaska Heritage Tours (☑877-777-2805, 777-2805; www.alaskaheritagetours.com)

Alaska Wildland Adventures (☑800-334-8730; www.alaskawildland.com)

Gray Line (☑800-478-6388; www.graylineofalaska.com)

Green Tortoise Alternative Travel (☑800-867-8647, 415-956-7500; www.greentortoise.com)

Knightly Tours (☑800-426-2123, 206-938-8567; www.knightlytours.com)

GETTING AROUND

Traveling around Alaska is unlike traveling in any other US state. The overwhelming distances between regions and the fledgling public transportation system make getting around Alaska almost as hard as it is to get there in the first place. Come with a sense of adventure and be patient!

Air

As a general rule, if there are regularly scheduled flights to your destination, they will be far cheaper than charter flights on the small airplanes known in Alaska as 'bush planes.' This is especially true for **Alaska Airlines** (☑800-426-0333; www.alaskaair.com).

Other regional carriers:

Era Aviation (☑800-866-8394; www.flyera.com) Southcentral Alaska, Fairbanks, Bush Alaska and Kodiak.

PenAir (☑800-448-4226;

www.penair.com) Aleutian Islands, Alaska Peninsula and Bristol Bay.

Wings of Alaska (☑789-0790; www.wingsofalaska.com) Southeast Alaska.

Bush Planes

With 75% of the state inaccessible by road, small, single-engine planes known as 'bush planes' are the backbone of intrastate transport. They carry residents and supplies to desolate areas of the Bush, take anglers to some of the best fishing spots in the country and drop off backpackers in the middle of untouched wilderness.

In the larger cities of Anchorage, Fairbanks, Juneau and Ketchikan, it pays to compare prices before chartering a plane. In most small towns and villages, you'll be lucky if there's a choice. In the regional chapters, bush flights are listed under the town or area where they operate.

Bush aircraft include floatplanes, which land and take off on water, and beachlanders with oversized tires that can use rough gravel shorelines as air strips. Fares vary with the type of plane, its size, the number of passengers and the amount of flying time. On average, chartering a Cessna 185 that can carry three passengers and a limited amount of gear will cost up to $400 for an hour of flying time. A Cessna 206, a slightly larger plane that will hold four passengers, costs up to $400 to $450, while a Beaver, capable of hauling five passengers with gear, costs on average $500 to $550 an hour. When chartering a plane to drop you off in the wilderness, you must pay for both the air time to your drop-off point and for the return to the departure point.

Double-check all pickup times and places when flying to a wilderness area. Bush pilots fly over the pickup point and if you're not there, they usually return to base, call the authorities and still charge you for the flight. Always schedule extra days around a charter flight. It's not uncommon to be 'socked in' by weather for a day or two until a plane can fly in. Don't panic: they know you're there.

Bicycle

For those who want to bike it, Alaska offers a variety of cycling adventures on paved roads under the Arctic sun that allows you to peddle until midnight if you want. A bicycle can be carried on Alaska Marine Highway ferries for an additional fee and is a great way to explore small towns without renting a car.

Most road cyclists avoid gravel, but cycling the Alcan (an increasingly popular trip) does involve riding over some gravel breaks in the paved asphalt. Mountain bikers, on the other hand, are in heaven on gravel roads such as De-nali Hwy in the Interior.

Anchorage's **Arctic Bicycle Club** (☎566-0177; www.arcticbike.org) is Alaska's largest bicycle club and sponsors a wide variety of road-bike and mountain-bike tours during the summer. Its website includes a list of Alaska cycle shops.

If you arrive in Alaska without a bicycle, see the regional chapters for the towns with rentals and expect to pay $30 to $50 a day. Purchasing a bike and selling it at the end of a trip is not something often done by travelers. You can take your bicycle on the airlines for an excess luggage fee of $50 per flight or ship it in advance to **Chain Reaction Cycles** (☎336-0383; www.chainreactioncycles.us) in Anchorage, which will assemble your bicycle and hold it until you arrive.

Boat

Along with the Alaska Marine Highway (see p40), the Southeast is served by the **Inter-Island Ferry Authority** (☎866-308-4848; www.interislandferry.com), which connects Ketchikan with Prince of Wales Island (adult/child $37/18); and **Haines-Skagway Fast Ferry** (☎766-2100, 888-766-2103; www.hainesskagwayfastferry.com) servicing Skagway and Haines (adult/child $35/18).

Bus

Regular bus service within Alaska is very limited, and companies come and go with alarming frequency. The following companies have been around for a number of years. All fares are adult one way and do not include a fuel surcharge.

Alaska Direct Bus Line (☎277-6652, 800-770-6652; www.alaskadirectbusline.com) Anchorage to Glennallen ($55), Tok ($120), Haines Junction ($220) and Fairbanks ($135).

Alaska Park Connection (☎800-266-8625; www.alaskacoach.com) Anchorage to Seward ($65), Denali National Park ($90) and Talkeetna ($65).

Alaska/Yukon Trails (☎800-770-7275; www.alaskashuttle.com) Fairbanks to Denali National Park ($55), Anchorage ($99) and Dawson City ($169).

Dalton Highway Express (☎474-3555; www.daltonhighwayexpress.com) Fairbanks to Prudhoe Bay ($221).

Homer Stage Line (☎235-2252; stagelineinhomer.com) Homer to Anchorage ($90).

Seward Bus Line (☎563-0800, 888-420-7788; www.sewardbuslines.net) Anchorage to Seward ($50).

Yukon Alaska Tourist Tours (☎866-626-7383, in Whitehorse 867-668-5944; www.yukonalaskatouristtours.com) Skagway to Whitehorse ($60).

Car & Motorcycle

Not a lot of roads reach a lot of Alaska but what pavement there is leads to some seriously spectacular scenery. That's the best reason to tour the state in a car or motorcycle, whether you arrive with yours or rent one. With personal wheels you can stop and go at will and sneak away from the RVers and tour buses.

Automobile Associations

AAA (☎800-332-6119; www.aaa.com), the most widespread automobile association in the USA, has one office in Alaska, **Anchorage Service Center** (☎344-4310), which offers the usual including maps, discounts and emergency road service.

Fuel & Spare Parts

Gas is widely available on all the main highways and tourist routes in Alaska. In Anchorage and Fairbanks the cost of gas will only be 10¢ to 15¢ per gallon higher than in the rest of the country. Along the Alcan, in Bush communities such as Nome, and at that single gas station on a remote road, they will be shockingly high.

Along heavily traveled roads, most towns will have a car mechanic, though you might have to wait a day for a part to come up from Anchorage. In some small towns, you might be out of luck. For anybody driving to and around Alaska, a full-size spare tire and replacement belts are a must.

Insurance

Liability insurance – which covers damage you may cause to another vehicle in the event of an accident – is required when driving in Alaska but not always offered by rental agencies because most Americans are already covered by their regular car insurance. This is particularly true with many of the discount rental places listed in the On the Road chapters. Major car agencies offer Collision Damage Waiver (CDW) to cover damage to the rental car in case of an accident. This can up the rental fee by $15 a day or more and many have deductibles as high as $1000. It's better, and far cheaper, to arrive with rental car insurance obtained through your insurance company, as a member of AAA, or as a perk of many credit cards including American Express.

Rental & Purchase

For two or more people, car rental is an affordable way to travel, far less expensive than taking a bus or a train. At most rental agencies, you'll need a valid driver's license, a major credit card and you'll also need to be at least 21 years old. It is almost always cheaper to rent in town rather than at the airport because of extra taxes levied on airport rentals.

Read any rental contract carefully, especially when it comes to driving on gravel or dirt roads. Many agencies, particularly those in the Fairbanks area, will not allow their compacts on dirt roads. If you violate the contract and have an accident, insurance will not cover repairs. Also be conscious of the per-mile rate of a rental. Add up the mileage you aim to cover and then choose between the 100 free miles per day or the more expensive unlimited mileage plan.

Affordable car rental places, such as the following, are always heavily booked during the summer. Try to reserve these vehicles at least a month in advance.

Denali Car Rental (☎276-1230, 800-757-1230; Anchorage)

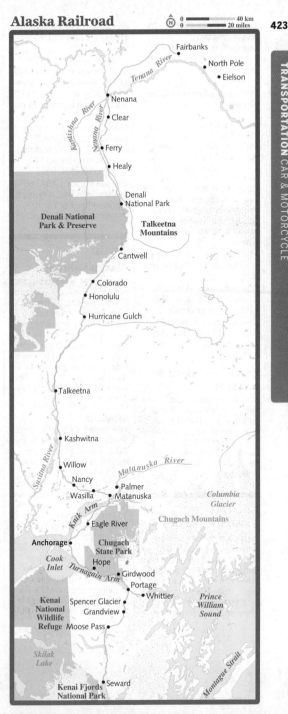

Fairbanks
North Pole
Eielson
Tenana River
Kantishna River
Nenana River
Nenana
Clear
Ferry
Healy
Denali National Park
Denali National Park & Preserve
Talkeetna Mountains
Cantwell
Colorado
Honolulu
Hurricane Gulch
Talkeetna
Kashwitna
Susitna River
Willow
Nancy
Wasilla
Matanuska River
Palmer
Matanuska
Columbia Glacier
Knik Arm
Eagle River
Chugach Mountains
Anchorage
Chugach State Park
Cook Inlet
Turnagain Arm
Hope
Girdwood
Portage
Whittier
Prince William Sound
Kenai National Wildlife Refuge
Spencer Glacier
Grandview
Moose Pass
Skilak Lake
Kenai Fjords National Park
Seward
Montague Strait

Rent-A-Wreck (☎800-478-1606; Fairbanks)

Midnight Sun Car & Van Rental (☎243-8806, 888-877-3585; Anchorage)

Valley Car Rental (☎775-2880; www.valleycarrental.com; Wasilla)

MOTORHOME

RVers flock to the land of the midnight sun in astounding numbers. This is the reason why more than a dozen companies, almost all of them based in Anchorage, will rent you a motorhome. Renting a recreational vehicle is so popular you have to reserve them four to five months in advance.

ABC Motorhomes (☎800-421-7456; www.abcmotorhome.com)

Clippership Motorhome Rentals (☎800-421-3456; www.clippershiprv.com)

Great Alaskan Holidays (☎248-7777, 888-225-2752; www.greatalaskanholidays.com)

Road Conditions & Hazards

For road conditions, closures and other travel advisories for the Alaska highway system, even while you're driving, contact the state's **Alaska511** (☎511, outside Alaska 866-282-7577; http://511.alaska.gov).

Local Transportation

In cities and most mid-size towns there will be taxi service, and at almost every Alaska Marine Highway port there'll be van service into town. There is also limited local bus service in some cities, with the most exten-

sive systems in Anchorage, Fairbanks, Juneau and Ketchikan.

Capital Transit (☎789-6901; www.juneau.org/capitaltransit) Juneau and Douglas.

Ketchikan Bus (☎225-8726; www.borough.ketchikan.ak.us/bus/info.htm)

Metropolitan Area Commuter System (MACS; ☎459-1011; www.co.fairbanks.ak.us/transportation) Fairbanks and North Pole.

People Mover (☎343-6544, Rideline 343-6543; www.muni.org/departments/transit/peoplemover) Anchorage.

Train

Alaska Railroad

It took eight years to build it, but today the Alaska Railroad (p176) stretches 470 miles from Seward to Fairbanks, through spectacular scenery. You'll save more money traveling by bus down the George Parks Hwy, but few travelers regret booking the Alaska Railroad and viewing pristine wilderness from its comfortable cars.

SERVICES

The Alaska Railroad operates a year-round service between Fairbanks and Anchorage, as well as summer services (from late May to mid-September) from Anchorage to Whittier and from Anchorage to Seward.

The most popular run is the 336-mile trip from Anchorage to Fairbanks, stopping at Denali National Park. Northbound, at Mile 279 the train passes within 46 miles of Mt McKinley, a stunning sight from the viewing domes on a clear day. It then slows down to cross the

918ft bridge over Hurricane Gulch.

The ride between Anchorage and Seward may be one of the most spectacular train trips in the world. From Anchorage, the 114-mile trip begins by skirting the 60-mile-long Turnagain Arm on Cook Inlet and then swings south, climbs over mountain passes, spans deep river gorges and comes within half a mile of three glaciers.

The Anchorage–Whittier service, which includes a stop in Girdwood and passes through two long tunnels, turns Whittier into a fun day trip. So does riding Alaska Railroad's *Hurricane Turn*, one of America's last flag-stop trains, which departs from Talkeetna.

RESERVATIONS

You can reserve a seat and purchase tickets, even online, through **Alaska Railroad** (☎800-544-0552; www.akrr.com); highly recommended for the Anchorage–Denali service in July and early August. See regional chapters for prices and departures.

White Pass & Yukon Route

Built during the height of the Klondike Gold Rush, the White Pass & Yukon Railroad (p147) is still the incredible ride it must have been for the miners. The narrow gauge line is seen mostly as a tour but can be used for transport to Whitehorse and by backpackers on the Chilkoot Trail.

Given all that, reservations are highly recommended any time during the summer. Contact **White Pass & Yukon Route** (☎800-343-7373; www.whitepassrailroad.com) for information.

Glossary

Alcan or **Alaska Hwy** – the main overland route into Alaska. Although the highway is almost entirely paved now, completing a journey along this legendary road is still a special accomplishment. The Alcan begins at the Mile 0 milepost in Dawson Creek (northeastern British Columbia, Canada), heads northwest through Whitehorse, the capital of the Yukon Territory (Canada), and officially ends at Delta Junction (Mile 1390), 101 miles southeast of Fairbanks.

AMS – acute mountain sickness; occurs at high altitudes and can be fatal

ANWR – Arctic National Wildlife Refuge; the 1.5-million-acre wilderness area that oil company officials and Alaskans have been pushing hard to open up for oil and gas drilling

ATV – all-terrain vehicle

aurora borealis or **northern lights** – the mystical snakes of light that weave across the sky from the northern horizon. It's a spectacular show on clear nights and can occur at almost any time of the year. The lights are the result of gas particles colliding with solar electrons and are best viewed from the Interior, away from city lights, between late summer and winter.

bidarka – a skin-covered sea kayak used by the Aleuts

BLM – Bureau of Land Management; the federal agency that maintains much of the wilderness around and north of Fairbanks, including cabins and campgrounds

blue cloud – what Southeasterners call a break in the clouds

breakup – when the ice on rivers suddenly begins to melt, breaks up and flows downstream; many residents also use this term to describe spring in Alaska, when the rain begins, the snow melts and everything turns to mud and slush

bunny boots – large, oversized and usually white plastic boots used extensively in subzero weather to prevent the feet from freezing

Bush, the – any area in the state that is not connected by road to Anchorage or is not part of the Alaska Marine Hwy

cabin fever – a winter condition in which Alaskans go stir-crazy in their one-room cabins because of too little sunlight and too much time spent indoors

cache – a small hut or storage room built high off the ground to keep supplies and spare food away from roaming bears and wolves; the term, however, has found its way on to the neon signs of everything from liquor stores to pizza parlors in the cities

calve – (of an ice mass) to separate or break so that a part of the ice becomes detached

capital move – the political issue that raged in the early 1980s, concerning moving the state capital from Juneau closer to Anchorage; although residents rejected funding the move north in a 1982 state election, the issue continues to divide Alaska

cheechako – tenderfoot, greenhorn or somebody trying to survive their first year in Alaska

chum – not your mate or good buddy, but a nickname for dog salmon

clear-cut – an area where loggers have cut every tree

d-2 – the lands issue of the late 1970s, which pitted environmentalists against developers over the federal government's preservation of 156,250 sq miles of Alaskan wilderness as wildlife reserves, forests and national parks

dividend days – the period in October when residents receive their Permanent Fund checks and Alaska goes on a spending spree

Eskimo ice cream – an Iñupiat food made of whipped animal fat, berries, seal oil and sometimes shredded caribou meat

fish wheel – a wooden trap powered by a river's current that scoops salmon or other large fish out of a river into a holding tank

freeze-up – the point in November or December when most rivers and lakes ice over, signaling to Alaskans that their long winter has started in earnest

humpie – a nickname for the humpback or pink salmon, the mainstay of the fishing industry in the Southeast

ice worm – a small, thin black worm that thrives in glacial ice and was made famous by a Robert Service poem

Iditarod – the 1049-mile sled-dog race run every March from Anchorage to Nome. The winner usually completes the course in less than 14 days and takes home $50,000

Lower 48 – an Alaskan term for continental USA

moose nuggets – hard, smooth droppings; some enterprising resident in Homer has capitalized on them by baking, varnishing and trimming them with evergreen leaves to sell during Christmas as Moostletoe

mukluks – lightweight boots of sealskin trimmed with fur, made by the Iñupiat

muktuk – whale skin and blubber; also known as *maktak*, it is a delicacy among Iñupiat and is eaten in a variety of ways, including raw, pickled and boiled

muskeg – the bogs in Alaska, where layers of matted plant life float on top of stagnant water; these are bad areas in which to hike

North Slope – the gentle plain that extends from the Brooks Range north to the Arctic Ocean

no-see-um – nickname for the tiny gnats found throughout much of the Alaskan wilderness, especially in the Interior and parts of the Brooks Range

NPS – National Park Service; administers 82,656 sq miles in Alaska and its 15 national parks include such popular units as Denali, Glacier Bay, Kenai Fjords and Klondike Gold Rush National Historical Park

Outside – to residents, any place that isn't Alaska
Outsider – to residents, anyone who isn't an Alaskan

permafrost – permanently frozen subsoil that covers two-thirds of the state but is disappearing due to global warming

petroglyphs – ancient rock carvings

portage – an area of land between waterways over which paddlers carry their boats

potlatch – a traditional gathering of indigenous people held to commemorate any memorable occasion

qiviut – the wool of the musk ox, often woven into garments

RVers – those folks who opt to travel in a motorhome

scat – animal droppings; however, the term is usually used to describe bear droppings. If the scat is dark brown or bluish and somewhat square in shape, a bear has passed by; if it is steaming, the bear is eating blueberries around the next bend.

scrimshaw – hand-carved ivory from walrus tusks or whale bones.

sourdough – any old-timer in the state who, it is said, is 'sour on the country but without enough dough to get out;' newer residents believe the term applies to anybody who has survived an Alaskan winter; the term also applies to a 'yeasty' mixture used to make bread or pancakes

Southeast sneakers – the tall, reddish-brown rubber boots that Southeast residents wear when it rains, and often when it doesn't; also known as 'Ketchikan tennis shoes,' 'Sitka slippers' and 'Petersburg pumps' among other names

squaw candy – salmon that has been dried or smoked into jerky

stinkhead – an Iñupiat 'treat' made by burying a salmon head in the sand; leave the head to ferment for up to 10 days then dig it up, wash off the sand and enjoy

taku wind – Juneau's sudden gusts of wind, which may exceed 100mph in the spring and fall; often the winds cause horizontal rain, which, as the name indicates, comes straight at you instead of falling on you; in Anchorage and throughout the Interior, these sudden rushes of air over or through mountain gaps are called 'williwaws'

tundra – vast, treeless plains

UA – University of Alaska
ulu – a fan-shaped knife that Alaska Natives traditionally use to chop and scrape meat; now used by gift shops to lure tourists

umiaks – leather boats made by the Iñupiat people

USFS – US Forest Service; oversees the Tongass and Chugach National Forests, and the 190 cabins, hiking trails, kayak routes and campgrounds within them

USFWS – US Fish & Wildlife Service; administers 16 federal wildlife refuges in Alaska, more than 120,312 sq miles

USGS – US Geological Society; makes topographic maps, including those covering almost every corner of Alaska

behind the scenes

SEND US YOUR FEEDBACK

We love to hear from travelers – your comments keep us on our toes and help make our books better. Our well-traveled team reads every word on what you loved or loathed about this book. Although we cannot reply individually to postal submissions, we always guarantee that your feedback goes straight to the appropriate authors, in time for the next edition. Each person who sends us information is thanked in the next edition – and the most useful submissions are rewarded with a free book.

Visit **lonelyplanet.com/contact** to submit your updates and suggestions or to ask for help. Our award-winning website also features inspirational travel stories, news and discussions.

Note: We may edit, reproduce and incorporate your comments in Lonely Planet products such as guidebooks, websites and digital products, so let us know if you don't want your comments reproduced or your name acknowledged. For a copy of our privacy policy visit lonelyplanet.com/privacy.

OUR READERS

Many thanks to the following travelers who used the last edition and wrote to us with helpful hints, useful advice and interesting anecdotes:

Deeanne Akerson, Garret Akerson, Jörg Berning, Laura Brumfield, Scott Donaldson, Michael Hentschke, Edward Hotchkiss, Anabelen Jimenez-Carro, Patrick Kabouw, Petra Meier, Trevor Miller, Gary Moore, Annie Patterson, Karl Rhoads, Stephen Rowe, Alice Savage, Kate Sullivan, Judith Thomas, Liesje Van Der Peet, Charles Warner, Martha Waters.

AUTHOR THANKS

Jim DuFresne

Thanks to my longtime Alaskan friends: Todd, Ed, Sue, Jeff, Dragon and Buckwheat for putting me up and putting up with me. I'll always be indebted to Annette, Dave, Aurora, Brian and the rest of the gang at the Clarkston Post Office for keeping the home front stable while I was gone. Finally here's to Postcard Margaret, Rachelle, Marlena and, most of all, my son Michael for high adventures on the Chilkoot and memorable evenings in Juneau.

Catherine Bodry

I'm very grateful to Cat Craddock-Carrillo for commissioning me and answering questions, as well as Anna Metcalfe. Robert Kelly was a co-author extraordinaire and totally on his game – thanks for all your help. On the road, I received an assortment of suggestions, couches, tips, support and more from, in particular: Mike and Lyn Perry, Alexandra Gutierrez, Jeff Dickrell and Kari Anderson. Will Schlein gets a special shout-out for research help and seeing me through to the deadline.

Robert Kelly

Many thanks to my co-authors, especially Catherine for letting me crash at her place. To the staff at so many park and visitor centers: your help was beyond what I expected. Countless Alaskans and travelers also deserve credit for answering questions, giving me feedback, and making me feel this work is valued. To Johnny Cash, the traveling cat, cheers for entertaining me in Fairbanks. Finally, to Huei-ming, thanks again for holding down the fort while I was gone.

ACKNOWLEDGMENTS

Climate map data adapted from Peel MC, Finlayson BL & McMahon TA (2007) 'Updated World Map of the Köppen-Geiger Climate Classification', *Hydrology and Earth System Sciences*, 11, 1633 44.

Cover photograph: Grizzly bear, Mt McKinley; Allen Prier/Photolibrary. Many of the images in this guide are available for licensing from Lonely Planet Images: www.lonelyplanet images.com.

THIS BOOK

This 10th edition of Lonely Planet's *Alaska* guidebook was researched and written by Jim DuFresne, Catherine Bodry and Robert Kelly. The previous edition was researched and written by Jim DuFresne, Greg Benchwick and Catherine Bodry. This guidebook was commissioned in Lonely Planet's Oakland office, and produced by the following:

Commissioning Editor
Catherine Craddock-Carrillo

Coordinating Editors
Lauren Hunt, Pat Kinsella

Coordinating Cartographer Julie Dodkins
Coordinating Layout Designer Mazzy Prinsep
Managing Editor Anna Metcalfe
Senior Editors Victoria Harrison, Susan Paterson, Angela Tinson
Managing Cartographers Shahara Ahmed, Alison Lyall, Andy Rojas
Managing Layout Designers Chris Girdler, Jane Hart

Assisting Editors Susie Ashworth, Janet Austin, Janice Bird, Amy Karafin
Assisting Cartographers Jane Chapman, Mick Garrett, Eve Kelly, Sophie Reed
Cover Research Naomi Parker
Internal Image Research Sabrina Dalbesio, Rebecca Skinner
Thanks to Lucy Birchley, Ryan Evans, Yvonne Kirk, Brigitte Ellemor, Trent Paton, Martine Power, Averil Robertson, Gerard Walker

index

000 Map pages
000 Photo pages

000 Map pages
000 Photo pages

how to use this book

These symbols will help you find the listings you want:

- 👁 Sights
- 🐾 Beaches
- 🏃 Activities
- 🛶 Courses

- 👉 Tours
- 🎊 Festivals & Events
- 🛏 Sleeping
- 🍴 Eating

- 🍷 Drinking
- ⭐ Entertainment
- 🛍 Shopping
- ℹ Information/Transport

These symbols give you the vital information for each listing:

- ☑ Telephone Numbers
- ⊙ Opening Hours
- Ⓟ Parking
- ⊝ Nonsmoking
- ❄ Air-Conditioning
- @ Internet Access

- 📶 Wi-Fi Access
- 🏊 Swimming Pool
- 🥗 Vegetarian Selection
- 📖 English-Language Menu
- 👪 Family-Friendly
- 🐾 Pet-Friendly

- 🚌 Bus
- ⛴ Ferry
- Ⓜ Metro
- Ⓢ Subway
- ⊖ London Tube
- 🚊 Tram
- 🚆 Train

Reviews are organised by author preference.

Map Legend

Sights
- 🏖 Beach
- ⚑ Buddhist
- 🏰 Castle
- ✟ Christian
- ☪ Hindu
- ☾ Islamic
- ✡ Jewish
- ❶ Monument
- 🏛 Museum/Gallery
- 🏚 Ruin
- 🍇 Winery/Vineyard
- 🐾 Zoo
- 👁 Other Sight

Activities, Courses & Tours
- Diving/Snorkelling
- Canoeing/Kayaking
- Skiing
- Surfing
- Swimming/Pool
- Walking
- Windsurfing
- Other Activity/Course/Tour

Sleeping
- 🛏 Sleeping
- ⛺ Camping

Eating
- 🍴 Eating

Drinking
- ☕ Drinking
- ☕ Cafe

Entertainment
- Entertainment

Shopping
- 🛍 Shopping

Information
- Post Office
- ℹ Tourist Information

Transport
- ✈ Airport
- Border Crossing
- Bus
- Cable Car/Funicular
- Cycling
- Ferry
- Ⓜ Metro
- Monorail
- Ⓟ Parking
- Ⓢ S-Bahn
- Taxi
- Train/Railway
- Tram
- Tube Station
- Ⓤ U-Bahn
- • Other Transport

Routes
- Tollway
- Freeway
- Primary
- Secondary
- Tertiary
- Lane
- Unsealed Road
- Plaza/Mall
- Steps
- Tunnel
- Pedestrian Overpass
- Walking Tour
- Walking Tour Detour
- Path

Boundaries
- International
- State/Province
- Disputed
- Regional/Suburb
- Marine Park
- Cliff
- Wall

Population
- ✪ Capital (National)
- ◉ Capital (State/Province)
- ● City/Large Town
- ● Town/Village

Geographic
- 🛖 Hut/Shelter
- Lighthouse
- Lookout
- ▲ Mountain/Volcano
- Oasis
- Park
-)(Pass
- Picnic Area
- Waterfall

Hydrography
- River/Creek
- Intermittent River
- Swamp/Mangrove
- Reef
- Canal
- Water
- Dry/Salt/Intermittent Lake
- Glacier

Areas
- Beach/Desert
- Cemetery (Christian)
- Cemetery (Other)
- Park/Forest
- Sportsground
- Sight (Building)
- Top Sight (Building)

OUR STORY

A beat-up old car, a few dollars in the pocket and a sense of adventure. In 1972 that's all Tony and Maureen Wheeler needed for the trip of a lifetime – across Europe and Asia overland to Australia. It took several months, and at the end – broke but inspired – they sat at their kitchen table writing and stapling together their first travel guide, *Across Asia on the Cheap*. Within a week they'd sold 1500 copies. Lonely Planet was born.

Today, Lonely Planet has offices in Melbourne, London and Oakland, with more than 600 staff and writers. We share Tony's belief that 'a great guidebook should do three things: inform, educate and amuse'.

OUR WRITERS

Jim DuFresne

Coordinating Author, Juneau & the Southeast, Anchorage & Around Jim has lived, worked and wandered all across Alaska and has had a hand in all 10 editions of Lonely Planet's *Alaska*. As the sports and outdoors editor of the *Juneau Empire*, he was the first Alaskan sportswriter to win a national award from Associated Press. As a guide for Alaska Discovery he has witnessed Hubbard Glacier shed icebergs the size of pick-up trucks. Jim now lives in Michigan where he is a regular contributor to www.michigantrailmaps.com, but regularly returns to the Far North to update his books.

Catherine Bodry

Prince William Sound, Kenai Peninsula, Kodiak, Katmai & Southwest Alaska Catherine has spent the bulk of her adult life rebelling from her suburban upbringing. She worked in Alaska during her summers in college, and then stayed to experience winter and go to grad school. She spent four years living in Seward and now calls Anchorage home. She's contributed to several Lonely Planet guides, including *Thailand*, *Canada*, *Discover Alaska* and *Pacific Northwest Trips*. When she's not on the road for Lonely Planet, she's usually running the trails in the Chugach or dodging moose on the bike trails in Anchorage.

Robert Kelly

Denali & the Interior, The Bush A native of Canada, Robert first hitchhiked north after high school and found that he was quite at home in unbounded wilderness. Later, a series of summer jobs in Dawson City allowed him plenty of time to cross borders into Alaska and pursue his passion for hiking and road trips. For research on this guide, Robert happily returned to some old haunts (Chicken, how little you've changed!), re-drove the sublime Richardson Hwy, and finally made it to the Arctic Ocean. Robert has been a freelance writer for the past decade and *Alaska* was his 7th guide for Lonely Planet.

Published by Lonely Planet Publications Pty Ltd
ABN 36 005 607 983
10th edition – April 2012
ISBN 978 1 74179 696 4
© Lonely Planet 2012   Photographs © as indicated 2012
10 9 8 7 6 5 4 3 2 1
Printed in China